Financial Market Integration and Growth

Paul J.J. Welfens • Cillian Ryan
Editors

Financial Market Integration and Growth

Structural Change and Economic Dynamics in the European Union

Springer

Editors
Prof. Dr. Paul J.J. Welfens
EIIW - European Institute for International Economic Relations
University of Wuppertal
Rainer-Gruenter-Str. 21
42119 Wuppertal
Germany
welfens@eiiw.uni-wuppertal.de

Prof. Dr. Cillian Ryan
Department of Economics
The University of Birmingham
Edgbaston
Birmingham, B15 2TT
United Kingdom
c.ryan@bham.ac.uk

ISBN 978-3-642-42365-9 ISBN 978-3-642-16274-9 (eBook)
DOI 10.1007/978-3-642-16274-9
Springer Heidelberg Dordrecht London New York

Cover design: WMX Design GmbH, Heidelberg, Germany

Printed on acid-free paper

Springer is part of Springer Science+Business Media (www.springer.com)

Contents

Introduction

While the determinants of structural change and economic growth in the EU are many, the role of financial capital, whether mediated through improved financial market processes or foreign direct investment, is clearly crucial. Over the last two decades the European Union has seen a variety of policy events which has influenced the structure of the market for financial capital among the original members and the incentive to invest in developing new-member economies. Thus, both globalization more generally and the EU Single Market Act and successive financial directives more specifically have influenced both the structure of the financial market in the EU15 and new member states and the incentive for firms to finance themselves in non-traditional ways. Similarly, enlargement to include developing economies, whether that be Ireland in the 1970s, Spain, Portugal and Greece in the 1980s or the more recent expansions of the last decade has provided important insights both on the evolution of financial markets and the incentive and mode of investment in such economies. Thus, new member countries not only represent a geographical enlargement of the Community but they also stand for a quasi-natural historical experiment in institutional changes and economic internationalization. However, while the Eastern enlargement thus presents welcome analytical challenges it is also crucial to understand the developments in EU-15 and the Euro zone, respectively over the last few decades. The unfolding of the Transatlantic Banking Crisis has undermined the stability of the Euro zone and the overall EU and indeed marks the historical shock to which policy makers so far hardly find adequate responses – understanding the role of banks, financial market integration and the overall EU single market developments is required as is the understanding of global international financial markets.

This volume thus aims to provides a timely study of the relevant European and global dynamics through a series of chapters which focus variously on the lessons which to be learnt from the current state of global banking; the evolution of, and degree of integration in, the original EU 15 single market; the impact of financial market development and/or FDI in the cohesion states of Portugal, Ireland, Greece and Spain; and, in turn, the experience of the new member states of the enlarged Union.

In their introductory chapter, Ryan and Horsewood explore the effects of EU enlargement via two distinct channels not previously distinguished in the EU integration literature. In general, market integration provides the opportunities associated with the standard gains from trade arguments for improved resource allocation, including the incentive for financial capital to move to those regions of Europe where it can yield the best returns. Ryan and Horsewood, however note that financial market integration provides potential additional effects in markets where investment has been constrained due to market information problems. They distinguish between the incentives for banks to provide credit finance to firms as a result of change in the perceived returns to firms trading in more internationalized markets (a change in project variance) on the one hand and the change in the portfolio variance experienced by banks due to the fact that the bank can now lend to a wider portfolio of international firms either directly or via a subsidiary on the other. The effect on credit financing of a change in the variance of project returns yields ambiguous results, not only due to potential differences in the way the distribution of shocks may affect liberalized markets (Newbury/Stiglitz versus Cole/Obstfeld) but also because the propensity to provide credit is sensitive to the shape of the return density function and the aggregate effect on the marginal borrower who the bank chooses or declines to finance. This result also applies to the additional impact of a reduction in firm-specific project variance on bank lending due to the elimination or decline in exchange rate fluctuations due to membership or shadowing of the Euro. The chapter goes on to shows that no such ambiguity applies to the impact of a reduction in portfolio variance from increased international lending and that this effect provides an unambiguous benefit from European financial integration. The chapter concludes by assessing the extent of the overall theoretical ambiguity via an econometric analysis of the entry of the Central and Eastern European Countries to the EU. The empirical findings suggest a strong role for openness in narrowing the interest rate margin, suggesting that at least on aggregate economic and financial integration work to enhance welfare, even where there are issues with asymmetric information and moral hazard in credit markets.

The contribution by Mevlud Islami investigates the interdependence between foreign exchange markets and stock markets in the case of four cohesion countries, Greece, Ireland, Portugal and Spain (prior to the introduction of the Euro) and four accession countries (Poland, Czech Republic, Slovenia, and Hungary). The analysis includes the basic theoretical approaches and the uses monthly data for the nominal stock market indices and nominal exchange rates. From the long-run co-integration analysis and short-term VAR analysis this chapter suggests that significant links exist between the stock market index and the exchange rate for Slovenia, Hungary, Ireland, Spain, and Greece whereas in the case of Poland there are short- and long-run links. The unambiguous result in all six cases that suggests that the exchange-rate movements are Granger caused by the stock market index is a surprise and contrasts with previous research on Asia. The European results might reflect a greater degree of market integration in Europe, both through FDI inflows to these countries, portfolio investments or simply financial market inflows in the light of improved investment and growth opportunities.

In the contribution of Paul Welfens the key dynamics of the transatlantic banking crisis are analyzed – with emphasis on the fact that the banking disaster of 2007/08 was not really a surprise, and five key requirements for restoring stability and efficiency in the EU/OECD banking sector are highlighted: Hedge funds should be regulated and be required to register with the Bank of International Settlements, which should have the right to tighten equity capital requirements if deemed necessary. The quality and comprehensiveness of banks' balance sheets must be radically improved and all off-balance sheet activities must be included in future total balance sheets (TBS). Securitization is a useful financial innovation, yet asset backed securities (ABS) should become more standardized and every bank selling ABS should declare its willingness to buy back this package at any point of time at a minimum of 50% of the initial transaction price. All credit default swaps (CDS) must be registered in a global database, and future transaction should go through a clearing house. Previous CDS transactions must also be recorded, since a critical veil of ignorance of counterparty risk would otherwise continue and hence the uncertainty about the valuation of large portfolio positions of banks, funds and insurance companies would continue. Financing of rating should be indirect, namely every country or company planning to place bonds in the market should pay fees into a pool, and this pool then finances the respective rating on a competitive basis. The analysis suggests that this two-stage approach of financing ratings would most likely eliminate the existing conflicts of interest in the present regime. Most important, however, is the proposal of a new tax regime designed to encourage bankers to take a more long term time horizon in decision-making and to reduce excessive risk-taking. Banks and funds should be taxed not only on the basis of profits but also on the basis of the variability – read variance – of the rate of return on equity: the higher the variability over time the higher the tax to be paid. The hybrid macro model presented sheds new light on the impact of the Transatlantic Banking Crisis; there is a broad range of new multipliers which underline the usefulness of the hybrid macromodel.

The contribution by Christian Schröder highlights the role of financial development in producing innovative products and services. After a general overview of the function of the financial structure as well as financial development in realizing product and service innovations, this work examines a financial intermediary which is particularly specialized to finance early-stage high-tech innovations – the venture capitalist (VC). The chapter employs a panel analysis to illustrate whether technical opportunities, taxes, stock market development, relative size of the banking sector, GDP growth and later-stage venture capital influence the level of early stage venture capital investments. The empirical analysis was conducted in EU 15 countries and looked at the period from 1995 to 2005. The results show that technical opportunities, size of the stock market and banking sector, interest rate growth and the amount of later-stage venture capital have a significant positive impact on the amount of early stage risk capital while the corporate tax rate has a negative impact. The structure of the national financial system seems not to have a significant influence.

Andy Mullineux, Victor Murinde and Rudra Sensarma examine the degree of convergence in corporate financing patterns in eight of the EU15 countries as means of gaining insights into the larger issue of European integration. Specifically, the paper seeks to determine whether the European economies are converging towards an Anglo-Saxon (capital-market-oriented) or a continental (bank-oriented) financial system. The study uses a series of modern panel unit root tests and generalized methods of moments (GMM) to test for convergence in panel data from 1972 to 2004 for Finland, France, Germany, Italy, The Netherlands, Spain, Sweden and the UK. For the panel unit root tests, the chapter finds evidence for convergence in bank and bond finance but does not obtain unambiguous results for equity and internal finance. The chapter then uses a panel variant of the Barro/Sala-i-Martin growth model to investigate convergence in the financing pattern of non-financial corporations (NCF's) and finds that they are increasingly using bond and equity markets for their financing needs. The paper thus concludes that the pattern of corporate financing in the EU mimics some elements of the pecking order theory of financing choices and that the EU financial system is converging on a variant of the Anglo-Saxon model, with heavy reliance on internal financing and direct financing from the capital market.

Antonia Calvo Hornero and Ignacio Garrido Sánchez consider to what extent lessons can be drawn for new member states from the experience of the financial system in Spain and Portugal's following their entrance into the EU in the 1980s. They present an in-depth comparative historical analysis of the two financial systems and analyse the changes that facilitated the deep transformation in the Spanish and Portuguese financial systems in the last two decades. The authors note that there are important distinctions to be drawn between the experience of Spain and Portugal and the new member states. Firstly, there was a well established banking system in existence prior to the accession, albeit one which was heavily regulated in both cases. However, both, but particularly Spain, had liberalised considerably prior to joining the EU which, crucially, at that stage was still characterised by a high degree of national-specific regulation both in relation to banking itself and to the mobility of capital. Thus the current wave of new member states are now attempting to harmonise with a much more highly integrated European financial market and thus they face more formidable challenges. In addition, the financial systems in new members states, by contrast with the long-established Iberian systems, were also really only evolving from the systems in place during the communist era and arguably, these had not reached a comparable steady state prior to accession of the new members to the EU. The authors argue that nevertheless there is much to be learnt by new member states from the Spanish experience in particular, which despite sharing some common elements of the Anglo-Saxon model (at least in relation to household mortgage lending) nevertheless avoided many of the pitfalls experienced by the US and UK in the current financial crisis. It therefore serves as a useful benchmark for new members.

Andy Mullineux's contribution considers the dynamics of liberalisation and regulation of financial markets. Banking trends since the liberalisation, re-regulation and the globalisation process accelerated in the 1970s are reviewed. The major international banks have responded to increasing competition and greater freedom by diversifying to form financial conglomerates – universal banking and bancassurance have become widespread. The implications for corporate governance of financial sector convergence in Europe is assessed. Global trends in corporate governance are reviewed and it is postulated that convergence on a hybrid financial model will lead to convergence of corporate governance mechanisms. The hybrid model will feature continental European universal banking and bancassurance alongside growing importance of Anglo-Saxon direct capital market finance. As a result, supported by the privatisation of pensions, non-bank institutional investors (pension and mutual funds and insurance companies) will play an increasingly important role in corporate governance worldwide.

The argument is that the drivers of change (liberalisation, re-regulation and globalisation), along with privatisation of pensions, are forcing convergence in the sense that bancassurance is becoming more universal and capital markets are increasing in importance. Globalisation has been facilitated by regulatory and supervisory harmonisation (Basle I and II, the development of International Accounting Standards, the Financial Stability Forum, replacement of Article 65 (Japan) and Glass-Steagall Act (US) etc.). Global wide banks, or financial conglomerates, are emerging (Citigroup, HSBC etc.).

Regulation and supervision can be regarded as part of the corporate governance mechanism for financial firms arising from their fiduciary duties to depositors and other investors (savers) in addition to their shareholders. The Anglo-Saxon and continental European corporate governance systems and the roles of banks and other financial firms therein, are compared and contrasted. It is then hypothesised that financial sector convergence will lead to a tendency for convergence in corporate governance mechanisms given the important and growing role played by the financial sector in corporate governance. Differences in legal systems notwithstanding, there are already some evidence of convergence given the acceptance of the OECDs best practice general principles. The EU continues to work towards greater convergence too. The question of what type of corporate governance system will emerge arises. Whatever the case, institutional investors seem set to play an increasing role. However, institutional investors themselves face conflicts of interest (e.g. through the desire to maintain mandates) and so issues relating to their corporate governance are coming to the fore.

Over two decades Ireland has attracted high FDI-inflows, which are investigated in the contribution of Mareike Koeller. Based on well-known theoretical models, some host country determinants for different modes of FDI are analysed. Koeller argues that the standard models for vertical and horizontal foreign direct investments can not sufficiently explain the high inflows to Ireland, thus another explanation has to be found. The inclusion of aspects of regional integration (membership of the EU) changes both the theoretically derived host country determinants and the real determinants in Ireland. This article shows that the export-platform-models and the new economic geography can explain FDI-inflows from third countries and from other EU member states to Ireland. Data on FDI-inflows and multinational enterprises is used to support the conclusions drawn.

Julius Horvath and Katarina Lukacsy address the issue of market integration within the EU by considering the relative degree of market integration across regions within a single country. The paper presents evidence about the extent of market integration within Slovakia for a range of products and the speed of convergence when price differentials exist. The evidence presented suggests that goods specifics are important with market integration being stronger for homogenous tradable products than for services and heterogeneous products. They also find evidence for convergence to the law of one price, however, the speed of convergence is relatively low by comparison with other international studies. The benefits of having these intra-national measures of market integration is that they allow us to assess the degree to which price differences within the EU can be ascribed to spatial separation as opposed to border effects. After reviewing the literature on market integration across borders, Horvarth and Lukacsy extend their intra-Slovakia discussion to consider the results from their recent work on the importance of the border effect between Slovakia and Hungary.

The main aim of the contribution of Kalman Dezseri is to shed some light on the possible trade, FDI and structural adjustment related effects of the process of joining of the new EU member states (EU-10) to the EMU. The analysis considers the nature and scale of the relocation of capital via FDI inflows into the central European new EU member states. Important aspects of this development are the already existing trends and future potential for relocations of capital from the old EU member states (EU-15) to the new member states in Central Europe. A particularly important issue are the changes in the structural characteristics of the relocation process and the groups of industries whose competitiveness and development benefit from it. The newly created production capacities of FDI have important trade creation and divertion effects. The most important ones are the structural changes of the economy and improvements in competitiveness.

The contributions presented are part of the scientific output of the EU-funded project (Financial Market Integration, Structural Change, Foreign Direct Investment and Economic Growth in the EU25; Agreement Number-2006-1623/001-001) The group of researchers from the University of Birmingham, Budapest (Central European University), the University of Wuppertal (European Institute for International Economic Relations/EIIW) and the Universidad Nacional de Educatión a Distancia. We are very grateful for the financial support from the Jean Monnet Programme. The analysis has shown that the financial market dynamics and the real economy create an impulse for expansion under normal circumstances – with different dynamics in EU member countries. While institutions, domestic and foreign capital accumulation, as well as trade creation have generally been supported in a favorable way, there are some doubts that integration dynamics have developed adequately to cope with periods of turbulence. The Transatlantic Banking Crisis has shed new light on the vulnerability of EU and global financial integration. Multinational companies are an important and stabilizing element of EU integration and there is little doubt that foreign direct investment has contributed to both efficiency gains and a more flexible overall economy in Europe. The challenges for economic policy makers are enormous, particularly in the field of regulation of financial markets.

We greatly appreciate the technical support by Deniz Erdem (European Institute for International Economic Relations, EIIW), Wuppertal and the editorial assistance provided by Michael Agner, Odense.

List of Tables

List of Figures

Contributors

Kalman Dezseri Department of European Integration, Institute for World Economics of the Hungarian Academy of Sciences, Budapest, Hungary

Antonia Calvo Hornero Universidad Nacional de Educación a Distancia (UNED), Madrid, Spain

Nicholas Horsewood European Research Institute and Department of Economics, College of Social Sciences, University of Birmingham, Birmingham, UK

Julius Horvath Central European University, Budapest, Hungary

Mevlud Islami European Institute for International Economic Relations, University of Wuppertal, Wuppertal, Germany

Mareike Koeller Georg-August-University Göttingen, Göttingen, Germany

Katarina Lukacsy Central European University, Budapest, Hungary

Andy Mullineux Birmingham Business School, University of Birmingham, Birmingham, UK

Victor Murinde Birmingham Business School, University of Birmingham, Birmingham, UK

Cillian Ryan European Research Institute and Department of Economics, College of Social Sciences, University of Birmingham, Birmingham, UK

Ignacio Garrido Sánchez Bank of Spain

Christian Schröder Researcher at the European Institute for International Economic Relations at the University of Wuppertal/Schumpeter School of Business and Economics, Rainer-Gruenter-Strasse 21, 42119 Wuppertal, Germany

Rudra Sensarma University of Hertfordshire Business School, Hertfordshire, UK

Paul J.J. Welfens European Institute for International Economic Relations, University of Wuppertal, Wuppertal, Germany

Chapter 1
The Role of Banks in Financial Integration: Some New Theory and Evidence from New EU Members*

Cillian Ryan and Nicholas Horsewood

1.1 Introduction

Over the last two decades, there have been major changes in the Central and Eastern European Countries (CEECs) as their economies collapsed and they undertook the journey from centralised economies to market-based systems. The initial effects of the transformation process involved substantial reductions in output and the need for a complete restructuring of industry. One of the main problems faced by the CEECs was the collapse of international trade as exports and imports were based on the Council of Mutual Economic Assistance, an economic organisation of command economies. The successful geographical reorientation of international trade required the economies of CEECs to face the competitive pressures of EU producers, which would hopefully lead to economic expansion and higher growth. There was concern that such a policy of openness would be inappropriate as the industries in the transition economies were inefficient and would result in further unemployment (Brenton and Gros 1997). However, these issues were successfully negotiated and eight CEECs gained accession to the European Union in May 2004.

The outcomes of the reforms depended upon the speed and sequencing of the restructuring process undertaken and differed between countries due to their starting positions and policies adopted. An integral pillar in the restructuring process was the establishment of a robust and efficient banking system, to enable resources to be allocated according to economic criteria. The financial infrastructure was required independently of whether the country adopted for promoting new private sector enterprises or for privatising the existing state firms. At the end of the

---

*The contribution is based on the paper: Ryan, C., Horsewood, N. (2009), The role of banks in financial integration: evidence from new EU members, *Journal of International Economics and Economic Policy*, *6*, Number 3/October 2009.

C. Ryan (✉) and N. Horsewood
European Research Institute and Department of Economics, College of Social Sciences, University of Birmingham, Birmingham, UK
e-mail: c.ryan@bham.ac.uk

P.J.J. Welfens and C. Ryan (eds.), *Financial Market Integration and Growth*,
DOI 10.1007/978-3-642-16274-9_1, © Springer-Verlag Berlin Heidelberg 2011

recovery, each former command economy needed to have in place credit institutions which could provide loans to private sector firms and maintain economic growth and development.

One issue was how to create a banking system from a very small or non-existent base. At the same time that the CEECs were undergoing the transition process, the banking system in the European Union was facing the Single Market Programme, part of which attempted to create a single banking market with a single banking license to operate across all member state. It was hoped that this policy change would encourage cross-border banking and stimulate cheaper lending within the EU. Concomitantly, developments in technology, in particular information processing, telecommunication and financial technology, facilitated cross-border banking. The extent to which this occurred is debatable [see Murinde et al. (2000)] however, towards the end of the 1990s financial intermediaries in the EU started to look towards the CEECs and opportunities available in those countries as we shall see below. As a result the banking system in the CEECs became financially integrated with EU institutions via cross-border activities.

The literature on banks as financial intermediaries is employed to examine the effect on financial aspects of market integration. The theoretical model analyses the impact on bank intermediation of the likely changes in the mean and variance of expected project returns due to the integration of both goods and financial markets and the reduction on exchange-rate risk following a move to the common Euro currency. It highlights the importance of these latter variance effects as potentially important variables in the movement of interest rates and lending volumes in the wake of increased real and financial integration.

Relatively little comparative research has been undertaken on the banking systems in CEECS. With the exception of Kasman and Yildirim (2006), few studies have attempted to take into account the different starting points of the countries in the transition process. This paper attempts to address the deficiency by consider key factors which are likely to influenced the process of financial integration in the banking sector across the CEECs. Rather than adopting a panel approach, the research will focus on analysing each country separately to investigate the determinants of the difference between borrowing and deposit interest rates, taken as one measure of the degree of integration in the banking sector. Such an approach will have important implications for economic policy as it should highlight the conditions necessary for an efficient financial system in the EU.

The remainder of the paper is organised as follows. Section 1.2 looks at the financial integration in Europe, in particular the penetration by foreign banks in CEECs. Section 1.3 develops a simple theoretical model of bank intermediation to highlight the effect of the integration of goods and financial markets on the banks and to identify the key factors affecting interest rate margins. Section 1.4 presents an overview of the pattern of interest rates in CEECs and describes the gap between the interest rate changed to borrowers and the rate paid to lenders. The following section contains the econometric analysis identifying the factors responsible for narrowing the gap. The final section concludes the analysis and presents some policy issues.

1.2 Financial Integration in EU Entrants

After the events in 1989, the CEECs embarked on the long road from command economies to market economies. The transition process to a market-based economy required major structural changes. The precise nature of the reform process differed between nations as it depended on the economic structures and relationships in place. However, most CEECs experienced considerable pain, witnessing high unemployment, high inflation and negative economic growth in the early 1990s.

A stable, efficient banking system was viewed as being one of the necessary pillars of a successful transition to a market-based economy. The financial markets were very inefficient, being dominated by the state monobank with funds not being allocated on economic terms. The banks possessed a large stock of bad debts, which restricted their lending behaviour in the transition process. This problem was partly a result of the inability to determine the creditworthiness of a company when prices were set centrally. There was preferential allocation of funds with governments identifying which industrial sectors should be given loans rather than the decision based on market criteria, such as net-present valuation. The problem was compounded as the pricing of loans was distortionary, frequently being set below the market interest rates and not incorporating risk (Perotti 1993; Roe et al. 2000).

A number of structural changes were proposed to create a more efficient and competitive banking system where funds were allocated according to economic criteria. The state monobanks should be broken down into a number of different financial intermediaries, with the interference from the state being removed. By breaking up the monopolies in the banking sector, the aim was to generate competition and increase efficiency. Some of these newly formed institutions were privatised at the beginning of the privatisation process, either by issuing shares to the nationals or allowing foreign banks to take a stake in them. The privatisation programme depended on the strength of the economy and the level of xenophobia in each CEEC. A number of licenses were granted to foreign banks to allow them to operate in a CEEC and vie with the domestic intermediaries for business. As well as providing competition, the entry of foreign banks was hoped to generate positive externalities, by providing knowledge and expertise in how to run a bank in a market economy (Thorne 1993).

The pressure to create a more sophisticated banking system in CEECs provided a strong incentive for cross-border intermediaries. Within existing EU countries, there were a number of factors encouraging banks to operate in different countries. The 1992 Single Market Programme attempted to create a single banking market among the 15 nations that were members of the EU prior to 2004. Prior to the implementation of the single market, measures of efficiency suggested widespread differences across member countries (up to 200%) even after making adjustments for differences in levels and types of services (see Ryan 1992, p. 103). The harmonisation of rules and regulations provided an incentive for banks to begin adopting a pan-EU view and operate in more than one country. In theory this enabled banks to develop know-how as to the optimal organisational structure to own and manage banks in other countries. However, Murinde et al. (2000) suggest that while levels of efficiency within the EU converged in the wake of the 1992 Single Market, the impetus for rationalisation and efficiency gains in the EU15 was due as much to the *threat* of mergers, acquisitions and new competition as it did to actual outside entrants. However, as Table 1.1 demonstrates, perhaps as a consequence of their improved efficiency or perhaps due to limited expansion possibilities in the EU 15 by 2000, EU banks started looking at entering CEECs due the perception of the large potential profits that could be made after the initial pain of the transition process. The introduction of the Euro further encouraged cross-border banking. The credit institutions no longer had to experience exchange rate risk when undertaking business in other Euro-based economies. How this impacted on financial intermediaries in CEECs and the possibility of foreign penetration depends upon a number of conflicting forces, for example the synchronisation of business cycles in the Euro-zone and between the Euro area and the CEECs. Positive spillovers from banking in the Euro-zone could encourage further expansion into other European countries, especially if there is an incentive to have a balanced portfolio of assets and loans.

The extent of the participation of foreign banks in CEECs between 1998 and 2008 is given in Tables 1.1a and 1.1b and the variation between the market structure of the banking system between countries can be observed. While in all the economies banks were largely domestic owned in 1998, by 2000 only Estonia still remained 100% domestic owned while in Latvia domestic banks were in a minority. Poland and Romania, two of the larger new (potential) members had reached 45 and 48% foreign ownership respectively. By 2004 only Croatia had a banking system with a dominant market share while Bulgaria and Estonia were evenly split.

This change in the ownership structure of CEEC banks was matched by a general trend in the growth of lending via subsidiaries (with the organisational structure apparently favouring subsidiaries over branches) with comparatively more modest growth in cross-border lending. Table 1.2 suggests that while cross-border lending

Table 1.1a Majority domestic owned versus majority international owned banks in selected emerging European countries

	Domestic Jan'98	Foreign Jan'98	Domestic Jan'00	Foreign Jan'00	Domestic Jan'04	Foreign Jan'04	Domestic Jan'08	Foreign Jan'08
Bulgaria	12	7	12	9	12	12	8	18
Croatia	37	8	32	7	17	13	18	19
Czech Rep	22	8	11	7	10	20	6	28
Estonia	11	0	4	0	3	3	2	8
Hungary	18	13	12	12	9	23	8	34
Latvia	17	7	4	6	8	9	9	11
Lithuania	9	2	7	2	3	6	3	8
Poland	29	17	21	17	11	26	11	45
Romania	8	6	13	12	8	16	6	27
Total	163	68	116	72	81	128	71	198

Source: Bankscope

Table 1.1b Majority domestic owned versus majority international owned banks in selected emerging European countries as a percentage of total banks

	Domestic Jan'98 (%)	Foreign Jan'98 (%)	Domestic Jan'00 (%)	Foreign Jan'00 (%)	Domestic Jan'04 (%)	Foreign Jan'04 (%)	Domestic Jan'08 (%)	Foreign Jan'08 (%)
Bulgaria	63	37	57	43	50	50	31	69
Croatia	82	18	82	18	57	43	49	51
Czech Rep	73	27	61	39	33	67	18	82
Estonia	100	0	100	0	50	50	20	80
Hungary	58	42	50	50	28	72	19	81
Latvia	71	29	40	60	47	53	45	55
Lithuania	82	18	78	22	33	67	27	73
Poland	63	37	55	45	30	70	20	80
Romania	57	43	52	48	33	67	18	82
Total	71	29	62	38	39	61	26	74

Source: Bankscope

in the EEA grew only marginally less than lending via subsidiaries, the growth in the latter was almost twice as strong in the CEEC's. Over the same period the cross-border activity to Commercial Presence Ratio (Table 1.3) fell from 6.3 to.1.6 in the CEES while in the EEA the figure, while it declined over the period was still 3.6. The preference for subsidiaries may be a result of the regulatory framework existing in each CEEC and the taxation treatment in the home country (Cerutti et al. 2007) or alternatively an indirect response to the first financial market crises, the GATS and BASEL II (Ryan and Murinde 2005).

Looking at the number of banks in CEECs can provide a false impression if the size of banks is not uniform in each nation. Table 1.4 presents information on the total assets of financial intermediaries in each CEEC. Given the size of its population, it is not surprising to find that financial intermediaries in Poland had the largest total assets and Lithuania the smallest in 2004. When looked at in terms of GDP, the Polish banking system does not appear as well developed and the share of financial sector in GDP in Hungary and the Czech Republic is greater. There is considerable variation in the proportion of total assets emanating from the European Economic Area (EEA), an area comprising the EU15 plus Norway, Iceland and Liechtenstein. In Estonia, the Czech Republic and Slovakia the proportion of bank assets being foreign owned are exceptionally high, being over 80 percent. Only Slovenia and Latvia have a percentage of assets from overseas below 50 percent, indicating the presence of foreign bank within CEECs. The corresponding figure for the EU15 was just 16.5 percent, which drops to 13.3 percent if the United Kingdom is excluded from the data set.

The majority of the assets from foreign banks are from the EEA countries, which reflects the importance of geographical proximity in cross-border banking. Only in the Polish banking system is the proportion of assets from foreign non-EEA nations above the figure for the EU15, and even then these are typically US and other major international banks with a significant market presence in the EU market. The high foreign bank share suggests that large banking institutions in nearby countries can

Table 1.2 Lending patterns by European banks

	Jun-98 (US$ bn)	Jun-00 (US$ bn)	Jun-02 (US$ bn)	Jun-04 (US$ bn)	Jun-06 (US$ bn)	Jun-08 (US$ bn)	Annual % growth (decline)					
							1998–2000	2000–2002 (%)	2002–2004 (%)	2004–2006 (%)	2006–2008 (%)	1998–2008 (%)
Europe												
Cross-border loans outstanding	n/a	4,214	5,238	7,324	10,469	15,988	n/a	11.49	18.25	19.56	23.58	18.14
Local loans by subsidiaries	n/a	806	1,012	1,519	2,367	4,475	n/a	12.05	22.51	24.83	37.50	23.90
Local liabilities of subsidiaries	n/a	832	854	1,378	2,617	3,577	n/a	1.31	27.03	37.81	16.91	20.00
Emerging Europe												
Cross-border loans outstanding	133	171	189	279	575	977	13.39%	5.13	21.50	43.56	30.35	22.07
Local loans by subsidiaries	21	43	103	163	298	665	43.10%	54.77	25.80	35.21	49.38	41.27
Local liabilities of subsidiaries	16	39	99	135	191	405	56.12%	59.33	16.77	18.95	45.62	38.14

Source: BIS (2008)

Table 1.3 Cross-border activity to commercial presence ratio[a]

	Jun-98	Jun-00	Jun-02	Jun-04	Jun-06	Jun-08
All developing countries	3.3	2.5	1.5	1.4	1.3	1.3
Emerging Europe	6.3	4.0	1.8	1.7	1.9	1.5
Developed countries	n/a	2.7	2.6	2.3	2.1	2.2
Europe	n/a	5.2	5.2	4.8	4.4	3.6

[a]Cross-border loans outstanding to lending by local subsidiaries
Source: BIS (2008)

Table 1.4 Foreign penetration in CEECs in 2004

Country	Total assets of credit institutions (€ mill)	Proportion in branches or subsidiaries from foreign EEA countries	Proportion in branches or subsidiaries from foreign non-EEA countries
Poland	131,904	0.588	0.087
Czech Rep.	86,525	0.869	0.050
Hungary	64,970	0.559	0.031
Slovakia	29,041	0.876	0.000
Slovenia	24,462	0.188	0.000
Latvia	11,167	0.394	0.041
Estonia	8,537	0.980	0.000
Lithuania	8,509	0.742	0.000
EU15	28,586,140	0.165	0.073

Source: Berger (2007)

supply the majority of banking needs, especially when the countries did not have a long history of financial intermediation.

1.3 The Effects of Market Integration When There Is Financial Intermediation

Although an increase in financial integration is commonly believed to have a positive influence on the banking system, the exact results need to be investigated, especially when there is financial intermediation. The effects on the credit markets will depend upon the economic environment that the banking systems are operating in, especially the initial conditions. The CEEC's are of particular interest as both their goods and banking markets were liberalised in a relatively short period, and to varying degrees these changes overlapped one another. The following theoretical analysis provides a framework to identify the outcome on the financial sector both when goods and banking markets are liberalised and where market integration is likely to influence the returns banks receive both on loans to enterprises and to investments in subsidiaries. The theoretical model of financial intermediation will be used to provide us with insight as to what happened in the banking sector when eight of the CEECs entered the European Union in May 2004.

1.3.1 Two Models of Banking Under Asymmetric Information[1]

Stiglitz and Weiss (1981) considered the case where borrowers' type or actions were not observable by banks, though the outcomes were. They showed that in this environment the standard debt contract creates different incentives for the bank and the borrowing firm. The form of the contract gives firms a larger share of the upside outcomes, while their downside risk is bounded by the potential loss of their collateral. The bank, by contrast, is interested in the return of the capital lent and the associated interest, and is thus more concerned with the lower end of the firm's distribution of returns when firms are more likely to default. The form of the contract thus causes risk-neutral firms to act as if' they are risk lovers, while risk-neutral banks act as if' they are risk averse. Thus, for example, in the case of their adverse selection model where firms differ according to risk (a characteristic which banks cannot observe in order to discriminate against riskier borrowers ex ante), banks are conscious that their choice of interest rate may affect the characteristics of the pool of borrowers which approaches them for loans. In particular, as the rate of interest rises, only the riskier firms have the incentive to borrow, while relatively safe firms drop out of the market.[2] Thus, while the higher borrowing rate of interest increases the expected return on all repaid loans, the bank's portfolio of loans will have a higher proportion of riskier projects (due to the nature of the debt contract) which will lower expected profits. This means that the total profit function may be a non-monotonic function of the borrowing interest rate. This paper employs the simple case where the bank's profit function has an internal maximum as a function of the borrowing interest rate, as in Fig. 1.1, and, since the borrowing interest rate cannot be raised to clear the market if demand for funds exceeds supply, credit-rationing occurs.[3]

By contrast, Williamson (1986) considers the case where the outcomes of projects are not costlessly observable by banks. Thus firms have an incentive to claim bankruptcy and banks must incur a cost in monitoring the outcomes of

[1]See Hillier and Ibrahimo (1993) for a comprehensive survey of this literature.

[2]In both Stiglitz–Weiss and Williamson, firms do not have an alternative source of additional funds.

[3]Whether there is rationing or not in this model depends on the amount of funds agents are willing to supply as a function of the zero-profit deposit interest rate implied by the maximum borrowing rate of interest. However, even if credit is not rationed the equilibrium level of investment will be less than the optimum (see Hillier & Ibrahimo op cit). While the analysis in this paper is presented in the context of equilibrium credit-rationing as in the original Stiglitz and Weiss and Williamson papers, it is easily extended to the case where rationing does not occur. In particular, the main results do not depend on the credit-rationing assumption [see Ryan (2007)].

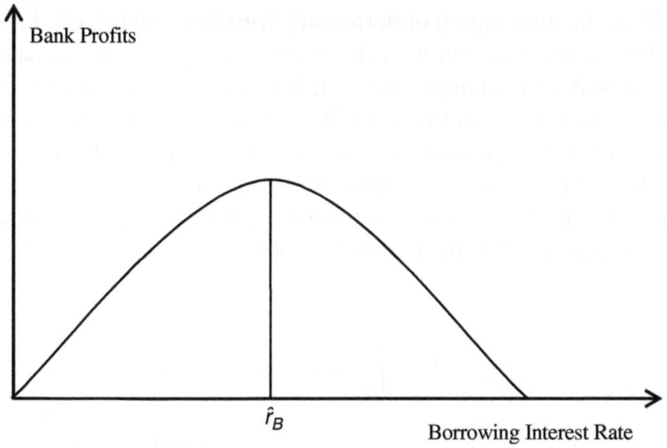

Fig. 1.1 Bank profits and borrowing interest rates

defaulting firms. In Williamson if a bank raises its interest rate, then this increases each firm's total repayment and hence the probability that it will claim that it cannot pay. At some point the costs incurred by the bank in monitoring the veracity of the defaulting firms' claims outweighs the revenue gains as a result of the interest rate rise, once again giving rise to a profit function like the one depicted in Fig. 1.1 above.

The key question addressed by the current paper is effectively: How does joining the EU Single Market for goods (strictly a move from autarky to free trade in goods) or allowing free trade in financial services (strictly allowing free trade in financial capital to purchase a share in an EU15/CEEC bank) affect this diagram and what are the implications of these shifts?

1.3.2 Freer Trade in Goods

In order to illustrate the basic point of this note first consider the case where trade in goods is liberalized in the Stiglitz–Weiss adverse selection model. Suppose initially that there are two autarkic economies populated by many firms with projects of varying risks, and in each country firms can borrow from one of the perfectly-competitive domestic banks in order to finance their project. The first issue we wish to consider is what happens when these firms are permitted to trade their goods more freely on the world market. In Cole and Obstfeld (1991), price-movements under freer trade provide insurance against industry-specific supply shocks and thus here we assume that a firm's return risk has an aggregate component that can be diversified by trade. Thus, trade reduces the variance of project returns of all firms in each industry. In this model, from the bank's perspective, this is equivalent to a left-ward shift in the distribution of borrowing firms indexed by risk. Free trade will also reduce the variance of returns if there are country-specific demand shocks as would the removal of exchange rate risk following the formation of a single-currency union. Newbery and Stiglitz (1983) essentially argue the converse case; that freer goods trade exposes domestic industries to the full effect of country-specific supply shocks in non-specialized industries; similarly, trade might increase aggregate uncertainty due to lack of information about foreign markets. However, the non-equivalence result to be derived below does not depend on which scenario prevails.[4]

$$\overline{\rho}(\hat{r}_B, r_D) = \int_{\hat{\phi}}^{\infty} \rho(\hat{r}_B, r_D, \phi) g(\phi) d\phi. \quad (1.1)$$

Total expected bank profits depend on the profitability of the loans to firms which choose to borrow, $\rho(\hat{r}_B, r_D, \phi)$, (where project risk is indexed by ϕ), and the density of these firms in the economy, $g(\phi)$, and greater ϕ corresponds to greater risk in the sense of mean-preserving spreads; $\hat{r}_B$ is the equilibrium borrowing rate of interest and r_D is the deposit rate of interest; and $\hat{\phi}$ is the critical level of riskiness such that a firm will only borrow from a bank if $\phi > \hat{\phi}$, and it rises as the borrowing rate of interest rises.

The effect of freer trade on the variance of project outcomes can be represented by inserting a shift parameter, η, in the distribution function G so that it takes the form:

$$G(\eta) = \int_{0}^{\infty} g(\phi, \eta) d\phi \quad (1.2)$$

and η captures the fact that the density (number) of firms with a given variance can change. The Cole–Obstfeld case of goods-market integration can thus be represented by a reduction in η where it is assumed that the distribution function $G(\eta)$ has the property that $G' \leq 0$, that is, for any given level of risk (variance), the cumulative density of the firms with risk greater than that level falls as the index of market segregation, η, falls (or the distribution function moves to the left).[5]

The initial impact on expected bank returns (holding the original borrowing interest rate $\hat{r}_B$ and hence the critical level of variance $\hat{\phi}$ constant) can be seen by differentiating (1.1) and (1.2) with respect to η, which yields:

[4]Stiglitz–Weiss actually use the average return for the bank, (their (1.7)). However, it is simpler to use the total profit function of the bank by including the cost to the bank of the loan in evaluating their return from a project, $\rho(\hat{r}_B, r_D, \phi)$. The competitive assumption requires that (1.1) should equal zero in equilibrium and thus determines the deposit interest rate, r_D, which will be exogenous for a representative bank.

[5]The existing degree of international asset trade (if any) is held constant in this exercise.

$$\left.\frac{d\overline{\rho}}{d\eta}\right|_{\hat{r}_B} = \int_{\hat{\phi}}^{\infty} \rho(\hat{r}_B, r_D, \phi) \frac{\partial g(\phi, \eta)}{\partial \eta} d\phi. \tag{1.3}$$

The term on the right-hand side of this expression is the change in the cumulative profitability (to the bank) of the firms now seeking funding. Its sign depends crucially on the form of the distribution function of firms indexed by risk, G. It essentially captures two effects and the intuition behind the ambiguity is as follows:

Recall that a bank's portfolio consists of some profitable and some unprofitable loans since it cannot discriminate (ex ante) on the basis of risk due to asymmetric information. Firstly, the reduction in the riskiness of firms' returns raises the expected payoff on all existing loans to the bank, but reduces it to firms, ceteris paribus. Secondly, and as a consequence of this, some firms will drop out of the credit market, and these firms will be the ones with the lower variance or the 'safer firms'. Thus, while the risk characteristics of all firms in the economy have fallen, the distribution of (ex ante identical) firms remaining in the market for funds *may* be such that those likely to pay positive profits are no longer sufficiently numerous to offset those likely to pay negative profits and, hence, total expected profits may fall from the banks' perspective.

Whether bank profits rise or fall initially is crucial as it ultimately determines whether there are welfare gains or losses as a consequence of trade liberalization. For example, if bank profits rise initially as a result of liberalization this induces a rise in the deposit interest rate until a new competitive equilibrium with zero profits is established. The rise in the deposit interest rate in turn increases the supply of deposits.[6] The overall welfare surplus (though not necessarily its distribution) is determined by the supply of these deposits in the same way as any quantitative restriction, such as a quota or VER, determines the surplus to be distributed in standard trade theory.[7] Thus, the induced rise in the supply of deposits is a sufficient condition for welfare gains.

Thus a rise in deposits supplied induced by the initial increase in bank profitability is a sufficient condition for welfare gains.

If returns per project are uniformly distributed over an interval and projects are uniformly distributed over an interval of risk, bank profits unambiguously rise. A counter example can easily be generated by employing a discrete distribution of firms and projects outcomes and details of both cases are included in Appendix 1.

In addition to the change in profits experienced by the bank as a result of trade liberalization, it can also respond to the shift in η by altering the borrowing interest

[6] Assuming a positively sloped supply of deposit funds.

[7] See Ryan (2007).

rate it charges, and consequently, the mix of applicants and the expected yield per loan. Differentiating (1.1) and (1.2) with respect to the interest rate yields an implicit function for $\hat{r}_B$,

$$\frac{d\overline{\rho}}{d\hat{r}_B} = -g(\hat{\phi},\eta)\rho(\hat{r}_B, r_D, \hat{\phi})\frac{d\hat{\phi}}{d\hat{r}_B} + \int_{\hat{\phi}}^{\infty} \frac{\partial \rho(\hat{r}_B, r_D, \hat{\phi})}{\partial r_B} g(\varphi,\eta) d\hat{\phi} = 0. \qquad (1.4)$$

This says that at the margin, the loss of the safe projects, due to the increase in r, must be equal to the extra profits from all remaining funded projects. Taking the total derivative of (1.4) yields:

$$\frac{\partial \hat{r}_B}{\partial \eta} = \frac{\hat{\rho}(\hat{r}_B, r_D, \hat{\phi})\frac{\partial g(\hat{\phi},\eta)}{\partial \eta}\frac{d\hat{\phi}}{d\hat{r}_B} - \int_{\hat{\phi}}^{\infty} \frac{\partial \rho(\hat{r}_B, r_D, \phi)}{\partial r_B}\frac{\partial g(\phi,\eta)]}{\partial \eta} d\phi}{\frac{\partial^2 \overline{\rho}}{\partial \hat{r}_B^2}}. \qquad (1.5)$$

The sign of this expression once again depends on the shape of the density function and the effect of the shift on it. The bank's marginal condition (1.4) sets the borrowing interest rate r_B such that the loss of the marginal safest projects, due to the increase in r_B, is offset by the additional interest payments on all remaining funded projects. A linear leftward-shift in the distribution, due to trade liberalization, reduces the number of projects to the right of $\hat{\phi}$ which can offset the loss of the marginal safe projects at $\hat{\phi}$, however, the density at every ϕ including $\hat{\phi}$ has also changed. It is obvious that any result can obtain and the precise effect depends on the exact distribution and the result is independent of the profit result. For the case where firms' profits and their risk are uniformly distributed, as in Appendix 1, the first term in (1.4) is zero and the second term is unaltered save for the loss of the marginal returns on the most risky projects which are no longer included as the distribution shifts left. Thus in this case and the case alluded to in footnote 7 banks reduce the borrowing interest rate.

However, for our purposes the change in the rate is not particularly important. As was pointed out above, if profits rise (fall) this results in a rise (fall) in r_D and an unambiguous rise (fall) in depositors and aggregate welfare. Whether or not borrowers as a group share in a welfare rise (fall) depends on what happens to their share of the surplus which, in turn, depends on the elasticity of the deposit supply curve and hence what happens to $\hat{r}_B$. Any change in the equilibrium borrowing interest rate merely determines how the total gains or losses are distributed between depositors, existing borrowers, new borrowers receiving a loan and the size of the pool of unsatisfied borrowers.

As we will see below, the key difference between liberalizing trade in goods and financial capital/assets is that here trade alters the distribution of the firms' returns and hence the incentive of safer firms to approach banks for debt and, as a consequence the banks' expected profits. Trade in financial capital does not affect the returns of firms, merely the bank's portfolio variance and, hence, there is no ambiguity in the results for freer trade in financial capital.[8] As a consequence, trades in goods and financial capital are not substitutes in this context. Furthermore, note that the ambiguous result does not depend on the *direction* which trade shifts the distribution of firms' returns. Thus, welfare can fall even if the variance of project returns falls (à la Cole–Obstfeld), and conversely it is possible for welfare to rise even though the variance of project returns rise (à la Newbery-Stiglitz).

Free trade in goods in the alternative Williamson model of financial intermediation can have also ambiguous results but in this case it depends exclusively on whether trade reduces or raises the variance of project outcomes.[9] If the effect of trade is as posited by Cole–Obstfeld and the variance of firms returns fall, then the probability of default falls and reduces the expected cost of monitoring. The consequent rise in bank profits results in a higher deposit interest rate, an increase in the supply of loans and a rise in welfare. If, however, freer trade leads to the Newbery–Stiglitz result, that is, the variance of project returns rises, then the converse results occur and welfare falls. Thus, despite the fact that freer trade in goods only affects the distribution of firms' returns and banks and firms are risk neutral, liberalization still affects welfare through its effect on banks' expected monitoring costs.

However, as was suggested at the outset, all three types of asymmetric information problems are likely to be present in the real world, and thus the Williamson result may be subservient to the Stiglitz–Weiss effect. That is, the bank may find that although the number of firms it has to monitor falls, the revenue from firms repaying has fallen by more as safer firms leave the market.

1.3.3 *Freer Trade in Intermediated Financial Capital*

The ambiguity of the results above contrasts with the effects of freer trade in intermediated financial capital. This may involve domestic banks directly lending to foreign enterprises from a domestic base or via a subsidiary branch located in the foreign market (freer trade being the right of establishment), lending to a domestic holding firm to purchase a foreign enterprise, or the purchase of shares in foreign banks.[10] In order to see the effect of this trade, suppose that both countries are completely identical, that the distribution of returns per project and the distribution of projects are the same across countries, but that there are specific shocks

[8]As we will see below the change in portfolio variance alleviates the asymmetric information problem and thus the banks' expected profit is still affected though in an entirely predictable way.

[9]The model is not presented in detail here as the result is effectively derived in Williamson (1986) pp. 176–177 and it is simply a matter of interpreting it in this context. Trade liberalization (when project variances fall) is effectively equivalent to his positive business cycle shock.

[10]For more on the trade related aspects of establishment versus direct lending as a means of servicing foreign markets see Jones and Ruane (1990).

associated with each project which are not perfectly correlated internationally. The absence of perfect correlation thus gives rise to the desire for international lending.[11] This section uses a very simple model to illustrate why goods and financial capital/asset trades are not substitutes and then goes on to show how risk-pooling can partially alleviate the asymmetric information problem.

Why are the two forms of trade not equivalent here? Assume initially that international asset trades are governed by capital controls in both countries which restrict the fraction of the total loan portfolio of a bank held in the form of foreign loans, α. Freer capital movement is then studied in the context of a relaxation of the (binding) constraint α.[12] Given the assumptions above, if there were no capital flow restrictions, banks would hold a perfectly diversified international portfolio of loans ($\alpha = 1/2$), and there would be a reduction in the variance of the profits on the bank's portfolio of projects. However, as we noted in Sect. 1.3 (i) above, in these models banks are risk neutral and, thus, while they care about the variance of *project* returns, since they affect the probability of repayment or monitoring and, thus, their expected return, they do not care about *portfolio* variance. Thus, freer trade in assets in this simple case does not affect interest rates or lending in any way. The key to the difference between the two different forms of liberalization is the fact that freer trade in goods affect project variances while freer trade in assets only affects a bank's portfolio variance (which in this simple case is irrelevant).

However, in general it is more plausible to assume that banks do in fact care about portfolio variance. What then is the effect of freer trade in financial capital? Risk-pooling as a result of liberalizing international lending offers a new source of gains from trade as it admits the possibility of a trade-off by the bank between lower portfolio variance and higher project variance.

One simple way of capturing risk-aversion here is to make the additional assumption that banks must keep reserves which are related to the degree of risk exposure of the bank.[13]

Thus (1.1) can be re-written as:

$$\overline{\rho}(r_B,\phi,\alpha) = \int_{\hat{\phi}}^{\infty} [(1-\alpha)\,\rho_H\,(r_B,\phi) + \alpha\,\rho_F\,(r_B,\phi)]g(\phi)d\phi - r_B\,k \times \left[\sigma_{\rho_I}{}^2\,(r_B,\alpha)\right] \tag{1.6}$$

[11]See French and Poterba (1991) on unexploited correlations in international returns.

[12]Alternatively, they may set up a foreign subsidiary or they can simply buy a share in a foreign bank.

[13]This of course admits the possibility that a lower portfolio variance will affect banks expected returns (rather than their welfare). Liberalising assets trades will have a direct effect on bank profits in addition to the possibility identified above as we will see shortly. Making banks explicitly risk averse would have similar results.

where the first term is the standard total expected profit on the portfolio of home and foreign loans indexed by the subscripts H and F respectively, and the second term is the opportunity cost to the bank of holding capital reserves, r_B, multiplied by the quantity of capital reserves k( ) it must hold.[14] The quantity of capital reserves a bank must hold is a function of its portfolio risk $\sigma_{\rho_I}{}^2(\hat{r}_B, \alpha)$. Portfolio risk is composed of two elements, a non-diversifiable element which is increasing in the riskiness of the projects funded (and thus $\hat{r}_B$), and a diversifiable element due to non-perfectly correlated international shocks and the risk depends negatively on the share of foreign assets in the total portfolio.[15]

The change in expected profits over all financed projects as a result of allowing increased domestic financing of foreign projects (a rise in α), holding the borrowing interest rate constant is:[16]

$$\left.\frac{d\bar{\rho}}{d\alpha}\right|_{\hat{r}_B, r_D} = -\hat{r}_B \frac{\partial k}{\partial \sigma_{\rho_I}{}^2} \frac{\partial \sigma_{\rho_I}{}^2}{\partial \alpha} \geq 0 \tag{1.7}$$

$$\left(\left.\frac{d\bar{\rho}}{d\alpha}\right|_{\hat{r}_B, r_D} = (-)(\hat{r}_B)(+)(-) \geq 0\right)$$

The effect of the regulatory relaxation is an increase in the share of foreign loans in the banks' portfolio, resulting in a lower portfolio variance and thus lower reserves and hence to a reduction in total reserve costs and higher bank profits.

[14] An alternative formulation would be to model a transactions cost on the acquisition and annual maintenance of foreign loans. Agents would then optimally choose α taking into consideration the additional cost of holding foreign loans as compared with their contribution to reducing the need for costly reserves. Asset trade liberalization can then be studied as a reduction in the transactions cost and the results, while more complicated, are essentially the same as the model considered here.

[15] The borrowing rate of interest is a determinant of the variance as a rise in the rate reduces the number of safe borrowers. This raises the portfolio variance for any given quantity of loans offered (which is determined exogenously by the supply of deposits given the deposit interest rate).

[16] Note that the effect of the change in α in the first term of the profit (1.4), can be ignored due to the symmetry in H and F and the fact that the weights sum to 1. Thus, in the subsequent analysis this term is written without reference to the weights or country subscript.

This initial effect on profits is a consequence of our method of modelling banks as caring about reserves rather than risk explicitly.

To see the additional effect identified at the outset of this section note that once again the bank can also respond to liberalization by altering the interest rate it charges. This effect can be deduced by differentiating the first order condition for the choice of $\hat{r}_B$, given profit maximization by the banks.

From (1.6) the first-order condition for a bank setting borrowing interest rates given a particular restriction on holding foreign loans is:

$$\begin{aligned} \frac{d\bar{\rho}_I}{d\hat{r}_B} = &- \rho(\hat{r}_B, \hat{\phi}) g(\hat{\phi}) \frac{\partial \phi}{\partial \hat{r}_B} + \int_{\hat{\phi}}^{\infty} \frac{\partial \rho(\hat{r}_B, \phi)}{\partial \hat{r}_B} g(\phi) d\phi \\ &- k({\sigma_{\rho_I}}^2) - \hat{r}_B \frac{\partial k}{\partial {\sigma_{\rho_I}}^2} \frac{\partial {\sigma_{\rho_I}}^2}{\partial \hat{r}_B} = 0. \end{aligned} \tag{1.8}$$

The first two terms of (1.8) are the standard (Stiglitz–Weiss) trade-off between safer firms opting-out of the loans market on the one hand, and higher profits per loan on the other. The final two terms are: the increased opportunity cost of holding existing reserves as r_B rises and, the increase in reserves required given that the quantity of loans on offer is now allocated to a pool of relatively more risky borrowers as safer borrowers leave the market. Note that these latter terms reduce the equilibrium choice of r_B here (and in equilibrium r_D), compared with the case where banks do not have to hold reserves and hence rationing is greater in this model as one would expect. The change in the equilibrium borrowing rate of interest as a consequence of liberalizing asset trade can be seen by taking the total derivative of (1.8), which yields:

$$\frac{\partial \hat{r}_B}{\partial \alpha} = \frac{\dfrac{\partial k}{\partial \left({\sigma_{\rho_I}}^2\right)} \dfrac{\partial \left({\sigma_{\rho_I}}^2\right)}{\partial \alpha} + \hat{r}_B \left[\dfrac{\partial^2 k}{\partial \left({\sigma_{\rho_I}}^2\right)^2} \dfrac{\partial \left({\sigma_{\rho_I}}^2\right)}{\partial \hat{r}_B} \dfrac{\partial \left({\sigma_{\rho_I}}^2\right)}{\partial \alpha} + \dfrac{\partial k}{\partial \left({\sigma_{\rho_I}}^2\right)} \dfrac{\partial^2 \left({\sigma_{\rho_I}}^2\right)}{\partial \hat{r}_B \partial \alpha} \right]}{\dfrac{\partial^2 \bar{\rho}_I}{\partial \hat{r}_B^2}} > 0. \tag{1.9}$$

The denominator is negative (from the second order conditions for the optimal choice of $\hat{r}_B$) as is the first term of the numerator which is the fall in reserves due to the increase in the share of foreign assets in the portfolio. The derivative as a whole will be positive, given the plausible assumptions that the *responsiveness* of the weighted portfolio variance to a rise in $\hat{r}_B$ is independent of the change in the international composition of the portfolio $\left(\dfrac{\partial^2 \left({\sigma_{\rho_I}}^2\right)}{\partial \hat{r}_B \, \partial \alpha} = 0 \right)$, and that the quantity of required reserves is either linear or rising in overall portfolio riskiness $\left(\frac{\partial^2 k}{\partial\left(\sigma_{\rho_I}{}^2\right)^2} \geq 0\right)$. Thus, $\left(\frac{\partial \hat{r}_B}{\partial \alpha} = \frac{(+)(-) + \hat{r}_B\left[(\geq 0)(+)(-) + (+)(=0)\right]}{(-)} > 0\right)$.

Thus, the relaxation of the foreign lending constraint induces banks to raise the borrowing rate, and hence the deposit rate and overall welfare. The explanation for the result is as follows: Prior to liberalizing financial capital/asset trades, if the bank increased its interest rate it had to balance higher returns on repaid loans against the fact that it was faced with proportionately more riskier borrowers as the safer firms dropped out of the market. With free trade in financial capital, it appears to the bank that its (international) portfolio of borrowing firms is now relatively safer than the domestic pool available before, and thus the loss of some safe borrowers at the margin (if it raises the interest rate) is less significant than before. Thus the banks have an incentive to raise the borrowing interest rate, and consequently the riskiness of project returns, as it can offset some of this additional risk due to the imperfect correlation of international project returns, and thus raise their expected profits.

Thus, freer trade in intermediated capital has two effects in general: It leads to a direct impact on welfare via a reduction in portfolio variance (and hence in this model on the need to hold risk-related reserves) and indirectly as it allows banks to trade off some of the reduction in risk for higher expected returns. Thus, freer trade in intermediated capital partially alleviates the asymmetric information problem since banks can attract more funds (offer a higher deposit interest rate) as a result of taking on a portfolio of (internationally, imperfectly-correlated) riskier loans and welfare rises.

In the specific example presented here, relaxing financial capital export controls leads to a reduction in portfolio variance (and hence a reduction in the reserve requirement) *and* a rise in the borrowing interest rate, both leading to a rise in profits and hence the deposit interest rate, a fall in credit rationing as the supply of credit is increased, and a rise in overall welfare. By contrast with the liberalization of trade in goods, the pooling of portfolio risk only affects the bank and does not induce any (first-order) response on the part of firms which can affect the pool of risky firms which banks face. Hence, there is no ambiguity about the results in this case.

1.4 Financial Integration in CEECs: The Law of One Price?

According the theoretical framework of financial intermediaries, there is some ambiguity of how the difference between the borrowing and lending rate of interest is affected by an increase in goods and capital market integration. The outcome will depend upon the characteristics of the banking sector in a country, in particular the effect of trade in goods on the returns of direct loans to enterprises by banks and on whether banks have been able to diversify internationally and improve the portfolio of borrowers via the removal of constraints on international markets.

Financial integration is not directly observable but most proxies are based on the law of one price, for example the cross-sectional variation of interest rates across countries (Baele et al. 2004). While the European Central Bank provides this information for the EU(15), little attention has been given to the new entrants to the European Union and the standard deviation of interest rates across countries is not readily available.

The banking sectors of the accession countries are still rather underdeveloped, although entry into the European Union should have provided some impetus for financial integration. However, it is generally recognised that the retail lending industry is less susceptible to international competition as there are advantages to being located close to the borrowers. Table 1.5 provides an overview of the average interest rates charged to lenders over three periods: 1994–1998, 1999–2003 and 2004–2008. The three epochs have been chosen to capture the various stages of the development process impacting on the banking sectors on each CEEC. During the first period the majority of the new entrants were undergoing the transition to a market economy and as a consequence their retail lending sectors were underdeveloped, with a considerable amount of risk associated with lending business. Only in Malta and Cyprus were rates approaching those of the EU average, which due to data availability are represented by France and The Netherlands.

The second group of years is from 1999 to 2003, thought of as the consolidation period, and there was a reduction in the costs of borrowing in all economies. The largest reductions were in those countries in the second wave of entrants into the EU, Bulgaria and Romania. The banks in the Baltic States reduced the interest rates by the largest proportions, with the cost of credit in Latvia and Lithuania being approximately 30% of the rate in the first period. Borrower interest rates again fell in the third period, by a greater proportion than in the EU15. However, the size of the decrease was greatly reduced as most of the countries had undergone the major

Table 1.5 Rate of interest for borrowers in new EU countries

	1994–1998	1999–2003	2004–2008
Bulgaria	171.49	10.74	9.36
Cyprus	8.48	7.52	6.99
Czech Republic	12.92	7.14	5.87
Estonia	17.58	7.70	5.97
Hungary	27.27	12.17	9.62
Latvia	32.86	10.12	8.41
Lithuania	31.33	9.51	6.11
Malta	7.91	6.75	5.74
Poland	31.68	14.93	6.63
Romania	67.19	45.15	17.52
Slovak Republic	15.99	13.18	7.53
Slovenia	26.21	13.42	7.31
France	7.28	6.65	6.60
Netherlands	6.88	4.04	3.64

Source: see Data Appendix

Table 1.6 Deposit rate of interest in new EU countries

	1994–1998	1999–2003	2004–2008
Bulgaria	42.32	3.00	3.37
Cyprus	6.32	5.37	3.58
Czech Republic	7.32	2.82	1.30
Estonia	8.11	3.42	3.30
Hungary	19.62	9.09	7.46
Latvia	13.88	4.18	4.20
Lithuania	19.26	2.95	2.89
Malta	4.54	4.42	2.93
Poland	23.52	9.42	2.91
Romania	46.42	27.22	7.56
Slovak Republic	11.46	8.25	3.53
Slovenia	16.46	8.26	3.46
France	3.88	2.80	2.53
Netherlands	3.78	2.80	3.11

Source: see Data Appendix

changes to market economies and they were beginning to undertake policies required for accession to EU membership. The borrowing rates in Poland, Slovakia, Slovenia and Romania were below 60% of those in the previous period.

The interest rates on savings accounts (Table 1.6) varied in the CEECs during the first stage of the transition period, with the rates paid in Bulgaria, Romania and Poland being over 20%. The Czech Republic and Estonia appear to be outliers as the deposit rates are similar to those in Cyprus and Malta. During the period of 1999–2003 only Romania had lending rates over 10% and six nations experienced rates below 5%, suggesting that convergence in financial markets.

Although interest rates in Hungary and Romania appear to be significantly above the rest of the transition economies, the deposit rates in 7 CEECs had approached the rates on the EU15 average by the time the first wave of countries had entered the EU in 2004. Financial intermediaries in Bulgaria and Latvia were higher in the final period than between 1999 and 2003, similar to the pattern witnessed in the Netherlands. The deposit interest rates in Poland, Lithuania were below those in the Netherlands but not the average in France. This provides *prima facia* evidence that the transition process of the banking sector had been mainly completed by the time the first wave of countries joined the European Union.

1.5 Econometric Results

The interest rate margin, the difference between the lending and borrowing interest rates, appears to not to be uniform among CEECs even though the each country's banking systems was becoming financially integrated with the old members of the European Union. The aim of the empirical research is to investigate whether the cause of variations in the interest margin, both between countries and over time, can be explained using quarterly data from *IMF Financial Statistics*. Although higher frequency data were available, a number of the potential explanatory variables only existed quarterly, for example trade data and GDP.

The general model considered is

$$(r_B - r_D)_t = \beta_0 + \beta_1 \Delta_4 \text{In}GDP_t + \beta_2 \Delta_4 \text{In}P_t + \beta_3 Open_t + \beta_4 \Delta_4 \text{In}\left(\frac{SP}{P}\right)_t + \beta_5 DumEU_t + \varepsilon_t$$

where the interest differential $(r_B - r_D)$ is believed to be determined by the annual growth rate in the country, $\Delta_4\text{In}GDP_t$. Higher economic growth is expected to be a sign of greater economic progress and should result in a decrease in difference between the borrower and deposit interest rates. The rate of inflation should have a positive effect on the gap between interest rates as the cost of borrowing will be adjusted more quickly than the payment received by depositors. When available, the annual growth of real share prices is included as a regressor to capture the financial developments in each country. Capital gains in the stock market could also be a measure of financial wealth and used as collateral, which should narrow the gap between the two interest rates. The idea that economic integration is combined with financial integration is receiving some credence in the literature (Schiavo 2008). A measure of openness, the sum of exports and imports to GDP, is used to proxy the degree to which each economy is influenced by trade. As the theory indicates, there is some ambiguity as to the effect of economic integration on the interest rate differential and it is one of key issues investigated. The dummy variable, *DumEU*, represent full EU membership of the accession countries in May 2004. Although the dummy variable could be viewed as a relatively crude measure of the trade integration effects, it will also capture political commitment of the transition countries and provide an indication to the direction of future economic policy, which could influence the interest rates gap.

The aim of the econometric work is to identify if general economic variables play a role in determining the difference between the borrowing and lending interest rates. In particular, emphasis is placed on the sign of the effect of economic integration, captured by the trade-to-GDP ratio and EU membership, and whether the variables are statistically significant. Care has been taken when specifying the above equation to make sure that all the explanatory variables are stationary, which rules out including level variables, such as real GDP per capita, in the regression equation as the divergence between interest rates does not display signs of possessing a unit root.[17] Where possible, the model was estimated from first quarter 1996 to third quarter 2008 as the economic upheaval was assumed to be over by the start date. It was important to continue the sample period to as late as possible to see if any effects from the entry into the EU in May 2004. The estimated parameters for the CEECs are presented in Table 1.7, with t-statistics in parentheses.

[17] Augmented Dickey–Fuller tests and Phillips–Perron tests for all the series for each country are available from the authors on request.

Table 1.7 Estimated coefficients on the difference between borrower and lender interest rates

	Hungary	Czech Rep.	Poland	Slovakia	Slovenia	Latvia	Lithuania	Estonia
Constant	5.222	5.726	10.343	9.516	8.939	16.801	13.187	3.827
	(4.11)	(8.20)	(5.91)	(5.78)	(13.1)	(3.79)	(10.5)	(1.77)
$\Delta_4 lnGDP_t$	−0.197	0.171	0.189	−0.267	−0.349	0.156	−0.283	−0.274
	(−1.14)	(2.08)	(1.40)	(−1.75)	(−2.14)	(0.58)	(−2.65)	(−1.52)
$\Delta_4 lnP_t$	0.388	0.229	−0.051	0.124	−0.352	0.348	0.094	−0.296
	(5.03)	(4.12)	(−0.56)	(0.68)	(−2.70)	(1.34)	(1.92)	(−1.61)
$\Delta_4 ln(Ps/P)_t$			−0.048		0.0001	−0.064		−1.717
			(−3.13)		(−0.06)	(−3.74)		(−2.52)
$Open_t$	−2.264	−1.676	−8.308	−3.283	−33.856	−16.76	−7.445	1.754
	(−2.76)	(−2.76)	(−3.17)	(−2.83)	(−2.97)	(−2.43)	(−4.44)	(0.89)
$DumEU_t$	−0.118	0.350	0.159	0.720	−0.807	−0.366	−1.404	−1.652
	(−0.33)	(1.53)	(0.34)	(1.41)	(−1.95)	(−0.30)	(−2.86)	(−4.09)
R^2	0.582	0.523	0.725	0.324	0.718	0.525	0.829	0.639
SER	0.635	0.408	0.720	1.120	0.611	1.789	0.889	1.186
Sample	1996 (1) −2008 (2)	1996(1) −2007(2)	1996(1) −2006(4)	1996 (1) −2008 (3)	1998 (1) −2008 (3)	1997(3) −2008(3)	1996 (1) −2008 (3)	1998(1) −2008(3)

The effect of the annual growth of GDP on the difference between the borrowing and lending interest rate is mixed. This might not be surprising as the parameters should be viewed as coming from a reduced-form model of interest rate setting. Higher growth of income could increase the demand for loanable funds but it could also raise the supply of funds. The net effect will depend on the financial systems in each country, suggesting that it is unlikely that a pattern in the coefficients will be observed.

No discernible pattern can be observed for the effect of annual inflation. The outcome is likely to be dependent on the inertia in the financial markets and how quickly banks were able and prepared to adjust interest rates as inflation changed. This is an important issue as the majority of the accession countries suffered high and variable inflation rates in the transition process to a market economy. As the inflation experience differed between countries, it is unlikely for there to be a uniform effect of inflation on the interest rate gap; the high negative responses in Slovenia and Estonia appear surprising.

Unfortunately consistently measured share prices indices were only available for a limited number of countries for the sample period. While the data exist for the 2000s, it was decided to estimate the equations from the mid-1990s. In Poland, Slovenia, Latvia and Estonia the growth of real share prices led to a narrowing of the gap between borrowing and lending rates, with only the effect in Slovenia being statistically insignificant. One explanation could be that financial deregulation in financial markets resulted in a stockmarket boom and increased competition in the retail banking sector. Equally the annual growth of real share prices might be due to takeover activity, particularly by non-domestic firms, which could be a sign of economic and financial integration.

With the exception of Estonia, there is strong support for the hypothesis that economic integration via trade results in greater financial integration. The more open the accession country the narrower the gap between borrowing and lending interest rates, suggesting that freer trade complements financial integration as discussed in the theoretical framework. Only in the cases of Lithuania, Estonia and Slovenia did entry into the European Union have a statistically significantly effect of reducing the interest margin. The impact was positive for the Czech Republic, Poland and Slovakia, although not statistically significant. These mixed findings are not surprising given that the CEECs would have started implementing policies before accession and the dummy variable is a rather crude measure to capture the regime shift on financial intermediaries.

1.6 Conclusion

We have investigated the important research and policy issue of why there is variation in the gap between the interest rate paid charged to borrowers and the interest rate paid to borrowers in markets in new EU member states a new set of indicators suggested by our theoretical model of intermediation. Our empirical findings suggest a strong role for openness in narrowing the interest rate margin, indicating that economic integration compliments financial integration. Exactly how this process works could be an area for further research into the banking system in CEECs. The penetration of foreign firms in Eastern Europe is higher than that in the EU15 countries and cross-border banking might a conduit for trade integration. It is impossible to disentangle such effects when working with aggregate data.

There is little direct evidence pointing to the entry into the European Union of the first wave of accession countries had an impact on each nation's banking system. The main effects on the financial intermediaries would be the harmonisation of regulations and the removal of government barriers. However, a high proportion of total assets the CEECs banking sectors came from the EU, which would suggest that the degree of financial integration was relatively high before 2004.

The strength of other parts of the financial sector, proxied by the growth of real share prices, may be an important consideration when focusing on the difference between borrowing and lending rates of interest and is an area where further research is required. It may be that spillovers exist between various parts of financial business and that know-how and techniques in one sector can be applied to banking. An alternative explanation may that as financial markets become more developed, more transactions take place and both the banking sector and the stock market become more efficient.

The analysis into the determinants of interest rate margins in the banking sector has strong policy implications. It suggests that allowing the entry of foreign banks into a country may not by itself generate greater financial efficiency. Opening up the country to the influence of international trade as it is important in reducing the gap between the cost of borrowing and the payment to depositors. It is hoped that narrowing the gap should lead to a more efficient and robust banking sector, resulting a better allocation of resources.

Appendix 1: Two Examples of the Effect on Banks' Profits as a Result of Freer Trade in Goods

Case 1: A rise in bank profits.

Consider the case of projects which are linearly and uniformly distributed across an interval of ϕ, that is, $g(\phi+\eta)=k$ for $\phi\varepsilon\ [0<\phi_l+\eta, \phi_u+\eta<\infty]$ where k is a constant $g(\phi+\eta)=0$ otherwise, and $\frac{\delta\rho(\hat{r}_B, r_D, \phi, \eta)}{\delta\eta}=O$. In other words the fall in η simply shifts the distribution leftwards and the profitability of the new density of firms at each ϕ is unchanged (holding r constant). Thus, between $\hat{\phi}$ and ϕ^* (the level of risk above which firms would be expected to yield negative expected profits) the density and profitability of projects is unchanged, while the cumulative density of projects above ϕ^* has fallen.

Thus the derivative in (1.3) is unambiguously negative. Hence, in this example profits for the banks rise as a result of goods market integration.

Case 2: A fall in bank profits.

Consider, three sets of firms with projects denoted by subscript $i\ \varepsilon\{1,2,3\}$, where each project has four possible discrete outcomes. There are two states which yield good returns, high, H, and very high, H + x which arise with probability, $p - q_i$, and q_i respectively. There are also two states which yield returns which result in no profit to the firm (though there will be some payment to the bank), low, L, and very low, L − x, which occur with probabilities $1 - p - q_i$, and q_i respectively. Differences in risk are captured by varying q_i, and $q_2 > q_1$ indicates that type 2 projects represent a mean preserving spread of returns of type 1 projects. The size of the loan is B and the collateral is C, both exogenously given.

The return to a firm of type i and a bank from funding firm i are:

$$\begin{aligned} &a)\ \pi_i=[H+x-B(1+\hat{r}_B)]\,q_i+[H-B(1+\hat{r}_B)](p-q_i)-C(1-p)\\ &b)\ \rho_i=(C+L-x)\,q_i+(C+L)(1-p-q_i)+B(1+\hat{r}_B)p, \end{aligned} \tag{1.10}$$

and $\pi_2 - \pi_1 = \rho_1 - \rho_2 = x(q_2 - q_1) > 0$, thus firms with the riskier (type 3) project have higher expected profits while banks prefer firms with the safest (type 1) projects. In Stiglitz–Weiss a bank can extract all the expected profit from an enterprises for the set of marginal borrowers (those with $\phi=\hat{\phi}$). Assume that q_1 is such that type 1 firms are marginal then from (1.10)(a):

$$\hat{r}_B=\frac{(H-B)p+xq_1-C(1-p)}{Bp}. \tag{1.11}$$

Substituting back into the expression for bank profits from each type of project yields:

$$\rho_i = \mathrm{Hp} + (1-\mathrm{p})\mathrm{L} - \mathrm{x}(\mathrm{q_i}-\mathrm{q_1}). \tag{1.12}$$

If bank (net) profits for project 3 are positive then there is no credit rationing problem, thus expected profits from project 3 must be negative if banks are lending to all types and credit is rationed, and total expected bank profits, $\bar{\rho} = 13\{\text{Hp} + (1-\text{p})\text{L}\} - \text{x}(\text{q}_2 - \text{q}_1) - \text{x}(\text{q}_3 - \text{q}_1)$, must be less than $\rho_1 + \rho_2$.

Suppose trade in goods is now allowed between the two countries and that as a result the probabilities associated with the extreme results fall to $\text{q}_\text{i} - \eta$, while the less extreme probabilities rise to $\text{p} - \text{q}_\text{i} + \eta$ and $1 - \text{p} - \text{q}_\text{i} + \eta$, respectively. At the original interest rate, (1.12) becomes

$$\rho_\text{i}|_\text{r} = \text{Hp} + (1-\text{p})\text{L} - \text{x}(\text{q}_\text{i} - \eta - \text{q}_1), \tag{1.13}$$

raising expected profits from type 3 projects, but driving type 1 firms out of the market (since their expected profits are now negative). Total expected profits can now rise or fall depending on the extent of $\text{x}\eta$. If the change in risk is sufficiently large such that type 2 and 3 firms are now as risky as type 2 and 1 firm used to be, then expected profits rise (since there are now no negative expected return firms receiving a loan) and the story is the same as case 1 above. There is no reason for this to happen however, and for small changes in risk (small η), total expected profits fall and may even be negative. In this discrete example, the banks would lower the interest rate to recapture the safer borrowers, resulting in a lower deposit rate of interest, a fall in the supply of deposits and hence, welfare.[18]

Appendix 2: Data

Notation	Variable	Source
r_B	Borrowers' rate of interest	IMF financial statistics
r_D	Depositors' rate of interest	
GDP_t	Real GDP	
P_t	GDP deflator	
Ps_t	Stock market index	
Open_t	Measure of openness, calculated as the sum of imports and exports over GDP	
DumEU_t	Dummy variable for EU membership, having the value of 1 from 2004 second quarter and 0 before that date	

References

Baele, L., Ferrando, A., Hordahl, P., Krylova, E., & Monnet, C. (2004). Measuring European financial integration. *Oxford Review of Economic Policy, 20*(4), 509–530.

Berger, A. (2007). Obstacles to a global banking system: 'Old Europe' versus 'New Europe'. *Journal of Banking and Finance, 31*, 1955–1973.

[18]In the continuous analogue of this problem there is no reason why the optimal interest rate change should induce the re-entry of all previous borrowers.

Brenton, P., & Gros, D. (1997). Trade reorientation and recovery in transition economies. *Oxford Review of Economic Policy, 13*(2), 65–76.
Cerutti, E., Dell'Ariccia, G. A., & Martinez Peria, M. (2007). How banks go abroad: branches or subsidiaries? *Journal of Banking and Finance, 31*, 1669–1692.
Cole, H. L., & Obstfeld, M. (1991). Commodity trade and international risk sharing. *Journal of Monetary Economics, 28*, 3–24.
French, K.R. and Poterba, J.M. (1991), "Investor Diversification and International Equity Markets," *American Economic Review: Papers and Proceedings*, pp. 222–226.
Hillier, B., & Ibrahimo, M. V. (1993). Asymmetric information and models of credit rationing. *Bulletin of Economic Research, 45*(4), 271–304.
Jones, R. W., & Ruane, F. (1990). Appraising the options for international trade in services. *Oxford Economic Papers, 42*(4), 672–678.
Kasman, A., & Yildirim, C. (2006). Cost and profit efficiencies in transition banking: the case of new EU members. *Applied Economics, 38*(9), 1079–1090.
Murinde, V., Agung, J., & Mullineux, A. (2000). Convergence of European financial systems: banks or equity markets. In M. M. Fischer & P. Nijkamp (Eds.), *Spatial dynamics of European integration*. Berlin: Springer.
Newbery, D., & Stiglitz, J. E. (1983). Pareto inferior trade. *Review of Economic Studies, 51*, 1–12.
Perotti, E. (1993). Bank lending in transition economies. *Journal of Banking and Finance, 17*, 1021–1032.
Roe, A., Siegelbaum, P. & King, T. (2000) *Analysing Financial Sector Transition: With special reference to the former Soviet Union* (Working Paper No. 499). World Bank.
Ryan, C. (1992). The integration of financial services and economic welfare. In L. A. Winters (Ed.), *Trade flows and trade policy after 1992*. Cambridge: Cambridge University Press.
Ryan, C., & Murinde, V. (2005). International banking: the influence of GATS and international prudential regulation. In S. Chirathivat, F. Knipping, C. Ryan, & P. J. J. Welfens (Eds.), *European Union and ASEAN: historical dimensions. Comparative analysis and politico-economic dynamics*. Heidelberg: Springer-Verlag.
Ryan, C. (2007). *Freer trade when capital is intermediated in a world with asymmetric information*. Birmingham, UK: University of Birmingham, Dept. of Economics Working Paper.
Schiavo, S. (2008). Financial integration, GDP correlation and the endogeneity of optimum currency areas. *Economica, 75*, 168–189.
Stiglitz, J. E., & Weiss, A. (1981). Credit rationing in markets with imperfect information. *American Economic Review, 71*(3), 393–410.
Thorne, A. (1993). Eastern Europe's experience with banking reform: is there a role for banks in the transition? *Journal of Banking and Finance, 17*, 959–1000.
Williamson, S. D. (1986). Costly monitoring, financial intermediation and equilibrium credit rationing. *Journal of Monetary Economics, 18*, 159–176.

Chapter 2
Interdependence Between Foreign Exchange Markets and Stock Markets in Selected European Countries

Mevlud Islami

2.1 Introduction

Since the 1970s the discussion about the interdependence between foreign exchange markets and stock markets has been the subject of many studies. In the late 1990s, it even experienced a further intensification due to the financial and currency crisis in Asia, with fast and massive adjustments in both foreign exchange markets and stock markets being observed. The more traditional perspective was to assume that the exchange rate could influence both stock prices and stock market indices. An increasing significance of capital movements and its influence onexchange rates has already been taken into account in various theoretical approaches, e.g. in the theory of uncovered interest rate parity. Dominance of capital movements of financial transactions relative to trade is obvious in many countries, and as investment in stocks is a key element of international capital movements it is crucial to consider the potential interdependence between stock prices and the exchange rate.

Stock market capitalisation experienced a huge increase over the past decade, particularly in Eastern European countries due to high portfolio capital inflows and in particular due to high Foreign Direct Investments (FDI). The impact of stock markets on foreign exchange markets could be relatively strong in Eastern European emerging countries as these capital markets are relatively underdeveloped and strong capital inflows due to reduced capital flow barriers – or favourable changes in expectations – could temporarily have a significant influence on nominal and real exchange rate movements. If portfolio investments or foreign direct investments concerns firms listed in stock markets, then capital inflows will have an impact on stock markets. In like manner, capital inflows will have an indirect effect to the extent that interest rates fall and hence stock market prices will rise (in line with CAPM).

An analysis of cohesion countries and accession countries offers an interesting opportunity to explore the links between the two markets in the context of EU

M. Islami
European Institute for International Economic Relations, University of Wuppertal, Wuppertal, Germany

P.J.J. Welfens and C. Ryan (eds.), *Financial Market Integration and Growth*,
DOI 10.1007/978-3-642-16274-9_2,

eastern enlargement. Furthermore, the EU financial market is probably more integrated than, for example, the Asian financial markets. The impact of the EU single market in general and of financial market integration in particular implies a reduction of barriers to capital flows; hence stronger links between the foreign exchange market and the stock market could result. As regards comparable newly industrialised Asian countries, significant results for such type of linkages were found in many studies (e.g. Granger et al. 2000; Amare and Mohsin 2000). Against this background it is interesting to analyze eastern European EU countries whose capital markets are still in a catching up process. Stronger links imply that central banks must also take this aspect into account when making decisions in terms of interest rate and money supply, as these decisions can have undesired impacts on the whole financial market. The links between the foreign exchange rate and stock market prices are particularly important in the context of the growing openness of eastern European countries and also because capital accumulation in the context of capital accumulation and catching-up will be reflected in the dynamics of large and medium firms quoted on the stock market.

In the following analysis the focus is on EU cohesion countries and selected post-socialist transition economies. The results of the subsequent analysis show that significant links exist for five countries (Ireland, Spain, Greece, Poland, and Hungary) in the short-term, where the stock market index Granger-causes the exchange rate. Thus the main channel for the eight countries considered is an impulse which runs from the stock market to the foreign exchange market. For Poland, additional long-term links exist with the same direction of causation.

The subsequent analysis is divided as follows: After the introduction a selective review of important literature is given in Sect. 2.2 before theoretical foundations and methods employed are discussed in Sects. 2.3 and 2.4, respectively. In Sect. 2.5, empirical results are presented with respect to the analysis of long-term and short-term links between foreign exchange markets and stock markets in selected cohesion and accession countries. Finally, the paper ends with a summary and some concluding remarks.

2.2 Selected Review of the Literature

Most of the analyses on the links between foreign exchange markets and stock markets have focussed either on the US during the 1980s and 1990s, the most developed capital market, or on South Eastern and South Asian countries (especially after the East-Asian crisis in 1997). During this time, both foreign exchange markets and stock markets experienced huge volatility.

The first study on the interdependence between foreign exchange markets and stock markets was carried out by Franck and Young (1972) who based their study on a simple correlation and regression analysis. They examined the repercussion of strong exchange rate volatility of foreign currencies with respect to the US dollar on stock prices of selected US multinational firms included in the S&P 500 and Dow-Jones index. No significant results could be found. After the collapse of the Bretton Woods System and therefore the correspondingly more volatile exchange rates, research on this topic advanced in various ways – e.g. the noteworthy study of Aggarwal (1981). The intuition for a link between the exchange rate and the stock market assumes that a devaluation or depreciation of the currency makes exports more profitable and as most major exporters are quoted on the stock market, one will see a rise in stock market prices. For the period between January 1974 and December 1978, positive long term and short term links were found. These links, however, were stronger in the short term.

Soennen and Hennigar (1988) used the real effective exchange rate of the US dollar and stock prices. They found strong negative links between the changes of the US dollar and the changes of stock prices of US enterprises for the period 1980–1986. Bahmani-Oskooee and Sohrabian (1992) applied the cointegration concept and Granger causality tests in order to study any potential links between foreign exchange rates and stock prices. They were also the first to research for a reverse relation. They applied monthly data for the period between July 1973 and December 1988 for the S&P 500 index and the effective exchange rate of the dollar, finding that both variables have an influence on each other. However, they were unable to find any long-term links.

After the Asian crisis, there were also various studies about the interdependence between foreign exchange and stock markets for Asian countries. Particularly important studies include that of Abdalla and Murinde (1997), who considered in their analysis South Korea, Pakistan, India and the Philippines by looking at the real effective exchange rates of these countries for the period from January 1985 to July 1994. Long-term links were tested using cointegration concept and short-term links with Granger causality tests. Only for India and the Philippines could long term links be found. Using an error correction model (ECM) for India and the Philippines implied for the former that the exchange rate indeed influences the stock market index; for the latter the reverse relation resulted. For South Korea and Pakistan, positive short term links have been found, where the exchange rate is causal – in the Granger sense – to the stock market index. Amare and Mohsin (2000) included nine Asian countries (Hong Kong, Indonesia, Japan, Malaysia, The Philippines, Singapore, South Korea, Taiwan and Thailand) in their study. They employed the cointegration concept to examine potential long-term links between the two markets. Long-term links could be confirmed only for the Philippines and Singapore. The inclusion of the additional variable "interest rate" led to the result that for six of nine countries, long term links could be confirmed. Granger et al. (2000) considered Hong Kong, Indonesia, Japan, Malaysia, the Philippines, Singapore, South Korea, Taiwan and Thailand by employing the cointegration concept and Granger causality tests. In order to filter out the shocks of the 1987 crash and the avian flu crisis in Asia, the time series were divided into three parts. They therefore used daily data of different time series' length (altogether from 3 January 1987 to 14 November 1997, i.e. 3,097 observations). Except for Japan, Singapore and Thailand significant links were found. These results effectively demonstrate that bi-directional links do exist. However, during the currency crisis – i.e., in the short-run – it holds that in most cases stock prices have an influence on exchange rates.

Muhammad and Rasheed (2003) considered Bangladesh, India, Pakistan and Sri Lanka for the period from 1994 to 2000, also employing the cointegration concept and Granger causality tests. For India and Pakistan they could find neither short-term nor long-term links. However, for Bangladesh and Sri Lanka, bi-directional (positive) links could be confirmed. Stavárek (2005) examined the interdependence between the stock market index and the real effective exchange rates of four veteran EU members – Germany, France, Austria and the UK – four new EU members – Poland, Slovakia, Czech Republic and Hungary – as well as the USA for the periods 1970–1992 and 1993–2003; he employed the cointegration concept, Vector ECM (VECM) and the Granger causality test. For the veteran EU member countries and the US, both long-term and short-term links were found, but the direction of causality is not uniform for all countries. Conversely, for the new members merely short term links resulted.

2.3 Theoretical Foundation

In the literature there are not many attempts to incorporate the stock market and foreign exchange market in a single model; the links between the two markets certainly exist, but they are not as obvious and unambiguous as, for example, the link between the interest rate and the exchange rate. Jarchow (1999) incorporates the stock market in a modified Mundell–Fleming model based on the idea of representing the stock price in the sense of Tobin's q and a variable price level. The ratio q consists of existing real capital p^A and newly produced real capital p. Hence, q can be interpreted as the real stock price.

The portfolio balance approach is a model which, besides the foreign exchange market, also incorporates the money market and the market of domestic and foreign securities (Branson 1977). Market participants possess a wealth stock – with given stocks of nominal money, domestic bonds and foreign bonds – for which investors choose the preferred portfolio structure, namely based on (expected) returns of the alternative assets. The demand for domestic money, foreign securities or domestic securities depend both on domestic interest rate i and the yield on foreign bonds (i^f which is the foreign interest rate plus the expected devaluation rate). The asset markets included in this model are represented by the equations:

$$M = w_1 \cdot \underset{(+)(-)(-)}{(W, i, i^f)}$$

$$B = w_2 \cdot \underset{(+)(+)(-)}{(W, i, i^f)}$$

$$e \cdot F = w_3 \cdot \underset{(+)(-)(+)}{(W, i, i^f)},$$

where

$$W = M + B + eF$$

Total wealth W is the sum of money M, domestic bonds B, and foreign bonds eF (F is the stock of foreign bonds – denominated in foreign currency – in the country considered; e is the exchange rate in price notation). The signs given below the equations indicate the influence of the corresponding variables on the demand of M, B and eF, respectively. In an e-i-space, the equilibrium loci for foreign bonds (FF) and domestic bonds (BB) are both negatively sloped. The slope of the MM curve – portraying equilibrium in the money market – is positive. The securities considered in this model represent bonds with very short maturities. In a modified version of the portfolio balance approach, Welfens (2007) includes the stock market instead of the domestic bonds market (for further Branson-type models, where beside the stock market also the oil market is incorporated as an additional asset market, see Welfens (2008)). In this model, the supply side of the stock market is given as the product of the real stock market index P′/P and capital stock K. The demand for stocks (also for foreign bonds and money) depends on marginal utility of money, capital productivity, expected growth rate of the stock market price, and the sum of foreign bonds' interest rate and expected depreciation rate of the exchange rate. In an e-P' space, the KK curve and FF curve are both positively sloped and the MM curve is negatively sloped.

These approaches emphasize stocks while flows are considered by Reitz et al. (2007). This flow-approach considers the aggregation of end-user order flows, which contain different information from different types of customers with respect to the expected fundamental value of the exchange rate. (A financial customer is much more engaged in exchange rate research than a commercial customer, as the latter only intends to hedge its money amounts resulting from exports or imports.) In particular, short-term deviations of the exchange rate from its fundamental value should be explained with this approach as traditional models do not offer satisfactory results.

Adler and Dumas (1984) capture the link between enterprise return and its exposure vis-à-vis relative exchange rate change in a single factor model which is given by the equation

$$r_i = a_i + b_i d + \varepsilon_i. \tag{2.1}$$

The slope coefficient b_i expresses the exchange rate exposure of enterprise i (i = 1, ..., n), a_i denotes the constant and ε_i the error term (where ε_i ~ white-noise). The variable d represents exchange rate return and r_i the return of enterprise i.

Bodnar and Wong (2003) proposed an augmented market model (a two-factor model) which subdivides the risk exposure of enterprises into two components (factors): the overall market exposure – i.e. the risk an enterprise is exposed to the total stock market – and exchange rate exposure. The modified equation

$$r_{it} = a_i + b_i d_t + \beta_i r_{mt} + \varepsilon_{it} \tag{2.2}$$

can be estimated as usual with the OLS method. β_i now represents the "stock market risk", i.e. the β-factor known from the standard Capital Asset Pricing Model (CAPM), with r_m expressing the stock market return and b_i representing the exchange rate exposure (see also Entorf and Jamin 2007).

The factor models presented above presume that the variable exchange rate is the explanatory variable, and the variable stock price (at enterprise level) is the explained variable. Making some reflections about the linkage between the two variables lead to the realization that both variables can actually have an impact on each other at the macro level, as Bahmani-Oskooee and Sohrabian (1992) for example have emphasized. Two possible channels will be explained through which links between the two markets can result.

The exchange rate has an impact on stock prices particularly on export-oriented enterprises. An increase of the exchange rate, i.e. a depreciation of the domestic currency, favours exports, therefore stock prices of enterprises should increase. Moreover, Froot and Stein (1991) emphasized particularly that foreign direct investments (FDI's) are also influenced by real exchange rate as real devaluation of domestic currency stimulates net inflows – the latter in turn will affect trade balance in the medium term. The Froot–Stein model emphasizes the role of imperfect capital markets.

The influence of the stock (market) price on exchange rate can be taken into account through including transactions in the stock market in the money demand function. Referring to the 1920s onset of the Great Depression in the United States, Field (1984) emphasizes the importance of considering the significant impact of stock trading's value on the demand to hold cash balances. He asserts that the fact of having not recognized stock trading as a relevant argument in the demand for money (an expansion of the money supply could be misjudged as expansionary while it might be neutral or even restrictive, namely if rising turnover figures in asset markets fully absorb the additional liquidity) led indirectly to the Great Depression, as the nature of monetary policy was misjudged – it was less expensive than the FED thought. Hence, he incorporates the stock market in his augmented money demand function – namely, the transaction volume of stock markets multiplied by the stock price.

In a modern version of the Field argument, one may argue with respect to FDI that the demand for domestic money increases if foreign investors invest in domestic enterprises and raise the nominal amount of stock market transactions. On the one hand, stock price increases, on the other hand the interest rate increases as a consequence of increased money demand. Therefore capital inflows are additionally favoured, and domestic currency will appreciate under flexible exchange rate. In case of fixed exchange rate, stock market prices should consequently have no influence on exchange rates but may have an impact on foreign exchange reserves of the central bank, which is committed to preserving the current value of the exchange rate. If domestic currency appreciates, the central bank is obliged to perform foreign exchange interventions.

Obviously the exchange rate can have a strong impact on the stock price at the micro level. However, at the macro level the impact could be weaker or even non-existent, as a stock market index actually measures the performance of a "diversified portfolio". In other words, enterprises – weighted by their capital stock – of several industries are incorporated in a stock market index. The exchange rate should have a greater impact on a stock market index when more export-oriented enterprises are represented in the stock market index. Hence, the composition of a stock market index is a crucial hint when it comes to the question as to whether the exchange rate does indeed have a significant impact on the stock market index.

At the macro level, capital (in)flows (e.g. due to investments in securities) can have a strong impact on the exchange rate as well. Investments in securities can be made either in bonds or in shares. Hence exchange rates are not only affected through foreign investments on domestic bonds but also through foreign investments on listed domestic enterprises. As the equity markets in emerging countries are relatively underdeveloped the effect of stock markets can be much higher than in highly developed capital markets. Moreover, emerging markets are quite interesting for investors, as high returns can often be obtained even though the risk is higher. According to the Capital Asset Pricing Model (CAPM), however, the investor is willing to bear a higher risk if he or she expects an enterprise return which is at least as high as its corresponding β (Sharpe et al. 1995). Hence, the security market line (SML) can be used to assess shares and is thus quite a useful instrument in making decisions on investments. Another reason for investments in these countries is that emerging markets do not strongly correlate with highly developed stock markets. Hence, portfolios can further be diversified.

2.4 Data and Methods Employed

2.4.1 Data and Countries

In the subsequent analysis, four accession countries (Poland, Czech Republic, Slovenia, and Hungary) and four cohesion countries (Ireland, Portugal, Spain, and Greece) are included in the analysis. Monthly (average) data (from Eurostat.; Index, 1995 = 100) of nominal stock market indices and nominal bilateral exchange rates (denominated as domestic currency per US dollar unit (for which time series data had to first be transformed)) will be used. The time series applied to the accession countries are considered until March 2008, but the initial values of the time series vary for both country groups due to a lack of data (initial values depend on the countries included in the analysis, i.e. initial values correspond to the initial values available at the data source mentioned above). The introduction of the Euro poses an additionally strong restriction for the applied data of the cohesion countries concerning the data length. For this reason, cohesion countries are considered until December 1998 (Greece until December 2000). The initial values of the cohesion countries are given as follows: Greece: 09-1988; Ireland: 12-1986; Portugal: 12-1992; Spain: 01-1987, and those of the accession countries: Poland: 04-1991; Slovenia: 01-1994; Czech Republic: 04-1994; Hungary: 01-1991.

2.4.2 *Methods Employed*

For the further analysis, it is important to examine whether the time series applied fulfil the property of stationarity. An appropriate unit root test must be carried out, as this property decides whether long-term or short-term links between variables can be examined. The Augmented Dickey Fuller (ADF) test is a quite powerful test, and it will therefore be employed in this analysis. This test is based on the following regression:

$$\Delta y_t = \delta y_{t-1} + \sum_{j=1}^{m} \alpha_j \Delta y_{t-j} + u_t, \tag{2.3}$$

where Δ represent the difference operator. The null hypothesis, y_t contains a unit root (i.e. $\delta = 0$), will be rejected if the t-value is less than the critical ADF value. Since autocorrelation of Δy_t is taken into account, the u_t must now fulfil the property of white-noise, otherwise the lag-length must be optimized until it does. The equation can adequately be estimated with the OLS method.

The links between distinct variables can be explored either in the short-term or in the long-term. The latter can be carried out by using the cointegration concept. The precondition for the employment of this approach is that all considered time series must be nonstationary and integrated of the same order. Cointegration means that time series have at least one common stochastic trend except for some temporarily deviations. According to Engle and Granger (1987), cointegration is defined as follows:

Let Y be a vector of k variables which are all integrated of order d. The components of Y are then cointegrated of order (d, c) in case of the existence of at least one linear combination z of these variables. The variable z is then integrated of order d–c ($d \geq c > 0$), i.e.

$$\beta' Y = z \sim I(d - c) \tag{2.4}$$

In other words, if the variables are integrated of order 1 – for economic variables this is often the case – then the residuals (resulting from the regression equations) must be of minor order, i.e. I(0) (Engle and Granger 1987).

The vector β is denoted as cointegrating vector. The number of linear independent cointegrating vectors represents the cointegration rank r. In case of $r = k$ the system consists of k stationary variables – i.e., the cointegration concept cannot be employed. If $r = 0$, a long-term relationship does not exist due to a lack of at least one stationary linear combination for these variables – i.e., cointegration exists only in the case of $0 < r < k$ (Enders 1995; Kirchgässner and Wolters 2007).

Both long-term and short-term links can also be explored simultaneously in case of the existence of a cointegrating relationship between the considered variables. In this case, an Error Correction Model (ECM) can be employed. In a two-variable case, a very simple two-step procedure could be carried out. The first step would be to regress each variable on the other if the property of nonstationarity for both variables is given, i.e.:

$$y_t = a_0 + b_0 x_t + z_t^y \tag{2.5}$$

$$x_t = a_1 + b_1 y_t + z_t^x. \tag{2.6}$$

In the second step, the transformation into an ECM follows. According to the Granger representation theorem, an existing cointegration relationship always contains an equivalent ECM (and the reverse), and this can be expressed with the following equations:

$$\Delta y_t = \gamma_0^y - \gamma_y \underbrace{(y_{t-1} - a_0 - b_0 x_{t-1})}_{=z_{t-1}^y} + \sum_{j=1}^{n_x} a_{xj}\Delta x_{t-j} + \sum_{j=1}^{n_y} a_{yj}\Delta y_{t-j} + u_{yt} \tag{2.7}$$

$$\Delta x_t = \gamma_0^x + \gamma_x \underbrace{(y_{t-1} - a_1 - b_1 x_{t-1})}_{=z_{t-1}^x} + \sum_{j=1}^{n_x} b_{xj}\Delta x_{t-j} + \sum_{j=1}^{n_y} b_{yj}\Delta y_{t-j} + u_{xt}. \tag{2.8}$$

The parameters γ_y and γ_x give information about long-term links (speed of adjustment toward the long-term equilibrium) between the variables y_t and x_t. If at least one of these parameters is significantly different from zero, a long-term link then exists between the considered variables. The parameters a_{xj}, a_{yj}, b_{xj} and b_{yj} represent short-term links. Furthermore, if the parameter γ_y (γ_x), and at least one a_{xj} (b_{yj}) is significantly different from zero – b_{yj} (a_{xj}) is not significantly different from zero – the variable x_t (y_t) is said to Granger cause y_t (x_t). The advantage of this approach is that the information lost through differentiating the data in level can be taken into account in differenced data.

A problem arises in this context with testing the property of stationarity of the residuals, as the common unit root tests are thought to be employed for realised but not generated time series. The critical values of the ADF test are therefore not valid, and other critical values must be considered (Mackinnon 1991). Furthermore, in case of more variables, two problems can emerge. On the one hand, multiple cointegration relations can exist, and on the other hand, the endogenous variable cannot be fixed a priori. If a cointegrating relation for the considered n variables exists, each variable should be exchangeable as an endogenous and exogenous variable and also be significantly different from zero. Often, however, exactly this anomalous feature emerges. Therefore a more powerful test is needed. The Johansen approach, based on a VAR, can overcome these problems. The starting-point is the following VAR without a deterministic trend (Johansen and Juselius 1988):

$$Y_t = A_1 Y_{t-1} + A_2 Y_{t-2} + \cdots + A_p Y_{t-p} + U_t. \tag{2.9}$$

The variables are I(1), and they may be cointegrated. Subtraction of both sides with Y_{t-1} and rearrangement of (2.9) leads to the Vector Error Correction Model (VECM)

$$\Delta Y_t = -\ \Pi Y_{t-1} + A_1^* \Delta Y_{t-1} + A_2^* \Delta Y_{t-2} + \cdots + A_{p-1}^* \Delta Y_{t-p+1} + U_t, \tag{2.10}$$

with

$$\Pi = I - \sum_{j=1}^{p} A_j \text{ and } A_j^* = -\sum_{i=j+1}^{p} A_i,\ j = 1, 2, \ldots, p-1.$$

The matrix I denotes the identity matrix and Π contains the long-term links between the included variables. Tests for cointegration can be carried out through examining the rank of the matrix Π (i.e. testing whether the eigenvalues λ_i are significant different from zero). The number of significant eigenvalues is equivalent to the rank of the matrix Π (Lütkepohl and Krätzig 2004). The idea is the same as in the case of the ADF test. The difference is that unit root is tested in a multi-equation case.

Considering the eigenvalues, two tests can be generated:

$$Tr(r) = \sum_{i=r+1}^{k} \ln(1 - \hat{\lambda}_i)(\text{trace} - \text{test})$$

with the hypothesis

H_0: the number of positive eigenvalues is at most r vs. H_1: there are more than r ($r < k$) positive eigenvalues.

$$\lambda_{max}(r, r+1) = -\ T\ln(1 - \hat{\lambda}_{r+1})\ (\lambda_{max} - \text{test})$$

However, the hypotheses of the λ_{max} − test are constructed as follows:

H_0: the number of positive eigenvalues is exactly r vs. H_1: there are exactly $r + 1$ positive eigenvalues.

The sequences of tests start with $r = 0$ and end when the null hypothesis cannot be rejected any more. The cointegration rank is then equivalent to the value at which the null hypothesis could not be rejected (Brooks 2003). The null hypothesis will be rejected if the value of the test statistic is larger then the critical value.

If the attempt of detection of any long-term links between variables fails, an alternative would be to ascertain whether at least short-term links can be found. Short-term links can be explored by employing VAR models for variables, which has been induced to stationarity. In a VAR model, the dependence of a variable to itself is considered up to the lag p and to other variables as well (SIMS 1980). A VAR without deterministic trend is given in (2.9), where in this case – short-term links are explored – all variables must be stationary. These models can easily be estimated with the OLS method. The correct specification of the model can be checked with the usual instruments, i.e. checking whether the residuals fulfil the property of white-noise or may be serially autocorrelated (e.g., using the Q statistics for each single equation).

Finally, the interdependencies should adequately be specified. The VAR process is not able to specify which variable is exogenous and which one is endogenous. Hence, Granger-causality tests will be employed. A variable, say x_t, is said to Granger-cause the other variable, say y_t, if the inclusion of x_t improves the forecast of y_t and vice versa. If both variables Granger cause each other, a feedback relationship is given.

Considering

$$\begin{pmatrix} x_t \\ y_t \end{pmatrix} = \sum_{i=1}^{p} \begin{pmatrix} \alpha_{11,i} & \alpha_{12,i} \\ \alpha_{21,i} & \alpha_{22,i} \end{pmatrix} \begin{pmatrix} x_{t-i} \\ y_{t-i} \end{pmatrix} + u_t \tag{2.11}$$

then in a bivariate VAR x_t Granger causes y_t if $\alpha_{21,i} \neq 0$ for at least one i ($i = 1, 2, ..., p$) and $\alpha_{12,i} = 0$ ($\forall i = 1, ..., p$) and y_t Granger causes x_t if $\alpha_{12,i} \neq 0$ for at least one i ($i = 1, .., p$) and $\alpha_{21,i} = 0$ ($\forall i = 1, ..., p$).

In this test the significance of lags of the considered variables is examined by using F-tests in order to ascertain whether the whole parameters of the lags are insignificant or at least one parameter is significantly different from zero. Therefore variables must fulfil the property of stationarity.

2.5 Empirical Results

2.5.1 Unit Root Test

The first step in the analysis consists of testing time series to determine whether they fulfil the property of non-stationarity as it is a requirement for the employment of the cointegration concept. Therefore, the ADF test will be employed in level and in first differences. For the sake of clarity, the presentation of the results will be divided into two groups, the group of cohesion countries, and the group of accession countries.

The ADF test critical values depend on selected lag length; for this reason, the optimal lag length must be determined somehow. In a univariate autoregressive process, the number of lag p is chosen, for example, by the Akaike Information Criterion (AIC) or Schwartz Bayesian Criterion (SBC). Furthermore, the lag length is augmented if significant serial autocorrelation for the residuals is indicated (e.g., through the Durbin–Watson statistic). In this analysis, both the multivariate AIC (MAIC) and the multivariate SBC (MSBC) are employed. The variable SP expresses the nominal stock market index and EXR the nominal exchange rate. DSP and DEXR express the differenced variables of SP and EXR, respectively.

2.5.1.1 Cohesion Countries

The results show that except for the exchange rate in case of Ireland, both stock market indices and exchange rates are nonstationary for all considered time series. Hence, the requirement of employing the cointegration concept is not fulfilled for Ireland. A VAR in first differences must therefore be employed (Table 2.1).

2.5.1.2 Accession Countries

Obviously all time series are I(1) according to the ADF test, i.e. stationarity will be induced after first differences. All accession countries included in the analysis can therefore be taken into account for testing long-term links between the two variables (Table 2.2).

Table 2.1 Results of ADF test

Country	Variable	t-Stat.	Test critical values	
Ireland	SP	0.7125	1%	−3.4768
	DSP	−3.1375	5%	−2.8818
	EXR	−3.2895	10%	−2.5777
	DEXR	−5.9077		
Portugal	SP	−0.9946	1%	−3.5285
	DSP	−4.7437	5%	−2.9042
	EXR	−2.3184	10%	−2.5896
	DEXR	−6.0621		
Spain	SP	0.4635	1%	−3.4775
	DSP	−6.2969	5%	−2.8821
	EXR	−0.6409	10%	−2.5778
	DEXR	−8.3412		
Greece	SP	−1.3650	1%	−3.4775
	DSP	−3.8481	5%	−2.8821
	EXR	0.5620	10%	−2.5778
	DEXR	−8.5979		

Null hypothesis: . . . has a unit root

Table 2.2 Results of ADF test

Country	Variable	t-Stat.	Test critical values	
Poland	SP	−0.3558	1%	−3.4627
	DSP	−11.7245	5%	−2.8757
	EXR	−2.0019	10%	−2.5744
	DEXR	−10.1764		
Slovenia	SP	1.9228	1%	−3.4731
	DSP	−8.7503	5%	−2.8802
	EXR	−1.3872	10%	−2.5768
	DEXR	−8.4053		
Czech Rep.	SP	−0.0969	1%	−3.4699
	DSP	−9.5093	5%	−2.8788
	EXR	−0.1042	10%	−2.5761
	DEXR	−9.4750		
Hungary	SP	−1.1418	1%	−3.4632
	DSP	−3.0379	5%	−2.8759
	EXR	−1.7570	10%	−2.5745
	DEXR	−11.4651		

Null hypothesis: ... has a unit root

2.5.2 Long Term Links

In the second part of the analysis, the cointegration concept is employed. In a two-variable case the Engle–Granger two-step approach could be employed. Obviously, the Johansen approach is a more sophisticated approach and at the same time it is more pleasant in implementation even in a two-variable case. The transformation into a Vector Error Correction Model (VECM) leads to a quasi VAR anyway.

As the results of the Johansen approach depend on selected lag order of the VAR, the optimal lag has to be determined by an appropriate information criterion. In this analysis, the multivariate AIC will be employed. Nevertheless, the lag length may need to be augmented if serial correlation does not disappear.

Tables 2.3 and 2.4 show that except for Poland, stock market indices and exchange rates are not cointegrated for any of the countries, as the critical values are not exceeded by the test statistic values; in other words, there are no long term links for seven of the eight countries under consideration.

2.5.3 Short Term Links

In the next step short term links are explored. An appropriate approach for this purpose is a bivariate VAR(p). A VAR process presumes that all variables depend on each other, i.e. there is no exogenous variable given. A suitable property of this approach is that, on one hand, the own endogenous structure of a variable is considered; on the other hand, interdependence to the other variables is also taken into account up to the lag p.

Table 2.3 Results of the cointegration test (cohesion countries)

Country					
Ireland	Lags	–	Statistic	Critical value	prob.[a]
	None			–	
	At most	1			
Portugal	Lags	5	Statistic	Critical value	prob.[a]
	None		13.2342	0.1065	
	At most	1	0.2063	3.8415	0.6497
Spain	Lags	6	Statistic	Critical value	prob.[a]
	None		11.4983	15.4947	0.1826
	At most	1	1.6909	3.8415	0.1935
Greece	Lags	2	Statistic	Critical value	prob.[a]
	None		7.0238	15.4947	0.5749
	At most	1	0.0011	3.8415	0.9735

[a]MacKinnon-Haugh-Michelis (1999) p-values

Table 2.4 Results of the cointegration test (accession countries)

Country					
Poland	Lags	4	Statistic	Critical value	prob.[a]
	None		17.8659	0.0216	
	At most	1	0.0570	3.8415	0.8112
Czech Rep.	Lags	2	Statistic	Critical value	prob.[a]
	None		5.3659	15.4947	0.7688
	At most		0.8128	3.8415	0.3673
Slovenia	Lags	2	Statistic	Critical value	prob.[a]
	None		6.7315	15.4947	0.6091
	At most		0.0435	3.8415	0.8347
Hungary	Lags	3	Statistic	Critical value	prob.[a]
	None		6.9283	15.4947	0.5860
	At most	1	0.1633	3.8415	0.6861

[a]MacKinnon-Haugh-Michelis (1999) p-values

2.5.3.1 Cohesion Countries

The results show that for Ireland significant links between the nominal stock market index and the nominal exchange rate can be confirmed until the second lag. Obviously the direction of causation is from stock market index (DSP) to exchange rate (DEXR). For Spain and Greece, significant links can be confirmed, while for Greece a feedback relationship seems to exist. Conversely, the stock market index and the exchange rate for Portugal do not depend on each other. An explanation for this could be the small number of observations included in the analysis (73 observations). It would be desirable to have a time series length of at least 10 years as monthly data are used. The data length may be one explanation for the lack of significance interdependence between the exchange rate and stock market index in Portugal.

From the VAR analysis, we can conclude that for the cohesion countries, three of the four countries considered are interrelated where the foreign exchange market seems to be influenced by the stock market. For Greece, a bi-directional link seems to exist. In order to ensure whether DSP or DEXR can be regarded as the exogenous variable – especially for Greece, as a lack of clarity remains – Granger causality tests must be employed (Tables 2.5–2.8).

Table 2.5 Results of VAR estimation for Ireland

Ireland	DEXR	DSP
Constant	0.2193	1.0268
	[0.8697]	[1.6816]
DEXR(-1)	0.3236	0.1406
	[3.2927]	[0.5909]
DEXR(-2)	−0.2511	0.4228
	[−2.4509]	[1.7043]
DEXR(-3)	0.1986	−0.0828
	[1.8360]	[−0.3160]
DEXR(-4)	−0.1523	0.1051
	[−1.3820]	[0.3939]
DEXR(-5)	0.0342	0.3031
	[0.3072]	[1.1229]
DEXR(-6)	−0.0391	0.0161
	[−0.3579]	[0.0608]
DEXR(-7)	−0.0736	0.3772
	[−0.6814]	[1.4422]
DEXR(-8)	0.0445	−0.2713
	[0.4273]	[−1.0757]
DEXR(-9)	0.1295	0.2492
	[1.3706]	[1.0890]
DSP(-1)	0.0855	0.4807
	[2.2058]	[5.1217]
DSP(-2)	−0.0965	−0.4156
	[−2.2197]	[−3.9469]
DSP(-3)	0.0564	0.2214
	[1.2503]	[2.0259]
DSP(-4)	−0.0186	−0.0570
	[−0.4000]	[−0.5063]
DSP(-5)	0.0340	-0.0699
	[0.6911]	[−0.5871]
DSP(-6)	−0.0620	−0.3022
	[−1.1911]	[−2.3978]
DSP(-7)	0.0336	0.0537
	[0.6217]	[0.4106]
DSP(-8)	−0.0895	−0.1961
	[−1.6853]	[−1.5254]
DSP(-9)	−0.0888	0.3906
	[−1.6853]	[3.1613]
R-squared	0.2853	0.3726
Adj. R-squared	0.1744	0.2752

t-statistics in [ ]

Table 2.6 Results of VAR estimation for Portugal

Portugal	DEXR	DSP
Constant	0.1192	1.6797
	[0.4104]	[1.1943]
DEXR(-1)	0.2747	0.0735
	[2.1891]	[0.1210]
DSP(-1)	0.0161	0.3726
	[0.6321]	[3.0263]
R-squared	0.1003	0.1431
Adj. R-squared	0.0738	0.1179

t-statistics in [ ]

Table 2.7 Results of VAR estimation for Spain

Spain	DEXR	DSP
Constant	0.4704	1.3903
	[2.6694]	[1.8770]
DEXR(-1)	0.3303	0.0323
	[3.9449]	[0.0918]
DEXR(-2)	−0.0359	−0.1302
	[−0.4242]	[−0.3662]
DSP(-1)	0.0079	0.4760
	[0.4172]	[5.9731]
DSP(-2)	−0.0527	−0.3928
	[−2.6164]	[−4.6434]
R-squared	0.1556	0.2423
Adj. R-squared	0.1308	0.2200

t-statistics in [ ]

Granger causality tests show that the hypothesis "DSP does not Granger cause DEXR" can be rejected for three of four countries, i.e. Ireland (can be rejected at 5.7% significance level), Spain, and Greece. The reverse direction cannot be confirmed for any of the cohesion countries. The selected lag length is equivalent to the lag length of the VAR model as it is intended to ascertain whether the interdependent links confirmed with the VAR approach can be specified with respect to the direction of causation (Table 2.9).

2.5.3.2 Accession Countries

The results of the VAR model for the accession countries are similar to those of the cohesion countries. Absolute changes of exchange rates and stock market indices show significant interdependence for Hungary and Slovenia. For the Czech Republic, exchange rate and stock market indices seem to be independent. For Poland, a VECM is employed as long-term links could be confirmed. From the VECM, short-term links become obvious. As in the equation of DEXR, both the adjustment parameter and the parameter of DSP in $t - 2$ are significant. It can thus be concluded that the

Table 2.8 Results of VAR estimation for Greece

Greece	DEXR	DSP
Constant	0.3719	4.6308
	[1.3522]	[2.0124]
DEXR(-1)	0.3125	−0.6183
	[3.0411]	[−0.7192]
DEXR(-2)	−0.146005	−0.1392
	[−1.3449]	[−0.1532]
DEXR(-3)	0.1019	0.6011
	[0.9593]	[0.6761]
DEXR(-4)	−0.2281	−0.8151
	[−2.1588]	[−0.9220]
DEXR(-5)	0.0284	0.2385
	[0.2794]	[0.2805]
DEXR(-6)	0.0130	−2.4684
	[0.1281]	[−2.8991]
DEXR(-7)	−0.1111	0.0960
	[−1.0113]	[0.1045]
DEXR(-8)	0.1650	−0.3674
	[1.4721]	[−0.3917]
DEXR(-9)	−0.6719	−0.2897
	[−1.7562]	[−0.3091]
DEXR(-10)	0.1269	0.5066
	[1.1226]	[0.5357]
DEXR(-11)	−0.1869	−0.6081
	[−1.6666]	[−0.6481]
DEXR(-12)	0.1246	−0.8881
	[1.1849]	[−1.0091]
DSP(-1)	0.0030	0.3343
	[0.2575]	[3.4354]
DSP(-2)	−0.0042	0.0460
	[−0.3546]	[0.4629]
DSP(-3)	0.0119	−0.0093
	[0.9971]	[−0.0931]
DSP(-4)	−0.0166	0.2274
	[−1.3265]	[2.1688]
DSP(-5)	−0.0186	−0.3381
	[−1.4020]	[−3.0454]
DSP(-6)	0.0166	−0.0310
	[1.2173]	[−0.2713]
DSP(-7)	−0.0010	0.1905
	[−0.0770]	[1.6784]
DSP(-8)	0.0241	0.0316
	[1.8345]	[0.2871]
DSP(-9)	−0.0281	0.0861
	[−2.1219]	[0.7760]
DSP(-10)	0.0119	−0.0538
	[0.8544]	[−0.4613]
DSP(-11)	0.0274	−0.3269
	[1.9270]	[−2.7499]
DSP(-12)	0.0404	0.1915
	[2.8277]	[1.6028]
R-squared	0.4025	0.3399
Adj. R-squared	0.2721	0.1959

t-statistics in [ ]

Table 2.9 Results of Granger causality tests for the cohesion countries

Country	Null hypothesis:	F-Statistic	Probability
Ireland Lags: 2	DSP does not Granger cause DEXR	2.9305	0.0567
	DEXR does not Granger cause DSP	1.1458	0.3210
Portugal Lags: 1	DSP does not Granger cause DEXR	0.3995	0.5295
	DEXR does not Granger cause DSP	0.0147	0.9040
Spain Lags: 2	DSP does not Granger cause DEXR	3.5551	0.0313
	DEXR does not Granger cause DSP	0.0674	0.9348
Greece Lags: 12	DSP does not Granger cause DEXR	3.2995	0.0004
	DEXR does not Granger cause DSP	1.2089	0.2860

Table 2.10 Results of VECM estimation for Poland

Poland		
Cointegrating eq.:		
EXR(-1)	1	
SP(-1)	0.7030	
	[3.7432]	
Constant	−296.6521	
Error correction: DEXR DSP		
CointEq.	−0.0071	0.0063
	[−4.1854]	[0.5642]
DEXR(-1)	0.3088	0.7094
	[4.1702]	[1.4679]
DEXR(-2)	−0.2456	0.4111
	[−3.1263]	[0.8019]
DEXR(-3)	0.0350	−0.0909
	[0.4557]	[−0.1814]
DEXR(-4)	−0.1133	0.7011
	[−1.5644]	[1.4831]
DSP(-1)	0.0041	0.1721
	[0.3559]	[2.2964]
DSP(-2)	0.0303	0.1052
	[2.6010]	[1.3830]
DSP(-3)	0.0115	−0.0407
	[0.9069]	[−0.4930]
DSP(-4)	0.0079	−0.0257
	[0.6378]	[−0.3192]
C	0.0719	1.8182
	[0.3153]	[1.2214]
R-squared	0.2333	0.0683
Adj. R-squared	0.1968	0.0240

t-statistics in [ ]

stock market index Granger causes the exchange rate (i.e. SP $\rightarrow$ EXR). In case of the other countries, Granger causality tests confirm that there is a significant link between stock market and foreign exchange market for Slovenia, where SP $\rightarrow$ EXR (Table 2.10).

For Hungary a significant impact of stock market on the foreign exchange market can only be confirmed at 10% (exactly at 7%) significance level. The reason for the weaker links between the two markets in comparison to the cohesion countries may be based upon the fact that financial markets (especially stock markets) in Eastern Europe are still underdeveloped as confirmed in the analysis of Köke and Schröder (2003). Moreover, Holtemöller (2005) confirmed that many accession countries – inter alia the accession countries considered in this analysis – exhibit a very low monetary integration. As a measurement of monetary integration, the interest rate spreads of the countries considered vis-à-vis the Euro interest rate and country specific risk premium volatility were used. An important reason in this context could also be the fact that the currencies of these countries – except for Poland – do not float freely but within currency bands (managed floating). For this reason, "true" links may become blurred (Tables 2.11–2.13).

Nevertheless, the results of both country groups are quite surprising in comparison with previous research on this aspect. Moreover, the results are not in consensus with part of traditional theory as exchange rate is assumed to influence stock price. It is also astonishing that the results do not show bi-directional links but an unambiguous direction of causation from stock market to foreign exchange market. The arising question is now how to explain this result.

Table 2.11 Results of VAR estimation for accession countries (Slovenia and Czech Rep)

Slovenia	DEXR	DSP	Czech Rep.	DEXR	DSP
Constant	0.3320	1.8974	Constant	−0.2183	0.7170
	[1.1182]	[2.5173]		[−0.9565]	[0.9616]
DEXR(-1)	0.3320	−0.0654	DEXR(-1)	0.2890	0.0390
	[4.7664]	[−0.3436]		[3.8422]	[0.1588]
DSP(-1)	−0.0700	0.3042	DSP(-1)	0.0064	0.3153
	[−2.2303]	[3.8168]		[0.2875]	[4.3665]
R-squared	0.1575	0.0890	R-squared	0.0836	0.1050
Adj. R-squared	0.1464	0.0770	Adj. R-squared	0.0724	0.0940

Table 2.12 Results of VAR estimation for Hungary

Hungary	DEXR	DSP
Constant	0.1650	5.6226
	[0.6080]	[1.6571]
DEXR(-1)	0.2726	1.6353
	[3.7638]	[1.8062]
DEXR(-2)	−0.0832	−0.3223
	[−1.1378]	[−0.3526]
DSP(-1)	0.0030	0.1823
	[0.5008]	[2.4706]
DSP(-2)	0.0126	−0.0547
	[2.1595]	[−0.7472]
R-squared	0.0921	0.0393
Adj. R-squared	0.0738	0.0201

Table 2.13 Results of Granger causality tests for the accession countries

Country	Null hypothesis:	F-Statistic	Probability
Czech Rep. Lags: 1	DSP does not Granger cause DEXR	0.0827	0.7740
	DEXR does not Granger cause DSP	0.0253	0.8740
Slovenia Lags: 1	DSP does not Granger cause DEXR	4.9744	0.0272
	DEXR does not Granger cause DSP	0.1181	0.7316
Hungary Lags: 2	DSP does not Granger cause DEXR	2.7010	0.0696
	DEXR does not Granger cause DSP	1.6446	0.1957

The unusual and a priori unexpected results of unidirectional causality link from SP to EXR could be explained with high capital inflows (i.e. portfolio investments and FDI) in these countries during their catching up process. For investors, it is quite attractive to invest in these countries as high marginal product of capital can be expected. Another explanation could be based upon capital market liberalization. It certainly facilitates cross border investments, and this can lead to an increasing movement of capital across countries. Hence, financial market integration could be one reason with respect to facilitation of cross border investments. Under these circumstances, a unidirectional causation from stock market to foreign exchange market is possible. Indeed, these countries experienced much FDI during this time, but not simultaneously. (Hungary and the Czech Republic, for instance, attracted high FDI inflows relative to GDP in early 1990s, but Poland later.) This could also be a reason for the different results within the accession countries. If there are strong portfolio adjustments, the exchange rate could also be affected. Furthermore, capital market liberalization could induce increasing speculations on stock markets and foreign exchange markets, which also may have an impact on the interdependence between these two markets. The results support the assumptions made in the Dornbusch model, for example, that short-term deviations from the long-term equilibrium are mainly caused by the fact that financial market prices are flexible and prices of goods are sticky in the short-term (Dornbusch 1976).

2.6 Concluding Remarks

In this analysis, four cohesion countries (Ireland, Portugal, Spain, Greece) and four accession countries (Poland, Czech Rep., Slovenia, Hungary) have been considered in order to examine any potential links between nominal stock market index and nominal exchange rate. For this purpose, monthly data were used, where the cohesion countries were taken into account until the introduction of the Euro. The cointegration concept was employed for testing on long-term links and the VAR approach for short-term links. Finally, Granger causality tests were employed for determination of the exogenous and endogenous variable. The results show that for five countries, significant links exist between the stock market index and foreign exchange rate, where for

Poland both long-term and short-term links exist. An unambiguous result with respect to the direction of causation, from stock market index to the foreign exchange market is a surprise. It could be partly explained by high incipient capital inflows. Comparable analyses for emerging Asian countries showed different results. The results of the analysis presented could largely be explained by high capital inflows – through FDI inflows and portfolio investments – in these countries. Increased financial market integration in Europe could be another reason, as it implies free trade and free movement of capital – with higher capital inflows anticipated, markets will react. This fact could have strengthened the "latent" links between the two markets.

References

Abdalla, I., & Murinde, V. (1997). Exchange rate and stock price interactions in emerging financial markets: evidence on India, Korea, Pakistan and the Philippines. *Applied Financial Economics, 7*, 25–35.

Adler, M., & Dumas, B. (1984). Exposure to currency risk: definition and measurement. *Financial Management, 13*, 41–50.

Aggarwal, R. (1981). Exchange rates and stock prices: a study of U.S. capital market under floating exchange rates. *Akron Business and Economic Review, 12*, 7–12.

Amare, T., & Mohsin, M. (2000). Stock prices and exchange rates in leading Asian economies: short run versus long run dynamics. *Singapore Economic Review, 45*(2), 165–181.

Bahmani-Oskooee, M., & Sohrabian, A. (1992). Stock prices and the effective exchange rate of the dollar. *Applied Economics, 24*, 459–464.

Bodnar, G. M., & Wong, M. H. F. (2003). Estimating exchange rate exposure: issue in model structure. *Financial Management, 32*, 35–67.

Branson, W. H. (1977). Asset markets and relative prices in exchange rate determination. *Sozialwissenschaftliche Annalen, 1*, 69–89.

Brooks, C. (2003). *Introductory econometrics for finance*. Cambridge: Cambridge University Press.

Dornbusch, R. (1976). Expectations and exchange rate dynamics. *Journal of Political Economy, 84*, 1161–1176.

Enders, W. (1995). *Applied econometric time series*. New York: Wiley.

Engle, R. F., & Granger, C. W. J. (1987). Co-integration and error correction: representation. *Estimation, and Testing, Econometrica, 55*, 251–276.

Entorf, H., & Jamin, G. (2007). German exchange rate exposure at DAX and aggregate level, international trade, and the role of exchange rate adjustment costs. *German Economic Review, 8*(3), 344–374.

Field, A. J. (1984). A new interpretation of the onset of the great depression. *Journal of Economic History, 44*, 489–498.

Franck, P., & Young, A. (1972). Stock price reaction of multinational firms to exchange realignments. *Financial Management, 1*, 66–73.

Froot, K. A., & Stein, J. C. (1991). Exchange rates and foreign direct investment: an imperfect capital markets approach. *Quarterly Journal of Economics, 106*, 1191–1217.

Granger, C. (1969). Investigating causal relations by econometric models and cross spectral methods. *Econometrica, 37*, 424–438.

Granger, C., Huang, B.-N., & Yang, C.-W. (2000). A bivariate causality between stock prices and exchange rates: evidence from recent Asian flu. *The Quarterly Journal of Economics and Finance, 40*, 337–354.

Holtemöller, O. (2005). Uncovered interest rate parity and analysis of monetary convergence of potential EMU accession countries. *International Economics and Economic Policy, 2*, 33–63.

Jarchow, H.-J. (1999), Eine offene Volkswirtschaft unter Berücksichtigung des Aktienmarkts, *CeGE-Discussion Paper* No. 2.

Johansen, S., & Juselius, K. (1990). Maximum likelihood estimation and inference on cointegration-with applications to the demand for money. *Oxford Bulletin of Economics and Statistics, 52*, 169–210.

Kirchgässner, G., & Wolters, J. (2007). *Introduction to modern time series analysis.* Heidelberg: Springer.

Köke, J., & Schröder, M. (2003). The prospect of capital markets in central and eastern Europe. *Eastern European Economics, 41*(4), 5–37.

Lütkepohl, H., & Krätzig, M. (2004). *Applied time series econometrics.* Cambridge: Cambridge University Press.

Mackinnon, J. G. (1991). Critical values for co-integration tests. In R. F. Engle & C. W. J. Granger (Eds.), *Long-run economic relationships* (pp. 267–276). Oxford: Oxford University Press.

Muhammad, N., Rasheed, A. (2003), Stock Prices and Exchange Rates: Are they related? Evidence from South Asian Countries, This paper was presented at the 18th Annual General Meeting and Conference of the Pakistan Society of Development Economists on January 2003, www:http://www.pide.org.pk/PSDE/Stock%20Prices%20and%20Exchange%20Rates.pdf.

Reitz, S.; Schmidt, M.A., Taylor, M.P. (2007), End-User Flow and Exchange Rate Dynamics, *Deutsche Bundesbank*, Discussion Paper, 5/2007.

Sharpe W, Gordon A, Bailey J.V. (1995), Investments, 5th edition, Englewood Cliffs: Prentice Hall.

Sims, C. A. (1980). Macroeconomics and reality. *Econometrica, 48*, 1–48.

Soennen, L., & Hennigar, E. (1988). An analysis of exchange rate and stock prices – the U.S. experience between 1980 and 1986. *Akron Business and Economic Review, 19*, 7–16.

Stavárek, D. (2005). Stock prices and exchange rates in the EU and the United States: evidence on their mutual interactions. *Czech Journal of Economics and Finance, 55*(3–4), 141–161.

Welfens, P. J. J. (2007). *Innovations in macroeconomics.* Heidelberg: Springer.

Welfens P.J.J. (2008), Portfolio Modelling and Growth, *EIIW Discussion Papers* 159.

Chapter 3
The Transatlantic Banking Crisis: Lessons, EU Reforms and G20 Issues

Paul J. J. Welfens

3.1 Introduction

Financial market globalization was reinforced in the decade following 1995, and one might expect major benefits from sustainable globalization. There is no doubt that securitization of loans and foreign direct investment of banks as well as internationalization of the banking business has intensified over time (Deutsche 2008; ECB 2008); the home bias in the use of savings – emphasized in earlier empirical analysis of Feldstein and Horioka (1980) – has reduced over time, particularly in the EU (Jungmittag and Untiedt 2002). While one should expect considerable benefits from financial globalization organized in a consistent framework, such globalization can have negative national and international collateral effects if the institutional framework is incomplete and inconsistent: a low degree of transparency resulting from this could raise systemic risks and generate negative international external effects. The international banking crisis which started in 2007 in the US subprime mortgage market shows that the institutional framework is incomplete and that there is a broad challenge for the EU countries and other OECD countries as well as China, India and other NICs in implementing a new global financial architecture. At the same time the US, the euro zone and other countries will have to adopt reforms in the domestic sphere. For the euro zone, the transatlantic banking crisis is a welcome test for its institutional set up, and it seems that the euro zone countries are doing rather well in the difficult transatlantic crisis; the ECB and several central banks deserve credit for flexible and rather consistent crisis management in 2008, although the crisis has not yet been fully resolved (Table 3.1).

The standard perception up to the US financial market crisis was that the US had the most integrated and liquid financial markets in the world. Due to the combination of the EU single market and the start of the Euro, the Euro zone

P.J.J. Welfens
European Institute for International Economic Relations, University of Wuppertal, Wuppertal, Germany

P.J.J. Welfens and C. Ryan (eds.), *Financial Market Integration and Growth*,
DOI 10.1007/978-3-642-16274-9_3, © Springer-Verlag Berlin Heidelberg 2011

Table 3.1 FDIC-insured institutions by asset size categories: numbers, and return on assets in percentage (1998–2008)

Institutions/ asset size	1999	2000	2001	2002	2003	2004	2005	2006	2007	2008	2009[a]
Greater than	76	82	80	106	110	117	118	119	119	114	104
$ 10 Billion	1.28	1.16	1.13	1.31	1.42	1.28	1.30	1.32	0.82	0.13	1.12 (1.22)
$ 1 billion to	318	313	320	450	471	480	512	530	549	562	451
$ 10 Billion	1.49	1.29	1.31	1.45	1.42	1.44	1.28	1.22	0.99	−0.15	1.17 (1.32)
$ 100 million to	3,029	3,078	3,194	4,118	4,211	4,285	4,339	4,399	4,425	4,498	3,958
$ 1 Billion	1.36	1.28	1.20	1.17	1.18	1.19	1.24	1.17	0.99	0.33	1.11 (1.06)
Less than	5,157	4,842	4,486	4,680	4,390	4,093	3,863	3,633	3,440	3,131	4,171
$ 100 mil.	1.01	1.01	0.91	1.00	0.95	1.01	1.00	0.93	0.75	0.31	0.88 (0.95)
Total/weighted	8,580	8,315	8,080	9,354	9,182	8,975	8,832	8,681	8,533	8,305	
average	1.27	1.19	1.16	1.31	1.38	1.29	1.28	1.28	0.86	0.12	

Source: FDIC Quarterly Banking Profile (1999–2008)
http://www2.fdic.gov/qbp/1999dec/qbp.pdf through http://www2.fdic.gov/qbp/12008dec/qbp.pdf
[a]Figure in brackets is without 2008

has made progress in financial integration. Just a few years after the start of the Euro zone and the ECB, it was argued by Gilchrist et al. (2002, p. 10) that risk-free financial markets had fully converged within the Euro zone so that a unique risk-free market had emerged. Still financial markets – broadly defined – remained somewhat fragmented (Gros and Lannoo 1999), and compared to the US, there was a predominance of bank credits relative to securities. In the Euro zone, economic activities rely more on bank credits than in the UK or the US. Hurst et al. (1999) have shown that banking credit accounts for more than 50% of financial intermediation in the Euro zone, which clearly exceeds the UK and US figures of 32% and 20%, respectively. Cecchetti (1999) has highlighted considerable differences across countries in the Euro zone. For example, banking credits represented 80% of financial intermediation in Ireland and 39% in Finland. Hence, the structure of financial systems differs across countries in the Euro zone, which should in turn affect the transmission of monetary policy. To the extent that frictions in financial markets exist – a prominent topic since the transatlantic banking crisis – there could indeed be negative impulses from disturbances in the financial sector to the real economy; in principle, the financial accelerator (Bernanke et al. 1999) could thus play a role in the Euro zone (Gilchrist et al. 2002). However, the European Commission to some extent has tried to create a more homogeneous EU single financial market, namely by adopting the Basel II rules which emphasize minimum capital requirements of banks based on risk-weighted liability indicators.

The US postponed adoption of Basel II until 2009/2010 and thus in the run up to the banking crisis 2007/2008 was on the standard capital requirement of the Basel I rules. At first sight, even under Basel I rules there should not be much reason to worry about the stability of the banking system, since regulations require internationally active banks to fulfill a minimum equity capital–loan ratio of 8%. However, the 8% requirement is costly for banks in the sense that bank managers might wish a higher leverage – thus raising the rate of return on equity – as adequate and therefore could seek raising the share of off-balance sheet activities as attractive. This problem indeed occurred in the run-up to US banking crisis and the international banking crisis. Few economists have considered the role of bank regulation on macroeconomic development. For instance, Blum and Hellwig (1995) have presented a model in which a negative shock to aggregate demand lowers the ability of firms to service their debts to banks, and this in turn could reduce equity capital of banks and – because of capital adequacy requirements – thus reduce bank lending and investment of industry. Under Basel II, there is a more differentiated approach in the field of minimum capital requirement. The new approach measures bank capital and portfolios on the basis of risks so that 8% applies to a risk-weighted portfolio of the bank. Moreover, there is a distinction between tier 1 capital (in the EU usually 4%, in the UK 6%), tier 2 capital (8% requirement) and tier 3 capital. Based on the method chosen for risk assessment – external rating or two alternative internal rating approaches – the capital requirements will slightly differ.

The basic logic of the Basel I/II approach is that an individual bank will face favorable survival prospects if its equity capital–loan ratio is sufficiently high; as regards an individual bank a high equity ratio is considered to serve as a cushion against adverse shocks. This logic, however, is flawed at the aggregate level as can be shown easily (see Appendix 5). Changing the Basel equity requirements is at least as important as the issue of pro-cyclicality of Basel II rules. The basic point is that raising the equity–loan ratio does not only improve the air bag of the individual bank, rather at the aggregate level it is prone to bring about an increase in the ratio of the credit multiplier to the money multiplier, which implies a greater likelihood of increasing and excessive volatility of asset prices and hence of risk. By implication, minimum equity capital requirement should be carefully redefined under Basel III, and there is indeed an optimum capital requirement in a macroeconomic perspective. However, the main focus of the subsequent analysis is on overcoming the existing banking crisis, and several institutional innovations will be suggested as new remedies.

The USA has faced a banking crisis in 2007/2008 which spilled over to Europe and later to the whole world. This major crisis brought about enormous depreciations on portfolios of banks and funds and could entail a new Great Depression as the real economies in OECD countries, Russia, China and elsewhere face a simultaneous decline in 2009/2010. In September/October 2008, the US government and European governments organized multi-billion dollar rescue packages to recapitalize banks, but national governments have not addressed the true structural problems. Iceland, Hungary, the Ukraine, Estonia and Latvia were among the countries facing balance-of-payments financing problems in October 2008. The euro zone's financial market stability was relatively satisfactory, while the epicenter of the banking crisis was in the US and to some extent in the UK, where banking supervisors had followed a similar benign neglect-attitude as their counterparts in the US. In the euro zone, Spain (Calvo-Hornero and Sanchez 2008) and to some extent Italy pursued rather strict regulatory approaches, which have helped them avoid facing major subprime problems. The US subprime mortgage markets were the trigger of the financial market crisis in August 2007, but there is no doubt that the whole US banking system was off-course with respect to sustainable banking in 2007. It is quite important to understand what went wrong, since successfully fighting the crisis requires measures based on adequate theoretical analysis. While the G20 meeting in Washington DC in November 2008 came up with a long list of 47 measures to be considered, it is doubtful that the key reform elements necessary were on the radar screen of policymakers. Overcoming the strange confidence crisis among banks is one of the key challenges as is a more realistic and more long-term profit maximization strategy of banks and other actors in financial markets. Better regulation and more regulation for big banks in the US and other OECD countries are also high on the agenda. Beyond the financial sector – shaped by high innovation dynamics, high volatility in 2008 and declining confidence among banks – the focus of policymakers is on the real economy with consensus forecasts for 2009 being rather bleak. This holds despite the big interest rate cuts of OECD central banks in the second half of 2008, which were designed to contain the turbulence to financial markets and to avoid a big recession.

Financial markets are crucial for financing investment and innovation, thus they are indispensible for economic growth (Saint-Paul 1992). Asymmetric information and moral hazard problems are specific aspects of financial markets and thus financial markets are not working perfectly. There could be credit rationing under specific circumstances (Stieglitz and Weiss 1981). The risk of bank runs is specific to the banking sector and hence the confidence of depositors and depositor protection are crucial elements of the institutional setup in the banking industry (Diamond and Dybvig 1983). From a theoretical perspective, there are sound arguments for why there should be ex-ante rules – regulations – for banks (Dewatripont and Tirole 1995) and not simply an application of the general competition law whose rules apply ex post, except for the field of merger control. Central banks are interested in systemic stability, as turbulences could undermine the effectiveness of monetary policy, and certainly investors and the general public have a strong interest in systemic stability (De Bandt and Hartmann 2000). For EU countries eager to create capital-based pension systems – as a complementary element to pay-as-you-go systems – the stability of financial markets is also quite crucial. While many banks run stress tests, it is unclear to which extent such tests are tailored adequately. From an economist's perspective, one may wonder whether prudential supervisors run simulations on the bankruptcy of individual banks. Part of the Economics research community was not really good in understanding the problems of the US subprime financing. For example, Peek and Wilcox (2006) argued on the basis of empirical analysis that the growth of asset backed securities markets had contributed to stabilizing housing investment in the US.

An important aspect of financial market developments concerns the links between financial innovations, investment and instability which is a Schumpeterian perspective on financial and real instability (Minsky 1990). Financial innovation such as securitization and asset-splitting had already been created in the 1980s (BIS 1986). An increasing role for private equity funds has been observed since the 1990s, and such funds have reinforced the adjustment and innovation pressure on firms. In certain cases, however, they have also weakened the long term ability of firms acquired to survive in the market (Van Den Burg and Rasmussen 2007). The innovation dynamics of the real sector in turn affects asset markets, in particular stock markets; patents affect the stock market prices significantly (Griliches et al. 1991). In imperfect capital markets, equity capital is important not least for financing international M&As, and a real depreciation of the currency – implying that foreign investors have a larger amount of equity capital expressed in the currency of the target country – will bring about higher foreign direct investment inflows relative to GDP (for the case of the US see Froot and Stein 1991). Thus, the international banking crisis must be explained in a broader context. An interesting feature of the US crisis is the fact that the US could still attract high capital inflows in 2007/2008, although its current account-deficit GDP ratio had reached 5–6% in that period. While conventional modeling suggests that high cumulated current account deficits imply a depreciation of the exchange rate (Hansen and Röger 2000), the US has experienced a rather strong appreciation of its currency in the second half of 2008, where a nominal appreciation reinforced the effect from the rise in the price level (followed by more deflationary pressure in 2009).

These puzzling effects as well as other issues must be analyzed, and one may ask to which extent the US is able to stabilize its economic system. While the US as a large economy should indeed be able to stabilize its banking system (paradoxically, part of the US automotive industry, including GM, is an element of the banking sector) through adequate policy measures, it is nevertheless obvious that a further acceleration of the banking crisis in 2009/2010 – fuelled by a strong US recession weakening banks further – could bring serious problems, as neither private US investors nor private investors from OECD countries are likely to be willing to recapitalize US banks on a broad scale. The US government had more or less provided \$200 billion as a government capital injection – financed through the \$700 billion TARP program – into US banks in late 2008, but already by early June 2009, the new US Administration allowed major banks to repay \$68 billion. Since most banks had favorably passed stress tests organized by the government and the US Central Bank, banks anticipated opportunities to tap the stock market. Moreover, they wanted to get rid of the restrictions on manager contracts which were part of the strings attached to government capital injections. Such strings were unwelcome, as foreign competitors not relying on US government capital injections could exploit the crisis, namely luring away skilled traders and top managers from major US banks.

If there should be further need to strengthen the capital basis of US banks, the US government and US banks would have to approach sovereign investment funds abroad, which would politically be a conflict-prone alternative. Another option would be further capital injections through the government, but such state-ownership of banks stands in sharp contrast to the principles of the US system. The options for international bank refinancing in the OECD are also weak, and this is largely due to the disaster with the bankruptcy of Lehman Brothers. For ideological reasons, the

Bush Administration had decided that there should be no further case like Bear Stearns which had been rescued in March 2008 with a guarantee of the US FED. Yet the decision to let Lehman go into Chap. 11 destroyed confidence in all major OECD markets; the interbank markets dried out in the following months in the US and the EU, so that the US government had generated serious negative transatlantic and indeed global spillover effects. The fact that the Bush Administration – and possibly also Congress – was unwilling to shore up guarantees from the FED for Barclays Bank, the only bidder left to take over Lehman Brothers on the weekend prior to September 15 – shows that economic nationalism is a vivid phenomenon in the US and that such political nationalism is indeed counter to the requirements of sustainable financial globalization.

The transatlantic banking crisis intensified after the US decided to let Lehman Brothers go bankrupt on September 15: a decision which was totally inconsistent given the previous bailout of the smaller investment bank Bear Stearns in March 2008; and taking into account that a few days later AIG, the giant insurance company, had been saved by the US government. The bankruptcy of Lehman in the midst of the banking crisis has fully destroyed confidence in OECD interbank markets and thus represents an irresponsible step on the part of the Bush administration. Freddie Mac and Fannie Mae had been rescued by government, not least under the pressure of China whose central bank held large amounts of bonds issues by those two semi-public mortgage banks. It seems that neither the EU nor Japan had warned the US not to let Lehman Brothers go bankrupt – the large majority of unsecured claims against Lehman Brothers was in Japan and the EU, while the US share was only about 10%. While the US government might have speculated that Lehman Brothers would be a cheap case of bankruptcy for the US, it was in effect the ultimate impulse for wiping out confidence in interbank markets of OECD countries. Thus the Bush administration committed a serious policy failure with large global negative external effects – with costs greatly exceeding simply the wiping out of international claims vis-à-vis Lehman Brothers. Lehman Brothers going under Chap. 11 signaled that no bank in the US was safe; and a fortiori, no bank in Europe.

As regards the starting dynamics of the banking crisis, one may well ask whether a broader perspective is adequate:

- The global imbalances in general and the high US current account deficit – partly reflecting high Chinese net exports of goods and services (and hence an excess of China's savings over domestic investment) – raise the question as to why so much capital was flowing towards the US. To some extent it was the mirror of current account surpluses of China, Japan and OPEC countries, but there is also a broad perception that the US financial system was the global leader in intermediation and that US leadership in financial innovations – including credit default swaps (CDS are a kind of insurance for loans and bonds, respectively, namely for the case that interest and principal might not be paid under adverse conditions). The US insurance company AIG had become one of the leading global underwriters of such CDS as became fully apparent when AIG – already rescued by the US government – was paying about €10 billion each to Deutsche Bank and Société Génerale in spring 2009 (smaller amounts to other EU banks and larger amounts to US banks; Goldman Sachs being the No. 1 in the US). It is clear that the Bush Administration had to rescue AIG since the option of non-rescuing would have implied large write-downs of portfolios in US banks and EU banks; some of those might have gone bankrupt within months after a fall of AIG. However, it is not clear that the US really has a comparative advantage in the CDS business. If one assumes that there are large national negative external effects in US CDS markets, the implication is that international services were much distorted. With internalization of such effects, the US might well have been a net importer of CDS and not a net exporter (see Appendix). If there were symmetric negative external effects in risk markets both in the US and the EU, the volume of CDS markets in the decade prior to 2007/2008 was much too high.

- Financial innovations played a strong role in the US banking system and the British banking system as well as part of the Euro zone banking system. Securitization became a broad phenomenon in the 1990s – beyond traditional government loans of developing countries. Banks in the US and the EU encouraged firms to place bonds which later allowed banks to repackage millions of corporate bonds into new bonds where part of those bonds obtained top ratings and thus could easily be sold in the capital market. Banks eager to obtain higher rates of return on equity often sold bundles of loans under the heading "originate-to-distribute" to special investment vehicles (SIVs), whose activities were not covered by banks' balance sheets. With such shadow banking increasing over time, bank depositors, investors and prudential supervisors understood less and less how big the true exposure of banks to risks really was. SIVs in turn relied on short-term refinancing. A full consolidation would have revealed that there was considerable balance-sheet mismatch. With increasing shadow banking (which formally required no bank equity capital under the regulations in most OECD countries), capital market signals became more and more unclear which might have caused efficiency losses. At the same time, it is quite unclear why prudential supervisors in the US and most European OECD countries – not in Spain and Italy – apparently ignored the fact that a rising share of banking activities were concealed from supervisory agencies. With banks chasing high rates of return on equity, there was a higher propensity to risk. However, risk management in several leading banks of the OECD area was apparently weak. In a paper on stress testing, the Bank of International Settlement noted that some banks did not even have professional risk management (BIS 2000), but such bad news had no visible consequence on the side of national supervisors in OECD countries.
- Trade in risk became a new growth area of both insurance companies and banks. Typically, a bank would buy a CDS from a large insurance company (or an investment bank), and often the respective bank would later sell the CDS in the global capital market. Almost all business was over the counter and thus opaque. There was no centralized registration on the CDS business and for unclear

reasons, prudential supervisors considered it normal that they had no idea where the CDS really were. Such a view was irresponsible since this blind spot of capital markets and supervisors implied that there could be large counterparty risks which would have gone unnoted, although a rise in counterparty risk always implies that the exposure of the underlying loans is rising. Worse, a bank which had bought CDS for a large portfolio of loans might have argued that there was no risk in its loan position and that the loans were highly liquid once they were repacked into a security – assuming here that the respective loan bundle and the associated asset-backed security had an A-rating. It could, however, happen that the respective bank would give a loan to a hedge fund which used the load to buy a "CDO squared" which would contain CDS originally bought by that bank. Why prudential supervisors in most OECD countries were allowing that under the heading of financial innovation market transparency and why the allocation of risk became increasingly opaque is rather unclear. One simple explanation is that supervisors have a mainly legal approach to supervision and are rather blind to the economic aspects of both financial innovations and supervision.

- Toxic assets – largely illiquid assets with doubtful ratings – became a major problem of many big banks during the 2007/2008 financial market crisis in OECD countries and governments in several countries have established a bad bank, which buys up some or most of the toxic assets of those banks. The assumption is that removing toxic assets from the banks' balance sheets will allow banks to function in a normal way, namely to finance investment and innovation projects. The British government has created a bad bank which has allowed British banks to largely exchange toxic assets against liquid government securities. The Obama Administration also has created a kind of bad bank approach which combines private sector money and government money – effectively subsidies for banks – to take care of toxic assets. Toxic assets were a major driver of high write-downs and losses of banks and insurance companies in the US and the EU in 2007/2008 ($180 billion for Freddie Mae and Fannie Mac, two semi-private US mortgage banks which effectively were nationalized in 2008; Bank of America, Wachovia and Citigroup had slightly above $100 billion in losses between 2007 and spring 2009; HSBC $42 billion, RBS $31 billion, HBOS $26 billion; AIG saw $90 billion, and in Germany, Deutsche Bank, Bayern LB and IKB recorded $19, 16 and 14 billion, respectively). Banks, funds and insurance companies had recorded losses of $1,471 billion in the period 2007 to May 2009, of which $1,236 billion could be recapitalized. The gap of $235 billion is noteworthy, and if one assumes that typically $1 equity capital of a bank finances $20 of investment there could be a global (cumulated) bank loan and hence investment gap of some $4,500 billion, which is almost twice the GDP of Germany. In early 2009, it also became apparent that world trade was suffering directly from the lack of international trade financing; risk premia had increased strongly in 2008/2009, and international trade to some extent fell victim to this development.

- As regards Germany, the country was facing one of the most difficult challenges in the OECD countries since a high share of Germany's exports consists of machinery and capital equipment. With investment – and real income – falling in most OECD countries in 2008/2009, it was clear that the German economy would face particular economic problems. Both in Germany and abroad, firms adopted major cuts in investment planning, partly because of the apparent world recession, partly because there was an increasing fear of a credit crunch. Firms eager to survive could not simply wait until central bank surveys would finally show a serious credit crunch. A modest increase in the probability of a future credit crunch might often be sufficient to cause big cuts in investment budgets in OECD countries. From there, a negative multiplier-accelerator mechanism could easily undermine economic recovery – not least since the world recession implied further downwrites on asset positions of banks. Increased uncertainty about future income in turn will translate into reduced current consumption spending, and hence a rapid rise in unemployment rates might occur. Generous government provisions and public funds earmarked for subsidizing temporary work during recession periods has helped employment in Germany to fall only gradually after the 2007/2008 transatlantic banking crisis.
- Central banks in the US and the UK have reduced interest rates to low record levels of close to zero in early 2009 and both central banks have adopted nontraditional instruments by directly acquiring part of the toxic assets of banks. The ECB has been somewhat more hesitant with extreme reductions of the interest rate and also quantitative easing has been adopted in a hesitant manner – largely because there is fear of losing central bank reputation and fuelling inflationary expectations in the medium term. As regards the short run (2009/2010), there is little doubt that the main transitory problem in OECD countries will not be inflation but rather deflation as high global excess supply in the tradables markets implies a sharp downward pressure on goods prices and the overall price levels. Moreover, as real estate prices have fallen strongly in the US, the US, Spain, France, Italy – less so in Germany – there is also downward pressure on the price level through falling rental prices. Many observers argued in early 2009 that there could be a quick economic recovery in OECD countries, however, one may raise some doubts about overly optimistic scenarios. The IMF's estimate in its spring 2009 Financial Stability Report that global downwrites in the financial industry in the end will reach about $4,000 billion implies that the second half of downward adjustment in banks is still to come. OECD governments have facilitated window-dressing in balance sheets since banks now can switch – from one quarter to the next – between fair value method and valuation on the basis of acquisition prices. This might have created an optimistic mood among capital market actors, however, window dressing should not be confused with really sorting out key problems. One unsolved problem is the poor information quality of balance sheets and the new valuation options compound the problem

mentioned. Thus the quality uncertainty about the banks' balances is reinforced so that the market-for-lemon-problems will persist in most OECD countries.

- The London G-20 summit of April 2, 2009 is historic, since it implies that the traditional global governance structure – the G-8 club – is no longer capable of sorting out critical issues. While the G-20 summit has promised to adopt stricter regulation of banks and hedge funds, one may doubt that all countries which have signed the London Declaration will really implement the measures necessary to implement the reforms promised. One also may raise the issue to which extent an adequate balance between more competition – and possibly less regulation – and more regulation, namely for few big banks (with the official label too big to fail) will be found. There also is the question whether one can find a way back to a normal economic situation with price stability, sustained growth and full employment and stable government finances. Moreover, one must raise the question as to whether sustainable financial globalization – assuming that it could generate net global economic benefits – is a realistic goal in the present global politico-economic system.
- The amounts mobilized to save the banking system and to stabilize the economy are very high: 10% deficit–GDP ratios (as expected for 2009) in the US and the UK are absolutely exceptional for times of peace, and it is hard to imagine that a strong increase of debt–GDP ratios in these two countries will not go along with higher real interest rates in the medium run and higher inflation rates in the long run – not so much because a high debt–GDP ratio causes inflation, rather the incentive for government to inflate away the burden of higher debt might be rather strong in the long run. The pressure towards higher inflation rates is not necessarily linked to the enormous creation of liquidity of central banks in the US and the UK – plus the Eurozone – in the aftermath of the collapse of interbank markets, but it simply reflects empirical findings about the long term link between the size of the debt–GDP ratio and the political propensity in favor of inflationary policies.

Since banks no longer trust each other, the refinancing of banks through state-guaranteed bonds is one of the few alternatives for restarting both the interbank market and the capital market. This will go along with mergers and acquisitions and government participation in major banks as well as other bail-out measures of governments. The governments of the US and of many EU countries have strongly intervened in the banking markets, creating thereby bigger banks as part of the rescue operations in the US. Such developments are, however, in contrast to what structural reforms require, namely more competition among private banks and dismemberment of large banks in order to bring about effective competition. The following analysis takes a look at the dynamics of the banking crisis (Sect. 3.2), considers some key theoretical aspects (Sect. 3.3) and suggests necessary reforms in the EU and at the global policy level (Sect. 3.4). In appendix serious doubts about Basel regulatory equity rules are raised: the Basel I-rule as well as the Basel II-rule raise the likelihood of a banking crisis.

3.2 The Dynamics of the Banking Crisis

At first glance, the US banking crisis started in subprime mortgage financing, as house prices started to fall in 2007. This implied serious doubts about the value of mortgage-backed securities largely held by special purpose vehicles (SPVs) of banks which had organized increasing off-balance sheet activities through SPV. Most SPVs held large positions of asset-backed securities (ABS) which represented loan portfolios which had been sold in national and international capital markets. The originate-to-distribute model which became popular in the late 1990s assumed that banks could easily sell loan portfolios in the capital market; banks created SPVs to unload ABS and to widen off-balance sheet activities. Hence the incentive for banks to broaden risk management was weakened and this held all the more as banks alternatively could not sell a loan portfolio but rather only the risk associated with that portfolio (we will refer to the relevant credit default swaps – the insurance instruments part of which was traded in the market – subsequently). As SPVs relied on refinancing through short-term commercial papers, the collapse of the US commercial paper market in summer 2007 forced banks to take the portfolios of their respective SPVs back into their own books – the credit lines which banks had given to their respective SPVs when setting up the SPVs were enormous and had not really been meant to be drawn upon. The very purpose of the large credit line was to get a top rating for the SPV and to thereby make sure that the SPV had low refinancing costs.

Falling house prices in the US had undermined confidence of investors into mortgage-based securities (MBS) held by SPVs and problems with refinancing MBS indicated serious problems in the ABS market. The price of portfolios representing MBS related to the mortgage subprime market in the US fell quickly in summer 2007. However, the crisis was not confined to the US. In the UK, a bank run on Northern Rock occurred in 2007, and the government quickly decided to save the bank whose problems could have been anticipated if the regulator had more carefully studied the aggressive expansion strategy of that mortgage bank (Mullineux 2007). In early 2008 the UK government decided to nationalize Northern Rock and this became the starting point to heavy government involvement in the UK banking crisis. British banks had largely adopted similar business models as their US counterparts and several banks were involved in the markets for MBS/ABS. As refinancing of SPVs became more and more difficult in summer and autumn 2007 the prices of the respective assets fell strongly: lack of liquidity in the markets became a major problem. The British financial markets were largely following the US market developments; British banks were strongly active in the US, but London also was the place where AIG FP, an AIG subsidiary specialized in CDS transactions was most active: Selling CDS for a bundle of loans – not for individual loans – had become a new business of AIG in 1998 (with Gary Gorton from the University of Pennsylvania being a major advisor for calculating CDS prices) and a few years later US investment banks were eager to get CDS for Collateralized Debt Obligations which in effect stands for a bundle of a bundle of loans: In the notes to the 2007 balance sheet one finds the information that AIG FP has sold a large volume of CDS: $ 562 billion. It was only in October 2005 that AIG managers in New York became suspicious about AIG FP activities whose CDS transaction included about $ 80 bill. on CDOs partly associated with subprime loans; while AIG FP stopped the subprime business in late 2005 other AIG subsidiaries continued with subprime investment – poor governance of AIG is visible here and the largest quarterly loss ever recorded in the US one of the results of weak management: $ 617 bill. in 2007.IV. The US government had to take over AIG in September 2008, the federal government invested 85 bill. in the first round and more in the year following so that the price tag for the US taxpayer figured about 180 bill. in early 2009 (the market value stood at only $ 6 bill. in mid-2009 which is a large discount compared to the top value of a market capitalization of $ 240 bill. on December 2000). AIG had grown partly on the back of temporary hyper growth of US investment banking.

In 2004, Wall Street Investment Bankers achieved a softening of SEC regulations, namely that the permissible leverage ratio was raised to 40 – but in the end this softening only raised the speed of high-risk investment banking, and all major investment banks went under or were merged with traditional banks in 2008. There are serious doubts that value-added of investment banks on Wall Street were positive in the period 2002–2008; the losses incurred and losses imposed on other banks, firms and countries most likely have exceeded profits and wages paid in that period. Moreover, big banks in the US – all too big to fail – obtained government capital and thus it seemed that those banks faced a soft budget constraint, a phenomenon which had been emphasized by Kornai (1980) in his book about socialist command economies. While his argument referred to banks and firms, the US case is mainly limited to the banking system, but if ailing automotive firms and other sectors would also come under the umbrella of the US government, the soft budget phenomenon would gain in relevance. The $700 billion rescue package offered by the US Congress for saving the banks and insurance companies – to this sum one must also add some $250 billion for rescuing Bear Stearns and Fannie Mae and Freddie Mac – will have been spent by mid-2009, and there is some risk that the US government will have to come up with even higher amounts of capital injections, guarantees and subsidies in the coming years. The recession of 2008/2009 will aggravate the problems of banks and insurance companies, and depreciations of portfolios will become a serious problem again.

The IMF (2008) warned early that depreciations of banks and hedge funds and investment funds could reach about $1,000 bill. worldwide, while updates of the IMF in the spring 2009 suggested even figures around $4,000 bill. The Stability Report of the Bank of England (2008) in autumn 2008 had already warned that depreciations could reach even $2.8 trillion. Such depreciations would partly reflect the impact of the recessions in the US, the UK and other countries affected by the international banking crisis. This crisis which apparently started in the US subprime mortgage market in 2007 and caused major problems in the interbank market accelerated in the summer of 2008 – with the collapse of the US investment bank Lehman Brothers on September 15 causing market panic.

In a historical perspective, the US banking crisis is the most severe crisis since the Great Depression, and the enormous international collateral damages and high costs to the US economy – facing recession in 2008/2009 – raises the question about the causes of this disaster, the impact of the international banking crisis and the options for dealing with the crisis. As regards the latter, one should clearly make a distinction between crisis management necessary to overcome the banking crisis in the short run and the structural reforms required in the context of more long-term systemic changes.

In the short run it will be necessary to save the banking systems in the US, the UK and the euro zone. Without a stable banking system there is a serious risk of another Great Depression. Governments have offered multi-billion dollar packages for partial nationalization of banks – read recapitalization of banks – and guarantees for banks which want to sell bonds in a shaky securities market and an almost non-existent interbank market. Given the small number of big US banks, competition among banks is rather weak as there is a rather general 'too big to fail problem' in the US (provided that the bank considered faces a large share of unsecured claims of US private and corporate citizens; hence the Lehman Brothers case is not really a counter-example).

Banks have lost confidence in each other, and the starting point was the growing tendency of bankers in the US (and Europe) to avoid regulatory equity requirements by transforming loans into asset-backed securities which could be sold in the capital market and often ended up in the special investment vehicles created by the banks themselves. The banks' expansion of off-balance sheet activities have thus created a market-for-lemons problem; that is, there was increasing quality uncertainty among bankers who could no longer draw reliable information from balance sheets about the financial status of potential partner banks. The classical lemons problem (Akerlof 1970) which had been identified as a potential source for market failure in goods markets is now visible in financial markets; with confidence among banks declining liquidity for many products has dried up.

In a similar way Taylor (2009) has argued that crisis management of the FED should be guided by clear principles and that the FED's policy to simply swamp markets with central bank liquidity is doubtful in a situation in which confidence problems in interbank markets signal that solvency problems in the banking sector are part and parcel of the problem: This can be seem from the spread between the 3 month LIBOR (relevant for short-term interbank lending) and the Overnight Index Swap (proxy for expected central bank rate in the coming 3 months): The spread was minimal – 0.1% points – in early summer 2007, in August it jumped and reached about 1% point as confidence among banks fell sharply, in October 2008, after the Lehman shock, it had reached 3.5% point, by January 2009 the spread had fallen to 0.92%. Solvency problems cannot be solved by massive liquidity injections of the central bank, rather recapitalization of banks and measures that improve the quality of financial reporting of banks are required – the latter has not been emphasized by the G20 on the London summit of April 2, 2009, indeed, several OECD countries have softened accounting standards which artificially raise equity capital and create 'accounting uncertainty' as banks are allowed to switch from quarter to quarter between different valuation standards. Even with some banks reporting profits in early 2009 one cannot be sure that this is reflecting sound banking since at the beginning of the twenty-first century Credit Default Swap growth was enormous – with the US company AIG being a global leader in the CDS market (CDS cover default risks in loan markets), while risk pricing was distorted (Goodhart 2007). High capital inflows in the US and expansionary monetary policy also have played a role here.

The US banking crisis is serious and has undermined the stability of the US and the transatlantic financial system. While the FED – through cutting interest rates sharply – and the US government have taken emergency measures to stabilize the economy, there is no sign that the US has adopted adequate structural reforms. With the quasi-nationalization of Fannie Mae and Freddie Mac (plus Citibank), the US has indeed paid a high prize for the lingering mismanagement of the banking crisis and for years of insufficient prudential supervision as well as a framework which allows rating firms to effectively operate on very weak professional standards (Ussec 2008). The latter has contributed to the subprime crisis and the collapse of the interbank markets in the US and Europe. Moreover, there were strange developments which have almost fully eliminated the normal risk premia – e.g., measured through the spread between corporate bonds with A-rating and government bond yields – in the US from 2003 to 2006 (Goodhart 2007). Too many A-rated subprime bonds were unloaded in financial markets and for unclear reasons, the senior tranches of almost all mortgage-based securities, exploding in volume between 2002 and 2006, could easily obtain an A rating in the US.

It is widely accepted that the US banking crisis started in the summer of 2007 when the housing prices started to fall and doubts about the substance of mortgage-based securities (MBS) spread, thus making the refinancing of special investment vehicles – with a strong focus on asset-backed securities (ABS)/MBO – increasingly difficult. However, the sources of the fragility of US banks and financial markets dates back to the late 1990s when hedge funds with high rates of return on equity created enormous pressure for Wall Street Banks.

- The unregulated hedge funds with their high rates of return – about 20% in the late 1990s – put enormous pressure on banks to come up with similar rates of return on equity. Twenty-five percent became a kind of magic number announced by top managers of US banks and with some delay also by bankers in the EU. Raising the return on equity became a top priority of bankers and stock markets, and the owners of banks quoted on the stock market cheered when top managers announced ever higher target rates of return – although basic Economics suggests that even a rate of return on equity of 15% would be quite remarkable if achieved over an extended period of time. The UBS in the US has indeed created its own hedge funds. Many banks in the US and the EU created off-balance sheet activities and special purpose vehicles to raise the rate of return; SPVs invested in ABS/MBS and collateralized debt obligation (CDOs) – CDO are repacked bundles of ABS with specific tranches in terms of risk profiles – and relied on short term commercial paper for refinancing.

This model collapsed once the participants in commercial paper market faced doubts about the inherent value of mortgage-based securities (MBS). With US real estate prices falling in 2007, doubts emerged quickly, and banks had to take the papers of their respective SPVs back into the balance sheet. The basic point is not that house prices can fall over time; the key problem is that hedge funds were unregulated and their indirect role for systemic instability was not recognized. Most critics looked only at the problem of leverage in hedge funds, but the associated high pressure on banks to come up with higher returns was largely ignored.

- A very serious problem is the market for lemons problems created by banks themselves. With increasing off-balance sheet activities, effective banking operations could no longer be monitored through balance sheets. As rumors about problems in off-balance activities became wide-spread, the confidence in banks generally declined. A second problem is the lack of transparency and the incompleteness of balance sheets. To achieve this goal, banks created off-balance sheet activities, largely in the form of special investment vehicles, which bought long-term asset-backed securities and hoped to easily refinance those portfolios through short-term commercial papers; many banks had created ABS, since an expansion of the loan business could thus be reconciled with regulatory capital requirements. In order to get a top rating for the SPV and hence low financing costs, the respective SPV typically obtained a large credit line from the parent bank. Banks did not have to put up any equity capital for such credit lines under Basel I rules.
- Banks packed dozens of loans in asset-backed securities and sold ABS and related papers in the capital market. In many cases, the banks wanted to maintain the loans on their books but wanted to get rid of the risk associated with the loans; the financial innovation used for this purposed were the Credit Default Swaps, which banks bought from special service providers and insurance companies – but CDS in term were traded in the capital market, mostly in the over the counter market. This market lacks transparency for both the prudential authorities and for the market as such. Regulators indeed allowed the CDSs to be sold around the world, and no one kept track of these transactions, although it would be wise to know those market participants representing the counterparty risk and whether they would be able to fully pay once the insurance case became reality. As lack of prudential supervision created a global veil of ignorance with respect to the allocation of CDS – there was no clearing house or global registry – currency markets and bonds markets are not only facing an impossible challenge, namely to correctly assess risk premia for various countries (it makes a big difference if most CDS were held within the US, the euro zone, the UK or China). Moreover, the market value of the underlying loan portfolios also became difficult to assess as it makes a big difference whether there is credible insurance for the loan. Allocation of CDS across countries remained opaque, and hence the efficiency of financial market pricing remained low. While the US recorded high growth rates of credit in the period from 2000 to 2006, the risk premia in credit markets declined to nearly zero in the period from

2003 to 2006, which was quite an abnormal situation. Part of this phenomenon could be explained by overgenerous rating agencies which accorded top ratings to too many financial products and business models, including SPVs.

- Rating agencies often came up with fantasy ratings which were much too good to be true – e.g., even 2 days before Lehman went bankrupt, the leading US rating agencies had almost top ratings for the bank. Many ABS/MBS had top ratings, although it seems that the rating agencies' methods were highly doubtful. In the context of Basel II, external ratings have a quasi-official status, and it is of paramount importance to make sure that ratings are carefully awarded and also swiftly corrected if needed over time. As long as ratings are flawed, there will be misjudgement of risks in capital markets and an underpricing of risks. US prudential supervision remained quite weak under the Bush administration. The USSEC – responsible for investment banks – was mainly interested in investor risk. However, it did not consider systemic risk issues, and the number of employees dealing with risk management fell dramatically under the presidency of George W. Bush. The Fed which was in charge of traditional banks (bank holdings) had adopted a laisser-faire-attitude under Chairman Greenspan; banks in the US and in the EU could incur increasing risks without regulators requiring enhanced risk management. Stability Reports of various central banks (Bank of England; ECB) warned about the rising risk banks were taking within OECD countries, but the regulators and the banks ignored such warnings. Moreover, the IMF's Financial Sector Assessment Program analyzed many crucial OECD countries, except for the US. It was only in 2006 that the US government agreed to a report being published on the US system in 2009.
- Time horizons of managers and traders were rather short, and there were inadequate incentives for long term investment horizons in banks. Many top bankers pursued high risk strategies and generated high bonus payments for managers and traders as long as the economic boom – along with rising asset prices – continued in the US and Europe. In the medium term – as asset prices fell – many banks, however, suffered high depreciations and losses from such 'front-loaded' investment strategies. The typical assumption of most textbook Economics – namely that investors maximize a profit function over a very long (infinite) time horizon – was not realistic, rather a hit and retire approach was often observed. As long as the boom continued, one could hit high goals, and once a crisis befell the market, early retirement was the ideal option for managers naturally willing to incur big risks for their respective banks.

The following figure summarizes the key dynamics of the US banking crisis which resulted not only in the collapse of the commercial paper market and the interbank market in late 2007, but also in the US central bank and the ECB providing emergency liquidity to banks which no longer could obtain loans in the money market and the interbank market. Mistrust among banks in the euro zone is so great that more than €100 billion in excess reserves were kept at the ECB during several weeks in 2008, although market rates in the interbank markets were higher

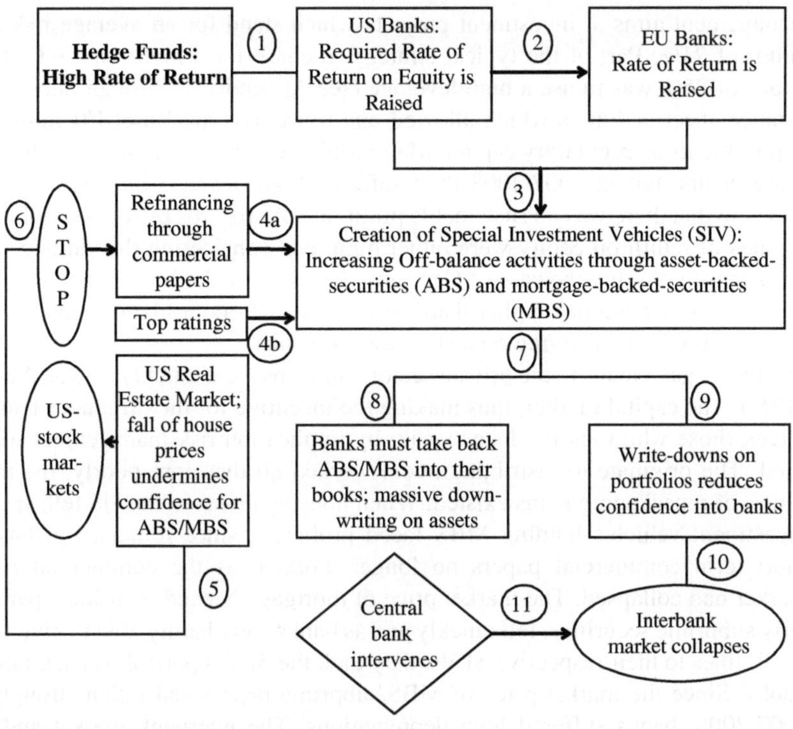

Fig. 3.1 Dynamics of the interbank market

than what could be earned at the ECB account. It is not surprising that the problems in US real estate market and US banks brought about a fall of the stock market price index in 2008; stock market prices in the euro zone also fell strongly in autumn 2008 (Fig. 3.1).

Coping successfully with the banking crisis and avoiding repeating this crisis within a few years can only be achieved if the causes of the banking crisis are recognized and adequate policy reforms be adopted. The problems in the US and European banking sectors are not really surprising if one considers the early warnings emphasizing the risk of falling house prices in the US – and Artus and Virard (2005), who warned that high rates of return on equity implied a high risk premium and hence incurring high risks.

- The laws of Economics imply that in the long run the nominal interest rate i must be equal to the sum of the inflation rate and the real interest rate (r), and r must be equal to the growth rate of real output (g_Y). The rate of return on capital in turn should be equal to the risk free government bond interest rate i plus a risk premium Ω – in the stock market being equal to the price of risk times the variance of the stock market price. If the risk free nominal interest rate is 4% and the required rate of return on equity is 25% the implication is that the bank management aims at investment projects which stand for an average risk premium of 21%. Part of the typical strategy to chase for a high required rate of return of 25% was to use a high leverage (see Appendix 3) through raising off-balance sheet activities which allowed one to by-pass the Basel I/II minimum requirements on regulatory capital. Many banks achieved 25% rates of return for a few years, but in 2007/2008 they suffered high depreciations and massive losses so that there was no sustainable profit rate. As regards big banks' volatility of rates of return on equity were rather high; e.g. considering the variance as a measure of volatility the case of Germany shows that volatility of rates of return of big banks were much higher than the volatility of savings banks, cooperative banks or Landesbanken/regional state-owned banks.

- The banks gave loans to the private sector, but loans were quickly sold as ABS or MBS in the capital market, thus making the incentive for the originator bank to screen those who took the loans weak; by implication risk management weakened. The originate-to-distribute model worked all the more poorly, the more stages of repackaging loans existed. When housing prices in the US fell, special investment vehicles holding MBS faced problems, since refinancing through short term commercial papers no longer worked, as the commercial paper market had collapsed. The market price of mortgage backed securities, particularly subprime securities, fell quickly and as banks were hardly able to give large credit lines to their respective SPVs, they took the SPV's portfolios back into its books. Since the market price of MBS/subprime papers had fallen strongly in 2007/2008, banks suffered high depreciations. The interbank market and the money market collapsed in 2008 as banks lost confidence in each other (this is the Akerlof problem already mentioned) – not knowing how large off-balance stakes were on the one hand and how big risks associated with various portfolio positions, often involving previous CDS transactions, really were on the other hand. Banks stopped lending to each other or did so only against collateral which was unusual hitherto. In the euro zone, moreover, banks with high liquidity would rather channel excess liquidity into the accounts of the ECB than offer such liquidity overnight to banks at interest rates well above the central bank's deposit rate.

In fact the banking crisis is not a real surprise, and one has to blame both banks themselves and prudential supervisors in the US and the EU to have allowed such chaos in financial markets to emerge. The US dynamics largely show that the big banks no longer understood the system they had created and for that US policymakers had failed to implement a clear system of supervision – instead the US had refused to adopt the Basel II rules which would have imposed at least a small amount of equity capital for extending large credit lines to special investment vehicles (in this perspective the UK banking sector looks better positioned than the US). By refusing to adopt Basel II, the US not only created an uneven transatlantic playing field for banks, but it also prevented greater transparency – in a world economy with high growth – from being achieved.

The priority reforms are therefore obvious; they must correspond to the problems identified and should be adopted by the relevant policy layers:

- Regulation of hedge funds: Hedge funds – largely active from tax havens – with more than €1 billion should be required to register with the Bank of International Settlements; BIS must reserve the right to raise equity requirements if deemed necessary, and trading in CDS could be restricted. Hedge funds which do not comply with BIS rules must not be permitted to trade government bonds in any member country of the IMF; this clause might require that government bonds be traded only through international clearinghouses, thus excluding over-the counter trade – in this manner, tax havens would be subject to rules and guidelines set at the European and global policy level.
- Banks must establish fully consolidated balance sheets, in the sense that a total balance sheet includes all off-balance sheet activities; banks which do not comply must face sharply restricted access to central bank liquidity. The ECB (the central bank) should encourage interbank activities by according different discount rates, namely a low discount rate to banks strongly active in the interbank market; banks with low activities in the interbank market would face higher discount rates. Thus one would have an incentive for banks to engage in the interbank market. The enormous expansion of ECB liquidity provision in euro zone interbank markets is a doubtful exercise if it were to continue in the long run; this would undermine both the efficiency of monetary policy and the incentive of banks to engage in the interbank market, which is normally a market important for the efficiency of the banking system – monitoring and signaling are crucial elements of the normal competition process in the interbank market.
- A strange problem of the transatlantic banking crisis concerns the uncertainties about valuation of assets and the opaque term toxic assets clouds the serious problem that financial markets are expected to price assets perfectly as markets are efficient – but all of a sudden bankers have told the general public that no (adequate) price can be found for many financial assets, some of which are allegedly 'too complex'. The critical economist understands, of course, that poor incentives for bank managers result from the standard procedure that bankers quickly repackage loans and sell them in the market under the ABS heading. What could be done to cope with the various problems? ABS products should be standardized in order to avoid complex pricing problems, and all CDS should be registered in a global data bank; a bank issuing ABS should keep 20% of the equity tranche in its books (this gives a strong incentive to really consider the risks contained in the loans which back the ABS) and declare its willingness to buy back the ABS product at 50% of the original price at any point in time, thereby avoiding pricing uncertainty even in the critical case that markets for specific financial products should collapse; the underestimation of liquidity risks, which was a serious element of the US/transatlantic banking crisis, must be avoided in the future. The 50% rule gives a strong incentive to bankers to carefully consider which loans they are bundling into a particular package and to whom the product is sold. New transactions with CDS should be possible only

through a clearinghouse, and previous CDS transactions should be required to register worldwide – otherwise, confidence in financial markets cannot be restored (the EU and the US have adopted steps into this direction in 2009).

- Rating agencies must face new rules and should be required to obtain a license as proposed by the European Commission; in addition, there should be random checks and fines for poor rating accuracy. Conflicts of interests (in the traditional regime, banks placing a bond issue have paid the respective rating agency) must be avoided. Specifically, a two-stage financing procedure would be useful; banks, firms or governments wanting to place bonds in the market should pay into a pool, and this pool then would finance the rating process on the basis of competitive tenders. At the bottom line, fees to be paid should reflect market shares of issuers – with a top-up for weak ratings of the respective placement of bonds. Thus, the information derived from ratings should be considered as a public rather than a private good. It would be useful if the EU or the ECB would encourage the creation of at least one major European rating agency.
- A new tax regime is necessary for banks, funds and insurance companies. Taxing the profits (Π) of banks should be only one basis for taxation; in addition, the variability of the rate of return on equity should be considered. The higher the variance ('V') on the rate of return, the higher the overall tax rate to be applied should be. The tax to be paid by an individual bank j would thus be given by subset formula (Π stands for profit, : τ is the income tax rate relevant for profits and τ^V is the tax rate applied to the variance). The tax formula would apply only for the profit exceeding one currency unit as the $\ln\Pi$ is the tax base for the variance tax – one element behind this formula is that an excessive variance translates into an unnormally high profit. Banks anticipating such a tax burden would have an incentive to take a more long-term view – in the long term, the variability should be smaller than in the short term, and bank managers can influence the variance of the respective bank's rate of return (Fig. 3.2).

(1) $T = \tau\Pi + \tau^V\ [V''\ln\Pi]$; marginal tax rate $dT/d\Pi$ will approach τ with $\Pi \rightarrow \infty$

A variance tax would be a true innovation in the OECD tax systems, but such a tax is indeed quite useful since it would help to avoid excessive short-term decision-making which results in excessive risk-taking and high negative national or international external effects (i.e., international instability spillovers and problems related to systemic instability causes by non-sustainable bankers' strategies). Indeed, a variance tax could be considered a special PIGOU tax which helps to internalize negative external effects. There could be a minor problem in recessions when the rate of return on equity falls, hence making the variance tax pro-cyclical; however, government could introduce a partial or full waiver for variance taxation in recessions.

Taking stock of the key elements of the banking crisis identifies seven areas of weaknesses: (1) deficiencies of US banking regulation; the Paulson reform program, which suggests that the FED should have a larger role in regulation, is a doubtful program given the fact that the FED has not used existing regulatory

Priority Reforms for Overcoming the International Banking Crisis				
Hedge Funds: must register with BIS; equity requirement; hedge funds which do not comply with rules cannot trade in government bonds markets	Balance Sheets: Full disclosure of bank's activities: including all off-shore balance activities	ABS and CDS: Standardization of ABS products; 20% of the equity tranche remains at the bank and bank must declare that it is willing to buy back the ABS at 50% of the original price	Rating Agencies: Agencies should face new rules such as obtaining a licence; agencies should be subject to random checks, fines for poor work; two-stage financing	New Tax Regime: Taxing profits and taxing the variability (variance) of the rate of return on equity
AIM: Controlling Risk from HFs	AIM: Restoring Confidence	AIM: Transparency, reduced transaction costs	AIM: Improving the quality of the ratings process; raising the quality of information	AIM: Encouraging long term time horizon of banks, funds and insurance companies (avoid short-term hit and retire strategy & inadequate bonus systems)

Fig. 3.2 Structural reforms to be adopted

power – its board has made clear for years that the best regulation effectively is no regulation. (2) There is a sustained problem of market failure in the US interbank markets and in EU interbank markets in 2007/2008, which represents a self-imposed market-for-lemon problem caused by insufficient financial reporting and opaque balance sheets. (3) Special problems of interbank market failure in the US have emerged, namely to the extent that EU banks were squeezed out of the market – somewhat remedied by the transatlantic swap operations organized by the FED and its counterparts in Europe; the swap operations allow EU banks with US subsidiaries – they were effectively locked out of the US interbank market after the summer of 2007 – to obtain dollar loans from the ECB, which in turn has obtained a dollar loan from the FED. The European bank will then send the dollar liquidity to its US subsidiary, which is a very strange indicator of discrimination of foreign banks in the US interbank market. This could be understood as being counter to the GATS rules of the WTO. (4) From 2002 to 2006, leading US rating agencies have partly done sloppy work as the report by the USSEC (2008) has shown, and it is absolutely unclear why Basel II gives those rating agencies even more power – external ratings have an official status for risk management of banks – while not imposing decent standards and responsibilities. (5) The trigger for the banking crisis was not the subprime crisis but the strange increase in the required rate of return on capital on Wall Street at the beginning of the twenty-first century. EU banks were afraid of being taken over by US banks if they could not match the new Wall Street benchmarks. (6) To a limited extent, the financial innovations adopted in the OECD banking world in the context of the originate-and-distribute approach is a useful way to deal with risk, but the excessive creation of A-rated ABS is doubtful, and systematic failure to consider liquidity risk raises doubts about the overall framework within which banks operate; (7) in Germany, there are major weaknesses in the field of banking supervision, and costs for the taxpayer of dealing with the IKB problems and part of the Landesbanken are already high – here, national reforms and EU reforms are necessary.

The reforms suggested in the context of this analysis are urgent and will help to sort out the mess in the US financial markets and elsewhere. While overregulation should be avoided, there is a need for more and better regulation. Basically, there are seven key proposals for solving the banking crisis: (i) The interbank market is fully restored by forcing banks to disclose their positions in structured products and off-balance sheet activities. In particular, banks must fully disclose all off-balance sheet investments in the notes to the balance sheet; moreover, from a specific target rate on, banks must hold 20% of the equity part of asset-backed securities; litigation among banks, which has increased in 2007/2008 and increasingly destroys confidence in the markets, should be minimized and conflicts be sorted out quickly outside courtrooms to the greatest extent possible; (ii) only those banks which have met the new disclosure procedures and take full commitment to the equity part investment in ABS will get full access to central bank refinancing. These measures will restore confidence in the interbank market. In the EU, a new European Banking Standard Council should be established which monitors banks' behaviour in world capital markets; strange behaviour and obvious problems in meeting legal requirements – e.g., UBS in the US from 1999 to 2008 – will have consequences, namely that banks considered in breach of critical rules and standards are excluded for at least 5 years from all transactions in the context of the emission of government bonds in the EU/euro zone. (iii) As regards the EU, greater efforts in terms of harmonizing national prudential supervision should be adopted; so far, the EU indeed offers a bewildering range of institutional arrangements – e.g., the central bank is involved in some countries, in some countries it is not involved at all and in still other countries it has exclusive competence for the supervision of banks and financial markets. (iv) The European Commission should publish regular reports on the banking systems in EU countries, and member countries should quantify the welfare costs of major banking crisis; in such a way, a new field of benchmarking would be established. Medium-sized and large hedge funds should become more involved in reporting as soon as they have the needed leverage, and an option should also be introduced for central banks to impose a maximum leverage ratio. In 2006/2007, the IMF did a poor job in economic policy assessment; its lukewarm reports on the US economy were not in line with what sober analysis of the US economy and US economic policy – required as part of regular surveillance of IMF member countries – would have shown, namely critical faults in US prudential supervision and massive growth of credit along with strongly declining risk premia in US bonds markets from 2003 to 2006. The reporting procedures in the IMF should therefore be adjusted in a way which enables external experts to contribute to surveillance activities. Finally, within the WTO, it remains to be analyzed to which extent the asymmetric collapse of the US interbank market represents a discrimination: subsidiaries of foreign banks could not obtain loans in the interbank market while the system still worked for US banks (e.g. subsidiaries of Eurozone banks would have to turn to their parent banks which in turn obtained $ liquidity from the ECB which had concluded swap arrangements with the FED).

An important issue concerns the question as to why the real interest rate in OECD countries (measured by government bond yields minus inflation rate) fell so dramatically in the crisis 2007/2008. In a standard portfolio model with stocks (expected stochastic yield is μ^R; variance is σ^R) and risk-free government bonds (yield r), the equilibrium of the investor – assuming a utility function $U = \alpha \ln\mu' - \alpha' \ln\sigma'$ (where α and α' are positive parameters, μ' and σ' denote the expectation value of the portfolio yield and the variance of the portfolio yield, respectively) – the equilibrium is given by the condition $\alpha'\mu'/(\alpha'\sigma') = [(\mu^R - r)/\sigma^R]$ which implies that the real interest rate is given by

(1) $r = \mu^R - [(\alpha'\mu'\sigma^R]/(\alpha\sigma')]$

In a world recession the expected yield on stocks (μ^R) will be relatively low. At the same time, it seems that investors are characterized by a preference shock in the sense that the degree of risk aversion as measured by the ratio α'/α has increased to the point that indeed many individuals might reconsider the weight attached to risk. (Such a shock to preferences is not a standard element of textbook Economics, however, the transatlantic banking crisis has been such an economic, political and social earthquake in the US, the UK and some other European countries starting with Iceland, Switzerland, Ireland, the Baltic countries and many other east European countries.) Moreover, the volatility of the yield of stocks has temporarily increased as a result of the crisis and thus it should not be surprising if there is both a temporary fall of r and a long term – preference-driven – fall in government bond yields. The latter would make financing and refinancing of government debt easier.

As regards the massive and sudden economic downturn in the US and the EU in the fourth quarter of 2008 and in 2009, one may emphasize several points:

- The downturn was not part of the forecast of standard macroeconomic models; a major reason for this ‘forecasting failure’ was that the US government’s decision to send Lehman Brothers into Chap. 11 in mid-September 2008 was a politico-economic shock whose economic significance probably was difficult to understand in the short run – however, the enormous immediate rise in spreads of the bond markets indicated that the case of Lehman Brothers was a serious shock; order inflow data were becoming doubtful in the fourth quarter of 2008, since order cancellations became a widespread phenomenon not covered in the official statistics. The international discussion about the macroeconomic impact of the banking crisis also was not always convincing. The IMF’s October 2008

Economic Outlook is a rather strange document in the sense that its forecast for the Eurozone predicts a fall in economic growth rates, but not a recession; the report presents some discussion about historical lessons from the banking crisis in Sweden, Norway and other individual OECD countries, however implicit and explicit event studies along these lines are not very useful since the crucial trait of the 2007/2008 transatlantic banking crisis concerns the fact that many OECD countries – including the US, the UK and Germany – faced massive problems in the banking sector at the same time; here a two-country perspective is adequate, i.e., an analytical view which takes into account the effect of the banking crisis in both countries and the international effects plus the negative repercussion effects.

- A confusing issue is the discussion about the role of a credit crunch. Most central banks of OECD countries have pointed out that surveys conducted show no evidence about a credit crunch; this finding typically is presented as a comforting message while in reality it is not. Investors which set up an investment project over an investment cycle of 4–8 years will not only be interested in current investment financing but also in the probability of getting adequate refinancing in the future. Fear of a credit crunch among a large share of investors is enough for a negative macroeconomic punch. Those countries which are heavily specialized in the production and export of machinery and equipment – in Europe, countries such as Germany, France and the Netherlands – will then face massive contraction of GDP since not only domestic investment is falling but exports as well. One may note that reduced exports of machinery and equipment also imply a fall in complementary knowledge-intensive services exports. If firms in manufacturing industry are characterized by fear of refinancing in the future – that is anticipation of a credit crunch – traditional surveys of central banks are a doubtful exercise. Rather international organizations should conduct a survey among investors and industrial firms, respectively (here the wording will be crucial: a typical question like 'are you afraid of a credit crunch' might bring biased answers while the question 'do you expect that fear of a credit crunch will affect your competitors investment decisions negatively' is more useful; the EU or the OECD should quickly introduce this type of survey in order to get a more sound decision basis for monetary policy and fiscal policy).
- Traditional models using a Taylor rule for monetary policy face some problems in the context of the world recession 2008/2009, since the nominal central bank interest rate implied is typically negative (in the NIGEM model, about 5%). To some extent such problems with the Taylor rule are not surprising, since the world recession represents a serious global shock; at the same time, one may raise the question as to whether one can find a more sophisticated monetary policy rule which can accommodate even extreme economic situations.
- To the extent that New Keynesian Macroeconomic models explain the deviation from an exogenous, steady-state equilibrium, the transatlantic banking crisis in combination with the world recession raises doubts whether the assumption of an exogenous, long-run equilibrium is useful. If the rate of technological progress should fall as a consequence of the transatlantic banking crisis (US and

EU venture capital markets certainly have suffered from the banking crisis, although it is unclear whether there will be a permanent negative effect), a standard neoclassical model implies that there will be a once-and-for-all rise in the level of the growth path plus a fall in the trend growth rate. In reality there will be a superposition of such negative supply-dynamics with negative demand-side shocks – for a new approach to cover such twin dynamics see Welfens (2007b). Moreover, it is unclear whether rational expectations can be a useful ingredient of models explaining bubble-type financial market dynamics.

- The size of necessary structural corrections is considerable in the US and Europe. The ability to maintain a rigid fixed exchange rate system in such a setting is quite doubtful and hence Latvia, Estonia and Lithuania should carefully consider their respective policy options. It is, however, hardly acceptable that these countries stick to a rigid parity while hoping for more and more bail-out money from the IMF, the EBRD or the EIB. The European Commission would be wise to push for a strong devaluation that would nurture – in combination with adequate national policy measures and supporting policy from the EU – expected currency appreciation. The alternative to devaluation are strong nominal wage cuts which are likely to be large in the tradables sector which is exposed to global competition but weak in the nontradables sector; a relative rise of the nontradables price will undermine the incentives to raise net exports of goods and services – a switch which is urgently needed in the Baltic countries with their huge current account deficits relative to GDP. A real devaluation would not only stimulate exports it also would reduce demand for consumption in the nontradables sector since households with loans denominated in foreign currency face a loss of net wealth and thus will cut consumption across the board which should help to avoid the problem of a rise of the tradables price ratio.
- The artificial reduction of risk premia in the US in the period 2003–2006 raised the speed of economic growth in OECD countries. From a theoretical perspective, there is no reason not to assume that 'growth speeding' will not face an implicit penalty function, namely in the sense that the period of excessive growth will be followed by a period of depressed growth that will bring the economy back to its normal 'natural' growth path. If long run equilibrium is characterized by the condition that the growth rate of output g_Y is equal to the real interest rate 'growth speeding' would be neutral if raising economic growth in period I is followed by an offsetting fall of the growth rate in period II; however, it could also happen that the long run growth rate would fall for a certain time period (Fig. 3.3). To the extent that there is an offsetting correction process, it is doubtful that fiscal policy or monetary policy would try to artificially raise the output development. Unfortunately, the theoretical underpinning of such a penalty function – not found in macro models thus far – is rather unclear except that one may argue that had investors known the true risk of many investment projects undertaken in the decade after 1995, they would have wanted lower investment–output ratios than those realized. The 2009/2010 crisis is thus a difficult challenge for policy makers, since a structural growth overhang is combined with a cyclical downswing in many countries.

3.3 Theoretical Aspects of Sustainable Financial Market Globalization

International capital flows and financial market globalization is widely expected to stand for an efficient process which raises economic welfare worldwide. Should one have some doubts here given the many distortions that have become apparent in the transatlantic banking crisis? Empirical evidence has to be established, but some theoretical reflections also are useful here.

Let us consider a simple two-country approach to risk markets (a special niche of insurance markets: think of the CDS markets) where demand in country 1 is given by DD_0 (see Fig. 3.4) and supply by SS_0; in country 2 demand and supply are given by DD_0^* and SS^*_0. There is a market for risk (σ) in the home country (panel a) and a market for risk in the foreign country (panel b). Under autarchy, the price of risk p in the home country (country 1; e.g., the US) is p_0 and p^*_0 in country 2. If countries should open up for both trade and capital flows, there will be excess supply in country 1 and excess demand in country 2. The world market price for risk – for credit default swaps for bundles of securities packaged in banks – is p^W_0. Country 1's insurance industry has expanded (q_2 is the supply instead of q_0 in the closed economy). However, if there are negative national external effects in country 1 – e.g., due to inadequate regulation – the social costs of providing insurance against risk is given by SS_{01} instead of SS_0, and hence the optimal allocation of resources would be different (at the initial global price for risk the welfare loss in country 1 is given by the area KJBA). Instead of being a net exporter of risk insurance services country 1 would be net importer of insurance services. Country 2 would be a net exporter. Moreover, the price of risk under efficient international

$$\int_0^T \left(\frac{d\ln Y}{dt} - r_0\right) e^{-rt}\, dt = \alpha \int_T^{T'} \left(r_0 - \frac{d\ln Y}{dt}\right) e^{-rt}\, dt$$

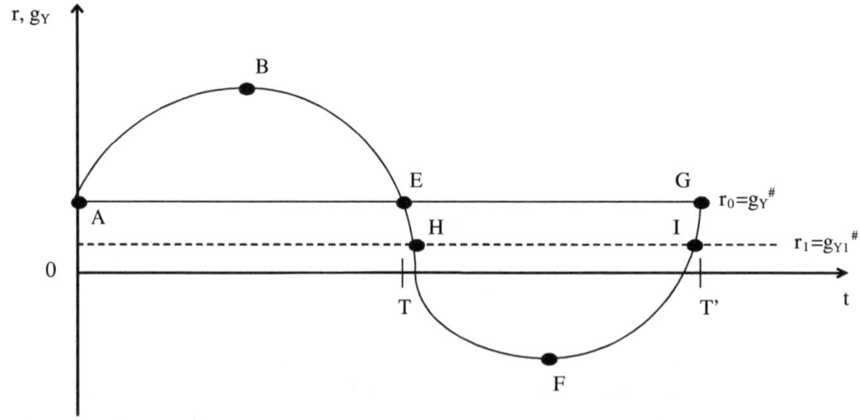

Fig. 3.3 Artificial growth acceleration

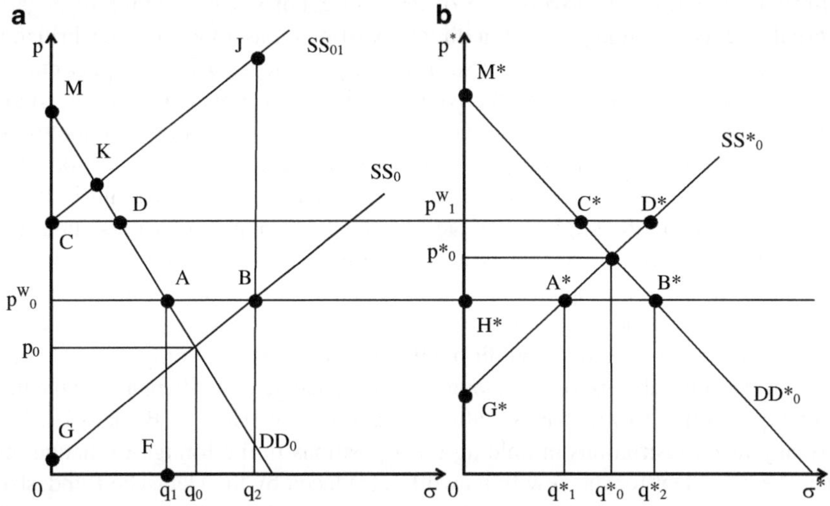

Fig. 3.4 Asymmetric negative external effects and international capital flows

allocation of resources would increase, the new price is $p_1{}^W$ (one also may note: an efficient allocation of resources implies a real devaluation of the currency of country 1 which makes FDI inflows into country 2 more likely; this atleast is in line with the standard argument of Froot and Stein (1991) on the link between FDI inflows and the real exchange rate). If country 2 would like to offset the negative external effect in country 1, it might consider subsidization of the supply side in country 2. The problem is that the effect of this kind of quasi-internalization leads to a fall in the price of risk. To the extent that risk premia in various asset markets are interdependent, such a solution would cause an artificially low risk premium in the stock market and hence there would be overinvestment. In a two-country model, the negative external effect in country 1 potentially implies a negative external effect in country 2 since comparing the social surplus at the initial world market price with the situation in which the price is $p_1{}^W$ implies that the consumer surplus is reduced by A*E*B* while the producer surplus is raised by E*C*D*. There is a redistribution effect between consumer surplus and producer surplus which is equal to the area $P^*{}_0{}^*E^*C^*p_1{}^W$; this effect is, of course, not neutral in terms of economic welfare if the risk insurance industry in country 2 is fully owned by firms from country 1 (to consider a special case which is quite interesting). As the supply curve in country 2 starts at a point G* which is above point G in country 1 the implication is that the cost competitiveness of country 1 is superior to country 2 – as long as negative external effects in country 1 are not internalized. As long as there is no internalization in country 1 one may assume that there is a considerable likelihood that insurance firms from country 1 take over firms from country 2 (recall the logic of the Froot and Stein argument). This is inefficient in a crucial sense; corporate governance from firms from country 1 will dominate the initial type of governance in firms in country 2. If governance of firms in country 1 is a source of negative external effects in country 1 foreign direct investment has now become a bridge for creating negative external effects also in country 2 (the associated supply curve is not shown in the diagram). If ineffective regulation of the financial sector in country 1 is the source of negative externality, international regulatory competition – assuming dominance of country 1 – will transmit the externality to country 2. Therefore the standard question in the international regulatory debate is flawed, namely whether there might be a race to the bottom in terms of standards or regulation. The more important issue is whether or not a regime with negative external effects has the opportunity to dominate other regimes with no or small external effects. In the context of a system with flexible exchange rates, there are specific risks to be considered additionally. This concerns not only the problem of potential (Dornbusch-type) overshooting of the exchange rate. There also is the more general question as to why banks – after the failure of the Herstatt Bank in 1974 – in Germany faced restrictions in holding open positions in the foreign exchange markets: The argument for the new framework introduced by the Deutsche Bundesbank obviously emphasized the risk of foreign currency speculation. From this perspective, it is absolutely unclear why individuals in EU accession countries could obviously take major exchange rate risks when taking loans in foreign currencies such as Euro or Swiss Franc (the majority of those financing cars or homes certainly are risk-averse, and thus it is absolutely unclear why banks would sell a loan denominated in a foreign currency – unless one assumes that banks have speculated that liability rules in the banking sector are not valid). Depreciations and in particular exchange rate overshooting could bring illiquidity, which for some individuals or firms indeed can bring insolvency once spreads are sharply increasing in destabilized markets (indeed in a global market system in which one finds a strange phenomenon such as 'distressed markets' – dead markets – which, according to standard theory of a market economy, should not exist at all).

If there is no level international playing field of financial services and if there is a serious too big to fail problem in many countries, the banks from the biggest country are likely to dominate with their standards the world economy. The role of the home bias in financial market services implies that the size of the home market will matter and the more economies of scale play a role in banking, the role of large banks from big countries is more important (the UK would have a larger home market if it were part of the euro zone). It is not obvious that big banks really have economies of scale or other advantages which generate a systematic advantage in terms of the rate of return on capital as the following figures for the US suggest – the rate of return on assets was highest for medium-sized banks, not for the big banks in the period 1999–2007 (except for 2005 and 2006). Big banks might have advantages in the sense that they are politically well connected and thus the survival probability is higher than for small and medium-sized banks. Moreover, it is rather surprising to see that during the banking crisis the US dollar has weakened only transitorily – save heaven effects paradoxically support the source country of the transatlantic banking crisis (see the modified Branson model in Appendix which also highlights some aspects of quantitative easing).

The US banks have dominated international financial markets for decades and the Washington consensus – as long as it was relevant (until the US banking crisis) – has reinforced the role of US banks. Asian countries and other countries were pushed to open up for banks from the US and other countries and US banks were often strong enough to impose their standards – some weak ones, some good ones – on banks abroad. In a world with open capital markets, banks in the rest of the world will always face the challenge of being taken over by leading competitors, and for decades, the US conveyed the impression that US banks were global leaders. Since the US banking crisis of 2007/2008, there have been serious doubts about this view; the fact that US investment banks were almost completely eliminated in 2008 – and that value-added in this sector probably was negative in the decade following 1998 (taking into account all negative external effects) – is an indicator that the US banking system faced considerable inefficiencies.

Will there be a sustained globalization process if the US banking system is so unstable and if the deleveraging of banks forces so many banks to cut back on the international business? A stable global market economy might be achieved if one has at least four ingredients:

- A stable political system in major countries – this question is partly related to economic stability and sustained growth in the respective countries.
- Clear property rights and full competition, including in the banking sector. There are considerable doubts that full competition in the banking sector can be established within the OECD or even worldwide. Larger integrated markets typically go along with bigger banks and if the too big to fail argument holds for many big banks in such markets, there is no effective competition. Rather bank managers will have every incentive to take big risks – while hunting for high rates of return on equity – and speculate that 'adverse market developments' will open up the option to save the bank by economic nationalization through taxpayers' money. The allocation of resources in such a setup will be inefficient, and it is doubtful that liberalization of capital flows under such conditions brings major economic benefits. One must consider the problem that there could be an increased problem of negative international spillover effects which might fully offset the traditional benefits from free capital flows.
- Clear liability rules so that incentives encourage efficient allocation of resources. Liability rules in the US system of mortgage financing are incomplete since home owners simply can move out and leave the key at the bank once the market value of the house is exceeding the mortgage. With 19 million empty houses at the end of 2008, the US economy represents an abnormally large excess supply in the housing market, and many of these houses will disintegrate over time as no responsible owner takes care of the house – in terms of economic welfare, the US would have been better off if one had built fewer houses in the decade after 1997 than actually was the case. Strangely, during this decade the relative price of houses strongly increased in the US (to some extent it is, of course, in line with the logic of the market that more houses are built if the relative price of houses is rising). In the EU those who by a house with a mortgage would face the risk that

the bank can put claims on part of labor income earned by the buyer of the house if he/she fails to serve the mortgage. Nontransparent mortgages at low initial teaser interest rates and other marketing tricks common in nontransparent US mortgage markets represent doubtful developments in US real estate and mortgage markets.

- Internalization of internationally relevant external effects should be realized. Markets can be quite useful as a means of internalizing certain external effects as is known, for example, from trading CO_2 emission certificates. However, such internalization could not take place without governments adopting a broad international agreement under the heading of the Kyoto Protocol in a first step and the EU (and some other OECD countries) setting rules for trading of emission certificates. Emission certificate trading amounts to a market-driven flexible international Pigou tax which normally could not be imposed as government from country I (II) cannot tax producers or consumers in country II (I). To the extent that inadequate national regulations of financial markets leads to distorted market signals and hence negative international external effects, it is desirable to adjust national regulations in such a way that national and international negative external effects are internalized.
- In the context of financial markets, part of the problem with regulation concerns potentially large international external effects which could, for instance, occur in the course of a bankruptcy of a major international bank. A full theoretical understanding of competition dynamics must include the probability of future bankruptcy and the direct and indirect effects of bankruptcy rules. There is an interesting paper available from the Swiss Banking Commission which has warned that the current rules and regulations in place within banks in OECD countries imply massive international negative external effects if there were a bankruptcy of any major bank with strong international business (Eidgenössische Bankenkommission 2008).

As regards sustainable financial market integration, one can expect long term globalization only under certain conditions. Financial market integration can generate considerable benefits by reducing international transactions costs, stimulating financial product innovations and efficiency gains as well as through a better diversification of risks. However, those benefits will not be generated automatically; in a multi-country world economy, the leading countries must implement a consistent international framework which creates a competitive level playing field on the one hand and establishes clear responsibilities on the other hand; the requirements for sustainable globalization are as follows:

- Long term benefits on the basis of a consistent institutional framework and clear responsibilities can be expected; this implies that no major player in the world economy imposes large negative external effects on other countries – as it was the case with the US in 2007/2008. The US policy in 2008 brought about a rise in the US inflation rate; about 5% was reached in summer 2008, and this imposes an inflation tax on those countries holding foreign reserves in US $; while one might argue that most foreign reserves are in dollar-denominated bonds, it is clear that the interest rate on US bonds is not really rising in parallel with the inflation rate; one may argue that the crisis-induced rise in the inflation rate was 4% points. With about $6,000 billion reserves worldwide in 2008, the depreciation effect on reserves is $240 billion in that year; as regards the EU there are additional costs for the Community in the form of a fall of real output which is roughly 1% points in 2009 compared to the business-as-usual scenario – to this effect of a fall in output of about $ 180 bill. one would have to add the drop in real output in other trading partners of the US. This is an international resource transfer in favor of the US amounting to about 2–3% of the rest of the world's GDP, and this is more than the $300 billion the US taxpayer is likely to pay for the rescue of Fannie Mae and Freddie Mac plus the costs of Lehman Brothers in 2008/2009. It could well be that the rest of the world will face higher costs from the US banking crisis than the US itself. The key players in the world economy will hardly be willing to accept a US-led financial globalization process if it turns out that it imposes major costs on non-US countries.

- The cost of achieving political consensus at the international level will affect the ability to cope with international crises. If there is a consistent mix of regional organizations (responsibilities) and global organizations, international frictions in running the global system will be relatively low. In this perspective, the EU principle of home country supervision for bank affiliates abroad – in other EU countries and the European Economic Space – is doubtful, as the ongoing internationalization of the intra-EU banking business means that national regulators face an increasingly tough challenge for effective regulation of banks. Moreover, banks from non-EU countries can easily set up a subsidiary in an EU country and subsequently engage in bank business in all EU countries through affiliates. If banks create a separate legal entity, a true subsidiary in another EU country, the host country's supervisors will be responsible for supervision. However, this leaves a difficult moral hazard problem on the part of supervisors, since the supervisor in the host country has a relatively weak incentive to effectively supervise the subsidiary. If the subsidiary is in trouble, the parent bank in any case will have to foot the bill, and if not the parent bank then it will be the ministry of finance of the headquartering country. Creating colleges of supervisors – as suggested by the European Commission for big banks with international operations – is rather strange as well. A better system would follow the logic of regulations in telecommunications in the EU, that is, by establishing a supranational framework and making sure that national regulators have to adopt a combined legal and economic analysis while notifying key approaches to the European Commission which will produce a comparative report on prudential supervision in each EU country. National central banks – politically independent and not directly involved in monetary policy – should be involved in prudential supervision, and ideally, the national supervisory agency would have a similar institutional setup across the Euro zone countries.
- Effective crisis management in an international crisis of financial markets is crucial. It is rather doubtful that the world economy has an institutional platform for effective crisis management. The interplay between the BIS and the IMF is

rather unclear; while the Bank of International Settlements has an analytical focus on world capital markets and also is home to the Basel Group of Supervisors; the BIS has an incomplete global coverage of (member) countries, while the IMF has no real competence in prudential supervision. It could have at least some reporting competence if the IMF statutes were changed in such a way as to require member countries to accept regular Financial Sector Assessment Programs, whose results would then be published. The OECD could also play a more important role, namely by conducting more research on financial market stability, prudential supervision and financial innovations. As regards the OECD reports of 2007/2008, one may argue that there is neither much theoretical reflection nor can one identify a critical assessment of the USA (see the OECD's 2007 opaque country report on the USA).

- An international system can be sustainable only if there is acceptance of burden sharing. In other words, the costs of a major crisis must be shared in a way which is politically acceptable and gives no perverse incentives (e.g., for countries to ignore international external costs of domestic policy pitfalls). To some extent, one might argue that the IMF will be in charge of helping countries with high current account deficits and problems occurring in the context of massive exchange rate swings. However, the case of an international banking crisis has not really been defined within the mission of the IMF, although it seems to be logical that the organization which is in charge of maintaining the international payments system should have certain competences here as well. The IMF should create a special facility for helping countries which are subject to an external shock from a major banking crisis; the World Bank, which is engaged in financial institution building in developing countries, should offer particular support for very poor countries and help to convey best practice in prudential supervision, namely in the context of international benchmarking.
- Leadership in the global economy's governance is crucial in the standard model of the international system dominated by a large economy – in the second half of the twenty-first century, the USA was the dominant country and its share of world GDP was still close to 30% at the beginning of the twenty-first century; this is much above the 20% of the EU. Figures based on PPP look smaller for the USA, namely 20% (in 1929 the nominal share of the US in world GDP was 38%, but considering the fact that US multinational companies subsidiaries abroad are more important for GDP outside the US in 2008 than in 1929 one may assume that the economic impact of the effective US economy has not reduced). However, with the rapid rise of China, there is no doubt that the exclusive leadership role of the US becomes less credible and legitimate over time. The alternative to a global system shaped by dominance would be one of joint leadership through an institutionalized policy club such as the G8 or the G20. Indeed, the meeting of the G20 in Washington in November 2008 suggests that the broader international G20 policy club is a feasible platform. The G20 policy club is relatively complex to organize since it has a relatively large number of member countries which have relatively heterogeneous characteristics. Given the fact that Chinese bankers – in Hong Kong and Shanghai (and in Singapore) – are

quite experienced and influential, one will probably have to deal with certain global governance issues at the level of the G20 or a future G25 which should additionally include Spain. The G8/G20 is the group of policymakers which most likely will discuss the need for global reforms in prudential supervision. The IMF (Strauss-Kahn 2008) also plays an important role.

While the IMF effectively is in charge of designing a new architecture of the global financial system, it is not fully clear why more regulation in banking sectors is really needed. One may argue that the basic alternative is to engage in broad national or international dismemberment of big banks and thus to reinforce competition in the banking sector of each country (dismemberment could be realized after nationalization of banks: privatization gives an ideal starting point for splitting up banks which have exceeded a critical size); with smaller banks we have less problems of the too-big-to-fail type, and competition would therefore be relatively strong – and hence light regulation is appropriate. If, however, there is no dismemberment of big banks (and possibly insurance companies) in most countries, competition will be relatively weak and in this case stricter regulation is necessary. Strict regulation is the natural policy response to a system characterized by a few big banks, which are all too big to fail. In this perspective, the US government under President Bush pursued an inconsistent policy: Bank mergers had brought about a system of Wall Street banks which were too big to fail, and at the same time, the government was not eager to implement strict regulation.

It is noteworthy that the biggest US banks – by size of assets – were not the most profitable. Thus, the dismemberment of banks might be considered as part of structural reforms in the banking sector. This, however, does not rule out that big banks nevertheless might have a critical function for the economy, for example in terms of innovation dynamics (in the banking sector or in other sectors), so that one has to carefully look into the issue of dismemberment of banks. One also cannot advocate a general expansion of regulation; for banks facing sustained competition and facing high transparency standards in terms of financial disclosure and balance-sheets, respectively, there is no need for strong regulation.

To the extent that regulation is implemented in a consistent and effective way, one may expect that financial markets could largely be efficient, and thus – from a theoretical point – it would suffice to consider only one asset price, say the short term interest rate which then is the benchmark for other assets. For example, the long term interest rates can be understood to be composed of the current short term interest rate plus the effect of expected future short-term interest rates. However, even in a setup with efficient markets a period of booming stock markets there will be an analytical challenge in the field of monetary policy, namely to the extent that not only transactions in goods markets are financed through money but also transactions in assets markets (or for simplicity only stock markets – as considered subsequently). FIELD (1984) has pointed out the basic analytical challenge in the context of the Great Depression and the empirical findings of FIELD suggest that the demand for money for $1 of transactions in financial markets is roughly 1/5 of the demand for money for $1 of transactions in goods markets. The US Federal

Reserve – according to FIELD – had overestimated the degree of expansiveness of monetary policy in the late 1920s as it did not take into account the fact that part of the money supply was effectively absorbed by transactions on the stock market. Thus the FED was relatively reluctant to adopt a more expansionary monetary policy stance in the early stage of the crisis. One may adopt a simple broad modeling approach on the basis of the quantity theory to highlight the basic analytical challenge. We will consider a simple approach and assume – in line with Welfens (2007b) – that velocity V is a negative function of the nominal interest rate i (K denoting the capital stock, P′ the stock market price, P the output price level and θ the frequency of asset turnover in the portfolio considered, ψ is a positive parameter) and that the implicit real demand for money is given by $m^d V(i) = Y + [K\theta P'/P]^{\psi}$ so that money market equilibrium (with $Q := P'/P$) can be stated as

(2) $[M/P]V(i) = Y + [QK\theta]^{\psi}$

Assuming that real output is given by a Cobb–Douglas function $Y = K^{ß}(AL)^{1-ß}$ – with Y denoting real output, A the stock of knowledge, L labor and ß the output elasticity of capital – we can write (with $ß' := [1 - ß]/ß$ and assuming for simplicity that $1/ß = \psi$):

(3) $[M/P]V(i) = Y\{1 + (AL)^{\psi ß'}[Q\theta]^{\psi}\}$;

Here K has been replaced by an adequate expression from the production function. Differentiating with respect to time and assuming that the expression is close to zero we can use the approximation $\ln(1 + x) \approx x$ so that we get – with $E_{V,i}$ denoting the positive elasticity of V with respect to i – for the inflation rate dlnP/dt:

(4) $\mathrm{dlnP/dt} \approx [\mathrm{dlnM/dt} - \mathrm{dlnY/dt}] + E_{V,i}\,\mathrm{dlni/dt} - d\{(AL)^{\psi ß'}[Q\theta]^{\psi}\}/dt$

For long run equilibrium one will set dlni/dt = 0 and the real stock market price P′/P (Tobin's Q) also should be constant. Here we take a look at the medium term policy perspective. The medium term inflation rate – according to the above inflation – is thus not only determined by the difference of the growth rate of the money supply rate and the growth rate of output; the inflation rate will rise if the nominal interest rate rises or if the growth of the labor supply in efficiency units or Q or the frequency rate of the portfolio turnover falls. There is no doubt that during the stock market boom 2002–2007 the real price of stocks increased as the turnover frequency in portfolios increased, which might partly explain the unusually low inflation rate in the years prior to the transatlantic banking crisis. To the extent that the turnover frequency should fall during the financial market crisis, a given growth rate of the money supply will become more inflationary than under normal economic conditions.

3.3.1 *Global Deflation Risks?*

While many observers have raised the issue whether deflation is going to be a serious challenge in the global recession in certain countries in 2009/2010, one might instead look at the development of the global price level, namely in the context of a simple two-country model. The two country approach basically allows one to consider the case that one of the countries faces deflation or that both countries are in deflation – and analytical links between price dynamics in both countries are interesting. The analytical discussion about deflation has been rather limited thus far and the main concern is that deflation encourages households to postpone consumption and that firms face high levels of real debt – given nominal debt dynamics – so that investment will have to be reduced.

A simple analytical step to understand the basic analytics of deflation becomes obvious from expressing the world price level P^W through a combination of the price level of country I (say the US) as well as that of country II. The price level in both countries is assumed to be composed of a price index (P^T) of tradables and nontradables (PN); country 1 is the home country; P^{T*} measures the price index of tradables abroad (in country 2: rest of the world). The price level thus can be written, on the one hand, on the basis of the relative price of tradables at home and abroad. On the other hand, the price index of nontradables in both countries plus the nominal exchange rate is crucial elements. A world recession will typically create an excess supply in the tradables markets so that the relative price of tradables will fall in both countries. If the world recession is combined with an excess supply in the real estate market – this dampens rents – the price index of nontrables might fall in both markets in absolute terms. A nominal depreciation, that is rise in e* in the rest of the world (country 2), will reinforce the global deflationary impulse during a global recession as e falls. It is appropriate to state the world price index in a common currency and as long as the dollar clearly dominates global currency markets, an appreciation of the dollar is what EU countries should fear in a situation of a serious world recession. However, we can focus in more detail on the elements in world price index $P^W := (P)^{\alpha}(eP*)^{1-\alpha}$; P is the price index, e the nominal exchange rate and * denotes foreign variables (as defined in the subsequent formula).

If relative tradable prices are the same across countries – implying in a Balassa–Samuelson context that both countries have very similar per capita incomes y and y*, respectively (the relative tradable price is a negative function of per capita income since one assumes that the demand for nontradables is a positive function of real income; moreover productivity growth in the nontradables sector is assumed to be lower than in the tradables sector), the world price level P^W will fall – at a given exchange rate – if:

- The relative price of tradables falls: from a theoretical perspective this will happen if there is a global demand shock, that is, if there a world recession which simultaneously affects both countries.
- The absolute price of nontradables falls, which in a traditional perspective depends on the excess supply in the nontradables sector in each country. However, while the traditional view would emphasize that there is no link between the nontradables market in country 1 and the nontradables market in country 2, a comprehensive analytical approach would consider the role of asset

markets which are internationally integrated. Assume that the nontradables market consists only of the price of rents in housing markets. If investors from country 2 have invested in the housing markets of both countries and a major banking crisis/ financial crisis occurs in country 1, investors from country 2 face a loss of financial wealth and thus will want to reduce – at given expected rates of return in domestic and foreign asset markets – the amount of real capital, including real estate, in the portfolio. This mechanism is standard in portfolio models of open economies. While machinery and equipment are to some extent tradable (e.g., a machine from country 1 could be redeployed in country 2), real estate is totally immobile. If investors from country 1 want to sell real estate in countries 1 and 2, the only short-term effect will be a fall in the price level of real estate and hence rents in both countries will fall. Thus the excess supply in the asset markets in both countries depresses the nontradables price index in both countries. At a given nominal exchange rate, a world recession in combination with a global financial market crisis will bring about deflation in the sense that the world price level will fall. This then will raise the level of real world debt and thus could reinforce the recession.

$$P^W = P^\alpha (eP^*)^{(1-\alpha)} \quad \text{where } \alpha \in]0,1[$$

We have

$$P^* = \left(P^{T*}\right)^{\alpha/*} \cdot \left(P^{N*}\right)^{(1-\alpha'*)}$$
$$P = \left(P^T\right)^{\alpha'} \cdot \left(P^N\right)^{(1-\alpha')}$$
$$P^T = eP^{T*}$$

1. $P^\alpha = \left(\left(P^T\right)^{\alpha/} \cdot \left(P^N\right)^{(1-\alpha/)}\right)^\alpha = \left(\left(P^T\right)^{\alpha'} \cdot P^N \left(P^N\right)^{-\alpha/}\right)^\alpha = \left(P^N \left(\frac{P^T}{P^N}\right)^{\alpha/}\right)^\alpha$
2. $(eP^*)^{(1-\alpha)} = \left(e\left(P^{T*}\right)^{\alpha/*} \cdot \left(P^{N*}\right)^{(1-\alpha/*)}\right)^{(1-\alpha)}$
3. $= \left(eP^{N*}\left(\frac{P^{T*}}{P^{N*}}\right)^{\alpha/*}\right)^{(1-\alpha)}$

Therefore the world price index is given by P^W

$$P^W = \left(P^N \left(\frac{P^T}{P^N}\right)^{\alpha/}\right)^\alpha \left(eP^{N*}\left(\frac{P^{T*}}{P^{N*}}\right)^{\alpha'*}\right)^{(1-\alpha)}$$

3.4 Global and EU Policy Options

The international banking crisis started in the US, whose banking market has dominated the international developments for decades – sometimes joined by British banks which benefitted from deregulation in the 1980s. While the internationalization of banking intensified in the 1990s – in Europe through the creation of the EU single market in 1992 – the world's leading economy, the US, has allowed effective regulation to weaken over time; the personnel for risk management in the USSEC declined dramatically under the Bush administration, surprisingly in a period in which the investment banks for which the USSEC is the relevant supervisor expanded heavily. The FED has held the view – under Greenspan and also under Bernanke – that reducing regulation should be the appropriate policy approach for traditional banks (bank holdings). The result has been insufficient equity capital for the growing risks taken by big banks in New York. Some of the Wall Street Investment banks were major players in the subprime mortgage market. There were also some banks from the UK, Germany, the Netherlands and France as well as Switzerland active in that market. As regards Germany, IKB Deutsche Industriebank and SachsenLB were among the large players in the US markets; the absolute volume of subprime deals represented by these two medium-size German banks was larger than that of the German leader, Deutsche Bank. The IKB had no clear idea of the type of business it was undertaking; indeed, on its website it explained the role of special investment vehicles and it claimed that investment in ABS are 'in the short run an almost risk-free investment' (see Appendix 4). In its 2006 annual report, IKB claimed that it had adopted a conservative strategy in the field of risk – one may argue that this is a straightforward lie. Interestingly, faulty statements in company reports are not liable. From this perspective, a key element of EU reforms should be to require company statements in the annual reports to incur a specific liability if key statements are wrong – statements about the risk strategy should be earmarked as being of particular sensitivity, and it would be useful to develop a new indicator system by which one could measure the degree of risk incurred. A new EU directive is urgent here and it is obvious that intra-EU capital flows are distorted by misleading statements of bankers with respect to risk and risk management, respectively. One also should note that the EU single banking market will be distorted by asymmetric government-led bank recapitalization in individual member countries; here the European Commission has an important task in pushing for common principles for recapitalization of banks.

As regards cooperation between the EU and the US, it would be useful to establish a transatlantic and global parliamentary debate on financial globalization. The Bank of International Settlements should become the core of enhanced financial regulation in a global context: This will require broadening membership on the one hand. On the other hand, the BIS should be subject to special international parliamentary control. Selected members of the European Parliament, the US House, and other parliaments should be delegates of a newly established Parliamentary Assembly at BIS. The OECD Development Centre also could be used as a forum for a policy debate involving industrialized countries, Brazil, China and other newly industrialized countries. Thus the pressure on the BIS to come up with better and more consistent work could be reinforced, and this would reinforce global governance. The IMF will have a crucial role for stabilizing countries facing sudden strong capital outflows and hence high devaluations; a particular problem will occur in countries with high foreign debt. Eastern European EU accession countries could face serious problems in 2009/2010 as a decline of the real economy could overlap with a second wave of the banking crisis and high capital outflows or reduced capital inflows. Individual EU countries as well as the Community should help eastern European accession countries. As regards Island – a country in the European Economic Space – the EU should also help the country since there is a global fragility which implies that bankruptcy of any country in Europe would be a signal for investors worldwide that countries in Europe could indeed go bankrupt: Country risk premia would increase while the US would benefit in such a situation from higher capital inflows driven by save-heaven considerations (Appendix 1 presents theoretical reflections which highlight the impact of financial market integration and changes in risk premia, respectively). As regards the euro zone one may emphasize that membership of the euro zone is quite useful for some Mediterranean countries; without the euro zone and ECB all EU countries would be part of the European Monetary System (EMS I) and there is no doubt that the international banking crisis would have created enormous tensions on the continent – with Greece, Italy and Portugal being among the prime targets for speculative attacks.

As regards the EU one may conclude that the best way to reform the system of prudential supervision is to combine stricter national regulations with a new EU-based complementary framework on prudential supervision. There are good arguments why an integrated financial EU market requires European supervision to some extent (Priesemann 1997; Welfens 2007a, b, c, 2008a, b; Wolf 2007). If the UK should be reluctant to support an EU-wide framework regulation of financial markets, the euro zone countries should undertake their own policy initiative. It should be possible to create a euro zone-wide regulatory framework quickly, namely through a treaty among central banks of member countries of the euro zone; this would be in line with the creation of the European Monetary System in 1979 when heads of states were skeptical that a traditional international treaty – requiring ratification in parliaments of all EU member countries – could work. Thus, the EMS was created on the basis of a treaty among EU central banks.

Better regulation is required to overcome the banking crisis of 2007/2008 (which could be reinforced by a global recession in 2009). Several principles should be emphasized here as elements of a solution:

- Typical remedies for coping with the market for lemons problem considered in the relevant goods market (e.g., used automobiles) should also be applied in the interbank market. Guarantees or warranties are one element, carefully building up reputation a second, while conveying quality signals are a third aspect. One should note that a quality control system can be developed by the banking industry itself, it is not really necessary for government to do this; rather government could encourage banks to develop quality signals, guarantee schemes, etc.
- A useful new rule should stipulate that banks creating an ABS or similar financial papers must declare that they will be willing to buy back the assets at

any point of time for no less than 50% of the initial market price. Such a clause would avoid uncertainties about valuation in an economic crisis. At the same time banks, would have a strong incentive to carefully consider the creation of markets and the range of partners involved in ABS transactions. Banks launching ABS should maintain a 20% stake in the equity tranche so that the respective banks have a strong motivation to carefully consider the risks involved in loan portfolios and securitization. (The German Minister of Finance has also advocated for such a 20% rule.)

- As regards revitalizing the interbank market, it is obvious that the mega rescue packages and guarantee schemes implemented by many OECD countries are a rather artificial way to jump-start the interbank markets. The rescue packages of September and October 2008 could be useful to some extent and are indeed helpful in creating some extra time to come up with truly adequate reform initiatives. However, it will be necessary to give incentives to banks to become more active again in the interbank market. The ECB should give preferential interest rates for access to central bank liquidity to those banks which are active in the interbank market; banks which are more active in the medium term should have more favorable access than banks which are mainly in the short term interbank market.
- As creating trust among banks is quite difficult, it could be useful to encourage the creation of small homogenous groups of banks which are willing to resume interbank lending. Such arrangements could indeed be encouraged both by central banks and the ECB. In a second step the regional clubs of banks could be merged in order to create a euro zone-wide banking community which is active in the interbank markets.

There is some risk that the global G20 deliberations will lead to discussions about a very long list of reform steps which are difficult to implement and which effectively create more confusion than progress in solving the critical problems. A very long and complex list of measures invites external pressure for delaying the process through confusing and complex debates. Thus, setting priorities is quite important, and five priorities have been highlighted here. A new regulatory approach in financial markets should follow the successful example of telecommunications markets; benchmarking, EU regulatory reviews and an ongoing dialogue with scientific experts are indispensible elements. The European Parliament should restore the EP's research service (former DG-IV of the EP), which is quite crucial for optimal legislation in an increasingly complex world economy.

If the US should fail to adopt Basel II rules – plus some additional key regulations for banks, hedge funds and insurance companies – the EU should consider imposing restrictions on transatlantic capital flows. It is not in the interest of the EU (nor of the world economy) that in the context of uneven regulatory conditions for banks, insurance companies and the like, capital from the EU flows to the US with its partly artificially high rates of return on equity. At least in the run-up to the banking crisis, many banks and other financial companies enjoyed a cost-advantage by not having to comply with Basel II rules. A US system which has neither consistent domestic regulation nor Basel II rules is creating negative external effects through the chaos the US banking crisis of 2007/2008 has created in international financial markets. This is neither a level playing field nor a system in line with basic requirements for efficiency and stability. One should note that imposing capital export taxes on investments of EU firms with realized plans for portfolio investment in the US simply reflects a type of PIGOU tax which is designed to help internalize negative external (international) effects. It is up to the US to avoid such effective barriers for international capital flows.

The EU should push for the creation of a formal Group of International Supervisors (GIS), which would become a twin organization to the existing BIS. The GIS should include supervisors from all countries of the world and be mainly organized in regional groupings (e.g., EU, NAFTA, MERCOSUR, ASEAN). The BIS/GIS should be subject to direct international parliamentary control in order to avoid bureaucratic inefficiencies and lack of transparency.

The IMF could have a new role, namely in organizing global annual meetings of GIS/BIS along with the World Bank and WTO. In such a manner, one could look more deeply into the interdependencies of setting international rules for the world economy. One could thereby create a more consistent international division of labor across international organizations.

Thus we can summarize the overall analysis as follows. The diagnostic part of the US banking crisis is obvious (1) The optimum (national) size of banks grows along with the volume of global financial markets; the rapid expansion and internationalization of financial markets after 1991 increased the size of banks and insurance companies in the US as well as in Europe. (2) Once certain banks and insurance companies obtained critical size, the potential risk of bankruptcy for each represents a systemic risk. The managers of these banks and insurance companies can then pursue strategies of excessive risk-taking in the context of chasing higher expected rates of return on equity – those managers can bet on a bail-out through the government in the case of bankruptcy, and therefore the competition process is seriously weakened. For example, as long as the bank was not on the brink of bankruptcy, the investment bank Goldman Sachs could pay its 26,000 employees $16 billion in bonus payments during 2006. Raising the required rate of return on equity to 25% at the beginning of the twenty-first century set in Wall Street – and in other OECD banking centers – an illusionary target, which testifies to the ignorance of top managers about firmly-established laws in Economics. With a 4% rate of return on risk-free government bonds, the target ratio of 25% implied a risk premium of 21% and hence implied furthermore that bankers were chasing very risky deals. (3) In the case of a banking crisis, major banks can obviously blackmail government and prudential authorities to impose a ban on short sales of banking stocks. In the US, Secretary of the Treasury Paulson imposed such a ban in September 2008 (possibly after a call from the boss of Morgan Stanley). (4) While it is true that the US administration did not bail out Lehman Brothers – it filed for protection under Chap. 11 – no big bank or insurance company faces a credible threat of bankruptcy as there is a visible 'too-big-to-fail problem.' Thus, competition in the banking sector is weakened; and in other sectors linked to the banking system directly (e.g. the US automotive firms and their respective banks which represent themselves high stocks of asset-backed securities/ABS, collateralized debt oligations/CDOs – a mixture of various ABS – and credit default swaps/ CDS which are a kind of insurance for loan packages). The government's bail out of the big insurance company, AIG, provides more evidence of this problem; indeed, it had to be saved once Lehman Brothers was pushed towards Chap. 11, because AIG sits on an enormous stock of credit default swaps, including those which cover part of the claims against Lehman Brothers. AIG also had to be saved, because its high stock of CDS would have been worthless once AIG had gone bankrupt. As CDS provides coverage against 'failure of bonds/loans packaged in ABS,' it is clear that enormous depreciation on portfolios in many banks and insurance companies would have been triggered once CDS of AIGs had become worthless. It is noteworthy that CDS and credit derivatives were sold worldwide at the beginning of the twenty-first century. For example, even Allianz probably had about €1,000 billion of CDS on its books at the end of 2007. As there is no global inventory list on CDS, it is absolutely unclear which countries – and to what extent – are infected through toxic CDS. This, in turn, reinforces the lack of confidence in financial markets in general and in interbank markets in particular. (5) At the bottom line the big banks, big funds and big insurance companies are in a situation coined in a phrase by Janos Kornai – there is 'soft budget constraint', as government bail-out is fully anticipated for the case that anything goes seriously wrong (Kornai's soft budget constraint originally referred to socialist countries where central banks had to ratify whatever overruns in costs in state-owned firms occurred). As the threat of bankruptcy is not faced by managers of these companies, there are poor incentives for good governance. Moreover, the incentive to take excessive risks is strong. It is strange that the phenomenon of the soft budget constraint once used by Kornai to discuss the notorious inefficiency of socialist command economies must now be discussed in the context of the 2007/2008 crisis of the US financial system. (6) The work of rating agencies has been poor and implies that financial market actors suffer from opaque signalling in bonds markets. (7) From the above list of problems and weaknesses, the necessary remedies for coping with the crisis and for avoiding future crises can be derived. The world economy needs competitive and efficient banks acting within a more long-term framework of open competitive markets.

Government bail-outs of major US banks and US insurance companies – or nationalization – is only one element of solving the crisis where we assume that those firms will be restructured and privatized in the long run. Other necessary reform elements are: a) restrictions on the size of banks and insurance companies – and even dismemberment of oversized firms which exhibit the 'too-big-to-fail problem'; in the absence of dismemberment stricter regulation is absolutely necessary. Insurance companies with standard insurance business should not be allowed to be active in the CDS market and related fields, as this pillar of potentially very large risks could easily undermine the stability of the respective insurance companies; (b) taxing banks, funds and insurance companies on the basis of both profits and volatility of rates of return (the higher the volatility, the higher the tax rate), so that the apparently short-term bonus/profit maximization strategies no longer look attractive; banks which sell asset-backed securities must keep 20% on their books and guarantee that they will buy back the assets sold for at least half of the selling price; (c) the large US rating agencies which represented – according to an SEC Report – such visible lack of proficiency should become subject to a licensing procedure while imposing random testing of the quality of rating projects; a group of experts should conduct regular testing, and at the same time, high fines must be imposed for faulty ratings and insufficient documentation of rating decision-making; (d) comprehensive regulations for banks and hedge funds as well as related actors in financial markets are needed, and prudential supervisory bodies should be more professionally organized in terms of research and a scientific advisory body (Germany's BaFin is a relevant, weak example in this field, and it should indeed be reorganized); (e) all CDS contracts should be registered in a global database, and regulators should adopt broad requirements in terms of transparency, on the one hand, and restrictions, on the other; for example, CDS contracts should not be accumulated by banks or insurance companies on a large scale, which effectively implies that they would no longer face any threat of bankruptcy (since they signify a systemic risk in case of bankruptcy); (f) rating agencies will no longer obtain fees directly from the issuing of bonds; instead, there should be a two-stage pool financing, according to which rating firms obtain fees only from a large pool within which all companies issuing bonds should contribute; (g) as regards prudential supervision, a Europeanization of the process is advisable to make sure that crisis management in the EU single financial market can be organized effectively; there is also a need to somewhat restrict regulatory arbitrage within the EU.

These minimum reform agendas for the USA – and also for the EU – should not be understood as simply reflecting a new policy fad with a bias in favour of regulation and control. Rather, this agenda is the logical response to the problem of a soft budget constraint on the part of the banking and insurance sector in OECD countries; too-big-to-fail has become a serious challenge. This clear preference in favour of more and better regulation can partly be justified by referring to arguments by Cooter and Schaefer (2008), who discuss the role of regulation for the specific case of (developing) countries with weak rule-of-law. With such a weakness, it is quite useful to have regulations as a kind of general remedy. In the US and the EU, one should realistically consider that the soft budget constraint of big banks and big insurance companies is an important problem and that market discipline and competition forces are often rather weak. Hence tighter regulations – and, in some cases, dismemberment of companies – are preferred policy options for coping with the problem of too-big-to-fail. It is noteworthy that ongoing financial market globalization will reinforce the tendency for a growing role of big banks and big insurance companies. Such growth dynamics are only acceptable by policymakers if there are strict regulation or remedies in favor of more competition (e.g., a fall of sunk costs and hence a greater likelihood of newcomers entering the market). The visible tendency of the US to internationally externalize a considerable share of the costs of its banking crisis makes reforms urgent, which helps to internalize negative external effects.

It is not implausible to assume that the rest of the world bears a larger share of the costs of the US banking crisis than the US itself.

Without better regulations or more competition in the banking sector – as well as better prudential supervision, which should follow a more economic approach as compared to the largely legalistic approach traditionally applied – no internationalization of the EU CO_2 emission certificate markets should take place. Similarly, there could also be no feasible pension reforms in Europe which would encourage individuals to embark more on private retirement savings. The apparent knowledge gap of bankers in some big banks suggest that compulsory retraining of managers would be useful; as much as retraining among medical doctors is standard, there is an equal need to make sure managers understand through teaching units – provided by independent universities and institutes – the challenges they face. Moral hazard remains a big problem.

The ECB should exploit opportunities for reducing the interest rate. Such a step is unlikely to directly stimulate economic expansion, but it would reinforce profitability of banks in the euro zone which face considerable problems with respect to profitability (see Appendix 2 for regressions on banks' profitability in the US, Switzerland, Germany, the UK and the EU, respectively). Banks in the euro zone will welcome profits from intermediation in a situation where high depreciations on portfolios of banks are common. With lower short term interest rates it could be possible to avoid an inverse yield structure; such a yield structure already has been observed in the US where save-heaven effects have channeled a high share of savings and capital inflows into long term government bonds. Profitability of banks is a key for revitalizing the banks' loan business in the medium and long run.

The EU would be wise to adopt an expansionary fiscal policy in 2009, namely in a situation in which monetary policy has lost its effectiveness (partly because banks hardly pass on the ECB's reduction of the central bank interest rate to the banks' clients; problems with the Keynesian liquidity trap could also play a role). Many countries simultaneously face a recession, and the recession could be unusually deep judging by forecasts of the IMF, the EU and the Deutsche Bundesbank in November 2008. In such a situation one should consider options for expansionary fiscal policy with a clear focus on stimulating innovation and investments; in some countries, measures to stimulate consumption could also be adequate. The EU countries should spend more money on improving infrastructure. This should include modern telecommunications, and here it would be quite useful for the European Commission to remove unnecessary (regulatory) obstacles for higher investment. The EU should try to enhance cooperation with the new US administration; on both sides of the Atlantic, an expansionary fiscal policy with a strong focus on green IT could be useful. The new US administration will consider climate policy as a more important field than the Bush administration has, falling more in line with the EU countries' year-long emphasis on fighting global warming. Thus it seems attractive to consider a joint expansionary policy with a triple focus on green IT, infrastructure modernization and selected impulses for higher innovation and investment. At the bottom line, it should be emphasized that restoring confidence in the interbank market is of paramount importance for overcoming the US and global crisis.

As regards sustainable long term rates of return in industry OECD countries have shown that about 16% can be considered as a normal gross rate of return (see Appendix 6); assuming a capital depreciation rate of 10% one may argue that Schumpeterian innovation rents of investors in industry reflect hard earned risk premiums. Thus there are few arguments why banks should be able to fetch much higher gross rates of return without incurring much higher risks. If hedge funds remain unregulated there is, however, a potential stimulus for a new wave of illusory yield expectations in financial markets. From a policy perspective the negative national and international external effects associated with behavior of unregulated hedge funds and big banks calls for a PIGOU tax or, alternatively, regulations which help to avoid negative external effects.

Once the banking crisis translates into a massive recession, one may expect a rapid rise in the unemployment rate in the US and the UK where labor markets are rather unregulated (Addison and Welfens 2003, 2009). As yields on investment of many US and British pension funds have fallen dramatically in 2008/2009, there will be an unusual labor supply effect among the elderly which could translate into a modest rise in national output – provided that wages are sufficiently flexible. In the euro zone, the rise in unemployment rates among member countries could be considerable once firms can no longer rely on the instrument of transitory reduced working hours, which are an option in all EU countries.

From an EU perspective, a serious challenge is faced in eastern European accession countries. People in those countries which are not a member of the euro zone face high depreciation rates of the currency, as safe heaven aspects drive many international investors to pull out of eastern Europe. The effect of the devaluation is a rise in foreign indebtedness and thus the problem looks somewhat similar to the Asian crisis of 1997/1998. Beyond the currency mismatch there also is the problem of maturity mismatch – partly in the banking sector, partly in industry. While labor market flexibility in Eastern Europe partly is below that of ASEAN countries, one may nevertheless recall some key findings for labor markets dynamics in the Asian crisis (Fallon and Lucas 2002): Employment fell less than output, countries with sharp depreciations faced high real wage rate cuts which in turn dampened the rise in unemployment rates. The fall of the real exchange rate should lead to a medium term rise in foreign direct investment if one follows the Froot–Stein argument who have argued that a real depreciation will stimulate foreign direct investment, namely in the context of imperfect capital markets. However, the transatlantic banking crisis raises specific concerns, namely that lack of bank capital in EU15 countries which were major investors in banking sectors of accession countries could undermine the viability of financial markets in Eastern Europe. Whether expansionary fiscal policy in OECD countries will be an adequate policy response remains to be seen. New Keynesian Models might not give an adequate answer to the issues at hand, since NKM assumes a given steady state output trajectory. However, the financial market tsunami of 2008/2009 is likely to affect the steady state value of both output and the unemployment rate.

There are few doubts that part of the original crisis dynamics in the US are linked to the high US current account deficit which was not sustainable. The high current account deficit was financed through high net US capital imports, partly based on expected rates of returns which were illusory (and tilted also by fraud of the type visible in the Madoff Ponzi scheme). High current account surpluses of Germany, Japan, China, Switzerland and several resource exporters were the mirror of the high US current account deficit. To the extent that the US banking crisis and the global recession signal that the previous economic pattern of international resource allocation – including the high US current account deficit – is not sustainable, there are new challenges for countries with a structural surplus in the current account. If the US savings rate should increase in the medium term, surplus countries such as Germany, China and Japan will face declining export growth. From this perspective, fiscal policy packages in these countries should consider a specific focus on the expansion of the nontradables sector, that is measures which raise the relative price of nontradable products. The medium term structure of employment in terms of the breakdown nontradables/tradables will have to adjust accordingly. In countries which are considered structural net exporters, fiscal stimulus packages should thus contain elements which reinforce expansion of the nontradables sector – for example, there could be specific measures in favor of an expansion of the health care sector, the education sector and construction activities. Such measures should help to raise the price of nontradables relative to that of tradables; thus production in the tradables sector would decline and net exports reduce. As regards the fiscal stimulus packages in structural net exporter countries, there is insufficient focus on the nontradables sector. At the bottom line, one may emphasize that the task of restoring a functional banking sector cannot be substituted fiscal policy packages. Thus, structural reforms are indispensible.

In the epilogue The Age of Turbulence, Alan Greenspan (Greenspan 2008, p. 522) argues that the underpricing of risk observed in the US in the bubble had to collide with innate human risk-aversion. This implies that the FED had recognized the problem, particularly that the situation was not sustainable. More interestingly, Greenspan (2008, p. 523) states: 'But I am also increasingly persuaded that governments and central bank could not have importantly altered the course of the boom either. To do so, they have had to induce a degree of economic contraction sufficient to nip the budding euphoria. I have seen no evidence, however, that electorates in modern democratic societies would tolerate such severity in macroeconomic policy to combat a problem that might not even materialize.' This view is strange and if applied to pilots steering an airplane, clearly ill-founded. If pilots note that they have different indicators on their flight instruments before take-off, they would not even be allowed to take-off and if such problems occur during flight – showing anomalies with respect to parameters – they have to consider an emergency landing. If bankers want to pursue financial engineering, we need to apply the rigorous testing and standard-setting of engineers, not the chaotic innovation system organized on Wall Street. From a Rawlsian perspective, it also seems clear that voters would rather have liked the FED to avoid an excessive boom and the following economic collapse – such as the situation of 1928/1929 in the US (followed by a cumulative fall of output by 27%), not to mention 2005/2006. Central banks which recognize underpricing of risk to occur over more than 1 year should be mandated by law to take steps to correct the market anomalies. Imposing capital export controls should be considered a legitimate policy option of countries whose central banks have identified sustained underpricing of risk in a situation in which the central bank of the country concerned has not taken steps to correct the market anomaly. Globalization can be a long term success story, but financial globalization without consistent rules is dangerous. Better democratic control of globalization is needed.

Beyond reform requirements for a more stable and efficient international financial system, one may raise three questions:

- Which economic development of the world economy would one have witnessed if the underpricing of risk and the institutional deficiencies of OECD financial markets would have been avoided? The basic hypothesis here is that economic growth would have been lower in the world economy, volatility of asset prices lower and the rise in unemployment in the global economy would have been largely avoided.
- Why is the market economy so weak in establishing responsibilities in the financial market system? Probably because it is quite complex and because 'big banks' are so well connected to parties and the political system that the pressure to cover up responsibilities is enormous. Economists who have learned that one has to distinguish allocation via markets and via alternative institutions (e.g., hierarchies, political voting systems) should be alarmed when bankers coin a word such as 'distressed markets.' Those who are active in financial markets and launch financial product innovations are responsible for markets that work. No financial innovation should be launched in any country without prior testing and careful simulation analysis. Governments and international institutions – the latter associated with independent research institutes – should present regular analysis on international financial market developments. A situation in which almost all OECD member countries have been analyzed by the OECD under the heading of Financial Sector Assessment Program – while the largest OECD country, the US, has not – is unacceptable and should not have been tolerated by EU countries. External effects of the US system probably are a problem (see Appendix)
- Economists have to develop better macro models – which must include an explicit banking system – if Economics as a science does not want to suffer a serious blow to its reputation. The inability of major macro forecasters to understand in late 2007 that a serious US banking crisis would have negative international spillovers and in the end would have negative real effects is disappointing and suggests that too many model-builders ignore even the most basic links between the monetary economy and the real economy. New Keynesian Macroeconomics which largely puts the focus on the deviation from an exogenous, long-term equilibrium is doubtful to the extent that the financial market crisis will undermine the existing long run equilibrium.

- There is some doubt that central banks can easily respond to a bubble in asset markets. However, the goal of central banks – often exclusively focused on maintaining price stability – could be adjusted in a way that the central bank should present regular analyses on the potential size of medium term bubbles: Given the experience of the early 1930s and 2007–2009, namely that the collapse of a major bubble goes along with deflationary pressure the central bank should have the mandate to fight excessive asset prices. Avoiding future deflation thus would be part of the goal to maintain price stability. In an open economy with integrated capital markets a single central bank is unable – perhaps except that of the US – to stop a bubble, but international joint intervention of major central banks should be able to avoid major bubble problems. At the same time governments should create the option to introduce a temporary sales tax in asset markets so that tax-based government interventions to tame a bubble in asset markets are an alternative or complementary policy option. As regards the development of the world price level a simple two country approach – with tradables and nontradables – implies that with given relative prices of tradables at home and abroad the decisive influences will come from the level of the nontradables price index at home and abroad and the nominal exchange rate (see Appendix 7). An excess supply in the housing market will reduce the price of nontradables – rents will fall along with the housing price index. From a Eurozone perspective an appreciation of the Euro implies that the world price index will fall (assuming that this exchange rate movement will have neither an impact on relative prices nor nontradables prices expressed in national currency). An important issue concerns the question how expansionary monetary policy really is if one takes into account that money is used not only for financing transactions in good markets but also for financing transaction in asset markets; with respect to the 1,920th and the great depression this issue was empirically analyzed by Field (1984) – for a more general analysis see Welfens (2007b).

As regards policy makers, there are new key issues for monetary policy. In the US there might be quantitative easing – the FED would acquire large amounts of bonds held by banks – which, however, are likely to bring a devaluation of the US dollar; the devaluation reflects fear of future inflation (this does not rule out short-term deflationary impulses in the context of a global recession). The higher the expected devaluation rate of the US $, the lower US portfolio inflows will be and this in turn could put pressure on the FED to raise interest rates in the medium term. Moreover, the more toxic assets the FED buys from big banks, the more those banks might be tempted to embark on a new expansion wave of securitization. If this should take place under unchanged institutional rules, a new stock of toxic assets will be created. In the euro zone, the ECB still has some room to cut interest rates, and this could help the ECB avoid embarking strongly on a path of quantitative easing. In the EU, one conclusion could be that the euro zone can cope more successfully with the international banking crisis than the UK and other non-euro EU member countries. At the same time, there is some risk that instabilities in

Eastern Europe could put additional pressure on both the European Commission and the ECB.

The large international current account imbalances might remain on the policy agenda for many years to come, although the short-run increase in the US savings rate has contributed over the medium term to reducing this international problem. However, one should not underestimate that part of the rise in the savings rate of US households was less the result of long term equilibrium adjustment but rather reflected the sudden cuts in lending of banks and the general rise of required equity capital ratios. There are serious doubts that in a world economy with high (cumulated) foreign direct investment real, exchange rate changes will easily contribute to current account adjustment (Welfens 2009a). If one assumes that imports of goods are proportionate to gross national income – and not to GDP as often is assumed in macro models – one has to consider the fact that gross national income (Z) is the sum of GDP plus net factor income from abroad; in the case of inward foreign direct investment and outward foreign direct investment and assuming that both countries considered (foreign country variables carry a*, Y is GDP, α is the share of the foreign capital stock owned by investors from country I, the home country; α^* is the share of capital K in country I owned by investors from country II; ß is the output elasticity of capital) are producing according to a Cobb–Douglas production function we have $Z = Y(1-\alpha^*ß) + \alpha ß^*\ q^*Y^*$ and similarly one can state Z* for country II. Looking at X:= exports/imports, one can show that under specific assumptions – e.g., with symmetric foreign direct investment – the condition for the current account to improve is not that the sum of absolute import elasticities abroad and at home must exceed unity, rather the sum of absolute elasticities must 2 and this condition obviously is more difficult to meet than the standard Marshall Lerner condition suggests (see Appendix).

Stabilizing the US economy is critical for the world economy, and the US government has adopted a series of measures to achieve such stabilization. The US might, however, be weakened after the crisis since it will take time to rebuild confidence in the US financial system and in the US economy and the political system. There is long term contradiction in the field of financial globalization, namely that the US political system favors such globalization while the US Congress would not be willing to even accept that a British bank acquire – with a guarantee of the FED – a nearly bankrupt US investment bank. Such contradiction between economic globalization and political nationalism bodes ill for sustainable financial globalization. The reaction patterns in the EU during the banking crisis were not more internationally minded that those visible in the US. It remains to be seen whether a new global financial architecture and effective global governance can be established under the heading of the G20. The EU should do its homework and try to establish enhanced networking across integration areas in the field of prudential supervision of major actors in international financial markets. The EU should also consider facilitating fiscal policy cooperation in periods of economic crisis; even a larger EU budget might be considered for the long run, provided that government outlays at the national layer will reduce. The Stability and Growth Pact is an important element of policy-making that should be useful to limit deficits and to enhance the credibility of both the EU and Eurozone.

Monetary policy has no room to maneuver in the US and the UK as interest rates are close to zero. Very low interest rates of central banks are not so much helping investors in the real economy – low capacity utilization and the fear of a credit crunch has depressed investment in many OECD countries – but banks' profits will benefit from expansionary monetary policy as is shown in the empirical analysis in Appendix.

The G20 group might find it difficult to deliver on the promises made at the G20 summit in London on April 2, 2009. In the wider public the meeting was understood as a fresh start towards more and better regulation, broader international policy cooperation and a bigger role of the IMF whose role still should be to convey a kind of Washington consensus. However, there is no long such a consensus since raising the capital of the IMF means to raise the profile of China, India and many other countries while weakening the role of the US. More regulation on paper is likely to come, however, implementation is the big problem and here governments in many countries can be expected to be quite hesitant if more regulation means a lower survival probability of big private or public banks. Some countries also will want to water down proposals for new regulation as they are afraid to be a loser in the quest for mobile investors in the banking sector. The quality of regulation matters and here regulation should indeed remain focused mainly on big banks – those banks which face little competition. Regulatory institution need more staff and staff must be paid better if better regulation is really a serious goal. New credit registers have been proposed and probably they will be established; while this is useful the more important issue is a regulation of the CDS business and insurance companies, respectively. Insurance companies such as AIG should not be allowed to be in the CDS business unless they have invested in reinsurance contracts; primary insurance companies seeking reinsurance face high equity stakes as asymmetric information and moral hazard are well known problems in that sector. Regulation on insurance companies, in particular on all actors active in the CDS markets, is needed and it would be useful to consider global coordination here. This point has not been considered in the G20 meeting in London, but future G20 summits should indeed pick it up urgently.

The world recession following the transatlantic banking crisis will further undermine assets of banks and consolidation of the banking sector will continue – but this does not necessarily mean more competition in the EU banking sector, the US banking sector or the global banking sector. Moreover, governments have injected large amounts of capital in many banks, but it is neither clear that management quality of those banks will be improved nor that the quality of financial innovation dynamics will be better in the future. It will be quite important that the Eurozone and the EU, respectively, take the lessons from the banking crisis.

What happens if the US current account deficit and the Chinese surplus continue? Part of the international financial market instabilities might continue as the US banking sector would be swamped with capital from China. It is doubtful that a real exchange rate appreciation of the Chinese currency alone could reduce China's export surplus (in a model with foreign direct investment – quite adequate for the case of China and the US – one can derive a modified Marshall Lerner condition which is stricter than the standard Marshall Lerner condition: see Welfens 2009b); domestic demand should increase – savings should reduce; here reforms of China's social security systems are important. While EU countries have spent about 20% of GDP on social security at the beginning of the twenty-first century, China's government has earmarked only 6%. From a European perspective this suggests that the international debate on the social market economy should be intensified. While Obama Administration in the US has adopted a broader reform of the US health insurance system – making the US look more European – the Chinese government is still hesitant to adopt a broader system of social security. If such a system were implemented the private savings rate in China would reduce and hence China's high current account surplus would fall. In the Eurozone Germany's high current account surplus is a problem to some extent as is the mirror problem of high current account deficits in Spain and Portugal and some other Mediterranean countries. While Germany's economy is likely to strongly benefit from economic upswing in the world economy once the banking crisis is over – more investment in the world economy will mean higher exports of Germany's exporters in the machinery and equipment industry – it might be useful to consider stimulating the German nontradables sector in the medium term: modernizing the education sector and the health care system could temporarily raise the relative price of nontradables and thus reduce the medium net exports of goods and services (somewhat higher wage growth thus also would result). As government is strongly involved in both sectors the crisis might be considered as a welcome starting point for modernization of the supply side of the economy; in the long run this should indeed help to raise long term economic growth as investing in education and human capital formation, respectively, will raise the progress rate and output growth. There is some risk that rising debt–GDP ratios of government in many EU countries – often related to banking crisis (see table: Appendix) – will encourage policymakers to raise income tax rates which in turn will undermine economic growth and thus certainly would make it even more difficult to stabilize the debt–GDP ratios.

The transatlantic banking crisis should be taken seriously, and adopting key reforms is urgent for both OECD countries and the global economy. If such reforms are not adopted in a timely fashion, there could be a backlash in globalization, and indeed some backlash in financial globalization has already become visible. As regards shoring up the shaky US housing market, the proposal of Feldstein (2008) should be realized quickly. With respect to the costs of the US banking crisis, a preliminary assessment is that the per-capita-cost for every American is about $1,000 (mainly related to the Freddie Mae, Fannie Mac and Lehman Brothers failures), whereas the international external costs are about $360 billion annually in 2008 and 2009, which in turn is equivalent to $1,200 per US citizen. Such large external international costs are unacceptable in a fair global economic framework. The world economy is paying high costs for the lack of a consistent US regulatory framework. Financial globalization implies that sorting out the problems in the US banking market will be much more complex than the case of the BCCI bankruptcy in 1991.

The banking rescue packages designed by the UK, Germany, France plus other EU countries and the US will hardly work, as they help to stabilize the banking systems only transitorily. As long as confidence in the interbank market is not restored, there is a risk of silent socialization of the banking system through ever-increasing liquidity injections from the central banks (plus explicit socialization through governments buying stocks and warrants of banks). Confidence in the interbank market can only be restored if parliaments in OECD countries adopt laws which force banks, hedge funds and the like to sell all products with CDS elements to a clearing house, which in turn then reallocates the CDS in a transparent way. Bank mergers sometimes could be a hidden avenue to raise the silent risk exposure of banks, as merging bank I and II typically implies that the bank taken over could have large stakes of CDOs part of which are a combination of ABS and CDS – products difficult to evaluate; such intransparency cannot be accepted and bank supervisory agencies and merger commissions should carefully look into the merger dynamics. The short-term options of saving the banking system – including M&As – are absolutely in contrast to what a solid efficient banking system looks like: smaller banks in a more competitive environment; the more mega banks (representing the ominous too-big-to-fail) there are, the more stricter regulations will have to be imposed. If the US does not accept Basel II+, there can be no free capital movement as the distorted US system would continue to create big international negative external effects.

3.5 Euro Crisis as a Starting Point for the Break-Up of the EU?[1]

The Eurozone was formed in 1999 and the Euro and the European Central Bank have served well during the Transatlantic Banking Crisis; moreover, the inflation rate in the first decade was close to 1.7%, but nevertheless the Eurozone is on the brink of collapse in the spring of 2010 – hardly 2 years after the Transatlantic Banking Crisis and only a year after the first global recession since the 1930s. Rising interest rate spreads for Greece in late 2009 and early 2010 have signaled that risk premiums for this country and other 'Club-Med countries' have increased strongly; indeed, when the new Greek socialist government announced in March 2010 that the deficit–GDP ratio for 2009 had been close to 12% instead of the 5%, which had been indicated by the outgoing conservative government in summer of that year, a confidence crisis rattled international capital markets; the massive upward revision was bad news, which fit into a multi-year series of upward revisions of Greek statistics on government deficits. When Standard and Poor's massively reduced the rating of the Greek sovereign debt to below investor-grade in

[1] See also the paper: Welfens (2010).

April 2010, pensions funds and insurance companies had to sell Greek bonds held in their respective portfolios; this implied considerable losses and stimulated nervous reactions in financial markets: Fear started to spread that other countries of the Eurozone, including Portugal, Spain and Ireland – all with high deficit–GDP ratios and a share of foreign debt of 50% of GDP or more – might soon face similar problems and could fall victim to speculative attacks: above all, Portugal was top of the list as the country was known for weak economic growth, high deficits and a series of high current account deficits; and all of these problems were reinforced during the Transatlantic Banking Crisis, which had generally strongly raised the debt–GDP ratios in OECD countries. In this situation – with Greece being the first EU country to face massive speculative attacks – governments of the EU should have expected to come up with a broad rescue package quickly, mainly guarantees of sovereign debt of the 'Club-Med countries'. Instead, Germany's chancellor, Angela Merkel, tried to postpone key decisions on a first rescue package for Greece and by doing so she has stimulated xenophobic and nationalist reactions in the German boulevard papers, raised the cost of stabilization and stimulated a broader speculative attack against the Eurozone. There was insufficient leadership from Germany, France and other countries during the crisis; the European Commission under Mr. Barroso also showed weakness in its strongest form.

It was only on May 9/10 that the head of governments of the Eurozone and the French president – as well as the ministers of finance from the Euro group – agreed in an emergency meeting in Brussels on a broader package of guarantees for countries of the Eurozone who are facing major problems with refinancing government debt. There would be a € 750 billion package of which the Eurozone states would provide € 440 bill. as loan guarantees for countries facing serious problems; € 250 bill. would be available from the IMF and another € 60 bill. from a broadened EU balance of payments facility. This hastily organized package will fence off speculators for a few months at best, but it is no solution to the partly real, partly fictitious problems of the Eurozone, whose debt–GDP ratio is slightly below that of the US in 2010. As with the Transatlantic Banking crisis, it seems again that policymakers and economists have faced adverse surprise movements in markets; but the Euro crisis could indeed be worse as such a serious crisis of the Eurozone could cause the break-up of this integration club and indeed of the whole EU. A serious sovereign bonds crisis of the Club-Med countries would trigger a new banking crisis in these countries and the OECD group, respectively and since the Transatlantic Banking Crisis of 2008/2009 has already raised debt–GDP ratios in the US and most EU countries by about 20% points (read: by 1/4 of the pre-crisis level), the remaining fiscal room to maneuver during a new international banking crisis would be so small that a new World Depression cannot be ruled out.

Was the Greek crisis really so surprising? It is noteworthy Welfens in his recent book (Transatlantische Bankenkrise, p. 168–169) precisely anticipated such a scenario – the text written in October 2008 and published in early 2009 reads as follows: 'The Eurozone could face serious problems if the risk premiums for such countries as Greece, Italy, Spain or Portugal should increase. Considering that Greece and Italy face high debt–GDP ratios and high deficits plus high foreign indebtedness one cannot rule out that during a temporary accentuation of the global financial crisis it will no be longer possible for these countries to get refinancing from markets. In such a situation, the no-bail-out clause of the Maastricht Treaty should not be applied if indeed a country such as Greece should face serious problems in the aftermath of impulses from the US banking crisis. Rather, member countries of the Eurozone should support member countries with refinancing problems in the spirit of solidarity and responsibility. Similar to the massive guarantees of EU countries for their respective banks, they should come up with guarantee packages for countries with serious refinancing problems. It should also be considered that the European Investment Bank – an EU institution – also gives particular guarantees for several years. It would not be adequate during a global financial crisis to apply the rules of the Maastricht Treaty established for the case of a normal world. This, however, is not to say that EU countries should excuse lax fiscal policies and high deficit GDP as a new loose fiscal framework. Given the fact that monetary integration and monetary union, respectively, have proven to be useful in the Transatlantic Crisis, it would be quite insensible to undermine the Economic and Monetary Union through an overly strict interpretation of the Maastricht Treaty' Welfens (2009). Interestingly, this analysis has been known to the chancellor's key economic advisor who obviously did not consider relevant conclusions and instead seems to have adopted a wait-and-see-attitude, which is reflecting the general crisis of a broader part of the Economics profession – those who have uncritically praised the alleged wonderful wisdom of free capital markets and free capital flows for so many years. It is also noteworthy that rather ignorant TV news coverage – in Germany and in other countries – about the Transatlantic Banking Crisis and the Greek/Eurozone crisis contributes to the destabilization of the economy as negative rumors and pessimistic expectations are spreading at a massive speed. While public TV channels in Germany have a clear mandate to inform the public through news, the information offered in many news channels are often incorrect and contribute very little to make financial market dynamics understandable to the wider public; this poor pattern of news coverage repeats what could already be witnessed during the banking crisis.

With Greece facing illiquidity and the brink of bankruptcy in early 2010, the Eurozone and the EU, respectively, are facing a serious test that should have been avoided:

- It was clear that a normalization of risk premiums – artificially low in 2003–2007 – would bring higher interest rates for many countries and that following the Transatlantic Banking Crisis there would be a new challenge for whole economies to face the survival test in capital markets. The debt–GDP ratio of Greece had reached 115% in 2009; however, the downgrading of Greek sovereign debt was mainly triggered by the enormous upward revisions of the deficit–GDP ratio. The confidence crisis triggered by Greece brought speculative attacks against the country and several banks started to sell large amounts of CDS related to Greece. As neither the EU nor the USA had adopted adequate reforms by late 2009, one can only guess how large the volume of CDS really is – failing to clean up the banking crisis has ushered in the financial system crisis 2.0.

- The joint Eurozone-IMF rescue package – mobilizing guarantees and indirectly loans for Greece (formally avoiding the breach of the bail-out clause) – has amounted to € 110 bill. of which about € 30 bill. are from the IMF, € 22.4 bill. from Germany and the rest from other Eurozone countries. The 3-year-package will most likely be too small to cover the needs of Greece, which is bound to face a sharp recession in 2010–2012. This alone will raise the debt–GDP ratio by about ten points. On top of this, the impact of the deficit–GDP ratio will come, which is unlikely to fall as strongly as promised by the Greek government; the government announced that the deficit–GDP ratio would be reduced by roughly 13% points in the period 2010–2013. Assuming that the debt–GDP ratio of Greece will stand at 140% of GDP in 2013, there will be an unsustainable situation – not least if one assumes that the interest rates will have risen in the US and Europe by then. This also makes clear that the adjustment period envisaged, namely 3 years, is much too short to remedy the problem. If the rescue package for Greece should work, it might help Portugal and Spain who have suffered a downgrade of sovereign rating through Standard & Poor's in April 2010. However, as foreign debt relative to GDP has reached about 100% in Portugal and thus is even higher than in Greece, where it stood at about 70% of GDP in 2009; as is in Spain. The government in Lisbon is going to face tough problems. Taking into account the experience of the Asian crisis, it would have been wise to come up with a broader Eurozone approach from the outset, shoring up all cohesion countries – read: Spain, Portugal, Greece and Ireland.
- It is noteworthy that Germany allocated about € 100 bill. in guarantees to the Hypo Real Estate bank alone and had injected € 6 bill. – as of March 31, 2010 – government capital into the ailing bank, which was nationalized in 2008. A more appropriate approach to the Greek crisis would have consisted not only of a faster reaction from the side of Germany but also of a broader regional stabilization package for all cohesion countries: Greece, Portugal, Spain, Ireland; and it is also clear that all EU member countries – not just Eurozone countries – should have contributed to such a rescue package since it is not just the Eurozone that is at stake through the Greek crisis. The fact that the EU does not really show solidarity during a historical crisis suggests that the political consensus is weak and that the EU will not survive in the medium term.
- A useful innovation would be a project of several small EU countries that agrees on the joint creation of a major state-owned bank, which would reinforce the rating of both governments and private banks in the respective countries. The German bank, KfW, is an example of a large state-owned bank with top rating, which only partly reflects the rating of Germany. The idea of such a joint state-owned bank is to allow investors interested in diversification to get such benefit even if they buy bonds from small EU member countries. Such a project would also reinforce economic policy cooperation among the countries involved. Greece, Portugal and Spain should put more emphasis on improving international competitiveness; the current account deficits have been much too

high for many years – and the European Commission has not pointed to this problem in an adequate manner.

- The Stability and Growth Pact is neither credible nor useful unless the requirement that governments must achieve a budget surplus in boom periods is to be imposed (say during at least four quarters), while facing automatic sanctions in the form of reduced allocations of structural funds or equivalent penalty payments in the case of a violation of this condition. Greece has not achieved any budget surplus in more than a decade of healthy growth after 1998. Achieving a budget surplus during a boom is a key requirement to shift cumulated deficit–GDP ratios downwards over time.

The rescue package for Greece is too small to achieve sustained stabilization; in a similar way, one might soon find out that the rescue package of the Eurozone from early May 2010 is insufficient. If the rescue packages should fail, one likely option for the larger EU countries is to leave the Community and to create a new continental EU economic and political union. Part of the turbulences in markets is caused by the leading three rating agencies that stand for a rather inefficient oligopoly. In any case, the creation of an independent EU rating agency is desirable; it testifies to the enormous weakness of leadership of the European Commission and the leading EU countries that, even 1½ years after the first G20 crisis meeting, the EU has not created a new rating agency that could reinforce competition and contribute to a higher quality of the rating process. It also would be useful to organize an EU information counter-attack against the wave of destabilizing rumors about the Eurozone countries; the main purpose of such rumors and strange dubbing "PIIGS" for the group (Portugal, Ireland, Italy, Greece and Spain) is to reinforce the momentum of profitable speculative attacks against the Eurozone; massive devaluation, government bankruptcy – not due to insolvency but due to illiquidity – rising interest rates and massive recessions could be the collateral damage of such speculative attacks. Taking a careful look at the ratio of interest rate payments on sovereign debt relative to GDP says that all member countries of the Eurozone face a serious improvement relative to the years immediately prior to the start of the Economic and Monetary Union. While the Eurozone has been able to strongly increase employment in the 5 years prior to the Transatlantic Banking Crisis – even more jobs were created than in the US in that time – the international banking crisis has seriously destabilized economic systems in the OECD. Three G20 meetings with historical press declarations have taken place, but neither the US nor the UK have delivered in the field of financial market reform.

If the US should be unwilling to regulate Wall Street in an adequate way, the EU should consider capital controls, as this is the only way to minimize negative transatlantic economic spillovers. However, the European Commission and the EU member countries are weak as there are no longer any clear policy principles and there is also a broad lack in terms of a sense of responsibility. The IMF continues to not publish the long overdue Financial Sector Assessment Program Report on the US, which is completely unacceptable since the IMF Statutes clearly state that policy surveillance is a key field of the IMF mandate – the foot-dragging

Bush Administration has agreed in 2007 that in 2009 the FSAP should be made, but even in spring 2010 there is no report. It is also noteworthy that the EU is becoming inconsistent by calling on banks that they should maintain Greek bonds in their portfolios while the high volatility of those bonds clearly suggests that responsible risk management should reduce the share of Greek bonds in banks' portfolios. Moreover, there are massive tendencies of populist politicians in the EU who argue that banks should face new levies now, however, few politicians seem to understand that at this critical juncture, pension funds and insurance companies had to sell Greek bonds at a steep loss and only banks and hedge funds are left as institutions that might be willing to hold such bonds; if Greece is to refinance sovereign debt in the medium term – the support package of the Eurozone countries is only for 3 years – one should rather make sure that banks continue to hold government bonds in Greece and other Club Med countries. A potential way out of much of the core problems in government debt financing in the Eurozone could be the creation of an EU euro bond agency; while this is not fully in line with the principle of subsidiaries and the non-bail-out clause of the Maastricht Treaty, the creation of such an agency that would place the bonds of all member countries of the Eurozone in international markets seems to be the only viable policy option for restoring stability. If the Eurozone should disintegrate and the EU should fall apart, Germany will push for a German Europe and this will lead back to political conflicts and disasters of a type encountered in the nineteenth century.

Other necessary measures, which the author has outlined in the journal International Economics, and Economic Policy (http://www.econ-international.net; issue No. 1 of 2010) have also not been adopted; this includes a two-stage financing of rating agencies so that there is no longer a conflict of interest in rating. If policy-makers in the EU and the US, as well as Japan, should fail to understand that stability in the Eurozone is an international public good and if European authorities should continue to not implement adequate reforms in financial markets – while improving fiscal policy regimes – the Eurozone and the EU will disintegrate within a few years, followed by a massive global economic crisis and possibly the collapse of Japan where the high debt–GDP ratio of more than 200% in 2011 bounds ill for future fiscal stability. Since Japan's sovereign debt is mainly domestically financed, Japan has fewer problems than the Club-Med countries in Europe, but there is no doubt that a massive destabilization of the Eurozone will undermine stability in Japan, the UK and the US. The natural winner of such a western doom scenario will be China where members of the Communist Party can only smile at how stupidly OECD country governments act as they continue to allow speculators to experiment with even the most lunatic financial weapons, such as 'wash sales' – one sells assets (including credit default swaps) in future markets while not yet holding the respective assets- in a disorganized and largely non-transparent OECD financial market system.

As regards the overall comparison of the USA and the Eurozone, the debt–GDP ratio of the Eurozone in 2010 will be 85%, while that of the US will be 94%. The figure for the UK will be 79%, which is roughly double the ratio within 4 years. The debt–GDP ratio of the US will exceed 100% in 2011. As regards the deficit dynamics of the Eurozone, the primary deficit–GDP ratio (considers deficits without interest payments) switched from a surplus of 1% in 2008 to a ratio of −3.5% in 2009; since the fiscal expenditure impulse reached 1.5% of GDP in 2008/2009 about two thirds of the swing of the deficit–GDP ratio is due to reduced revenues. With respect to the fear of rising inflationary pressures in the Eurozone – partly related to the ECB buying government bonds of Club Med countries one may point out that such anticipations are not reasonable since the European Central Bank can sterilize part of the impact on monetary growth. However, there would be a serious problem of an inflationary increase of the monetary base if the Eurozone countries were to go bankrupt, resulting in massive depreciations of the ECB's assets – to the extent that this is monetized, there would be an impulse for inflation which might be reinforced by a sudden fall in output. This points to the need to design rescue packages for Greece and other countries more carefully: the present ad hoc approach to come up with a rescue package on the basis of emergency meetings is not what is required to restore confidence on the basis of the realistic medium-term adjustment program. If EU countries and OECD countries respectively are not able to come up with consistent rescue packages and adequate structural reforms, the western world will be the loser of modern globalization. This again points to the need to carefully implement adequate reforms for global financial markets. Here, the US and Europe are a historical joint responsibility.

Appendix 1: Theoretical Analysis: Modified Branson Model and the Banking Crisis

Financial market globalization is related to regional monetary integration – see particularly the case of the euro zone – and to financial product innovations, which amounts to raising the marginal utility of financial instruments. In integrated markets, the fixed costs of financial innovations could be more easily spread across world markets than in a world economy with fragmented markets. Hence integrated financial markets should generate a higher rate of product innovations. At the same time, one may emphasize that the financial market crisis of 2007/2008 amounts to some transatlantic disintegration of both financial markets and banking services, not least since EU banks' subsidiaries in the US could no longer get refinancing in the US in 2007 – to some extent this could be considered discrimination against EU banks in the US. (Since December 2007, transatlantic swap agreements between the FED and the ECB had to make sure that European banks could get sufficient dollar liquidity. The FED gives a US$ loan to the ECB, which thus can give a dollar loan to big EU banks – with a subsidiary in the US. The European bank's respective headquarters then gives a US$ loan to its subsidiary in the US.)

The Branson model is a useful analytical starting point to understand some of the key aspects of financial market integration and disintegration. The model determines the nominal interest rate i and the nominal exchange rate e – denoted here in price notation – in a system of flexible exchange rates. It is a short-term model with three assets, namely (short-term) domestic bonds whose stock is B; money M and foreign bonds F (denominated in foreign currency). The desired share of each asset in total wealth (real wealth is A') is denoted as b, n and f, respectively, and each asset demand is assumed to be proportionate A'. We can thus state the equilibrium conditions for money market, the domestic bonds market and the foreign bonds market as follows ($i^{*\prime}$ denotes the sum of the exogenous foreign interest rate i* and the exogenous expected depreciation rate a^E):

(1) $M/P = n(i, i^{*\prime})A'$ MM curve
(2) $B/P = b(i, i^{*\prime})A'$ BB curve
(3) $eF/P = f(i, i^{*\prime})A'$ FF curve
(4) $A' = M/P + B/P + eF/P$

The budget constraint (4) implies that only two of the three equations are independent. As n and f are a negative function of i, while b is a positive function of i, the MM curve has a positive slope in e-i-space. The BB curve and the FF curve have a negative slope, but the FF curve is steeper than the BB curve. B, F and M are given in the short run. F will increase if there is a current account surplus; B will increase if there is a budget deficit. For simplicity, one may assume that we initially have neither a budget deficit nor a current account deficit. In the medium term the current account will react to a change in the real exchange rate. (As the price level at home and abroad is assumed to be constant, we can consider changes in the nominal exchange rate as a change in the real exchange rate.) Here we emphasize that a change of the exogenous variables will shift the BB curve or the FF curve or the MM curve; in some cases all curves will shift. If we consider an expansionary open market policy ($dM = -dB$: thus real wealth is not changing in the short term), the MM curve does not shifting, but the BB curve shifts to the left. The short-term reaction is a depreciation and a fall in the interest rate (see point E_1), which brings about a medium term improvement of the current account as exports of goods will increase and imports will decline as a consequence of the rise in the exchange rate. This in turn will cause a downward shift of the FF curve (this current account effect is neglected in the traditional Branson model), so that the FF line runs through the intersection of the BB_1 curve and the MM_0 curve. Note also that the diagram b) contains an additional MNI curve which indicates monetary neutrality in the sense that – following the logic of the monetary condition index – a real depreciation and a fall in the real interest rate are expansionary with respect to real GDP. Point E_1 is above the line for the monetary neutrality index (MNI_0 line which has a negative slope) and thus real income increases. With a given capital stock K the implication is that average capital productivity will increase, and if we consider a Cobb–Douglas production function it is clear that the marginal product of capital has also increased, which in turn stimulates investment and will increase both the real interest rate r and the nominal interest rate i. We leave it open here how the long run adjustment will be, but one may emphasize that even economic growth can be considered in a modified Branson model (Fig. 3.5).

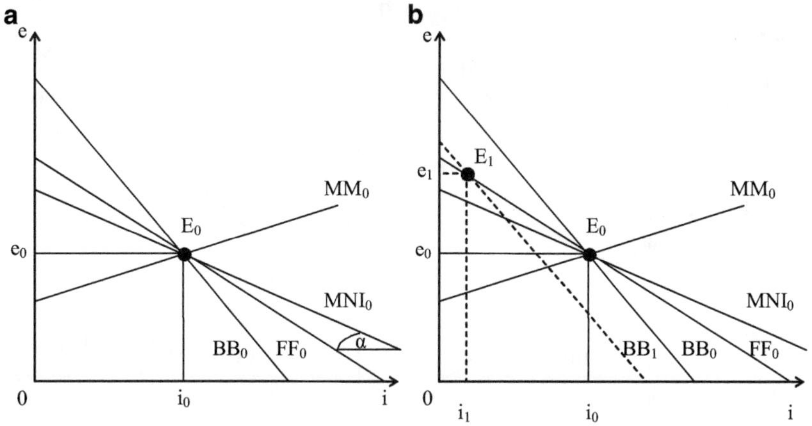

Fig. 3.5 Branson model (**a**) and expansionary open market policy (**b**)

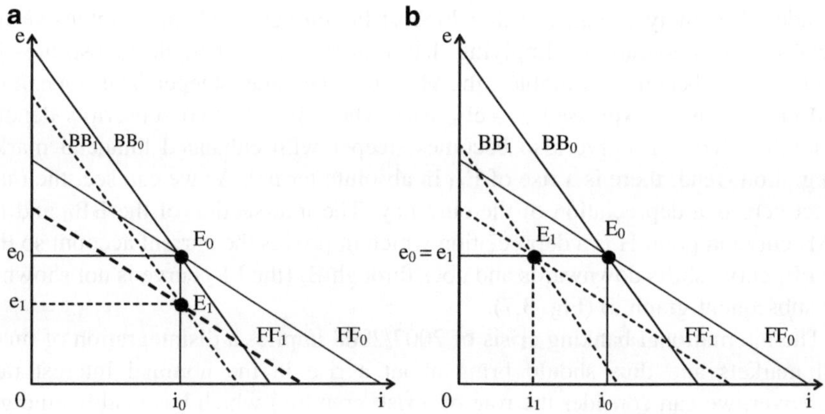

Fig. 3.6 Effects of a fall of the foreign interest rate under weak (**a**) and strong financial market integration (**b**)

Next we consider a fall in the foreign interest rate. The leftward shift of the BB curve is given by $-b_{i*}/b_i$ (b_{i*} and b_i denote the partial derivative of b with respect to i and i*, respectively) and thus becomes stronger with increased financial market integration, as b_{i*} will rises in absolute terms through integration. The leftward shift of the FF curve is indicated by f_{i*}/f_i, and as financial market integration implies that f_i will rise in absolute terms, the leftward shift of the FF curve is smaller under strong integration than under weak integration. Thus the following graph with case (b) is more typical for the case of international financial market integration than case (a): a fall in the foreign interest rate will thus entail a fall in the interest rate (Fig. 3.6).

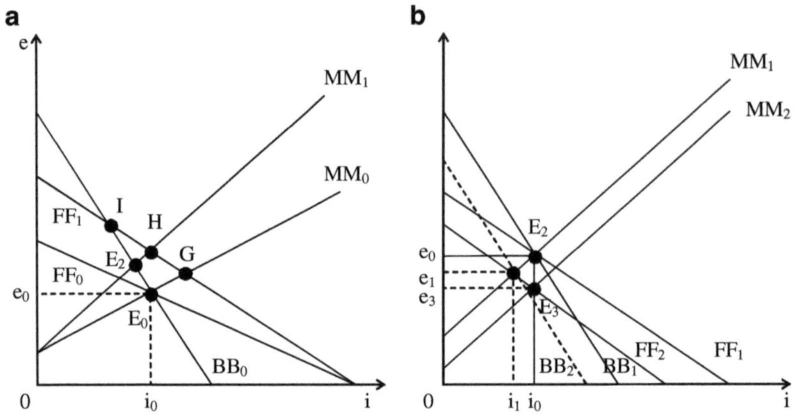

Fig. 3.7 Enhanced financial market integration (**a**) and role of risk premium (**b**)

There is an additional aspect of financial market integration that has to be considered, namely changes in the slope of the curves. With more intensive financial market integration – implying that a larger range of liquid (substitutes for money) assets becomes available – the MM curve becomes steeper. The slope of the MM curve can be expressed as $-eE_{n,i}/(fi)$, where E with two subscripts denotes elasticities. The FF curve also becomes steeper with enhanced financial market integration (read: there is a rise of $E_{f,i}$ in absolute terms). As we can see, the main effect here is a depreciation of the currency. The intersection of the BB_0 and the MM_1 curve in point H is a depreciation which improves the current account so that the FF_1 curve shifts downwards and goes through E_2 (the FF_2 curve is not shown in the subsequent graph a) (Fig. 3.7).

The international banking crisis of 2007/2008 implies a disintegration of financial markets and thus should bring about a rise in the nominal interest rate. Moreover, we can consider the role of a risk premium which has visibly emerged in 2008 – after a strange period 2003–2006 in which the risk premia in US markets declined. Let us assume that B represents only government bonds and F are foreign bonds (could include bonds placed by foreign multinational companies). In a period of high market turbulence and a rising risk premium, we may consider the following modified model where Ω denotes risk premium:

(1) $M/P = n(i, i^{*\prime}, \Omega)A'$ MM curve
(2) $B/P = b(i, i^{*\prime}, \Omega)A'$ BB curve
(3) $eF/P = f(i, i^{*\prime}, \Omega)A'$ FF curve

The demand for money is a positive function of the risk premium, and the demand for domestic government bonds is also a positive function of Ω; hence the MM curve shifts downwards and the BB curve to the left. The demand for foreign bonds declines if the exogenous Ω increases and hence we get a leftward shift of the FF curve (FF2 instead of FF1): a fall of e implies that there is a negative net supply effect (gross supply eF minus induced demand from the change of e which related to A′). The higher risk premium thus brings about a nominal – and real appreciation. Taking the US as the relevant country to be considered, one may argue that the $ appreciation in the autumn 2008 can thus be explained. There is a caveat in that the US represents a large economy and therefore a two country model would be more appropriate than the simple approach presented here. However, the qualitative results would not really change in a two country model. For all countries with high foreign debt – denominated in US$ – this implies additional problems, as foreign debt expressed in domestic currency will rise.

Appendix 2: Regression Results for Banks' Profits

The following analysis looks at the profits of banks in the period 1980–2007 (annual data). To the extent that there are no lags of endogenous variables, we use the Durbin Watson test to check for auto-correlation. If there are lags of endogenous variables to be considered, we use the relevant Ljung-Box Q-statistics. A straightforward hypothesis is to assume that profits are negatively influenced by the central bank interest rate and the interest structure (3-month interest rate/long term rate: this ratio indicates the profit potential from intermediation); in like manner, profits should positively depend on stock market volumes and nominal GDP. As regards Switzerland, the central bank rate has a significant negative impact, but the interest rate structure has a positive sign; the adjusted R^2 (0.56) is relatively high. For the UK, it is rather difficult to find a good fit, as stock market volumes are neither significant on a current basis nor on the basis of lags. As regards the US, the equation with the two variables discount rate and GDP presents a good fit and R^2 is 0.82. In the case of Germany, we have two relevant variables, namely the discount rate and the interest rate structure – both with the theoretically correct sign; also the stock market volume is significant. For the EU15, the equation shows a relatively low R^2, the stock market volume positively affects profits, and the discount rate has a negative impact on profits. The EU15 equation might be blurred by exchange rate changes which could particularly affect figures for the UK. If the banking sector is to be stabilized in Germany, it would be important to avoid an inverse yield structure.

Dependent Variable: DBG			Switzerland
Included observations: 17 after adjustments			
Variable	Coefficient	t-Statistic	prob.
C	1.898177	1.412786	0.1831
DDISCR(−1)	−2.065266	−2.387576	**0.0343**
DGDP	0.744485	2.360272	**0.036**
DIG_RATIO	7.366168	2.216426	**0.0467**
DSMV	−0.010434	−1.334539	0.2068
R-Squared	0.667601		
Adjusted R-squared	0.556801		

Dependent Variable: DBG			UK
Included observations: 16 after adjustments			
Variable	Coefficient	t-Statistic	prob.
DIR_RATIO	67.21117	1.504203	0.1584
DIR_RATIO(−1)	−68.26024	−1.511647	0.1565
DSMV	0.207897	0.246016	0.8098
DSMV(−1)	0.71439	0.777999	0.4516
R-Squared	0.322577		
Adjusted R-squared	0.153221		

Dependent Variable: DBG			US
Included observations: 17 after adjustments			
Variable	Coefficient	t-Statistic	Prob.
DDISCR	−1.102426	−1.939272	**0.0715**
DGDP	1.174455	9.029179	**0**
R-squared	0.834837		
Adjusted R-squared	0.823826		
Durbin-Watson stat	2.250786		

Dependent Variable: DBG			EU15
Included observations: 17 after adjustments			
Variable	Coefficient	t-Statistic	Prob.
C	2.141516	1.353922	0.1972
DDISCR(-1)	−2.048125	−2.452928	**0.0279**
DSMV	0.2099	1.920008	**0.0755**
R-squared	0.341618		
Adjusted R-squared	0.247563		

Dependent Variable: DBG			GER
Included observations: 17 after adjustments			
Variable	Coefficient	t-Statistic	Prob.
C	13.95844	2.742814	**0.0168**
DISCR	−2.167209	−1.938802	**0.0745**
DIR_RATIO	−50.72781	−4.416443	**0.0007**
DSMV	0.16535	3.570429	**0.0034**
R-squared	0.707515		
Adjusted R-squared	0.640019		
Durbin-Watson stat	1.781588		

Definition of variables: D: differentiated variable (first time difference), DBG: bank profits (first difference), DISCR: discount rate (central bank rate), DDISCR: discount rate (first time difference), DGDP: GDP (first time difference), IR_Ratio: 3 months interest rate relative to 10 year bond rate, DIRRatio: first difference of IR_Ratio, SMV: stock market volume, DSMV: first difference of stock market volume

Appendix 3: Rate of Return on Equity and Leverage

Raising the required rate of return (E′) on equity is a typical challenge for managers. If a banker wants to raise that rate of return he/she will consider the following equation (i is the interest rate, α the ratio of equity capital to total capital, R' is the total rate of return on capital):

(1) $R' = \alpha E' + (1 - \alpha)i$
(2) $E' = (1/\alpha)R' - [(1 - \alpha)/\alpha]i$
(3) $E' = (1/\alpha)R' + [1 - (1/\alpha)]i$
(4) $E' = i + (1/\alpha)(R' - i)$

Hence the rate of return on equity can be raised by lowering the equity-capital ratio α as long as there is a positive difference between R' and i; alternatively the bank can try to raise the differential $R' - i$. In a system of perfect capital markets (along the logic of the Modigliani–Miller theorem which argues that the structure of capital is irrelevant for the rate of return on equity) the strategy of raising the leverage, namely reducing α, will bring about a rise of the bank-specific interest rate which simply offsets the initially favorable effect of lowering the equity-capital ratio: The rise of the bank-specific risk premium will neutralize the impact of a lower α. If, however, the capital markets are imperfect – and this is the more realistic perspective – the bank, starting with $\alpha = 1/10$ and $i = 5\%$ and R' as 6%, can raise the initial rate of return on equity of 15% by a higher leverage: the equity-capital ratio will be reduced to 1/20 and thus the required rate of return on equity will rise from 15 to 25%. Alternatively, the bank could maintain $\alpha = 1/10$ and try to widen to differential from the initial 1 to 2%. This also would raise the rate of return to 25%.

However, 25% is quite an unrealistic target in the long run since a market economy will face standard economic laws:

- The nominal interest rate should be equal to the real interest rate r plus the inflation rate π.
- The real interest rate r should be equal to the growth rate g_Y of output (Y).

Thus the real rate of return on equity $E'' := E' - \pi$ is given by:

(5) $E'' = g_Y + (1/\alpha)[R' - (g_Y + \pi)]$

Let us denote the real rate of return $R'' = R' - \pi$, then we can write – assuming a function $R''(\ldots)$:

(6) $E'' = [1 - (1/\alpha)]g_Y + [1/\alpha]R''(Z, g_Y, a, \ldots)$

For the sake of simplicity we assume that the overall rate of return on capital R'' depends on the risk premium Z – incurred by the representative bank – the real growth rate of the market (assume that this growth rate is equal to gY) and the rate of technological progress in banking we can use a linearized function $R'' = q'Z + q''g_Y + q'''a$ (the parameters $q' > 0, q'' > 0, q''' > 0$) so that we get for the case $q'' > 1$ that output growth always has a positive impact on E'':

(7) $E'' = [1 - (1/\alpha)(1 - q'')]g_Y + [1/\alpha]q'Z + q'''a$

A period with a strong expansion of modern information and communication technology (ICT) could go along with a rise of the progress rate a and this in turn will raise the real rate of return for the representative bank. A critical issue is the risk premium Z.

In the context of the capital asset pricing model we have for the rate of return on stocks $v = r+\Omega\sigma$ where r is the real rate of return on government bonds, Ω is the price of risk and σ the volatility of the respective stock index. If the price of risk should fall artificially – through financial innovations – one would get a rise of the investment output ratio provided that σ is not rising.

Appendix 4: Information for IKB Clients (From the Website of IKB Deutsche Industriebank); IKB-Kundeninformation (IKB, 2005)

This document explains to the reader the advantages of ABS and of special purpose vehicles where the authors argue that Rhineland Funding Capital Corporation. It had been created by the IKB Deutsche Industriebank as a special purpose vehicle; Rhineland Funding had received \$ 8.1 bill. as a credit line from IKB in order to make sure that Rhineland Funding would get a top rating and hence low refinancing costs; IKB invested heavily in subprime products – most of which were rate triple A, but this, of course, did not mean absence of liquidity risk. Rhineland Funding went bankrupt in 2008 and investors received 55% of the money invested; the main prudential supervisory agency in Germany, the BaFin, was fully aware of all the transactions of IKB and obviously did not disapprove them although IKB's subprime exposure in absolute terms exceeded that of Deutsche Bank in 2006 – IKB had equity of less than € 2 bill. BaFin in its annual report 2008 declared in the preface that it was totally surprised by all the financial market developments in the US and did not have a real idea of what was going on the US. This is a strange statement for the prudential supervisor of the ECB's largest financial market and has remained without any consequences). The IKB information shows that the bank had not fully understood its own product – liquidity aspects were not considered and hence it was argued that the product was 'without any risk in the short term'; the website info states (page 3;

translated by the author – the website info was deleted from the bank's website in September 2008):

„Das SPV refinanziert den Kauf des Forderungsportfolios z.B. durch die Emission von Commercial Papers. Hierbei handelt es sich um Wertpapiere mit kurzen Laufzeiten von in der Regel 30 bis 60 Tagen, die durch das Forderungsportfolio (deshalb ‚Asset Backed´ Commercial Papers) besichert sind. Um das notwendige Rating für eine Emission zu erreichen, bedarf es häufig einer zusätzlichen Sicherheitenverstärkung (Credit Enhancement). Hierbei wird z.B. ein Abschlag auf den Kaufpreis als Besicherungs-‚Überhang´ (Over-Collateralisation) vereinbart und zusätzlich eine Liquiditätslinie durch eine Bank mit einem entsprechend guten Rating gestellt. Überdies lassen sich ABS auch mittels einer Warenkreditversicherung zusätzlich absichern. Aus Sicht der institutionellen Investoren handelt es sich hierbei also um eine sehr sichere Kurzfristanlage.

(SPV refinanced acquisition of portfolios of claims, for example through issuing commercial papers. Those papers have short maturities, typically in the range of 30–60 days; commercial papers are backed through the loan portfolio – [thus they are dubbed asset backed commercial papers]; often one tries to achieve an adequate rating for a placement, namely through credit enhancement. This amounts to considering a price line below the market price so that there is over-collateralisation, and in addition one obtains a credit line from a bank with a top rating. Moreover, one could additionally reduce the risk of ABS through an insurance on the loan portfolio. From the perspective of an institutional investor such a model stands for an almost riskless short term investment. The document was available for about 3 years under the following address: http://www.ikb.de/content/de/produkte/inland/abs_publikationen/11_03_Mittelstandsfin.pdf.

Appendix 5: Serious Doubts About Basel Rules for Required Equity Capital

The Basel I rules as well as the Basel II rules impose a required ratio of equity capital to total capital for every bank. Regulatory actors argue that a high equity ratio improves the survival prospects of a bank in periods of negative shocks (read: high depreciations and losses, respectively). This view, however, is seriously mistaken as will be shown here in the context of banks' consolidated balance sheets. The following presentation is based on Kath (1992), who derives – based on the standard Brunner–Meltzer approach – the multipliers for the money supply (M_1) and for credit supply (KR^s). However, the analysis of Kath ignores equity capital. In the following analysis equity capital is included on the liability side (equity capital is not considered in Kath 1992) of the banks' consolidated balance sheet, which is shown here along with the balance sheet of the central bank:

Balance Sheet of Central Bank

Foreign Reserves	B1	Cash	Bc
Government Bonds	B2	Deposits of Banks (Reserves)	TR
Refinancing Component	RF		
Monetary Base (Source Side) B		Monetary Base (Uses Side)	B

Consolidated Balance of Banks

Credit to Nonbanks	KR	Sight Deposits of Nonbanks	D1
Deposits with Central Bank	TR	Term Deposits of Nonbanks	D2
		Loans from Central Banks	RF

The Basel rules require – among other things – that the equity ratio of a bank should exceed 8%. Denoting deposits at a bank by D, loans from the central bank by RF and equity capital by E′ the above requirement says for an individual bank j that the ratio E'_j to credits KR_j must exceed a critical ratio; the basic argument is that a high ratio of equity to credits serves as a cushion for adverse shocks (high allowances or even losses in periods of adverse shocks).

Let us now consider the aggregate perspective for the banking sector. For simplicity we can consider the Basel requirement as

(I) $E' = \alpha' KR$(parameter α' is in the range between zero and unity);

The consolidated balance sheet of all banks has on the asset side the credits to nonbanks KR and the banks' deposits with the central bank (reserves of banks: TR). On the liability side we have deposits of nonbanks, namely sight deposits D_1 and term deposits D_2 plus the credits obtained from the central bank (RF) plus equity capital E′. Hence we have the following identity from the balance sheet:

(II) $KR + TR = D_1 + D_2 + RF + E'$

Taking into account the regulatory requirement that $E' = \alpha' KR$ we can write:

(III) $KR + TR = D_1 + D_2 + RF + \alpha' KR$

Hence we obtain:

(IV) $KR(1 - \alpha') + TR = D_1 + D_2 + RF$

Standard banking theory assumes that banks will want to have a certain ratio (tr) of reserves at the central bank to total deposits ($D = D_1 + D_2$). Hence the reserve coefficient is defined as:

(V) $tr = TR/(D_1+D_2)$

Similarly one may define a desired reserve coefficient rf:

(VI) $rf = RF/(D_1+D_2)$

Let d denote the discount rate, i the interest rate on loans and rr the reserve ratio required by the central bank one may assume the following function (we indicate negative partial derivatives only, e.g. $tr_i := \partial tr/\partial i$; those not indicated explicitly have a positive sign):

(VII) $tr = tr(rr, i, d)$, where $tr_i < 0$
(VIII) $rf = rf(rr, i, d)$, where $rf_d < 0$.

Furthermore, one may define (with C^P denoting cash held by nonbanks) the cash balance ratio $bk := C^P/D_1$ and $t' = D_2/D_1$ – we assume $t'(i', Y_K)$, where $t'_{YK} < 0$ (i′ is the interest rate on deposits at the bank, Y_K is the marginal product of capital) – then the definition of the monetary base $B = C^P + TR$ gives a money supply multiplier m_1 for $M_1 := C^P + D_1$: The multiplier is defined as

(IX) $m_1 = M_1/B = (C^P+D_1)/(C^P+TR)$

Dividing the expressions in the numerator and the denominator by D_1 (and writing TR/D_1 as $[(TR/D)(D_1+D_2)/D_1]$ while taking into account $D_2 = t'D_1$ and $D_2/D_1 = t'$, respectively) we can write:

(X) $m_1 = (bk + 1)/\{bk + [(TR/D)(D_1+D_2)/D_1]\}$

Thus the money supply multiplier can conveniently be expressed as

(XI) $m_1 = (1 + bk)/(bk + tr(1 + t'))$

Next we define the exogenous monetary base B^{ex} in a suitable way

(XII) $B^{ex} = C^P + TR - RF$

Taking into account that $RF = b'(D_1+D_2)$ we obtain (in analogy to the procedure above) the following multiplier for the exogenous monetary base:

(XIII) $m^{ex} = (1 + bk)/[bk + (tr - b')(1 - t')]$

Thus the money supply function can be expressed as:

(XIV) $M_1 = m_1{}^{ex}(i, d, rr, i', Y_K)B^{ex}$

If the multiplier were homogeneous of degree one in Y_K and production would be characterized by a Cobb–Douglas production function $Y = K^{ß}(AL)^{1-ß}$ – where K is capital, A knowledge and L labor (0<ß<1) – we could simplify the equation by scaling both sides by Y and K, respectively; this holds because $Y_K = ßY/K$. Note also that we can divide both sides of the equation by the price level P so that the left hand side would ride (M/P)/Y which is the inverse of the average productivity of real money balances while $(B^{ex}/P)/K$ is the real exogenous monetary base per unit of real capital.

The partial derivatives with respect to d and rr are negative, those with respect to the marginal product of capital (Y_K) and the deposit interest rate i′ also if $(tr - b') < 0$. Up to this point the analysis is fairly standard. However, the following considerations for the credit multiplier contain crucial – and paradox – new aspects about the role of equity capital in the banking system. The analysis sheds new light on the importance of making a distinction between the perspective of the individual bank and the overall banking system. We will basically argue that the Basel rules in the field of equity requirement strengthen the ability of individual banks to cope with bad weather, but that the same rules also raise the probability of bad weather so that one may raise doubts about the Basel I/II rules; revisions of non-optimal rules – while ignoring the weakness of the Basel I/II approach – therefore could undermine the stability of banks rather than reinforce the resilience and stability of the system.

Credit Supply Multiplier

Based on equation (IV) one can derive a credit multiplier which implicitly is defined through the ratio of credit supply (KR^s) and the exogenous monetary base; the multiplier is denoted as a^{ex}:

(XV) $KR^s/B^{ex} = a^{ex}$
(XVI) $a^{ex} = KR/B^{ex} = [D_1 + D_2 - TR + RF]/\{(1-\alpha')[C^P + TR - RF]\}$

In the following expression we have taken into account the regulatory requirement that equity capital $E' = \alpha' KR$. Thus we obtain an expression whose denominator is identical to that of the money supply multiplier. More importantly, the regulatory parameter α'

(XVII) $a^{ex} = \{(1+t')(1-(tr-b'))/(1-\alpha')\}/[bk + (tr-b')(1+t')]$

We thus can write

(XVIII) $KR^s = a^{ex}(\alpha', i, d, rr, i', Y_K)B^{ex}$

The partial derivatives of the credit multiplier are negative with respect to d, rr and Y_K, and α, positive for i and i′. The higher the required α' the lower is $1 - \alpha'$. The higher α' the higher is the credit multiplier. If a high leverage of investment – broadly defined – entails a high volatility of asset prices and hence high risk for investors and banks, respectively, one should not be surprised that a high required α could raise macroeconomic instability since the macroeconomic effect of a higher credit multiplier could offset the (microeconomic) cushioning effect of a high equity ratio of individual banks. The hypothesis that a higher equity ratio E′/KR could entail a higher macroeconomic volatility implies that there is an optimum E′/KR which maximizes long term bank survival $S'_j = [1 - f(\sigma)]/F(\sigma)$ where F(.) is a function describing macroeconomic volatility σ and f(.)

a function – defined in the range (0, 1) – which represents the individual bank's absorption of macroeconomic shocks. The individual bank will go bankrupt if S'_j reaches a critical threshold as depositors will want to withdraw their deposits immediately.

We may particularly state the hypothesis that a rise of KR^s/M_1 above a natural (long term) level will raise macroeconomic volatility. Note that the multipliers for the credit supply and the money supply have identical denominators so that we can conveniently express the ratio $KR^s/M_1 := \Omega'$ as:

(XIX) $\Omega' = \{(1 + t')(1 - (tr - b'))/(1 - \alpha')\}/(1 + bk)$

Here we have used $\ln(1 + x) \approx x$ which is a good approximation for x close to zero. Assuming that all parameters on the right-hand side of the equation are close to zero we can use the convient approximation:

(XX) $\ln \Omega' \approx t' - (tr - b') + \alpha' - bk$

Let us denote the degree of confidence loss in the interbanking market by σ' – which indeed is the risk not to find liquidity in the market – and assume that t′ is a negative function of the lack of confidence in the interbank market (the private sector will substitute short-term deposits D1 for term deposits D2) and that b′ is a positive function of the lack of confidence (as banks will want to rely more one central bank loans in a period of liquidity crisis and as the central bank is expected to be a lender of last resort), then we can write

(XXI) $\ln \Omega' \approx t'(\sigma') - tr(rr, i, d) + b'(\sigma') + \alpha' - bk(i');$

Note that we also have assumed that $bk := C^P/D1$ is a negative function of the deposit interest rate i′. Recall that $\partial tr/\partial i<0, \partial tr/\partial rr>0, \partial tr/\partial d>0$ so that a fall of the discount rate will reduce the ratio of credit supply to money supply. In a situation of a non-elastic relative credit demand – in a period of a strong economic boom – the above equation implicitly determines i/i′ and hence the profitability of banks (one also may argue that the equation determines the slope of the yield curve, assuming that banks lends long term and have medium term and short term deposits). The impact of the confidence parameter σ' on the relative loan supply is ambiguous so that empirical analysis of t′(.) and b′(.) is necessary to determine the impact of a confidence shock.

Next we consider the fact that a rise of the required equity ratio raises the ratio of loans to the money supply. This rise of Ω' will bring about increased investment in assets – in particular if the relative demand for loans is highly elastic (hence in the early economic upswing). If we assume for simplicity that the demand for money is proportionate to nominal output and that there is equilibrium in the money market at any time we will have a real rise of asset prices, namely to the extent that one may assume that loans are used only to a small extent to buy new goods and services, but rather loans are used to buy existing stocks of capital and real estate. The consequence will be asset price inflation (indeed pure asset price inflation if the output price level is constant). Real asset prices will be driven above long term equilibrium levels and this implies an asset price bubble – a period of rapidly rising asset prices later fallowed by a sharp decline in asset prices. This implies that a rise of the ratio KR^s/M brings about higher volatility of asset prices and hence higher risk which in turn makes the banking sector more vulnerable. While the rise of required regulatory equity capital ratio reinforces the ability of banks to weather stormy weather in the market the same rise of that ratio also raises the probability that stormy weather will occur. This raises the issue about an optimum equity capital ratio. An alternative to the existing regulations could be to require within a new approach Basel III that $E = \alpha''D + \alpha'FK$ where the first new element would reinforce the individual bank's ability to absorb adverse shocks while not raising the credit multiplier in the case of a rise of α'' (defined in the range 0.1). This can be seen be only looking at the case $E' = \alpha''D$ which gives a new multiplier for the credit supply:

$$\text{(XXII)}\ a^{ex\prime} = (1+t')[1-tr(1+\alpha'')-b']/(bk+(tr-b')(1+t'))$$

Thus one may raise serious doubts about the existing Basel rules in the field of required equity capital. Carefully adjusting the framework for banks will be crucial for achieving stability.

Real Credit Demand and the Relative Price of Stocks and Real Estate

Let us consider a setup without inflation and assume that nominal credit demand is given by the following simple function

$$\text{(XXIII)}\ H^d = \eta(YP + P'K + P''K'')/(\psi r)$$

where P' is the stock market price index and η and K, respectively, stand for a positive parameter and the physical capital stock; K'' is the stock of real estate capital and ψ is a parameter which indicates the responsiveness of credit demand with respect to the real interest rate r. The credit demand function specified assumes that for producing (nominal) output and for holding stocks and real estate loans are taken.

By implication the real credit demand can be written as $H/P = \eta(Y + q'K + q''K'')/(\psi r)$ where $q' := P'/P$ and q'' denotes the relative price P''/P (P'' is the price index of real estate). Next we divide both sides of the real credit demand equation by AL (A denotes knowledge, L labor). If real credit supply $KR/P = a^{ex}B^{ex}/P$ and $M_1{}^s/P = m^{ex}B^{ex}/P$ we can obviously write $KR/P = (a^{ex}/m^{ex})(M/P)$. Taking into account the production function $Y = K^{\beta}(AL)^{1-\beta}$ credit market equilibrium – namely $(H^d/P)/K = (H^s/P)/K$ – thus can be written as

$$\text{(XXIV)}\ (a^{ex}/m^{ex})(M/P)/K = (\eta/(\psi r)](K^{\beta}(AL)^{1-\beta} + q'K + q''K'')/K$$

or with $k' := K/(AL)$

(XXV) $(a^{ex}/m^{ex})(M/P)/K = \eta(k'^{ß-1} + q' + q''K''/K)/(\psi r)$

If one solves for r and assume for the sake of simplicity that the ratio (a^{ex}/m^{ex}) is exogenous and also that q' is exogenous (an alternative assumption would be $q' = 1$ if new investment goods and existing capital K are perfect substitutes in the medium term) we get the medium term equilibrium real interest rate:

(XXVI) $r = (m^{ex}/a^{ex})\eta(k'^{ß-1} + q' + q''K''/K)/\{[(M/P)/K]\psi\}$

The higher the credit multiplier and the monetary policy target ratio (M/P)/K are the lower is the real interest rate; the true policy variable is M/K. The price level P will result from the excess demand in the goods market. Let us denote the expected inflation rate as π'. If one assumes that $Y^d = [M^d\psi''(r + \pi\prime)]/P$ – this implicitly reflects a money demand function $M^d = YP/[\psi''(r + \pi')]$ – and consider the price adjustment function $dP/dt = h''[Y^d/(AL) - Y\#/(AL)]$ we will get (with the steady state income Y# relative to labor in efficiency units AL) the following solution for a non-inflationary price level: $P = [M/(AL)]\psi''r/(s/(n + a))^{ß/1-ß}$. Note that we have replaced $k'\# := K'/(AL)\text{by}[s/(n + a)]^{ß/1-ß}$ which is the standard result from neoclassical growth theory under the assumption that the savings rate s and the progress rate $a(a := d\ln A/dt)$ as well as the growth rate of labor $(n : = d\ln L/dt)$ are exogenous. The production function used here is, of course, the Cobb–Douglas function.

The above equation can be interpreted alternatively in a different way. Assume that (M/P)/K is determined by monetary policy preferences and that K″/K is given; if $r = ßY/K = ßk'^{ß-1}$ – reflecting profit maximization of firms (assuming that the capital depreciation is zero) – the implication is that Tobin's q will rise if k′ is raised. Despite a rise of k′ the variables q′ and q″ could rise if there is a sufficiently strong increase of a^{ex}/m^{ex}. Thus a relatively strong increase of the (relative) credit multiplier could raise the real price of stocks and the relative price of real estate. Financial innovations and a relative rise of the credit multiplier thus could raise q′ and q″. This points to some of the problems in the US banking crisis 2007/2008. Note that k′ in the long run can be replaced – within a neoclassical growth model – by the steady state solution $[s/(a + n)]^{1/1-ß}$. If one assumes that $q'' = \Omega''q'$ – so that Ω″ is the relative price P″/P′ – we can rewrite the equation as

(XXVII) $(a^{ex}/m^{ex})(M/P)/K = \eta(k'^{ß-1} + q' + q'\Omega''K''/K)/(\psi ßk'^{ß-1})$
(XXVIII) $(a^{ex}/m^{ex})(M/P)/K = [\eta/(\psi ß)]\{\psi ß + [q'(1 + \Omega''K''/K)/k'^{ß-1}$

Here the implication clearly is that a rise of the (relative) credit multiplier will raise the real price of stocks P′/P. Parallel to the rise of P′/P there will be a rise of P″/P.

Appendix 6: Rate of Return to Real Capital (Including Depreciation Rate)

Table 3.2 Rates of return on capital in the business sector[a]

	1960–1969	1970–1979	1980–1989	1992	1993	1994	1990–1994
United States	17.1	15.7	14.9	17.1	18.1	18.8	17.4
Japan	24.8[b]	17.9	14.3	14.0	13.8	13.4	14.2
Germany	16.3	13.5	11.9	13.7	13.2	13.8	13.7
France	11.9[c]	12.8	11.9	14.6	14.3	14.7	14.5
Italy	12.7	11.8	13.6	14.5	14.6	15.2	14.7
United Kingdom	11.8[c]	10.2	9.6	9.9	10.9	11.5	10.2
Canada	12.4[d]	14.2	17.1	16.1	16.4	17.1	16.5
Netherlands	n.a.	13.9	16.3	17.4	16.7	17.9	17.9
Belgium	n.a.	12.7	11.7	12.5	12.1	12.4	12.7
Sweden	13.2[b]	10.7	10.0	11.1	12.0	12.6	11.0
Switzerland	15.6	11.1	8.9	8.5	9.3	10.4	9.4
G-10 weighted average	17.0	14.8	13.8	15.1	15.5	16.0	15.3

[a]Gross output of the business sector minus net indirect taxes and labor income, all divided by non-residential capital stock excluding land
[b]1965–1969
[c]1963–1969
[d]1966–1969
Source: OECD (1995)

Appendix 7: Global Price Level

(A1) $P^W = P^{\alpha}(eP^*)^{(1-\alpha)}$ where $\alpha \in]0,1[$

The world price level P^W thus is defined as an index composed of the price index of country 1 (home country) and country 2 (foreign country); α is the weight attached to the price index of country 1. The price index in each country is composed of sub-indices for the tradables sector and the non-tradables sector where weights in the two countries considered are α' and $\alpha'*$ for the tradables sector. It will be assumed that the low of one price holds for the tradables sector so that $P^T = eP^T*$.

Let us denote the price index of tradeables and non-tradeables as P^T and P^N, respectively; e is the nominal exchange rate, P the aggregate price level.

We have
$$P^* = \left(P^{T^*}\right)^{\alpha'^*} \cdot \left(P^{N^*}\right)^{(1-\alpha'^*)}$$
$$P = \left(P^T\right)^{\alpha'} \cdot \left(P^N\right)^{(1-\alpha')}$$
$$P^T = eP^{T^*}$$

$$\text{(A2)}\quad P^{\alpha} = \left(\left(P^{T}\right)^{\alpha'} \cdot \left(P^{N}\right)^{(1-\alpha')}\right)^{\alpha}$$
$$= \left(\left(P^{T}\right)^{\alpha'} \cdot P^{N}\left(P^{N}\right)^{-\alpha'}\right)^{\alpha}$$
$$= \left(P^{N}\left(\frac{P^{T}}{P^{N}}\right)^{\alpha'}\right)^{\alpha}$$

$$\text{(A3)}\quad \left(eP^{*}\right)^{(1-\alpha)} = \left(e\left(P^{T^*}\right)^{\alpha'^*} \cdot \left(P^{N^*}\right)^{(1-\alpha'^*)}\right)^{(1-\alpha)}$$
$$= \left(eP^{N^*}\left(\frac{P^{T^*}}{P^{N^*}}\right)^{\alpha'^*}\right)^{(1-\alpha)}$$

Therefore the world price index is given by P^{W}

$$\text{(A4)}\ P^{W} = \left(P^{N}\left(\frac{P^{T}}{P^{N}}\right)^{\alpha'}\right)^{\alpha}\left(eP^{N^*}\left(\frac{P^{T^*}}{P^{N^*}}\right)^{\alpha'^*}\right)^{(1-\alpha)}$$

Let us define

$$\text{(A5)}\ \varphi := \frac{P^{T}}{P^{N}}$$

and

$$\text{(A6)}\ \varphi^{*} := \frac{P^{T^*}}{P^{N^*}}$$

So we get:

$$\text{(A7)}\quad P^{W} = \left(P^{N}\varphi^{\alpha'}\right)^{\alpha}\left(eP^{N^*}\varphi*^{\alpha'^*}\right)^{(1-\alpha)}$$
$$= \left(P^{N}\right)^{\alpha}\left(\varphi^{\alpha'}\right)^{\alpha}\left(eP^{N^*}\right)^{(1-\alpha)}\varphi^{*}\alpha'^{*(1-\alpha)}$$
$$= eP^{N^*}\left(\frac{P^{N}}{eP^{N^*}}\right)^{\alpha}\varphi^{\alpha'\alpha}\varphi^{*\alpha'*(1-\alpha)}$$

The growth rate of the world price level can be obtained from (4) or (3); if one considers (3) we get for the global inflation rate (with a′ denoting the depreciation rate of country 1's currency, π'' denoting the inflation rate of the nontradables price index and using the definition of the relative tradables price):

$$\text{(5)}\ \pi^{W} = \alpha\pi'' + (1-\alpha)\pi''^{*} + \alpha\alpha' g_{\varphi} + \alpha\alpha' a' + (1-\alpha)\alpha'^{*} g_{\varphi}$$

At first one may assume that the exchange rate is constant and – also for simplicity – we assume that the growth rate of the relative price change is the same in both countries. Thus we will get deflation if

- The relative price of the tradables is falling: This may be expected in the case of an excess supply in the world economy (the world recession 2009 corresponds to this situation); and

- The non-tradables price index in both countries is falling: This may be expected in the case of an excess supply in the non-tradables sector – however, this also may be expected if there is a strong fall of the nominal price index of the housing market which in turn could be triggered by falling financial asset prices in both countries. The latter is the case of the transatlantic banking crisis.

In this short-term perspective it is easy to understand that for 2009/2010 one should rather anticipate deflation than inflation although the medium term analysis cannot ignore the role of a rather strong growth of the money supply in the world economy. In a medium term full employment perspective one may argue that the relative price of tradables is determined by productivity growth in the tradables sector and the nontradables sector, respectively; at the same time one may argue that the absolute price level of the nontradables is determined by aggregate demand which is proportionate to the stock of money M as can be derived from the quantity equation in the version (with velocity V assumed to be constant):

$$MV = [P^N]^{(1-\alpha')}\varphi^{\alpha'}[N(\varphi) + \varphi T(\varphi)]$$

We denote the growth rate of the money supply by μ and thus can derive the following equation for the growth rate of π'':

Appendix 8: Structural Unemployment Rate, Growth and Technological Progress

Let us briefly take a look at a growth model with a structural unemployment rate (u) – which might rise in a period of unstable financial markets-, a given rate of capital depreciation (δ) and a given output elasticity of capital (ß). One may note that a standard neoclassical growth model (with a Cobb–Douglas production function $Y = K^{ß}(AL)^{1-ß}$; K is capital, A knowledge which growth at an exogenous growth rate a, L labor which growth at the exogenous growth rate n) in combination with a modified savings function – namely savings $S = sY(1-\tau)(1-u)$ – and a technological progress function $a = a' - a''u$ (where s, a′ and a″ are positive parameters, τ is the income tax rate and u the unemployment rate; s is in the interval (0,1)) gives the following solution for output Y relative to labor in efficiency units (AL):

(I) $y'(t) = \{C_0 e'^{-(a'-a''u+n+\delta)(1-ß)t} + s(1-\tau)(1-u)/(a'-a''u+n+\delta)\}^{ß/1ß}$

Here y′ denotes the ratio Y/(AL) while C_0 is to be determined by the initial conditions, e′ is the Euler number and t the time index. In such a setup the unemployment rate negatively affects the transitory growth rate and the steady state growth rate, respectively. Moreover, the unemployment rate affects the level of the growth path – but the impact is somewhat unclear as u is both in the numerator expression and in the denominator of the steady state (denoted by #) values which is

(II) $y'\# = [s(1-\tau)(1-u)/(a' - a''u + n + \delta)]^{ß/1ß}$

In such a setup an NKM model would be inadequate because the steady state solution is not independent of the unemployment rate. It also is noteworthy that Y/L will grow in the steady state with rate $a = a' - a''u$; the term a' is exogenous, $a''u$ reflects the assumption made, namely that a higher unemployment rate pushes the growth rate of knowledge below its natural level (which is a'). Thus there is a double need to consider both the dynamics of the level of the growth path and the trend growth rate of output; both the level of the growth path and the trend growth rate of output are influenced by both u and a. Explaining only the deviation of output from trend thus analytically is not satisfactory. As regards the budget constraint of government one should consider that government real consumption G relative to AL is given (with v denoting an indicator for the replacement ratio of income for those receiving unemployment compensation) by

(III) $G/(AL) = \tau y' + vu$

As G/(AL) is considered as exogenous – and denoted by γ – the tax rate τ obviously is endogenous and can be written in the steady state as:

(IV) $(\gamma' - vu)/\{(s(1-\tau)(1-u)/(a' - a''u + n + \delta)\}^{ß/1-ß} = \tau$

Let us define $\gamma' = 1 - \gamma''$ where γ'' is a proxy for the degree of political conservatism (assuming that conservative voters prefer a small ratio of government expenditures to output). Assume furthermore that $n + \delta$ is equal to unity so that we can use the approximation $\ln(1 + x) \approx x$ – provided that x is close to zero. Hence taking logarithms gives (with $ß' := ß/(1 - ß)$; it is assumed that $0<ß'<1$):

(V) $-ß'\ln s + (ß' - v + a'')u - a' - \gamma'' \approx \tau(1 - ß')$

The tax rate is a positive function of u provided that $ß' + a'' - v$; and it is a negative function of the savings rate, the autonomous progress rate a' and the conservatism proxy γ''.

(VI) $-ß'\ln s + (ß' - v + a'')u - a' - \gamma'' \approx \tau(1 - ß')$

Let us define $1 - ß' := ß''$ and we can write:

(VII) $-(ß'/ß'')\ln s + [(ß' - v + a'')/ß'']u - a'/ß'' - \gamma''/ß'' \approx \tau$

From this equation we conclude that the explicit solution of the steady state is given by the equation (for the special case that $n + \delta = 1$):

(VIII)

$y'\# = \{[s(1 + (ß'/ß''))]\ln s - [(ß' - v + a'')/ß'']u + a'/ß'' + \gamma''/ß'')](1-u)/(a' - a''u + n + \delta)\}^{ß/1ß}$

References

Addison, J., & Welfens, P. J. J. (Eds.). (2009). *Innovation, employment and growth policy issues in the EU and the US*. Heidelberg: Springer.

Addison, J., & Welfens, P. J. J. (Eds.). (2003). *Labor markets and social security* (2nd ed.). Heidelberg: Springer.

Akerlof, G. A. (1970). The market for "lemons": quality uncertainty and the market mechanisms. *The Quarterly Journal of Economics, 84*(3), 488–500.

Artus, P., & Virard, M.-P. (2005). *Le capitalisme est en train de s'autodétruire (Capitalism is on its way to self-destrcution)*. Paris: Editions La Découverte.

Bank of England (2008), Financial Stability Report – Rebuilding Confidence in the Financial System, Issue 24, London.

Bernanke B., Gertler, M.; Gilchrist, S. (1999) The financial accelerator in a quantitative business cycle" In J.B. Taylor and M. Woodford (Eds), Handbook of macroeconomics, North-Holland.

BIS (1986), Recent innovations in international banking, Basel.

Blum, J., & Hellwig, M. (1995). The macroeconomic implications of capital adequacy requirements for banks. *European Economic Review, 39*, 739–749.

Calvo-Hornero, A.; Sanchez, I.G. (2008), The Financial System in Spain and Portugal: Institutions and Structure of the Market, paper presented at the Jean Monnet Workshop "Financial Market Integration, Structural Change, Foreign Direct Investment and Growth in the EU25", Brussels, April 25; in Welfens, P.J.J. et al., (Ed.), EU Financial Markets, Structural Change and Economic Growth, Springer, New York, Berlin.

Cooter, R. & Schaefer, H.-B. (2008), Law and the Poverty of Nations, Mercatus Center, George Mason University, mimeo.

Cecchetti, S. (1999) Legal Structure, Financial Structure and the Monetary Policy Transmission Mechanism, Federal Reserve Bank of New York Economic Policy Review, July, 9–28.

De Bandt, O., & Hartmann, P. (2000), Systemic Risk. A Survey, ECB Working Paper, No. 35, Frankfurt/M.

Deutsche Bundesbank (2007), Finanzstabilitätsbericht der Deutschen Bundesbank (Financial Stability Review of Deutsche Bundesbank), Frankfurt/M.

Deutsche Bundesbank (2008), Neuere Entwicklungen im internationalen Finanzsystem (Recent Developments in the International Financial System), Monatsbericht, July 2008, Frankfurt/M, 15–31.

Dewatripont, M., & Tirole, J. (1995). *The prudential regulation of banks*. Cambridge: MIT Press.

Diamond, D., & Dybvig, P. (1983). Banks runs, deposit insurance, and liquidity. *Journal of Political Economics, 91*, 401–419.

ECB (2008), 10th Anniversary of the ECB, Monthly Report, Frankfurt/M.

Eidgenössische Bankenkommission. (2008). *Bankinsolvenz*. Bern: Situation in der Schweiz und auf internationaler Ebene.

Fallon, P. R., & Lucas, R. E. B. (2002). The impact of financial crises on labor markets, household incomes and poverty: a review of evidence. *The World Bank Research Observer, 17*, 21–45.

FDIC Quarterly Banking Profile, 1999–2008 Table III-A December 31, http://www2.fdic.gov/qbp/1999dec/qbp.pdf through http://www2.fdic.gov/qbp/12008dec/qbp.pdf.

Feldstein, M., & Horioka, C. (1980). Domestic savings and international capital flows. *Economic Journal, June*, 314–329.

Feldstein, M. (2008). How to shore up America's crumbling housing market. *Financial Times, 27* (2008), 9.

Field, A. J. (1984). A new interpretation of the onset of the great depression. *Journal of Economic History, 44*, 489–498.

Froot, K. A., & Stein, J. C. (1991). Exchange rates and foreign direct investment: an imperfect capital markets approach. *Quarterly Journal of Economics, November*, 1217.

Gilchrist S.; Herault J.-O.; Kempf H. (2002), Monetary policy and the financial accelerator in a monetary union, European Central Bank Working Paper Series Nr. 175, 2002.

Goodhart, C. A. E. (2007). The background to the 2007 financial crisis. *International Economics and Economic Policy, 4*, 331–339.

Greenspan, A. (2008). *The age of turbulence* (2nd ed.). London: Penguin Books.

Griliches, Z., Hall, B. H., & Pakes, A. (1991). R&D, patents, and market value revisited: is there a second (technological opportunity) factor? *Economics of Innovation and New Technology, 1*, 183–202.

Gros, D., & Lannoo, K. (1999). The structure of financial systems and macroeconomic instability. *EIB Economic Papers, 4*, 61–69.

Hansen, J., & Röger, W. (2000). *Estimation of real equilibrium exchange rates*. No: European Commission Economic Paper. 144.

Hurst, C., Pere, H., & Fischbach, M. (1999). On the road to wonderland? Bank restructuring after EMU. *EIB Economic Papers, 4*, 83–103.

IKB (2005), Asset Securitisation für den Mittelstand – Finanzoptimierung durch Forderungsverbriefung im Fokus Mittelstandsfinanzierung: http://www.ikb.de/content/de/produkte/inland/abs_publikationen/11_03_Mittelstandsfin.pdf.

IMF (2008), Global Financial Stability Report, Washington DC.

Jungmittag, A., & Untiedt, G. (2002). Kapitalmobilität in Europa aus empirischer Sicht: Befunde und wirtschaftspolitische Implikationen (Capital Mobility in Europe: Empirical Findings and Implications for Economic Policy). *Jahrbücher für Nationalökonomie und Statistik, 222*, 42–63.

Kath, D. (1992); Geld und Kredit (Money and Credit), Vahlens Kompendium der Wirtschaftstheorie und Wirtschaftspolitik, Bd. 1, 5.A., München: Vahlen, 175–218.

Kornai, J. (1980). *The Economics of shortage* (Vol. I and II). Amsterdam: North Holland.

Minsky, H. (1990). Schumpeter: finance and evolution. In A. Heertje & M. Perlman (Eds.), *Evolving technology and market structure* (pp. 51–77). Michigan: The University of Michigan Press.

Mullineux, A. (2007). British banking regulation and supervision: between a rock and a hard place. *International Economics and Economic Policy, 4*, 350–357.

OECD (1995), Saving, Investment, and Real Interest Rates, A Study for the Ministers and Governors by the Group of Deputies, Paris, October 1995, Paris.

Peek, J., & Wilcox, J. A. (2006). Housing, credit constraints, and macro stability: the secondary mortgage market and reduced cyclicality of residential investment. *American Economic Review, 96*(2), 135–140.

Priesemann, J. (1997). Policy options for prudential supervision in stage three of monetary union. In P. J. J. Welfens & H. Wolf (Eds.), *Banking, international capital flows and growth in Europe* (pp. 81–120). Heidelberg: Springer.

Saint-Paul, G. (1992). Technological choice financial markets and economic development. *European Economic Review, 36*, 763–781.

Stieglitz, J. E., & Weiss, A. (1981). Credit rationing in markets with imperfect information. *The American Economic Review, 71*, 393–410.

Strauss-Kahn, D. (2008), Mut zum Eingreifen (Courage to Intervene), Financial Times Deutschland, 23.09.08, 26.

Taylor, J.B. (2009), The Financial Crisis and the Policy Responses: An Empirical Analysis of What Went Wrong, NBER Working Paper No. 14631.

USSEC (2008), Summary Report of Issues Identified in the Commission Staff's Examinations of Select Credit Rating Agencies, United States Securities and Exchange Commission, Washington, DC.

Van Den Burg, I., & Rasmussen, P. (2007). *Hedge funds and private equity – a critical analysis*. Brüssel: Socialist Group in the European Parliament.

Welfens, P. J. J. (2007a). Banking crisis and prudential supervision: a European perspective. *International Economics and Economic Policy, 4*, 358–367.

Welfens, P. J. J. (2007b). *Innovations in macroeconomics*. Heidelberg: Springer. 2nd revised and enlarged edition 2008.

Welfens, P. J. J. (2007c). Reform der Bankenaufsicht – ein internationales Politikthema (Reforming Prudential Supervision – an International Policy Topic). *Wirtschaftsdienst, 10*(2007), 648–652.

Welfens, P. J. J. (2008a). *Transatlantische Bankenkrise (Transatlantic Banking Crisis).* Stuttgart: Lucius.

Welfens, P.J.J. (2008b), Financial Market Integration, Stability and Economic Growth in Europe, Paper Presented at the Jean Monnet Workshop, Financial Market Integration, Structural Change, Foreign Direct Investment and Economic Growth in the EU25, Brussels, DG II/ European Commission, April 28, 2008, forthcoming in: WELFENS, P.J.J. ET AL., (Eds.) (2008), EU Financial Market Integration, Stability and Growth, Heidelberg and New York: Springer.

Welfens, P.J.J. (2009). *Transatlantische Bankenkrise*, Lucius&Lucius, Stuttgart.

Welfens, P. J. J. (2009a). *Financial markets and instability: theory and policy issues*. Heidelberg: Springer (forthcoming).

Welfens, P.J.J. (2009b), Marshall-Lerner Condition and Economic Globalization, EIIW Working Paper No. 168, EIIW at the University of Wuppertal.

Wolf, H. (2007). Rethinking banking supervision in the EU. *International Economics and Economic Policy, 4*, 368–373.

Welfens, P. J. J. (2010). Transatlantic banking crisis: analysis, rating, policy issues. *Journal of International Economics and Economic Policy, 7*(1), 3–48.

Chapter 4
Financial System and Innovations: Determinants of Early Stage Venture Capital in Europe

Christian Schröder

4.1 Introduction

From the 1990s until now, the most developed economies in Europe have significantly lower GDP growth rates than the US. These considerable lower growth rates go along with lower productivity growth and a poor development on the labour markets in the most European countries, especially in the large economies like Germany, France and Italy. One main challenge which faces the EU-15 economies is to be more innovative in terms of goods and services in order to counter the pressure of labour costs in EU-15 for unskilled labour triggered from the new EU member states and developing countries worldwide. Other than flexible institutions and less bureaucracy (see e.g. Alesina et al. 2003; Klapper et al. 2004), small- and medium-sized enterprises face one major hindrance to unlock their full innovative ability: access to capital. Improving SMEs' access to finance is one of the key factors for more innovative business start-ups with high growth perspectives. Thus, the financial environment plays a crucial role in promote innovation.

The Lisbon Programme notes that the limited availability of finance is an obstacle in setting up and developing businesses in Europe. A Eurobarometer poll published in 2005 showed that many small- and medium-sized enterprises (SMEs) find it increasingly difficult to obtain bank loans. In response to the question as to what would best assure the development of their company, 14% of 3,047 interviewed SMEs in the EU-15 stated easier access to means of financing.[1] The results of the fourth community innovation survey (2004) support country specific surveys and shows that 23.6% of a sample of 70,623 interviewed innovative firms in the

[1]Eurobarometer: http://europa.eu.int/comm/enterprise/entrepreneurship/financing/surveys.htm.

C. Schröder
Researcher at the European Institute for International Economic Relations at the University of Wuppertal/Schumpeter School of Business and Economics, Rainer-Gruenter-Strasse 21, 42119 Wuppertal, Germany
e-mail: schroeder@eiiw.uni-wuppertal.de

P.J.J. Welfens and C. Ryan (eds.), *Financial Market Integration and Growth*,
DOI 10.1007/978-3-642-16274-9_4, © Springer-Verlag Berlin Heidelberg 2011

EU-27 complain about innovation costs being much too high; thus this is an important factor of hampering innovation activities.[2]

In the traditional perfect market approach to the analysis of financial markets, services are bought and sold in an anonymous manner, and the only information transfer consists of signals given by movements in prices. In this Arrow–Debreu world there is no need for financial intermediaries, as borrowers would obtain their loans directly from depositors. We have learned from Modigliani and Miller (1958) that in such a world, the financial structure of a firm does not matter. Nevertheless, one can find in the literature many reasons why the Modigliani and Miller theorem does not hold in the real world especially in financing innovations, e.g. Stoneman (2001):

- The completeness of a capital market concerns issues relating to the diversity of capital instruments available. There could be a lack of such instruments, e.g. venture capital in underdeveloped financial markets, and affect the innovative entrepreneur or R&D investments of firms.
- A perfect market needs high numbers of participants on both the demand and the supply side. Even with offers on the supply side in certain areas, the financial services could have a monopolistic structure and thus avoid the development of a culture of innovative entrepreneurship.
- Financing innovative projects that have not yet been undertaken elsewhere, it may be particularly difficult to observe the systematic risk of similar projects in other firms (Goodacre and Tonks 1995) and thus difficult to determine the appropriate discount rate.
- Moral hazard problem in R&D investment arises in the usual way: modern industrial firms normally have separation of ownership and management. This leads to a principal-agent problem when the goals of the two conflicts, which can result in investment strategies that do not share value maximizing (Hall 2002).
- The asymmetric information problem refers to the fact that an inventor frequently has better information about the likelihood of success and the nature of the contemplated innovation project than potential investors. Therefore, the marketplace for financing the development of innovative ideas looks like the "lemon" market modelled by Akerlof (Hall 2002).
- Risk assessment on the stock market might be determined not by future, long term potentials of the firm, but rather by the psychologically determined peculiarities of the stock market (e.g., the stock market bubbles in Europe and US from 1998 to 2001).
- Financing decisions will be based upon after-tax costs and returns. The tax environment will thus have considerable influence upon the degree of investment and the means of financing investment. As tax regimes, especially in Europe, differ across countries, one may expect to find inter-country differences on preferred finance structures and financial instruments.

---

[2]http://epp.eurostat.ec.europa.eu/extraction/retrieve/en/theme9/inn/inn_cis4_ham?OutputDir=EJ OutputDir_428&user=unknown&clientsessionid=36B5ACB284DB9EF789B3402F5C84B21D. extraction-worker-1&OutputFile=inn_cis4_ham.htm&OutputMode=U&NumberOfCells=28 &Language=en&OutputMime=text%2Fhtml&.

- For innovative projects, assets are highly specific and difficult to resell and thus bankruptcy costs are high. The difference between R&D investments and real capital goods are that the former has an essential higher rate of personnel costs (e.g., for R&D, construction, design, training and market launch). In Germany in 2004, only one-third of knowledge intensive goods and services fall upon real assets (KfW 2006).
- The knowledge one earns from research is often implicit and it is not possible to codify the new knowledge; moreover, if research staff leaves the firm the new knowledge is lost for the company.

In this context one kind of financial intermediary has been well-established in the US and has successfully dealt with the problems of financing innovative projects: venture capitalists (VCs). VCs mediate risk capital normally from institutional investors like pension funds, insurance companies, banks, funds of funds, etc. Institutional investors manage large amounts of assets which are well-diversified. These investors then seek additional returns and are thus willing to allocate a small fraction of their capital in riskier investments. They use VCs normally specialized in one specific sector to screen the market for promising companies with extraordinary high growth opportunities. VCs bring supply and demand of risk capital together. The success of the VCs depends not only on their experience and ability to find adequate enterprises, but also on the economic environment as a whole.

This paper examines factors which could influence the relative amount of early stage Venture Capital (VC) investments within Europe from a macroeconomic view. Early Stage VC means VC which is provided in the beginning of the firm's business cycle the so-called seed (or pre-seed) and start up phase which is critical, as very often no final product exists. This investment stage is obviously risky but provides potentially high returns in the case of a successful firm development. The less risky later stage VC investments which encompass expansion and replacement investments could be more attractive for VCs. So the financing gap exists especially in the start up phase. The difference of the early stage VC investments relative to GDP between the European countries is tremendous. In addition to the already existing analysis of Gompers and Lerner (1998), Jeng and Wells (2000), Schertler (2003, 2004), Romain and Van Pottelsberghe (2004a, b) in terms of the level of (early stage) VC, I use for the most part other variables, in particular the inclusion of the financial system of each country is new. Aside from the technology capability, high skilled human capital stock, company tax rates, entrepreneurship, labor costs and growth opportunities, the panel data analysis of 15 European countries includes variables which indicate whether the financial system is more bank-based or market-based. The existing literature suggests that VC investments are affected by the financial system and could be one reason for different VC investment levels. A market-based system may be more suitable than a bank-based system for VC investments, since an IPO is the most profitable exit strategy.

In the following section, I show some arguments why VCs are successful in establishing young firms. Section 4.3 provides arguments in the literature as to which financial system – a bank-or market-based system – may be more efficient in promoting innovative firms. This may be useful in two respects. On the one hand, the existence of financial intermediaries needs to be justified in economic terms, and on the other hand, the arguments made for both systems make clear why VC is especially efficient in fostering innovation or in other words market failure in financing innovations occur in both kind of financial system and so affects the demand and supply function of VC. I derive my main hypotheses that a market-based system fosters and a bank-based system rather prevents early-stage VC investment in the context of the arguments the literature is providing. However, the literature provides comprehensible arguments for both a bank- and a market based system to boost innovations, but a market-based system creates an environment which attracts early-stage VC as banks seem instead to be substitutes for VC due to their similar business model. The panel analysis in Sect. 4.4 supports this view. Section 4.5 closes with some concluding remarks.

4.2 Venture Capital and Innovative Firms

VC is primarily funding provided to young and typically innovative companies not quoted on the stock market, but it is provided in return for a share of equity in the company. The investors normally have a time horizon of 3–7 years, but sometimes as many as 10 years is allowed.[3] Frequently VCs support the nascent entrepreneur not only with capital but also with advice and management expertise. VCs may sit on boards of directors to valuable governance and advisory support (Romain and Van Pottelsberghe 2004b). VC companies are typically specialized in very few or one industry sector. This specialization deepens technical knowledge and enables the VCs to select risky investments more efficiently. Fenn et al. (1995) estimate that only 1% of all firms seeking capital obtain venture capital financing. Gebhardt and Schmidt (2001) also conclude that VC promotes less than 5% of all potential projects. Even actual data of National-, European- and US Private Equity and VC Associations confirm this ratio. As a result of such a stringent selection process, Kortum and Lerner (2000) find out for the US that increases in VC activity are associated with significant increases in patent rates. Moreover, they show that VC investments are three times more effective in generating industrial innovation than R&D expenditures. A very similar study for Europe by Popov and Rosenboom (2009) discovers that the impact of €1 of private equity[4] relative to €1 of industrial R&D expenditures is 2.6 times more effective in terms of producing innovations measured by patents.

Hellmann and Puri (2002) discover that a start-up company financed by VCs needs less time to bring a product to the market. However, their survey contains 149

[3]Along DiMasi et al. (2003) e.g. the development process of biopharmaceuticals demands on average 12 years and 100 million US $ R&D expenditures with only one out of 5,000 initial drug candidates reaching market launch (Evans and Varaiya 2003).

[4]Private Equity includes beside VC also management buyins (MBI) and management buyouts (MBO). A management buyout (MBO) is a form of acquisition where a company's existing managers acquire a large part or all of the company and a MBI occurs when a manager or a management team from outside the company raises the necessary finance, buys it, and becomes the company's new management. In general MBIs and MBOs are financed by debt and occur in less risky and therefore often less innovative industry sectors which are characterized by relative stable cash flows.

recently-formed firms in the Silicon Valley, and this local concentration should be taken into account before interpreting their results.

Baumol (2002) argues that entrepreneurial activity may account for a significant part of the 'unexplained' proportion of the historical growth output. Empirical evidence shows that VC-backed firms grow much faster at least in the beginning than non-VC-backed firms (Engel 2002; Engel and Keilbach 2007). Berger and Udell (1998) and Gompers and Lerner (1999) emphasize that venture-backed firms outperform non-venture-backed firms because of their willingness to conduct pre-investment screening and their special ability to monitor and assess value added.

On further aspect is that the VCs does not make an investment all at once. Instead, capital is provided in stages, and the entrepreneur only receives enough funding to reach the next stage. An important theoretical prediction is that the objective of the first stage is to provide capital to a cash-constrained entrepreneur. After this first round, an agency relationship is established between the entrepreneur and the investor. Follow-up rounds are intended to mitigate the agency costs associated with this relationship. Objectives other than removing a cash constraint take precedence in follow up rounds. Davila et al. (2003) deliver empirical results which go along with the theoretical prediction.

If performance objectives are not met, the VCs must make a decision: should the firm's strategy be reconsidered or must the management be changed (Gorman and Sahlman 1989)? Hellmann and Puri (1999) show that VCs replace the founder twice as often as non VC-backed firms. In the worst case, the venture capitalist stops his activity. Even if the venture capitalist decides to continue the project, he or she demands a greater participation on the part of the firm. So the venture capitalist has a powerful position. The venture capitalist usually receives convertible preferred stock. Like a debt contract, preferred stock requires the firm to make fixed payments to the shareholders whereas the promised payments must be made before any common shareholder gets dividend payments and impeded in that way that the entrepreneur is not paying himself high dividends (Berlin 1998). When a venture capitalist holds the shares of a young firm, which means the shares are not marketable to other investors, the venture capital investor avoids the free-rider problem. The investor is able to earn profit from its monitoring activities and relieve the information costs of moral hazard (Hubbard 2008, p. 240). VCs in the US are able to efficiently invest in young innovative firms due to their selection process, specialization, know-how and financial instruments. However, the early-stage market in Europe is very heterogeneous in terms of the (early-stage) investment levels and underdeveloped in the most countries in comparison to the US.

4.2.1 Early Stage Venture Capital in Europe

According to the OECD assessment lack of an equity investment culture, information problems, and market volatility especially from mid-2000 to 2003 hinder the development of early-stage financing in many European countries (OECD 2003). In

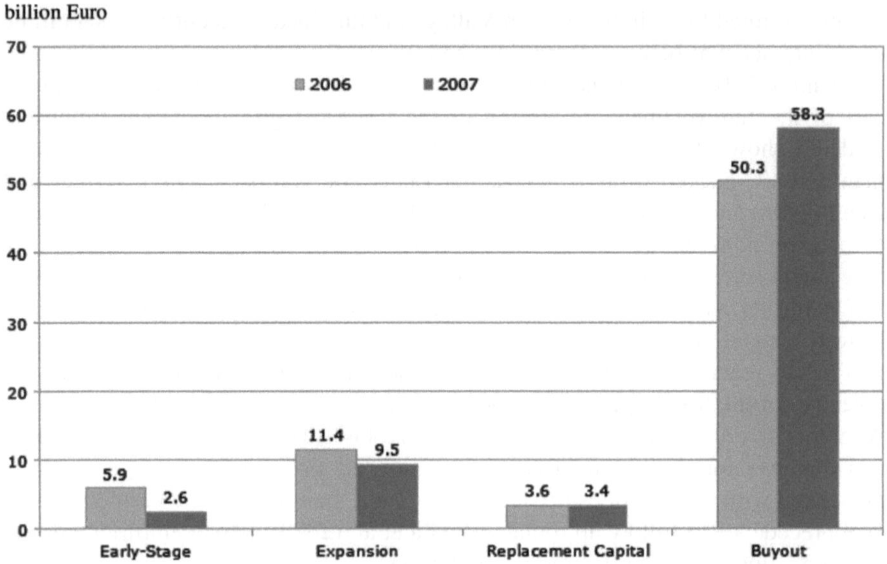

Fig. 4.1 Stage distribution of investments in Europe
Source: EVCA

spite of the existence of VC, the so-called seed (or pre-seed) and start up stage is critical. The less risky later stage VC investments which encompass expansion and replacement investments could be more attractive for VCs. The costly and time consuming phase for due diligence in seed and early-stage deals often makes these investments less profitable compared to later stage VC investment deals that provide more attractive risk-return profiles (European Commission 2005b). Therefore, the so-called business angels and early stage VCs play a crucial role to fill the capital gap in the seed stage.[5]

European early stage venture capital represents only a small fraction of all private equity invested in Europe. The amount of Leverage Buyouts (LBOs) and Management Buyouts (MBOs) is ten times higher than in early stage venture capital (Fig. 4.1).

Storey (1995) and Murray (1998) describe the difficulties in financing especially young high-tech firms as follows:

- It is difficult for outside investors to make reliable assessments of demand for the products/services in highly immature markets.

[5]Business angels are wealthy private persons with normally successful experience as an entrepreneur or a manager. They contribute their network of personal contacts in business and company finance circles. In addition to their experience, they also provide capital for young entrepreneurs with convincing business ideas. The European Business Angel Network (EBAN) reports that in the US, 250,000 angels invested $24 billion in 2005 in comparison to 75,000 angels who invested only €2-3 billion in Europe (http://www.eban.org/download/Standard%20EBAN%20Presentation_2007.ppt#287,18,Benchmarking angel activity).

- The investments frequently encompass the research and developmental costs and high expenditure in the marketing phases.
- The authors also point out that the threat of accelerated redundancy in rapidly changing technology-based sectors remains.
- The entrepreneurial recipients of the investors' funds frequently lack the managerial experience and therefore the ability to exploit the advantages of the new technological innovation.

Young and fast growing firms often need years to reach the break-even point. These firms have negative cash flow and need a developed venture capital market. A developed VC market means that there are enough independent VCs which are specialized in specific sectors and have built up both reputation and experience (the so called track record) to attract potential investors for high-risk investments.

The next section devotes some attention to the role of the financial systems in fostering innovations. The following remarks should clarify why market failure in financing innovative firms occurs in both market- and bank-based financial systems. This market failure creates demand for risk capital in the high income countries I consider in the empirical analysis. One could argue that a market-based system creates a better risk/return ratio by means of the most lucrative exit strategy for VCs via IPO, but on the other hand, one could argue that bank-based systems additionally influence the amount of early-stage VC investment negatively due their similar business model. Through the competitive situation between banks and VCs, the latter could be underdeveloped in terms of their relative size. In the end of the following section I derive my hypotheses as to which determinants may stimulate early stage VC investments in Europe and showing the empirical results in Sect. 4.4.

4.3 Financial System, Venture Capital and Innovations

Financial constraints have a large and significant impact on investments in innovative projects. Schumpeter (1911) was one of the first to discuss the importance of credit in the process of innovation. According to Schumpeter, the entrepreneur is the driving force behind the process of innovation, and he considers the lender's assessment of the borrower to set the limit of credit expansion. In a further step, Pagano (1993) employs a simple endogenous AK growth model to illustrate how financial development can influence growth through the enhanced accumulation of capital through higher savings (Hicks 1969) and the improved ability of the financial sector to increase technological progress through the efficient selection, funding and monitoring of projects. On the one hand, larger volumes of financial funds saved promote growth as more savings are available to fund investment projects. This effect relates to the Hicksian view that better developed financial systems are those which channel higher quantities from savers to investors. On the other hand, an improved quality of intermediation can both enhance factor productivity and reduce the fraction of savings that are foregone due to suboptimal production plans of financial agents.

Both effects resemble the Schumpetrian view, with better financial systems fostering capital by investing in more profitable projects (Koetter and Wedow 2006). In this context, Levine (2004) and Ang (2008) deliver a useful summary about the functions and recent developments in the finance and growth literature.

Debt financing of R&D projects could be difficult because of the above-mentioned characteristics of financing innovations. The Flash EB Report (European Commission 2005a, p. 25) seems to support this view. Answers to the claim that banks do not want to take risks in lending provide insight into the reasons why many SMEs are sceptical about access to financing through banks. Seventy one percent of SMEs totally agree or tend to agree with the statement that banks do not want to take risks in lending to companies and only 23% disagree with it.

There are some further problems which especially banks face. Due to fixed interest payments, banks do not participate in the high returns of successful outcome. They are therefore more concerned with the probability of failure when calculating the price of a loan. In this context, Stiglitz and Weiss (1981) analyze why it could come to credit rationing instead of a higher interest rate which clears the market. The effects of moral hazard and adverse selection in debt markets explain why lenders may deny a loan agreement even if the project is profitable. Because of asymmetric distributed information about the risk characteristics and default probabilities of firm's investment projects, lenders may ration credit rather than accept a higher interest rate to clear the market, because increases in the interest rate induce low-risk borrowers to exit the pool of applicants first. In addition, borrowers whose actions cannot be monitored by lenders have an intrinsic incentive to invest in risky, higher-return projects that increase the probability of bankruptcy. It is primarily for this moral hazard problem that equity rather than debt is considered the natural source of external finance for firms investing in risky R&D projects (Kukuk and Stadler 2001).

Allen (1993) argues that such a system which aggregates diverse views of many market participants is appropriate where are legitimate grounds for differences in views with respect to the investment decision. Levine (2001) and Levine and Zervos (1998) maintain that market-based systems create more suitable conditions in enhancing risk management, information dissemination, corporate control and capital allocation. Powerful banks use their close relationships to well established firms in order to prevent the entrance of newcomer. Hence, established firms are protected due to higher entrance barriers (Hellwig 1991). Dispersed shareholders can more credibly commit to not interfering in the running of firms than can dedicated owners.

Despite this and the argument of credit rationing, one can also find arguments which emphasize the role of banks in financing innovative projects. Stiglitz (1985) himself argues that well developed stock markets reveal information very quickly and they therefore reducing incentives for individual investors to invest in innovative projects. Gerschenkron (1963) and Boot et al. (1993) argue in this context that banks could mitigate that problem by building up long-run relationships to firms. A further argument could be the ability of banks to realize economies of scales in monitoring firms (Carlin and Mayer 2000). Stulz (2000) claims that banks are more effective in financing innovative activities that require staged financing, because banks can credibly commit to making additional funding available as the project develops (Beck and

Levine 2002). Myers and Majluf (1984) explained in their so called pecking order theory, why firms may be forced to issue new shares at a discount for financing R&D or be forced to self-finance their R&D projects because of the adverse selection problems.

Taking these arguments in account, firms often rely on internal funds as a consequence of imperfect capital markets. Empirical studies provide results demonstrating that R&D expenditures will be determined by available cash flow (e.g. Hall 1992; Himmelberg and Peterson 1994; Harhoff 1998). However, the effect differs between countries (Mulkay et al. 2001). Empirically, results dedicated to young firms show that they are more financially constrained because they cannot use earlier profit accumulations for financing their R&D projects (Moore 1994; Petersen and Rajan 1995; Berger and Udell 2002; Carpenter and Petersen 2002; Czarnitzki 2006). Moreover, older firms could benefit from their established relationships to banks and therefore reduce problems of asymmetric information. There are higher exit rates for young companies because of inexperienced management, problems of developing a costumer base and problems of establishing the product in the market (Mueller and Zimmermann 2006, p.4). Link and Bozeman (1991) highlight the differences among small innovative companies with respect to different competition environments which could affect their financial decision. Boyd and Smith (1998) do not argument in such a controversial way; banks and markets might act as complements in providing financial services.

The aim of the VCs is to create value and to exit via buyout or initial public offering (IPO). The exit via IPO is to some extent the most profitable option for the investor and the entrepreneur. Black and Gilson (1997) stress this view. They highlight the role of stock markets and their complementary role as regards venture capital. This could be one determinant as to why the VC industry has more weight in the US than in Europe. The stock market for young, high-tech firms in the US is much better developed and enables many more IPOs than in Europe. This ensures much higher average returns on VC investments in the US than in Europe. On average a VC in the US yields returns of 26% p.a. for a 10-year investment to 31 December 2004 in comparison to 6.3% in Europe (EVCA, NVCA). A study of Hege et al. (2006, 2009) supports the these results and show that US venture capital firms show a significantly higher performance on average than their European counterparts, both in terms of type of exit and of rate of return. The study finds that US venture capitalists outperformed their market benchmark by a median annualised return of 63%, whereas their European counterparts underperformed their benchmark by 20% (Hege et al. 2006, p. 543). In this context I enunciate my first hypothesis.

Hypothesis 1: Market-based financial systems stimulate vc investments

Audretsch and Lehmann (2004) empirically analyzed whether debt and equity are complements or rather substitutes in financing young and high-tech firms. The results provided from Audretsch and Lehmann confirm the view of Black and Gilson. Using a data set of the firms listed on the Neuer Markt in Germany reveals that they suffer from lower performance as long as finance is restricted to traditional banks. They also point out the necessity for institutions such as the former Neuer Markt, because venture capital and debt provided by banks is found not to be complements but rather substitutes. I follow their approach and think that banks and

VCs are rivals in terms of their business model. To find out whether these results hold for other European countries, I include the size of the banking sector of each country in the panel analysis and derive the second hypothesis.

Hypothesis 2: Bank-based systems prevent VC investments as banks are to some extent substitutes

The third hypothesis considers other macroeconomic factors which may influence the level of early stage VC investments. VCs companies are interested in a strong demand for VC that means they are interested in a huge human capital stock of highly skilled people willing to start a business. The stock of knowledge depends i.a. on the educational system, the (international) networks of companies and R&D expenditures. VCs prefer also low company tax rates and labour costs which enhance their portfolio value. High GDP growth rate supports the demand for VC and may influence the survival rate of portfolio companies. All these factors are interrelated. The innovation system which Metcalfe (1995) defines as a "… set of distinct institutions which jointly and individually contribute to the development and diffusion of new technologies and which provides the framework within which governments form and implement policies to influence the innovation process. As such it is a system of interconnected institutions to create, store and transfer the knowledge, skills and artefacts which define new technologies" clarify that the mentioned factors interact. For example the causality between finance and the genesis of innovation or growth is unambiguously (Fig. 4.2).

Hypothesis 3: The existing stock of later stage VC, qualified human capital, growth opportunities, entrepreneurship, interest rates, and technology capabilities positively influence early stage VC levels while the corporate tax rate and labor costs negatively affect early stage VC investments.

The following section deepens some aspects concerning the third Hypothesis as I explain the used variables.

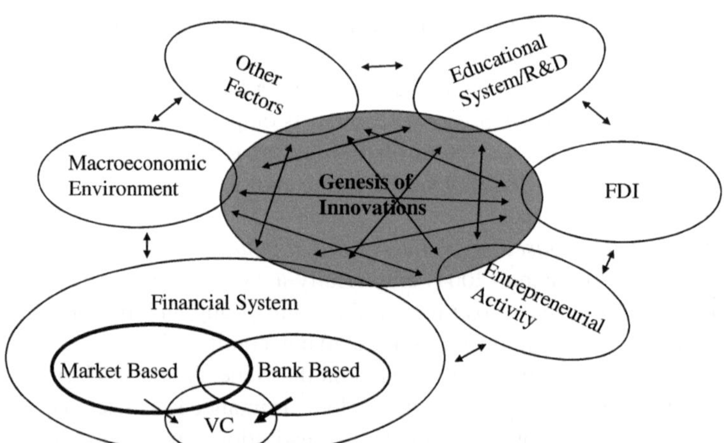

Fig. 4.2 Innovation system

4.4 Empirical Analysis

Empirical results from a macroeconomic perspective which explain determinants of VC via panel analysis are relatively scarce. Jeng and Wells 2000; Schertler 2003, 2004; Romain and Van Pottelsberghe 2004a, b have done similar analysis, but for different countries, time periods and for the most part, different variables. Nevertheless, the following panel analysis follows their approach.

4.4.1 Descriptive Statistics

As mentioned above, early-stage VC capital investments raised from 1995 to 2005 in Europe differ profoundly across the European countries. In Denmark and Sweden, early-stage VC investments in 2005 amount to upwards of 0.051 and 0.052% of GDP, respectively; in Greece, early stage VC scarcely exits. I apply a GLS panel analysis to find out if the determinants formulated by the three hypotheses are responsible for such huge differences in the amount of early-stage risk capital in 15 European countries. The analysis includes the countries Austria, Belgium, Germany, Denmark, Finland, France, Greece, Ireland, Italy, Netherlands, Norway, Portugal, Spain, Sweden, and the United Kingdom from 1995 to 2005. These countries have been selected because of their similar per capita income, available data and the fact that an analysis of this country sample has never been done before. In Eastern Europe, VC hardly plays a role in the observed time period (Fig. 4.3).

4.4.2 Variables[6]

The dependent variable is early-stage VC investments. The VC data are available at Eurostat.[7] Hence, following their definition, early-stage means the sum of seed and start-up risk capital. The variable is scaled by gross domestic product at market prices.

The explanatory variables are proxies for the technological and growth opportunities, qualified human capital stock, macroeconomic and entrepreneurial environment as well as the financial system. Including the amount of VC investments in the later-stage (expansion and replacement capital) also makes sense considering the evolution of the VC markets. Evolution of a VC market means it seems logical to assume that in the beginning, VCs prefer to invest in less risky projects such as already-existing firms, which have a successful business model and need VC to assure growth opportunities. VCs need time to build expertise and confidence. Building a track record (e.g., building trust) is essential for convincing potential investors to commit money to a venture capitalist (Schertler 2002). Successful exits

[6]For a more detailed data definition see Appendix.

[7]http://epp.eurostat.ec.europa.eu/tgm/web/table/description.jsp.

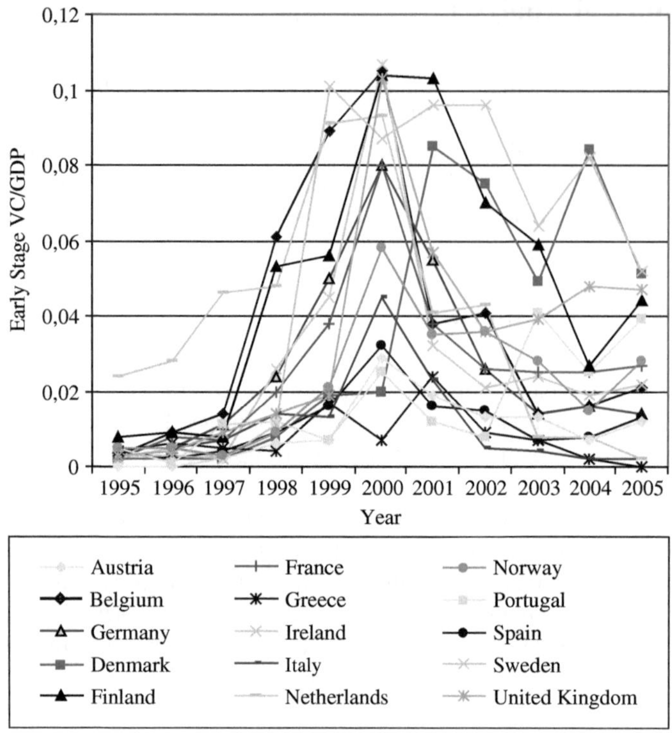

Fig. 4.3 Early stage VC investments in selected EU countries
Source: Eurostat

of portfolio firms build reputation, enable economies of scale and syndicate with other VCs, thus allowing the venture capitalist to invest in risky, early-stage investments. Zarutskie (2006) determines that in seed stage VC funds, having a founding venture capitalist team with both venture investing experience and experience managing a start-up is the strongest predictor of fund performance. First-time seed stage funds with such founding teams strongly outperform their counterparts. An additional aspect is that in a more mature VC market as in the US, the VC portfolios are on average larger and provide better options for diversifying portfolios in early and later stage VC investments.

The banking sector and stock market developments represent the financial system. Stock market development also affects the exit strategy and therefore the returns of VCs. To measure the weight of the banking sector, I follow the approach of Levine and Zervos (1998). The variable banking sector equals the value of loans made by banks to private enterprises divided by GDP. Specifically, I divided line 22d by 99b from the IMF´s International Financial Statistics. The market capitalization of listed companies (% of GDP) represents the size of the market-based system. Market capitalization (also known as market value) is the share price times the number of shares outstanding. Listed domestic companies are the domestically incorporated companies listed on the country's stock exchange(s) at the end of the year. Listed companies do not include investment companies, mutual funds, or other collective investment vehicles. I also include the stock turnover into the regression in order to measure the liquidity of the national stock markets. The turnover ratio is the total value of shares traded during the period divided by the average market capitalization for the period. Average market capitalization is calculated as the average of the end-of-period values for the current period and the previous period.

High-tech patent applications, foreign direct investment inflows (FDI) and research and development (R&D) expenditures represent both technological ability and innovation activities. Patents reflect a country's inventive activity. Patents also show the country's capacity to exploit knowledge and translate it into potential economic gains. In this context, indicators based on patent statistics are widely used to assess the inventive performance of countries (Eurostat). I differentiate the variable patent applications in the way that I use high-tech patent applications to the European Patent Office scaled by population assuming the later delivers better results to explain early stage VC investment, since VCs are interested in investing in fast growing high-tech sectors like information and communication technologies, biotechnology, and nanotechnology. R&D expenditures of the public and private sector represent the creation of new knowledge. In addition, I add FDI inflows which can permanently increase knowledge spillovers and the transfer and diffusion of technologies, ideas, management and organizational processes. In the regression, (high-tech) patent application, R&D expenditures and FDI represent the technological opportunities (TO) of each country. FDIs inflows represent also potential networks to foreign multi national enterprises and can be seen as an indirect measurement of labour market rigidities.

New technologies are being developed and applied, in many cases very quickly. An increasingly skilled and effective workforce will be required if countries are to negotiate the rapid change and new challenges emerging in science and technology (S&T). Human resources in science and technology (HRST) signify the stock of human capital which fulfils one or other of the following conditions: successfully completed education at the third level in a S&T field of study; not formally qualified as above, but employed in a science and technology occupation where the above qualifications are normally required. The share of HRST of the whole work force may also be a proxy of potential entrepreneurs in high-tech sectors and therefore even a driver for the demand of VC (Table 4.1).

I use the self-employment rates as a percentage of total civilian employment to measure entrepreneurial activity or spirit. One has to handle this proxy with care since it contains all kinds of self-employment. Numerous entrepreneurs are not relevant for the demand of VC because of their less innovative business model. Moreover, becoming an entrepreneur can be triggered from the demand or the supply side of entrepreneurship. Being involved in entrepreneurial activity could be a necessity; there are simply no other options for earning a living, and there is no comparative assessment to be made. However, the countries in the panel analysis are high-income countries, and we can assume that the perception of people who start a business is opportunity-driven in the sense that they have the opportunity of an alternative occupation as an employee.

Table 4.1 Descriptive statistic of used variables

	VC early stage[a]	*VC later stage*[a]	*High-tech patents*[b]	*FDI*[a]	*R&D expenditure*[a]	*Stock-marketcap*[a]	*Banking sector*[d]
Mean	0.028	0.076	19.953	4.66	1.688	73.125	0.882
Median	0.019	0.055	11.891	2.15	1.72	61.793	0.831
Maximum	0.107	0.351	124.435	92.67	4.250	271.11	1.730
Minimum	0.000	0.000	0.05	14.73	0.433	12.688	0.306
Std. Dev.	0.028	0.0654	25.675	9.645	0.903	46.442	0.345
Sum	4.718	12.632	3292.36	768.9	278.62	12065.63	145.554
Sum Sq. Dev.	0.131	0.702	108112.5	15258.5	133.94	353735.9	19.572
Observations	165	165	165	165	165	165	165
Cross sections	15	15	15	15	15	15	15

	GDP growth[c]	*Corporate tax rate*[c]	*Interests*[c]	*Stock-turnover*[a]	*Laborcosts*[e]	*HRST*[f]	*Self-employment*[g]
Mean	3.053	33.136	5.759	55.47	0.577	34.91	18.938
Median	3.032	34.00	5.055	37.57	0.596	35.15	14.10
Maximum	11.681	53.20	17.270	257.94	0.705	49.77	46.10
Minimum	−1.119	12.50	3.320	2.80	0.338	16.15	7.10
Std. Dev.	1.911	5.839	2.311	48.92	0.081	8.830	10.809
Sum	503.76	5467.54	950.39	9153.27	95.29	5760.4	3124.8
Sum Sq. Dev.	599.28	5592.05	876.42	392575.8	1.098	12788.3	19162.33
Observations	165	165	165	165	165	165	165
Cross sections	15	15	15	15	15	15	15

[a]In % of GDP
[b]Per million inhabitants
[c]In %
[d]Value of loans made by banks to private enterprises/GDP
[e]Annual labor costs calculated as total labor costs/real output
[f]% of active persons in the age class of 25–64 years
[g]% of total civilian employment

The corporate tax rate negatively influences the value of the potential portfolio company as future gains have a higher discount rate and could affect the supply side of VC negatively. I also expect such a negative effect for the labour costs on early stage VC investments. Annual unit labour costs (ULCs) are calculated as the quotient of total labour costs and real output.

An increase in interest rates should positively affect the demand from entrepreneurs for early-stage VC. Otherwise if the supply effect is higher – i.e., the VCs invest more when interest rates fall – the coefficient should be negative. I use the logarithm of the interest rates of 10 year government bonds and expect a positive sign as Romain and Van Pottelsberghe (2004b) already show in their analysis based on a panel data set of 16 OECD countries from 1990 to 2000. I use the logarithm as I assume a non linear correlation of VC investments and interest rates. The expansion of an economy, measured as real GDP per capita growth, should affect the opportunities of firm growth and the survival rate of potential portfolio companies.

4.4.3 Model

Following the model of Jeng and Wells (2000) and Romain and Van Pottelsberghe (2004b), I create a supply and a demand function of early-stage venture capital. I assume the early stage venture capital supply (4.1) is driven by the level of later-stage VC investments, the corporate tax rate, the relatively size of the stock market capitalization and liquidity, labor costs, and banking sector as well as GDP growth. Equation (4.2) shows the demand function. I expect the later-stage VC, the corporate tax rates, technical opportunities, stock market developments, GDP growth, the stock of qualified human capital, entrepreneurial activity and the growth of interest rates influence the demand of early-stage VC. The variable technical opportunity is measured by FDI inflows, high-tech patent applications and all R&D expenditures.

$$\begin{aligned} VC^{S}_{early_{it}} &= a_0 + a_1 Returnpercentage + a_2 VC_{later_{it}} + a_3 Tax_{it} + a_4 Stockmarket_{it} \\ &\quad + a_5 Stockturnover_{it} + a_6 GDPGrowth_{it} + a_7 Labor\cos ts_{it} \end{aligned} \tag{4.1}$$

$$\begin{aligned} VC^{D}_{early_{it}} &= b_0 + b_1 Returnpercentage + b_2 VC_{later_{it}} + b_3 Tax_{it} + b_4 TO_{it} \\ &\quad + b_5 Stockmarket_{it} + b_6 Stockturnover_{it} + b_7 GDPGrowth_{it} + b_8 HRST_{it} \\ &\quad + b_9 Banks_{it} + b_{10} Selfemployment_{it} + b_{11} \log(Interest_{it}) \end{aligned} \tag{4.2}$$

where in the equilibrium

$$VC^{S}_{early_{it}} = VC^{D}_{early_{it}} = VC_{early_{it}} funds \tag{4.3}$$

hence the regression equation

$$VC_{early}funds_{it} = \gamma_0 + \gamma_1 VC_{later_{it}} + \gamma_2 Tax_{it} + \gamma_3 TO_{it} + \gamma_4 HRST_{it} + \gamma_5 Stockmarket_{it} + \gamma_6 Stockturnover_{it} + \gamma_7 GDPGrowth_{it} + \gamma_8 Labor\cos ts_{it} + \gamma_9 Banks_{it} + \gamma_{10} Selfemployment_{it} + \gamma_{11} \log(Interest_{it}) + \mu_i + \varepsilon_{it} \tag{4.4}$$

To obtain (4.4), I solve the supply equation for the return percentage, and substitute this expression into the demand equation. The index i represents the country and t time; μ_i is a country specific unobserved fixed effect (see Wooldridge 2002). One should expect positive signs for all γ, except for γ_2, γ_8, and γ_9 in the case that the panel analysis is able to support the three hypotheses I have formulated. Before starting the regression analysis, I apply the panel-based unit root test of Levin et al. (2002). As one can see (in Table 4.5 in Appendix) that the test fails to reject the presence of a unit root of the variables banking (sector) and labor costs, I modify the regression and take into account the first differences of the two relevant variables:

4.4.4 Model 1

$$VC_{early}funds_{it} = \gamma_0 + \gamma_1 VC_{later_{it}} + \gamma_2 Tax_{it} + \gamma_3 TO_{it} + \gamma_4 HRST_{it} + \gamma_5 Stockmarket_{it} + \gamma_6 Stockturnover_{it} + \gamma_7 GDPGrowth_{it} + \gamma_8 d(Labor\cos ts_{it}) + \gamma_9 d(Banks_{it}) + \gamma_{10} Selfemployment_{it} + \gamma_{11} \log(Interest_{it}) + \mu_i + \varepsilon_{it} \tag{4.5}$$

It is also worth noting that d represents the first differences. Table 4.6 in Appendix makes clear that after taking first differences for the two relevant variables the test does not fail to reject the presence of a unit root for all variables any more. In the second model presented in Table 4.3, I include lags where it seems to be reasonable in an economic sense.[8]

Model 2 (including lags for the variables R&D, high-tech patent application, self-employment and GDP growth):

$$VC_{early}funds_{it} = \gamma_0 + \gamma_1 VClater_{it} + \gamma_2 Tax_{it} + \gamma_3 TO_{it-1} + \gamma_4 HRST_{it} + \gamma_5 Stockmarket_{it} + \gamma_6 Stockturnover_{it} + \gamma_7 GDPGrowth_{it-1} + \gamma_8 d(Labor\cos ts_{it}) + \gamma_9 d(Banks_{it}) + \gamma_{10} Selfemployment_{it-1} + \gamma_{11} \log(Interest_{it}) + \mu_i + \varepsilon_{it} \tag{4.6}$$

[8]It needs time before R&D expenditures as well as patent applications become marketable products.

4.4.5 Regression Results

The regressions results for models 1 and 2 are presented in Tables 4.2 and 4.3. All variables which are considered as insignificant were taken out so as not to distort the R-squared or Durbin-Watson value. To estimate the regression, I use the Estimated Pooled General Least Square Method (EGLS) with country-specific fixed effects. Using a heteroksedasticity consistent covariance matrix estimator which provides correct estimates of the coefficient covariances in the presence of heteroskedasticity, derived from White (1980), the tables accordingly present a weighted and unweighted estimation test result. The Durbin Watson test indicates no linear association between adjacent residuals from the regression models. Table 4.7 shows that the test values of 1.68 for model 1 and 1.61 for model 2 denote no autocorrelation of the residuals at the 1% level. Using the White covariance estimator, there is not much of a difference in the p-values in the t-tests. The weighted values of the particular model, 1.6 and 1.55, lies between the critical Durbin Watson significance values from 1.50 to 1.75 for model 1 and 1.48 to 1.77 for model 2 along the corresponding test statistic. Even the charts of the residuals for each country illustrate this fact (see Appendix Figs. 4.4 and 4.5).

The stock market capitalization and the stock turnover as a sign for the liquidity of the stock market seem to be important determinants in explaining early stage VC investments since both are significant in both models between the 1 and 3% level. This result goes along with Hypothesis 1 and other already existing empirical results which show that vibrant stock markets are important due the higher chance of a lucrative exit strategy for VCs. However, the most important outcome is that the size of the banking sector could have a negative impact on early-stage risk capital investments. It appears that along the lines of Audretsch and Lehmann, the volume of credits to firms guaranteed from banks substitutes early-stage VC investments. This interesting empirical result supports the strand of financial literature which postulates that a market-based financial system is more appropriate to finance innovations if one believes that VCs are really more efficient in selecting and financing young and innovative entrepreneurs, because a market-based system creates an environment which attracts VCs. A further reason for the negative coefficient could be that one can observe an increasing number of bank-dependent VCs in Europe. Hirsch and Walz (2006) and Hellmann et al. (2008) observed that bank-dependent VCs invest in early investment stages less often.[9] However in model 2 the coefficient of the banking becomes less significant. A longer time

[9] Hellmann et al. (2008) simply show that the probability is higher that independent VCs invest in early stage deals in comparison to bank dependent VCs. In absolute terms early stage VC deals or investments can increase with an increasing number of bank depending VCs.

Table 4.2 Regression results model 1

Dependent variable: VC early stage funds				
Method: pooled EGLS (cross-section weights)				
Sample (adjusted): 1996 2005				
Included observations: 10 after adjustments				
Cross-sections included: 15				
Total pool (balanced) observations: 150				
Linear estimation after one-step weighting matrix				
White diagonal standard errors and covariance (no d.f. correction)				
Variable	Coefficient	Std. Error	t-Statistic	Prob.
C	−0.082927	0.020864	−3.974549	0.0001
VC later stage	0.159797	0.041449	3.855318	0.0002
FDI	0.000780	0.000152	5.132427	0.0000
Banking sector	−0.036393	0.014346	−2.536744	0.0124
Stockmarket	0.000154	7.30E-05	2.110038	0.0368
Stockturnover	0.000167	6.48E-05	2.585072	0.0109
Log interests	0.022036	0.007028	3.135439	0.0021
Corporate tax rate	−0.000640	0.000331	−1.934749	0.0553
R&D expenditure	0.036127	0.008657	4.173218	0.0001
Laborcosts	−0.235038	0.126356	−1.860122	0.0652
Fixed effects (Cross)				
Austria-C	−0.000798			
Belgium-C	0.001936			
Germany-C	0.007772			
Denmark-C	0.001937			
Finland-C	−0.045558			
France-C	−0.009654			
Greece-C	0.056389			
Ireland-C	0.025554			
Italy-C	0.026525			
Netherlands-C	−0.019440			
Norway-C	0.002405			
Portugal-C	0.046571			
Spain-C	0.008155			
Sweden-C	−0.069562			
United Kingdom-C	−0.032232			
	Effects specification			
Cross-section fixed (dummy variables)				
	Weighted Statistics			
R-squared	0.654581	Mean dependent var		0.031804
Adjusted R-squared	0.591529	S.D. dependent var		0.026261
S.E. of regression	0.018740	Sum squared resid		0.044252
F-statistic	10.38151	Durbin-Watson stat		1.606942
Prob(F-statistic)	0.000000			
	Unweighted statistics			
R-squared	0.626970	Mean dependent var		0.031460
Sum squared resid	0.047431	Durbin-Watson stat		1.679994

Table 4.3 Regression results model 2 (including lags)

Dependent variable: VC early stage funds				
Method: pooled EGLS (Cross-section weights)				
Date: 08/13/09 time: 16:13				
Sample (adjusted): 1996 2005				
Included observations: 10 after adjustments				
Cross-sections included: 15				
Total pool (balanced) observations: 150				
Linear estimation after one-step weighting matrix				
White diagonal standard errors and covariance (no d.f. correction)				
Variable	Coefficient	Std. Error	t-Statistic	Prob.
C	−0.072305	0.021504	−3.362486	0.0010
VC later stage	0.157951	0.041436	3.811909	0.0002
FDI	0.000782	0.000154	5.083583	0.0000
Banking sector	−0.028905	0.017043	−1.695949	0.0924
Stockmarket	0.000162	7.10E-05	2.284764	0.0240
Stockturnover	0.000139	6.20E-05	2.244956	0.0265
Log interests	0.022689	0.007087	3.201373	0.0017
Corporate tax rate	−0.000667	0.000327	−2.039043	0.0436
R&D expenditures(-1)	0.026337	0.009203	2.861645	0.0049
Laborcosts	−0.216935	0.127478	−1.701750	0.0913
High-tech patents (-1)	0.000303	0.000143	2.120515	0.0359
Fixed effects (Cross)				
Austria-C	0.004759			
Belgium-C	0.002975			
Germany-C	0.010988			
Denmark-C	0.003546			
Finland-C	−0.052554			
France-C	−0.006184			
Greece-C	0.051050			
Ireland-C	0.021863			
Italy-C	0.025017			
Netherlands-C	−0.027821			
Norway-C	0.003402			
Portugal-C	0.042980			
Spain-C	0.008698			
Sweden-C	−0.057451			
United Kingdom-C	−0.031269			
	Effects specification			
Cross-section fixed (dummy variables)				

	Weighted statistics		
R-squared	0.667583	Mean dependent var	0.031788
Adjusted R-squared	0.603759	S.D. dependent var	0.026176
S.E. of regression	0.018505	Sum squared resid	0.042804
F-statistic	10.45974	Durbin-Watson stat	1.547431
Prob(F-statistic)	0.000000		
	Unweighted Statistics		
R-squared	0.636740	Mean dependent var	0.031460
Sum squared resid	0.046189	Durbin-Watson stat	1.610536

series would be helpful to clarify whether hypothesis 2 becomes more or less empirical support.

The panel analysis also supports the view that later-stage VC is a precondition for early-stage VC. The negative coefficients of the corporate tax rate and laborcosts indicate that the entrepreneurial environment counters. It is worth to mention that the lagged selfemployment rate and GDP growth rate both indicate a 11% probability to be "significant" which is very close to be statistically significant on a low level and it might be that a proxy which measures only the founders of high-tech firms delivers better results. And so I cannot clearly support Jeng and Wells (2000) and Romain and Van Pottelsberghe (2004b) which determined that GDP growth has a positive impact on early-stage investment, probably as I did not use time proxies for the bubble on the stock market in 1999 and 2000.

Table 4.2 shows that two of the three proxies for the technological and innovation capacity, namely R&D expenditures and FDI inflows, are highly significant. In model 1 (without lags), the coefficient of high-tech patent applications is not significant, but in the model within which I have lagged this variable back to 1 year, the coefficient becomes significant.

Human Resources in Science & Technology (HRST) as a percentage of active persons in the age class of 25–64 year is the sole variable which is far away to deliver significant results in either model. However the panel analysis supported for the most part the three hypotheses formulated in this paper. The R-squared suggests that the independent variables might explain more than 65% of the variance of early stage VC.

4.5 Concluding Remarks

In Europe young firms and firms with between 10 and 49 employees face specific challenges in obtaining capital for achieving their innovative ideas in marketable goods and services due to moral hazard, adverse selection and lack of collaterals. VC is appropriate to alleviate these problems. However, the difference between European countries in terms of early-stage VC in terms of the relative size is enormous.

This paper is an attempt to analyze possible determinants that could influence the level of early-stage VC. The empirical results in this paper suggest that the technological capability, low corporate taxes and labor costs, interest growth rates as well as later-stage capital enhance the activities of early-stage venture capital investments. One further aspect might be responsible for the relatively poor development of early stage VC in the most European countries in comparison to the US VC market. The financial system could play a significant role in attracting early-stage VC. While it might be unsurprising that developed stock markets go along with high investment activities, the fact that the size of the banking sector has a significant negative impact is striking. The hypothesis that banks substitute VC due to their similar business models might be an explanation, but one must nevertheless be careful when interpreting these results. The analysis does not take into account which kind of firm receives capital. The applied variable banking sector does not divide between the size and innovation activities of companies obtaining bank credits. Moreover the industry structure remains unconsidered and following studies in this direction might deliver a more differentiate picture concerning the impact of financial systems on VC.

Nevertheless the results suggest that goal of policy makers should be to support a single European stock market, which is appropriate for an investment exit via IPO to achieve higher investment returns for VC investments in Europe. A European stock market segment like the AIM in UK, where investors have essential tax benefits if they invest in companies traded on AIM, is achievable. One adequate instrument to spur early-stage investments which follows the same goal is to implement low tax rates for potential portfolio firms. This also enhances the value of the firm and makes it more attractive for venture capitalists to invest in Europe. This strategy seems to be more effective than a direct subsidy for innovative SMEs. A uniform tax regulation for Europe might enhance transparency, but it impedes competition for a best practice solution and does not account for country-specific conditions. The strategic objectives of the Lisbon Agenda (e.g., enhancing R&D expenditures) seems to be appropriate, even though the presented analysis is of course no cost-benefit analysis, and it remains unconsidered that the marginal costs could be higher than the marginal benefits. Moreover the considered variables interact and potential efficiency gains can be realized by an improved networking of the institution within the innovation system, e.g. between universities, Greenfield investments and VC companies.

An interesting aspect in terms of stimulating early stage venture capital markets is to examine the role of government programmes or public depending VCs. Are publically funded VCs adequate at stimulating the VC market? If publically funded VC is required to develop VC markets, at which time would public help be useful and when could it become redundant? Depending on the composition of VC providers in different countries, one could expect varying risk profiles in investment behaviour and government structures to protect investors. In the case of Germany, Becker and Hellmann (2005) have analysed the clash of the WGF, the first German VC fund, determining that German norms on contracting and corporate governance provided insufficient investor protection, especially for the financing of early-stage, high-risk ventures. More research may be done in this direction to learn more about VCs and their role in pushing innovations especially in Europe with heterogeneous conditions in the different countries. This heterogeneity may be helpful for finding the most appropriate solutions.

Appendix

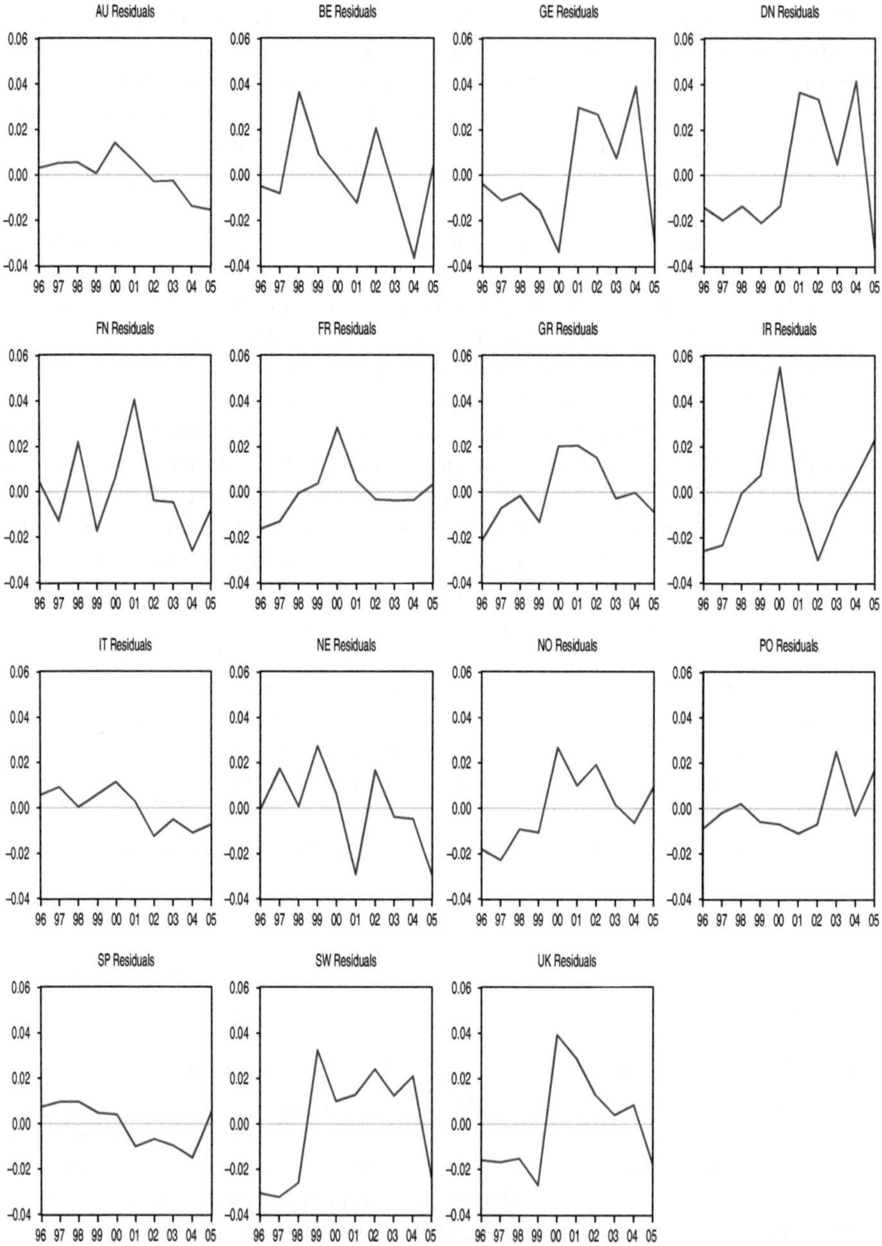

Fig. 4.4 Residual plots (of the regression presented in Table 4.2)

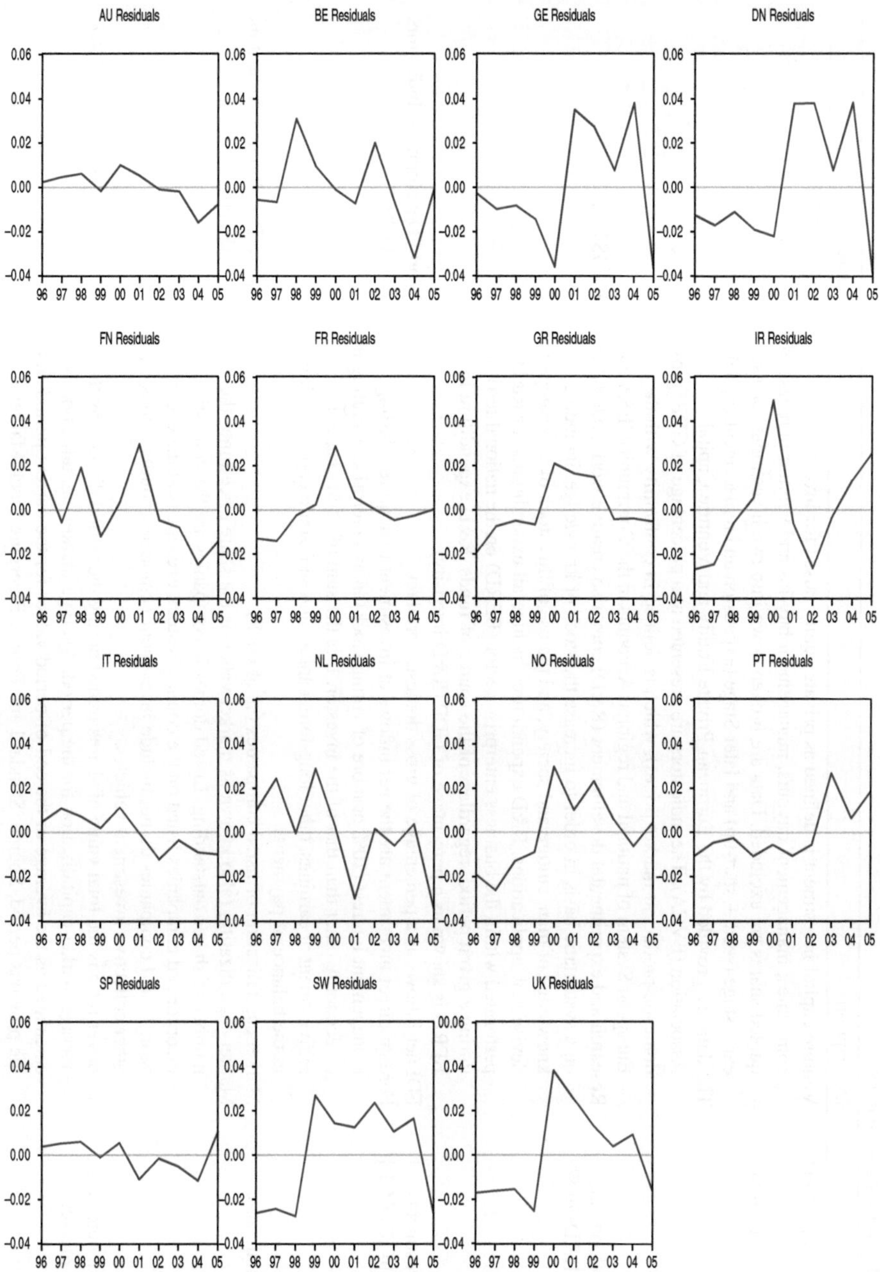

Fig. 4.5 Residual plots (of the regression presented in Table 4.3)

Table 4.4 Data definitions and sources

Variable	Description	Source
Early stage venture capital in % of GDP Later stage venture capital in % of GDP	Venture capital investment is defined as private equity raised for investment in companies; management buyouts, management buy-ins and venture purchase of quoted shares are excluded. Data are broken down into two investment stages: early stage (seed + start-up) and later Stage (expansion and replacement capital). The data are provided by the European Private Equity and Venture Capital Association (EVCA). The indicators are presented as a percentage of GDP (gross domestic product at market prices), which is defined in conformity with the European System of national and regional Accounts in the Community (ESA 95).	EUROSTAT
Research and development expenditures (R&D) in % of GDP	Research and experimental development (R&D) comprise creative work undertaken on a systematic basis in order to increase the stock of knowledge, including knowledge of man, culture and society, and the use of this stock of knowledge to devise new applications. R&D expenditures include all expenditures for R&D performed within the business enterprise sector (BERD) on the national territory during a given period, regardless of the source of funds. R&D expenditure in BERD is shown as a percentage of GDP (R&D intensity).	EUOSTAT
Foreign direct investments (FDI) inflows in % of GDP	FDI net inflows as a percentage of gross domestic product Foreign direct investment are the net inflows of investment to acquire a lasting management interest (10% or more of voting stock) in an enterprise operating in an economy other than that of the investor. It is the sum of equity capital, reinvestment of earnings, other long-term capital, and short-term capital as shown in the balance of payments.	World Development Indicators CD 2007
Stock market capitalization in % of GDP	Market capitalization of listed companies (% of GDP) Market capitalization (also known as market value) is the share price times the number of shares outstanding. Listed domestic companies are the domestically incorporated companies listed on the country's stock exchanges at the end of the year. Listed companies do not include investment companies, mutual funds, or other collective investment vehicles.	World Development Indicators CD 2007
Stock turnover as a percentage of the average market capitalization	Turnover ratio is the total value of shares traded during the period divided by the average market capitalization for the period. Average market capitalization is calculated as the average of the end-of-period values for the current period and the previous period. Source: Standard and Poor's, Emerging Stock Markets Factbook and supplemental S&P data.	World Development CD 2007

Banking sector (Loans/GDP)	To measure the weight of the banking sector I follow the approach of Levine and Zervos (1998). The variable banking sector equals the value of loans made by banks to private enterprises divided by GDP. Specifically, I divided line 22d by 99b from the IMF´s International Financial Statistics	International Financial Statistics from the International Monetary Fund (Yearbook 2006)
Corporate tax rate in %	The basic combined central and sub-central (statutory) corporate income tax rate given by the adjusted central government rate plus the sub-central rate.	OECD Tax Database
Gross domestic product growth (gdpgrowth) in %	GDP growth (annual %) Annual percentage growth rate of GDP at market prices based on constant local currency. Aggregates are based on constant 2000 U.S. dollars. GDP is the sum of gross value added by all resident producers in the economy plus any product taxes and minus any subsidies not included in the value of the products. It is calculated without making deductions for depreciation of fabricated assets or for depletion and degradation of natural resources.	World Development Indicators CD 2007
Hightech patent applications to the EPO per million inhabitants	The data refers to the ratio of patent applications made directly to the European Patent Office (EPO) or via the Patent Cooperation Treaty and designating the EPO (Euro-PCT), in the field of high-technology patents per million inhabitants of a country. The definition of high-technology patents uses specific subclasses of the International Patent Classification (IPC) as defined in the trilateral statistical report of the EPO, JPO and USPTO.	EUROSTAT
Human resources in science & technology (HRST) as a percentage of active persons in the age class of 25–64 years	Data examines the existing labour market stocks of HRST at national and regional levels. Unless otherwise stated, data is collected in line with the recommendations laid down in The Manual on the Measurement of Human Resources devoted to S&T (Canberra Manual) issued in 1995 by the OECD. HRST are people who fulfil one or other of the following conditions: • Have successfully completed a tertiary level education or; • Are not formally qualified as above but employed in a S&T occupation where the above qualifications are normally required. The conditions of the above educational or occupational requirements are considered according to the internationally harmonised standards ISCED and ISCO. Eurostat does not include managers (ISCO 1) in the HRST population.	EUROSTAT

(continued)

Table 4.4 (continued)

Variable	Description	Source
Annual unit labor costs (Business Sector excl. Agriculture	Annual unit labour costs (ULCs) are calculated as the quotient of total labour costs and real output. For more information on the OECD System of Unit Labour Cost, see http://stats.oecd.org/mei/	OECD statistics
Self-employment rates as a percentage of total civilian employment	Self-employment jobs re those jobs where the remuneration is directly dependent upon the profits (or the potential for profits) derived from the goods or services produced (where own consumption is considered to be part of profits). The incumbents make the operational decisions affecting the enterprise, or delegates such decisions while retaining responsibility for the welfare of the enterprise.In this context "enterprise" includes one-person operations.	OECD Factbook 2009: Economic, Environmental and Social Statistics
Interest rates in %	Long term (in most cases 10 year) government bonds are the instrument whose yield is used as the representative 'interest rate' for each country. Generally the yield is calculated at the pre-tax level and before deductions for brokerage costs and commissions and is derived from the relationship between the present market value of the bond and that at maturity, taking into account also interest payments paid through to maturity.	OECD Statistics

Table 4.5 Common pool unit root test results/LEVIN, LIN, CHU method

Variable	Statistic	Probability[a]
Venture capital early stage	−2.34291	0.0096
Venture capital later stage	−3.66284	0.0001
Hight tech patent application	−6.45178	0.0000
Foreign direct investment inflows	3.27781	0.0005
R&D expenditures	3.74187	0.0001
Stock market capitalization	5.47631	0.0000
Stockturnover	3.53733	0.0002
GDP growth	3.06084	0.0011
Corporate tax rate	−6.33028	0.0000
Interests rate	−10.2301	0.0000
Banking sector	1.64344	0.9499
HRST	−4.94271	0.0000
Self employment	3.82449	0.0001
Labor costs	−1.12914	0.1294

[a]Probabilities are computed assuming asymptotic normality
Sample: 1995, 2005
Exogenous variables: individual effects
User-specified lags: 1 and Bartlett kernel
Total (balanced) observations: 135
Cross-sections included: 15

Table 4.6 Common pool unit root test results/LEVIN, LIN, CHU method (first differences)

Variable	Statistic	Probability[a]
Venture capital early stage	−3.59301	0.0002
Venture capital later stage	−2.18883	0.0143
High tech patent application	−9.75054	0.0000
Foreign direct investment inflows	−4.39294	0.0000
R&D expenditures	−4.59215	0.0000
Stock market capitalization	−4.01439	0.0000
Stock turnover	−3.52805	0.0002
GDP growth	−5.84061	0.0000
Corporate tax rate	−5.34751	0.0000
Interests rate	−5.25741	0.0000
Banking sector	−3.67208	0.0001
HRST	−10.8963	0.0000
Self employment	−3.14969	0.0008
Labor costs	−5.36502	0.0000

[a]Probabilities are computed assuming asymptotic normality
Sample: 1995, 2005
Exogenous variables: Individual effects
User-specified lags: 1 and Bartlett kernel
Total (balanced) observations: 112
Cross-sections included: 14

Table 4.7 Durbin-Watson statistic: 1% significance points of dL and dU (models with an intercept)

	$k^a=1$		$k=2$		$k=3$		$k=4$		$k=5$		$k=6$		$k=7$		$k=8$		$k=9$		$k=10$	
n	dL	dU	dL	dU	dL	dU	dL	dU	dL	dU	dL	dU	dL	dU	dL	dU	dL	dU	dL	dU
6	0.390	1.142	-----	-----	-----	-----	-----	-----	-----	-----	-----	-----	-----	-----	-----	-----	-----	-----	-----	-----
7	0.435	1.036	0.294	1.676	-----	-----	-----	-----	-----	-----	-----	-----	-----	-----	-----	-----	-----	-----	-----	-----
8	0.497	1.003	0.345	1.489	0.229	2.102	-----	-----	-----	-----	-----	-----	-----	-----	-----	-----	-----	-----	-----	-----
9	0.554	0.998	0.408	1.389	0.279	1.875	0.183	2.433	-----	-----	-----	-----	-----	-----	-----	-----	-----	-----	-----	-----
10	0.604	1.001	0.466	1.333	0.340	1.733	0.230	2.193	0.150	2.690	-----	-----	-----	-----	-----	-----	-----	-----	-----	-----
11	0.653	1.010	0.519	1.297	0.396	1.640	0.286	2.030	0.193	2.453	0.124	2.892	-----	-----	-----	-----	-----	-----	-----	-----
12	0.697	1.023	0.569	1.274	0.449	1.575	0.339	1.913	0.244	2.280	0.164	2.665	0.105	3.053	-----	-----	-----	-----	-----	-----
13	0.738	1.038	0.616	1.261	0.499	1.526	0.391	1.826	0.294	2.150	0.211	2.490	0.140	2.838	0.090	3.182	-----	-----	-----	-----
14	0.776	1.054	0.660	1.254	0.547	1.490	0.441	1.757	0.343	2.049	0.257	2.354	0.183	2.667	0.122	2.981	0.078	3.287	-----	-----
15	0.811	1.070	0.700	1.252	0.591	1.465	0.487	1.705	0.390	1.967	0.303	2.244	0.226	2.530	0.161	2.817	0.107	3.101	0.068	3.374
16	0.844	1.086	0.738	1.253	0.633	1.447	0.532	1.664	0.437	1.901	0.349	2.153	0.269	2.416	0.200	2.681	0.142	2.944	0.094	3.201
17	0.873	1.102	0.773	1.255	0.672	1.432	0.574	1.631	0.481	1.847	0.393	2.078	0.313	2.319	0.241	2.566	0.179	2.811	0.127	3.053
18	0.902	1.118	0.805	1.259	0.708	1.422	0.614	1.604	0.522	1.803	0.435	2.015	0.355	2.238	0.282	2.467	0.216	2.697	0.160	2.925
19	0.928	1.133	0.835	1.264	0.742	1.416	0.650	1.583	0.561	1.767	0.476	1.963	0.396	2.169	0.322	2.381	0.255	2.597	0.196	2.813
20	0.952	1.147	0.862	1.270	0.774	1.410	0.684	1.567	0.598	1.736	0.515	1.918	0.436	2.110	0.362	2.308	0.294	2.510	0.232	2.174
21	0.975	1.161	0.889	1.276	0.803	1.408	0.718	1.554	0.634	1.712	0.552	1.881	0.474	2.059	0.400	2.244	0.331	2.434	0.268	2.625
22	0.997	1.174	0.915	1.284	0.832	1.407	0.748	1.543	0.666	1.691	0.587	1.849	0.510	2.015	0.437	2.188	0.368	2.367	0.304	2.548
23	1.017	1.186	0.938	1.290	0.858	1.407	0.777	1.535	0.699	1.674	0.620	1.821	0.545	1.977	0.473	2.140	0.404	2.308	0.340	2.479
24	1.037	1.199	0.959	1.298	0.881	1.407	0.805	1.527	0.728	1.659	0.652	1.797	0.578	1.944	0.507	2.097	0.439	2.255	0.375	2.417
25	1.055	1.210	0.981	1.305	0.906	1.408	0.832	1.521	0.756	1.645	0.682	1.776	0.610	1.915	0.540	2.059	0.473	2.209	0.409	2.362
26	1.072	1.222	1.000	1.311	0.928	1.410	0.855	1.517	0.782	1.635	0.711	1.759	0.640	1.889	0.572	2.026	0.505	2.168	0.441	2.313
27	1.088	1.232	1.019	1.318	0.948	1.413	0.878	1.514	0.808	1.625	0.738	1.743	0.669	1.867	0.602	1.997	0.536	2.131	0.473	2.269
28	1.104	1.244	1.036	1.325	0.969	1.414	0.901	1.512	0.832	1.618	0.764	1.729	0.696	1.847	0.630	1.970	0.566	2.098	0.504	2.229
29	1.119	1.254	1.053	1.332	0.988	1.418	0.921	1.511	0.855	1.611	0.788	1.718	0.723	1.830	0.658	1.947	0.595	2.068	0.533	2.193
30	1.134	1.264	1.070	1.339	1.006	1.421	0.941	1.510	0.877	1.606	0.812	1.707	0.748	1.814	0.684	1.925	0.622	2.041	0.562	2.160
31	1.147	1.274	1.085	1.345	1.022	1.425	0.960	1.509	0.897	1.601	0.834	1.698	0.772	1.800	0.710	1.906	0.649	2.017	0.589	2.131
32	1.160	1.283	1.100	1.351	1.039	1.428	0.978	1.509	0.917	1.597	0.856	1.690	0.794	1.788	0.734	1.889	0.674	1.995	0.615	2.104
33	1.171	1.291	1.114	1.358	1.055	1.432	0.995	1.510	0.935	1.594	0.876	1.683	0.816	1.776	0.757	1.874	0.698	1.975	0.641	2.080
34	1.184	1.298	1.128	1.364	1.070	1.436	1.012	1.511	0.954	1.591	0.896	1.677	0.837	1.766	0.779	1.860	0.722	1.957	0.665	2.057
35	1.195	1.307	1.141	1.370	1.085	1.439	1.028	1.512	0.971	1.589	0.914	1.671	0.857	1.757	0.800	1.847	0.744	1.940	0.689	2.037
36	1.205	1.315	1.153	1.376	1.098	1.442	1.043	1.513	0.987	1.587	0.932	1.666	0.877	1.749	0.821	1.836	0.766	1.925	0.711	2.018
37	1.217	1.322	1.164	1.383	1.112	1.446	1.058	1.514	1.004	1.585	0.950	1.662	0.895	1.742	0.841	1.825	0.787	1.911	0.733	2.001
38	1.227	1.330	1.176	1.388	1.124	1.449	1.072	1.515	1.019	1.584	0.966	1.658	0.913	1.735	0.860	1.816	0.807	1.899	0.754	1.985
39	1.237	1.337	1.187	1.392	1.137	1.452	1.085	1.517	1.033	1.583	0.982	1.655	0.930	1.729	0.878	1.807	0.826	1.887	0.774	1.970
40	1.246	1.344	1.197	1.398	1.149	1.456	1.098	1.518	1.047	1.583	0.997	1.652	0.946	1.724	0.895	1.799	0.844	1.876	0.749	1.956
45	1.288	1.376	1.245	1.424	1.201	1.474	1.156	1.528	1.111	1.583	1.065	1.643	1.019	1.704	0.974	1.768	0.927	1.834	0.881	1.902
50	1.324	1.403	1.285	1.445	1.245	1.491	1.206	1.537	1.164	1.587	1.123	1.639	1.081	1.692	1.039	1.748	0.997	1.805	0.955	1.864
55	1.356	1.428	1.320	1.466	1.284	1.505	1.246	1.548	1.209	1.592	1.172	1.638	1.134	1.685	1.095	1.734	1.057	1.785	1.018	1.837
60	1.382	1.449	1.351	1.484	1.317	1.520	1.283	1.559	1.248	1.598	1.214	1.639	1.179	1.682	1.144	1.726	1.108	1.771	1.072	1.817
65	1.407	1.467	1.377	1.500	1.346	1.534	1.314	1.568	1.283	1.604	1.251	1.642	1.218	1.680	1.186	1.720	1.153	1.761	1.120	1.802
70	1.429	1.485	1.400	1.514	1.372	1.546	1.343	1.577	1.313	1.611	1.283	1.645	1.253	1.680	1.223	1.716	1.192	1.754	1.162	1.792
75	1.448	1.501	1.422	1.529	1.395	1.557	1.368	1.586	1.340	1.617	1.313	1.649	1.284	1.682	1.256	1.714	1.227	1.748	1.199	1.783
80	1.465	1.514	1.440	1.541	1.416	1.568	1.390	1.595	1.364	1.624	1.338	1.653	1.312	1.683	1.285	1.714	1.259	1.745	1.232	1.777
85	1.481	1.529	1.458	1.553	1.434	1.577	1.411	1.603	1.386	1.630	1.362	1.657	1.337	1.685	1.312	1.714	1.287	1.743	1.262	1.773
90	1.496	1.541	1.474	1.563	1.452	1.587	1.429	1.611	1.406	1.636	1.383	1.661	1.360	1.687	1.336	1.714	1.312	1.741	1.288	1.769
95	1.510	1.552	1.489	1.573	1.468	1.596	1.446	1.618	1.425	1.641	1.403	1.666	1.381	1.690	1.358	1.715	1.336	1.741	1.313	1.767
100	1.522	1.562	1.502	1.582	1.482	1.604	1.461	1.625	1.441	1.647	1.421	1.670	1.400	1.693	1.378	1.717	1.357	1.741	1.335	1.765
150	1.611	1.637	1.598	1.651	1.584	1.665	1.571	1.679	1.557	1.693	1.543	1.708	1.530	1.722	1.515	1.737	1.501	1.752	1.486	1.767
200	1.664	1.684	1.653	1.693	1.643	1.704	1.633	1.715	1.623	1.725	1.613	1.735	1.603	1.746	1.592	1.757	1.582	1.768	1.571	1.779

[a]k is the number of regressors excluding the intercept

Source: based on Savin and White (1977)

Acknowledgements This article is part of a Jean Monnet research project (Project No.:-2006-1623/001-001-001-JMO-JMO) financed by the European Commission.

I would like to thank Prof. Dr. Paul J.J. Welfens, Prof. Dr. Werner Bönte, Jens Perret, Mevlud Islami, Thomas Domeratzki, Deniz Erdem and the participants of the FIRB-RISC conference on Research and Entrepreneurship in the knowledge-based economy in Milano at the Bocconi University in September 2009 for their useful comments. I am also grateful to Michael Agner for his patient help to correct the numerous errors in my translation.

References

Alesina, A., Ardagna, S., Nicoletti, ,G., Schiantarelli, F. (2003). Regulation and Investment. NBER Working Paper No. 9560.

Allen, F. (1993). Stock markets and resource allocation. In C. Mayer & X. Vives (Eds.), *Capital markets and financial intermediation* (pp. 81–108). Cambridge: Cambridge University Press.

Ang, J. (2008). A survey of recent developments in the literature of finance and growth. *Journal of Economic Survey, 22*(3), 536–576.

Audretsch, D., & Lehmann, E. (2004). Debt or equity, the role of venture capital in financing high-tech firms in Germany. *Schmalenbach Business Review, 56*, 340–357.

Baumol, W. J. (2002). *Free market innovation machine: analyzing the growth miracle of capitalism.* NJ, USA: Princeton University Press.

Beck, T., & Levine, R. (2002). Industry growth and capital allocation, does having a market- or bank-based system matter? *Journal of Financial Economics, 64*, 147–180.

Becker, R., & Hellmann, T. (2005). The genesis of venture capital: lessons from the German experience. In C. Keuschnigg & V. Kanniainen (Eds.), *Venture capital, entrepreneurship, and public policy* (pp. 33–67). Cambridge: MIT Press.

Berger, A., & Udell, G. (1998). The economics of small business finance: the roles of private equity and debt markets in the financial growth cycle. *Journal of Finance, 22*, 613–673.

Berger, A., & Udell, G. (2002). Small business credit availability and relationship lending: the importance of bank organizational structure. *Economic Journal, 112*, 32–53.

Berlin, M. (1998). *That thing venture capitalists do business review. january/february* (pp. 15–27). Philadelphia: Federal Reserve Bank of Philadelphia.

Black, B., & Gilson, R. (1997). Venture capital and the structure of capital markets: banks versus stock markets. *Journal of Financial Economics, 47*, 243–277.

Boot, A., Greenbaum, S., & Thakor, A. (1993). Reputation and discretion in financial contracting. *American Economic Review, 83*, 1165–1183.

Boyd, J., & Smith, B. (1998). The evolution of debt and equity markets in economic development. *Economic Theory, 12*, 519–560.

Carlin, W., & Mayer, C. (2000). How do financial systems affect economic performance? In X. Vives (Ed.), *Corporate governance: theoretical and empirical perspectives* (pp. 137–168). Cambridge: Cambridge University Press.

Carpenter, R., & Petersen, B. (2002). Capital market imperfections, high-tech investment, and new equity financing. *The Economic Journal, 112*, 54–72.

Clarysse, B., Knockaert, M., Lockett, A. (2005). How do early stage high technology investors select their investments? Working Paper 2005/297, Ghent University.

Czarnitzki, D. (2006). Research and development in small- and medium-sized enterprises: the role of financial constraints and public funding. *Scottish Journal of Political Economy, 53*(3), 257–335.

Davila, A., Foster, G., & Gupta, M. (2003). Venture capital financing and the growth of startup firms. *Journal of Business Venturing, 18*, 689–708.

Davis, E. (2000). Pension Funds, Financial Intermediation and the New Financial Landscape, Discussion Paper PI-0010. The Pension Institute, UK, London.
DiMasi, J., Hansen, R., & Grabowski, H. (2003). The price of innovation: new estimates of drug development costs. *Journal of Health Economics, 22*, 151–185.
Engel, D. (2002). The Impact of Venture Capital on Firm Growth: An Empirical Investigation. ZEW Discussion Paper No. 02-02.
Engel, D., & Keilbach, M. (2007). Firm-level implications of early stage venture capital investment – an empirical investigation. *Journal of Empirical Finance, 14*(2), 150–167.
European Commission (2005a). SME Access to Finance. Flash Eurobarometer 174.
European Commission (2005b). Best practices of public support for early-stage equity finance, Final report of the expert group. Resource Document. Directorate-General for Enterprise and Industry. http://ec.europa.eu/enterprise/entrepreneurship/financing/docs/report_early-stage_equity_finance.pdf. Accessed 20 May 2008.
European Commission (2006). SME Access to Finance in the New Member States, Flash Eurobarometer 184. The Gallup Organization.
Evans, A., & Varaiya, N. (2003). Assessment of a biotechnology market opportunity. *Entrepreneurship Theory and Practice, 28*(1), 19. 87–105.
Fenn, G., Liang, N., & Prowse, S. (1995). *The economics of the private equity market. Stuff study 168*. Washington, DC: Board of Governors of the Federal Reserve System.
Gebhardt, G., & Schmidt, K. (2001). Der Markt für Venture Capital: Anreizprobleme, Governance Strukturen und staatliche Interventionen. *Perspektiven der Wirtschaftspolitik, 3*(3), 235–255.
Gerschenkron, A. (1963). *Economic backwardness in theoretical perspective*. Cambridge: Harvard University Press.
Gompers, P., & Lerner, J. (1998). What drives venture capital fundraising? *Brookings Papers on Economic Activity Microeconomics, 1998*, 149–204.
Gompers, P., & Lerner, J. (1999). *The venture capital cycle*. Cambridge, MA: The MIT Press.
Goodacre, A., & Tonks, I. (1995). Finance and technological change. In P. Stoneman (Ed.), *Handbook of the economics of innovation and technological change* (pp. 298–341). Oxford: Basil Blackwell.
Gorman, M., & Sahlman, W. (1989). What do venture capitalists do? *Journal of Business Venturing, 4*, 231–248.
Hall, B. (1992). Research and development at the firm level: Does the source of financing matter? NBER Working Paper No. 4096.
Hall, B. (2002). The financing of research and development. *Oxford Review of Economic Policy, 18*(1), 35–51.
Harhoff, D. (1998). Are there financing constraints for R&D and investment in German manufacturing firms? *Annales d'Economie et de Statistique, 49*(50), 421–456.
Hege, U., Da Rin, M., Llobet, G., & Walz, U. (2006). The law and finance of venture capital financing in Europe: findings from the RICAFE research project. *European Business Organization Law Review, 7*, 525–547.
Hege, U., Palomino, F., & Schwienbacher, A. (2009). Venture capital performance: the disparity between Europe and the United States. *Revue de l'association française de finance, 30*(1), 7–50.
Hellmann, T., Lindsey, L., & Puri, M. (2008). Building relationships early: banks in venture capital. *The Review of Financial Studies, 21*(2), 513–541.
Hellmann, T., & Puri, M. (2002). Venture capital and the professionalization of start-up firms: empirical evidence. *Journal of Finance, 57*(1), 169–197.
Hellwig, M. (1991). Banking, financial intermediation, and corporate finance. In A. Giovanni & C. Mayer (Eds.), *European financial intermediation* (pp. 35–63). Cambridge: Cambridge University Press.
Hicks, J. (1969). *A theory of economic history*. Oxford: Clarendon Press.
Himmelberg, C., & Peterson, B. (1994). R&D and internal finance: a panel study of small firms in high-tech industries. *Review of Economics and Statistics, 76*, 38–51.

Hirsch, J., Walz, U. (2006). Why Do Contracts Differ between VC Types? Market Segmentation versus Corporate Governance Varieties. Center for Financial Studies, Discussion Paper No. 2006/12.

Hubbard, R. G. (2008). *Money, the financial system, and the economy* (6th ed.). New York: Pearson.

Jeng, A., & Wells, C. (2000). The determinants of venture capital funding: evidence across countries. *Journal of Corporate Finance, 6*(3), 241–289.

KfW Bankengruppe (2006). Mittelstands- und Strukturpolitik Nr. 37. Sonderband "Innovationen im Mittelstand", Frankfurt.

Klapper, L., Leaeven, L., & Rajan, R. (2004). *Business environment and firm entry: evidence from international data*. Working Paper: World Bank Policy Research. 3232.

Koetter, M., Wedow, M. (2006). Finance and Growth in a Bank-based Economy: Is it Quantity or Quality that matters? Discussion Paper Series 2: Banking and Financial Studies No. 02/006.

Kortum, S., & Lerner, J. (2000). Assessing the contribution of venture capital to innovation. *RAND Journal of Economics, 31*(4), 674–692.

Kukuk, M., & Stadler, M. (2001). Financing constraints and the timing of innovations in the German service sector. *Empirica, 28*, 277–292.

Levin, A., Lin, C., & Chu, C. (2002). Unit root tests in panel data: asymptotic and finite-sample properties. *Journal of Econometrics, 108*, 1–24.

Levine, R. (2001). Bank-based or market-based financial system: which is better? *Journal of Financial Intermediation, 11*(4), 398–428.

Levine, R. (2004). Finance and Growth: Theory and Evidence. NBER Working Paper No. 10766.

Levine, R., & Zervos, S. (1998). Stock markets, banks, and economic growth. *American Economic Review, 88*, 537–558.

Link, A., & Bozeman, B. (1991). Innovative behavior in small-sized firms. *Small Business Economics, 3*, 179–184.

Maddala, G., & Wu, S. (1999). A comparative study of unit root tests with panel data and a new simple test. *Oxford Bulletin of Economics and Statistics, 61*, 631–652.

Metcalfe, S. (1995). The economic foundations of technology policy: equilibrium and evolutionary perspectives. In P. Stoneman (Ed.), *Handbook of the economics of innovation and technical change* (pp. 409–512). London: Blackwell.

Modigliani, F., & Miller, M. (1958). The cost of capital, corporation finance and the theory of investment. *American Economic Review, 48*, 261–297.

Moore, B. (1994). Financial constraints to the growth and development of small high-technology firms. In A. Hughes & D. J. Storey (Eds.), *Finance and the small firm* (pp. 112–144). London: Routledge.

Mueller, E., Zimmermann, V., (2006). The Importance of Equity Finance for R&D Activity – Are There Differences Between Young and Old Companies? ZEW (Centre for European Economic Research) Discussion Paper No. 06-014.

Mulkay, B., Hall, B., & Mairesse, J. (2001). Investment and R&D in France and in the United States. In D. Bundesbank (Ed.), *Investing today for the world of tomorrow* (pp. 229–273). Heidelberg: Springer.

Murray, G. (1998). Early-stage venture capital funds, scale economies and public support. *Venture Capital, 1*(4), 351–384.

Myers, S., & Majluf, N. (1984). Corporate financing and investment decisions when firms have information that investors do not. *Journal of Financial Economics, 13*, 187–221.

National Venture Capital Association (2008). Venture Capital Performance. Resource Document. EVCA http://www.nvca.org/index.php?option=com_docman&task=doc_download&gid=503&ItemId=. Accessed 09 January 2010.

OECD (2003). Venture Capital: Trends and Policy Recommendations. Science Technology Industry. Resource Document. http://www.oecd.org/dataoecd/4/11/28881195.pdf. Accessed 10 June 2008.

Pagano, M. (1993). Financial markets and growth: an overview. *European Economic Review, 37*, 613–622.
Petersen, M., & Rajan, R. (1995). The effect of credit market competition on lending relationships: evidence from small business data. *Journal of Finance, 49*, 3–37.
Popov, A.; Rosenboom, P (2009). Does Private Equity Spur Innovation? Evidence from Europe. ECB Working Paper Series No. 1063.
Romain, A., Van Pottelsberghe, B. (2004a). The Economic Impact of Venture Capital, Deutsch Bank Discussion Paper Series 1, Studies of the Economic Research Centre No. 18/2004.
Romain, A., Van Pottelsberghe, B. (2004b). The Determinants of Venture Capital: Additional Evidence. Deutsch Bank Discussion Paper Series 1, Studies of the Economic Research Centre No. 19/2004.
Savin, N., & White, K. (1977). The Durbin–Watson test for serial correlation with extreme sample sizes or many regressors. *Econometrica, 45*, 1989–1996.
Schertler, A. (2002). Under What Conditions Do Venture Capital Markets Emerge? Kiel Working Paper No. 119.
Schertler, A. (2003). Driving Forces of Venture Capital Investments in Europe: A Dynamic Panel Data Analysis. Kiel Institute for World Economics, Working Paper No. 03-27.
Schertler, A. (2004). Explaining cross-country variations in venture capital investments: theory and empirical evidence. *Kredit und Kapital, 37*(3), 297–328.
Schertler, A. (2007). Knowledge capital and venture capital investments: new evidence from European panel data. *German Economic Review, 8*(1), 64–88.
Schumpeter, J., (1911). *Theorie der wirtschaftlichen Entwicklung,* Eine Untersuchung über Unternehmergewinn, Kapital, Kredit, Zins und den Konjunkturzyklus, 7. Auflage (1987). Berlin: Dunker & Humblot.
Stiglitz, J., & Weiss, A. (1981). Credit rationing in markets with imperfect information. *American Economic Review, 71*, 393–410.
Stiglitz, J. (1985). Credit markets and the control of capital. *Journal of Money, Credit and Banking, 17*(2), 133–152.
Stoneman, P. (2001), Heterogeneity and Change in European Financial Environments, EIFC Working Paper No. 01-7.
Storey, D. J. (1995). *The financing of new and small enterprises in the OECD countries.* Coventry: SME Centre, Warwick Business School.
Stulz, R. (2000). Financial structure, corporate finance, and economic growth. *International Review of Finance, 1*(1), 11–38.
Tiwari, A., Mohnen, P., Palm, F., Van der Loeff, S. (2007), Financial Constraint and R&D Investment: Evidence from CIS. Working Paper 2007-011, Maastricht: United Nations University.
Ueda, M. (2004). Banks versus venture capital: project evaluation, screening, and expropriation. *Journal of Finance, 59*, 601–621.
White, H. (1980). A heteroskedasticity-consistent covariance matrix and a direct test for heteroskedasticity. *Econometrica, 48*, 817–838.
Wooldridge, J. (2002). *Econometric analysis of cross section and panel data.* Cambridge, MA: The MIT Press.

Chapter 5
Evolving Corporate Financing Patterns in Europe: Is There Convergence?

Andy Mullineux, Victor Murinde, and Rudra Sensarma

5.1 Introduction

One of the main objectives behind the formation of the European Union (EU) is attainment of financial integration among member countries. Greater financial integration is expected to facilitate financial sector efficiency, macroeconomic stability and effective implementation of monetary policy in the EU (Trichet 2006). While there have been several attempts at assessing the progress of financial integration in the EU,[1] one important aspect of the process, namely corporate financing, has been largely under-researched. This paper attempts to investigate convergence in corporate financing patterns in the EU and thereby provide insights into the larger issue of European integration. In this respect, the paper extends the work of Murinde et al. (2004), which tested for convergence in corporate financing patterns in the EU using a 1972–1996 dataset, by using more recent data for 1972–2004 and by studying a slightly larger set of EU countries, namely Finland, France, Germany, Italy, The Netherlands, Spain, Sweden and the UK.[2] In addition, this study invokes more innovative econometric techniques by using modern panel unit root tests, following Evans and Karras (1996), and further by employing more appropriate (GMM) methodology for testing convergence in panel data, following Islam (1995) and Nerlove (1996).

In a previous study, Murinde et al. found little evidence of convergence in bank and bond finance and some evidence of convergence in equity and internal

[1]See for example, Hartmann et al. (2003) and Guiso et al. (2004).

[2]The sample selection is driven by data availability. The chosen countries are the only ones for which sufficient data was available for the period studied. Data beyond 2004 was not available for most countries.

A. Mullineux (✉)
Birmingham Business School, University of Birmingham, Birmingham, UK
e-mail: a.w.mullineux@bham.ac.uk

V. Murinde
Birmingham Business School, University of Birmingham, Birmingham, UK

R. Sensarma
University of Hertfordshire Business School, Hertfordshire, UK

P.J.J. Welfens and C. Ryan (eds.), *Financial Market Integration and Growth*,
DOI 10.1007/978-3-642-16274-9_5,

Fig. 5.1 Evolving corporate financing patterns in the EU
Note: Mean values are plotted for each year. Leverage refers to the ratio of debt (bank + bond) financing to equity financing; bank to market financing ratio refers to the ratio of bank financing to market (equity + bond) financing

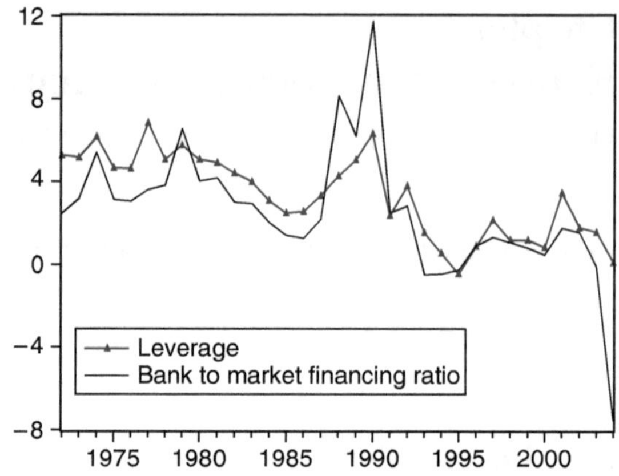

corporate finance, with strong growth in the latter in line with other previous studies (Bertero 1994; Corbett and Jenkinson 1996). Our extended dataset, as summarized in Fig. 5.1, indicates that the EU has continued to witness convergence in corporate financing with a clear shift from bank financing towards market based financing. The graphs suggest an ongoing switch from bank to equity and bond debt finance and indicate that internal finance is no longer growing strongly. In this paper we undertake formal empirical testing to confirm the above convergence.

Mullineux (2007, 2010) *inter alia* examines the impact of financial sector convergence, postulating the evolution of a hybrid model in which financial conglomerates have evolved in the US and Japan (where they were prohibited by regulations until the regulatory reform in those countries in the mid to late 1990s) similar to the prevailing European universal banking and bancassurance models. And capital markets have become more important in Europe and Japan, leading to some catch up with the US (and the UK). The euro denominated corporate bond market has grown rapidly, since the introduction of the euro in 1999 and overtook the US dollar (USD) denominated market in the middle of the subsequent decade. By 2007 it was approximately 50% bigger in the USD market.

Our findings confirm the growth in the NFC bond financing and suggest that it is at the expense of bank financing. A similar disintermediation ('securitisation') involving a switch by large corporates (but not bank dependent SMEs) from bank loan to bond (and shorter term rate and commerce paper) finance can be seen in Japan and the US. The situation of medium sized companies is under-researched and more complex as they are gaining access to alternatives to bank finance through the issuance of 'junk' (below investment grade) bonds and venture capital. However our data set pertains to NFCs of all size classes since the disaggregated data by asset size was not available.

The observed convergence on a hybrid model ('hybridisation') consisting of large global financial conglomerate banks (and smaller local banks and specialist institutions), is increasingly market orientated and thus a less bank orientated (insider) and more market orientated (outsider) system of corporate governance is evolving (Mullineux 2007). Precisely, corporate governance is becoming more Anglo-Saxon. However, the term 'Anglo-Saxon' itself is a bit of a misnomer if it is taken to include both the US and the UK since their corporate governance models are very different (Mullineux 2010) and indeed the UK system is now closer to that of the rest of Europe, in terms of the role of institutional shareholders in the corporate governance system, than to the US; which is increasingly looking like an outlier. Indeed since the passing of the Sarbanes-Oxley Act in 2002, which was necessary to underpin internal controls after the Enron debacle, New York appears to be losing business to London, which has a lighter corporate regulatory and corporate governance regime. Regulation in the UK is conducted by the Financial Services Authority on a 'risk-based' basis. London's success is not entirely driven by its low regulatory 'tax', it is also at the centre of the rapid growth in euro denominated financial markets and is laying claim to the Islamic bond market too. The lack of institutional shareholder proxy voting rights in the US may also be putting New York at a disadvantage and the regulator, the Securities and Exchange Commission was reviewing the situation in 2007.

More generally, financial sector integration is being encouraged in the EU as a way of improving financial service provision, deepening markets and reducing the cost of capital, including the cost of payments and settlement. The introduction of the euro in 1999, aimed to facilitate this process, along with the Financial Services Act Plan (FSAP) adopted by the European Council in March 2000. Thirty eight of its 42 members had been widely adopted by the end of 2004. There is some frustration about the continuing high costs of cross-border payments, but the EC is pressing for a single European Payment Area (SEPA) to be completed before the end of the decade. The European Central Bank (ECB) is seeking permission to launch a Europe-wide system itself, as a means of bypassing the obstacles. It should be noted that the FSAP and SEPA cover retail banking initiatives as well as corporate finance (cost of capital and money and capital market liquidity) issues. European regulatory convergence was achieved to a large extent before the end of the 1990s. Revisions are underway in preparation for the implementation of Basel II and there remains a concern that the country level regulatory and supervisory authorities may not implement the EU level regulation conformably. Significant tax differences also remain.

The development of a single European financial market, to the extent that remains possible under globalization, also has implications for the conduct of monetary policy (Trichet 2006). Changes in interest rates have more similar effects in the various parts of the EU. Harmonisation of home loan markets may reduce financial instability and lower costs of capital may increase investment and growth. Therefore, financial integration in the EU can be expected to boost economic growth and aid financial stability. In this context, the issue of whether financial systems across EU countries are converging becomes important.

The remainder of the paper is organized as follows. Section 5.2 provides an overview of empirical modeling of convergence. Section 5.3 presents the results from panel unit root tests of convergence followed by the results from GMM regressions in Sect. 5.4. Finally, Sect. 5.5 summarizes and concludes the paper.

5.2 Modeling Convergence

Bulk of the literature on convergence can be traced back to Barro and Sala-i-Martin (1992) who developed regression based tests for growth convergence. Subsequent developments in the convergence literature have proceeded in two broad directions. The first is the approach of Evans and Karras (1996) who developed a formal test of convergence that is based on panel unit root tests. The second is the work by Islam (1995) and Nerlove (1996) who extended the Barro and Salai-i-Martin framework to allow for testing of convergence in a panel framework. We conduct both the above types of tests in this paper and hence provide a brief overview of each.

While the classical growth regression approach is quite popular in the literature, it has faced criticism on account of ignoring time-series properties of the data. Evans (1996) recommended exploiting both the time-series and the cross-section information provided by panel data in order to evaluate the convergence hypothesis. Evans and Karras (1996) showed that, economies can be said to converge if and only if there exists a common trend such that $\mathrm{E_t}\,(\mathrm{y_{n,t+1}} - \mathrm{a_{t+1}}) = \mu_\mathrm{n}$, where a_t is the common trend and μ_n is a constant. Evans and Karras (1996) posited this question as a test of stationarity of the mean-differenced series, $y_{n,t+i} - \bar{y}_{t+i}$. In this paper we employ a variety of modern panel unit root tests to conduct tests of convergence on the mean-differenced data on bank financing, equity financing, bond financing and internal financing respectively for the EU countries in our data-set where we consider the share of each mode of financing in total financing as the relevant endogenous variable.

For conducting panel unit root tests, we first use the test given by Levin, Lin and Chu (LLC 2002). This is essentially a pooled Augmented Dickey-Fuller (ADF) test but is general enough to allow for individual fixed effects as well as time effects. Next we employ Breitung's (2000) test which is similar to LLC expect for the way in which it uses proxies to estimate the auto-regressive coefficients. However the major limitation of these tests is that each cross-section in the panel is assumed to share the same auto-regressive coefficient. Thus rejection of the null of non-stationarity implies that the rate of convergence is same across all units. This assumed homogeneity of the unit root was overcome by Im et al. (2003, 1997) who estimated individual-specific ADF tests and then computed the mean of the different t-statistics. Thus, the IPS test does not assume that all series are stationary under the alternative, but is consistent under the alternative that only some of the series are stationary. Therefore, we employ the IPS test as a robust means of testing our convergence hypothesis. We also use the Fisher-ADF test and the Fisher-PP test (Madalla and Wu 1999; Choi 2001). The Fisher tests are similar to the IPS test in the sense that they combine independent unit root tests (conducted as chi-square tests in this case) of the individual series.

Finally, we apply a stationarity test, viz. the Hadri test (Hadri 2000) which is a residual based Lagrange multiplier test with the null hypothesis of stationarity of the series. This test has high power and has the advantage of being robust to non-normality. We also provide results from a variant of the Hadri test that is heteroscedasticity consistent. In sum, we employ five panel unit root tests and two panel stationarity tests.

However the above framework provides only an examination of unconditional convergence where different initial conditions among the countries cannot be controlled for. The classical growth regression approach of Barro and Sala-i-Martin allows testing for conditional as well as unconditional convergence and the original framework was extended by Islam (1995) and Nerlove (1996) to fit panel data. Their framework starts by defining a Cobb–Douglas production function, $y = A^{1-\alpha}k^{\alpha}$, where y is the per capita output, k is the capital intensity and A denotes productivity. Following the Solow model's equality between savings and investment, we can derive the following formulation:

$$\log y_t = \frac{\alpha(1-\gamma)}{1-\alpha}[\log s - \log(n+g+\delta)] + (1-\gamma)\log A_t + \gamma \log y_{t-1} \quad (5.1)$$

where s is the savings rate, n is the population growth rate, g is the productivity growth rate and δ is the depreciation rate of capital stock. It can be shown that the rate of convergence of per capita output to the equilibrium level is inversely proportional to γ. If γ is smaller than 1 then there is such convergence, and convergence speed increases as γ decreases. The model yields the following estimable formulation:

$$y_{it} = \gamma y_{it-1} + x'_{it}\beta + \mu_i + u_{it} \quad (5.2)$$

where $t = 1$ to T, represents year and $i = 1$ to N represents country; y_{it} stands for GDP per capita for country i in year t; x_{it} stands for all the determinants of growth; μ_{it} represents the country-specific effects; and u_{it} is white noise.

In this paper, our objective is to adopt the above framework for testing convergence in growth rates of corporate financing patterns of EU countries. The flow of funds data that we use decomposes the aggregate economic activity of a country to the flow of funds in the government, private, household and financial sectors. Therefore, a convergence in national economic growths does not automatically imply that there will be convergence in each of the disaggregated sectors of the economy. This motivates the modeling of convergence in the disaggregated components of the aggregate economy, i.e. financial sector in our case. Analogous to the neo-classical production function that is typically assumed for the macro-economy, we conceptualise the economic activity in the financial sector in terms of corporate financing being produced by employing different inputs such as those implied by monetary policy and other control variables (Murinde et al. 2004). Therefore, we replace GDP per capita in the traditional growth model by the types of corporate financing. In other words, in (5.2) we replace y_{it} by the share of corporate financing from a particular source. Consequently, we are able to test for convergence among EU countries in terms of their corporate financing patterns.

However the main problem with the model outlined in (5.2) is that the lagged dependent variable y_{it-1} and the country-specific effects μ_{it} are correlated, which means that the usual panel estimators are biased and inconsistent. The Generalized Method of Moments (GMM) methodology is a convenient means of estimating this model where instrument variables are used for y_{it-1} and moment conditions are exploited in the estimation (Hansen 1982; Arellano and Bond 1991). In this paper we follow Arellano and Bover's (1995) methodology of orthogonal deviation that removes the unobserved country-specific effects. The orthogonal deviation transformation expresses each observation as the deviation from the mean of future observations for the same country and it weights each deviation to standardize the variance. The advantage of using this transformation is that the transformed errors will be serially uncorrelated and homoskedastic.

We apply the above methodology to estimate four different equations. First, we estimate the convergence model for bank financing based on the following equation:

$$BANK_{it} = \gamma BANK_{it-1} + \beta_1 BMY_{it} + \beta_2 ER_{it} + \beta_3 IR_{it} + \beta_4 OPEN_{it} + +u_{it} \quad (5.3)$$

where BANK is bank financing by the NFCs, BMY is a financial deepening variable calculated as the ratio of money supply to GDP, ER is the nominal exchange rate, IR is the nominal interest rate and OPEN is a measures of the degree of openness calculated as the ratio of exports and imports to GDP. While the control variables BMY and IR are proxies for monetary policy and are consistent with the idea of monetary convergence as stipulated by the European Commission (Murinde et al. 2004), ER and OPEN are expected to control for the influence of trade policy and terms of trade on corporate financing. In the above equation, if the estimated γ turns out to be less than one, then we can deduce that there is convergence in bank financing by the NFCs across the countries in our sample and over the time period considered. Moreover, the inverse of γ indicates the speed of convergence.The second equation that we estimate is based on the role of equity markets in providing finance to NFCs:

$$EQUITY_{it} = \gamma EQUITY_{it-1} + \beta_1 BMY_{it} + \beta_2 ER_{it} + \beta_3 IR_{it} + \beta_4 OPEN_{it} + +u_{it} \quad (5.4)$$

where EQUITY is equity financing by the NFCs and the control variables are the same as before. We also estimate an equation based on bond financing of NFCs:

$$BOND_{it} = \gamma BOND_{it-1} + \beta_1 BMY_{it} + \beta_2 ER_{it} + \beta_3 IR_{it} + \beta_4 OPEN_{it} + +u_{it} \quad (5.5)$$

where BOND is bond financing by the NFCs and the control variables are the same as before. Finally, we test convergence in the use of internal finance by NFCs by estimating the following equation:

$$INTERN_{it} = \gamma INTERN_{it-1} + \beta_1 BMY_{it} + \beta_2 ER_{it} + \beta_3 IR_{it} + \beta_4 OPEN_{it} + +u_{it} \quad (5.6)$$

Table 5.1 Correlation matrix of corporate financing and macroeconomic variables for eight EU countries, 1972–2004

	Bank	Equity	Bond	Intern	BMY	ER	IR	Open
Bank	1.000							
Equity	0.360	1.000						
Bond	0.293	0.634	1.000					
Intern	−0.866	−0.770	−0.606	1.000				
BMY	−0.076	0.113	0.204	−0.025	1.000			
ER	−0.054	−0.149	−0.143	0.121	−0.150	1.000		
IR	0.232	0.028	0.008	−0.168	−0.110	−0.179	1.000	
Open	−0.125	−0.270	−0.179	0.228	−0.212	0.203	−0.429	1.000

Note: Bank bank financing by the NFCs to total financing, Equity equity financing by NFCs to total financing, Bond is bond financing by NFCs to total financing, Intern internal financing by NFCs to total financing, BMY the ratio of money supply to GDP, ER is the nominal exchange rate, IR is the nominal interest rate and Open the ratio of exports and imports to GDP

where INTERN is internal financing by the NFCs and the control variables are the same as before.

The data for this study are taken from the OECD flow-of-funds tables and covers the period 1972–2004 for eight EU member countries, viz. Finland, France, Germany, Italy, the Netherlands, Spain, Sweden and the UK. We define the financing variables as percentages of the total. The data on macroeconomic variables are collected from IMF's International Financial Statistics database. Mean values of the corporate finance data are plotted in Fig. 5.1. The evolving pattern provides preliminary indication of a shift from bank based financing to market sources. Table 5.1 presents a correlation matrix of all the main variables that we study.

5.3 Results from Panel Unit Root Tests

Panel unit root tests have the advantage that they take account of time-series properties of the variables while examining convergence. Thus we employ a variety of panel unit root tests for convergence in corporate financing in the EU. Accordingly we conduct five panel unit root tests and two panel stationarity tests on each corporate financing variable and the results for all the eight countries in our sample are presented in Table 5.2. For bank financing, the results are overwhelmingly in favour of convergence as the null hypothesis of non-stationarity of the data gets rejected by all the five unit root tests (albeit marginally for the LLC test at the level of 10%). Furthermore, the Hadri tests of stationarity do not reject the null hypothesis of stationarity. However for equity financing, the results do not indicate convergence. Although the Fisher-PP test rejects the null hypothesis, however the rest of the tests do not provide evidence to suggest a convergence in equity financing among the sample countries.

Table 5.2 Panel unit root and stationarity tests: results for eight EU countries, 1972–2004

Method	Bank		Equity		Bond		Intern	
	Statistic	P-value	Statistic	P-value	Statistic	P-value	Statistic	P-value
Null: Unit root (assumes common unit root process)								
Levin, Lin and Chu	−1.39695	0.0812	0.27109	0.6068	−8.12964	0.0000	−1.10692	0.1342
Breitung t-stat	−4.16643	0.0000	−1.16491	0.1220	−4.20111	0.0000	−2.28877	0.0110
Null: Unit root (assumes individual unit root process)								
Im, Pesaran and Shin W-stat	−3.40697	0.0003	−0.39352	0.3470	−7.77701	0.0000	−2.10592	0.0176
ADF – Fisher Chi-square	41.5028	0.0005	16.5072	0.4182	86.8901	0.0000	26.3358	0.0495
PP – Fisher Chi-square	32.8367	0.0078	26.7665	0.0442	67.7155	0.0000	23.5700	0.0993
Null: No unit root (assumes common unit root process)								
Hadri Z-stat	0.84747	0.1984	0.47226	0.3184	1.42700	0.0768	2.08913	0.0183
Hadri Heteroscedasticity Consistent Z-stat	0.90051	0.1839	1.09923	0.1358	1.03987	0.1492	0.71894	0.2361

Note: The regression for the unit root tests follows from Evans and Karras (1996)

The bond financing results are in favour of convergence as indicated by the unanimous rejection of the null hypothesis in all the unit root tests. It may be noted that although the Hadri test rejects the null hypothesis of stationarity at the 10% level, the heteroscedasticy consistent version of the test provides evidence for convergence. The results for internal finance are not entirely unanimous. While the LLC test fails to reject the null hypothesis of non-stationarity, the Fisher-PP test rejects it only at the 10% level of significance. However all the other tests provide results to indicate convergence in internal financing. In sum, the above tests strongly indicate that there has been convergence in the corporate financing patterns of the EU countries in terms of bank and bond financing. Our results provide weak evidence in favour of convergence in terms of equity and internal financing.

We also conduct the panel unit root tests for only the countries that have adopted euro as their currency. The results are presented in the Appendix Table 5.6. The results are almost similar to those obtained for the full sample, except for mixed results in the case of equity financing. Hence, the convergence hypothesis appears to hold for bank finance and bond finance whereas the results are mixed for equity finance and internal finance (the Hadri tests of stationarity indicate convergence whereas the unit root tests do not). These results reinforce our earlier findings for the EU countries. Hence, our results strongly suggest that NFCs in euro countries have converged in terms of their bank and bond financing patterns, whereas the results for equity and internal finance are mixed. Finally we conduct the panel unit root tests on our sample only for the countries that were EU members from the beginning of our data period, i.e. 1972. Hence, we leave out the new entrants, viz. Finland, Spain and Sweden, from our sample. The results are presented in Table 5.7. These results suggest that these countries exhibited convergence in terms of bank finance and bond finance, thereby re-affirming our previous results.

$$\Delta CORPFIN_{it} = \beta CORPFIN_{t-1} + \sum_{j=1} \lambda_j \Delta CORPFIN_{t-j} + \alpha_i + u_{it},$$

where CORPFIN is the mean differenced endogenous variable for corporate financing measured as bank financing, equity financing, bond financing and internal financing by NFCs as a ratio of total financing. We employ a variety of modern panel unit root tests based on the above formulation. Probabilities for Fisher tests are computed using an asymptotic Chi-square distribution. All other tests assume asymptotic normality.

To summarize, our panel unit root tests indicate that the EU countries have exhibited convergence in their corporate financing patterns in terms of their bank financing and equity financing. This pattern of convergence has been consistent across the countries that have adopted the euro as their currency as well as for the founder EU member countries.

5.4 Results from GMM Regressions

While the above tests examined financial convergence only in an unconditional sense, we now move to the formal testing for convergence based on the modification of the classical regression approach as outlined in (5.3)–(5.6). These set of regressions, based on the dynamic panel GMM methodology, allow us to assess unconditional as well as conditional convergence. The results of the estimation of (5.3)–(5.6) all the eight countries in our sample are presented in Table 5.3. The coefficients of the lagged financing variables are less than one in all cases except for internal financing. This indicates that there has been convergence in corporate financing patterns in terms of bank, equity and bond financing across the eight countries in our sample over the period 1972–2004. However, the speed of convergence varies across the source of finance. Considering un-conditional convergence, bond finance appears to have exhibited the quickest convergence followed by equity and bank finance in that order. This pattern is repeated even when factors affecting financial convergence are controlled for, i.e. in the case of conditional convergence once again it is bond finance that exhibits the fastest convergence followed by equity and bank finance in that order. Our results indicating slow convergence of bank finance are comparable with the results of Murinde et al. (2004) who observed a lack of convergence in financing from this source.

Therefore, based on a more recent and expanded dataset, we observe that the EU countries have begun to converge in terms of the use of bank financing by NFCs, although the speed of convergence is the slowest for this source of finance. Another interesting finding is that EU countries exhibit convergence in bond financing and in fact this variable shows the fastest conditional as well as unconditional convergence, whereas Murinde et al. (2004) did not observe any convergence in financing from this source. This indicates that in recent years, NFCs in European countries have shown a tendency to source similar proportions of their total financing requirements from the bond markets. Our GMM results indicate convergence in equity financing whereas the panel unit root tests do not suggest convergence in this source of financing. Hence, while EU countries did not exhibit a common trend in

Table 5.3 GMM estimation results for eight EU countries 1972–2004

	Bank(-1)	*Equity(-1)*	*BMY*	*ER*	*IR*	*Open*	*Eurodum*	*Entrydum*	*Sargan*	*d.f.*
Bank models	0.781								30.60	31
	(0.00)									
	0.784		−0.079						22.12	30
	(0.00)		(0.10)							
	0.787			−0.026					29.76	32
	(0.00)			(0.00)						
	0.773				0.006				25.82	32
	(0.00)				(0.00)					
	0.774					−0.233			30.09	32
	(0.00)					(0.00)				
	0.756		0.135	−0.006	0.012	−0.361			19.22	33
	(0.00)		(0.25)	(0.61)	(0.00)	(0.00)				
	0.753		0.132	−0.004	0.012	−0.374	0.078		18.81	34
	(0.00)		(0.22)	(0.78)	(0.00)	(0.03)	(0.00)			
	0.758		0.136	−0.002	0.012	−0.369		0.087	19.68	34
(0.00)		(0.24)	(0.81)	(0.00)	(0.00)		(0.39)			
Equity models		0.753							31.31	31
		(0.00)								
		0.704	0.099						23.44	30
		(0.00)	(0.01)							
		0.750		0.008					31.32	32
		(0.00)		(0.00)						
		0.748			0.001				23.78	32
		(0.00)			(0.03)					
		0.750				0.083			27.37	32
		(0.00)				(0.00)				
		0.690	0.162	0.043	0.003	−0.302			23.91	33
		(0.00)	(0.00)	(0.00)	(0.00)	(0.00)				
		0.684	0.141	0.043	0.003	−0.308	0.249		23.20	34
		(0.00)	(0.01)	(0.00)	(0.00)	(0.00)	(0.00)			
		0.723	0.129	0.024	0.002	−0.168		−0.377	24.19	34
		(0.00)	(0.02)	(0.03)	(0.00)	(0.00)		(0.00)		

Bond models	0.356								29.68	31
	(0.00)		(0.00)							
	0.348			0.005					29.40	32
	(0.00)			(0.18)						
	0.361				0.002				27.89	32
	(0.00)				(0.00)					
	0.344					−0.044			28.19	32
	(0.00)					(0.10)				
	0.231		0.170	0.048	0.002	−0.273			24.86	33
	(0.00)		(0.00)	(0.00)	(0.03)	(0.00)				
	0.210		0.167	0.045	0.002	−0.273	0.132		25.83	34
	(0.00)		(0.00)	(0.00)	(0.00)	(0.00)	(0.00)			
	0.232		0.169	0.048	0.002	−0.262		0.014	25.62	34
	(0.00)		(0.00)	(0.00)	(0.03)	(0.00)		(0.82)		
Intern models		1.001							21.68	31
		(0.00)								
		1.060	0.242						14.96	30
		(0.00)	(0.03)							
		1.010		0.031					21.77	32
		(0.00)		(0.03)						
		1.023			−0.007				20.52	32
		(0.00)			(0.00)					
		1.009				0.261			20.17	32
		(0.00)				(0.00)				
		1.047	0.175	0.047	−0.009	−0.233			15.24	33
		(0.00)	(0.28)	(0.00)	(0.01)	(0.18)				
		1.035	0.169	0.047	−0.010	−0.215	−0.286		15.35	34
		(0.00)	(0.27)	(0.00)	(0.00)	(0.20)	(0.00)			
		1.014	0.159	0.042	−0.009	−0.186		−0.240	15.36	34
		(0.00)	(0.31)	(0.00)	(0.00)	(0.28)		(0.58)		

Note: Sargan denotes the test for validity of instruments (instruments are the second lags of corporate financing variables). The numbers in parentheses are p-values

terms of equity financing, there was convergence in the sense suggested by the growth regression approach, i.e. countries with lower initial levels of equity financing exhibited higher growth in financing from this source.

The role played by introduction of the euro in 1999 in the patterns of corporate financing is examined by including a dummy variable (EURODUM) for the year 1999 in the above specifications.[3] For the bank finance models, the results for the impact of the introduction of the euro suggests that while there has been convergence in bank financing, the introduction of the euro has actually led to an increase in dependence on bank borrowings. Similarly, the coefficient of the dummy variable is positive and significant in all cases of the equity financing and bond financing models suggesting that NFCs in the European countries increased their financing from equity issues and bond markets subsequent to the introduction of the Euro. However the introduction of the euro appears to have reduced the dependence on internal financing. These results indicate a convergence towards a variant of the Anglo-Saxon model of corporate financing characterized by increased importance of market based sources of finance and reduced role of internal finances in providing funds to the NFCs.

Whether entry of a country into the EU mattered in terms of the patterns of corporate financing is examined by including a dummy variable (ENTRYDUM) for the years of EU entry in the above specifications. While the results for the bank finance, bond finance and internal finance models do not show any impact of entry, the coefficient of the dummy variable is negative and significant in almost all specifications of the equity finance models. These results indicate that entry into the EU was characterized by NFCs of member countries reducing their dependence on equity financing. One possible explanation for this is that membership of the EU provided countries with an immediate reduction in risk premium thereby making debt financing less expensive.

We also re-estimate the model specifications only for the countries that have adopted the euro thus leaving out Sweden and UK in these set of estimations. The results from these estimations are reported in Table 5.4. The results are almost the same as obtained for the entire sample earlier. Hence, the euro countries have exhibited both unconditional and conditional convergence in their corporate financing patterns. Bond finance appears to have exhibited the quickest convergence, in this case followed by bank finance and equity finance in that order.

We then re-estimate the model specifications only for the countries that were EU members from the beginning of our data period, i.e. we leave out Finland, Spain and Sweden, from our sample. See Table 5.5. Once again we observe that there has been convergence in corporate financing patterns across this sample of countries,

[3]We have experimented with other regulatory and policy change variables such as a dummy for the year 1993 (launch of a single European market) and 2000 (adoption of the FSAP) but the convergence results were qualitatively similar to those reported in the paper. Moreover we controlled for structural breaks in the series (detected by Andrews-Quandt tests for unknown break points) but once again the convergence results were qualitatively similar to those reported in the paper.

Table 5.4 GMM estimation results excluding non-Euro EU countries, 1972–2004

	Bank(-1)	*Equity(-1)*	*BMY*	*ER*	*IR*	*Open*	*Sargan*	*d.f.*
Bank models	0.797						22.83	31
	(0.00)							
	0.796		−0.222				15.16	26
	(0.00)		(0.00)					
	0.803			−0.120			21.79	32
	(0.00)			(0.00)				
	0.773				0.010		20.62	32
	(0.00)				(0.00)			
	0.787					−0.371	20.61	32
	(0.00)					(0.00)		
	0.711		−0.213	−0.366	0.029	−0.782	14.81	29
	(0.00)		(0.00)	(0.00)	(0.00)	(0.00)		
Equity models		0.844					31.23	31
		(0.00)						
		0.826	0.043				12.35	26
		(0.00)	(0.00)					
		0.841		0.058			29.47	32
		(0.00)		(0.00)				
		0.836			0.003		19.62	32
		(0.00)			(0.00)			
		0.836				−0.106	20.27	32
		(0.00)				(0.00)		
		0.749	0.427	0.340	0.005	−0.686	14.56	29
		(0.00)	(0.00)	(0.00)	(0.00)	(0.00)		
	Bond models	*Intern models*	*BMY*	*ER*	*IR*	*OPEN*	*Sargan*	*d.f.*
Bond models	0.303						23.40	31
	(0.00)							
	0.227		0.056				16.66	26
	(0.00)		(0.01)					
	0.302			0.035			26.17	32
	(0.00)			(0.00)				
	0.264				0.003		23.16	32
	(0.00)				(0.00)			
	0.298					−0.075	22.21	32
	(0.00)					(0.00)		
	0.018		0.371	0.260	0.005	−0.627	17.74	29
	(0.00)		(0.00)	(0.00)	(0.00)	(0.00)		
Intern models		1.024					20.56	31
		(0.00)		0.078				
		1.044	0.325	(0.00)			23.78	32
		(0.00)	(0.00)		−0.010			
		1.031			(0.00)		19.75	32
		(0.00)						
		1.015				0.305	19.37	32
		(0.00)				(0.00)		
		1.022		0.291	−0.016	−0.060	12.60	29
		(0.00)		(0.00)	(0.00)	(0.66)		
		1.004	0.502					
		(0.00)	(0.00)					

Note: Sargan denotes the test for validity of instruments (instruments are the second lags of corporate financing variables). The numbers in parentheses are p-values

Table 5.5 GMM estimation results for expanded EU, 1972–2004

	Bank(-1)	*Equity(-1)*	*BMY*	*ER*	*IR*	*Open*	*Sargan*	*d.f.*
Bank models	0.839						22.02	31
	(0.00)							
	0.818		0.070				13.91	27
	(0.00)		(0.00)					
	0.841			−0.004			21.08	32
	(0.00)			(0.00)				
	0.852				0.001		20.23	32
	(0.00)				(0.00)			
	0.817					−0.140	17.19	32
	(0.00)					(0.00)		
	0.826		0.090	0.015	0.001	−0.009	14.44	30
	(0.00)		(0.01)	(0.15)	(0.00)	(0.32)		
Equity models		0.629					24.60	31
		(0.00)						
		0.569	0.140				15.83	27
		(0.00)	(0.00)					
		0.624		0.063			23.86	32
		(0.00)		(0.00)				
		0.634			0.001		19.07	32
		(0.00)			(0.00)			
		0.628				0.040	19.21	32
		(0.00)				(0.00)		
		0.547	0.275	0.200	0.001	−0.287	15.41	30
		(0.00)	(0.00)	(0.00)	(0.00)	(0.00)		
	Bond(-1)	*Intern models*	*BMY*	*ER*	*IR*	*Open*	*Sargan*	*d.f.*
Bond models	0.544						18.86	31
	(0.00)							
	0.472		0.075				16.37	27
	(0.00)		(0.00)					
	0.532			0.035			19.09	32
	(0.00)			(0.00)				
	0.571				0.001		18.62	32
	(0.00)				(0.00)			
	0.546					0.001	18.15	32
	(0.00)					(0.85)		
	0.406		0.144	0.108	0.002	−0.171	17.47	30
	(0.00)		(0.00)	(0.00)	(0.00)	(0.00)		
Intern models		0.794					20.46	31
		(0.00)						
		0.843	−0.114				13.94	27
		(0.00)	(0.02)					
		0.784		−0.096			19.25	32
		(0.00)		(0.00)				
		0.846			−0.060		17.98	32
		(0.00)			(0.00)			
		0.836				0.156	17.49	32
		(0.00)				(0.00)		
		0.860	−0.221	−0.165	−0.007	0.074	15.74	30
		(0.00)	(0.00)	(0.00)	(0.00)	(0.52)		

Note: Sargan denotes the test for validity of instruments (instruments are the second lags of corporate financing variables). The numbers in parentheses are p-values

including internal financing in this case. Considering un-conditional or conditional convergence, bond finance appears to have exhibited the quickest convergence followed by equity finance, bank finance and internal finance in that order.

5.5 Concluding Remarks

Recent studies, based on micro as well as macro level approaches have shown that the EU is undergoing financial integration (Baele et al. 2004; Gaspar et al. 2003; Kiehlborn and Mietzner 2005). In this context, the present paper examines a particular aspect of the financial integration process, namely corporate financing patterns. We examine convergence in the corporate financing patterns of European countries during the period 1972–2004. Employing a number of modern panel unit root tests, we find evidence for convergence in bank and bond finance, but we do not obtain unanimous results for equity finance and internal finance. We then apply the dynamic panel variant of the traditional growth regression approach.

Our results suggest that NFCs in Europe are converging in terms of the proportion of funds they access from banks, equity issues and bond markets. In sum, it appears that financial integration in EU has been characterized by NFCs increasingly taking recourse to bond and equity markets for their financing needs. Hence to some extent this indicates a move from bank-based financing to the Anglo-Saxon mode of market based financing. Whether this has also been accompanied by a shared reduction in internal financing is however not consistently borne out by our results.

Appendix

Table 5.6 Panel unit root and stationarity tests: results excluding non-Euro EU countries, 1972–2004

Method	Bank		Equity		Bond		Intern	
	Statistic	P-value	Statistic	P-value	Statistic	P-value	Statistic	P-value
Null: Unit root (assumes common unit root process)								
Levin, Lin & Chu	−1.49589	0.0673	−0.89357	0.1858	−8.44002	0.0000	−0.11152	0.4556
Breitung t-stat	−4.01631	0.0000	−1.05775	0.1451	−4.72845	0.0000	−1.12894	0.1295
Null: unit root (assumes individual unit root process)								
Im, Pesaran and Shin W-stat	−3.02376	0.0012	−1.00445	0.1576	−8.2134	0.0000	−1.08854	0.1382
ADF – Fisher Chi-square	29.4868	0.0033	14.5715	0.2657	80.4060	0.0000	14.5814	0.2651
PP – Fisher Chi-square	23.1257	0.0267	13.9236	0.3056	63.9975	0.0000	12.1041	0.4374
Null: No unit root (assumes common unit root process)								
Hadri Z-stat	0.39561	0.3462	0.32403	0.3730	0.15628	0.4379	1.20426	0.1142
Hadri Heteroscedasticity Consistent Z-stat	1.46572	0.0714	0.52801	0.2987	0.30316	0.3809	0.52862	0.2985

Note: See Table 5.2

Table 5.7 Panel unit root and stationarity tests: results for expanded EU, 1972–2004

Method	Bank		Equity		Bond		Intern	
	Statistic	P-value	Statistic	P-value	Statistic	P-value	Statistic	P-value
Null: Unit root (assumes common unit root process)								
Levin, Lin & Chu	−1.55054	0.0605	−0.43768	0.3308	−4.68723	0.0000	−1.58974	0.0559
Breitung t-stat	−3.23386	0.0006	−1.5777	0.0573	−3.86892	0.0001	−1.95092	0.0255
Null: Unit root (assumes individual unit root process)								
Im, Pesaran and Shin W-stat	−3.12549	0.0009	−0.76531	0.2220	−4.29365	0.0000	−3.1005	0.0010
ADF – Fisher Chi-square	38.0153	0.0000	14.9266	0.1348	38.5545	0.0000	29.8815	0.0009
PP – Fisher Chi-square	22.0669	0.0148	27.7755	0.0020	30.5764	0.0007	22.5056	0.0127
Hadri Z-stat	3.72672	0.0001	0.57174	0.2838	1.40502	0.0800	1.36157	0.0867
Hadri Heteroscedasticity Consistent Z-stat	1.46576	0.0714	1.53405	0.0625	1.45977	0.0722	2.05805	0.0198

Note: See Table 5.2.

References

Arellano, M., & Bond, S. (1991). Some tests of specification for panel data: Monte Carlo evidence and an application to employment equations, *Review of Economic Studies, 58,* 277–297.

Arellano, M., & Bover, O. (1995). Another look at the instrumental variable estimation of error-components models, *Journal of Econometrics, 68,* 29–51.

Baele, L., Ferrando, A., Hördahl, P., Krylova, E. and Monnet, C. (2004), Measuring financial integration in the euro area, Occasional Paper Series 14, European Central Bank.

Barro, R., & Sala-i-Martin, X. (1992). Convergence. *Journal of Political Economy, 100,* 223–251.

Bertero, E. (1994). The banking system, financial markets and capital structure: some evidence from France. *Oxford Review of Economic Policy, 1014,* 68–78.

Breitung, J. (2000). The local power of some unit root tests for panel data. In B. Baltagi (Ed.), *Nonstationary panels, panel cointegration, and dynamic panels, advances in econometrics* (Vol. 15). Amsterdam: JAI.

Choi, I. (2001). Unit root tests for panel data. *Journal of International Money and Finance, 20,* 249–272.

Corbett, J., & Jenkinson, T. (1996). The financing of industry, 1970–1989: an international comparison. *Journal of the Japanese and International Economies, 10*(1), 71–96.

Evans, P. (1996). Using cross-country variances to evaluate growth theories. *Journal of Economic Dynamics and Control, 20*(6–7), 1027–1049.

Evans, P., & Karras, G. (1996). Do economies converge? Evidence from a panel of U.S. States. *Review of Economics and Statistics, 78*(3), 384–388.

Gaspar, V., Hartmann, P., & Sleijpen, O. (2003). The transformation of the European financial system, Frankfurt: ECB.

Guiso, L., Jappelli, T., Padula, M., & Pagano, M. (2004). Financial market integration and economic growth in the EU. *Economic Policy, 19*(40), 523–577.

Hadri, K. (2000). Testing for stationarity in heterogeneous panel data, *Econometrics Journal, 3*(2), 148–161.

Hansen, L. P. (1982). Large sample properties of generalized method of moment estimators. *Econometrica, 50,* 1029–1054.

Hartmann, P., Maddaloni, A., & Manganelli, S. (2003). The euro-area financial system: structure, integration, and policy initiatives. *Oxford Review of Economic Policy, 19*(1), 180–213.

Islam, N. (1995). Growth empirics: a panel data approach. *Quarterly Journal of Economics, 110,* 1127–1170.

Kiehlborn, T., & Mietzner, M. (2005). *Is there a 'core' Europe? Evidence from a cluster-based approach*. Frankfurt: University of Goethe Working Paper.

Maddala, G. S., & Wu, S. (1999). A Comparative study of unit root tests with panel data and a new simple test, *Oxford Bulletin of Economics and Statistics, 61,* Special Issue, 631–652.

Mullineux, A. (2007). Financial sector convergence and corporate governance. *Journal of Financial Regulation and Control, 15*(11), 1358–1988.

Mullineux, A. (2010). Is there an Anglo-Saxon Corporate Governance Model? *Journal of International Economics and Economic Policy*, *7*(4), 437–448.

Murinde, V., Agung, J., & Mullineux, A. (2004). Patterns of corporate financing and financial system convergence in Europe. *Review of International Economics, 12*(4), 693–705.

Nerlove, M. (1996). *Growth rate convergence, fact or artifact? Manuscript*. MD, USA: University of Maryland.

Trichet, J-C. (2006), The process of European financial integration: where do we stand?, Speech delivered at WHU Otto Beisheim School of Management, Vallendar, 13 January.

Chapter 6
The Financial System in Spain and Portugal: Institutions and Structure of the Market

Antonia Calvo Hornero and Ignacio Garrido Sánchez*

6.1 Introduction

In the EU, there is a general consensus about the need for greater financial integration. It is regarded as beneficial for the improved efficiency of the financial systems of the individual member states, as well as being a factor in promoting greater European integration. It is therefore not surprising that financial integration has been one of the priority areas within the schedule of projects and reforms in the EU.

However, due to the differences between countries it is difficult to identify the precise mechanisms through which the benefits of financial integration accrue and to compare these between countries. The benefits will vary from country to county and will depend on the economic situation of each country, the extent to which it is already integrated within the European financial market and the level of financial development within the economy.

The degree of financial integration is also important for other reasons, in particular its influence of the operation of monetary policy, insofar as it is channelled through the financial system, and the need to guarantee the stability and cohesion of the financial system. Furthermore, financial integration is seen as a key component of the EU single market project, which is further consolidated by the implementation of a single currency, providing more opportunities, greater diversification and better capital allocation. Finally, other potential benefits are the exploitation of economies of scale and scope in the financial sector as well as an increase of the competence of financial intermediaries.

---

*The last version of this paper was closed as of March 2008. Collaboration in this paper by: Mª Ángeles Rodríguez Santos (UNED), Rosa Mª Fernández Martín (UNED), Raquel Marban Flores (UNED) and Ana Fernández-Ardavín Martínez (Rey Juan Carlos University).

A.C. Hornero (✉)
Universidad Nacional de Educación a Distancia (UNED), Madrid, Spain
e-mail: mcalvo@cee.uned.es

I.G. Sánchez*
Bank of Spain

P.J.J. Welfens and C. Ryan (eds.), *Financial Market Integration and Growth*,
DOI 10.1007/978-3-642-16274-9_6, © Springer-Verlag Berlin Heidelberg 2011

However, even if financial integration is not enough to make the resulting markets more efficient, there can be no doubt that with increased globalization, technological changes, the implementation of a single currency and the increase in competition, the EU needs to guarantee a more effective financial system, able to respond to the increase in international competition. Until the mid 1970s, the Spanish financial system, especially the banking system, was highly regulated, concentrated and subject to government intervention. This was a reflection of the development model prevailing in Spain, in spite of the fact that there has been some experimentation with liberalisation following the 1959 Stabilisation Plan of the Spanish Economy.

Spain and Portugal joined the European Economic Community in January 1986 simultaneously. At that time the efforts of the Union to implement the Internal Common Market in goods had been considerably more fruitful than the integration of service industries. The process of integration in services, and in particular financial services, was still in its infancy although the legal basis went back to the 1960s. The need for renewed action on service-sector integration was repeatedly signalled by the European Council in the first half of the 1980s. Finally, at meeting in Brussels at the end of March 1985, it was "called upon the Commission to draw up a detailed program with a specific timetable before its next meeting" to "achieve a single large market by 1992". The Financial Integrated Area was firstly envisaged in the Commission's White Paper of June 1985 "Completing the Internal Market" in which a detail program and timetable was proposed, to be adopted a month later by the European Council at the meeting to be held in Milan. At that moment, the Commission was already aware of the fact that to attain the objective by 1992, it "was necessary to draw the lessons from the setbacks and delays of the pas" and presupposed "that Member States will agree on the abolition of barriers of all kinds, harmonization of rules, approximation of legislation and tax structures, strengthening of monetary cooperation and the necessary flanking measures". Twenty two years have passed since that program was adopted and a lot of "flanking measures" have had to be adopted, including the monetary integration process, to reach the current stage where it might be argued that we are now on track to achieve the integration envisaged in the 1992 Single Market exercise.

The fact that convergence in the main body of European financial markets took so long is relevant to the degree of convergence that could be expected to have been attained by Spain and Portugal in 1986 when they joined the EU. Their financial systems were clearly less integrated when compared with the degree of convergence achieved by the East European member states when they joined; or the degree of convergence that can be expected from future members.

There are several reasons for the differences on accession between Spain and Portugal and the new Eastern European members. On the one hand, the huge progress in the integration of the Union, including in the monetary and financial fields, has produced corresponding development of the "acquis communautaire" in the financial sector of the economy, enabling new member states to take appropriate action to ensure convergence in advance of membership. In parallel, the international community has developed a whole host of standards for good practices covering virtually every aspect of the financial sector management, which was implemented through the International Monetary Fund's and World Bank's Financial Sector Assessment Programme, through a highly comprehensive, integrated and standardised evaluation processes. The result of which is that there is a wealth of new knowledge and regulatory guidance at the disposal of national authorities and in the information-flow reaching the market.

The embodiment of this institutional, juridical and information wealth provided to candidates before their accession to the EU has been extraordinary effective in bringing their economies onto a much healthier path, in terms of monetary stability, fiscal soundness and financial freedom. On the other hand, the market expectations of the beneficial effects of these institutional changes bring a sizable proportion of the medium-term results forward, particularly in interest rates levels and credibility of financial policies, which are to be expected of the new institutional and policy-making framework after a particular country joins the EU, Finally, unlike in 1986, there is now a significant flow of foreign direct investment channelled into the financial and real sectors of new member states, in order to exploit the emerging opportunities in the newly integrated markets. In parallel with this financial flow, comes a whole host of practical know-how in bank and financial sector management, better practices in control, regulation and supervision, applied technology, etc.

It is necessary to note that the available statistics have set a time limit on the possibility of bringing the analysis and/or the information back until Spain and Portugal join the European Union. This shortcoming is due to the significant revision of the time series which is currently underway, as a result of the new accounting rules to be implemented after the adoption of the International Financial Reporting Standard (IFRS), and after some changes were made to the National Account time base.

6.2 The Financial System in Spain and Portugal Before Entering the EU

6.2.1 Spain

The banking sector enjoyed a privileged situation with easy terms to obtain liquidity in compensation for their credit transactions. In exchange, the banks and saving banks had to contribute to the financing of the government deficit and to the treatment of certain sectors of economic activity; granting credits on more favourable terms.

The Bank of Spain, the core of the Spanish financial system, was established on 2 June 1782, by a Royal Warrant of King Charles III as the *Banco Nacional de San Carlos*. It was the first modern Spanish bank, its capital was private and it can be considered as the forerunner of the present Bank of Spain. The Bank Ordinance Law of 1921 regulated the relationship between the Bank of Spain and the private banks for the first time with the aim of converting the bank of issue into a Central Bank. The Law of Bank Ordinance of 31 December 1946, in the middle of the autarchy period, assigned most of the powers over monetary policy to the government, making the

Bank of Spain dependent on the Treasury. With the Stabilization Plan of 1959 an opening-up and modernization process of the Spanish economy started. As part of this opening-up process it was considered necessary to modernize the legal regulations of the financial system and with the law to regulate Credit and Banks of 14 April 1962, the foundations of the new model of the Spanish financial system were laid. The essential aspects of this law were the nationalization of the Bank of Spain, which until then kept private participation and was dependent on the government through the Treasury. The nationalization of the official credit banks (except for the *Banco Exterior de España* – Spanish Bank for International Trade and the *Caja Postal* – Postal Savings Bank) continued depending on the Ministry of Transport, through the application of a bank specialization model (Commercial banking, Industrial banking and Merchant banking) and the adoption of a closed financing model, similar to the one adopted in France after World War II. With the Government Decree of 7 June 1962, on Nationalization and Reorganization of the Bank of Spain, this entity stopped being a private corporation. Over the 1970s, a decisive reform of the Spanish financial system was carried out, in 1977 and in 1981, liberalizing the sector and bringing it closer to the European operational ways. The entry into the EU constituted of the definitive step towards the liberalization of the Spanish economy and financial system. Spain's entry into the EU was going to force the Spanish financial system to adapt itself to the Community rules and requirements of a single financial space. As a consequence, in the 1980s and at the beginning of the 1990s, the Spanish financial system experienced a deep transformation due to the deregulation and liberalization of the system, with the complete elimination of the minimum investment rate and the restrictions on the setting of interest rates.

The creation of the single market for financial services, after joining the EU, caused the progressive consolidation of the banking system, and even though it may happen that an excessive consolidation in a market segment might affect the competition, the financial liberalization experimented in Spain did not produce a reduction in the competition level, rather on the contrary. The competition in the banking system increased when the business expanded towards other activities, away from the traditional ones, based on attracting savings and interest rates applied to their transactions.

6.2.1.1 Savings Banks and Cooperative Credit Associations

The origin of the Savings banks dates back to around the middle of the eighteenth century. The first institutions appeared in Germany and Switzerland. In Spain, the first Savings Bank was in Jerez in 1834. In 1838 a Royal Decree gave origin to the Savings Bank of Madrid (Caja de Ahorros de Madrid), with the aim of attracting savings and placing them in the "Mount of Piety" (pawnbroker establishment), for investment in credit transactions against a collateral in pawn. After the creation of the Savings Bank of Madrid appeared: The Savings Bank of Granada (1839), Santander (1839), Sagunto (1841), Valladolid (1841), Sevilla (1842), La Coruña (1842), Barcelona (1849–1844) and Valencia (1851) were established.

The Royal Decree of 29 June 1953 established that there should be a savings bank in the capital of every province, with branch offices in those towns where, to the discretion of the respective Governors and councils, it would be advisable. The Act of 29 June 1880 had an opposite nature to the previous one, overriding the standardized aspects and respecting the diverse reality in the management and promotion of savings banks.

In 1962, the Law to regulate Credit and Banks strengthened the spirit of control over the savings banks. The regulatory law brought the novelty of financing the small- and medium-size enterprises (SMEs), as well as financing small savers so they could gain housing access. This intervention was made based on the compulsory investment ratio that regulated the kind of assets and the percentages of their resources to be invested.

Until 1977, with the Royal Decree of 2290/1977, the savings banks' transactions were not yet comparable in scale with those of the banks. The savings banks kept a different treatment with respect to their geographical growth. They could not operate outside the province in which their head office was located. With the commencement of the Ministerial order of 20 December 1979, the savings banks ceased to be bound to the territory and could expand all over Spain.

Among the main characteristics of the Spanish savings banks are the following:

- Their private legal nature.
- They maintain a foundation-like legal status. They do not fully fit with today's existing models of foundations since they are exploited through their social works.
- They develop an economic-lending activity matching up with a foundation-enterprise.

In addition to savings banks, cooperative credit associations also operate in the Spanish financial system, that are companies incorporated according to the law 13/1989 of 26 May, whose social aim is to satisfy the financial needs of their partners and third parties through the exercise of activities typical of credit entities.

The number of partners is limited and their responsibility varies according to their investment value. The characteristics of these entities are the following:

- Rural banks or Agricultural Credit Cooperatives:
  - Rural nature; can be local, regional or provincial.
  - Generally they are promoted by country cooperatives and agricultural societies.
  - The final objective is to finance agriculture, cattle raising, the timber industry and activities that may improve the living conditions in the rural community.
- Non-agricultural credit cooperatives:
  - Industrial and urban nature.
  - Were created from trade and professional associations and cooperatives.

The importance of the savings banks in the financial system can be measured by their participation rate in the total bank deposits. In the case of the EU countries the rates are the following:

- Germany, 47.7%
- Italy, 13.7%
- France, 14.7%
- Spain, 10.3%
- Belgium, 6.5%

6.2.1.2 The Stock Market

Madrid's stock market was created in 1831 by King Ferdinand VII, the first trading day being held on October 20. Its first operating stage was interrupted by the Civil war outburst, which provoked its closing in 1936 until 1940. The real trading boom, after the long post-war, took place with the Spanish economy takeoff after the Stabilization Plan of 1959. The development of the Spanish economy and its opening to the foreign trade promoted a significant rise of the Spanish stock market, which went on until the 1970s.

In the 1960s a reform of the Spanish financial system was carried out through the perfection of the intervention systems. The pivotal reform was the Law to regulate Credit and Banks of 1962. With regards to the stock market, the market development issue was established and the creation of Societies and Real State investment trusts were supported. The aim of this was to increase stock-market investments. However, these first attempts did not produce the anticipated results, since the stock market continued to be underdeveloped and it was confined to the share market. That is how a vague period started that lasted until the 1960s, when a decisive reform of the Spanish financial system was launched, that continued until the following decade. In this period the reform of 1977 (Fuentes Quintana Reform) and the reform of 1981 were both crucial. Both resulted in greater liberalisation of the sector, bringing it closer to the European environment.

The modernization of the Spanish capital market is closely bound to the Spanish entry in the EU in 1986. However, it should not be forgotten that Spain then already had a capital market in operation and therefore it did not start from scratch, unlike the cohesion countries. In the Spanish case, the entry in the EU definitively sealed the end of the autarchy to which the passage of the Law on Stock Markets contributed in 1988. This law allowed a notable change in the stock market and the start of its definitive, but gradual, modernization and integration into the European market of financial services.

6.2.1.3 Other Financial Institutions

Mutual Guarantee Societies

The schemes of mutual guarantees were born in the different Community countries with the aim of facilitating the access of small entrepreneurs to bank credits and although, at first, its objective was to grant guarantees, its activities actually comprise a larger range. There is a great heterogeneity in Europe regarding the situation of the companies of mutual guarantee, given the differences in structure, organization and legal systems.

Mutual guarantee companies started working in Spain after the Economic Reform and Reorganization Programme of 1977. They intended to be the answer to the financing problems of the small and medium size businesses; given their small size, they had difficulties in accessing the capital market and medium- and long-term financing. This, together with the scarcity of guarantees to backup their credit needs, the problem worsened by the widespread practice of the financial institutions of subordinating the risks underwriting to the personal assets of the entrepreneur instead of the company's assets. We can distinguish some phases in the development of these kinds of institutions: The initial phase was characterized by the creation of new institutions and plentiful lawmaking, in which the supervision was carried out by the IMPI (Institute of Small and Medium Size Industry), which participated as a protective partner. This phase ended with a crisis period between 1982 and 1986, caused by the economic crisis, which also affected these societies by the lack of experience of its managers. Part of the societies created so far disappeared. There was an attempt to solve the problem by making the guarantee cost cheaper, which made the entrepreneurs reluctant to use the system.

Venture Capital Firms

The activities of venture capital arise, like with the MGS, as a way of financing the Small and Medium-size Enterprises, especially in their initial phase, trying to solve their access problem to the credit as well as its high cost. In Spain, the first venture capital entity was founded in 1972. The main feature, in the initial phase of these activities in Spain, besides the slowness of the process, was the strong predominance of the public initiative; which explained why a high percentage of the investments were placed in early start-up and seed stage companies, to revitalize the entrepreneurial tissue of the autonomous region in which the respective institution was located.

There are two types of institutions carrying out venture capital activities in Spain:

- Venture capital companies (VCC): Public limited companies whose main corporate purpose consists of acquiring temporary stakes in the capital of non-financial companies whose shares are not quoted on the stock market. They can supply mezzanine financing or carry out other financing ways, as well as to provide advisory services.
- Venture capital funds (VCF): Are investment funds managed by a Management Company, which has the aforementioned main corporate purpose of venture capital companies, being the Management Company who carries out the advisory services.

The Management Companies of Venture Capital Bodies (MCVCB) are public limited companies whose main corporate purpose is the management and administration of Venture capital funds and assets of Venture Capital Companies; complementarily they can carry out advisory services.

The Leasing Sector

In Spain, the financial leasing companies are gathered into the CILRO's collective (Credit Institutions with a Limited Range of Operations) since 1977. Its supervision was dependent on the Department of Economic Affairs and Finance. In Portugal's case, we cannot talk about the situation of the Mutual Guarantee Societies or Capital Venture before its incorporation to the European Community, given that they started to operate later. It can be said that the Portuguese financial system is not as developed in those points as the Spanish; in fact, it has attempted to follow in its steps.

6.2.2 Portugal

The Portuguese financial system was a traditionally highly regulated system, with a significant presence of the public sector, scarce activity and reduced efficiency. Its evolution is bound to a political event with important financial repercussions, The Carnation revolution of 1974, to the effects of the financial crisis of the 1970s and beginning of the 1980s; and above all, to Portugal's entry into the EU. In 1983 a gradual liberalization process started, principally in the banking sector, although the benefits also extended to the stock market, becoming more liquid and with greater portfolio diversification.

Until the end of the 1950s, the legal framework that regulated the commercial activity of the commercial banks and other credit institutions was not created. The existence of a budgetary surplus allowed and ensured the viability and passivity of the monetary policy until mid 1970s. The Carnation revolution in 1974 caused significant changes, among them, the nationalization of the Bank of Portugal, which until then had operated as a Public Limited company and to a great extent, was privately owned. The Bank of Portugal that had been founded on 19 November 1846, at first acted like a commercial and issuing bank. Its statute was reformed in June 1931, to hold the Government financing and as an attempt to exercise a greater monetary control. Later on, the capital movements and the trade were liberalized. During that period, the functions of the Bank of Portugal changed, extending to a context of international settlements and reserve management.

The Constitutional Act of 15 November 1975 redefined the Statutes of the Bank of Portugal and for the first time it was given the task of supervising the banking system. The greater responsibilities taken on by the Bank of Portugal in the monetary and credit control and the organization and regulation of the money market; and above all, the entry of the country into the EU in 1986, has transformed Portugal's financial system.

During World War II and the post-war period, restrictions over the international transactions were introduced, thus developing a complex system of exchange control. From 1957 to 1960, Portuguese law forced the banks to hold minimum cash reserves, entrusting the Bank of Portugal with greater responsibilities and an increasing intervention in the credit control and ascertainment of interest rates.

6.2.2.1 Savings Banks

The birth of the savings banks in Portugal was characterised for being a product of the private initiative: The institutions of mutual nature reinforced their activity, creating the "Caixas económicas" and being bound to the "Mounts of Piety" to prevent the economic shortage of the most underprivileged.

Historically they have devoted themselves mainly to attract savings, more than to grant loans or credits. Until the Decree-law of 13 May 1979, these institutions were considered as special, like the investment banks, cooperative credit associations or the General Portuguese "PREDIAL" Credit Company. The Portuguese savings banks have had a significant bound with mutual insurance companies and charitable institutions of local nature, in part due to its savings attracting nature and in part, for its link with the "Mounts of Piety".

The evolution of the savings banks in this country present a double model, the public and the private:

- Savings banks of public nature, represented by the "Caixa Geral de Depósitos" were founded in 1876. Its activity is oriented towards:
  - Granting loans to local corporations
  - Collecting and managing the deposits claimed by the Law or the Courts of Justice
  - Acting as Mortgage Institution and financing the industry and the agriculture.
- Savings banks with a private nature that pertain to the "Caixas económicas". Actually their number is reduced to two, a public limited company and another related to the Mutual Relief Associations and Charitable Institutions.

6.2.2.2 The Stock Market

The financial system in Spain and Portugal has gone through deep change in the last two decades. In particular, the capital market has acquired a greater dimension and scope of influence.

Until its entry in the EU the financial market and especially the capital market was a highly regulated system, with a considerable weight on the public sector. Its development was marked by (1) a happening of political nature but with financial consequences, 1974 revolution and; (2) the financial crisis of the 1970s and the beginning of the 1980s.

A gradual liberalization started in 1983, but its main figure was the banking sector. However, said reform was also favourable for the capital market that attained a greater portfolio diversification and more market liquidity.

6.2.2.3 Insurance and Pension Funds Sector in Spain and Portugal

In a society characterised by the social changes and the ageing population, the insurances provide an efficient way of supporting a country in its pensions, health and social security coverage. The insurances and the pension funds propitiate the generation of long-term savings. For this reason, they have a significant role in financing the economy and actually it can be said that they are the foundation of the complementary social welfare. In this sense, the insurance sector plays a basic role in the economy, contributing to the economic growth and the structural development through several channels:

1. Providing a larger coverage to the companies, improving their financial steadiness.
2. Intensifying the entrepreneurial activity, stimulating investments, innovations and competition.
3. Offering social protection.
4. Intensifying the financial intermediation, creating liquidity and mobilising the savings.
5. Promoting a risk sensitive management in shareholders and enterprises, contributing to a responsible and sustainable development.

Traditionally, the European insurance industry has been very regulated and characterised by the absence of community harmonization. Although with some differences among countries, the deregulation and liberalization process of this industry started around the middle of the 1980s. In Spain, the regulation was quite restrictive, compared to other European countries. However, the increasing competition, together with the gradual deregulation of the financial activity and the progressive liberalization of the capital movements would make a reorganization of the insurance sector necessary.

In the EU, the development of the complementary pension schemes is structured in three mainstays (Lovaina's approach):

1. Social Security public system.
2. The private and supplementary occupational or employment schemes arising in the entrepreneurial and labour relations context.
3. The individual decisions with regard to savings.

This frame determinates the development of the pension funds and insurances in Spain and Portugal. In Spain, the historical antecedent of government intervention in insurance activity is on 1570s Ordinance, by Felipe II, where the obligation to register all the insurance contracts formalized was established, considering those not registered as null. During the second half of the nineteenth century and the first third of the twentieth century, the first special rules appear that regulate the activity of insurance companies (Portugal, 1907; Spain, 1908). In Spain, the first insurance Law was that of 14 May 1908. Later on, other laws were published but it was necessary to wait until Law 50/1980 of October 17 to establish the regulation over Insurance Contract.

Social Security moves a big amount of financial resources out of reach for financial sector entities (banks, savings banks, insurance companies and other institutions). In Spain and Portugal, social security systems have a characteristic to be distribution systems. Each year they distribute the assets obtained from both employers' and employees' contributions.

6.2.2.4 Social Security in Spain

In 1963 the Social Security Base Law is established with the aim of establishing an integrated and united model of social protection, with a distribution financial base, public management and Government participation on its financing. Trying to solve the problem of superimposed organisms, in 1972, the Protective Action Financing and Improvement Law is put into place. Its failure will make it necessary to wait until Constitution approval to proceed with the most important review, the publishing of the Royal Decree Law 26/1978. With the Toledo Pact signature in 1995, a work plan is established to ensure the financial stability and future assistance of Social Security. Currently, Social Security in Spain is regulated by the Royal Decree 1/1994 of June 20, which includes the approval of the Social Security General Law. Affiliation is mandatory and unique for each person's whole life and for the whole system, and payment of the instalments is also mandatory from the moment that a new activity begins its development. It applies to people who practise their activity in national territory.

6.2.2.5 Social Security: Institutional Organization in Spain

- Social Security National Institute. It has its own legal status and it is in charge of economic assistance management and the administration of the social security public system and of the acknowledgement of the health assistance right.
- National Health Institute. It was created in 1978, as a free health assistance entity, when the National Precaution Institute was withdrawn. After the competences transferred to the Autonomous Regions, during the period 1981–2002, it was reorganized and replaced by the Health Management National Institute (INGESA) in 2002. It depends on the Health and Consumption Ministry.
- Social Services National Institute administers social services and later on it is called the Elders and Social Services Institute.
- Navy Social Institute, for sea workers.

– Social Security General Treasury. It is the system-united cash. This Treasury unifies all of the economic resources and financial administration of social security, it has its own legal status, and it acts under the financial solidarity principle (Fig. 6.1; Table 6.1).

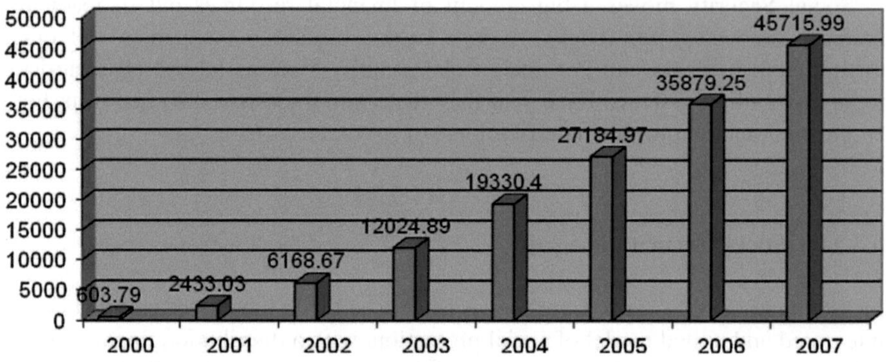

Fig. 6.1 General evolution of reserve fund (Euro millions)
Source: Social Security Secretary of State, Spain

Table 6.1 Reserve fund profitability evolution, 2000–2007

Year	T.G.R, maturity Cumulative	Profitability	Cumulative profitability, p.m.
2000	4.78	4.78	3.37
2001	4.44	4.32	6.04
2002	4.35	3.27	5.89
2003	3.81	2.31	5.18
2004	3.60	2.02	5.18
2005	3.37	2.02	4.92
2006	3.51	2.77	4.21
2007	3.75	3.79	3.99

Source: Social Security Secretary of State, Spain

6.2.2.6 Social Security in Portugal

In Portugal, first step on public assistance was given in the eighteenth century, with the foundation of *Casa Pia de Lisboa*. Insufficient social protection made *Caixas de Aposentaçoes* appear at the end of the nineteenth century. Publication of *Estatuto do Trabalho Nacional* in 1935 established the basis for social protection organization.

Social Security reform took place with the publication of Law No. 2115, in June 1962 and Decree No. 45266 in September 1963.

In Portugal, the insurance companies were nationalised in 1975 and the foreign companies had to accept government representatives among their executives. The Law enacted in 1983 allowed the private sector to enter into the national insurance sector again. Because of the weakness of the re-privatisation process of the insurance industry, many companies established alliances with banks. This circumstance hindered the entry into the sector of new companies, mainly from foreign countries. However, the market opened up after Portugal's entry into the Economic Community. From 1977 onwards, they started working on the establishment of a unified and decentralized Social Security system, through a new organic structure. In 1984, the Social Security Base Law in Portugal, Law No. 28/84, was approved.

With global character, Portuguese Social Security is financed through contributions from workers and companies, and through government or other public entities' transfers. More precisely, the general system is financed by workers' contributions; in the case of employees, by employers' contributions. The non-contributive system is financed by government transfers, as is most of the social action.

6.2.2.7 Social Security: Institutional Organization in Portugal

- At the national level:
  - *Instituto de Gestao Financeira da Segurança Social,*
  - *Centro Nacional de Pensoes, Departamento Relaçoes Inaternacionais da Segurança Social*
  - *Centro Nacional de Protecçao Contra os Riscos Profissionais.*
- At the regional level, they established *Centros Regionais de Segurança Social*

The *Instituto de Gestao Financeira da Segurança Social (Social Security Finance Management Institute)*, was created in 1977, with financial and administrative independence, and its own legal status and wealth. It is in charge of financial management of economic resources assigned on social security budget. Currently it is regulated by Decree-Law No. 215/2007 of May 29. It holds the function of only treasury of the Portuguese social security system, and it administers, among others, the *Fundo de Garantia Salarial* and the *Fundo de Socorro Social*. This institute also tries to obtain profitability from cash surplus through the market.

The first Portuguese legal reference relating to the pension funds is found in the Act 2/71 of 12 April 1971, but it did not have any practical effect. In 1984, the Social Security Act 28/84 of August 14 established the structure of the complementary pension schemes. The management of those pension schemes was entrusted to insurance companies and other entities established for this purpose. In 1985, with the Decree-law 325/85 of August 6, the first legislation of some importance for the pension funds is established. However, the lack of tax incentives made the regulation go unnoticed. The new legislation enacted in 1986 (Decree-law 396/86 of November 25) allowed the pension funds to be managed by companies created for this aim, as well as by life assurance companies. Later, in 1987 tax incentives were introduced for the holders of pension funds.

6.3 Adaptation Process to the Community Regulations

The international financial transactions have experienced an unparalleled expansion since the 1970s. The technological innovations and the progresses in telecommunications allowed brokers and financial institutions to operate quickly and effectively in a more and more integrated and universalised market.

In the EU, the first steps were not easy. The Directive of 28 June 1973, had been proposed in July 1965, and it took all those years to discuss it. The directive regulated, for the financial activities altogether, the right of establishment and the freedom to provide services, laying down the non-discrimination among the national and community institutions as a principle. Nevertheless, the freedom to provide services remained limited to the services related with the liberalised capital movements according to the two directives enacted by the Council in 1960 and 1962. Those two directives were joined by two judgements of the European Court, in 1974 (Rayners' Judgement) on establishment and the judgement (Van Bins Bergen's Judgement) in December of that same year, on freedom to provide services. Those two judgements meant that Articles 52 and 59 were directly applicable at the end of the transitory period established by the treaty, without the need for a new directive.

The banking sector has traditionally been one of the most regulated sectors. All of the member states have regulated the access to this sector and have supervised the entities, although the control method changes from one member state to another. Until 1985, when the White Paper was approved, the community harmonisation in the banking sector was based on the almost total harmonisation of national legislations. The existence of different national laws and the difficulty in the decision making in the EU, due to the existing unanimity principle, kept advancements in the banking sector to a minimum. From 1985 and before the impossibility of ensuring the total legislative harmonisation, the Commission adopted a more pragmatic approach with minimum harmonisation of the different national laws and the mutual recognition. In this way, agreements on essential aspects of the financial services were reached and at the end of 1989 two basic directives were approved: the Second Banking Co-ordination Directive and the own funds and solvency ratio Directives.

Before approving the White Paper on the single market in 1985, the community regulations in banking affairs was materialised in only three Directives. In 1974, the Commission proposed the first Directive on Co-ordination (adopted by the Council on 12 December 1977). This Directive was not addressed to the financing institutions, only to the credit institutions and it is regarded as the first step for providing the host country with supervising means. The proceeding to authorise the establishment of credit entities was established, and a set of minimum requirements were fixed, leaving plenty of freedom to the national authorities. The aim of the second Directive, on bank co-ordination, 89/646/EEC of 15 December, was to encourage the free implantation of EU banks in the community, limiting the legal barriers as much as possible. It established the Single Banking licence or single passport that allowed the free provision of financial services all over the community.

The Directive 83/350/EEC was adopted by the Council on 13 June, 1983 and laid down the foundations for the banking control on a consolidated basis, forcing the national supervising authorities to watch over the foreign branches of the banks located in their territory. The third directive was adopted in 1986, on the banks' and other financial institutions' annual consolidated accounts. The two first directives contributed nothing to the free provision of services, only to the right of establishment of the credit entities. In 1983, the Council presented a Communication on the financial integration, which launched a discussion at a community level, including a series of directives, to co-ordinate the establishment and operating conditions of life assurance, other underwriters, and credit institutions.

Jacques Delors' appointment as President of the European Commission in 1985 gave a great boost to the community integration, including financial issues. The Single European Act was signed in February 1986, the year in which Spain and Portugal joined the EU. In that same year, on December 8, the Directive that harmonises the rules of presentation of the annual and consolidated accounts of banks and other financial institutions, as well as their profit and loss account, are adopted. Some days later, on the 22nd of that month, the Commission published two recommendations as regards to banks, one related to the great credit risks and the other to the integration of the deposit-guarantee plan. One of the milestones of the financial system liberalisation in Europe is the free capital movements. The approval in June 1988 of the Directive 88/361/EEC on the free movement of capital (in force since the 1 of July 1990) laid the foundations for the free movement. Spain and Portugal, together with Ireland and Greece, were conceded with a temporary derogation, with a maximum time limit until 31 December 1995.

6.3.1 Spain: General Overview

The Spanish financial sector has experienced a deep transformation and expansion since the accession to the European Union. Taking the evolution of the financial balance sheet of the Financial National Account as a reference, the ratio of the domestic sector's total assets to GDP, both at current prices, has passed from 4.2 in 1889 to 4.7 in 1995 and to7.9 in 2006. The ratio of liabilities has expanded even more from 4.3 to 4.9 and to 8.5 in the same years, showing a growing dependence of the Spanish economy on the external saving during that period. To get a more precise assessment of the depth and width of this process, it is necessary to bear in mind that the GDP increased 3.5 times in that period and that this quantitative evolution was doubled by a remarkable qualitative transformation. This transformation was not so intense in the types of existing agents as in the relative importance of each one and in the palette of instruments offered to investors. Particularly intense was disintermediation and the financial innovation processes during these years that went hand in hand with the liberalisation that took place both in the domestic and in the international systems.

Deposits and loans approximately double their weight in relation to GDP, and the same increase was experienced by the financial entities as a whole; but the bigger expansion was registered directly or indirectly in capital market instruments and in the institutions providing them: Investment trust, pension funds and insurance companies. It does not mean that the banking system has lost his prominent position in the Spanish financial system, given that the expanding entities mentioned were parts of financial groups or conglomerates headed by banking character institutions.

As far as the three final sectors are concerned: Households, non-financial corporations and government, it has to be signalled that the former one has slightly increased its strong surplus position in terms of percentage of the GDP to 95%, although it has more then doubled its liabilities ratio from 42.6% to 85.6% in relation to the GDP. The non-financial corporation more than doubled its deficit position till −129.6 % of the GDP, having increased its liabilities over the second half of the period in a similar amount as the entire financial system did, showing the intense investment process developed over the long expansive phase of the present Spanish economy cycle. The General Government position moved rather inversely to those of households and non-financial companies. In the first half of the period, the recessive situation of the economy underpinned a steep increase in the negative net financial position that decreased from −31.9% of the GDP to −50.7% in 1995, and starting a steady redressing afterward that brought the ratio to −25.3% in 2006. Looking closer, the result of the powers devolution process from the Central

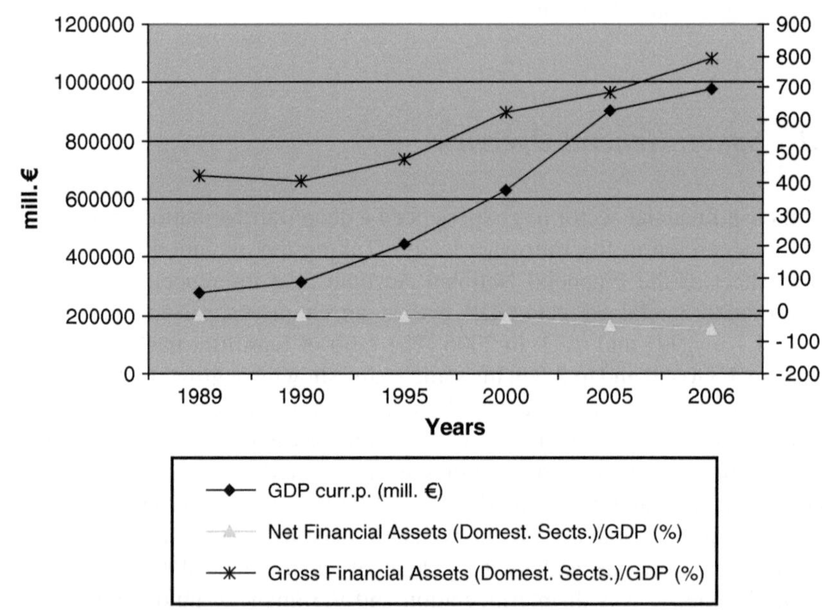

Fig. 6.2 Financial assets holdings by agents
Source: National Financial Account, Bank of Spain

government to the Regional and Local governments that took place in Spain during the period could be observed. This process resulted in growing deficit net position of the three levels of Government and of the Social Security during the recessive first half of the period and then, in the expansive second half, a steeper reduction of the deficit net position of the Central Government took place, with the Social Security changing from net deficit position into a net surplus one and the Local, and above all Regional Governments' grosso modo, maintaining their net deficit positions (Figs. 6.2–6.4; Tables 6.2 and 6.3).

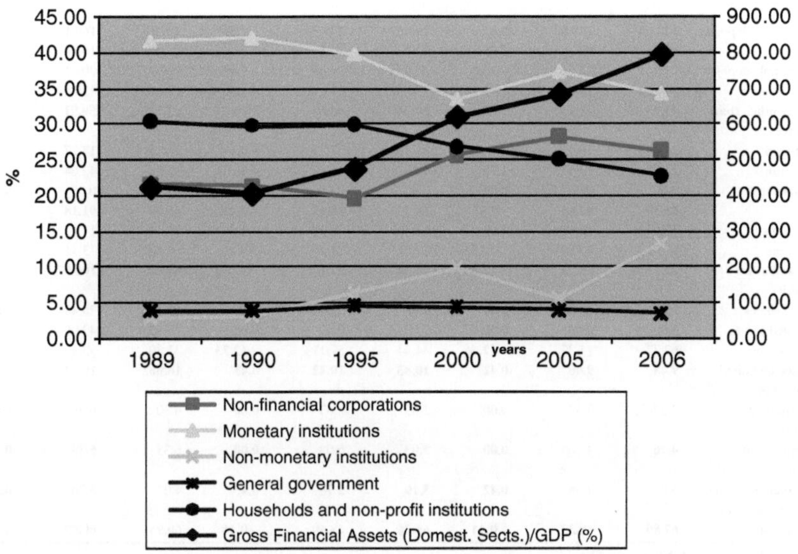

Fig. 6.3 Financial assets structure by agents
Source: National Financial Account, Bank of Spain

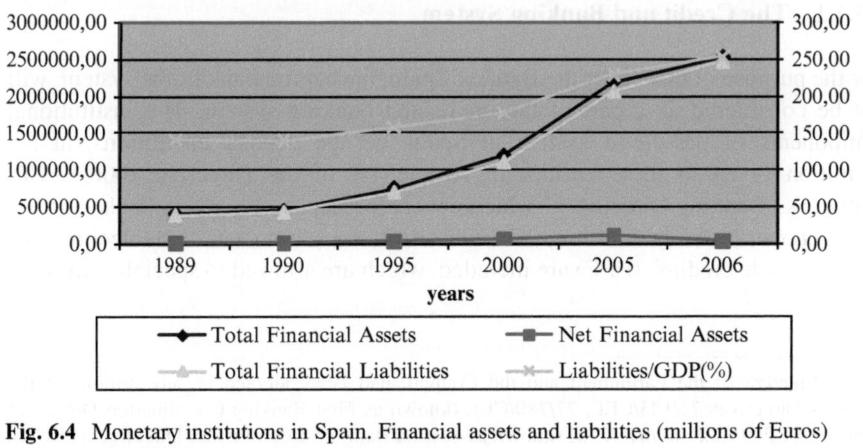

Fig. 6.4 Monetary institutions in Spain. Financial assets and liabilities (millions of Euros)
Source: National Financial Account, Bank of Spain

Table 6.2 Financial assets and liabilities in Spanish economy by assets

	1989			1990			1995		
GDP curr.p. (mill. €)	280488			312425			447205		
Net Financial Assets (Dom. Sects.)/GDP (%)	−10,50			−12,46			−20,54		
	Assets	Liabilities	Net	Assets	Liabilities	Net	Assets	Liabilities	Net
Assets and liabilities (Dom. Sects.) Mill.€	1,187,507.8	1,216,950.7	−29,442.9	1,265,725.8	1,304,665.0	−38,939.2	2,118,241.3	2,210,108.4	−91,867.1
Assets and liabilities (Dom. Sects.)/ GDP (%)	423.37	433.87	−10.50	405.13	417.59	−12.46	473.66	494.20	−20.54
Monetary gold and SDRs	1.14	0.00	1.14	1.05	0.00	1.05	0.63	0.00	0.63
Currency and deposits	148.64	147.82	0.82	143.63	145.99	−2.36	167.67	160.13	7.54
Currency	9.16	9.11	0.05	9.63	9.58	0.04	10.89	10.84	0.05
Transferable deposits	21.44	22.51	−1.07	23.95	24.99	−1.04	19.69	20.61	−0.92
Other deposits	118.04	116.20	1.84	110.05	111.42	−1.37	137.08	128.68	8.40
Securities other than shares	47.95	45.76	2.18	50.34	46.65	3.69	52.52	59.91	−7.39
Short term	25.63	26.15	−0.52	26.76	27.22	−0.46	16.71	17.27	−0.56
Long term	22.32	19.61	2.70	23.57	19.43	4.15	35.81	42.64	−6.83
Derivatives	0.00	0.00	0.00	0.00	0.00	0.00	0.00	0.00	0.00
Loans	85.50	87.66	−2.15	86.57	88.67	−2.11	86.00	91.18	−5.18
Short term	17.93	16.85	1.08	18.36	17.32	1.04	19.47	17.77	1.70
Long term	67.57	70.80	−3.23	68.21	71.35	−3.15	66.53	73.41	−6.88
Shares and other equity	62.77	75.23	−12.46	44.44	57.17	−12.73	89.22	105.97	−16.74
Quoted shares	0.00	0.00	0.00	0.00	0.00	0.00	17.48	25.48	−8.00
Unquoted shares	0.00	0.00	0.00	0.00	0.00	0.00	40.45	47.00	−6.55
Other equity	62.77	75.23	−12.46	44.44	57.17	−12.73	31.30	33.49	−2.19
Insurance technical reserves	9.48	9.06	0.42	10.85	10.42	0.43	16.66	16.33	0.32
Life insurance reserves	2.32	2.32	0.00	2.63	2.63	0.00	6.30	6.30	0.00
Pension Funds reserves	4.16	4.16	0.00	5.03	5.03	0.00	6.33	6.33	0.00
Prep. premiums and claims reserves	3.00	2.58	0.42	3.19	2.75	0.43	4.03	3.70	0.32
Other accounts	67.89	68.33	−0.44	68.26	68.69	−0.44	60.96	60.69	0.27

Source: Financial National Accounts

6.3.1.1 The Credit and Banking System

For the purpose of this paper the Bank of Spain, the central bank of the system, will not be considered as a part of the credit and banking system. The institutional components of the credit system in Spain are the deposit institutions, in the definition given to these entities in Article 1.1 of the Directive 2000/12/CE, known as "Banking Directive",[1] which covers the banks, the saving banks and the credit cooperatives. In addition, the credit institutions known as "Establecimientos financieros de crédito" (EFC) are included, which are allowed to specialise in some

[1]This Directive of the Parliament and the Council, had been adopted in substitution for the previous Directives 73/183/CEE, 77/780/CEE (known as First Banking Coordination Directive) (1BCD), 89/299/CEE, 89/646/CEE (known as Second Banking Coordination Directive) (2BCD), 89/647/CEE, 92/30/CEE and 92/121/CEE and their amendments.

Table 6.2 (continued)

2000			2005			2006		
630263			905455			976189		
−25,13			−48,49			−59,55		
Assets	Liabilities	Net	Assets	Liabilities	Net	Assets	Liabilities	Net
3,910,186.5	**4,068,567.0**	**−158,380.5**	**6,659,938.8**	**7,098,972.7**	**−439,033.9**	**7,752,024.1**	**8,333,366.3**	**−581,342.2**
620.41	**645.53**	**−25.13**	**735.54**	**784.02**	**−48.49**	**794.11**	**853.66**	**−59.55**
0.83	**0.00**	**0.83**	**0.74**	**0.00**	**0.74**	**0.69**	**0.00**	**0.69**
150.34	**159.56**	**−9.22**	**172.32**	**189.55**	**−17.23**	**190.18**	**200.85**	**−10.67**
9.54	9.49	**0.06**	10.62	9.17	**1.45**	10.82	9.22	**1.59**
27.05	28.05	**−1.00**	49.34	50.61	**−1.27**	51.88	53.08	**−1.20**
113.75	122.03	**−8.28**	112.36	129.78	**−17.42**	127.48	138.54	**−11.06**
64.39	**67.43**	**−3.04**	**85.47**	**100.17**	**−14.70**	**79.87**	**115.75**	**−35.87**
8.48	9.29	**−0.81**	8.94	9.73	**−0.79**	8.86	10.62	**−1.76**
55.91	58.14	**−2.23**	75.58	89.70	**−14.11**	69.05	102.79	**−33.74**
0.00	0.00	**0.00**	0.95	0.74	**0.20**	1.96	2.33	**−0.37**
109.66	**117.99**	**−8.33**	**157.17**	**171.51**	**−14.34**	**180.79**	**195.40**	**−14.61**
22.26	23.45	**−1.19**	26.08	25.95	**0.13**	29.08	28.15	**0.93**
87.41	94.54	**−7.13**	131.09	145.55	**−14.47**	151.71	167.25	**−15.53**
194.64	**200.50**	**−5.86**	**219.65**	**223.26**	**−3.61**	**236.94**	**236.57**	**0.37**
58.64	68.57	**−9.93**	51.78	61.87	**−10.08**	62.53	73.73	**−11.20**
76.37	71.09	**5.28**	90.25	84.74	**5.51**	98.84	89.25	**9.59**
59.62	60.83	**−1.21**	77.62	76.65	**0.97**	75.57	73.59	**1.98**
26.11	**25.83**	**0.28**	**29.16**	**28.77**	**0.38**	**29.14**	**28.77**	**0.36**
11.31	11.31	**0.00**	12.11	12.11	**0.00**	11.86	11.86	**0.00**
9.70	9.70	**0.00**	10.79	10.79	**0.00**	11.11	11.11	**0.00**
5.10	4.82	**0.28**	6.26	5.88	**0.38**	6.17	5.81	**0.36**
74.43	**74.22**	**0.21**	**71.03**	**70.76**	**0.27**	**76.51**	**76.33**	**0.18**

specific types of credit financing, but without making recourse to deposits taking to finance their activity.[2, 3]

The regulation of Spanish credit institutions was gradually liberalised since the early 1960s[4] through to the 1970s, – opening the possibility of creating new deposit institutions, equalisation of the operational capacity and regulatory and fiscal treatment of banks and saving banks, nationalisation of the Bank of Spain and attribution

[2]These institutions, regulated by the Law 3/1994, of April 14, were created in substitution for a bunch of specialised credit entities known collectively as "Entidades de capacidad operative limitada" (ECAOL).

[3]It has also the nature of credit institution The Instituto de Crédito Oficial, which has the character of State's Financial Agency. As such, it is subject to a specific regulation.

[4]The Law 2/1962, of April 14, set the bases for the new, modern, regulation of credit and banking activity, nationalized the Bank of Spain and assigned to him the banking supervision of private banks. It was necessary to wait till 1971 to have the savings banks supervision also attributed to the Bank of Spain and till 1977 to have banks and saving banks on an equal legal operational capacity.

Table 6.3 Financial assets and liabilities in the Spanish economy by agents

	1989			1990			1995		
GDP curr.p. (mill. €)	**280488**			**312425**			**447205**		
Net financial assets (Dom. Sects.)/GDP (%)	**−10,50**			**−12,46**			**−20,54**		
	Assets	Liabilities	Net	Assets	Liabilities	Net	Assets	Liabilities	Net
Assets–liabilities (Dom. Sects.) Mill.€	**1,187,507.8**	**1,216,950.7**	**−29,442.9**	**1,265,725.8**	**1,304,665.0**	**−38,939.2**	**2,118,241.3**	**2,210,108.4**	**−91,867.1**
Assets–liabilities (Dom. Sects.)/GDP(%)	**423.37**	**433.87**	**−10.50**	**405.13**	**417.59**	**−12.46**	**473.66**	**494.20**	**−20.54**
Non-financial corporations	**91.17**	**149.20**	**−58.03**	**86.63**	**139.94**	**−53.31**	**92.88**	**163.68**	**−70.81**
Financial institutions	**187.71**	**194.18**	**−6.47**	**182.72**	**185.28**	**−2.56**	**217.92**	**217.85**	**0.08**
Monetary institutions	*176.00*	*181.02*	−5.02	*170.14*	*171.77*	−1.63	*188.06*	*187.60*	0.46
Bank of Spain	23.01	23.19	−0.18	21.65	21.80	−0.16	19.13	19.13	0.00
Other monetary institutions	152.98	157.83	−4.84	148.49	149.96	−1.47	168.93	168.47	0.46
Non–monetary institutions	*11.72*	*13.16*	−1.45	*12.58*	*13.51*	−0.93	*29.86*	*30.24*	−0.38
Other financial intermediaries	2.73	2.83	−0.10	2.68	2.79	−0.12	11.79	12.10	−0.31
Financial auxiliaries	1.17	0.95	0.22	1.12	0.75	0.37	1.44	1.02	0.42
Insurance Companies and Pension Funds	7.82	9.38	−1.56	8.79	9.97	−1.18	16.64	17.13	−0.49
General government	**16.02**	**47.90**	**−31.88**	**15.39**	**49.85**	**−34.46**	**21.43**	**72.15**	**−50.72**
Central government	*9.53*	*36.69*	−27.16	*9.78*	*38.65*	−28.86	*15.88*	*55.56*	−39.68
Regional government	*1.25*	*2.79*	−1.54	*1.18*	*3.61*	−2.43	*1.91*	*7.21*	−5.30
Local government	*3.42*	*6.99*	−3.57	*2.61*	*6.10*	−3.50	*1.49*	*5.54*	−4.05
Social Security	*1.81*	*1.42*	0.39	*1.82*	*1.49*	0.33	*2.15*	*3.84*	−1.69
Households and non-profit institutions	**128.47**	**42.59**	**85.88**	**120.40**	**42.53**	**77.86**	**141.43**	**40.53**	**100.90**

Source: Financial National Accounts

of the deposit institutions' supervision, barred since 1940, opening the possibility for foreign banks to be created in Spain. After the accession to the European Union, the banking regulation was very rapidly fully aligned with that of the European Union, with the exception of a transitory period until 1992, during which the Spanish authorities were allowed to invoke the "economic necessity" criterion to object to a bank creation application. It should be pointed out that in some cases, when the Union regulation has the character of "minimum", the Spanish regulation is more stringent. This is true for the case of the minimum capital needed to create a bank, the provisioning policy or the regulatory capital, temporary restrictions for new banks to freely attribute profits in order to reinforce their equity, etc.

The two main components of the Spanish banking and credit system are the banks and the saving banks. At the end of 2005 the banks accounted for 55.6% and the saving banks for 38.0% of the credit system's total balance sheet. The credit cooperatives accounted for 3.8% and the EFC for 2.6%. There is a tendency for the saving banks to catch up with the banks in domestic activity and even to overtake them in certain meaningful items, like the mortgage credit to households for home buying. By contrast, the international activity of the Spanish credit institution and the physical presence in foreign markets through mergers and acquisitions is actually almost limited to banks until now.

In Spain, the free movement of capitals for residents was liberalised on 18 April 1991. In February 1992, Spain incorporated the countries with full

Table 6.3 (continued)

2000			2005			2006		
630263			905455			976189		
−25,13			−48,49			−59,55		
Assets	Liabilities	Net	Assets	Liabilities	Net	Assets	Liabilities	Net
3,910,186.5	**4,068,567.0**	**−158,380.5**	**6,659,938.8**	**7,098,972.7**	**−439,033.9**	**7,752,024.1**	**8,333,366.3**	**−581,342.2**
620.41	**645.53**	**−25.13**	**735.54**	**784.02**	**−48.49**	**794.11**	**853.66**	**−59.55**
158.94	**253.94**	**−95.00**	**192.51**	**307.73**	**−115.22**	**207.92**	**337.55**	**−129.63**
268.27	**266.24**	**2.02**	**345.32**	**341.88**	**3.44**	**378.17**	**377.86**	**0.30**
207.05	*205.30*	1.75	*254.82*	*253.82*	1.00	*271.60*	*273.34*	−1.74
18.29	18.33	−0.04	13.69	13.72	−0.03	14.02	14.04	−0.02
188.75	186.97	1.79	241.13	240.10	1.03	257.58	259.30	−1.72
61.22	*60.95*	0.27	*90.50*	*88.06*	2.45	*106.57*	*104.52*	2.05
32.26	32.85	−0.58	55.60	56.37	−0.77	71.81	72.62	−0.81
1.57	0.90	0.66	1.45	0.73	0.73	1.60	1.05	0.55
27.39	27.19	0.20	33.45	30.96	2.49	33.16	30.85	2.31
26.87	**71.07**	**−44.20**	**26.48**	**56.92**	**−30.44**	**27.37**	**52.69**	**−25.32**
19.90	*53.89*	−33.98	*15.07*	*41.25*	−26.18	*14.67*	*36.92*	−22.25
1.80	*7.74*	−5.95	*2.90*	*8.23*	−5.33	*3.28*	*8.20*	−4.92
1.66	*4.39*	−2.73	*2.11*	*4.24*	−2.12	*2.43*	*4.65*	−2.22
3.51	*5.05*	−1.54	*6.40*	*3.21*	3.19	*7.00*	*2.93*	4.07
166.33	**54.29**	**112.04**	**171.22**	**77.49**	**93.73**	**180.65**	**85.56**	**95.09**

liberalisation of the movement of capital, getting ahead of the temporary derogation deadline. The only condition that was maintained was the obligation of operating with banks resident in Spain. In order to count with a mechanism of information, for tax and statistics purposes, the obligation to inform to the competent authorities about the movement of accounts abroad was determined. The possibility of carrying a maximum amount of 10 millions of pesetas physically on hand was also signalled.

Although the reform of the Spanish financial system in the 1960s had been carried out through the perfecting of the intervention schemes with the basic law adopted in that period, the Law to regulate Credit and Banks of 1962; it is in the 1970s when the most decisive reform is carried out (the reforms of 1977 and 1981) that would continue in the decade of the 1980s, deepening into the financial sector and bringing it closer to the EU.

In the evolution of the financial market in Portugal, the revolution in 1974 had a great influence, which, even though was an eminently political event, it had important financial consequences and the influence that the different financial crises of the 1970s and 1980s had in its development. However, it is in 1983, when a gradual liberalization process is carried out, the banking sector being the core of the reform.

With the entry into the EU, the regulation of the credit activity in Spain was organised based on several law requirements, among which the following can be highlighted:

- Royal Legislative Decree 1298/1986 of June 28
- Law 26/1988 of June 29
- Act 3/1994 of April 14

With the Royal legislative Decree of 28 June the Spanish laws on the First Directive of Banking Co-ordination (77/780/EEC) were adopted, the credit institutions were defined and the type of institutions included under this definition. With the Act of 29 June 1988 on the discipline and intervention of the credit institutions, a common system for supervising credit institutions was established and the general framework for credit institutions' performance took shape. The implementation of the Second Banking Co-ordination Directive (89/646/EEC) was carried out by means of the Act of 14 April 1994.

Following these rules, the Spanish credit system is organised according to the following institutions:

- Banks
- Savings banks
- Co-operative bank
- Official Credit Institute (ICO)

Credit institutions were added to those institutions until the 31 December 1996 with a limited range of operations (ECAOL) made up by a heterogeneous group of entities and associations of mortgage loans, financial leasing, factoring and other financial institutions, specialised by products that were unable to attract sights deposits or short-term deposits (less than one year). However, if we consider the banking system in the strict sense of the word, made up of the entities authorised to attract reimbursable funds, i.e. deposits from the public, the system would only be made up of banks, savings banks and co-operative banks.

Among the most important transformations of the financial legislation in Spain, it can be mentioned:

- Act 37/1998, of 16 November, on the Stock market Law reform
- Act 46/1998, of 17 November, on the introduction of the Euro
- Act on Financial System Reform measures (Financial Act), 44/2002 of 22 November, to improve competitiveness in the Spanish financial sector. With this Act it was intended to:
  - To achieve a greater efficiency and protection of the customers
  - To adapt to the community framework (Tables 6.4–6.6)

Savings Banks

Since Spain's entry into the EU, the number of savings banks has decreased from 77 savings banks at the moment of the Accession Treaty signature, to 47 nowadays. The sector concentration took place mainly in the 1980s through a taking-over and merging process (Figs. 6.5–6.7; Tables 6.7–6.9).

Table 6.4 Evolution of the number of credit entities recorded in Spain, 2001–2006

	2001	2002	2003	2004	2005	2006
Credit entities	364	361	350	348	350	355
Deposit-taking-institution	–	278	272	269	272	276
Banks	145	144	139	137	140	144
Domestic	62	61	56	53	53	54
Foreign	–	83	83	84	87	90
Branches	56	–	58	61	65	71
Subsidiaries	27	24	25	23	22	19
Savings banks	47	47	47	47	47	47
Co-operative banks	88	87	86	85	85	85
Financial-credit establishments (FCE)	84	83	78	79	78	79
Mergers and takeovers	–	7	6	6	3	2
Between banks	–	5	5	5	1	1
Between co-operatives	–	2	1	1	–	–
Between FCE	–	–	–	–	1	–
FCE taken-over by deposit-taking institutions	–	–	–	–	1	1

Source: Banking supervision statement of the Bank of Spain, 2001–2006

Unlike the rest of the financial organisations, savings banks allocate part of their benefits to social works. This social work is related to the origin of the savings banks bound with the "Mount of Piety", which appeared in the fifteenth century with the purpose of eradicating usury and facilitating the loans in species or metallic, in beneficial conditions as far as terms and collateral security. The "Mounts of Piety" also had an important repercussion not only in the case of Spain but also in other European countries like Italy, where the *Montes de Peruggia* appeared, considered to be one of the first of its kind.

The savings banks have devoted almost 30% of their net benefits to social works in the last 25 years. The endowment allocated to social works has almost tripled since 1995 until 2004. Nevertheless, this increase in the endowment is related to the increase of the savings banks' net benefits during the last years (Table 6.10).

Nowadays 46 is the number of savings banks operating in Spain and some of the savings banks have an important weight in the Spanish financial system (the Caixa and Caja Madrid are among the first five Spanish deposit-taking institutions with as far as total assets). For reasons of geographic proximity of economic influence, some savings banks are introducing themselves in other State members of the EU, especially in Portugal (Aforros de Vigo (Caixanova), Caja de Galicia, Caja de Ahorros de Salamanca and Soria and Caja Duero) (Table 6.11).

For the banking industry, in general and for the savings banks in particular, the technological innovation has been fundamental to continue the growth and internationalization process in other markets. Spain's entry in the EMU, together with the continuous need for incorporating new technologies into the industry, has influenced the rise of the number of credit and debit cards. The number of credit cards in Spain has increased from 16,060,000 in 2000 to 38,490,000 in 2006. In the case of the credit cards issued by the Spanish savings banks, it has also increased

Table 6.5 Credit institutions unconsolidated. Percentage structure of the financial balance sheet (%)

	1989	1990	1995	2000	2005	2006
Total financial assets	**100.00**	**100.00**	**100.00**	**100.00**	**100.00**	**100.00**
Currency and deposits	**28.52**	**27.24**	**32.62**	**19.70**	**16.21**	**15.38**
Securities other than shares	**15.66**	**16.02**	**15.61**	**12.81**	**14.88**	**10.01**
Short term	10.01	10.49	6.29	2.82	1.57	0.66
Long term	5.65	5.52	9.32	9.99	13.04	8.83
Derivatives	0.00	0.00	0.00	0.00	0.27	0.52
Loans	**51.28**	**52.56**	**44.26**	**50.50**	**57.98**	**62.99**
Short term	11.93	12.37	11.24	11.33	10.36	10.86
Long term	39.35	40.18	33.03	39.17	47.61	52.14
Shares and other equity	**0.11**	**0.12**	**4.91**	**14.77**	**9.47**	**9.94**
Quoted shares	0.00	0.00	1.40	3.19	2.80	3.40
Unquoted shares	0.00	0.00	3.39	11.44	6.36	6.24
Other equity	0.11	0.12	0.11	0.13	0.31	0.30
Other accounts	**4.43**	**4.06**	**2.60**	**2.22**	**1.47**	**1.67**
Net financial assets	**5.30**	**4.90**	**7.29**	**6.84**	**5.40**	**2.00**
Total financial liabilities	**100.00**	**100.00**	**100.00**	**100.00**	**100.00**	**100.00**
Currency and deposits	**87.99**	**88.99**	**89.47**	**80.92**	**77.01**	**73.81**
Transferable deposits	15.41	16.15	11.35	13.12	21.32	20.20
Other deposits	72.58	72.84	78.12	67.81	55.69	53.61
Securities other than shares	**3.48**	**3.58**	**3.16**	**4.97**	**13.23**	**15.54**
Short term	0.75	1.05	0.32	0.81	2.25	2.45
Long term	2.73	2.53	2.84	4.16	10.66	12.28
Derivatives	0.00	0.00	0.00	0.00	0.32	0.81
Loans	**3.37**	**2.73**	**1.02**	**0.14**	**0.08**	**0.08**
Short term	0.00	0.00	0.00	0.00	0.00	0.00
Long term	3.37	2.73	1.02	0.14	0.08	0.08
Shares and other equity	**0.50**	**0.54**	**4.78**	**11.73**	**7.98**	**8.62**
Quoted shares	0.00	0.00	4.56	11.40	7.86	8.51
Unquoted shares	0.50	0.54	0.23	0.32	0.12	0.12
Insurance technical reserves	**1.35**	**1.20**	**0.37**	**0.63**	**0.41**	**0.38**
Pension funds reserves	1.35	1.20	0.37	0.63	0.41	0.38
Other accounts	**3.30**	**2.96**	**1.20**	**1.62**	**1.29**	**1.56**
Pro Memoria: Liabilities/GDP	141.68	139.67	158.56	177.26	229.29	253.94

Source: National financial accounts, Bank of Spain

from 34,031 cards in year 2004 to 35,121 cards in 2006 (Figs. 6.8 and 6.9; Tables 6.12 and 6.13).

The number of cash dispensers also makes up part of the financial system's innovative processes, some of these institutions maintain a growth strategy based in technology. The number of cash dispensers in Spain has increased in the past years from 33,940 in 1997 to 51,978 dispensers in 2003.

The technological innovation in Spain can also be linked with the creation of the "*Portal móvil on line*" (Mobile Web portal on-line). Through this system, in year 2006, approximately 363,399 operations were carried out, of which, 6,715 were money transfers and 2,900 securities exchanges. With the web portal, the use of messages sent to mobile phones has increased. In 2006, 6,483,653 messages were

Table 6.6 Credit institutions unconsolidated financial balance sheet (Mill. €)

	1989	1990	1995	2000	2005	2006
Total Financial Assets	419,650.03	458,865.93	764,845.14	1,199,256.59	2,194,559.90	2,529,625.61
Currency and deposits	119,678.26	125,000.80	249,508.35	236,309.73	355,643.01	389,098.30
Securities other than shares	65,715.05	73,494.27	119,387.22	153,618.38	326,566.75	253,208.74
Short term	42,015.03	48,152.91	48,079.58	33,835.44	34,515.03	16,690.28
Long term	23,700.02	25,341.36	71,307.64	119,782.94	286,199.32	223,378.08
Derivatives	0.00	0.00	0.00	0.00	5,852.41	13,140.38
Loans	215,195.22	241,163.17	338,541.70	605,653.06	1,272,375.90	1,593,500.50
Short term	50,077.75	56,774.43	85,950.54	135,848.38	227,438.75	274,591.81
Long term	165,117.47	184,388.74	252,591.16	469,804.68	1,044,937.15	1,318,908.69
Shares and other equity	478.84	567.39	37,547.94	177,078.27	207,794.83	251,520.47
Quoted shares	0.00	0.00	10,724.70	38,262.83	61,410.86	86,111.46
Unquoted shares	0.00	0.00	25,954.70	137,232.02	139,523.09	157,939.49
Other equity	478.84	567.39	868.54	1,583.42	6,860.88	7,469.53
Other accounts	18,582.66	18,640.30	19,859.93	26,597.15	32,179.41	42,297.59
Net Financial Assets	22,246.07	22,500.76	55,763.44	82,053.70	118,418.14	50,709.96
Total Financial Liabilities	397,403.95	436,365.17	709,081.70	1,117,202.90	2,076,141.76	2,478,915.65
Currency and deposits	349,661.34	388,303.01	634,402.82	904,072.51	1,598,887.4	1,829,616.9
Transferable deposits	61,226.416	70,458.28	80,481.856	146,532.29	442,589.63	500,658.24
Other deposits	288,434.91	317,844.74	553,920.96	757,540.22	1,156,297.9	1,328,958.7
Securities other than shares	13,834.528	15,604.601	22,398.296	55,473.248	274,759.55	385,285.76
Short term	2,977.923	4,575.482	2,251.994	9,040.456	46,711.944	60,779.6
Long term	10,856.605	11,029.119	20,146.302	46,432.792	221,307.86	304,331.9
Derivatives	0.00	0.00	0.00	0.00	6,739.74	20,174.27
Loans	13,407.91	11,932.72	7,224.54	1,536.46	1,735.13	2,090.46
Short term	0.00	0.00	0.00	0.00	0.00	0.00
Long term	13,407.91	11,932.72	7,224.54	1,536.46	1,735.13	2,090.46
Shares and other equity	2,003.26	2,373.33	33,909.32	130,997.93	165,639.03	213,752.25
Quoted shares	0.00	0.00	32,302.80	127,370.00	163,142.00	210,899.01
Unquoted shares	2,003.26	2,373.33	1,606.52	3,627.93	2,497.03	2,853.24
Insurance technical reserves	5,375.10	5,234.26	2,633.49	7,035.03	8,432.00	9,471.00
Pension funds reserves	5,375.10	5,234.26	2,633.49	7,035.03	8,432.00	9,471.00
Other accounts	13,121.82	12,917.24	8,513.24	18,087.72	26,688.65	38,699.28
Pro memoria: GDP m.p.	280,488	312,425	447,205	630,263	905,455	976,189

Source: National Financial Accounts, Bank of Spain

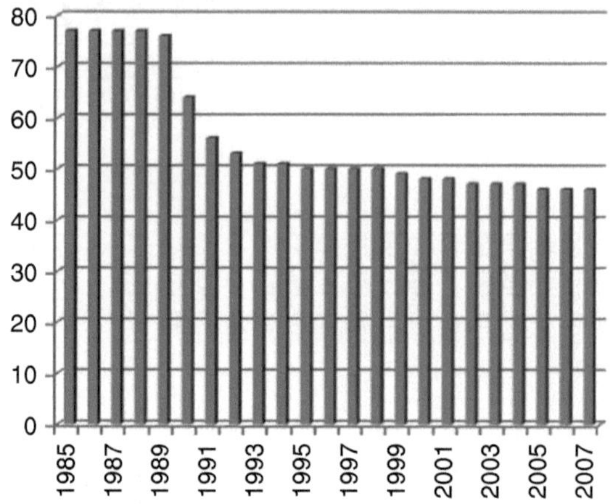

Fig. 6.5 Number of saving banks in Spain

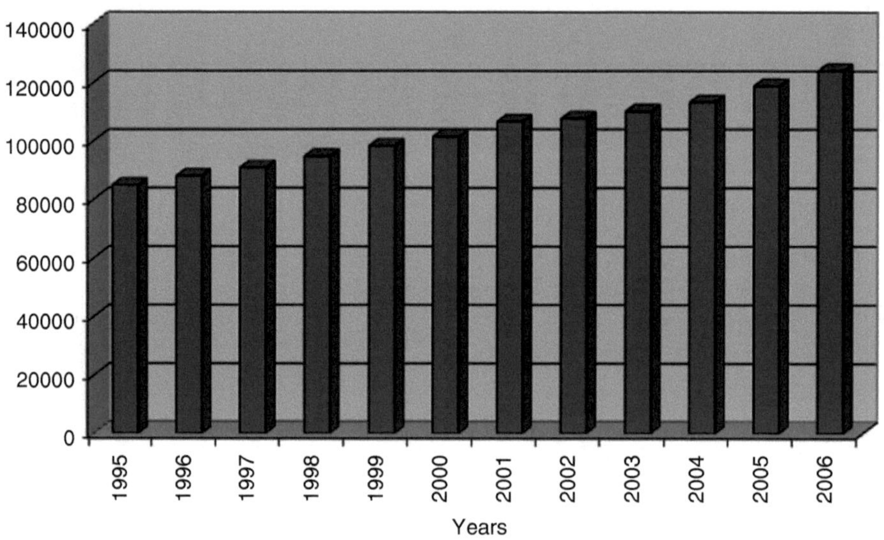

Fig. 6.6 Number of savings banks branches in Spain

sent to mobiles, from the 28 savings banks taking part in this portal to its clients. This "Search engine" is not related with the entry in the EMU, rather with the technological innovation present in the financial industry.

Furthermore, European savings banks take part in the Pan-European service of Direct Debits. Actually, there are 21 savings banks from countries like Germany, Italy and France in this service. The operated sum in 2006 amounts to €5,451,222.

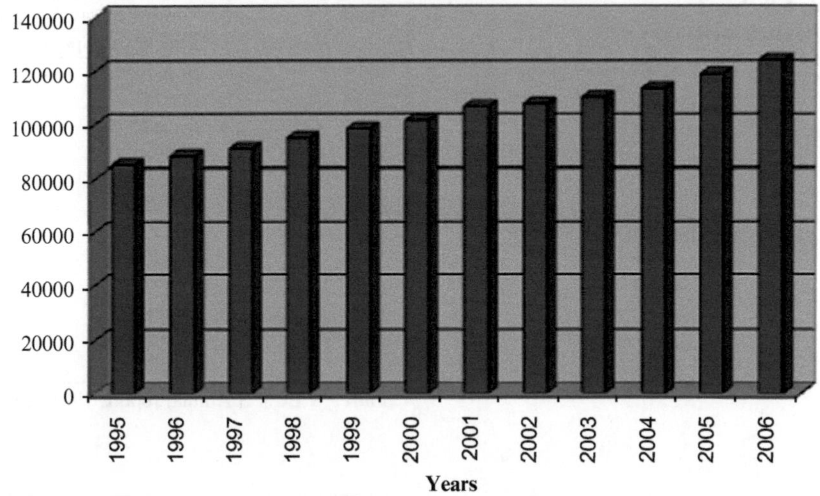

Fig. 6.7 Number of savings banks employees in Spain
Source: FUNCAS' Annual Statement, 1985–2007

Table 6.7 Number of saving banks in Spain

Years	Total savings banks
1985	77
1986	77
1987	77
1988	77
1989	76
1990	64
1991	56
1992	53
1993	51
1994	50
1995	50
1996	50
1997	50
1998	50
1999	49
2000	48
2001	48
2002	47
2003	47
2004	47
2005	46
2006	46

Source: CECA'S Annual report, 1985–2007

6.3.1.2 Stock Market

Euro has outstandingly contributed to the modernisation of the European Union's securities and derivatives markets. Strengthened by the market forces, the European

Table 6.8 Number of savings banks branches in Spain

Years	Number of savings banks branches in Spain
1995	15,010
1996	15,874
1997	16,647
1998	17,598
1999	18,350
2000	19,297
2001	19,842
2002	20,349
2003	20,893
2004	21,528
2005	22,863
2006	23,457

Source: CECA'S Annual report, 1985–2007

Table 6.9 Number of savings banks employees in Spain

Years	Number of employees
1984	63,213
1995	84,866
1996	88,060
1997	90,853
1998	94,846
1999	98,372
2000	101,462
2001	106,684
2002	107,745
2003	110,243
2004	113,408
2005	118,971
2006	124,139

Source: FUNCAS' Annual Statement, 1985–2007

Table 6.10 Social works endowment in savings banks

Years	Social works endowment (millions of Euros)
1995	414
1996	515
1997	620
1998	722
1999	770
2000	867
2001	867
2002	983
2003	1,043
2004	1,190
2005	1,374
2006	1,693

Source: FUNCAS' Annual Report, 1985–2007

Table 6.11 Size indicators of the Spanish deposit-taking institutions according to equity volume to total assets, July 2005

Institutions	Million of dollars	Ranking in Spain
BSCH	783,707	1
BBVA	423,689	2
La Caixa	154,068	3
Caja Madrid	117,588	4
Banco Popular	85,456	5
Grupo Bancaja	59,082	6
Banco Sabadell	57,606	7
Caixa Catalunya	48,799	8
Bankinter	40,052	9
Caixa Galicia	37,503	10
Caja del Mediterráneo	31,030	11
Ibercaja	28,970	12
Unicaja	25,953	13
BBK	22,419	14
Caja Spain	20,303	15

Source: "The top one thousand World banks". The Banker, July 2005

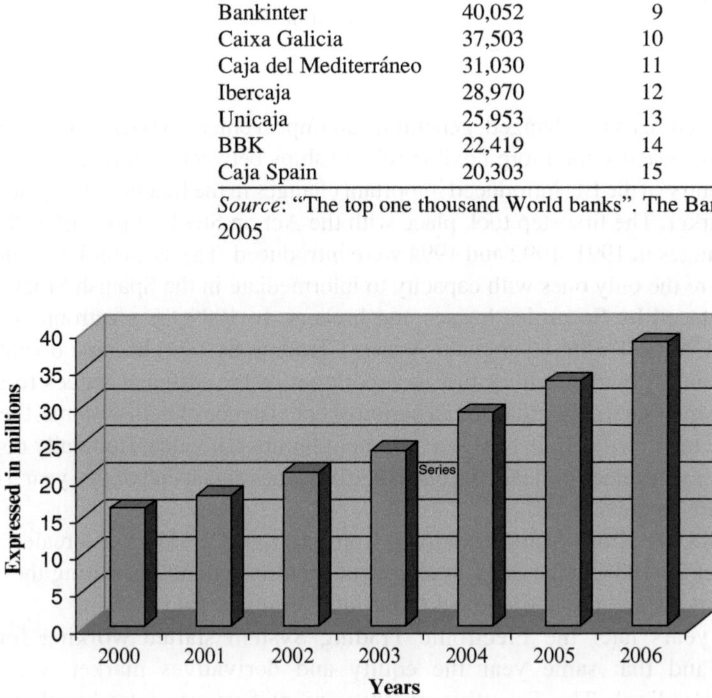

Fig. 6.8 Active cards in Spain issued by the financial institutions

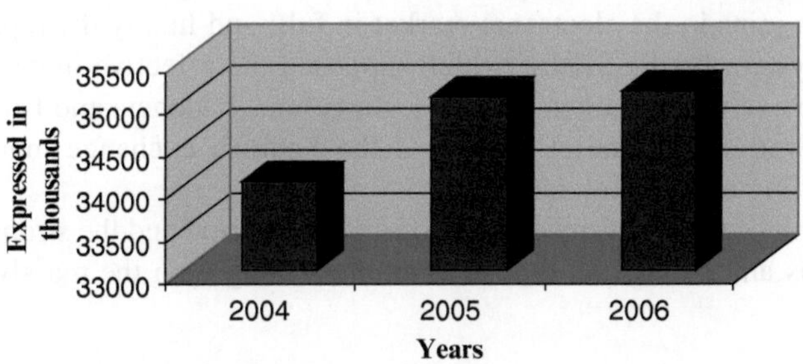

Fig. 6.9 Credit cards issued by the savings banks in Spain

Table 6.12 Active cards in Spain issued by financial institutions (expressed in millions)

Years	2000	2001	2002	2003	2004	2005	2006
Number of cards	16.06	17.75	20.95	23.86	28.98	33.25	38.49

Source: Report form the Bank of Spain, 2000–2006

Table 6.13 Credit cards issued by the savings banks in Spain

Year 2004	Year 2005	Year 2006
34,031	35,039	35,121

Source: Report form the Bank of Spain and FUNCAS, 2004 to 2006

financial centres have changed, generating an improvement in payment and securities settlement systems and more flexible relationships between different stock markets. Spain's entry in the EU introduced important changes in the functioning of the Spanish stock market. The first step took place with the Act on Stock Market of 1988. Later, other changes in 1991, 1992 and 1994 were introduced. The stockbrokers, who, up to 1998, were the only ones with capacity to intermediate in the Spanish Stock Market, were replaced by Securities houses and brokers. In 1989 the electronic system of trading (CATS: Toronto Computer Assisted Trading System) became operative and the continuous market with a fast incorporation of the different values to the new mechanism in such a way that after a period of coexistence of both systems, the trading floor was restricted definitively to a minimum number of values, to finally disappear. In 1989, seven values initiated the exchange of values and at end of this year 51 values had already been indexed.

In 1988, the Stock Market National Commission (CNMV) was created according to Act 24/1988 as the body in charge of monitoring and inspecting the Spanish stock markets and the activities of those intervening in said market.

Two years later the Electronic Trading System started working for fixed-income and that same year the equity and derivatives market was created (MEFF Holding). The Directive on Investment Services introduced the single passport and the mutual recognition that were already consolidated in the banking industry. The 1990s will be marked by the incorporation of technological innovations; like the new clearing and settlement system, which gave origin to the book-entry clearing system; the disappearance of the trading floor for Fixed-income issues which joins in the electronic market in full; and finally the replacement of the CATS system by the SIBE,[5] which supposed the effective integration of the four Spanish exchange markets (Madrid, Barcelona, Valencia and Bilbao), which in turn allowed an unparallel growth of the Spanish exchange market both in terms of trading and capitalization.

The growth of the Spanish economy during this period and the strong process of privatizations and listings on the stock market, along with the massive arrival of

[5]Stock market Interconnection System or continuous market.

foreign investors turned the investment values in a possibility within reach of the Spanish population, attaining the record number of eight million Spanish investors in the Exchange market. It is necessary to emphasise that without the technological innovations aforementioned it would not have been possible to reach these figures. The Euro being the catalyst for a market-driven modernisation of the European securities and derivatives markets: The implantation of the Euro in 1999 hardly had any influence in the growth of the Spanish stock exchange. Its greater repercussion took place in the monetary markets. In 1999, the Financial Services Action Plan was approved (FSAP), among which is the objective of developing the retail markets.

Gradually, new contributions were introduced in order to provide the Spanish market with sufficient stance to compete in the international markets and particularly, to become a market of reference in Europe. Thus, a new index started up, the Latibex, relating to the market of Latin American capitals in Euros. In addition, the "new market" for fast growing companies was created. From 1999 on, all of the securities of the Spanish market were negotiated exclusively in Euros.[6]

In 2003, the Act on Transparency was approved, and like in other countries, the idea was to provide an answer to foreseeable financial scandals like the one involving the Enron Corporation in the United States in 2001. It could be said that after its entry into the European Community in 1986, Spain has made an important effort to adapt and liberalise its economy in general and its financial system in particular. This has supposed, among other achievements, that in the last years, the Spanish stock market has reached similar levels of capitalisation and trading volume as the rest of the European stock markets encompassed in Euronext. The communitarian regulations have been incorporated into Spanish Law, and maybe the most important and definitive was the adaptation of the Spanish Stock Market Law to the Directive on Investment Services, which caused significant changes in its performance. The implantation of the single currency and the coordination of the time zones have acted very positively in the interconnection of the Spanish market with the rest of the European markets and have favoured, without a doubt, the integration of the Spanish stock market in the European financial panorama (Table 6.14).

The Spanish market capitalization in 2005 broke an historical record. 2005 was the third consecutive year of excellent results in the Spanish Stock exchange, thus, the main Spanish indicator; the IBEX35 experienced an 18.20% rise. In 2006 it increased to 26.5% until reaching €831,577.6 million, in spite of the entry of new companies in the market. Furthermore, the new issuances were complemented by the price rise of the shares (Tables 6.15 and 6.16).

The growth of the electronic trading volume exceeded the main European markets, London stock Exchange, Euronext, German and Italian stock Exchange in 2005 according to the Federation of European Securities Exchanges data (Table 6.17).

[6]Even though it wasn't until 1 January 2002, when the Euro started to circulate in the member countries of the EUM.

Table 6.14 Rule-box 1. Directives incorporated in the corpus of Spanish law

Directive scope	Commencement
Coordinating the conditions for the admission of securities to official stock exchange listing	1981
Investment services in the securities field	1996
Prudential requirements	1996
Investors protection	1999

Source: Own making

Table 6.15 Issuances and public offering of transferable securities (millions of Euros)

	2003	2004	2005	2006
Net domestic issue	77,578.1	146,570.7	184,373.5	231,291.3
Fixed-income	75,801.6	129,008.4	180,141.1	223,660.1
Central government	327.7	6,650.1	3,890.0	−4,789.1
AATT	1,784.3	1,533.0	2,792.0	2,055.1
Monetary financial institutions	42,910.9	61,363.6	78,042.4	96,667.6
Other financial intermediaries	31,892.6	59,591.0	95,522.1	128,677.8
Non-financial corporations	−1,113.9	−129.3	−105.4	1,048.7
Variable income	1,776.5	17,562.3	4,232.4	7,631.2
Monetary financial institutions	248.2	15,786.9	1,272.4	2,921.2
Other financial intermediaries	62.4	486.3	−4.7	90.8
Non-financial corporations	1,465.8	1,289.1	2,964.7	4,616.1
Public offering	417.4	2,557.0	157.1	2,485.4
Pro memoria				−6,304.4
Net abroad subsidiaries issue	12,473.2	−30,336.2	−20,652.3	−320.4
Financial institutions	8,325.1	−26,744.3	−15,496.9	−320.4
Non-financial corporations	4,148.1	−3,591.9	−5,155.4	−5,984.0

Source: Bank of Spain, Annual report (2006)

Table 6.16 Capitalisation of the Spanish stock exchange

Capitalization per sector	2004	2005	% 05/04
Oil and energy	90,012	114,965	27.72
Basic materials, Ind. Y Con.	36,858	57,626	56.34
Consumer goods	32,509	40,513	24.62
Consumer services	44,795	48,036	7.23
Financial and real state services	173,241	207,852	19.98
Technology and telecommunications	112,627	103,848	−7.79
Foreign values	182,192	282,471	55.04
Total sectors	672,235	855,311	27.23
Effective figures for each year in million of Euros			

Source: CNMV

The evolution of the Spanish market from the 1990s onwards has been quite notorious. This evolution coincides with the consolidation of the Spanish Stock market reform and the almost complete implementation of the European regulations (Table 6.18).

All of these transformations of the Spanish market have allowed it to acquire a big enough size to compete in the European market, becoming one of the biggest with regards to GDP. Nevertheless, the Spanish stock market is still a narrow

Table 6.17 Average of the last 18 years. Evolution of the stock markets of Spain, United Kingdom and Germany

	Spain		United Kingdom		Germany	
	Dec-12-05	Average 18 years	Dec-31-05	Average 18 years	Dec-31-05	Average 18 years
Ratio price/book value	2.9	1.9	2.6	2.4	1.8	2.2
PER	16.6	16.5	13.9	16.3	17.4	24
Rate of return per dividend	2.9	3.2	3.2	3.7	2.1	2.7

	Italy		France		USA	
	Dec-12-05	Average 18 years	Dec-31-05	Average 18 years	Dec-31-05	Average 18 years
Ratio price/book value	2.3	2.3	2.3	2.2	3	3.1
PER	16.1	16.1	14.5	24.8	18.6	21.2
Rate of return per dividend	3.4	3.4	2.2	2.9	1.8	2.3

Source: Morgan Stanlay Cap. Int

Table 6.18 Volume traded in the secondary and derivative markets

	2003	2004	2005	2006
Public debt book-entry market	21,290,331	22,833,682	22,219,946	22,615,358
Cash	2,246,882	2,136,698	2,338,208	2,903,145
Repos and simultaneous	18,979,902	20,584,242	19,571,854	19,384,782
Term bond	63,547	112,743	309,884	327,432
AIAF fixed-income market	380,197	566,580	872,297	900,202
Promissory notes	261,526	286,468	404,380	481,596
Government and securitisation bonds	86,498	217,368	371,769	324,895
Rents	32,173	62,743	96,148	93,711
Fixed-income exchange market	74,346	82,790	93,191	93,449
Equity exchange market	499,745	643,542	853,971	1,155,682
Derivative MEFF market	292,539	393,666	583,839	933,973
Fixed-income	138	5	0	0
Ibex 35	268,879	371,494	544,064	883,472
Share options	12,714	12,014	16,861	22,936
Futures contracts	10,808	10,152	22,914	27,565

Source: Bank of Spain, Annual report (2006)

market with an important concentration on a few values. In definitive, although it has been spared no effort, there is still a long way left, both in the Spanish stock exchanges and in the EU itself, for the development and competition of other financial markets (Table 6.19).

6.3.1.3 Insurances and Pension Funds Sectors

Article 8.A of the EEC Treaty establishes the creation of an internal market for Insurance Companies. First with the EEC Treaty, and later with the Single

Table 6.19 Rule-box 2 Main facts of the Spanish stock market

Year	Events
1831	Foundation of Madrid's stock market
1868	Creation of the peseta
1936–1940	Closing of the stock market as a consequence of the Civil War
1959	Stabilisation plan
1974	New book-entry system
1988	Spain incorporated into the EMS. The Stock Market Law is approved. Creation of the CNMV (National Commission of Stock Markets), Securitises houses and brokers, and governing bodies.
1991	MEFF Holding is created. The Fixed-income electronic trading system begins to operate. The investor protection is created
1992	Start-up of the new clearing and settlement service
1993	All Fixed-income issues start being traded in the electronic system. Approval of the Investment services directive
1994	CATs is replaced by SIBE
1996	Spain meets Maastricht criteria
1998	The record figure of 8 million of Spanish investors is reached. European Cardiff Council commissions the Financial Services Action Plan
1999	Birth of Latibex. All trading is made in Euros
2001	Stockholm European Council approves Lamfalussy Report
2002	"Bolsa y Mercados Españoles" birth. Euro coins and bills start circulating. Creation of the European Securities Committee and the European Securities Regulators Committee
2003	Transparency Act is enacted
2004	IBEX surges above the 9,000 points barrier. The new Act on Collective Investment Undertaking comes into force. Europe approves the integration of ten new members

Source: Own making

European Act, the aim was to make the citizens gain access to a greater product range regarding insurances, ensuring the legal and financial protection of the operations. The purpose was to guarantee that any insurance agency authorised by a State member could settle down and offer its services in any state member. All things considered, the establishment of a single Insurance market in the European Union (EU) requires the establishment of a structure allowing the insurance companies to operate in all of the Union territory, providing its services freely. The main advances to establish a single insurance market started from the judgement of the European Court of Justice of 1986. The European Single Act and the liberalisation of the movement of capitals on 1 July 1990 (Directive 88/361/EEC) constitute of definitive advances for the constitution of a single insurance market. From the signing of the Treaty of Rome, in 1957, to the ratification of the European Single Act, in 1987, the first directives relating to insurances were approved. The insurance market was opened to the trans-boundary services on 1 July 1991, date on which the third directives on life and non-life insurances took effect.

In the life assurance field, the first directive's objective on the coordination of direct life assurance business (Directive 79/267/EEC) of 11 May 1979 was to supervise the restrictions on the payments for the provision of services.

This directive was amended by a second directive (90/619/EEC) in order to lay down the necessary foundations to facilitate the development of the effective exercise of the free provision of services. In December, 1992 the third directive (Directive 92/49/EEC) was adopted whose objective was to achieve the internal market in direct life assurance, applying the principle of single passport and the supervision of the insurance business by the member state authorities where said insurance company has its registered office.

In the non-life insurances context, the first directive (73/239/EEC) established the legal framework for the set up of the freedom of establishment right in the direct non-life insurance sector. A second directive (88/357/EEC) dealt with the free provision of services in the non-life insurance and had a wide coverage. The third coordination directive on the non-life insurance (92/96/EEC) proposed to coordinate the national laws relating to assets investment, diversification and placement. Insurances other than life assurances, like motor vehicle insurances, have been legislated in the EU independently. With this regulation in the insurance industry, the annual individual and consolidated accounts, as well as the technical provisions of the insurance companies, were harmonised. The Insurance Committee, a consulting body, as well as a forum for the information exchange, the Conference of Insurance Supervisory Authorities of the EU member states was created.

The regulations transformation in the context of the pension funds was more delayed due to different difficulties, among them and fundamentally due to the strategic nature that the insurance industry and the pension funds in some member states had for their social nature. The heterogeneity in the fiscal treatment, mainly in life assurances and pension funds, and certain legal loopholes are among those difficulties. In this sense, the EU was working in the European reinsurance and mutual company's context.

The first time that, in the context of a single market, the pension funds were incorporated into the communitarian lawmaking was in the Council directive 98/49/EC of 29 June 1998, on safeguarding the supplementary pension rights of employed and self-employed persons moving within the Community. Its reach was very limited with little practical effects. In Spain, this directive was added to the legal system through the Royal Decree 1588/1999 of 15 October 1999, on instrumentation of the pension commitments of the companies with their workers and beneficiaries.

On 23 April 2001, the Commission presented a *Communication on the elimination of tax obstacles to the cross-border provision of occupational pensions,* where it analyses the different fiscal treatments and the discriminatory situations, not only between State members, but also between different financial instruments within the same country. The Pension Forum, created by the decision of the European Commission of 9 July 2001, intended to collaborate with the Commission in solving problems related with the cross-border workers mobility in the context of supplementary pensions. It had to wait until 2003, when the first specific directive on activities and supervision of pension funds (2003/41/EC, on activities and supervision of institutions for occupational pensions) was put into place. This directive ensured the enjoyment of free movement of capital and freedom to provide services and guaranteed the protection of its members and beneficiaries.

However, with the aim of achieving a single market in financial services, the Committee of European Insurance and Occupational Pensions (retirement pensions) Supervisors (CEIOPS) and the European Insurance and Occupational Pensions Committee (EIOPC) were created on November 5 2003. Both Committees, closely related, must contribute to improving the regulations on insurance, reinsurance and occupational insurance. They are advisory bodies and are closely connected.

In Spain, the insurance business can only be carried out by private institutions adopting one of the following forms:

- Public limited company
- Mutual company
- Cooperative
- Provident mutual society

The pension funds manager institutions can also be classified into:

- Authorised public limited companies
- Authorised life assurance institutions

In addition, the pension funds and insurance industry in Spain can be classified as follows:

- General insurances (direct insurance other than life). The Private Insurance Regulation and the Supervision Act 30/1995 carries out a classification by class of insurances, based on the nature of the risks covered (accident insurance, disease, healthcare, damages related to transport on motor vehicles, persons, goods, fires and material losses, liability, credit and surety ship, pecuniary loss or loss of profits, personal assistance and death insurance).
- Life assurance. Life assurance plays a very important role in the medium and long-term savings formation. In addition, the flexibility of this product allows generating tailor-made insurances to the customer's measure.
- Pension funds. Pension funds are characterised for being a long-term savings instrument. They are instruments of supplementary prevision insofar as they offer coverage for the contingencies of retirement, invalidity and death, supplementary to the social security scheme.

Laws that have modified the insurance contract law

- Law 21/1990, of December 19th, adaptation of Spanish regulation to Directive 88/357/CEE on services freedom on insurance other than life and update of private insurance regulation (articles 3 and 6).
- Law 9/1992, of April 30th, mediation on private insurances (revoking resolution, section 3).
- Law 30/1995, of November 8th, ordering and surveillance of Private Insurances (sixth additional resolution).
- Law 18/1997, of May 13th, modifying article 8 of insurance Contract Law to guarantee full usage of all official languages when drawing up contracts.
- Law 44/2002, of November 22nd, financial system reform measures (art. 12). Order ECO/77/2002, of January 10th, develops some aspects of regulatory laws of private insurance and information obligations are established as a consequence of the introduction of the Euro.[a]

– Law 22/2003, of July 9th, competition (28th final resolution) – Law 34/2003 of November 4th modifies and adapt to Community Laws private insurances regulation (Second article).

Source: DGSFP[a]Law 44/2002 also involved the creation of Commissionaire for Insured and Pension Funds Participant Defence and the obligation for insurance entities to have a customer attention department or service in charge of solving claims and complaints

In Spain, a rise in demand in the insurance industry has been observed. The pension funds have also experienced an important development, although they are still halfway when compared with EU's most advanced countries. In the insurance field, the Financial Act (Act 44/2002, of 22 November) supposed the transposition of directive 2000/26/EC (on civil responsibility insurance derived from the circulation of motor vehicles). With this law, the Settlement Commission of Insurance Companies is suppressed, whose functions would be assumed by the Insurance Compensation Consortium.

With Act 34/2003 of 4 November, Spain incorporates and gets adapted to the communitarian regulations on the private insurances. This way, the Act 30/1995, of 8 November, on Private Insurances Regulation and Supervision was modified and Spain adapted itself to the directives 2001/17/EC of 19 March, relating to the winding-up and restructuring of insurance companies; directive 2002/13/EC of 5 March 2002 modified the directive 73/239/EEC (relating to solvency margins of the insurance companies other than life assurance); directive 2002/83/EC of 5 November on life assurance (which rewrites community rules on life insurance, including directive 2002/127CE of March 5th, through which directive 79/267/CEE was modified on requirements for reliability margin of life insurance companies) and lastly, directive 2002/65/CE about distance commercialisation of finance services for consumers, which modifies directive 90/619/CEE and directives 97/7/CE and 98/27/CE and includes a modification on directive 91/619/CEE about coordination of legal, regulatory and administrative resolutions related to direct life insurance.

6.3.1.4 Insurance Compensation Consortium

This Consortium complements private assurance activity, when there is no competition in the private sector. This way, protection of needs not covered by the private sector is guaranteed. From a legal point of view, it was consolidated with a law in 1954. With the Law 21/1990 that incorporated 88/357/CEE directive into Spanish law, its new legal statute was approved, somehow justified by the Spanish Accession Treaty to the EU. With the new statute, Consortium was not an autonomous organism anymore (depending on Insurance and Saving General Direction) and it became a government society. Though there have been later variations, the most remarkable ones have taken place in the current century and have been caused, in their majority, by international terrorist attacks.

6.3.1.5 CESCE

The Spanish Company of Export Insurance and Credit (Compañía Española de Seguros y Créditos a la Exportación (CESCE)) was established in 1970 as a public limited company, participated by the Spanish Government and the main Spanish banks and insurance companies. Its initial purpose was to help Spanish companies' internationalisation, and it currently offers credit and finance services through the bank channel, giving coverage to product and services credit sales in both national and foreign markets. Its most important associates are Spanish banks: Santander, BBVA, Sabadell and Popular.

Evolution of economic and politic situation in Spain caused the expansion and diversification of CESCE on the EU market during the 1990s. Later on, it began its expansion to the Latin-American market, creating the International Consortium of Credit Assurance, to which BBVA, Santander group and the German re-assurance company Munich Re also belong. In 2006, CESCE became the owner of 51% of the Mexican company, Seguros Bancomext, currently called Cescemex.

Nowadays, CESCE group offers:

- Credit insurance (CESCE: Spain, Portugal, France; Latin-America: CIAC and Morocco: SMAEX).
- Commercial, financial and marketing information of companies through the INFORMA database.
- Retrieve debts and unpaid instalments through Reintegra, established in 2001 for credit retrieval.
- Technology, through CTI (Cálculo y Tratamiento de la Información), established in 1968.

Within in its insurance activity, CESCE covers short-term commercial risks coming from credit operations between Spanish companies and private or public foreign purchasers. Through CESCE, the government also covers commercial risks on external operations with long-term financing, and extraordinary and political risks in all terms, coming from Spanish commerce and investments abroad (Figs. 6.10 and 6.11).

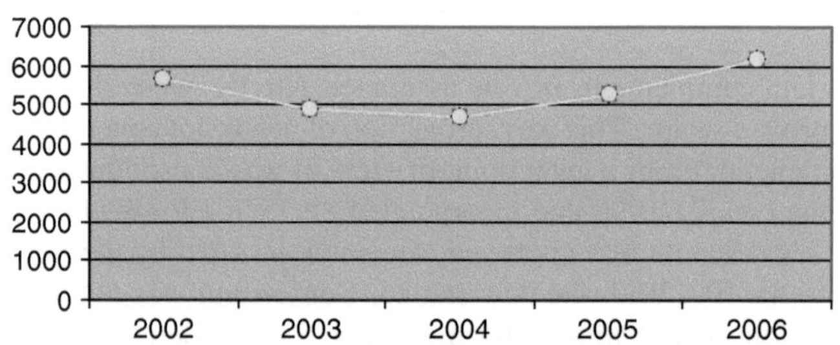

Fig. 6.10 Issued insurance [is the amount of financed credits (main amount plus interest rates, without insured personal participation)] by CESCE, 2002–2006 (figures in millions of Euros)
Source: CESCE

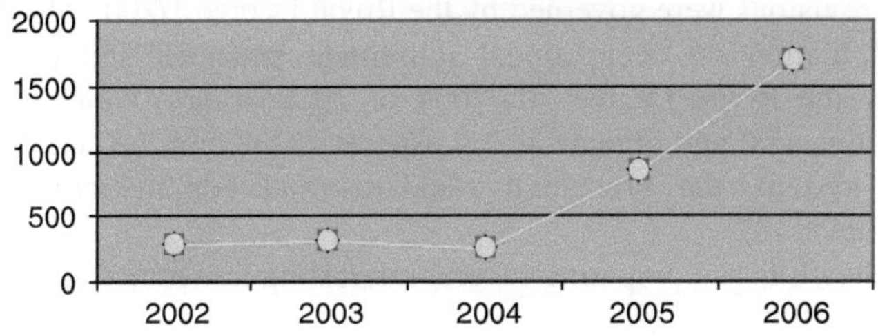

Fig. 6.11 Recoveries, 2002–2006 (figures in millions of Euros)
Source: CESCE

In Spain, the pension funds were regulated by the Act 8/1987 that was reformed in 2001 through 24/2001 Act on tax, administrative and social order measures (which integrates Laws 8/1987 and 30/1995 on Ordering and Surveillance of Private insurances). With this reform, the Spanish pension funds got adapted to the new financial framework, resulting from the establishment of the Economic and Monetary Union.

Law 62/2003 of December 30th, on Tax, Administrative and Social Measures in Spain, and especially the item related to insurance, pension plans and funds, involves modifications to the Pension Plans and Funds Law. Its purpose is that companies promoting employment pension funds can make the necessary contributions to guarantee the economic rights of favoured participants on plans that include definitive retirement assistance systems. It also involves the adaptation to the 2003/41/CE directive about pension funds surveillance and the 2001/65/CE directive of September 27th (which modifies directives 78/660/CEE, 83/349/CEE and 86/635/CEE).

With the Royal-Decree 1430/2002 of December 27th, the Social Precaution Mutual Companies Regulation was approved in Spain. Before that, Law 30/1995 involved full inclusion of social precaution mutual companies into insurance company rules, determining its social aim as exclusive assurance, together with the possibility to provide social assistance according to the entities' nature. New Regulation adjusts the foundation requirements of the social precaution of mutual companies, the insurance activity access procedure and the specialities of these entities. Later on, with Royal Decree 8/2004 of October 29th, the rewritten text of the Law about civil responsibility and insurance in engine vehicles circulation was approved.

Law 26/2006 of Private Assurance and Reassurance Mediation of July 17th involves the inclusion of 2002/92/CE Directive of December 9th, 2002 into Spanish laws about insurance mediation within the EU, which established the legal framework that allows insurance mediators to work freely in the EU. Evolution that has taken place on the mediation field has made new practises not included in Spanish rules till that moment appear (Law 9/1992, of April 30th), which are included in this new law, apart from guaranteeing transparency on the mediation sector.

Through the Act 11/2006 of 16 May, the adaptation of the Spanish Law to the directive 2003/41/EC of 3 June, on the activities and supervision of institutions for occupational retirement provisions took place. Until now laws relating to occupational retirement provisions were governed by the Royal Decree 1/2002 of 29 November and the Regulation on occupational retirement pensions and pension funds, approved by the Royal Decree 304/2004 of 20 February, which regulated the contractual, financial and organizational aspects of the pension schemes and pension funds system, the prudential standards and administrative supervision (Figs. 6.12 and 6.13).

In 2007 they finished preparing several interesting law projects:

- Law 21/2007 of July 11th, which modifies rewritten text of law about civil responsibility and insurance in engine vehicles circulation (approved by Royal Decree Law 8/2004) and rewritten text of Ordering and Surveillance of Private insurances, approved by Royal Decree 6/2004. This way 2005/14/CE Directive, of 11 May 2005 (which modifies directives 72/166/CEE, 84/5/CEE, 88/357/CEE, 90/232/CEE and 2000/26/CE) and directive 2005/68/CE about reassurance are included.
- Royal Decree 1684/2007 of December 14th, which modifies regulation of pension plans and funds, approved by Royal Decree 304/2004 of February 20th, and regulation on implementation of pension commitments by companies with workers and favoured, approved by Royal Decree 1588/1999.

The insurance business is experiencing important transformations. New risks have arisen that did not use to be the object of their business, risks specially related

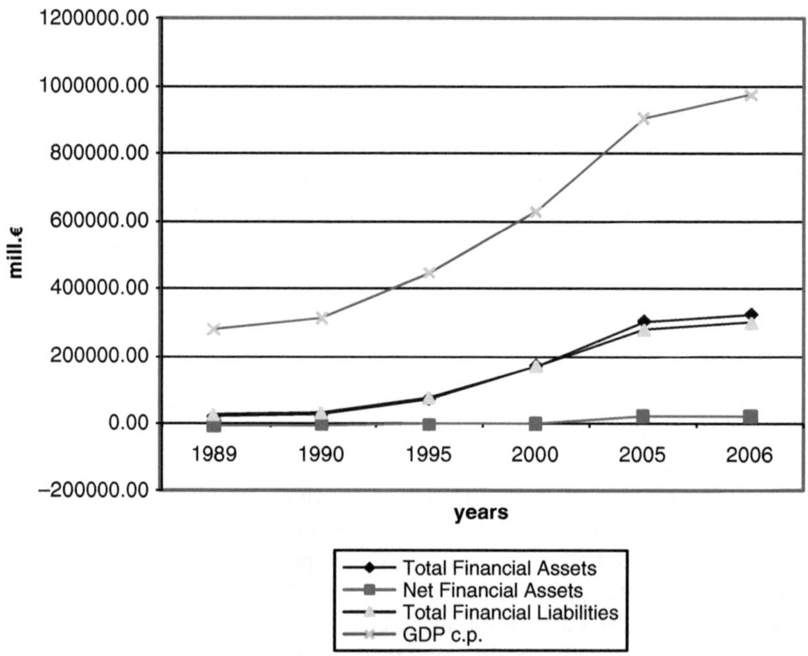

Fig. 6.12 Insurance companies and pension funds in Spain. Financial assets and liabilities
Source: Financial National Accounts. Bank of Spain

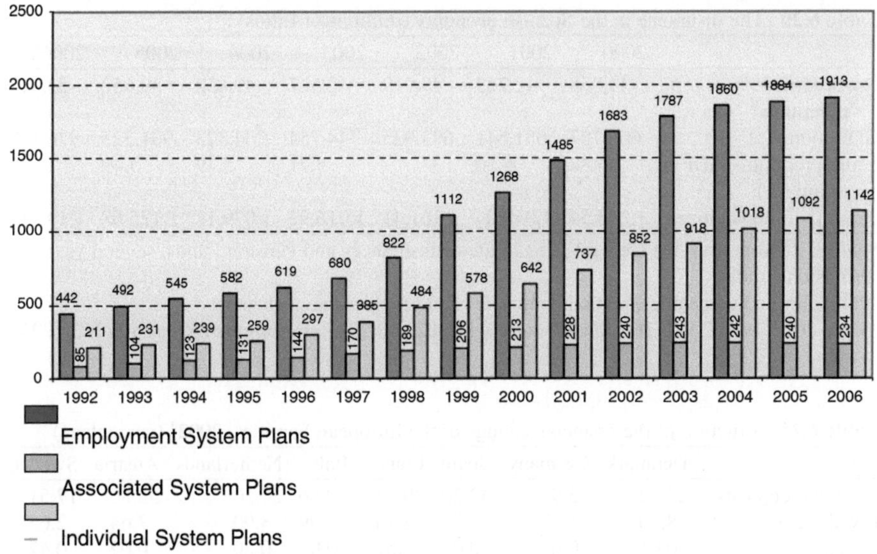

Fig. 6.13 Pension Plans Composition in Spain, 1992–2006, (number of pension plans)
Source: DGSFP, 2006

to the incorporation of new technologies, the appearance of financial products that are more and more sophisticated. Consequently, the insurance industry must adapt itself to the new environment without reducing the protection of the insured.

According to the reports that the General Directorate of Insurances and Pension funds (DGSFP) annually discloses, the private insurance market in Spain is more and more mature because there are less and less deviations from the activity programmes presented by the institutions. In 2006, the First DGSFP Modernisation Plan that had been developed during the four previous years was considered complete. However, the sector continues evolving as a result of the regulations adaptation and the boost of the electronic administration services. In general terms, the Spanish insurance industry has been displaying an upward tendency, experiencing growth rates over 5% of the GDP. In spite of this satisfactory evolution, Spain is below the average of the European markets, for that reason, its growth expectations are still high (Table 6.20).

The portfolio generated by the Spanish households on pure savings or savings insurance, that is, the sum of life assurances and pension schemes, is small if we compare it to the European levels. The Spanish saver is characterised for holding excessively liquid positions and products subject to volatility. This peculiarity can be due to the fact that in most European countries policies that encourage savings insurance, mostly through tax measures, have been developing for a longer time than in Spain. In the late 1980s, the situation in Spain began to improve when, as a result of pension funds and pension schemes tax benefits, an alignment with the most frequent taxation systems on savings insurance in Europe began. Moreover,

Table 6.20 The insurance in the Spanish economy (millions of Euros)

	2000	2001	2002	2003	2004	2005	2006[a]
Gross earned premiums[b]	41,858	42,763	49,919	42,547	49,652	49,652	53,923
GDP to mp[c]	608,787	651,641	693,925	744,754	904,323	904,323	976,189
Gross premiums/GDP to mp (%)	6.88	6.56	7	5.71	5.49	5.49	5.45
Gross premiums/citizen	1,033,54	1,040.04	1,161.41	1,016.92	1,079.17	1,125.68	1,191.15

Source: Reports from the General Directorate of Insurances and Pension Funds, several years
[a]Provisional data
[b]Public limited companies, mutual companies and provident mutual society
[c]Since 2002, base 2000. The data of exercises 2002 and 2003 are formulated based in NC 1995

Table 6.21 Structure of the financial savings of the European Families, 2002[a] (percentage)

	Denmark	Germany	Spain	France	Italy	Netherlands	Austria	Sweden
Cash and deposits	27.42	35.94	42.20	29.23	29.66	24.10	55.80	17.51
Fixed-income	8.90	11.27	1.77	2.10	24.99	3.90	7.64	2.65
Loans	0.01	0.0	0.0	0.61	0.0	0.20	0.02	0.42
Stock market and investment funds	18.66	21.01	36.81	38.58	29.90	11.78	13.53	30.43
Insurances and pension funds	46.65	30.19	15.48	26.42	14.84	57.38	22.25	40.09
Other	1.36	1.59	3.73	3.05	0.62	2.64	0.75	8.89

Source: Eurostat
[a]France data are from year 2001

Table 6.22 Private insurance institutions sorted by their legal form

	1999	2000	2001	2002	2003	2004	2005	2006
Direct insurance institutions								
Public limited companies	272	259	251	247	240	225	215	207
Mutual companies	55	52	51	47	45	44	40	38
Provident mutual society	78	69	70	65	63	59	55	51
Branch offices of foreign companies	39	39	37	37				
Total direct insurance	444	419	490	396	348	328	310	296
Reinsuring specialised institutions	4	4	3	3	2	2	2	2
Total insurance institutions	448	423	412	399	350	330	312	298

Source: Directorate General of Insurance and Pension Funds, several years

Spain is one of the few countries that has had a protection system for the policy-holder since 1985 (Table 6.21).

Another factor that differentiates the Spanish insurance industry, compared with other countries of the European Union (EU), is the reduced percentage that the fixed-income investments represent. However, the recovery of the variable income markets has resulted in a light increment of this activity weight over the past years (Table 6.22).

Also, the Spanish insurance industry is characterised for the coexistence of a high grade of concentration of the business volume in few entities, mainly in those that operate on highly competitive fields and modes (life, motor and multiple risk modes), which need great net worth and management resources with the dispersion of a minimum part of that business volume over a large number of entities that operate in other insurance modes, for which so many resources are not essential. An example of this fact is than in 2005, the fifteen first entities of the sector, representing 5.91% of the total number of entities, canalised almost half of the total output. This structural characteristic has become more acute in the last exercises due to bigger degrees of entrepreneurial competitiveness between the institutions of the national market and of the internationalisation process, which is taking place within this market. Furthermore, since the mid 1980s and as a consequence of the single market start-up, a process of mergers and acquisitions began in the insurance industry that still continues today.

With regard to the merging operations of underwriters pertaining to the EEA (European Economic Area) operating in a system of free provision of services or in a system of freedom of establishment, the Protocol of Collaboration between Control Authorities of the EEA stipulates that the respective authorities shall consult each other, following the same procedure as with cessions of portfolio (Table 6.23).

The structure of the private market of pension schemes and pension funds can be analysed through its main elements: schemes, pension funds and their management and depository entities. In Spain, the system called EET[7] is applied, which is also applied in most countries of the European Union and the developed world. It is based on the principle that income is taxable at its collection time, so in the assumption of deferred compensation and the pensions being both public and private, subject to the personal Income tax; the actual tax system respects the principle of tax neutrality that eliminates double taxation, paying taxes for those rents at the moment of their collection in the form of pension (Tables 6.24 and 6.25).

During the last years, the accrued worth of the pension funds in Spain has followed an upward trend, even in situations of high volatility of the financial markets. The growth of this social welfare instrument is, therefore, observed in absolute terms in spite of the financial context.

Table 6.23 Entities in merging, split or portfolio cession process

Entities	2001	2002	2003	2004	2005	2006
Intervening in the processes	37	30	26	31	23	30
Stop being operative or are cancelled	11	7	12	16	11	15

Source: Directorate General of Insurances and Pension funds, several years

[7]Exempt contributions, exempt investment income and capital gains of the pension institution, taxed benefits.

Table 6.24 Private market of pension funds and plans

	2005	2006	Absolute increase	In percentages
Pension schemes	3,216	3,289	73	2.2
Pension funds	1,255	1,340	85	6.7
Management Bodies	116	112	−4	−3.4
Depositary Institutions	108	100	−8	−7.4

Source: Directorate General of Insurances and Pension Funds, 2006

Table 6.25 Evolution of number and wealth of pension funds, 1988–2006

Years	Number of registered funds	% Change	Assets (equity) (€ millions)	% Change
1988	94		153.26	
1989	160	70.21	516.85	237.25
1990	296	85.00	3,214.21	521.86
1991	338	14.19	4,898.25	52.39
1992	349	3.25	6,384.95	30.35
1993	371	6.30	8,792.74	37.71
1994	386	4.04	10,517.48	19.62
1995	425	10.10	13,200.44	25.50
1996	445	4.71	17,530.61	32.80
1997	506	13.71	22,136.26	26.20
1998	558	10.28	27,487.25	24.18
1999	622	11.47	32,260.64	17.36
2000	711	14.31	38,979.45	20.83
2001	802	12.80	44,605.62	14.43
2002	917	23.53	46,609.91	11.22
2003	1,054	14.94	56,997.34	14.89
2004	1,163	10.34	63,786.80	11.91
2005	1,255	7.91	74,686.70	17.08
2006	1,340	6.77	82,660.50	10.68

Source: DGSFP, 2006

The portfolio structure of the pension funds has experienced great change moving from the domestic investment, and most of all, from fixed income investments, towards foreign and variable income investments. In this sense, the portfolio internationalisation of the Pension Funds was promoted during 2005, which had decreased in the period 2002–2004 due to the decrease in foreign variable income investments.

The reconstitution of families' savings, initiated in 2002 and consolidated in the last years, as a consequence of a deceleration of the families' consumption especially in durable goods, along with the good behaviour of the financial markets (USA, Europe and Japan), made 2006 a positive year for the pension funds, continuing the tendency of previous years. In this sense, it is foreseeable that the measures approved by the Spanish Parliament on taxes in 2002, correcting the personal Income Tax, the corporation tax and modifying the regulations of the pension schemes and pension funds Act, will result in a continued support towards the coverage of the supplementary pension schemes.

If the access of foreign companies to the Spanish insurance market is examined, two sides can be distinguished: On one hand, the institutions with registered offices in the European Economic Area (EEA): and, on the other hand, those proceeding from third countries, since the juridical regimen which they are subject to varies according to their origin. In general, the foreign insurance companies registered in Spain belong to EEA's countries. In year 2006, the foreign capital in Spanish Insurance Institutions represented 27.64%; it was somewhat lower in 2005, with 25.46% (Tables 6.26–6.28).

The portfolio cessions of EEA's Insurers operating under the system of free provision of services or under the system of right of establishment in Spain are subject to a special procedure. As a result, although the authorisation of the operation of cession corresponds to the country where the headquarters of the transferor is registered, the state where the risks are localised will have to give its conformity to the cession and, finally, publish the authorised cession. If the transferor is a subsidiary established in Spain of an insurance entity registered in another State

Table 6.26 Branches of foreign institutions in Spain

	2002	2003	2004	2005	2006
Third countries (USA)	2	2	2	2	2
Germany	6	6	7	7	7
Belgium	3	3	3	2	3
Denmark	1	1	1	1	1
France	9	9	12	12	13
Italy	1	1	1	1	1
Ireland	2	2	2	2	3
Luxemburg	0	1	1	1	1
Netherlands	1	1	1	1	1
Portugal	3	3	3	3	3
United Kingdom	9	12	14	18	21
Total EEA	35	39	45	48	54
Total	37	41	47	50	56

Source: Directorate General of Insurances and Pension Funds, several years

Table 6.27 Branches of Spanish institutions in the EEA

	2002	2003	2004	2005	2006
Germany	0	0	0	0	1
Belgium	3	4	3	3	2
France	6	6	6	6	3
Greece	1	1	1	1	1
Ireland	2	2	2	2	2
Italy	0	1	1	1	1
Portugal	29	27	27	26	16
United Kingdom	2	2	4	4	4
Hungary	0	0	1	1	1
Total	43	43	45	44	31

Source: Directorate General of Insurances and Pension Funds, several years

Table 6.28 Insurance institutions in Spain classified by activities and country of origin

	Registered on 31-12-2002	Registered on 31-12-2003	Registered on 31-12-2004	Registered on 31-12-2005	Registered on 31-12-2006
By activity					
Life	69	79	88	99	114
Non-life	265	284	315	357	387
Mixed	17	17	15	15	15
By country					
Austria	7	8	6	7	10
Germany	39	41	44	46	45
Belgium	23	23	24	24	29
Denmark	5	6	3	3	3
Finland	2	1	1	1	1
France	30	32	36	42	46
Greece	1	1	1	1	1
Ireland	53	63	74	84	92
Italy	34	33	32	34	36
Liechtenstein	5	6	9	11	13
Luxemburg	36	40	41	43	46
Norway	5	6	6	6	7
Netherlands	9	10	11	27	29
Portugal	5	6	6	7	7
UK	84	90	107	115	125
Sweden	13	14	17	18	18
Total	351	380	418	469	508

Source: Directorate General of Insurances and Pension Funds

member of the EEA, the Spanish department of Economic Affairs and Finance shall be consulted on the operation (Tables 6.29 and 6.30).

6.3.1.6 Mutual Guarantee Societies

There are two kinds of members in the mutual guarantee societies (MGS):

- Protector members who have no right to obtain a guarantee from the MGS, and are for the most part public institutions whose sole objective is to support SMEs.
- Participant members who have the right to ask for a guarantee and are partners exclusively for this purpose.

As the system develops, the protector partners' contribution decreases; except when a new MGS appears and the percentage of participant partners decreases. Among the protector partners there is majority participation from the autonomous regions and some private institutions relevant in the area of competence of each MGS, mainly savings banks (Table 6.31).

The Government has been guaranteeing, through the *Compañía Española de Reafianzamiento* (CERSA) "Spanish Counter-guarantee Company", MGSs

Table 6.29 Evolution of the size of pension funds relative to GDP, 2001–2005

OECD countries	Total investments of pension funds (in per cent of GDP)				
	2001	2002	2003	2004	2005
Australia	57.7	58.1	54.4	51.4	58.0
Austria	3.9	3.9	4.2	4.5	4.7
Belgium	5.5	4.9	3.9	4.1	4.2
Canada	53.3	47.8	52.1	48.9	50.4
Czech Republic	2.3	2.8	3.1	3.6	4.1
Denmark	27.2	25.5	27.4	29.8	33.6
Finland[a]	8.2	8.0	8.3	45.3	66.1
France	3.9	6.6	7.0	6.0	5.8
Germany	3.4	3.5	3.6	3.8	3.9
Greece	–	–	–	–	–
Hungary	4.0	4.5	5.3	6.9	8.5
Iceland	84.7	85.7	99.9	108.0	123.2
Ireland[b]	44.3	35.1	39.4	42.0	52.8
Italy	2.3	2.3	2.4	2.6	2.8
Japan[c]	13.9	14.1	15.3	15.2	18.8
Korea	–	1.5	1.6	1.7	1.9
Luxembourg	–	–	–	0.3	0.4
Mexico	4.3	5.2	5.8	6.3	7.2
Netherlands	102.6	85.5	101.3	108.7	124.9
New Zealand	14.7	13.0	11.3	11.3	11.3
Norway	4.0	4.0	4.6	6.6	6.8
Poland	2.5	4.0	5.5	7.0	8.7
Portugal	11.5	11.5	11.8	10.6	12.9
Slovak Republic[d]	0.0	0.0	0.0	0.0	0.6
Spain[e]	5.8	5.7	6.2	9.0	9.1
Sweden[f]	8.2	7.6	7.7	12.4	14.5
Switzerland	104.4	96.7	103.6	108.5	117.4
Turkey	–	–	–	0.1	0.3
United Kingdom[g]	72.5	68.9	65.1	68.8	70.1
United States	96.2	84.1	96.2	99.6	98.9
Total OECD	**86.7**	**75.5**	**84.8**	**87.3**	**87.6**

Source: OECD, Global pension statistics
Weighted total averages used
[a]Data for 2004 and 2005 include the statutory pension funds
[b]Source: Irish Association of Pensions Funds
[c]Data does not include Mutual Aid Trust; 2004 and 2005 data are estimates
[d]2004 pension assets data is from 2003
[e]Data for 2004 pension and 2005 include Mutual Funds
[f]Includes assets from the premium pension system for 2004 and 2005. 2005 data are estimates
[g]2005 pension assets data is staff estimates; 2002 pension assets data is 2001

warrants and guarantee operations, an activity that has widened and diversified since 2000 with the collaboration of the European Investment Fund (EIF); the collaboration of the Ministry of Science and Technology in the investment and innovation operations; and the collaboration of the Department of Agriculture, Fisheries and Food through the FROM program (Regulation and Organization Fund for the Fish and Marine Cultures Market) , in operations involving the fishing sector.

Table 6.30 Evolution of pension funds on international framework

Variable		1000: Investment									
Units		USD: US Dollars (millions)									
Years		1997	1998	1999	2000	2001	2002	2003	2004	2005	2006
Type	Country										
A1: Pension funds	Australia	–	–	–	–	268,181	281,376	348,860	341,355	415,299	492,338
	Austria	–	–	–	–	5,675	7,863	10,551	12,884	14,573	15,611
	Belgium	–	–	–	–	12,775	12,428	12,152	14,355	16,549	16,769
	Canada	–	–	–	–	351,615	355,922	410,224	477,439	570,385	678,952
	Czech Republic	–	–	–	–	1,404	2,053	2,852	3,884	5,152	6,462
	Denmark	–	–	–	–	43,639	45,288	60,646	75,328	87,032	89,570
	Finland	–	–	–	–	61,972	66,725	88,798	117,055	134,163	149,497
	France	–	–	–	–	–[d]	–[d]	22,595	24,849	24,856	25,094
	Germany	67,409	70,781	71,737	65,451	65,147	70,470	88,887	104,161	112,587	122,764
	Greece	–	–	–	–	–[d]	–[d]	–[d]	–[d]	–[d]	–[d]
	Hungary	–	–	–	–	2,071	2,976	4,397	6,989	9,338	10,978
	Iceland	–	–	–	–	6,636	7,481	10,781	14,103	19,517	21,672
	Ireland	–	–	–	–	45,807	42,231	62,645	77,447	96,856	110,093
	Italy	–	–	–	–	19,582[n]	21,751[n]	36,787	44,351	49,520	55,681
	Japan	–	–	–	–	580,519	561,645	477,322	373,380	301,994	–[d]
	Korea	–	–	–	–	–[d]	8,438	9,884	11,516	14,652	25,829
	Luxembourg	–	–	–	–	–[c]	–[c]	–[c]	116	398	455
	Mexico	–	–	–	–	26,600	33,643	37,213	42,718	76,409	96,470
	Netherlands	398,977	425,307	477,554	437,109	411,460	374,875	545,239	659,839	769,986	843,011
	New Zealand	–	–	–	–	7,687	7,865	9,094	11,157	12,446	13,120
	Norway	–	–	–	–	9,389	10,596	14,565	16,939	20,266	22,874
	Poland	–	–	548	2,222	4,624	7,623	11,560	17,140	26,513	37,964
	Portugal	–	–	13,622	12,677	13,278	14,657	18,396	18,868	23,591	26,581
	Slovak Republic	–	–	–	–	0	0	7	0	293	1,537
	Spain	–	–	–	–	35,072	39,061	54,778	69,147	81,551	92,527
	Sweden		–[d]	–[d]	–[d]	18,254	18,542	23,457	26,373	33,211	36,397
	Switzerland	251,728	278,354	299,454	275,649	261,357	267,554	334,829	389,497	434,746	465,497
	Turkey	–	–	–	–	–	–	–	1,539	3,245	3,965
	United Kingdom	–	–	–	–	1,040,472	930,832	1,175,335	1,467,118	1,763,762	2,003,503
	United States	6,238,456	6,976,063	7,786,730	7,639,718	7,207,878	6,593,058	7,913,957	8,599,308	8,979,361	9,721,120

Source: OECD Global Pension Statistics*c* Confidential; *d* No data; *n* Estimated at national level

Table 6.31 Partners' participation percentage of mutual guarantee societies

	1995	1996	1997	1998	1999	2000	2001	2002	2003	2004	2005	2006
Protector partners	52.3	51.5	50.9	48.6	47.9	47.2	44.5	42.8	44.2	41.6	38.0	40.8
Participant partners	47.7	48.5	49.1	51.4	52.1	52.8	55.5	57.2	55.9	58.4	62.0	59.2

Source: CESGAR and Bank of Spain

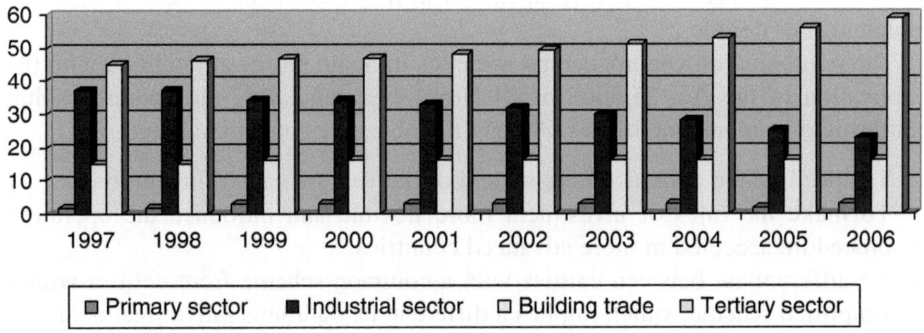

Fig. 6.14 Exposure per sectors (Percentage)
Source: Bank of Spain

Nowadays, 23 societies of reciprocal guarantee exist in Spain (one of them is being winded-up). In spite of the small number, it is a very heterogeneous sector, since the majority of them perform in a specific territorial base, restricted to an autonomous region or part of it, and the remaining are sectored, i.e. restricted to the transport sector or leisure and games sector. With the years, a decrease in the industrial sector's importance in favour of the tertiary sector has been observed (Fig. 6.14).

As from 1986, coinciding with Spain's entry into the European Union, the system of mutual guarantee began to fulfil the objectives, for which it was created. Nevertheless, after the Act 26/1988 on discipline and intervention of credit institutions, when a substantial change took place, the mutual guarantee societies passed to be under the supervision of the Bank of Spain. It is then that the deficiencies of the system started to reveal themselves at exercising a most thorough control. Some societies are unviable and in most of these societies, their own resources are not enough for bearing the assumed risk. The need to reform the system comes into question, in order to endow it bigger solvency and to make it more operative. The result is the enactment of Act 1/1994 of 11 March on the legal system of the mutual guarantee societies (currently in force), with which: the corporate purpose is enlarged to incorporate the provision of assistance and financial advising services to its members; the minimum capital amount rises substantially; and the guaranty fund is replaced by the technical reserve.

6.3.1.7 Venture Capital Firms

From 1987 to the early 1990s, this financial activity passed mainly to the private initiative, raising the existent societies spectacularly both in number and in resources. From then on, it can be said that the structure of the sector approaches the structure of the countries around us. The consolidation of these types of societies took place during the 1990s. The period of uncertainty produced by the technological values crisis in 2000 and the economic deceleration at the start of this decade affected the activity of these firms, certain recuperation in the sector being observed since the middle of this decade.

The regulation on venture capital societies in Spain has been modified with the publication of the Act 25/2005 of 24 November, regulating the venture capital entities and its managing bodies. Among the objectives of this Act are:

- To speed up the administrative system of the venture capital institutions.
- To make the rules of investment more flexible and introduce the operating procedure accepted in more advanced countries.
- To differentiate between entities with a common scheme from entities with a simplified scheme, which implies a differentiated administrative treatment.
- To enlarge the advising scope of the firms and their managing bodies.
- To allow venture capital firms' holdings in non-financial companies to be quoted in the first market with the aim of excluding them from the listing.

In spite of a favourable regulatory and tax framework, the countries with more weight in this industry are Greece, Ireland and Denmark. The investment directed towards the venture capital industry in Spain is still below the European average (4.5% against 6.4%) (Fig. 6.15).

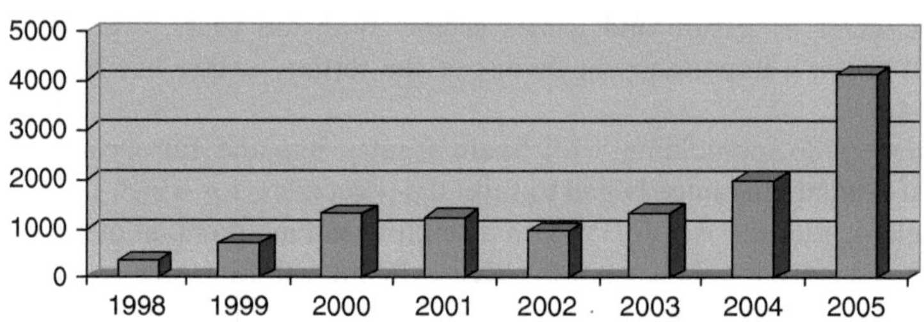

Fig. 6.15 Investments made in Spain (Millions of Euros)
Source: ASCRI (Spanish Venture Capital Association)

With the aim of encouraging the investment in this industry, the Spanish Government has incorporated some initiatives; among them the programme NEO-TEC Venture capital (New Technological Companies) stands out as a joint programme of the Centre for the Development of Industrial Technology (CDTI) and the European Investment Fund (EIF). The programme intents to invest

€176 million for its investment engaged during the period 2006–2010 (fast scenario) or 2006–2012 (slow scenario). With this, the aim is to contribute to the creation of a sound Spanish sector of venture capital in the segment of advanced technologies, avoiding fast answers in what should be a long-term activity, relying on the participation of the private financial and entrepreneurship industries.

At a European level, there are no specific directives for the mutual guarantee activities, venture capital or leasing, therefore, some directives that are more generic, relating to the financial system are applicable (Table 6.32).

Table 6.32 Rule-box 3 Applicable regulations: Mutual Guarantee Society – Venture capital society – Leasing Society

	Spanish regulations	European regulations	Level of adaptation (transposition)
Mutual Guarantee Societies	Act 1/1994 of 11 March. Mutual Guarantee Societies legal system Royal-decree 2345/1996 of 8 November. Standards on administrative authorisation and solvency requirements of the Mutual Guarantee Societies	Directive 2006/48/EC of 14 June 2006 on the taking-up and pursuit of the business of credit institutions	N/A
Venture capital societies	Act 25/2005, of 24 November, regulating venture capital firms and its managing companies		N/A
Financial leasing societies (leasing)	Act 3/1994 of 14 April, Adaptation of the Spanish Law with regards to credit Institutions to the second Banking Coordination Directive Law 26/1988 of 29 July. Discipline and Intervention on Credit Institutions	Directive 646/89/EEC. Second Banking Coordination Directive	N/A

Source: Bank of Spain and web page of the European Union

6.3.1.8 The Leasing Sector

Continuing with the ways in which the small and medium-sized enterprises can obtain financing, we find the sector of the financial leasing. The main advantage of leasing is that companies have access to technological innovations without being forced to lock up a significant amount of their capital, in addition to having a flexible financing modality that can be adapted to each particular case (Figs. 6.16–6.18).

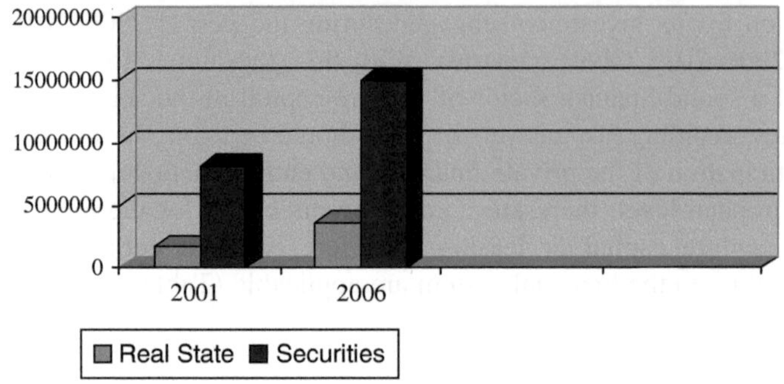

Fig. 6.16 New investments in leasing as of 31-12-2001 and as of 31-12-2006 (Thousands of Euros)
Source: Leasing Spanish Association

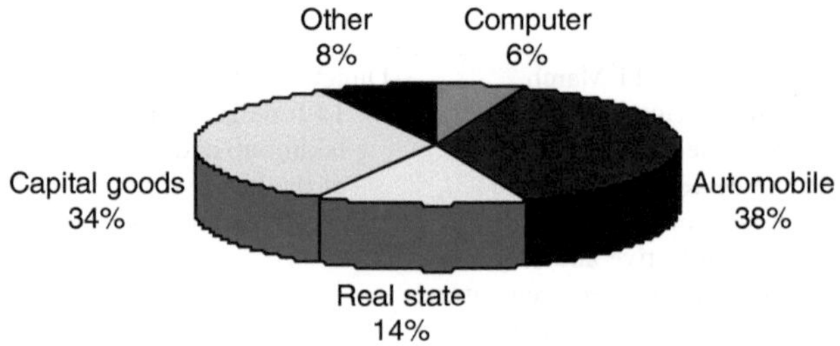

Fig. 6.17 New investment in leasing per sectors. 1996
Source: Leasing Spanish Association

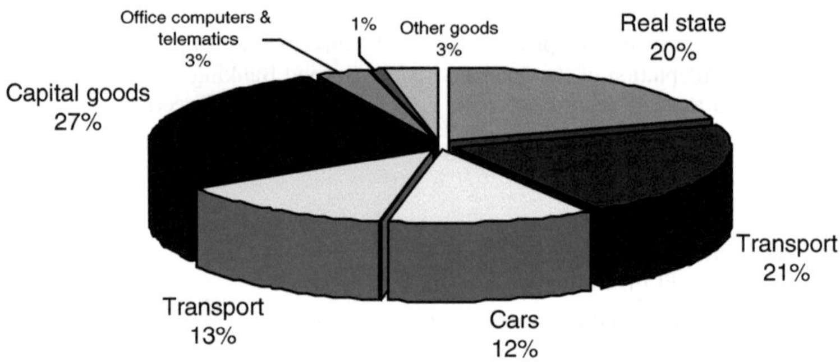

Fig. 6.18 New leasing investment per sectors. 2006
Source: Leasing Spanish Association

6.3.1.9 The Enterprise and the Technological Innovation

The Aid Scheme on Innovation for Small and Medium-Size Enterprises "InnoEmpresa" (2007–2013)

The SMEs in Spain represent a substantial part of the entrepreneurial framework. This programme takes advantage of the experience of a previous programme, the

Consolidation and Competitiveness Plan for SME (2001–2006), but it incorporates new aspects to be better adapted to the current conditions of the markets. It prioritises the following (1) Aid lines directly related with the improvement of the innovation capacity of the enterprises in a wide sense, not limited to technological innovations, (2) The opening of all aid lines at the direct request of the SME, (3) An increase in the aid limit for investments in tangible or intangible assets and (4) Specific attention to be paid to the projects to be developed by different companies and bodies in a collaboration or consortium regime.

The aid lines can be synthesised in three big groups:

– Organisational Innovation and Advanced Management
– Technological Innovation and Quality
– Joint or "consortium" Innovation projects

The beneficiaries of the aids are:

– Small and medium-size enterprises with one or more employees.
– Intermediate bodies (Public or private non-profit organisations that usually provide services to support SMEs' innovation and have enough material and human resources).

The Programme InnoEmpresa (2007–2013) has a budget estimated at €500 million for the period 2007–2013, taking the co-financing of the European Regional Development Fund (ERDF) of approximately €95 million into account, and the additional funding of those autonomous regions deciding to do so, within the framework of the Sectoral Conference on the small and medium-size enterprise. The number of projects and the number of enterprises that could benefit from the scheme are estimated at 11,000 and 60,000, respectively, as well as an induced private investment that could reach €1,500 million.

6.3.2 Portugal

In October 1990 the new constitutional law on the Bank of Portugal was published. Important innovations were introduced regarding the restrictions imposed over the financing of public deficits and other dispositions to ensure greater independence for the Bank of Portugal. In April 1992, the Portuguese escudo entered into the mechanism of Exchange Rates of the European Monetary System and in December of the same year, it was decided to complete the liberalisation of capital movement allowing the escudo to become completely convertible.

The prices stability began to become the principal objective of the Bank of Portugal while the independence of the monetary policy was intensified. In January 1998, the Bank of Portugal Constitutional law (approved through the Act 5/98 and amended through the Decree-Laws 118/2001 of 17 April, 50/2004 of 10 March, and 39/2007 of 20 March 2007) was modified again, reinforcing the independence of the institution with regards to participation in the third phase of the EMU (Economic and Monetary Union) and its integration in the European System of Central Banks (ESCB); effective since 1 June 1998. The amendments introduced in the Constitutional Law on Banks were effective since the beginning of the third phase of the EMU.

Portugal's commitment to participate in the EMU was incorporated in the Government programme approved by the Parliament on 14 November 1991. With the Portuguese escudo's entry into the European Monetary System (EMS) in April 1992, and the announcement of the full liberalisation of the capital movements, the necessary steps towards financial integration were taken. Through the Decree-law 298/92 of 31 December, Portugal incorporated the directives 77/780/EEC (on the coordination of laws, regulations and administrative provisions relating to the taking up and pursuit of the business of credit institutions), 89/646/EEC of 15 December 1989 (second directive on banking coordination that replaces directive 85/611/EEC) and 92/30/EEC of 6 April 1992 (on credit institutions supervision) into its legislation. That way an important reform of the Portuguese financial system was undertaken, except the insurance and pension funds sector. With the later amendments to the Decree-law 298/92 of 31 December, with which the credit institutions and financial enterprises' legal structure in Portugal[8] was approved, the Portuguese legislation incorporated:

- Directive 2000/12/EC of March 2000[9] that replaced directive 93/22/EEC of May 1993, on investment services with regards to transferable securities.
- Directive 2000/28/EC of 18 September 2000 that modified directive 2000/12/EC.
- Directive 2001/107/EC that modifies the directive 85/611/EEC on the coordination of laws, regulations and administrative provisions relating to undertakings for collective investment in transferable securities (UCITS), with regards to the regulation of the management companies and simplified prospectuses.

According to the Decree-law 298/92 and its later amendments, the Portuguese credit system is structured as follows:

- Banks
- *Caixas* económicas
- *Caixa Central* De Crédito Agrícola Mútuo and *caixas* of crédito agricola mutuo
- Financial credit institutions
- *Leasing* companies
- *Factoring* companies
- Credit purchase financing companies
- Companies of mutual guarantee
- Institutions of electronic money

The Directive regarding the valuation rules for the annual and consolidated accounts of certain types of companies, as well as of banks and other financial institutions (2001/65/EC), has involved the introduction of new regulations in

[8]Decree-laws 246/95 of 14 September, 232/96 of 5 December, 222/99 of 22 June 250/2000 of 13 October, 285/2001 of 3 November, 201/2002 of 26 December, 319/2002 of 28 December and 252/2003 of 17 October.

[9]Directive on the taking-up and pursuit of the credit institutions.

Portugal. Within the areas of competence of the Bank of Portugal, this directive has materialised itself in the Proceedings 11/2003 and 12/2003 for credit institutions and financial companies. The Insurance Institute of Portugal has involved the introduction of the regulatory rule 4/2003 for the insurance companies. Finally, National Securities Market Commission embraced the Regulation 6/2002, applicable to the issuers admitted to quotation in the regulated market.

Fig. 6.19 Evolution of financial saving of institutional sectors
Source: Bank of Portugal, 2007

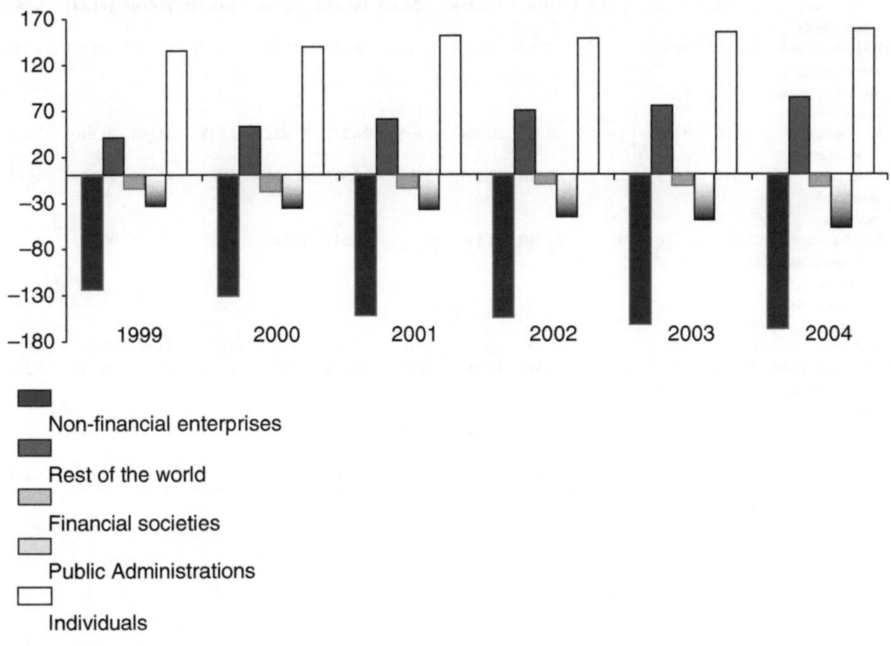

Fig. 6.20 Evolution of financial assets of institutional sectors, 1999–2004 (thousand million Euros)
Source: Bank of Portugal, 2007

Table 6.33 National financial accounts – Financial assets and liabilities, total economy, consolidated values in million Euros

	1999			2000			2001			2002		
	Assets	Liabilities	Net	Assets	Liabilities	Net	Assets	Liabilities	Net	Assets	Liabilities	Net
BF.90 Net financial worth	**578.208**	**613.974**	**−35.766**	**663.011**	**708363**	**−45.352**	**748.167**	**807.445**	**−59.277**	**756.343**	**829.750**	**−73.407**
Memo item: in percentage of GDP									−45.8			−54.2
AF.1 Monetary gold and SDR	**5.961**	**0**	**5.961**	**5.773**		**5.773**	**6.215**	**0**	**6.215**	**6.291**	**0**	**6.291**
AF.2 Currency and deposits	**166.465**	**180.314**	**−13.849**	**182.535**	**209.859**	**−27.324**	**188.921**	**223.714**	**−34.793**	**191.036**	**226.717**	**−35.681**
AF.21 Currency	5.876	5.673	203	5.710	5.425	285	4.811	4.509	302	5.012	4.464	548
AF.22+AF.29 Transferable deposits and other deposits	160.589	174.641	−14.052	176.825	204.434	−27.609	184.110	219.205	−35.095	186.024	222.254	−36.230
AF.3 Securities other than shares	**76.917**	**71.621**	**5.296**	**85.675**	**77.231**	**8.444**	**89.138**	**90.795**	**−1.657**	**93.930**	**100.911**	**−6.981**
AF.33 Securities other than shares, excluding financial derivatives	76.166	71.621	4.545	84.808	77.231	7.577	87.927	90.795	−2.868	93.354	100.910	−7.556
AF.331 Short-term	12.397	6.250	6.147	13.883	6.945	6.938	15.693	10.870	4.823	15.403	11.631	3.772
AF.332 Long term	63.769	65.372	−1.603	70.925	70.286	639	72.234	79.924	−7.690	77.951	89.279	−11.328
AF.34 Financial derivatives	751	0	751	867	0	867	1.211	0	1.211	576	1	575
AF.4 Loans	**128.934**	**137.317**	**−8.383**	**157.925**	**166.941**	**−9.016**	**192.729**	**204.840**	**−12.111**	**211.688**	**224.858**	**−13.170**
AF.41 Short-term	41.922	39.047	2.875	46.318	43.491	2.827	51.313	51.753	−440	53.194	52.981	213
AF.42 Long term	87.012	98.270	−11.258	111.607	123.450	−11.843	141.416	153.087	−11.671	158.494	171.877	−13.383
AF.5 Shares and other equity	**130.368**	**156.259**	**−25.891**	**150.033**	**174.418**	**−24.385**	**185.476**	**204.193**	**−18.717**	**165.066**	**191.647**	**−26.581**
AF.51 Shares and other equity, excluding mutual funds shares	108.102	135.612	−27.510	127.824	154.164	−26.340	161.205	182.767	−21.562	140.371	170.037	−29.666
AF.52 Mutual funds shares	22.266	20.648	1.618	22.209	20.254	1.955	24.271	21.426	2.845	24.695	21.610	3.085
AF.6 Insurance technical reserves	**33.199**	**32.815**	**384**	**37.678**	**37.285**	**393**	**42.343**	**41.873**	**470**	**45.438**	**44.979**	**459**
AF.61 Net equity of households in life ins. and pension funds reserves	28.460	28.460	0	32.359	32.359	0	36.544	36.544	0	39.441	39.441	0
AF.62 Other	4.739	4.355	384	5.319	4.926	393	5.799	5.328	471	5.998	5.539	459
AF.7 Other accounts receivable and payable	**36.634**	**35.648**	**986**	**43.391**	**42.630**	**761**	**43.346**	**42.030**	**1.316**	**42.892**	**40.637**	**2.255**
AF.71 Trade credits and advances	19.617	20.219	−602	22.568	23.147	−579	24.363	24.798	−435	23.126	23.030	96
AF.79 Other	17.018	15.429	1.589	20.823	19.483	1.340	18.983	17.232	1.751	19.766	17.607	2.159

Source: Bank of Portugal

Table 6.33 (continued)

2003			2004			2005			2006		
Assets	Liabilities	Net	Assets	Liabilities	Net	Assets	Liabilities	Net	Assets	Liabilities	Net
823.032	**902.836**	**−79.804**	**876.217**	**966.288**	**−90.071**	**939.862**	**1.040.449**	**−100.587**	**1.017.679**	**1.135.835**	**−118.157**
		−57.6			−62.5			−67.6			−76.2
5.565	**0**	**5.565**	**4.855**	**0**	**4.855**	**5.924**	**0**	**5.924**	**6.023**	**0**	**6.023**
198.464	**232.296**	**−33.832**	**202.729**	**244.811**	**−42.082**	**215.459**	**264.483**	**−49.024**	**234.769**	**286.210**	**−51.441**
5.131	4.127	1.004	5.502	4.078	1.424	5.916	4.215	1.701	5.460	3.466	1.994
193.333	228.169	−34.836	197.227	240.733	−43.506	209.543	260.268	−50.725	229.309	282.744	−53.435
105.185	**104.113**	**1.072**	**115.533**	**111.449**	**4.084**	**133.405**	**123.525**	**9.880**	**134.994**	**131.257**	**3.737**
105.144	104.068	1.076	116.026	111.352	4.674	133.449	123.518	9.931	135.127	131.454	3.673
17.334	14.399	2.935	16.329	21.474	−5.145	21.161	26.975	−5.814	19.753	24.910	−5.157
87.811	89.669	−1.858	99.697	89.877	9.820	112.287	96.542	15.745	115.374	106.544	8.830
41	45	−4	−493	98	−591	−44	7	−51	−133	−197	64
227.237	**247.747**	**−20.510**	**237.969**	**257.262**	**−19.293**	**252.234**	**276.625**	**−24.391**	**271.716**	**299.248**	**−27.532**
54.719	53.455	1.264	53.736	53.117	619	55.371	53.330	2.041	53.952	54.082	−130
172.518	194.292	−21.774	184.233	204.145	−19.912	196.863	223.295	−26.432	217.764	245.166	−27.402
190.981	**226.009**	**−35.028**	**216.065**	**255.602**	**−39.537**	**231.654**	**277.598**	**−45.944**	**259.655**	**312.818**	**−53.163**
163.234	201.100	−37.866	185.834	228.399	−42.565	196.156	246.727	−50.571	221.912	280.372	−58.460
27.747	24.909	2.838	30.231	27.203	3.028	35.498	30.871	4.627	37.743	32.446	5.297
49.249	**48.630**	**619**	**51.470**	**51.072**	**398**	**60.123**	**59.654**	**469**	**65.625**	**65.084**	**541**
42.878	42.878	0	45.100	45.100	0	53.225	53.225	0	58.339	58.339	0
6.371	5.752	619	6.370	5.971	399	6.899	6.429	470	7.286	6.745	541
46.350	**44.041**	**2.309**	**47.597**	**46.091**	**1.506**	**41.062**	**38.563**	**2.499**	**44.898**	**41.218**	**3.680**
27.231	27.011	220	27.691	28.103	−412	26.867	26.507	360	26.656	25.023	1.633
19.119	17.030	2.089	19.905	17.988	1.917	14.195	12.056	2.139	18.242	16.195	2.047

The Directive 2001/97/EC that amends the Directive on the laundering of capitals 91/308/EEC was incorporated to the Portuguese law through the Act 11/2004 of 27 March. The Bank of Portugal and the National Securities Market Commission reached an agreement for the presentation of an Act on preliminary transposition with regards to the Directive on markets in financial instruments (2004/39/EC) (Figs. 6.19 and 6.20; Table 6.33).

6.3.2.1 Savings Banks

Unlike what happened in Spain, in Portugal, the number of employees in savings banks has decreased by 20% since Portugal entrance into the EU (Table 6.34). This drop is the consequence of the concentration process, which the Portuguese savings banks have undergone. This drop in the number of savings banks (only three nowadays) is in part due to the association of 104 savings banks in Caixa Central de Crédito Agrícola Mutuo (Table 6.34).

The banking institutions in Spain keep a growing evolution with respect to the number of cash dispensers, which have gone from 33,940 in 1997 to 51,978 dispensers in 2003. In the case of Portugal, the number of cash dispensers has grown but not at the same level as in Spain (Fig. 6.21; Table 6.35).

The Portuguese savings banks are not under the obligation of allocating part of their benefits to the charity social works unlike the Spanish savings banks. Some of them, like the "Caixa Económica Montepío Geral", are a mutual society and are inside the social economy, although their characteristics are more similar to those of the credit unions than saving banks.

As it has been previously said, in Portugal they operate three important savings banks, two of them of private nature and a public one. All of them were founded at the end of the nineteenth century, created for social purposes based in loans or savings attracting, but nowadays, they have diversified their business and are also devoted to other activities like the insurance industry, for instance (Table 6.36).

Table 6.34 Evolution of the number of employees of credit institutions in Portugal

Years	Portugal
1985	67,647
1990	74,796
1995	75,395
1996	74,871
1997	64,965
1998	61,965
1999	61,319
2000	58,097
2001	55,538
2002	55,260
2003	53,931

Source: ESBG calculations based on data from the ECB and Eurostat for the years 1985 until 1996. From 1997 onwards: "Report on EU Banking Structure", ECB, November 2004

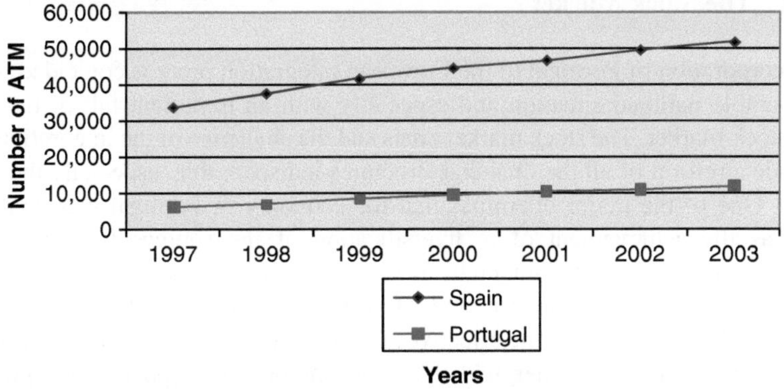

Fig. 6.21 Evaluation of number of ATMs in Spain and Portugal
Source: ESBG calculations based on data from the ECB and Eurostat for the years 1985 until 1996. From 1997 onwards: "Report on EU Banking Structure", ECB, November 2004

Table 6.35 Evaluation of number of ATMs in Spain and Portugal

Years	1997	1998	1999	2000	2001	2002	2003
Spain	33,940	37,893	41,871	44,851	46,990	49,876	51,978
Portugal	6,280	7,081	8,506	9,701	10,524	11,117	11,985

Source: ESBG calculations on the basis of data from the ECB and Eurostat for the years 1985 until 1996. From 1997 onwards: "Report on EU Banking Structure", ECB, November 2004

Table 6.36 Rule box 4

The three Portuguese savings banks:

- Caixa Central de Créditos Agrícola Mutuo
  Unites 104 caixas associated in the whole Portuguese Area
  This saving bank has the main aim of providing economic–financial advice and consultancy services. The advice is related to capital management and the diversification in the insurance field
- Caixa Económica Montepío General
  It was created in 1840 with a mutual's spirit, it is the largest mutual and financial institution of private capital in Portugal, and is the only one related to the socially oriented economy of that country. Its members have preferred terms in: Caixa Económica Montepío Geral (Loans), Leacok (insurances) and Futuros (funds subscription). The private social welfare institution whose objective is the reciprocal assistance in the interest of its members and their families.
- Caixa General de Depósito
  Founded on 10 April 1876 during the reign of D. Luis, in 1896 it became an autonomous entity of the Public Credit Board. In 1969 it is transformed into a Public Company with the Decree-law 48/953 of 3 April 1969. In 1993, it became a public limited company. Currently, the CGD is present in the banking business (Investment bank), venture capital, real estate, insurance, asset management, specialised credits, e-commerce and cultural activities. This savings bank is carrying out an expansion process in several member States of the EU and overseas

6.3.2.2 The Stock Market

The incorporation of Portugal to the European integration process coincided with an unfavourable national situation and especially with an important fall of the Portuguese stock market. The stock market crisis and the challenge of the integration in the EU made a reform of all the financial structures indispensable, especially the capital market. One of the major dilemmas that the economy of Portugal was confronted with was the achievement of a diversification of the sources for financing its enterprises, until then, fundamentally banking, in order to make them competitive in a liberalised European environment. However, it is not until 1991 when the new Securities Market Code became effective. This new regulation constituted the core of a larger reform that, together with some technological improvements, gradually enabled the evolution toward a continuous market, with a subsequent decrease in the verbal market.

The reform of the market was also fostered by the reform of other segments of the financial market (it is pertinent to mention the New Bank of Portugal Constitutional Law and the new regulation on foreign investors). An important fragmentation added up to this, not only of the stock market, but also of the financial system in general, accompanied by a strong apathy of the small investors and the scarce number of institutional investors. All this increased the already strong exposition of the market to the movements of the international investors, in a market characterised by excessive volatility of prices and low liquidity. In addition to these belated reforms, the Implementation of the White Paper of 1992 on the financial system is still under discussion, which helps us to get an idea of the delay of the Portuguese market, compared with other European markets.

The PSI 20 Index is an index made up of the 20 securities quoted in the Lisbon Official Stock Exchange. The PSI 20 index has a double finality: on the one hand to serve as an average indicator of the market evolution in Portugal and on the other hand to be the support for the trading of options and futures contracts (Table 6.37).

The Portuguese stock market has experienced an outstanding development since its accession to the EU. In terms of capitalisation, in 1995, it represented less than 20% of the GNP, coming to represent 60% in 1999. In spite of the good evolution of the market, as a result of the liberalising process, it is still ranking below the average market size of the Euro-zone. The end of the privatising process that came together with market liberalisation and its own fluctuations due to the volatility of the international markets has propitiated the evolution of the Portuguese stock market in consonance with the rest of the stock markets, especially since 2000. The number of companies quoted on the Portuguese stock market is not significant. The increase in the competition due to the liberalisation and opening of the market and the process of concentration due to mergers and acquisitions has also propitiated to the drop in the number of quoted companies. Nevertheless, this drop in quoted companies was not matched by an equivalent drop in capitalisation. It is necessary to highlight the absence of foreign companies quoted on the Portuguese market. In 2000, the Lisbon Stock Exchange and the Oporto Derivative Exchange formed a joint stock company called BVLP (Managing Body of the Regulated Markets, S.A).

Table 6.37 Capitalization of the main Exchange markets

Markets	DEC- 01	DEC- 02	DEC- 03	DEC- 04	DEC- 05	DEC- 06
Germany	1,203,681	658,573	855,452	878,806	1,035,254	1,241,963
Ireland	84,568	57,540	67,444	83,933	96,722	123,824
Italy	592,319	457,992	487,446	580,881	676,606	778,501
Ljubljana				7,115	6,697	778,501
London	2,414,105	1,713,791	1,974,460	2,071,775	2,592,623	2,873,541
Luxemburg	25,506	23,569	23,596	36,891	43,448	66,290
Malta	N/A	N/A	N/A	2,089	3,474	3,411
Prague	N/A	N/A	N/A	21,720	31,059	34,693
Spain	525,839	443,097	575,766	692,053	813,812	1,003,299
Warsaw				51,888	79,353	112,672
Vienna	28,307	32,235	44,811	64,577	107,085	146,197
NASDAQ	3,253,459	1,914,714	2,314,987	2,634,928	3,055,458	2,927,080
NYSE	12,383,882	8,654,560	9,221,026	9,477,609	11,284,720	11,678,898
Japan	2,543,291	1,936,527	2,403,629	2,653,397	3,876,905	3,494,368

Source: Comissao do Mercado de Valores Mobiliarios "Relatorio sobre a situaçao de valores mobiliarios" (several years)

The BVLP manages and governs the cash and derivatives markets in Portugal since 28 February 2000. All stock markets must be registered in the CNVM (National Securities Commission).

6.3.2.3 Insurance and Pension Funds

In 1989, the scope of the pension funds expanded to the private savings with the establishment of the Decree-law 205/89 of 27 June (Retirement Saving Plans). Those pension funds enjoyed a very favourable tax treatment. In 1991, the Decree-law 415/91 of 25 October, attempted to amend the deficiencies that still remained in the Portuguese pension funds' legal framework. This new law, among other aspects, reduced the bureaucratic steps necessary to constitute a pension fund, introduced an increased flexibility in the payments and it enabled the participation of more than one manager in a pension fund. In addition, a differentiation between the closed pension funds and the open pension funds was introduced. In 1995, the *Equity Savings Plans* (Decree-law 204/95) was created in order to strengthen the market.

Through the Decree-law 12/2006 of 20 January, Portugal undertook the transposition of the Directive 2003/41/EC on the activities and supervision of institutions for occupational retirement provision. The incorporation of the Directive on the supplementary supervision of credit institutions, insurance undertakings and investment firms in a financial conglomerate (2002/87/EC) to the Portuguese law was not exempt from problems. The proposed Decree-law for that Directive's transposition was sent to the Ministry of Finance in May 2004, together with the proposed law that authorised the government to extend its application to the holdings and mixed financial companies subject to the supervision of the Portuguese Insurance Institute (Decree-law 94-B of 17 April). After the approval of the legal instruments involved in the transposition, the groups rated as financial conglomerates, as well as the designation that would receive the groups not included under that denomination, were defined.

The insurance and pension funds industry plays an important role in the national economy and the social protection of the Portuguese people, contributing to the profitability of the capital market and, as a result, to the increment of confidence indexes of the economic agents. The global evolution of the economic and financial activity has conditioned the development of insurances and pension funds in Portugal through several factors (1) financial profits generated in the principal international exchange markets; (2) the entry into force of the international accounting standards for companies quoted on the stock markets; (3) the financing facilities as a consequence of the low interest rates and the extension of the loan amortisation periods; (4) the enactment of the European directive on savings tax and; (5) the stagnation of the Portuguese economy and the deterioration of its competitive capability (Tables 6.38 and 6.39).

The life insurance industry has largely contributed to the global increase in the number of contracts in this sector. This growth has been favoured by the increase in the working population with respect to the sustainability of the financing of the current Social Security benefit levels, besides the entrance into force of the Decree-law 62/2005 of 11 March, resulting from the transposition of the directive 2003/48/EC. For the next years, the following is expected: A moderate growth in premiums and amounts managed; a minor profitability of the capital markets, matched with a higher volatility of the prices and financial conditions, generally more restrictive;

Table 6.38 Main macroeconomic indicators of the Portuguese economy

	1999	2000	2001	2002	2003	2004	2005	2006
GDP (%)	3.8	3.7	1.8	0.5	−1.2	1.3	0.5	1.3
CPI[a] (%, annual average)	2.3	2.9	4.4	3.7	3.3	2.4	2.3	3.1
Current accounts balance[b] (% of GDP)		−10.4	−10.1	−7.6	−5.4	−7.7	−9.7	−9.5

[a]Within 1992–1997 CPI based on 1991*Source*: Annual reports of the Bank of Portugal

Table 6.39 Insurance and reinsurance companies in Portugal

	1998	1999	2000	2001	2002	2003	2004	2005	2006
Public limited companies	49	49	47	47	44	41	38	39	42
Life	16	16	15	15	15	14	14	14	15
Non-life	25	26	25	25	23	21	19	20	22
Mixed	8	7	7	7	6	6	5	5	5
Mutual	2	2	2	2	2	2	2	2	2
Branches of foreign companies	47	43	37	37	36	31	29	30	32
With headquarters in the EU	44	41	35	35	34	30	28	29	31
Life	14	12	11	9	10	10	9	9	9
Non-life	30	28	23	25	23	19	18	19	21
Mixed	0	1	1	1	1	1	1	1	1
UIT headquarters outside the EU	3	2	2	2	2	1	1	1	1
Life	1	1	1	1	1	0	0	0	0
Non-life	1	0	0	0	0	0	0	0	0
Mixed	1	1	1	1	1	1	1	1	1

Source: Portugal Institute of Insurances, Relatório do Sector Segurador e Fundos de Pensões, several years

that is, the type of conditions that intensify the market risk and the solvency requirements of the financial sector, increased by the requirements of the new solvency system of the European insurance market whose effects have been systematically anticipated by the markets (Solvency II).

With the aim of reinforcing the consumer protection; incrementing the professionalisation and assessment of the mediation activities; and improving the supervision efficiency, a reformulation of the legal system of the insurance mediation has been accomplished, which intends to contribute to the stability and good functioning of the insurance market.

The pension funds market is composed of pension funds in the banking industry and in the transport and communications sectors. The planned structural reforms can stimulate the market and alter its structure (Table 6.40).

The Portuguese pension funds sector is characterised by its high concentration level. As for its socioeconomic role, the importance of the pension funds as a supplementary financing instrument of the Social Security Tax benefits has to be highlighted.

The pension fund's growth is basically due to two factors: good profitability and a global revision of the method used for assessing responsibilities in the pension funds with regards to the budgets. This revision was essentially confirmed in the pension funds whose members were companies quoted on the exchange market and mainly affected the funds of the banking industry. By virtue of the increase in responsibilities due to the budgets review, the members will unquestionably have to contribute with much higher amounts (Fig. 6.22).

Table 6.40 Evolution of pension funds in Portugal

	1996	1997	1998	1999	2000	2001	2002	2003	2004	2005	2006
Number	237	237	233	238	244	236	231	229	221	223	227
Amount (millions of Euros)	8,232.2	10,059.8	11,577.6	12,911,1	13,766.5	14,807.9	15,880	16,283	15,186	18,982	21,185

Source: Portugal Insurance Institute, Relatório do Sector Segurador e Fundos de Pensões, several years

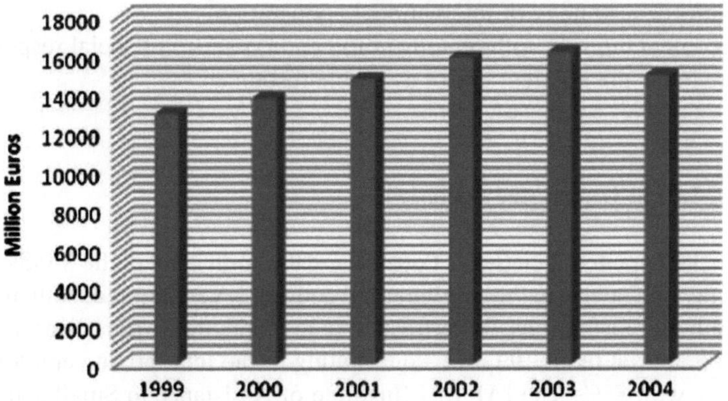

Fig. 6.22 Total value of the pension funds, 1999–2004
Source: Portugal Insurance Institute

The presence of Portuguese Institutions abroad has been stable during the last years and is not very active (Table 6.41).

Table 6.41 Branches of Portuguese institutions abroad

	2000	2001	2002	2003	2004	2005
Third countries (Macau)	2	1	1	1	1	1
Germany	1	1	–	–	–	–
Belgium	1	1	1	1	1	1
Spain	4	4	3	3	3	3
France	3	3	3	3	3	3
Greece	1	1	–	–	–	–
Holland	1	1	–	–	–	–
Luxembourg	1	1	1	1	1	1
United Kingdom	1	1	–	–	–	–
Total EU	13	13	8	8	8	8
Total	15	14	9	9	9	9

Source: Portugal Insurance Institute, Relatório do Sector Segurador e Fundos de Pensões, several years

In its valuation on the Portuguese financial industry, the Portuguese Insurance Institute has designed a strategic plan for the period 2007–2009 with the aim of ensuring the correct operation of the insurance and pension funds market in Portugal. The following points summarise the areas of performance gathered in this strategic plan:

1. To ensure the insurance agents' definition and compliance with suitable levels of financial soundness.
2. To achieve high behaviour patterns in insurance agents.
3. To foster the implementation of efficient management and control systems.
4. To contribute to the innovation and competitiveness of the insurance and pension funds market.
5. To inform the consumers on the functioning of the insurance and pension funds market.
6. To reinforce a strategy of international cooperation.
7. To become a referent with regards to the good practice of social responsibility.
8. To maximise the efficient use of available resources.

6.3.2.4 Mutual Guarantee Societies

The Mutual Guarantee societies in Portugal are the equivalent of the MGSs in Spain, although their existence in the neighbouring country is very limited, both in time and in the number of institutions. In Portugal, like in Spain, the SMEs constitute most of the entrepreneurial tissue (99.4%), contributing to the total private employment of the country with 85%. The IAPMEI (Institute of Assistance to Small and Medium Size Enterprises and to Investment) is the body of reference for the Portuguese SMEs. Since its creation in 1975, the IAPMEI has been focused on the industrial sector (18%) and services sector (24%). The mechanisms of assistance to the enterprises are carried out through grants, subsidies, financial interventions addressed in funds of venture capital and guarantees instruments. With regards to the guarantees, the IAPMEI promoted a pilot project in 1994, the creation of the first mutual guarantee society, *la Sociedade de Investimento* (SPGM).

La Sociedade de Investimento (SPMG) was created as a reaction to the competitive shock that implied the integration to the European Union and the resultant liberalising process. Its main objective was to strengthen the Portuguese SMEs, modernise them and improve their performance, thanks to the sustainability granted by the guarantees system. The preference to develop a system under the Spanish influence with technical support of the European Association of Mutual Guarantee Societies (AECM) was expressed. In 2002, the SPMG provided the financial resources necessary to create the Counter-guarantee Fund as well as the capital for the launching of some Mutual Guarantee societies. The finality, in all the cases, was to get completely integrated in a privately managed system, respecting the market requirements and rules. Thanks to the work of the SPMG, in January 2003, three Mutual Guarantee societies began to operate in Portugal, at a local level and directed towards small projects, although originally they were directed towards medium-size enterprises.

The SPMG was created with two kinds of shareholders, quite similar to the Spanish case:

- Founding shareholders (promoters): Public and private institutions that founded the society and cannot use their services directly. The finality of their holding is to support the creation and development of projects of prospect enterprises or to consolidate the performance of companies economically viable.
- Beneficiary shareholders: The companies that can use and benefit from the SPMG services, particularly the SME in need of guarantees and meeting the requirements to adhere to the system.

The operations that the Guarantee societies can guarantee are practically all those operations for which the financial system requires a guarantee from the company or its manager, particularly:

- Long and medium-term loans, associated with the funding of investment schemes or restructuring of financial liabilities.
- Short and medium-term funding, intended to cover cash requirements, associated with the previous ones.
- Financial guarantees and/or guarantees on a project's good performance, in the context of support programmes for enterprises.
- Technical guarantees, in the context of supply of raw materials, works, etc.
- Special credit operations:
  - Issuance of Commercial Paper Programs
  - Bondholder loans
  - Loans in foreign currency
  - Leasing contracts and in some cases, factoring contracts.

6.3.2.5 Venture Capital Firms

Venture capital firms' objectives in Portugal are to support and promote the investment and technological innovation in entrepreneurial projects or in existing companies through temporal stakes in their respective capital stock. As incidental object, and since those services are rendered to investee companies or undertakings with which they are developing a project, with the entry of venture capital in their capital stock in mind, these firms can:

- Provide assistance in the financial, technical, administrative and commercial management of the participated companies.
- Elaborate technical–economic studies on the viability of the companies or on new investment projects, as well as the conditions and modes of the according funding.

Nowadays, apart from the Venture capital firms (VCF), which are the ideal investment form, there are two collective investment instruments in venture capital: the venture Capital Funds (VCF) and the Funds for the Restructuring and Internationalisation of Enterprises (FRIEs).

In 1991, the first regulation of the venture capital industry took place in Portugal. Since then, there have been frequent changes in the legal regulations of these kinds of societies, whose activity is ruled by law and subject to the supervision of the Securities Market National Commission of Portugal. Until 2002, the venture capital activity could only be carried out by venture capital firms and their supervision was performed jointly with the Bank of Portugal. From 2001 on, the venture capital activities in Portugal experienced a downtrend that worried the economic authorities. A review of the sector performance was carried out and in 2002 some modifications were included in its regulation with the Decree-law 31/9/2002 of December 28th. The purpose was to promote venture capital activities and therefore the development and creation of new enterprises in sectors such as the technological, industrial components and biotechnological ones (Figs. 6.23 and 6.24; Table 6.42).

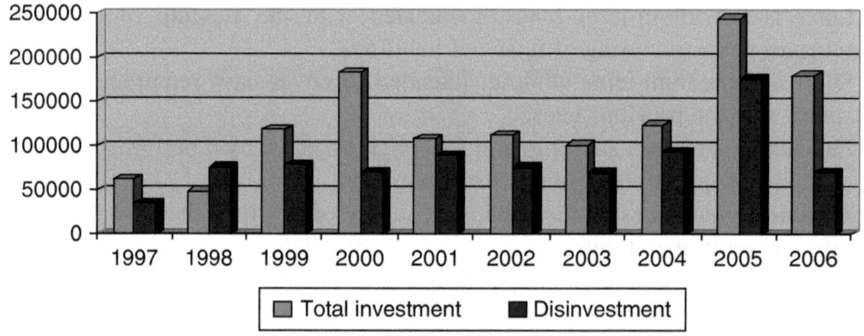

Fig. 6.23 Evolution of the venture capital activity in Portugal (thousand of Euros)
Source: APCRI (Portuguese Venture Capital Association)

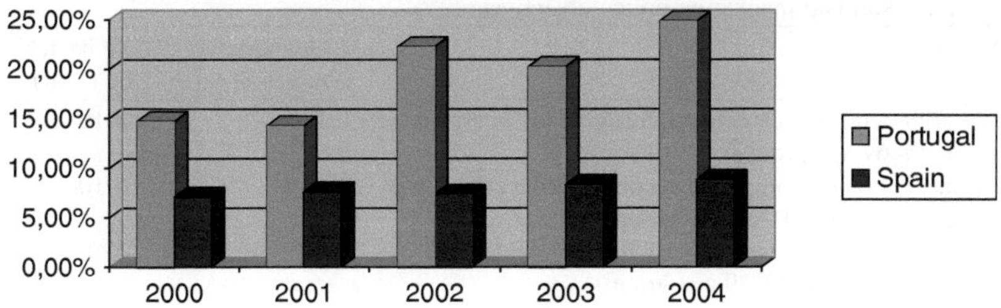

Fig. 6.24 Penetration ratio of the leasing sector
Source: Leaseurope

6.3.2.6 The Leasing Sector

In Portugal, the penetration ratio of this activity is higher than in Spain and the sector is more consolidated as a financing system.

Table 6.42 Evolution of the investment in leasing of movable and real estate assets, (million Euros)

		1998	1999	2000	2001	2002	2003	2004	2005
Portugal	Leasing movable assets	1,995	2,642	2,874	2,886	2,431	2,277	2,874.36	3,056
	Leasing real state	598	815	923	908	925	1,054	1,352.64	1,833
Spain	Leasing movable assets	5,552	6,809	7,102	8,006	7,972	9,324	10,866.6	13,834.5
	Leasing real state	850	1,240	1,387	1,655	1,699	2,391	3,113.3	3,604.9

Source: Leaseurope

6.3.2.7 The Enterprise and Technological Innovation

From the beginning of the current decade, Portugal has been experiencing lower levels of economic growth, loss of competitiveness in terms of labour costs and descent in productivity. In order to break this tendency and to stimulate the innovation, the Portuguese Government elaborated a technological plan to give a new turn to his policy on technological innovation. The Technological Plan constitutes a mainstay for the growth and competitiveness of the National Portuguese Reform Plan, named National Action Program for the Growth and Employment 2005–2008, which was approved in November 2005. The main objectives on innovation of the national policy can be found in this Technological Plan, where there are 21 specifically quantifiable objectives defined, to be attained in 2010, comprising: Government expenditure in R&D (to achieve 1% of the GDP), entrepreneurial expense in R&D (to achieve 1.8% of the GDP); employment in high-tech manufacturing and services (to achieve 4.7% and 1.8% of total

Table 6.43 National innovation policy objectives

Objective	Quantitative target (if set)	To be achieved by (year)
1. Population with tertiary education degree (as a percentage of the 25–64 age groups)	15%	2010
2. Population having completed secondary education (as a percentage of the 20–24 age group)	65%	2010
3. Population with a degree in S&T fields per thousand inhabitants (in the 20–29 age group)	12	2010
4. Researchers as a share of employed population (per thousand)	5.3	2010
5. Percentage of families with broadband Internet connection	50%	2010
6. Lifelong training	12.5%	2010
7. New S&T PhDs per thousand population (in the 25–34 age cohort)	0.45	2010
8. Scientific output per million population	609	2010
9. Full time equivalent people engaged in R&D activities (per thousand active population)	7.5	2010
10. Full time equivalent researchers (per thousand active population)	6.0	2010
11. Public R&D expenditures as a percentage of GDP	1.0%	2010
12. Business enterprise R&D expenditures as a percentage of GDP	0.8%	2010
13. Employment in medium hi-tech manufacturing (as a percentage of total employment)	4.7%	2010
14. Employment in hi-tech services (as a percentage of total employment)	1.8%	2010
15. Medium-high and High-tech manufacturing value added	6.2%	2010
16. High-tech services value added	6%	2010
17. High-tech product exports (as a percentage of total exports)	11.4%	2010
18. Firms created in medium-hi and high-tech industries (as a percentage of total number of firms created in the year)	12.5%	2010
19. EPO patents per million population	12	2010
20. Community trademarks per million population	50	2010
21. Venture capital investment as a percentage of GDP	0.15%	2010

Source: Technological Plan

population, respectively) and high-technology product exports (achieving 11.4% of total exports) (Table 6.43).

The Technological Plan is deemed an important step in some aspects, since it attempts to correct many weaknesses, for instance: the almost total lack of services extended to the SMEs, not only in the technological area, but also in strategic terms and in organisational and marketing problems; the limited scope of the initiatives to foster the employment of university graduates by the SMEs, and, at the same time, the low attraction level that the SMEs have for young graduates. Nevertheless, this last point has improved somewhat by the launching of the program INOV_JOVEM. Other aspects that still require improvement within the Plan are related to the difficulties arising from the management, given that the responsibilities are allocated among various ministries.

6.4 Regulation and Supervision of the Financial System

The establishment of the Single European Market was the catalyst for the harmonisation of the supervision cooperation rules in the EU. The EU formally took charge of the banking supervision by means of the First Directive on Banking Coordination (1977). With the second Directive on Banking Coordination (1989) the three performance principles of the single banking market were established (1) Minimum harmonisation; (2) Mutual recognition of the supervisory practices; and (3) Authorisation and control from home countries.

The freedom of establishment in the EU enables the credit institutions to provide their services in any member State but the supervision falls on the authorities of the country of origin of the institution. Nevertheless, for an effective financial supervision, an adequate legal framework for supervision is also necessary and enough powers to verify the compliance with the standards and to face security and legal protection, besides mechanisms for the confidential transmission of information between supervisors.

Based on this concern, in the Vienna Congress of December 1998, the Commission was invited to draw up a work programme to achieve the objectives set out in the framework for action, on which a consensus had emerged. The result was a plan captured in the Communication "Financial Services: building a framework for action". This action plan for financial services is also based on the discussions held within the Financial Services Policy Group (FSPG) composed by representatives of the Finance Ministers and the European Central Bank (ECB). Given the importance of the initiative, the European Council at its meeting in Cologne on 3 and 4 June 1999 requested the Commission to continue the work undertaken.

The Financial Services Action Plan (FPSA) proposes to achieve a single financial market in the EU based on three fundamental objectives:

– Establishing a single market in wholesale financial services
– Making retail markets open and secure
– Strengthening the rules on prudential supervision

The FPSA contains guiding priorities and a schedule of specific measures, adopted by the Commission in its summit of May 1999. Under this initiative, new directives have been developed, occasionally, amending previous ones. The slowness with which in some cases, the authorities of the member countries are undertaking the incorporation to their respective laws, hampering some of the main directives needs to be highlighted (Fig. 6.25; Table 6.44).

To be prepared for the challenges raised by the integration of the financial markets and given the existing institutional framework, it was considered

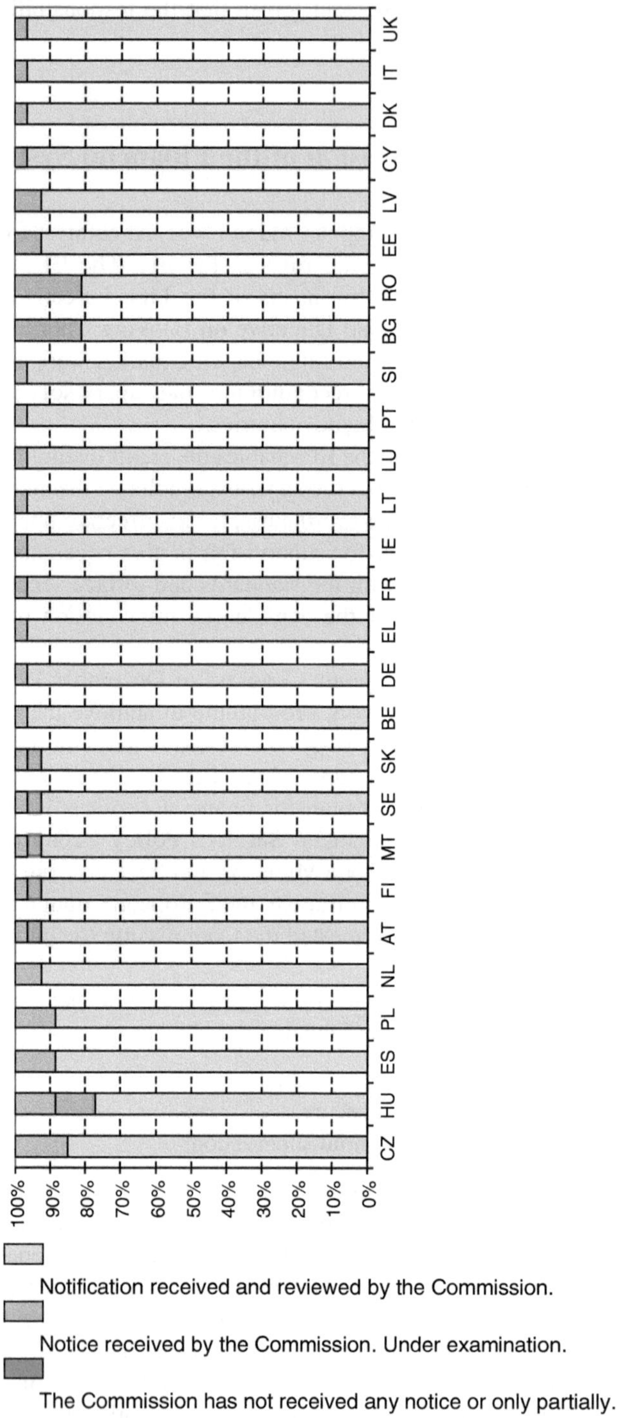

Fig. 6.25 Transposition of FSAP Directives for each member state. Situation as at 1 April 2008
Source: European Commission

Table 6.44 Rule-box 5 Directives included in Financial Services Action Plan (FSAP)

– Directive on the taking up, pursuit of and prudential supervision of the business of electronic money institutions	Directive 2000/46/EC
– Directive amending previous directives as regards exchange of information with third countries	Directive 2000/64/EC
– Directive on the reorganisation and winding-up of insurance undertakings	Directive 2001/17 CE
– Directive amending the directive on Money laundering	Directive 2001/97/EC
– Two directives on undertakings for collective investment in transferable securities (UCITS)	Directives 2001/107/EC and 2001/108/EC
– Directive amending the solvency margin requirements for insurance undertakings	Directive 2002/12/EC which revokes the Directives 2002/83/EC and 2002/13/EC
– Directive on Financial Collateral Arrangements	Directive 2002/47/EC
– Directive on the valuation rules for the annual and consolidated accounts of certain types of companies as well as of banks and other financial institutions	Directive 2001/65/EC
– Directive on taxation of savings income in the form of interest payments	Directive 2003/48/EC
– Directive on the reorganisation and winding up of banks	Directive 2001/24/EC
– Directive on the supplementary supervision of credit institutions, insurance undertakings and investment firms in a financial conglomerate	Directive 2002/87/EC
– Directive concerning the distance marketing of consumer financial services	Directive 2002/65/EC
– Directive supplementing the Statute for a European company with regards to the involvement of employees	Directive 2001/86/EC
– Directive on insider dealing and market manipulation (market abuse)	Directive 2003/6/EC
– Directive on the annual and consolidated accounts of certain types of companies, banks and other financial institutions and insurance undertakings	Directive 2003/51/EC
– Directive on markets of financial instruments	Directive 2004/39/CE
– Directive on transparency	Directive 2004/109/CE
– Directive on public takeovers	Directive 2004/25/CE
– Directive on demand and monitoring of credit institutions business	Directive 2006/48/CE
– Directive on investment companies and credit institutions capital suitability	Directive 2006/49/CE

indispensable to organise a committee of independent individuals (conclusions of the ECOFIN Council of 17 July 2000) to debate practical questions allowing to implement community standards, especially in certain regulatory areas (detail of companies, public offering of securities, etc).

The group of experts or group of wise men was established on 17 July 2000, with Alexandre Lamfalussy as chairman, ex–president of the European Monetary Institute (EMI). On 15 February 2001, a final report of the Committee (Lamfalussy Report) was presented where the Exchange market of the Union is analysed and the problems of the financial system are studied in depth, which are explained in part by the regulation complexity. The extrapolation of the Report's objective to the other sectors of the financial system was materialised with the creation of the European Banking Committee (EBC), the European Insurance and Occupational Pensions Committee (EIOPC), the European Financial Conglomerates Committee (EFCC), the Committee of European Banking Supervisors (CEBS), the Committee of European Insurance and Occupational Pensions Supervisors (CEIOPS) and the Financial Services Commission (FSC). The evaluation of the FSAP has been divided in two parts. The first part was completed in November 2005. The second part was to assess the economic and legal implications of the measures included in this program. Spain and Portugal have been adapting themselves to the legislative framework included in the FSAP.

Solvency II Project

Since the first years, the weaknesses of the solvency margin calculation model are evident. With directive 73/239/EEC, of 24 July 1973, the solvency margin was introduced in the European Insurance Industry for the first time. Later on, with the Directive 2002/83/CE, of 5 November 2002, the possibility of letting the solvency margin act as a "shock absorber" face to the eventual negative alterations of the industry was introduced. With the Solvency II Project, a revision of the actual directives of the insurance industry and the solvency system within the EU is being carried out. The aim is to provide an adequate protection to insurance policy holders in all the countries of the European Union, establishing a system to set the capital requirements adapted to the risk profile of each institution. The first stage of the Solvency II Project took place from 20 May 2001 until December 2002. During that stage, information was gathered to elaborate new supervisory procedures. Currently, the project is in its second stage, whose final objective is to elaborate a framework Directive.

It can be said that Solvency II is the equivalent of Basle II in the banking industry. The following are the pillars on which Solvency II is based:

- Pillar I: Own resources requirement.
- Pillar II: Supervisory processes.
- Pillar III: Market discipline.

The amendments that Solvency II will bring to the calculation system of the capital requirements will adapt better to the risks of the specific entity. In this sense, the supervisory processes will become more complex, requiring a greater co-operation among the supervising authorities of the member states, but attaining more transparency.

Risk Capital Action Plan

The interest on the performance of the venture capital societies within the EU and the achievement of a real single market for this kind of activities drove the heads of

State and the government to the Summit of Luxemburg in November 1997 to formally request the Commission to carry out a study on the barriers hindering the achievement of a single market in this industry. The outcome of such study, carried out by the Commission, was the Risk Capital Action Plan (RCAP), adopted in the Cardiff Summit of 15 and 16 June 1998. Among the barriers to be removed there were the following:

- Market fragmentation
- Institutional regulatory barriers
- Taxation
- Shortage of high-tech small businesses
- Human resources
- Cultural barriers

At the Lisbon Summit of 2000, it was decided to hasten the fulfilment of the Plan, so the end of 2003 was set as the deadline for its achievement. The results published yearly on the fulfilment level of the Plan so far have been positive, having achieved the political objectives and most of the technical targets. Although the EU is still far away from United States, this gap has been narrowed since 2000, having improved the venture capital sector within the EU.

6.4.1 Spain: Regulation and Supervision

In Spain, the bank of Spain is the entity in charge of supervising, monitoring and inspecting the credit institutions, and, likewise, the CNMV (National Securities Market Commission) on the exchange market. It was created on 2 June 1972 by a Royal Warrant from King Charles III under the name of *Banco Nacional de San Carlos*. Its legal status was modified by the Law on Autonomy of the Bank of Spain, 13/1994, of 1 June. The purpose of that law was to incorporate the terms of reference of the Maastricht Treaty on monetary policy and independency of central banks. Other changes put forward by the law were requirements related to the Bank's governing bodies, the new legal system for the Bank's acts and decisions for its budgetary situation and competences. The Bank's supervisory function regulated by the Act 26/1988 of 29 July, as well as other functions, was not modified (Table 6.45).

Regulation of the reliability margin and the guarantee fund has become an effective way to guarantee and survey entities' reliability. Spain had to complete adaptations to complementary rules. Directives on the reliability margin (2002/83/CE and 2002/13/CE) involve the regulation of a fundamental item related to insurance entities' surveillance. They were included in Spanish laws through the Royal Decree 3051/1982 of October 15th, formalised by Law33/1984 of August 2nd about Ordering Private Insurance.

With Act 5/2005 of 22 April, the transposition of Directive 2002/87/EC on the supervision of financial conglomerates is implemented in Spain (the Royal-decree

Table 6.45 Banking supervision in Spain and Portugal

	Authority in charge of the banking supervision	Situation with respect to the government	Composition of the managing bodies	Areas of competence in the supervisory context outside the banking industry	Central Bank's participation in the banking supervision	Formal agreements on co-ordination between the banking supervisory authorities and the central bank	Other authorities with competences in banking regulation	Other authorities taking part in bank licenses grant or revocation
Spain	Bank of Spain	Independent Central Bank	Bank of Spain Council	None	Full responsibility	Same authority	None	Department of Economic Affairs and Finance
Portugal	Bank of Portugal	Independent Central Bank	Bank of Portugal Council	Investment societies	Full responsibility	Same authority	Department of Economic Affairs	None

Source: ECB

1332/2005 of 11 November shall develop that act). In February 2006, an agreement was signed on financial stability, prevention and crisis management between the Department of Economic Affairs and Finance, the Bank of Spain and the National Securities Market Commission by which the Committee of Financial Stability was created in Spain.

The globalisation affects the financial stability to a great extent, given that the integration of inter-bank markets and capital markets generates a greater interrelation between institutions and financial intermediates. As a result of the financial crisis of the 1990s, the IMF and the WB jointly undertook a programme to evaluate the financial systems of the member countries, including all the financial institutions. This programme, known by its acronym FSAP or Financial Sector Assessment Program, is based on the idea that the stability is the result of a set of requirements and policies, not only economic ones; it also includes an institutional configuration, adequate design of institutions and markets and a regulatory framework for efficient supervision.

The financial and insurance industries in Spain and Portugal have been assessed by the FSAP. The related reports are on the IMEF's web page. In the case of Spain, the evolution of the implementation of the GAF's good practice code has not put the vision of the FSAP into effect but rather the more specific vision of the international organisation, in spite of being one of the most widely used codes. They also added the code on countering the Capital Laundering and the one that fights against Terrorism financing. That is due to the size and complexity of the Spanish financial system and the relative importance of its different segments and markets. Usually, once the respective specific missions are finished, the FSAP uses and integrates the outcome of the assessment carried out by the GAF, thus achieving to reduce costs, avoid overlapping and propitiating, which each institution conducts.

6.4.1.1 The Stock Market

In 1988 the National Securities Market Commission (CNMV) was created with the Act 24/1988 as the body in charge of the supervision and incorporation of the Spanish securities markets and the activities of those operating in such markets. The creation of the CNMV constituted a substantial reform of the Exchange markets and the Spanish financial system. The Act by which the CNMV was created has been used subsequently to adapt to the evolution and requirements of the EU, through the Acts 37/1998 and 44/2002, incorporating new investor protection measures. The transparency of the Spanish securities markets and the correct prices formation are part of the CNMV's targets. The information on the markets gathered by the CNMV is published in its official registers. The CNMV exercises a prudential supervision on the collective investment institutions and over the secondary securities markets. The societies that issue securities for public placement, the companies supplying investment services and collective investment institutions are the entities under the areas of competence of the CNMV. All the securities issued in Spain are assigned ISIN and CFF codes with international validity.

6.4.1.2 Insurance and Pension Funds

In Spain, the insurance and pension funds industries are under the supervision and control of the Directorate General of Insurances and Pension Funds (DGSFP), which depends on the Spanish Department of Economic Affairs (Royal Decree 1552/2004 of June 25th). This General Directorate is assigned functions related to private assurance and reassurance, insurance mediation, capitalisation and pension funds, except for those specifically assigned to the Economy and Tax Ministry.

The DGSFP is in charge of monitoring the good performance of the industry and providing an adequate protection to the insurance companies' customers, as well as, to those holding a pension fund. With this aim, it carries out activities of regulation, planning and supervision of the institutions that make up the industry. The supervisory activity is carried out in three stages (1) Statements analysis, (2) Inspection and (3) Follow-up of records and adoption of special monitoring measures. On the other hand, the market regulation of the DGSFP includes monitoring activities on the access to the insurance activity. But the control is not limited to the moment of the licence grant, it is also extended to the first exercises, verifying solvency and assessing the compliance degree of the forecasts presented in the programmes of activities.

6.4.1.3 Mutual Guarantee Societies

The Mutual guarantee societies have a legal status similar to that of the credit institutions, especially in subjects related to its supervision of financial institutions, even though they dispose of legal arrangements on administrative authorisation, solvency requirements and accounting standards adapted to their specific features. In this sense, their regulations have not been modified to adapt to the new IFRS (International Financial Reporting Standards).

Although their activity has developed in a significant way, the MGSs still represent a really low percentage of the risk with regards to the credit institutions (around 1.5% of the liabilities). They have focused on providing warrants and guarantees, highlighting the boost of technical warrants against the more moderate growth of those destined to investment loans.

6.4.1.4 The Leasing Sector

After Spain's entry in the EU and its adaptation to the community regulations, the monetary regulation and the functioning of the leasing sector in Spain were to experience substantial changes. In 1988, a qualitative change took place with the Act 26/1988 of 28 July, when from that date on, those entities were considered as credit institutions whose supervision was developed by the Bank of Spain, demanding discipline, prudential and supervisory rules from them, similar to those required from the deposit-taking institutions. The second enhancement came with the adaptation of the second Directive on Banking Coordination with the Act 3/1994 of 14 April, according to which it would not be necessary for a given bank or financial institution to have a specific leasing company with independent legal status, thus fostering many take-over mergers of leasing companies with their respective financial groups.

6.4.2 Portugal: Regulation and Supervision

Through the Law-decree 228/2000 of September 2000, the *Conselho Nacional de Supervisores Financieros* (CNSF) was created in Portugal. The National Council of Financial Supervisors (CNSF) is a forum for the supervision coordination of the financial system in Portugal. It groups the Bank of Portugal, the Insurance Institute of Portugal and the National Securities Commission. The Bank of Portugal is in charge of the prudential supervision of the credit institutions, the investment firms and other financial companies. The Insurance Institute of Portugal carries out the prudential supervision of insurance and reinsurance companies, insurance and pension funds' intermediaries and its managing bodies. Finally, the National Securities Commission is in charge of supervising the securities markets.

During these last years, the National Council of Financial Supervisors (CNSF) has focused on financial conglomerates, annual accounts, transposition of directives, preparing for the Financial Industry Evaluation Programme of the IMF, treatment of the legal concept of external auditor under the Portuguese law and the coordination of the supervisory actions undertaken by the competent authorities. The CNSF of Portugal also defined the necessary guides for the settlement of disputes within the framework of the Directive 2002/65/EC (Directive amending directives 90/619/EEC, 97/7/EC, and 98/27/EC.) concerning distance marketing of consumer financial services. As a result of the joint work of the three supervisory authorities of the financial system in Portugal, the CNSF defined the principles on transparency standards that were applicable to the new financial products, denominated as *Instrumentos de Captaçao de Aforro Estructurados* (Structured Savings Collection Instruments).[10] (Report 2000–2004)

[10]Press release 6/2002 of 18 September of the Bank of Portugal, Standard 05/2004 of 10 September of the Insurances Institute of Portugal complemented by the Law-decree 60/2004 of 22 March, and some rights incorporated in several regulations of the National Securities Commission.

Within the framework of Basle II, the directives 2006/48/EC (relating to the taking up and pursuit of the business of credit institutions) and 2006/49/EC (on the capital adequacy of investment firms and credit institutions) incorporated the legal framework of the New Basle Agreement into the community legislation. In Portugal, the incorporation of those two directives was carried out with the force of two Law-decrees, 103/2007 and 104/2007.

6.4.2.1 Stock Market

Coinciding with the start of the liberalisation and autonomy process of the securities market, the market in 1991 was equipped with a juridical statute, in accordance with its private nature and new forms of supervision and inspection. In Portugal, the National Council of Financial Supervisors (CNSF) defined the guidelines on the transposition process related to Undertakings for Collective Investment in Transferable Securities (UCITS) (2001/107/EC and 2001/108/EC) to the Portuguese law,[11] which includes the National Securities Commission and the Bank of Portugal. The combined work of both authorities gave rise to the enactment of the Law-decree 252/2003 of 17 October.

With regards to Directive 2003/71/EC on the Prospectus, the CNSF determined that the credit institutions could continue to be exempt from being obliged to publish a prospectus regarding securities issued in a continuous or repeated manner. The National Council of Financial Supervisors (CNSF), where the National Securities Commission and the Bank of Portugal are present, is in charge of establishing the guidelines for the transposition of the directives regarding the Undertakings for Collective Investment in Transferable Securities (2001/107/EC and 2001/108/EC amending Directive 85/611/EC). The Law-decree 252/2003 of 17 October has been one of the outcomes of the combined work of both authorities, the Bank of Portugal and the National Securities Commission (CNMV).

The jurisdiction over the market supervision falls on the National Commission of Market Securities (CNMV), which was created in 1991 as an independent body and responsible before the Accounts Tribunal.

Among the functions of the CNVM we find the regulation, supervision, inspection and promotion of securities markets and the activities developed by those markets, among them; regulation and supervision of investment services, directly or indirectly connected with securities; in addition to intermediaries professionally exercising their activity. It is also responsible for the supervision of intermediation activities, either carried out by banks or by investment societies. Furthermore, the

[11]Amending Directive 85/611/EEC.

CNVM advises the Government and co-operates with the pertinent authorities from other countries, essentially within the EU area.

The Commission is managed by a council of Directors, appointed through a resolution of the Council of Ministers, at the proposal of the Minister of Finance for a mandate of 5 years. The Council of Directors is composed of five members: The Chairman, Vice-Chairman and three Committee-men and it is assisted by an Advisory Council, which in turn, is composed OF representatives of all the relevant agents of the capital market and inspected by a Supervisory Commission.

Fundamentally, the following are subject to the CNVM:

- Securities issuers
- Financial intermediaries
- Managing societies and securities settlement societies.
- Institutional investors
- Investment funds
- Venture capital societies

The CNVM collaborates with other national regulatory institutions, like the Bank of Portugal and the Insurance Institute of Portugal. In the international context, it also co-operates with numerous institutions, like the International Organisation of Securities Commissions IOSCO, the Committee of Regulatory Authorities of the European Securities Markets, the IberoAmerican Institute of Stock Markets and furthermore, it collaborates in the projects of the EU institutions.

The commission issues regulatory rules and technical instruction necessary for the adequate development of the Exchange market, having issued more than 70 regulations on different subjects on investors' information, public offerings, admission to quote on the stock market, financial intermediaries, investment funds and organisation of derivatives markets (Table 6.46).

6.4.2.2 Insurance and Pension Funds

In Portugal, the Insurance Institute of Portugal (ISP) is in charge of regulating, inspecting and supervising the business of insurance, re-insurance, insurance intermediaries and pension funds. It is ruled by the Board of Governors and supported by the Advisory Committee. It enjoys financial autonomy and obtains its income through the exercise of its supervisory activity.

The IMF recommends a modification of the ISP's statutes in order to introduce a greater independency. It is necessary that Portugal intensifies its supervisory and regulatory activities for several reasons: asymmetrical information between operators and clients, growing complexity of the products, the need to converge towards international standards, greater transparency and communication, and a more risk-oriented approach.

Table 6.46 Rule box 6: Schedule for the incorporation of European directives into the Portuguese market

Directives	2005				2006				2007			
	1st TR	2nd TR	3rd TR	4th TR	1st TR	2nd TR	3rd TR	4th TR	1st TR	2nd TR	3rd TR	4th TR
Market abuse												
Law-decree # 52/2006, 15/3/06 Took effect on 30/3/2006												
Prospectus												
European Regulations in effect since 1/7/05												
Law-decree # 52/2006,15/3 In effect since 30/3/06												
Takeover bid												
Law-decree # 219/06 2 November In effect since / 11/06												
Transparency												
Transposition period 20/1/07												
Public consultation- between 26/06/06 and 20/07/06												
Markets and financial instruments												
Transposition period 31/1/2007												
Public consultation on draft Hill before 29/12/06												

Source: Comissao do Mercado de Valores Mobiliario "Annual report" (several years)

6.5 Foreign Direct Investment and the Financial System

6.5.1 *Spain*

The evolution of the foreign investment in Spain and Portugal is related to the opening and liberalisation process of both economies, and the confidence and security that this process has inspired in international investors. The internationalisation of the Spanish companies' activities, the liberalisation of the international economic relationship since the beginning of the 1980s and the anticipation effect produced in view of the certainty of Spain's accession to membership to the EU facilitated the capital income and the direct foreign investment directed towards the modernisation of the economy. In the 1990s, the laws were modified to make the country more attractive for investors. Also in that decade, an economic stagnation in industrialised countries took place, in such a way that there was a change in the trend of international capital flows. Spain was also affected by this stagnation and the foreign direct investment incomes that significantly decreased in this decade. Since 1996, a new wave of direct investment has taken place in Spain in consonance with what has happened at an international level, as well as the progress in the integration process of the Monetary Union, the liberalisation of some service activities and the development of new information technologies. Since 1992 Spain has eliminated the controls on exchange and capital. A full range of tax incentives, preferred access to official loans, subventions and many more benefits were offered at a regional, city and local level to attract foreign investment (Table 6.47).

In Spain the existing restrictions on direct foreign investment (DFI) have been gradually liberalised, and after the Decree 664/1999 of 23 April, DFI was allowed, subject only to ex-post notice. Investments from tax heavens or directly related with national security require previous notice. There are also specific restrictions on air transport, radio and TV, games, mining, hydrocarbons, pharmaceutical products, telecommunications and private security. The government may suspend the general rule in certain investments for public policy, security or public health reasons. Also, the restrictions on the acquisition of national companies have been liberalised. The securities market regulations require the investors to make a formal take-over offer if they want to acquire more than 50% of a Spanish company. After the privatisation process of the public Spanish companies, the government has kept a golden share in some of them that were not in use. In general, both public and private companies receive the same treatment with regards to their access to markets, loans, licences and supplies.

6.5.2 *Portugal*

Portugal, like Spain, fosters and promotes FDI inflows. The Portuguese system is based on the non-discrimination with regards to the investments' origin. The private

Table 6.47 Rule Box 7: Main legislations relating to FDI in Spain

– Corporations Law of 17 July 1951; amended by Royal Decree 1564 of 22 December 1989
– Private Limited Liability Companies Law 2 of 23 March 1995
– Mergers and Acquisitions Royal Decree 1080 of 1992
– Royal Decree Law 1676 of 1999 on Takeovers
– Competition Law 52 of 28 December 1999
– Urgent Measures to Intensify Competition in Goods and Services Markets. Royal Decree 6 of 23 June 2000
– Regulatory Details of the Bank of Spain's Powers (specifically regarding foreign investment in the bank sector). Royal Decree 1245 of 1995
– Authorisation of Investments in New Entities. Royal Decrees 622 and 623 of 27 March 1981
– Foreign Investment Royal Decree 664 of 23 April 1999
– Industrial Property Law 11 of 1986
– Royal Decree 441 of 1994 on procedures in industrial property
– Patents Law 11 of 20 March 1986. Application of Patents Law Royal Decree 2424 of 1986
– Intellectual Property Law 22 of 11 November 1987
– Intellectual Property, Law-out, Topographies of Semiconductor Products Protection Law 11 of 3 May 1988
– Software Protection Law 18 of 12 April 1996
– Trademarks Law 32 of 10 November 1988. Royal Decree 645 of 1990 on Trademarks Law
– Regulations for the Implementation of the Trademark Law
– Applicable Procedure in Industrial Property Royal Decree 441 of 1994
– Corporate Tax Law 43 of 27 November 1995
– Budget Act of 1991
– Foreign Exchange Royal Decree 1816 of 1991
– Urgent Fiscal Measures to Stimulate the Economy, Law 7 of 7 June 1996
– Urgent Fiscal Measures to Stimulate Savings and Small and Medium-sized Enterprises Law 6 of 13 December 2000
– Resolution of the Department of Trade Policy and Foreign Investment of 9 July 1996, applying articles 4, 5, 7 and 10 of the Minister of Economy and Finance of 27 December 1991 on Foreign Economic Transactions
– Hydrocarbons Law of 7 October 1998, effective: 8 October 1998
– Electrical Sector Law 54 of 1997
– New General Telecommunications Law 32/2003 of 3 November
– Tax Reform of 2003

Source: UNCTAD, 2005

investment is only limited when it involves certain economic activities, which include: exploitation, treatment and distribution of water for public consumption, postal services, train transport as public service and the running of seaports. Private companies can operate in those areas under the concession of a managing contract. The investment projects are subject to special legal requirements only if they somehow affect public policy, security or health; if they imply manufacturing arms, ammunitions or other military equipment; or if they imply the exercise of the public authority. The AICEP (Portuguese Trade and Investment Agency) is the institution responsible for the promotion of investment and investors support at a large scale in Portugal. The AICEP is the sole contact point for strategic investment projects in the country, providing a one-to-one service in the whole investment process. With regards to conditions on property and control, or operating ones, there are no applicable restrictions to FDI in Portugal. There is no restriction on the cross-border flow of capital either. Only under exceptional circumstances can the central bank impose temporary restrictions. The financial institutions must report their cross-border operations to the central bank for statistical purposes. Foreign investors are free to transfer and repatriate their investment (capital), benefits or revenues, royalties or fees after paying taxes accordingly.

Foreign investment in Spain has decreased gradually since 2003 up until now (Fig. 6.26; Tables 6.48 and 6.49).

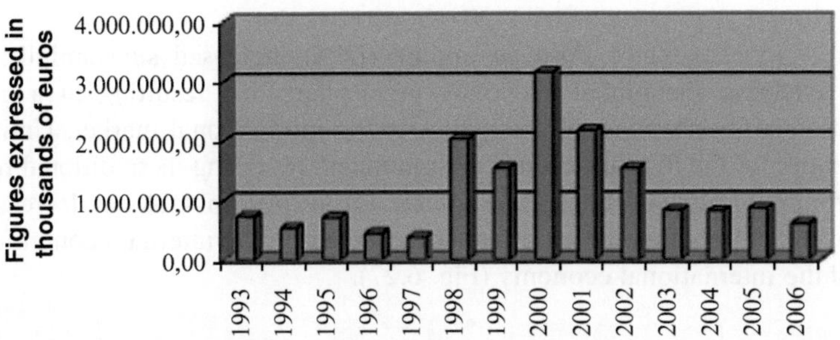

Fig. 6.26 FDI in Spain

Table 6.48 FDI in Spain

Years	Figures expressed in thousands of Euros
1993	723,667.56
1994	532,688.35
1995	706,064.88
1996	436,843.26
1997	375,821.92
1998	2,021,667.47
1999	1,536,792.40
2000	3,148,073.91
2001	2,169,390.04
2002	1,532,908.38
2003	822,732.87
2004	809,561.18
2005	858,506.85
2006	592,416.35

Source: Ministry of Industry, Tourism and Trade, Secretary of State of Industry, Tourism and Trade. Reports: 1993–2005

Table 6.49 FDI in Spain

Years	Net position (assets–liabilities)	From Spain abroad (assets)	From abroad to Spain (Liabilities)
1999	−7.3	117.5	124.8
2000	12.2	180.2	168
2001	16.3	217.5	201.1
2002	−22.1	223.1	245.2
2003	−37.4	231.6	268.9
2004	21.8	254.7	280.9
2005	1.1	301.4	302.6
2006	42.9	367.8	324.9
2007 (1st semester)	56.4	392.9	336.5

Source: Statistics from the Bank of Spain

6.5.2.1 Portugal Direct Investment Abroad

The direct investment of Portugal abroad (DIA) increased substantially in the 1990s, reflecting the global economic atmosphere and resulting in a growing implication of the Portuguese companies in the international market. Until 2000, the evolution of the FDI has been very significant, reversing its traditional role and transforming Portugal into a capital exporter. From 2001 on, DIA has decreased as a result of the entrepreneurial environment affected by the internal economic situation and the international economy (Fig. 6.27).

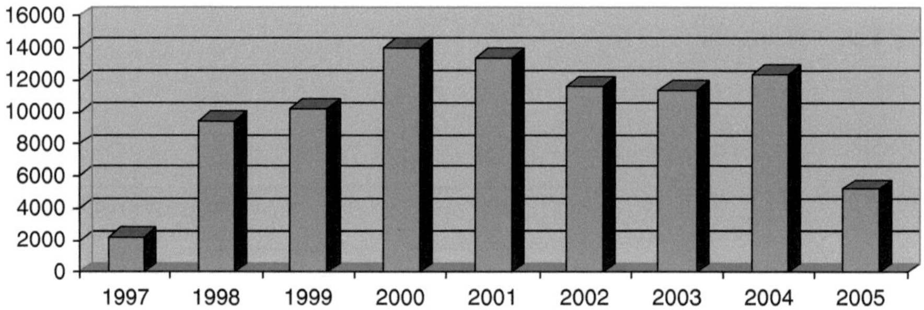

Fig. 6.27 Evolution of the direct investment of Portugal abroad (Gross investment in millions of Euros). Data available as of May 2006
Source: Bank of Portugal

Until 1990, the investment abroad was specially directed towards the United States and Europe, with special focus on the United Kingdom, Spain and France. Between 1991 and 1995 Spain was, by far, the first destination of the Portuguese outflows, representing more than 45% in 1995. Nevertheless, from 1996 on, the tendency changed, which was translated into a greater geographical diversification of DIA destinations. The EU quota decreased from 80% in 1995 to 46% in 2000. Brazil arose as the privileged market for Portuguese investors, reaching 40% of DIA in 1998. In 2001, a greater concentration of Portuguese investment in the EU markets took place, the Netherlands being the first destination, followed by Spain. Once again, the EU in 2001 represented 81% of DIA. The alterations are the product of the entrepreneurial strategies dynamic. This situation was due to a greater vulnerability of the investments in Latin America, therefore, investment in Brazil in 2001 dropped to 9%, much less than in previous years. In 2002, the first DIA destinations were also Spain and Netherlands, but Brazil recovered the third place. In 2004, the European Union's position became more pronounced, with Denmark, Netherlands and Spain in the first places, followed by Brazil. In 2005, the situation was very similar, with Netherlands, Spain and Greece, in the first place, followed by Canada and Brazil.

In the last years, a greater diversification of the Portuguese outflows destinations has been registered. In fact, Brazil's position has been replaced by countries from Central and East Europe, reflecting the will and capacity of developing a global stance. Portuguese investment in Portuguese-speaking African countries also resulted in DIA growth, mainly in Angola. The search of Portuguese companies for well-defined strategies of internationalisation, based on sound and sustainable foundations, will allow the promotion of Portugal and Portuguese products abroad, with advantageous consequences as far as an increase in revenues for the country, and dissemination of the good Portuguese name world-wide.

Between 1996 and 2003, the Portuguese investments per activity sector, have been mainly addressed to real estate activities, rents and services supplied to companies, which represent more than half of the total. These are followed by financial activities, transport, storage and communications, trade, repairs, lodging and restaurants. In 2004, DIA concentration was significant in real estate activities, rents and services supplied to companies (87% of the total), followed, by far, by trade, repairs, lodging and restaurants (4.2%), financial activities (4.1%) and the

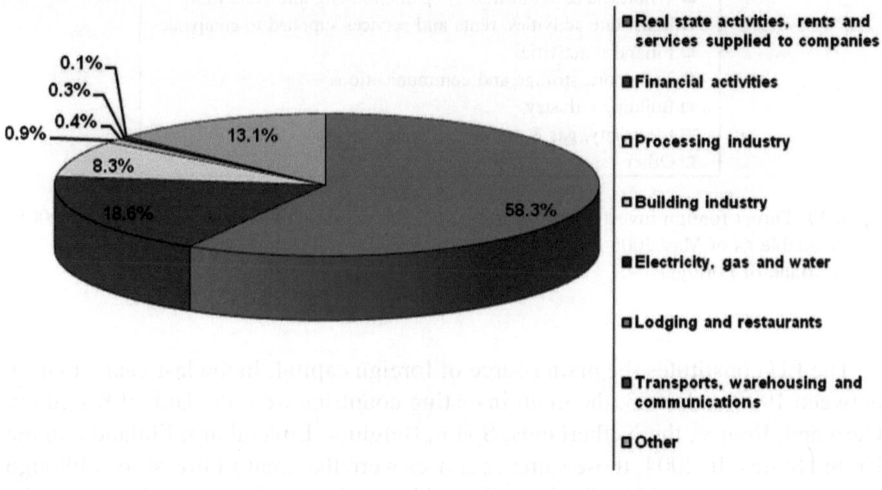

Fig. 6.28 Direct Investment of Portugal abroad per activity sectors. 2005
Source: Bank of Portugal, Data available as at May 2006

processing industry (2.1%). In 2005, real estate activities, rents and services supplied to companies had less weight (58.3%), but was still the most important. Financial activities gained relevance (18.6%) as well as the processing industry (8.3%) (Fig. 6.28).

6.5.2.2 Portugal: Direct Foreign Investment

Direct foreign investment in Portugal has grown intensely since the beginning of the 1990s, reaching high levels in 1993–1994. Coinciding with the project Autoeuropa, greater levels of direct foreign investment were reached in Portugal. Nevertheless, there was a decrease around the middle of the 1990s, followed by a recovery at the beginning of 2000 during the crucial moment of the international mergers and acquisitions. The atmosphere that had influenced the direct foreign investment in Portugal has been recovered, although in the last 3 years, there has been a downward inflection (Fig. 6.29).

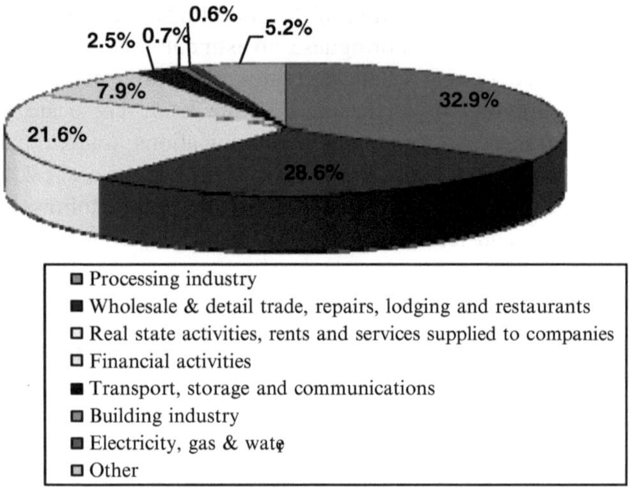

Fig. 6.29 Direct foreign investment in Portugal per sectors of activity (gross investment), 2005. Data available as of May 2006
Source: Bank of Portugal

The EU constitutes the main source of foreign capital. In the last years, mainly between 1996 and 2003, the main investing countries were the United Kingdom, Germany, France, the Netherlands, Spain, Belgium, Luxemburg, Finland and the United States. In 2004, those same countries were the greatest investors, although the first place was held by Spain, followed by the United Kingdom, Germany, the Netherlands, France, Finland, Belgium and the United States. In 2005, the main places were occupied once again by countries form the European Union: Germany in the first place, followed by the Netherlands, the United Kingdom, France and Spain.

In the distribution per sectors, the processing industry is the main investment sector. Between 1996 and 2003, the processing industry represented more than two fifths of the total invested amount, followed by real estate activities, rents and services supplied to companies, trade, repairs, lodging and restaurants, transport and communications and financial activities. In 2004, the processing industry continued leading the list (30.1%), followed by trade, repairs, lodging and restaurants (28.2%), real estate activities and services supplied to companies (24.1%) and financial activities (10.7%). As early as 2005, as it can be observed in the following graph, the position of the processing industry is strengthened; the trade maintains its weight, as much in wholesale as in retail, repairs, lodging and restaurants, and the real estate activities and services supplied to companies reduce their participation by a small amount. Also, the financial activities lose significance in 2005.

It has to be said that part of the decrease in direct foreign investment in Portugal has been due to the increment of international competition and the relocation flare-up of many companies to more competitive countries, mainly in Central and Eastern Europe and Asia. According to the National Budget for 2007, the Portuguese government would have actively promoted the creation of the necessary conditions for attracting initiatives of domestic or foreign investment in structures, that would connect with the entrepreneurial network (especially small and medium-size enterprises) and with the scientific and technological system of the country, thus contributing to the internationalisation of the Portuguese companies and the improvement of the specialisation profile of the national economy. In parallel, the Government would support and back the Portuguese investment dynamic abroad, endeavouring to combine economic efficiency with social effectiveness.

6.6 Conclusion

Both the Spanish and the Portuguese financial systems have traditionally been highly regulated and subject to government intervention. With heavily protected domestic economies and poor competitiveness, the financial system accurately reflected the general economic trend of both countries. In Spain, the Stabilisation Plan of 1959 implied significant changes in the Spanish economy, stimulating an opening and liberalisation process which was reflected in the financial system with the enactment of the Law regulating Credit and Banks of 1962. In the 1970s and beginning of the 1980s, a decisive reform of the Spanish financial system was carried out, liberalising and bringing it closer to the European performance. With its accession to the EU, Spain took the definitive step to liberalise its economy and financial system, when inevitably, it had to adapt to the Community Regulations and the requirements of the single financial area.

In the specific case of the Spanish financial system, even though it was directed towards the banking industry, non-banking intermediaries have acquired a significant role in recent years, which has favoured a greater development and diversification of the domestic financial market and greater opportunities to guide the domestic savings towards new financial products and services. The reasons for this change were mainly due to:

- The process of financial liberalisation carried out throughout the 1980s and at the beginning of the 1990s with the entry into the EU.
- The increase competition that has facilitated and encouraged the financial businesses' expansion in Spain.
- The creation and consolidation of the single market in financial services, which has fostered a process of banking concentration in Spain, that, instead of weakening the banking industry has strengthened and transformed it into a highly competitive industry inside and outside its frontiers.
- The financial globalisation, technological advancement and the internationalisation of the Spanish economy.
- The development and opening of the financial system in Spain, since the mid 1990s.
- The international expansion strategy of Spanish banking businesses, which turned to Europe in search of strategic alliances with European banks, as a first stage, and which was followed around the middle of the current decade, with trans-European mergers and acquisitions. Inside the national borders an important consolidation process took place, usually with internal restructurings of the big bank groups, especially between 1998 and 2000. The expansion strategy in Latin America has tended towards the direct presence of the Spanish banks in those countries.
- The EMU and the single currency that have combined and facilitated the virtuous circle of financial stability and budgetary prudence, with public deficit reduction, redirecting financial resources that used to go to the State towards private industry, thus favouring the development of the stock market.
- The flexibility demonstrated by the banking system in seeking new sources of income, after the EU moved to the third stage of EMU stage and the single currency, targeting new investment segments and income other than interest rates in order to maintain an acceptable rate of profitability in an environment where operating margins have narrowed.
- The cessation of political interference in the banking system. The official banks have practically privatised themselves. The Official Credit Institute (ICO) is the only official bank acting as a finance agency for the government and as a development bank.
- The quick expansion of the capital markets due to the financial deregulation and harmonisation process in the EU. In Portugal, the legal framework that

regulated the trading activity of banks and other credit institutions was not created until the final years of the 1950s. The most important changes took place in the 1970s, after the 1974 revolution and its effects on the financial system. At the beginning of the 1980s a gradual process of liberalisation began, whose main focus was the banking industry. Portugal's accession to membership of the EU, like Spain, was the definitive step for the liberalisation of the Portuguese economy.

Comparing the experience and evolution of Spain and Portugal with the transformation that the Eastern European cohesion states experienced, we can establish some parameters in order to answer the question raised at the beginning of this essay: Could the experience of the evolution of the financial markets in Spain and Portugal countries serve to inform the cohesion countries in their adaptation to financial globalisation and the EU single financial area? In answering this, we set out the operating framework in which Spain, Portugal and the cohesion countries have developed. In both groups of countries the first step for the economic–financial transformation has been linked with a political trigger. In Spain with the Stabilisation Plan in the midst of the autarchic period and the absence of liberties, and the need for a more open economy, scarcely political, but economically necessary; in Portugal with the revolution of the 1970s, and in the cohesion countries with the fall of the Berlin wall.

1. The economic situation of the world and the EU when Spain and Portugal joined the Union, is far from being comparable to the situation of the world and the EU economies when the cohesion countries joined, given both the evolution in the interim experienced by the international financial system and the evolution of the EU itself as far as the financial practices that have been developed and the current supervisory and regulatory standards.
2. When Spain and Portugal joined to the EU in 1986, the financial, technical and tax barriers hampering the existence of a single market in Europe had just been identified. In the White paper, approved in June 1985, the proposals to achieve a single internal market and a schedule were set out. Thus in 1986 the EU was only embarking on the single market project. By contrast, when the cohesion countries joined, the internal European market was under way with 11 years of experience; that is to say, they joined with an internal market in operation with free movement of capital, services, goods and, persons.
3. Although the free movement of capital can be deemed as the starting point of the EU financial system's liberalisation when Spain and Portugal joined the union, the directive 88/361/EEC had not yet been approved. The Rome Treaty considered that the complete liberalisation of the movements of capital was one of the fundamental freedoms, and that was one of the reasons why the Werner Report of 1970 is included among the necessary conditions for the Monetary Union (the second condition). The White paper programme included the expectation that the European financial system would to be transformed into a competitive and efficient system connecting savings and investment in a single market. But neither in the Rome Treaty, nor in the

community law nor in the Single European Act were movements of capital defined. Lists only existed about transactions liberalised or not yet liberalised, but did not say anything about what was understood by current payments and movements of capital. Only 2 years before Spain's and Portugal's entry into the EU, the EC Court of Justice recognised that gap and proposed a definition differentiating among current payments and movements of capital, and 2 years after the entry of both countries, the directive 88/361/EEC on the free movement of capital was approved in June 1988, being in force for residents in Spain since 18 April 1991 and definitively in February 1992. The barriers to Spanish investment abroad and the foreign investment in Spain were eliminated in May 1999. The control was reduced to a notification for statistical purposes (except in tax havens or foreign investment in the Spanish defence industry). The cohesion countries joined when all the member states of the Union had already completely incorporated the community regulations derived from directive 88/361/EEC.

4. The directive on capital liberalisation not only opened the way for the financial integration but it also placed the European Union in need of undertaking a decisive reform of the European Monetary System, leaving the central banks without a defence instrument when faced with the speculative attacks against their domestic currencies. Spain and Portugal joined the debate on the EMU and the Delors Report was approved in Madrid Summit 3 years after Spain became a member in June 1989. That is, when Spain and Portugal joined the EU, the discussion basis in the EU had not yet been foreseen. It would not be until years after they joined that the need for an Economic and Monetary Union in Europe started emerge. The idea of the single currency was still a long way off. By contrast, the cohesion countries joined with a completed EMU and a single currency, the Euro, in place. Their financial and economic systems have found themselves with a monetary scheme already established and with operating rules approved beforehand.
5. The cohesion countries had joined the EU when there was already an institutional monetary organisation in the EU with the European System of Central Banks (ESCB), the European Central Bank (ECB) and a monetary policy for the countries of the Euro zone. They have the opportunity of joining voluntarily, as member states subject to exception, to the new Exchange-rate mechanisms (ERM II) under economic and monetary behaviour rules that not only ensured convergence towards macroeconomic stability in order to incorporate the Euro, but which also protected them against unjustified turbulences and pressures in the currency markets. Spain and Portugal, because of the European Monetary System of 1992, suffered two devaluations of their respective currencies with the subsequent economic consequences.
6. International cooperation has intensified in recent last years, especially since the Asian crisis. The standards of good behaviour both at the sectoral level and at the joint level through the FSAPs, put into practice by the IMF and the World Bank, have substantially contributed to create a new performance framework not

only for EU member states but also for all the countries within the international community.

7. If the creation of a European financial area is directly related to the establishment of the single European market, Spain and Portugal joined the EU in the historic moment in which that single market was launched. Since 1983, when the Council presented a report on the widening of financial integration, the discussion at community level has progressed to include a series of directives to co-ordinate the establishment and operating conditions of the life assurance companies, other insurances and credit institutions, the advancement of the liberalisation process on services moved from the first directives on banking and insurances, and the free establishment towards the freedom to provide services, which was the objective of the Second banking co-ordination directive (1989) and the third insurances directive (1992).
8. The Second banking co-ordination directive, as well as the third insurance directive, and those proposed afterwards, were enacted when Spain and Portugal where already in the EU. The cohesion countries have found themselves with an established financial framework ready to be incorporated into their respective domestic legislations.
9. Finally, it could be concluded that the financial experience of Spain and Portugal with regards to the cohesion countries is quite different. The first two countries, especially Spain, have gone through a financial evolution prior to joining the EU, with decisive reforms of their financial systems and with previous solvency standards, so their adaptation to the community regulations did not involve a substantial alteration of their internal administration. This leads us to conclude that the Spanish financial experience is not comparable with that of the cohesion countries which lacked a financial background prior to joining the EU. However, we think that the developing countries or emerging countries who look at the EU as a regulatory and financial benchmark could use the experience and financial development of Spain, as well as the solvency standards that Spain has maintained throughout all this time, to avoid domestic and international financial turbulences.

Appendix 1. Spanish Direct Investment Abroad

Spanish Direct investment abroad: banking industry, other financial intermediaries, insurances, and pension plans (1993–2007)

(1000s of Euros)

Countries	1993	1994	1995	1996	1997	1998	1999
Andorra	2,950.66	22,044.93	808.91	3,568.94	76,100.20	5,587.77	
Angola	8,725.98	3,484.59	1,622.73				
Algeria			923.75	4,426.32	536.13	462.05	1,674.08
Argentina	138,057.72	608,145.49	283,691.16	1,560,085.63	4,246,638.40	1,758,122.98	
Aruba	1,033.76		9,223.40	0.92			1,636.41
Australia	2,291.52	7,115.98	18,455.88	1,102.95	5,040.81	2,889.55	6,006.06
Austria	577.90	0.00	3,032.76		113.00	1,483.62	76,544.48
Azerbaijan							
Bahamas	1,819.92		6,890.10	60.07	33.64		18,377.22
Bahrain		598.80		376.22	12.23		45.88
Belgium	123,334.13	41,905.72	52,521.76	38,267.26	9,784.92	689,717.63	96,598.76
Belize						2.40	0.00
Benin					31.79		
Bermudas	195.68	10.81		73.65	10,963.03	78.58	494,042.68
Belarus			150.25	1.06			
Bolivia	349.40	76.93	21.24	4,507.29	16,372.66	65,431.77	125,852.43
Brazil	52,593.30	45,070.21	72,656.10	594,958.54	1,120,824.47	5,654,022.74	8,558,237.98
British Virgin Islands	248,987.63	120,398.04	1,672,165.38	49,222.73	3,618.47	622.56	374,354.67
Canada	3,070.80		22,856.43	1,511.55	539.20	1,208.09	316,852.75
Chile	210,698.00	15,702.73	54,655.16	639,144.33	586,889.17	438,035.27	5,245,853.07
China	70.21	85.04	3,698.75	3,939.40	5,101.02	6,135.97	17,024.35
Colombia	10,661.34	30,588.68	38,848.62	54,910.78	1,641,506.88	423,262.88	741,304.79
Costa Rica	162.84	237.93	8.66	6,538.26	4,027.74	1,284.31	653.98
Croatia					11.39	2.09	1.58
Cuba	2.25	3,556.67	189.59		44,039.83	1,480.02	15,862.39
Czech Republic	96.15	603.72	730.10	3,506.52	1,777.62	6,338.28	12,796.52
Denmark					4,790.94	3.40	269,312.44
Ecuador	299.03	35,541.68	580.84	18,547.10	40,773.99	71,736.70	6,712.70
Equatorial Guinea		144.24			626.05	0.36	
Egypt			6,536.62		3.57		134.52
El Salvador	11.56		114.16		18.78	81,299.22	41,828.34
Estonia					0.38		
Filipinas	2,554.30		50,163.91	20,076.84	9,901.44	28,514.83	220,883.89
Finland				9.97			10,000.00
France	168,853.43	212,643.50	607,166.05	144,015.11	133,801.13	195,770.52	950,135.79
Gambia			869.67			3,320.59	0.00
Germany	55,221.39	32,867.95	227,314.28	189,861.24	184,516.50	357,856.65	2,556,040.32
Ghana				22.92	23.44	10,456.10	3.95
Gibraltar	2,862.80	343.54	1,080.67	4,401.01	9,846.93	302.73	291.51
Granada							
Greece	9.86	962.86	15,355.13	673.09	2,730.10	1,073.61	13,863.61
Guatemala	57.78	435.30		72.11	17.74	46.34	387,025.71
Guinea	1,460.46			0.05	1,613.42		
Guinea-Bissau		591.75	530.09		31.29		151.79
Honduras		2.10			19,184.31	38,733.17	5.43
Hong Kong	3,889.51	11,784.24	5,195.27	3,854.93	1,557.49	8,123.70	57,397.51
Hungary	1,538.03	3,079.27	4,326.85	2,526.89	490.97	9,880.98	28,946.86
Iceland		13.10					
India	248.98	195.87	52.25	20.01	2,785.47	925.90	1,280.56
Indonesia	17.28		2,226.15			806.81	1,018.34
Ireland	26,798.91	11,531.77	4,613.92	13,387.83	7,188.25	11,705.04	131,313.61
Islas Cayman	39,337.28	92,015.44	274,959.29	272,488.03	166,286.44	552,711.45	843,538.92
Islas Malvinas (Falklands)		783.72	599.98	411.30	8,355.18	3,244.96	5,493.54
Israel					9.02	4,984.90	5,451.43
Italy	69,202.01	120,844.47	42,653.37	64,637.85	44,026.61	177,257.77	1,380,312.21
Ivory Coast				124.27	7.54	1.50	
Jamaica			1.82	7.67			
Japan			1,267.22		8.90	2,348.62	18,486.05
Jersey	23,029.52	542.44	55,346.13	24,571.78	5,379.58	165,626.54	12.08
Lebanon		10.56					
Liberia	1.56						1,803.04
Libya	38.18	42.07	36.06		36.60		38.94
Liechtenstein	12,645.29	23.71	2,218.94	5,586.23	467.08	268.10	2,649.11

2000	2001	2002	2003	2004	2005	2006	2007 (January–March)
188,866.25	2,438.68	1,539.81	3,668.14	200.41	2,453.33	12,321.90	60.00
				19.48	126.01	119.92	
	246.41	119.88	1.16	240.72	2,226.90	83,179.53	368.58
3,458,075.73	2,163,558.49	1,552,114.53	484,168.82	225,674.90	2,483,301.64	375,465.49	64,868.20
0.00							
12,483.45	38,449.83	1,255,717.32	19,729.98	7,322.14	10,863.72	4,106.25	
6,300.86	70,466.31	89,990.49	175,763.40	47,546.47	41,190.52	709,124.59	2,850.43
19,952.97	1,174.42	180,068.67				14,519.24	
			1,238.46				
40,451.67	27,791.10	140,309.25	198,625.41	117,669.23	68,388.70	3,096,968.69	330,630.67
3.99		50.00	181.39	82.73	2,055.13	1,203.74	
12.19							
28,025.85	5,891.36		1,404.10	3,252.03	20,013.64	72,145.31	
14,788.72	2,595.66	93,831.59	152.22	15,256.35	4.17		
19,799,214.80	1,979,566.45	3,071,917.65	960,272.59	802,067.88	1,570,542.77	919,084.75	398,575.91
98,726.44	36,448.44	40,374.93	717.22	37,915.71	917.62	77,580.86	
8,544.40	17,122.84	198,787.61	59,741.52	536,508.02	185,687.46	32,222.02	205.47
1,022,764.98	1,431,899.73	443,261.44	1,971,892.21	703,108.70	531,548.80	131,183.71	6,849.93
43,020.45	18,037.14	22,031.53	27,053.60	68,661.97	60,753.68	90,010.68	990,928.73
637,404.77	361,946.89	146,234.03	192,016.43	273,935.20	15,053.19	32,242.33	4,379.27
4,745.46	6,415.47	5,566.63	6,841.11	12,608.61	7,636.58	3,797.27	
0.79	8,391.82	245.68			5.70	20,797.29	
773,193.73	23,131.98	1,024.00	3.20		2,024.01	2,976.36	
9,417.53	22,980.74	3,505.32	46,993.90	44,807.68	3,685,062.24	209,843.95	8,824.51
606,506.21	3,330.17	4,503.90	243,998.01	6,337.11	431,125.12	76,730.21	
1,466.93	5,645.70	40,850.87	8,324.72	4,403.06	1,288.03	8,590.45	326.52
300.51						1,800.00	6.00
28.61	6,610.71	8,668.04	214,681.92	7,846.74	374,558.15	3,432.83	1,836.84
40,155.23	36,772.60	73,527.02	2,410.05	13,853.07	28.94	807.42	
						1,022.17	
2,651.68	22,575.95		6,279.97	2,568.31			
15,748.06	500.00	9,300.00		38,130.99	104,006.40	40,629.06	37,295.86
1,946,422.87	943,141.35	655,140.37	1,002,767.52	3,340,698.47	5,747,625.19	4,967,979.63	1,192,923.34
1,727.52			3.02				
1,356,433.60	1,882,799.07	8,257,483.42	890,650.88	1,171,107.72	537,912.30	1,011,532.87	163,521.74
12,161.59	440.04		5,056.00	344.20	1,030.09		
1.59	1.64	2,148.34		1.56	10,777.96	0.14	
1,918.85	111,394.69	10,661.24	328,554.86	81,684.15	65,216.81	151,833.19	559,241.11
20,478.82	37,753.09	188,948.37	7,507.16	246.63	372.10	3,337.45	
	1,605.80				1,508.06		
				762.20			
132.85	1.60	127.69	24.30	1,081.20	94.66	237.19	
191,649.03	6,352.04	1,503.15	1,474.71	1,512.46	12,473.57	3,482.89	397.00
2,336,917.30	176,517.32	233,966.22	541,151.60	278,272.78	4,371,384.14	2,326,755.44	15,576.87
					2,359.20		
349.52	2,241.10	74,369.92	3,588.22	2,161.43	822.52	55,805.99	1.75
3,870.16	1,033.68	203.00	2,401.65	6,195.29	84.50	57.69	
285,383.78	7,014.48	461,511.77	1,350,282.93	594,392.27	69,723.26	264,675.86	25.00
831,444.77	263,192.27	29,690.68	450,553.97	326,137.59	35,970.90	157,691.01	3,087.86
2,811.63		1,734.21	1,668.95	2,408.82		4,582.07	
4,157.59	8,056.58		5,709.05		148.23	266.19	
476,365.17	2,190,191.48	164,297.89	1,006,879.31	2,461,019.49	613,008.19	1,278,014.31	735,995.20
	108.43		12,983.10	1,808.71			
	1.00		6,138.50		384.34	1,157.29	
11,252.55	994.42	10,840.06	1,871.18	78,887.15	57,934.33	27,492.76	
9,122.02	10,000.00	2,288.62	1,005.10	915.36	622.96	18,047.00	
20.69					593.37		
	3,833.50				1,150.93		
		4,500.00	4,500.00	3,867.93			
					6,404.00		

(*continued*)

Countries	1993	1994	1995	1996	1997	1998	1999
Luxemburg	23,126.72	394,827.34	47,630.45	23,899.95	47,747.06	113,577.30	38,400.45
Malaysia	172.65			490.66	10,512.59	1,081.08	336.48
Mali			477.70				
Malta				1.03			
Man Island		4.80	9.20				
Mauricio					2.60	93.10	99.35
Mauritania		416.93	6.01	22.56	260.83	1.35	
Mexico	43,123.18	77,836.77	150,325.38	72,048.27	318,122.33	560,112.86	1,464,014.27
Moldavia							0.27
Monaco			20,238.76	447.22	1,185.19		1,304.92
Morocco	66,516.52	5,258.10	29.,27.69	26,068.77	10,839.55	14,084.14	174,117.26
Mozambique	18.19		1,833.21		103.83	38.77	
Namibia	3,979.41	1,803.04	1,627.06	4,886.23	14,028.22	2,434.10	5,420.58
Netherlands	412,263.27	363,697.38	251,899.07	214,516.29	1,214,044.56	1,382,261.59	4,245,988.41
Netherlands Antilles	22.38	3,267.08	7,644.27	10,860.29	95,812.97	1,064.82	245,579.21
Nicaragua		7.51	7.59		6,167.55	4,269.73	131.30
Niger							
Nigeria				18.51			
Norway		76.40	954.30			432.48	2,720.28
Pakistan				172.43			
Panama	22,172.97	104,181.43	189,293.59	194,258.41	104,328.46	263,899.32	178,903.60
Paraguay	1,631.10	888.56	2,458.48	3,656.52	1,626.58	5,855.82	26,803.04
Peru	74.53	1.692,327.89	190,234.44	299,231.62	84,910.81	83,388.35	211,352.80
Poland	26,014.68	18,158.73	10,889.59	1,503.29	798.33	1,618.93	75,878.58
Portugal	495,067.76	674,154.86	2,439,042.91	533,474.92	773,223.79	828,914.54	1,111,327.99
Republic Of Cape Verde				796.57			2,377.81
Romania			468.94	19.50	123.17	2,724.31	10,706.32
Russia	128.42	17,950.61	228.70	240.86	10,223.73	1,005.02	1,797.00
Senegal		2.47	257.48	3.76	33.19	4,530.25	1.13
Serbia And Montenegro							
Singapore	0.00	16,856.76	1,589.00	103.31	874.71	717.10	728.69
Slovakia Republic				12.14	143.02		
Slovenia	0.23	28,126.16	5,524.17		337.12	540.43	
South Africa	2,319.92		1.50	676.30	274.37	1,381.95	21,678.26
South Korea	299.91				51.09	219.51	21,860.11
Sweden	895.75	5.35	805.27	8.17	1,998.37	3,891.39	778.96
Switzerland	2,962.83	3,459.23	2,522,699.84	71,766.01	22,024.04	596,050.67	1,815,416.13
Taiwan			416.01			398.38	
Thailand	3.49	11.42	296.74	58.54	5,283.10	21.92	5,927.70
Tunisia	429.76	873.64	295.39	392.14	411.92	136,454.22	24,677.83
Turkey	42.69	1,418.09	31,609.25	12,809.68	5,784.98	5,714.98	90,155.98
Ukraine	107.10	627.13	85.78		2.75	5,791.93	17.24
United Arab Emirates	48.71	57.70	1,451.63	210.35		239.25	
United Kingdom	23,086.16	25,382.03	58,836.37	119,156.18	272,282.00	694,211.05	485,188.56
United States De America	227,700.01	302,016.91	322,088.62	830,900.00	692,262.18	2,181,345.55	826,636.61
Uruguay	5,44.15	9,814.64	2,975.86	84,332.79	72,738.30	17,357.42	46,561.19
Venezuela	15,360.50	2,616.33	6,615.40	105,385.13	688,366.96	697,605.95	73,505.52

Source: Ministry of Industry, Tourism and Trade, Secretary of State for Industry, Tourism and Trade. Reports: 1993–2005

2000	2001	2002	2003	2004	2005	2006	2007 (January–March)
164,760.31	657,250.39	295,624.41	71,765.64	326,196.85	1,521,109.10	239,115.30	56,460.60
798.29		580.00	557.05	4,754.74	1,129.20	137.48	
			3.63	1.55			
295.83	126.23			1,710.99	26,842.88	59,453.10	
2,687.59	2,902.33	230.52				315.00	
		703.13	78,404.04	83.16	2,500.99	6,000.00	
1,142.95	1,990.28	755.00	72.00		0.00		
7,474,043.18	2,187,330.88	1,548,133.03	1,246,606.59	7,437,039.46	891,763.79	455,016.34	29,139.90
40,651.86				2,627.43			
	38,121.76	1,095.38	765.06		299.00		
49,607.08	28,606.46	185,724.17	1,397,537.68	23,418.06	81,479.87	437,420.29	5,521.82
1,859.51	405.18			2,885.76			
		0.04	6,005.26	20,428.51	57,935.46	46,914.49	
2,685,347.45	7,901,086.09	3,336,260.73	452,248.85	3,812,526.58	2,019,627.33	2,465,708.23	20,502.15
1,091.20	2,924.64	1,448.80	99.92	390.04	45.59	758.44	
135,307.01	6,409.74	226.20		106.47	13.95	5,173.50	
			15.01				
9,916.70	169.71	640.63	3,479.11	14.59			
978.82	2,448.93	6,212.39	3,553.49	1,017,102.90	107,775.82	546,162.48	
	157.54			315.48			
162,593.72	25,580.32	3,269.74	14,878.79	249,171.00	3,300.80	18,382.28	3,629.45
633.77	192.14	99.18	2,419.90		1,832.29		
797,945.39	463,700.60	212,301.45	24,114.33	21,420.45	23,508.82	4,203.81	1,018.33
75,357.22	30,773.83	35,801.88	119,803.14	184,915.97	232,505.76	221,530.56	7,695.24
6,543,972.11	913,187.69	1,420,470.76	2,549,559.32	2,267,683.56	1,519,297.83	2,600,669.44	86,375.91
453.45	3,533.69		299.28	9,672.09	8,903.75	56.77	
178.96	8,966.79	727.20	2,055.69	4,905.48	20,344.39	143,146.43	3,423.45
2,453.13	5,822.52	62,411.64	2,048.26	205,471.17	210,696.17	96,775.59	223.20
		78.40	1,846.80	4.50		2,000.00	
	133.62		20.56		9,238.88	2,060.00	
33,246.13		3,471.03	1,176.29	123.39	930.00	452.66	29.82
	1,264.61	1,851.04	2,576.76	10,960.15	29,917.90	7,027.13	1,038.16
150.00		9.22	990.70	2,800.00	480.00	3.00	
39,772.13	5,576.73	357,245.04	7,245.49	27,840.67	153,743.22	3,263.15	
209.57	1,152.80	284.07	8,360.00	10,079.86	15,872.46	787.57	
19,595.72	13,760.28	108,181.04	12,628.77	46,611.93	22,386.90	118,471.83	
3,437,763.72	1,264,409.99	1,541,916.41	16,983.22	62,223.50	1,073,558.78	40,803.66	1,062.84
		294.15		70.54	25.80	94.18	
3,142.74	14,385.81	1,045.22	804.88	5,847.98	1,480.33	445.81	
469.32	3,958.61	118,127.96	2,173.68		590.15	6.00	572.94
25,800.91	28,649.98	21,438.22	2,532.27	11,776.80	105,577.35	188,346.14	272,481.26
10,097.23	110.89	2.83	2,025.46		4,121.21	502.28	424.61
379.75	61.22	218.93	324.26	284.95	4,126.09	14,122.69	
1,357,792.62	650,885.18	983,911.03	3,649,801.91	26,978,804.50	3,303,747.07	31,655,435.35	127,529.58
10,405,306.60	2,900,741.84	2,473,858.24	1,937,367.32	1,103,336.26	2,928,628.22	10,856,096.14	914,811.04
307,701.01	217,086.44	624,387.72	94,521.55	108,683.66	58,664.98	22,997.80	36,340.50
113,233.88	2,279,188.64	45,600.66	24,637.47	170,256.94	30,884.97	106,827.46	6,650.71

Appendix 2. FDI Flows, by Type of Investment, of Spain, 1992–2003 (millions of Euros)

FDI flows, by type of investment, of Spain, 1992–2003 (millions of Euros)

Year	Inward investment				Outward investment			
	Equity	Reinvested earnings	Other	Total	Equity	Reinvested earnings	Other	Total
1992	4,821	–	3,395	8,216	1,118	–	218	1,336
1993	4,678	–	2,642	7,320	1,942	–	485	2,427
1994	6,084	–	1,385	7,468	3,470	–	−161	3,310
1995	3,008	–	1,702	4,710	2,590	–	526	3,116
1996	3,016	–	2,178	5,193	3,724	–	532	4,256
1997	3,810	–	1,811	5,620	9,623	–	1,417	11,041
1998	4,109	–	6,483	10,592	14,053	–	2,949	17,002
1999	10,267	–	4,524	14,791	37,987	–	1,514	39,501
2000	30,382	–	10,346	40,728	52,690	–	6,654	59,344
2001	15,524	–	15,771	31,296	29,549	–	7,433	36,982
2002	18,019	–	20,134	38,153	33,831	–	−348	33,483
2003	4,408	–	18,297	22,705	20,870	–	−160	20,709

Source: Bank of Spain, Balanza de Pagos

Note: Data on reinvested earnings are not available. Other capital includes intra-company loans. Due to rounding, the components may not add up to the total. In 1993, a new balance-of-payments data compilation system was introduced and therefore, data from 1993 onwards reflect this new methodology. However, only data for the year 1990–1992 were adjusted to this methodology resulting in a break in time series in 1990. Data might differ from those reported in 5–10 as updated information on FDI flows classified by region/economy and by sector/industry were not available

Appendix 3. FDI Flows, by Type of Investment of Portugal, 1992–2003, million dollars

Year	Inward investment				Outward investment			
	Equity	Reinvested earnings	Other	Total	Equity	Reinvested earnings	Other	Total
1992	1,825	47	2	1,873	614	–	73	687
1993	1,067	−2	469	1,534	50	11	86	147
1994	989	–	281	1,270	185	–	102	287
1995	150	–	535	685	476	1	211	688
1996	1,117	718	−132	1,703	694	55	223	972
1997	810	796	935	2,542	1,865	312	9	2,187
1998	1,356	809	987	3,151	3,148	316	387	3,851
1999	−576	1,059	752	1,235	2,598	414	7	3,019
2000	5,612	639	586	6,836	7,243	191	221	7,655
2001	1,415	835	3,572	5,822	5,665	281	1,651	7,597
2002	1,919	−510	382	1,790	1,415	46	2,001	3,462
2003	1,892	−132	−791	969	715	312	−901	125

Source: International Monetary Fund, balance-of-payments CD-ROM, March 05

Note: Due to rounding, the components may not add up to the total

Appendix 4. Investment Fund (million Euros, outstanding balances at the end of the period)

Total of assets and liabilities	Spain	Portugal
1998	175,550	26,877
1999	168,179	27,746
2000	165,822	25,442
2001	158,249	25,588
2002	144,150	25,421
2003	178,858	28,456
2004	207,570	31,261
2005	207,570	31,261
2006	305,716	40,566

Source: Bank of Spain. Statistics of the Euro area

Appendix 5. Debt in National Currency, Spain

Date	Bills				Bonds		Debentures	
	Up to 3 months	6 months	12 months	18 months	3 years	5 years	10 years	15 years
1987			15,254		12,582		4,654	
1988			21,984		18,826		4,450	
1989			32,477		20,938		4,009	
1990			44,368		24,940		3,904	
1991	2,378		43,971		26,565	8,158	6,551	
1992	8,047	5,895	44,894		21,701	13,332	13,143	
1993			64,449		26,431	32,253	25,490	1,959
1994		27,288	43,106		23,730	36,736	30,105	3,957
1995		4,049	66,558		27,023	40,811	42,993	5,800
1996		8,646	71,904		30,517	44,953	52,253	7,800
1997		8,687	33,663	29,440	33,030	50,184	63,946	12,785
1998		4,028	17,439	38,287	36,135	42,006	72,232	21,199
1999		2,885	18,189	32,068	39,291	49,462	81,784	25,066
2000		806	11,833	32,025	40,726	55,647	88,471	27,664
2001			12,306	23,278	36,655	53,978	101,337	29,369
2002			15,008	20,823	29,177	54,829	109,855	35,403
2003	1,053	2,476	12,366	22,871	21,988	54,609	111,747	36,938
2004	774	3,007	11,399	21,808	19,080	55,835	114,641	42,528
2005		1,720	9,584	21,990	23,904	45,562	119,649	43,733
2006			10,414	20,887	22,672	38,754	123,446	43,733
2007		3,089	22,266	7,090	11,604	35,529	128,558	43,733
2008								
January		3,672	25,093	7,090	15,848	37,319	112,331	43,733
February		3,672	26,425	4,613	15,848	37,319	117,331	43,733

Source: Bank of Spain, 2007

Appendix 6. Spain: Negotiation of Treasury Bills

	Account Owners				Third Parties					Stock Market	TOTAL NEGOTIATED			Pro-memory
Date	Outright	Repo Agreement	Sell/Buyback Transactions	TOTAL	Outright	Forward	Repo Agreement	Sell/Buyback Transactions	TOTAL	Outright	Outright	Rest**	TOTAL	BLIND MARKET***
1987	11	189		201	15		394		410		27	583	610	
1988	28	570		598	32		2,148		2,180		59	2,718	2,778	2
1989	69	832		905	93		3,440		3,533		165	4,273	4,438	7
1990	57	1,001		1,060	101		3,833		3,935		160	4,834	4,995	7
1991	116	1,227		1,344	231		4,051		4,282		348	5,278	5,626	6
1992	104	1,572		1,676	211		3,431		3,642		315	5,003	5,318	3
1993	131	1,566	1	1,699	324		2,853	82	3,259	1	457	4,502	4,959	6
1994	124	958	4	1,091	253	1	3,189	27	3,469	1	384	4,177	4,561	1
1995	196	855	4	1,063	321	5	3,084	43	3,453	2	531	3,987	4,518	1
1996	203	1,017	13	1,239	328	1	4,142	35	4,505	3	540	5,207	5,747	–.
1997	277	1,728	4	2,019	478	3	7,340	56	7,876	2	770	9,128	9,898	1
1998	160	1,144	88	1,398	244	2	6,089	14	6,349	1	412	7,335	7,747	
1999	126	301	1,374	1,810	193	5	7,977	29	8,203	0	332	9,681	10,013	
2000	89	173	1,479	1,749	236	2	8,110	117	8,465		334	9,880	10,214	
2001	85	87	1,764	1,937	144	1	8,523	118	8,785		230	10,492	10,722	
2002	59	37	802	898	101		7,909	7	8,018		160	8,756	8,915	8
2003	246	28	1,752	2,028	112	0	8,247	4	8,362		360	10,031	10,390	283
2004	333	8	1,511	1,853	118	1	6,936	7	7,062		453	8,462	8,915	269
2005	323	2	1,573	1,899	129	1	6,702	11	6,844		453	8,289	8,742	217
2006	251	0	1,634	1,886	114	0	4,648	1	4,764		367	6,283	6,650	101
January	332		1,612	1,943	85	1	5,284		5,370		418	6,896	7,314	166
February	230		1,904	2,134	113		5,384		5,498		343	7,288	7,631	105
March	263		2,569	2,832	73		5,605	0	5,678		336	8,174	8,511	195
April	343		2,342	2,686	174		5,259		5,433		518	7,601	8,119	178
May	308		1,792	2,118	134		4,653		4,787		460	6,445	6,905	116
June	274		1,830	2,107	107		4,704		4,811		384	6,534	6,919	73
July	304		1,214	1,518	156		4,240	5	4,401		460	5,459	5,919	113
August	200		1,060	1,260	130		4,058		4,188		330	5,119	5,449	83
September	258		988	1,246	138		3,982	10	4,130		396	4,980	5,376	69
October	208		1,331	1,539	132		3,942		4,074		340	5,273	5,613	20
November	126		1,555	1,681	34		4,404		4,437		159	5,959	6,118	55

December	169		1,472	1,641	110		4,335		4,445	279	5,807	6,086	37
2007	142	0	1,205	1,348	84	2	4,887	9	4,983	229	6,102	6,331	62
January	190		1,842	2,032	147	3	4,821	20	4,990	340	6,682	7,022	58
February	168		1,274	1,442	104	3	4,759	15	4,881	275	6,048	6,323	44
March	120		902	1,022	75		4,510	12	4,597	196	5,423	5,619	28
April	93		1,143	1,236	103	3	4,834	28	4,969	199	6,006	6,205	20
May	67		1,028	1,095	58	8	4,798	33	4,898	134	5,860	5,994	27
June	118		1,102	1,220	96	5	4,617	7	4,725	220	5,726	5,946	38
July	125		1,007	1,132	62	2	3,844	1	3,909	190	4,852	5,041	37
August	228		1,210	1,438	106	2	4,072		4,181	337	5,282	5,619	73
September	115		898	1,013	68	4	4,583		4,655	187	5,481	5,667	61
October	145		951	1,096	72		4,835		4,907	217	5,786	6,003	77
November	140		1,270	1,410	37		5,407		5,444	177	6,677	6,855	113
December	185		1,904	2,088	85		7,959		8,044	270	9,862	10,133	167
2008	216	0	2,409	2,625	127	0	8,106	0	8,234	344	10,515	10,859	119
January	265		2,312	2,577	143		7,630		7,773	408	9,942	10,350	158
February	165	0	2,510	2,675	110	1	8,606	0	8,716	276	11,116	11,392	79

Source: Bank of Spain, 2008

** All types of transactions excluded outright, spot and forward ones; that is to say: Repo agreements and Sell/Buyback transactions.

*** Wholesale market between market-makers through authorized dealers that conceal counterparties' identities to each other.

Appendix 7. Portugal: Public Debt

Government debt issues – Funded debt (in a calendar year perspective)									
EUR millions	1998	1999	2000	2001	2002	2003	2004	2005	2006
Treasury bonds (OT)[a]	8,517.5	9,078.8	7,673.7	8,643.5	12,998.0	7,571.5	6,700.0	16,742.2	13,911.4
5 years	287.2	0.0	0.0	0.0	0.0	5,071.5	4,200.0	1,800.0	0.0
5 years	2,860.7	3,536.8	2,526.9	3,385.9	5,817.0	0.0	0.0	3,000.0	3,000.0
10 years	3,014.8	5,000.0	5,146.8	5,257.6	5,036.0	2,500.0	2,500.0	5,855.7	5,800.0
15 years	2,354.8	542.0	0.0	0.0	2,145.0	0.0	0.0	6,086.5	0.0
30 years	0.0	0.0	0.0	0.0	0.0	0.0	0.0	0.0	5,111.4
Short term[b]	1,874.0	833.9	877.2	3,559.3	1,712.2	5,719.2	13,266.4	14,435.6	13,977.6
Saving certificates[c]	1,122.4	1,223.1	1,821.1	1,772.1	1,622.6	1,174.8	945.1	1,082.8	1,609.4
Other[d]	315.9	1,240.0	0.0	0.0	193.9	0.0	0.0	0.0	0.0
Total debt	11,829.9	12,375.7	10,372.0	13,974.9	16,526.6	14,465.5	20,911.5	32,260.5	29,498.5

Source: IGPC (Instituto de Gestao da Tesouraria e do Crédito Público)

[a]OT at nominal value and according to the original maturity. Includes EURO-OT in 1998

[b]Includes Treasury Bills, ECP, Repos and CEDIC at discounted value

[c]Excludes accrued interest[d]Excludes Promissory Notes

Bibliography

AECM. (Mayo, 2006). The prevention and resolution of defaults in Guarantee companies: A matter of professional management.
AEL. (2002). Estadísticas.
AEL. (2006). Estadísticas.
APCRI. (Abril, 2004). A Actividade de Capital de Risco em Portugal em 2003.
APCRI. (Mayo, 2005). A Actividade de Capital de Risco em Portugal, 2004.
APCRI. (Mayo, 2006). Actividade de Capital de Risco em Portugal, 2005.
APCRI. (Mayo, 2007). Actividade de Capital de Risco em Portugal, ano de 2006.
Avilés Palacios, C., & Guzmán Romero, I. La rentabilidad en cajas de ahorro y cooperativas de crédito: análisis comparativo. UNED, Centro Asociado de Jaén "Andrés de Vandelvira".
Banco De España. (Diciembre de 1999). Research Department. Has financial market integration increased during the nineties. Banco de España. Servicio de Estudios, documentos de trabajo, No. 9923.
Banco De España. (2005a). Memoria de supervisión bancaria en España.
Banco De España. (2005b). Informe Anual.
Banco De España. Boletín Económico. Julio-agosto 2001, julio-agosto 2002, junio 2003, junio 2004, junio 2005, mayo 2006.
Banco De Portugal. (Winter, 2006). Outlook for the portuguese Economy: 2007–2008. Boletín Económico, Economic Policy and Situation.
Banco De Portugal. Código de Conducta.
Barrios Pérez, V. (Septiembre de, 2000). La regulación del coeficiente de recursos propios en las Cajas de Ahorro españolas. Boletín Económico del ICE, No. 2662.
BCE. (Abril, 2000). La UEM y la supervisión bancaria. Boletín mensual.
BCE. (Octubre, 2003a). Evolución reciente de las estructuras financieras de la zona del euro. Boletín mensual.
BCE. (Octubre, 2003b). Integración de los mercados financieros europeos. Boletín mensual.
BCE. (Octubre 2005). Boletín Mensual.
BCE (Marzo, 2007). Financial integration in Europe.
Bernabé Pérez, M., & Marín Hernández, S. (Julio a septiembre de 2002). Aspectos conceptuales y tratamiento contable de la adecuación del capital en las entidades de crédito en los nuevos acuerdos regulatorios internacionales. Boletín del ICE, No. 2737.
Blanco Escolar, R. (1999). El mercado español de renta variable. Análisis de la liquidez e influencia del mercado de derivados. Servicio de Estudios Económicos, No. 66. Año publicación.
Blesa De La Parra, M. (2002). La internacionalización de las cajas de Ahorro españolas. Reflejo en Caja Madrid. *Revista de Economía, 799*, 115–118.
Bolsa De Madrid. (diciembre de, 1998). La moneda única trae novedades a la Bolsa. Resumen de Actividad No. 72.
Bolsa De Madrid. (2002). Dimensión, tecnología y competencia internacional.
Bolsa De Madrid. (diciembre de, 2003). Informe sobre la integración financiera europea en 2003: avances y proyecto. Editado por la Bolsa de Madrid.
Calvo Hornero, A. (2000). La Unión Europea. Mecanismos Financieros y Moneda Única. Madrid: CERASA.
Calvo Hornero, A. (coordinadora) (2006). *La Ampliación de la Unión Europea*. Madrid: Thomson.
Calvo Hornero, A. (2007). *Organización de la Unión Europea*. Madrid: CERASA.
CDTI. Qué es NEOTEC Capital Riesgo.
CEA. Insurers of Europe. Annual Report 2005–2006.
CECA. Informe, memoria. Año 2005.
Clarotti, P. (1988). Hacia un sistema financiero europeo. Papeles de Economía Española, No. 21.
CMVM. (Diciembre de, 2006). A reforma legislativa do mercado de capitais portugues no cuadro das novas directivas comunitárias.
CNMV. (Diciembre, 2006). Actividad de las entidades de capital riesgo en España.

Coello, J., & Ruza, C. (Septiembre, 1997). El arrendamiento financiero en España. Cuadernos de Información Económica. No. 126.
Comision De Las Comunidades Europeas. (2005a). Libro Verde sobre la política para los servicios financieros (2005–2010). Bruselas, 3.5.2005.
Comision De Las Comunidades Europeas. (2005b). Libro Blanco. Política de los servicios financieros 2005–2010. Bruselas, 1.12.2005.
Comision De Las Comunidades Europeas. (2007). Commission Staff Working document. Single Market in Financial Services Progress Report 2006. Bruselas (21.2.2007). SEC(2007)263.
Comisión Europea. (2006). European Trend Chart on Innovation. Annual Innovation Policy Trends and Appraisal Report. Portugal: Comisión Europea.
Deutsche Bank Research. (Junio de 2003). The new ISD-better regulations for EU investment services? EU Monitor. Financial Market Special.
Dirección General de Política de la Pequeña y Mediana Empresa. Programa de Apoyo a las Agrupaciones Empresariales Innovadoras. Orden ITC/2691/2006.
Dirección General de Política de la Pequeña y Mediana Empresa. Programa de Apoyo a la Innovación de las Pequeñas y Medianas Empresas "Innoempresa" (2007–2013).
Dirección General de Seguros y Fondos de Pensiones. Informe anual, varios años.
European Central Bank. (2002). Report on Financial Structure.
European Central Bank. (October, 2006). EU Banking Structures.
Fernández Gayoso, J. (1995). Las cajas de ahorro y economía real. Vinculaciones y dependencias. Papeles de Economía Española, No. 65. Madrid.
Fernández-Ardavín, A., & Rodriguez, M.A. (2006). El sector financiero de los nuevos Estados miembros de la UE: especial referencia al sector bancario. In A. Calvo (coord.), *La Ampliación de la Unión Europea* (pp 89–111). Madrid: Ed. Thomson.
Ferruz, L., López, A., & Sarto, J.L. (1995). Evolución y perspectivas del leasing en España. Papeles de Economía Española. No. 65.
Funcas. (1994). Sociedades de Garantía Recíproca. Perspectivas del sistema financiero. No. 47.
García Herrero, A., & Del Río López, P. (Agosto-Septiembre, 2003). La ampliación de la Unión Europea: La estabilidad macroeconómica, las reformas estructurales y el sistema financiero en el proceso de convergencia real. Boletín ICE No. 809.
Gelpi, R. M. (1992). Adaptación de las instituciones financieras al nuevo marco europeo: Riesgos y oportunidades. Papeles de Economía Española, No. 37.
Hilbers, P. El Programa de evaluación del Sector financiero por parte del Fondo Monetario Internacional y del Banco Mundial. FMI: Departamento de Asuntos Financieros y Cambiarios. http://www.imf.org.
Iapmei; Apcri. Guia Prático do Capital de Risco 2006.
IMF. (2005). Financial Sector Assessment Program. Background Paper.
IMF. (2006). Report on the Evaluation of the Financial Sector Assessment Program.
IMF; World Bank. Analytical tools of the FSAP. 24 febrero 2003.
IMF; World Bank. (6 abril 2005). Executive Board Reviews Experience with the Financial Sector Assessment Program.
IMF; World Bank. (January, 2007). Country Report no. 07/3. Portugal: FSAP-Detailed Assessment of Observance of IAIS Insurance Core Principles.
Instituto de Seguros de Portugal. Relatório do Sector Segurador e Fundos de Pensoes. Varios años.
Juan Pablo Olmo y Carmen Choclán Campaña. La supervisión en el sector asegurador.
Liso, J. M., Balaguer, T., & Soler, M. (1996). El sector bancario europeo: panorama y tendencias. Colección Estudios e Informes. No. 6 (La Caixa).
Martín Rodriguez, M. (1995). El sistema financiero y la financiación de las PYME. Papeles de Economía Española. No. 65.
Morant Vidal, J. (Mayo, 2002). El capital riesgo como instrumento de financiación de las pequeñas y medianas empresas. Noticias jurídicas.
Muñoz Guarasa, M. (Octubre, 2002). Deslocalización sectorial de la inversión directa extranjera en España. Boletín ICE Económico, No. 2744.

Página web del Deustche Bank Research. (2006). Evaluation of the FSAP's economic impact.
Pellicer, M. (1992). Los mercados financieros organizados en España. Banco de España. Servicio de Estudios Económicos, No. 50.
Perspectivas del Sistema Financiero No. 88. (2006). Integración y Consolidación Financiera en Europa.
Pilar González de Frutos. Hacia dónde va el seguro español.
Reform of EU regulatory and supervisory structures: progress report. (Deutsche Bank Research. 4 Julio 2003).
Revista ICE. No. 801. Regulación Sectorial (Agosto–Septiembre 2002).
Revista ICE. No. 833. El sector asegurador y de los planes y fondos de pensiones (Noviembre—Diciembre 2006).
Rodríguez Ruiz, O. (2006). El capital intelectual de las cajas de ahorro españolas. Cuadernos de Estudios Empresariales, Vol. 16.
Rodriguez Santos, M. A., & Fernández-Ardavin, A. (2006). El sector financiero de los nuevos Estados miembros de la UE: especial referencia al sector bancario. In: A. Calvo (coord.), *Aspectos económicos de la ampliación de la Unión Europea*. Madrid: Editorial Thomson.
Rubio Picón, C., & Díaz Fernández, M. Un estudio crítico de las configuraciones estructurales y las estrategias organizativas del sector bancario en España.
Sánchez De La Vega, J. C., & Buendía Azorín, J. D. (Marzo 2003). España en los mercados internacionales de capital. Análisis del grado de integración financiera. Boletín ICE No. 805.
Secretaría De Estado De Economía. Seguros y Fondos de Pensiones. Informe 2005.
Subdirección General de Inversiones Exteriores. (2006). Posición de España en inversión exterior directa. Boletín Económico ICE, No. 2898.
The Pfandbrief and other covered bonds in the EU capital market: development and regulation. (Deutsche Bank Research, 1 Octubre 2003).
UNCTAD, WID Country Profile: Spain. (September 2005). Country Fact Sheets. World Investment Directory on line.

Bibliography: Statitics

Bolsa de Madrid, *Estadísticas, Diciembre 2006*.
Estadística del Banco de España (2007), Informe Serie Estadística sobre la posición de la inversión internacional. http://www.bde.es/estadis/.
Leaseurope. Key Facts and Figures (2001).
Leaseurope. Key Facts and Figures (2002).
Leaseurope. Key Facts and Figures (2003).
Leaseurope. Key Facts and Figures (2004).
Leaseurope statistics. (1999).
Leaseurope statistics. (2000).
Leaseurope statistics. (2001).
Leaseurope statistics. (2002).
Leaseurope statistics. (2003).
Leaseurope statistics. (2004).
Leaseurope statistics. (2005).
Leaseurope statistics. 1st semester (2006).

Web pages

Banco de España. http://www.bde.es/.
Banco de Portugal: http://www.bportugal.pt/.

Bolsa de Madrid. http://www.bolsamadrid.es/esp/portada.htm.
Bolsa de Portugal. http://bolsami.com/port.htm.
Caixa Galicia. http://www.caixagalicia.es/comunidad.
Cajas de Ahorro Confederadas (CECA). http://www.ceca.es/CECA-CORPORATIVO/es/index.htm.
Crédito Agrícola. linhadirecta@creditoagricola.pt.
Dirección General de Mediana y Pequeña empresa, Ministerio de Industria. http://www.ipyme.org/IPYME/es-ES/AEI.
Dirección General de Seguros de Portugal. http://www.spgm.pt/abc.html.
Dirección General de Seguros y fondos de inversión. http://www.dgsfp.mineco.es/.
Fundación Cajas de Ahorro (FUNCAS). http://www.funcas.ceca.es/.
Ministerio de Industria, Turismo y Comercio de España. http://datainvex.comercio.es/index.htm.
SPMG. ABC Garantía Mútua. http://www.spmg.pt/abc.html.

Chapter 7
Corporate Governance and the 'Hybridisation' of Financial Sectors

Andy Mullineux

7.1 Banking Trends

7.1.1 An Overview

Since the early 1970s there has been substantial liberalisation of the banking sector and financial innovation. The process has been facilitated by re-regulation of banks (Mullineux 1987, pp. 30–63, 83–125, 126–153, 154–165), which continue to lie at the heart of all financial systems (Mishkin 2004, pp. 23–43), and necessitated ongoing revisions in prudential regulation, and monetary policy. The general trend has been away from proscriptive regulation of financial activities, quantitative control of bank lending in total (in pursuit of monetary control), directed lending to sectors of the economy (in pursuit of development policy), and qualitative controls and guidance; see (Hermes et al. 2000, p. 76). Quantitative and qualitative controls and guidance have been largely replaced in many countries with a price (interest rate) oriented monetary policy and general prudential regulations. The latter include: risk related capital adequacy requirements (CARs); deposit insurance schemes (also risk-related in the US); rules prohibiting overexposure (to individuals, sectors of the economy, or foreign exchange risk) in order to promote portfolio diversification and risk reduction; and rules requiring the holding of adequate reserves to assure liquidity and to make provisions against forecast bad or doubtful debts.

To inform supervision by the authorities, there are confidential disclosure requirements; and to facilitate monitoring by equity and bond holders, public disclosure and auditing requirements are also imposed. Finally, to aid comparison in the increasingly global environment, accounting and disclosure rules are in the process of being harmonised and country based supervisors are increasingly sharing information about banks and other financial firms. The general trend is towards establishing a set of rules that encourage banks and other financial institutions to

A. Mullineux
Birmingham Business School, University of Birmingham, Birmingham, Germany

P.J.J. Welfens and C. Ryan (eds.), *Financial Market Integration and Growth*,
DOI 10.1007/978-3-642-16274-9_7, © Springer-Verlag Berlin Heidelberg 2011

manage their asset and liability portfolio risks effectively. If banks achieve an appropriate balance between risk and return, then depositors will be protected and shareholders will earn an appropriate return. Systemic risk, the risk of destabilising crises in the whole banking or financial system, will be contained, and capital will be more efficiently allocated.

The banking and wider financial markets are rapidly being globalised. The process started in the 1970s with the internationalisation of banking (Pecchioli 1983, p. 1). This was followed in the 1980s by a period of rapid innovation in the capital markets, often dubbed securitisation. Securitisation involves disintermediation, the growth of non-bank-intermediated or direct (from the capital markets) finance, and a process of making loans tradeable on securities markets, using asset-backed securities. The securitisation process continued into the 1990s, and was enhanced by the rapid growth in the use of financial derivatives. In the first decade of the new millennium, securitisation and the use of derivatives look set to continue to grow and to become more widespread.

In the 1990s, there was also a progressive relaxation of capital controls. Some countries moved earlier than others, e.g. the UK in 1979, but relaxation of capital controls has been increasingly encouraged by the IMF as a means of stimulating inward portfolio and direct investment to facilitate economic development. The result has been a rapid growth in overseas portfolio investments by mutual, insurance and pensions funds, with UK and US institutional investors playing a prominent role. Further, the conclusion of the GATS agreement relating to financial services in the mid 1990s encourages the opening of financial sectors in countries around the world to entry by foreign financial institutions. Progress with European financial integration, including EMU and the creation of Euroland, through the Financial Services Action Plan, is encouraging more cross border activity in the financial service sector, including bank branching and cross border alliances and mergers. With some notable exceptions, the merger activity in Europe to date has largely entailed internal consolidation; leading more concentrated national banking systems. These have, however, increasingly faced greater competition from abroad. The US is probably experiencing the most rapid consolidation, but this is hardly surprising given the highly fragmented banking system that existed in their country at the beginning of the 1990s as a result of strict branching restrictions. At the end of the 1990s, consolidation also began in Japans banking and wider financial system as a means of resolving bank bad debt problems.

The picture seems to be one of the gradual evolution of global banks competing on a global stage. This is most advanced in the investment banking sphere, but is likely to become increasingly evident as a result of the internet revolution. Banks can now offer services across borders without a branch network. Entry is thus much easier and competition is consequently intensifying. Retail banks, engaged primarily in deposit taking, the provision of payments services and lending, face competition on both sides of the balance sheet and in service provision. Competition in the provision of loans (home, car etc.), including that from credit card companies, is clearly increasing. There is also growing competition in the savings market from internet based banks, mutual funds, and the providers of longer term savings investments, such as personal pension products. The big banks have already seen their share of the supply of debt finance to the larger firms decline as the latter switch increasingly to direct finance, tapping the capital (bonds) and money (commercial paper) markets. Increasingly, commercial or retail banks are left supplying commercial loans to small and medium sized enterprises (SMEs). Competition in SME financing is, however, also hotting up in the US as the big banks attempt to use mailshots based on the analyses of their growing data bases to cherry pick. However, the UK SME and broader retail banking market remains uncompetitive, (Competition Commission 2002, pp. 3–5; Mullineux and Terberger 2006, p. 11).

7.1.2 Strategic Responses

Banks have been forced to refocus their businesses. Many retail based banks have diversified into investment banking in order to help their large corporate clients access the money and capital markets. In so doing they have boosted their (broking and market making) fee income to compensate for declining interest-based earnings from loans. The combination of investment and retail banking is sometimes called universal banking. This has long been permitted in parts of Europe, but was not the custom in the UK (or France before the mid 1960s) and was prohibited in the US post 1933, and in post-war Japan. Japan is in the process of relaxing the restrictions introduced by the US administration after World War II, and the US repealed the 1933 Glass–Steagall Act, which separated investment and commercial banking, in 1999. Universal banking has long been the norm in Germany and Switzerland, for example.

German universal banks have traditionally held sizeable shareholdings in non-financial firms. Cross-shareholding between Japanese city banks and other keiretsu member firms are also significant, and cross-shareholding between banks, insurance companies and non-financial firms is also common in France and Italy, for example. Since the turn of the century bank shareholding in Japan and Germany and cross shareholdings have been reduced, in part to release capital for more profitable use. EU banking regulations limit the proportion of a banks capital that can be held as shareholdings in non-financial companies and the current trend is to reduce cross-shareholdings, which raise a number of issues for competition and prudential regulation policy (should banks own non-banks and vice versa?) There are also corporate governance issues and these have come to the fore in the 1990s, leading to pressure on banks to reduce their shareholdings in non-financial firms. The prudential concerns about non-financial firms owning banks relate to the risk of the owning firms exploiting bank depositors by forcing the banks to supply cheap finance and the risk that the owning firms might be brought into the lender of last resort and too big to be allowed to fail safety nets. This might also be true in cases where banks own non-financial firms, whose failure would undermine the banks.

It should also be noted that although financial conglomeration is becoming the norm in most national systems, especially amongst OECD countries, there are two main approaches to financial conglomerate structuring. The integrated firm approach has been common in mainland Europe, whilst the UK has tended to favour a holding company approach, and the US is set to do so too. Diversification in the US has hitherto been required to take place through separately capitalised subsidiaries in the hope of erecting fire-walls between them. These have yet to be rigorously tested and there is considerable doubt about their likely effectiveness in face of too big to fail considerations. There does, however, seem to be an emerging trend towards converting integrated universal banks into holding companies with specialist retail (including telephone and/or internet), corporate and investment, asset management and (see below) insurance subsidiaries.

The banks have sought to diversify their retail financial activities, often hoping to cross-sell products (e.g. house insurance on the back of home loans) or simply to exploit the information contained in enlarged data bases for marketing and product development purposes. They have thus diversified their loan portfolios and now commonly offer home loans, which were traditionally the preserve of specialist savings banks in many countries (savings and loans companies in the US, and building societies in the UK, for example). In addition, they have engaged in offering insurance and pension products, leading to the development of what has been called bancassurance companies. Many insurance companies are also in the process of entering banking; frequently through the internet or telephone-based services.

The development of global bancassurance firms providing retail banking, insurance, and asset management (pensions and mutual funds etc.), as well as investment banking services worldwide is thus on the verge of a reality. The large financial conglomerates will of course continue to compete with narrower specialist and domestically based institutions, some of which will be national champions formed through domestic mergers. Some big questions remain to be resolved.

7.1.3 Outstanding Issues

The globalisation process has been facilitated by regulatory and supervisory harmonisation. Initially this consisted of an attempt to create a level playing field for international banks through the 1988 Basle Concordat on risk related CARs and subsequent recommendations from the Basle Committee (BIS) (now incorporated in Basle II). The creation of the single market in the EU required the adoption of the second EC Banking Directive 1987. This consolidated the continental European model of universal banking, which combines investment and commercial banking, and permitted the development of bancassurance. Throughout most of the 1990s, Japan and the US maintained (though progressively relaxed, especially in the US) banking laws that separated investment and commercial banking and banking from insurance. In 1998 Japan introduced Big Bang legislation laying out a phased relaxation of these restrictions, and in 1999 liberalising legislation was passed in the US. As predicted in (Mullineux 1992, pp. 1–11), the drive to achieve international competitive equality has led to the adoption of the more liberal, in terms of the scope of banking activity, continental European regime. This has in turn increased the range and intensity of competition amongst the increasingly globalised large banks. In such a context, does the present, largely nationally based, regulatory system provide for adequate regulation supervision of the emerging global bancassurance companies and increasingly interlinked national capital market and the internet based financial markets and transactions?

The emergence of financial conglomerates or wide banks, also, raises the question of how they should be regulated. Commercial banks (banks engaged in lending and deposit taking businesses with personal and corporate customers) have traditionally been regarded as special. This is because: they are the dominant financial institutions in terms of repositories for savings and providers of finance; they are the main providers of payments services, which are infrastructural to modern commerce; and, amongst financial institutions, they alone have liabilities which are money and are thus the most important potential contributors to the inflation generating process. Thus banks have been regulated separately from other financial institutions in most countries. As banks have diversified, other formerly specialist financial institutions have entered into banking. Hence, the continuing need to regulate banks separately has been questioned. The UK, Sweden and Japan have already introduced FSAs.[1] In each country, providers of financial services have the same regulator and the regulator is a semi-autonomous government agency, which is not the central bank. Central banks, to the extent that they were responsible for bank and wider financial sector regulation and supervision, are now required to concentrate on inflation control and have been given independent (of the Finance Ministry/Treasury) power to set interest rates in pursuit of this goal, subject to an agreed level of accountability to the legislature. The US, with its complex array of bank and other financial regulators, each with their own vested interests, has yet to move in this direction, but Germany introduced a single financial sector regulator (BaFin) in 2002.

Moving to the global stage, the BIS has driven international bank regulatory and supervisory harmonisation, whilst the International Organisation of Security Commissions (IOSCO) has led harmonisation in the sphere of capital market regulation and supervision. There are numerous gaps in global cooperation, however, and there is no global (or EU-wide) regulatory and supervisory organisation. As a response to the Asian finance crisis of the late 1990s, however, the Financial Stability Forum has been established to promote international financial stability through enhanced information exchange and institutional cooperation in financial market supervision and surveillance. The International Monetary Fund (IMF), the International Bank for Reconstruction and Development (World Bank), the BIS, the

[1]The letters stand for different words in each country, Financial Services Authority in the UK, Financial Supervisory Agency in Japan, and Financial Supervisory Authority in Sweden, but the approach is similar.

Organisation for Economic Cooperation and Development (OECD), IOSCO and the International Association of Insurance Supervisors (IAIS) are all participating, along with representatives of offshore banking groupings. Meanwhile the EU has established under the Lamfalussy Process three separate bodies to help accelerate the creation of single markets in banking, securities and insurance.

More generally, banking in the new millennium will be directly influenced by the main developments in the last three decades: global regulatory harmonisation; financial sector and capital account liberalisation; and the computing and information technology revolution. All these developments increase the mobility of capital and facilitate the creation of a single global financial space. However, niche players and geographically segregated markets still exist in securities business, retail banking and SME banking. It should also be noted that securitisation and increasingly tradeable financial asset holdings by banks have complicated both prudential regulation in pursuit of financial stability and monetary policy in pursuit of price, and perhaps also (as in the US) general macroeconomic, stability.

7.2 European Financial System Convergence and Corporate Governance

A contrast is drawn between Anglo-Saxon (capital market oriented) financial systems, as represented by the UK, and continental (banking oriented) financial systems, as typified by Germany and much of continental Europe. The term 'banking oriented' alludes to bank lending via the creation of demand deposits in connection with a debt contract between the bank and the borrower. Nevertheless, it is noted in Sect. 7.1, that banks, especially in the EU, are increasingly engaging in both banking and securities business i.e. universal banking, fund management and, more recently, insurance business ('bancassurance' or 'Allfinance'). The term 'bank oriented', therefore, may have various interpretations. It could mean a system in which banks are the dominant institutions providing both indirect (or intermediated debt) finance and access to direct finance from the money and capital markets via instruments such as commercial bills and paper (money market debt finance), bonds and Euro-notes (capital market debt finance) or shares (capital market equity finance), inter alia. The key distinctions here are between direct and indirect finance and between debt and equity financing. Since banking fundamentally involves the provision of indirect or intermediated debt finance, 'bank oriented' could more narrowly be taken to mean that the most important source of external financing for non-financial companies (NFCs) is bank loans. If this is the case, then there are no capital market oriented systems, since even the US, the country with the most advance capital markets, remains bank oriented. The issue really is the extent to which countries systems are more or less bank (capital) market oriented i.e. the US is more capital market oriented than any other country, but still bank oriented (Mishkin 2004, pp. 169–200).

With reference to the EU, therefore, a bank oriented system could be viewed as one in which banks are the key financial institutions as regards corporate governance by virtue of being both providers of debt finance and the key institutional holders of equity, as in the universal banking system of Germany, and also to some extent in the French system (Mallin 2007, pp. 159–187). In contrast, in capital market oriented systems, the key institutional shareholders are pension and insurance funds. This is especially true in the UK, where share ownership is heavily concentrated (see Mallin 2007, pp. 80–100). Hitherto, the institutional shareholders in the UK have not exercised their voting rights (including proxy voting rights) as actively as the large German private sector banks, (Deutsche, Commerzbank, Dresdner etc.). The capital markets in the UK also influence management behaviour via the threat posed by aggressive mergers and acquisitions activity. In contrast, in continental Europe, unsolicited take-over bids have, atleast until recently, been largely unknown.

The 'battle of the systems', regarding the relative merits of the more bank oriented and more capital market oriented systems, is integral to the policy debates on the evolution of financial systems in the EU member countries. If direct financing is increasing relative to bank financing, the capital markets will have a greater role to play in the future. To the extent that more bank oriented systems are more 'long-termist', this trend may lead to a spread of 'short-termism' in investment and 'research and development' expenditure decisions. Counteracting this tendency, and helping to deepen capital markets in previously more bank-dominated systems, the privatisation of pensions, in response to ageing populations and increasing longevity and the associated budgetary pressures being caused by maintaining 'pay-as-you go' state pension schemes, will lead to a build up of pension funds. These funds are likely to increasingly invest in shares (equities) as restrictions requiring large proportions of the funds in domestic government bonds are removed in response to competitive pressures to achieve acceptable returns for the investors.[2] Because pension funds are dealing with long term savings, they should naturally take a strategic view and this should help counteract any bias towards short-termism. The trend toward greater transparency of pension fund managers decisions (including voting and stock picking behaviour) should reinforce this. The creation of the single currency area within the EU ('Euroland') has already boosted the development of a European corporate bond market. The continued rapid growth in the Euro-based corporate bond market should further reduce the role of bank loans as a source of corporate debt finance.

The question remains, however, whether the different financial systems in the EU have exhibited a tendency to converge over time, following the Single European Market initiative in 1993. In the context of EU financial systems and the patterns of corporate financing, the 'convergence criterion' reflects the expectations of EU

[2]The UK, where pension funds have traditionally invested heavily in equities may be an exception. A number of funds are trying to better match their assets and liabilities by reducing equity holdings and increasing bond holding of appropriate maturities.

member countries that the launching of a borderless Europe in January 1993 would impact on the financial systems of these economies by facilitating the achievement of a single financial space in the EU. The subsequent Financial Services Action Plan is aimed at accelerating this and it moved a significant step closer with the decision to proceed with the creation of a single currency adopted by most of the EU states in January 1999. In 'Euroland', convergence is expected to accelerate.

Murinde et al. 2004 (pp. 698–703) obtain results which suggest that over time and across the seven EU member countries NFCs have generally shifted towards the use of equity finance for new investment; the stock markets have also increasingly become important as a means of raising equity finance for new investment by NFCs. However, the UK remains a bit of an outlier. These results are interpreted as providing evidence that the EU member countries are converging towards a more capital market oriented system, in the context of an increase in the relative share of the equity market in the overall financing of new investment by NFCs. Further, there is evidence that there has been a tendency towards convergence among the EU member countries in terms of the increasing use of company bond finance by NFCs. Moreover, the formation of 'Euroland' can be expected to accelerate the growth of the Euro-dominated corporate bond market. The findings on convergence with respect to increasing use of internal finance are consistent with previous findings.

Thus, as they participate in a single market project inaugurated in 1993 and as a result of the ongoing restructuring of their banking systems, EU member countries may expect convergence of their financial systems on an evolving model with increasing reliance on internal financing, with bank intermediated lending decreasing in importance and direct financing via equity and bond markets (especially the Euro-note and bond markets) increasing in the generally declining market for the external financing of investment. A great leap forward occurred in the development of the corporate bond market following the adoption of the Euro in January 1999; further undermining the dominance of bank debt financing of large corporates and pointing to convergence on the US financial system, where the corporate bond markets have historically been much more developed. In a subsequent paper, Mullineux et al. (2010) (pp. 9–12) find further evidence of the growing role of corporate bonds relative to bank debt in Euroland. Throughout Europe, the banks are also progressively diversifying into the provision of underwriting and broking (of financial instruments) services to NFCs; replacing traditional bank loans with securities issuance.

All in all, the EU single market launched in 1993 and the ongoing restructuring of banking systems in most EU countries are expected to facilitate convergence of the financial systems in the EU towards the continental model, but with a marked increased in the role of capital markets. This is also true of the UK, given the virtual disappearance of indigenous independent investment banks. It is only in the US that investment banks flourish as separate entities. However, following the repeal of the Glass–Steagall Act in 1999, the US financial system is tending to converge on a similar model as large corporations seek both credit lines and the underwriting of securities issues from both their commercial and their investment bankers. In sum there is a process of 'hybridisation' underway whereby the US finance system is becoming more continental European (Citicorp is already one of the largest global 'bancassurance' firms and has rapidly developed its international banking capability since 1999) and the continental European system is becoming more like the US as the (euro dominated) corporate bond markets develop apace (and HSBC is a European based global player).

7.3 Trends in Corporate Governance

The competing financial systems (Anglo-Saxon vs. Germanic, or market vs. bank oriented) debate is often couched in terms of implications for corporate governance, and indeed society as a whole (Albert 1994, pp. 250–260). As noted above, the debate is frequently somewhat confused as a result of the influence of financial myths (Mishkin 2004, pp. 23–43). We have already noted that internal, rather than externally supplied, finance is the dominant source of investment finance for both large corporates and SMEs. It is also the case that in all countries SMEs are the largest employers and are largely dependent on banks for external finance, and that banks are the major suppliers of finance to the non financial business sector. Only in the US is the corporate bond market a major alternative to loans as a source of debt finance, although the introduction of the euro has resulted in a rapid acceleration of the development of European corporate bond markets. Even in the US, banks remain the main suppliers of debt finance, however, and it is only the larger firms that can tap the traditional bond market, whilst growth firms in the new technology sectors can increasingly tap the higher risk 'junk bond' market. Further, the equity market is primarily a market in second hand stocks through which ownership is transferred. In years of high merger and acquisition (including private equity led leveraged buy-outs (LBO)) activity and share buy-backs the net supply of new equity finance through the market is *negative* in the US and the UK. Markets specialising in financing new companies, again usually in the new technology sectors (e.g. Nasdaq in the US, and AIM in the UK), tend to be net suppliers of equity, but often as a result of replacing the investments of venture capitalists and private equity holders, as they exit from their investments. Venture capitalists and business angels have been growing in importance as alternatives to bank finance for early stage growth firms in the technology sector.

In sum, in Anglo-Saxon systems, banks remain the dominant source of external finance, and there dominance may actually be increasing as they diversify from making loans into wider, securities related, corporate finance. The bank vs. market dominated distinction has become unhelpful because the nature of banking has changed as a result of the generally liberalising, re-regulation of banks and other financial institutions, which is also driving convergence of the scope of banks and other financial institutions (on the continental European model). Hence the Germanic (Rhinish) vs. Anglo-Saxon distinction between financial systems is losing relevance too. Further, there is a growing realization that the Anglo-Saxon corporate governance model is also a myth. The UK and US are, at any rate very different (Mullineux 2010, pp. 437–448) and indeed there is growing competition between the 'rules based and litigious' US system and the more 'principles and risk-based', 'comply or explain' UK system. Indeed the success of the London Capital market in the mid 2000s in winning mandates the New York capital market might have expected to win has prompted a re-evaluation of the US regulatory auditing and governance systems. The UK system has been praised by prominent US officials, and an overhaul of the US system in response to the competition is underway.

It is however true that a larger proportion of indirect finance is, at least for the larger firms, being provided through bond (debt), equity and money (commercial paper and bills and notes) markets. As such, there is convergence on a hybrid 'Americanised' continental European system i.e. one in which the main players are diversified bank and insurance companies (and also some specialised investment banks, at least for a while yet) and mutual and pension *funds*, but financial markets are becoming increasingly important. The insurance, mutual and pension funds are, however, becoming the dominant institutional investors as pensions are progressively being privatised and banks disengage from cross-shareholdings in Japan and the EU (particularly Germany).

The convergence of financial systems or 'hybridisation' is leading to some convergence of corporate governance mechanisms. For the largely private SME sector, there is less change. Banks remain the key players in their governance unless management control is diluted by taking on equity finance from outside (from private equity and venture capital funds). For larger firms that have issued equity to the public and/or taken on bond financing, institutional investors can be expected to play an increasing role in governance relative to banks; but banks will also remain key actors. Given the, seemingly growing, importance of internal finance in larger firms, good corporate governance is required to ensure that efficient use is made of retained earnings. Here issues pertaining to the structure of management boards, the role of non-executive directors, and whether the roles of Chairman and Chief Executive Officer should be separated become increasingly important. Further, stock markets, and increasingly private equity funds, play a role in providing a market for corporate control to keep the managers on their toes as a result of the threat of takeovers or LBO. Behind the markets are the institutional shareholders and fund managers, who must decide which shares to hold in their portfolios and in what proportions.

Through the institutional shareholders and fund managers, the interests of small investors and pensioners are represented and legislation can be used to encourage investors to take account of social and environmental considerations in constructing their investment portfolios, as in the 1999 pensions fund legislation in the UK. The institutional investors can also influence business behaviour by voting their shareholdings and 'engaging' with management. The extent to which they do so is unclear because they tend to be secretive about their behaviour. However, a number of active fund managers (e.g. Hermes) are notable exceptions. Without cross-country data can institutional shareholder voting and wider engagement activity, it is difficult to assess the extent to which financial sector convergence is driving corporate governance convergence.

The rise of private equity led LBO activity raises the issue of whether institutional investor 'engagement' is in fact working. Tax issues aside, LBO targets could after all have been encouraged to adopt a more highly leveraged capital structure and more incentive compatible remuneration packages. The corporate governance and regulation of the investment funds themselves thus becomes an issue. The need for fund managers to compete for mandates may induce short-termism, for example, and pension fund trustees may lack the required level of training.

The interests of stakeholders other than shareholders can also be brought to bear through legislation on management board membership (e.g. requiring worker and/or consumer representation, as is the case in a number of countries). By such means the tiger of global capitalism can be tamed and capital directed in such a way as to ensure its most efficient (from social as well as financial or economic perspectives) use. Growth will be enhanced and poverty reduced as a result. Social auditing may increasingly complement traditional financial auditing. To achieve this, however, countries must adopt common accounting standards, and best practices in financial sector regulation and, partly as a result of the former, conformable corporate governance (including bankruptcy procedures) systems.

Thus we can anticipate that triple bottom line accounting (covering financial and social and environmental impacts), perhaps complemented by a further bottom line on corporate governance procedures, might emerge.

7.4 Concluding Remarks

The growth in the internal financing of investment through retained earnings exacerbates the principle-agent problem and makes good corporate governance key to assuring that capital is efficiently invested. The growth in direct (capital market) finance reduces the role of banks in corporate governance and this tendency is enhanced by their declining role as institutional investors through cross-shareholdings (particularly in Germany and Japan). Bondholders (often banks and other financial institutions), not just shareholders, are increasingly important and this leads to complications in procedures for temporarily protecting companies in financial difficulties from creditors (US, 'Chapter 11') and more general bankruptcy proceedings. However, banks remain the key monitors of SMEs. Stock markets, through secondary trading, takeover bids, LBOs and share buy-banks, are markets for corporate control as well as sources of new finance through initial public offerings (IPOs). Institutional shareholders (insurance, pension and mutual funds) and fund managers, including activist hedge funds, are increasingly the key players in corporate governance. They are playing a progressively more active role in ensuring that companies have good management structure and internal controls. However, the greater emphasis on shareholder-value may lead to short-termism, as opposed to the long termism associated with universal banking. Over the last decade in the US, however, the benefits of greater innovation and flexibility appear to have outweighed the costs of short-termism; although the jury is still out following the over-investment in communications and information technology that occurred in the late 1990s boom and the Enron/WorldCom debacles in 2001. Further, short-termism tends to increase pressure to distribute profits as dividends, reducing capital 'hoarding' for internal investment. Stakeholders other than shareholders may, however, need protecting. This could be done through social and corporate governance auditing; the US felt the need to legislate in the form of the Sarbanes–Oxley Act (2002), in order to strengthen internal controls. As a result the more rules based, litigious corporate governance system in the US contrasts starkly with the UK's principles based corporate governance, auditing and financial sector regulatory systems and its 'comply or explain' corporate governance system. Which system will prevail? London vs. New York is emerging as the new 'battle of the systems', unless the private equity revolution is pointing to a 'third way'.

References

Albert, M. (1994). *Capitalism against capitalisation*. London: Whurr Publishers.

Competition Commission. (2002). *The supply of banking services by clearing banks to small and medium sized enterprises, Cm 5319 (14/03/02)*. London: Competition Commission.

Hermes, N., Lensink, R., & Murinde, V. (2000). Capital flight and political risk. *Journal of International Money and Finance, 19*, 73–92.

Mallin, C. A. (2007). *Corporate governance* (2nd ed.). Oxford: Oxford University Press.

Mishkin, F. S. (2004). *The economics of money, banking and financial markets* (7th ed.). New York: Addison Wesley International.

Mullineux, A. W. (1987). *UK banking after deregulation*. London: Croom Helm.

Mullineux, A. W. (1992). *European banking*. Oxford: Blackwell.

Mullineux, A.W. (2010). Is There an Anglo-Saxon corporate governance model?, *Journal of International Economics and Economic Policy, 7*, 437–448.

Mullineux, A. W., Murinde, V., & Sensarma, R. (2010). Evolving corporate financing patterns in Europe: is there convergence? In P. J. J. Welfens & C. Ryan (Eds.), *EU financial market, structural change, economic growth, chapter F*. Berlin: Springer.

Mullineux, A.W. & Terberger, E. (2006). The British banking system: a good role model for Germany? Anglo-German Foundation Report, June 2006.

Murinde, V., Agung, J., & Mullineux, A. W. (2004). Patterns of corporate financing and financial system convergence in Europe. *Review of International Economics, 12*(4), 693–705.

Pecchioli, R. M. (1983). *The internationalisation of banking*. Paris: OECD.

Chapter 8
Different Modes of Foreign Direct Investment in Ireland: A Theoretical Analysis

Mareike Koeller

8.1 Introduction

A high inflow of Foreign Direct Investment (FDI) has been observed in Ireland in recent decades. The significance of foreign firms manifests itself in several key figures: the FDI inflows (as a percentage of the GDP) have been higher than the EU average since the beginning of the 1990s (Goerg and Ruane 2000, p. 408). The FDI stock per capita almost exceeded the EU average fivefold in the year 2000.[1] 47% of the Irish employees worked in foreign firms and 77% of the overall industrial output came from foreign firms in Ireland (Goerg and Ruane 2000, p. 405).[2] Ireland's remarkable development initiated a multitude of studies on the location advantages and specifics of the country with regard to its attractiveness for FDI (e.g. Barry 1999; Roller 1999; Gray 1997). However, they tend to regard FDI as uniform and neglect a differentiated consideration. For example, FDI for sales motives (horizontal FDI) are made under very different premises compared to FDI made for cost-orientated reasons (vertical FDI). The distinction between vertical and horizontal FDI is indeed addressed in some studies on Ireland (e.g. Barry 2004; Barry et al. 2003), but extensive consideration of the location factors in either forms or dependence on relevant FDI models are nevertheless lacking.

In FDI theory, a large number of models and approaches can be used to explain FDI. According to Dunning's 'eclectic theory' (Dunning 1981, 1993) an FDI decision requires three advantages: the FDI of a multinational enterprise (MNE) are determined firstly by the possession of firm-specific advantages (Hymer 1976), secondly by the consideration of internalising these advantages (Buckley and Casson 1976) and thirdly by the consideration of the profitability of the various production locations (Vernon 1966).

[1] See Fig. 8.1 in Appendix.

[2] The EU average of the share of workers in foreign firms is only 19%.

M. Koeller
Georg-August-University Göttingen, Göttingen, Germany

P.J.J. Welfens and C. Ryan (eds.), *Financial Market Integration and Growth*,
DOI 10.1007/978-3-642-16274-9_8, © Springer-Verlag Berlin Heidelberg 2011

Nevertheless, the decision regarding internalisation has already been made for an analysis of the FDI to Ireland and consequently a multinational enterprise's choice of location. FDI models from the new trade theory which highlight internationalisation strategies (e.g. exports versus FDI) are suitable for the consideration of location-specific determinants and consequently combine the firm-specific advantages with the location-specific determinants of a country.[3] Furthermore, FDI are differentiated in vertical and horizontal form in these models. This approach facilitates an accurate analysis of the location factors of the respective FDI forms.

In the following sections, the location-specific determinants will be selected from the models for vertical and horizontal FDI and these location factors applied to Ireland. Whether the firm- and industry-specific data supports these statements will also be examined. The inclusion of the regional integration and further considerations regarding the particularity of the European market alter the decision picture considerably and can reinforce the significance of the analysis.

8.2 Horizontal Foreign Direct Investment

FDI are classed as horizontal if a MNE carries out all or parts of the production process in the recipient country parallel to the donor country in order to be in a position to serve the local market. The primary reasons for the investment are the reduction of the costs of supplying the market and subsequently an improvement in the competitive position in the recipient country. However, in most cases it is assumed that certain headquarter activities in the donor country remain and are not duplicated to make use of the firm-specific advantages. Consequently, the aim of serving the market and the parallel production in several countries are crucial for horizontal FDI (Protsenko 2004, pp. 14).

One of the more general models regarding the development of horizontal FDI is the 'Proximity-Concentration Trade Off' (Brainard 1993).[4] Here, the MNE has to decide whether it wants to use the advantages of concentrated production or those offered by the proximity to the market. Under the assumption that the demand for and sale of the MNE product are independent of the form of market service, the amount of the trade costs t determines the form of internationalisation. Consequently, the gain function can be written as $\pi(t)$, in which all other determinants of the gain are included as fixed factors irrespective of the market service.

[3]The activities remain in both cases (Exports or FDI) inside the firm. Only a few papers of the New Trade Theory try to include internalisation aspects, see e.g. Ethier and Markusen (1996).

[4]This standard model is used by many authors. See e.g. Markusen (2002), Chap. 2.

Therefore, as regards the export strategy the MNE's gain function is $\prod_{Ex} = \pi(t)$.[5] However, for the FDI strategy the MNE does not incur any trade costs but rather additional fixed costs for the construction of the production affiliate and operating a plant in the recipient country. Here, the gain function reads: $\prod_{FDI} = \pi(0) - f$. The selection consequently depends upon the difference between the two profit opportunities (so-called 'tariff-jumping gain'):

$$\Pi_{FDI} - \Pi_{EX} = \pi(0) - f - \pi(t). \tag{8.1}$$

In all, the trade costs to serve the market are confronted with the costs of the geographic dispersion. Higher fixed costs of an affiliate thus lead to exports, higher trading (and other transaction) costs rather to an FDI decision by the MNE (Neary 2002, pp. 293).

The models of horizontal FDI explain multinational activities between similar countries in terms of size and factor endowment. If the two countries differed in size, an additional plant would not be profitable in the smaller country as the high fixed costs would exceed the savings from the trade costs of the low number of exports. In the case of countries of the same size but which differ in terms of factor endowments and subsequently have different factor costs, the FDI strategy would have the disadvantage that the MNE would also have to carry out production in the country with the marginally available and therefore more costly production factor (Protsenko 2004, pp. 16).

There are additional models for the development of horizontal FDI, all of which are based on the trade-off between the fixed costs and the trade costs. The Markusen (1984) model was one of the first to highlight the firm level economies of scale: the duplication of affiliates does not result in the duplication of the fixed costs in the construction of the production facilities through the firm level economies of scale (which are founded on the firm-specific advantages) and thus makes FDI feasible. Extensions can be found, for example, in Markusen and Venables (1998); Markusen and Venables (2000) or Helpman et al. (2004). Nevertheless, these extensions do not add any additional location-specific determinants for horizontal FDI.

In the case of the existing models, the geographic proximity to the sales market through FDI only constitutes using the savings of the trade costs. However, these savings have effects upon the equilibrium of the price and market shares of all firms in the market segment. As the MNE also has lower marginal costs in virtue of the lower trade costs, it can offer the product at a lower price and gain additional market shares. Additionally, the proximity to the customer, competitors and local suppliers is an argument for horizontal FDI in itself.[6] These extensions, not to mention the

[5]There are still fix costs by producing the additional export volume in the parent country, but these would arise in any internationalisation form and could be neglected. Additionally, we assume no capacity limit in the affiliates here and in following chapters.

[6]So, the tariff-jumping-gain is not any longer primary argument for horizontal FDI in many current papers, see for example Pontes (2001).

possibility of a production affiliate capacity threshold, would be even more likely to shift the internationalisation decision in favour of FDI.[7]

In all, certain location factors in the prospective host country can be selected from the models described: crucial factors are a large market, similar stage of development, similar factor endowment, high trade barriers and a relatively large geographic distance. Significant location advantages for all FDI forms – such as political stability, low exchange rate risk, agglomeration advantages or a good infrastructure[8] – are taken as read here but excluded in the considerations.

Furthermore, firm and industry-specific characteristics can increase the significance for examination in Ireland. The industry sectors, which are either influenced by the aforementioned location factors or primarily make horizontal FDI by virtue of their specific properties, are filtered out.

The plant-level economies of scale (in contrast to the high firm level economies of scale) have to be relatively low.[9] Should these also be high, a duplication of the production would be inefficient. Additionally, the product-specific transport costs have to be relatively high for the production locally to be worthwhile in contrast to transportation from a single production location (Barba Navaretti and Venables 2004, p. 31). Furthermore, the sectors tend to be found more in growth industries (as the high firm-specific advantages can be used the most effectively with this strategy) and in fields which require close proximity to the customer, as well as in many other service sectors (that are not or hardly tradable). Another important indicator is the export share of the production affiliate, especially the share back into the donor country: as in the case of horizontal FDI the production facilities were constructed to serve the market, a large portion of the production remains in the host country or sales region.

8.3 Vertical Foreign Direct Investment

In the case of vertical FDI, the focus is not the decision as to the kind of market service but rather the decision regarding the production process's degree of spatial concentration. Vertical FDI develop if the MNE separates individual production stages geographically in order to exploit the factor price differences between countries (Carr et al. 2001, p. 385).

The models on vertical FDI are primarily based upon Helpman (1984), whereby in contrast to the horizontal models perfect competition and constant returns to

[7]The existence of similar factor costs is necessary in simple models, but trade costs play only a secondary role in reaching customer proximity or securing and enlarging market shares. In these cases different factor costs between the countries are also possible.

[8]For more information about location advantages see e.g. UNCTAD (1998), Chap. 4.

[9]Thus, a distinction between plant level and firm level economies of scale is important.

scale are assumed.[10] Different factor intensities in the geographically separated production phases are crucial for the development of vertical FDI: if all production phases had the same factor intensities, a concentration of the production in the lowest cost country would take place in lieu of a geographic separation of the production phases in terms of vertical FDI.

In the simplest case, there are two production stages, the first of which remains in the mother country, much like in horizontal FDI, and purely involves headquarter activities; the second phase includes the production and is located wherever the production costs are at their lowest. Assuming that the prospective host country does not demand the manufactured product, the whole production is transferred back to the home country for sale.[11] Here, the production costs are not only determined by the trade costs but also by the local production costs which for simplification only comprise the labour costs. Assuming the production only requires one unit of labour for a final product, the production of the intermediate product costs the same amount in both forms of internationalisation and the transferral of the intermediate product in the case of a geographic separation does not incur any additional costs. As for the concentration of the production process in the home country, the gain function thus comprises: $\prod_K = \pi(w)$, with the labour costs w in the home country.[12] Alternatively, the gain function for a geographic separation comprises: $\prod_{FDI} = \pi(w^* + t) - f$. The MNE would have to carry lower costs w* for production in the lower cost country but additional trade costs to the amount of t and additional fixed costs due to the geographic separation. The MNE then opts for a geographic separation of the production process through vertical FDI if the following applies:

$$\prod_{FDI} - \prod_K = \pi(w^* + t) - f - \pi(w) > 0 \tag{8.2}$$

Vertical FDI thus become increasingly probable the higher the labour cost difference between the home and host countries and the lower the trading and additional fixed costs. On the other hand, relatively similar labour costs (and/or factor costs) do not lead to the possibility of exploiting differences in factor price and permit the concentration strategy to appear more advantageous. In contrast to horizontal FDI, high trade costs inhibit FDI here.

In most extensions, the significance of trade is ascertained[13] and further models – such as Zhang and Markusen (1998) – address the comparison between the stages of

[10] The Helpman-Model does not contain the assumptions of the OLI-Paradigm, but allows focusing on factor price differentiation and their effects.

[11] Under assumption of a lack of demand in the host country there are more than two production stages possible. In that case, the home country or a third country would process the production.

[12] All other gains of the firm are equal in all internationalisation decisions (similar to the horizontal FDI model), whereby they could be neglected.

[13] In the original paper of Helpman (1984) trade costs don't exist, the motivation for FDI is due to the lack of fully factor price equalization through trade.

development in the countries. In all, they confirm the significance of lower trade costs and different stages of development. However, a certain development level is necessary in a potential host country as foreign production in an extremely underdeveloped country would cause prohibitively high costs due to the lack of infrastructure and political stability (Zhang and Markusen 1998, p. 251).

If the host country of the vertical FDI demands a proportion of the final product, the country's relative market size would also enter into the decision: if only a part of the production were transferred back to the home country, the significance of the trade costs would decrease. However, as only the proportion of the vertical FDI constitutes the production of the final product and the greater part has to be exported completely owing to the processing, this scenario is very implausible. Consequently, a difference between the countries in the stage of development, low trade barriers, small geographic distances, different factor endowments and factor price differences can be worked out.

Further aspects can be determined by considering the firm-specific characteristics for vertical FDI. Here, the plant level economies of scale do not play a significant role as the production steps are not duplicated for either of the alternatives.[14] In this instance, the product-specific transport costs have to be relatively low as the geographic distribution of the production results in high import and export shares. Consequently, it also becomes clear that the export share of vertical FDI, especially back into the home country or in a handful of other countries, is very high (Barba Navaretti and Venables 2004, pp. 32). Another necessary condition has already been addressed above: for the MNE to be able to exploit factor price differences, different factor intensities in the individual production stages are vital.[15] As capital-intensive headquarter activities remain in the home country in most instances, the labour-intensive production processes are primarily relocated abroad. It is a question of simple production processes which have already been standardised and simple services.

In order to combine the models of vertical and horizontal FDI, the 'Knowledge-Capital Model' emerged (Markusen 2002). Here, the factor costs and market access are the driving forces, whereby both FDI types develop endogenously in a model. However, it does not add any further decisional factors for a MNE's selection of a location so that closer consideration does not seem necessary. In all, a clear separation of horizontal and vertical FDI is difficult as the foreign affiliate also receives certain headquarter operations from the parent firm in the case of horizontal FDI. Consequently, horizontal FDI also always have certain vertical features (Protsenko 2004, pp. 15).

The results of the location factors are summarised in Table 8.1. Most location factors influence both FDI types, although rarely in the same direction and weight.

[14]The firm level economies of scale could be relative high, but are not critical for the internationalisation decision.

[15]That shows certain parallels to horizontal FDI: there is a similar factor endowment necessary for duplicating some part of the production process in a second location.

Table 8.1 Location specific determinants – without integration effects

Determinants	Horizontal	Vertical
Market size	Large	~
Development stage	Similar	Different
Relative factor endowment	Similar	Different
Relative factor costs	~	Different
Trade barriers	High	Low
Geographical distance	High	Low

The results will be applied in the following section: do the location factors for one of the two FDI forms correspond with the Irish location advantages? What does this mean from the perspective of the foreign firm's structure in Ireland?

8.4 Location Determinants in Ireland

With a population of 4.1 million and a gross domestic product of 150 bn. € (at current prices) in 2004, Ireland is a relatively small country. Whilst both the GDP and the population have risen dramatically since 1990 (37 bn. € and 3.5 million respectively),[16] Ireland is classed as one of the smaller countries in both the EU and OECD.[17] As a result, the location factor large *market size* is not given in Ireland.

The country's *stage of development* has changed greatly, especially since its accession to the EU in 1973. The per-capita income (GNP per capita in PPP)[18] was around 65% of the UK but reached the EU average in 2000 and rocketed to second place behind Luxembourg with approx. 130% of the EU average in 2005.[19] Consequently, at the beginning of the 1990s the state of development was slightly below compared to potential donor countries such as the USA but a similar development stage can be posited from 1995 onwards. In addition, if we consider the standard of living as a measure for the stage of development, the rising costs of living in Ireland since 2000 reduces the high per-capita income somewhat.[20]

Investigating the relative *factor endowment* is not particularly easy. The proportion of qualified and unqualified labour can serve as a rudimentary factor. Ireland's endowment with labour is very similar to the rest of the EU: the proportion of the

[16]For the data see different publications of Central Statistics Office (CSO) Ireland.

[17]The population of Ireland has only a share of 1% of the whole EU population, the Irish GDP adds only 1.5% to the EU-GDP. See Eurostat data base.

[18]GNP is used here as it excludes the profits earned by foreign firms producing in Ireland. The GDP per head is still higher: Ireland has reached the EU average in GDP per capita since 1997.

[19]See European Commission, Eurostat Yearbooks in different years. The sharp increase in 2005 is partly due to the decrease of the EU average through the EU Enlargement in 2004.

[20]The average expenditures of a household are above EU average. See Eurostat data base.

Irish population with tertiary education corresponds to the OECD average; the proportion of the younger population, however, is even higher (OECD 2001, p. 25). As the potential donor countries are highly developed (e.g. Barba Navaretti and Venables 2004, pp. 5), a higher proportion of qualified labour can also be expected. Consequently, Ireland had a factor endowment with qualified and unqualified labour in 1990–2005 similar to that of the donor countries. In the case of a similar factor endowment, similar *factor costs* can also be expected. However, the wages in Ireland (for qualified and unqualified labour) are relatively low compared to the EU and the USA. In the 15 EU member states, the hourly labour costs are only lower in Greece and Portugal. In spite of the enormous economic and productivity growth, the wages have only increased moderately,[21] meaning that the relative unit labour costs have even decreased (OECD 2001, p. 22). As the factor costs largely comprise the labour costs, these conclusions also apply to the overall factor costs.

The *trade barriers* have been very low since Ireland's accession to the EU in 1973 and after the realization of the Common Market in particular. There are no trade barriers towards the member states for the period in question and the protectionist barriers towards third countries are marginal. This is also reflected in the country's degree of openness: it is considerably higher than that of the EU (Goerg and Ruane 2000, p. 409).

The home countries are crucial for the investigation of the *geographic distance/ proximity*. The foreign firms in Ireland's industrial sector primarily come from the USA and the EU.[22] In the case of FDI from the USA, it is a matter of geographic distance whereas the other EU countries – despite Ireland's peripheral location – boast a geographic proximity to the country. Finally, the location factors in Ireland are compared with the results from Sects. 2 and 3 in Table 8.2.

Table 8.2 Location specific determinants in Ireland – without integration effects

Determinants	Horizontal	Vertical	In Ireland
Market size	Large	~	Small
Development stage	Similar	Different	Similar
Relative factor endowment	Similar	Different	Similar
Relative factor costs	~	Different	Different
Trade barriers	High	Low	Low
Geographical distance	High	Low	High/low

[21]This development is partly due to an agreement between the government, firms and labour unions, which arranged wage restraints.

[22]In 2000, about 80% of the production of foreign firms are from US-firms, see Table A2 in Appendix. New Data of FDI shows the EU, in particular Netherlands, as the important FDI-donor. These inflows arise basically of a few banks. These utilize location advantages (particularly the low tax rate) in Ireland, but don't play a decisive role in production; employment and the Irish development as well as they can't explain the high FDI inflows in the 1990s.

8.5 Vertical or Horizontal Foreign Direct Investment in Ireland?

According to the theory, neither the market size, development state nor the trade barriers led to horizontal FDI in Ireland at the beginning of the 1990s. Only 5 years later, the per-capita income and relative factor endowment could be regarded as location advantages, although a definite reason for horizontal FDI cannot be found from the location factors.

The trade structure of the foreign firms in Ireland supports this thesis: on average, 90% of the foreign firms export their production and the import share is also considerably higher than in the domestic firms (UNCTAD 2002, pp. 172). The main sectors with foreign firms in Ireland are computers and software development, chemistry and pharmaceuticals, and financial services (O'connor 2001, pp. 33). These industries are all relatively research-intensive and contain high-tech areas which require qualified labour, a high developed country and, particularly in the case of financial services, proximity to the customers. However, according to the different industrial sectors, it does seem to be a matter of horizontal FDI in some parts. The large geographic distance of the US FDI supports this thesis. Subsequently, the high import share can also be explained through the Irish economic structure: the necessary inputs were not available in Ireland by virtue of the different economic structure of the domestic industry, especially at the beginning of the 1990s.

Equally, there is a divided picture for vertical FDI: relatively low cost production factors (esp. labour) and low trade barriers are to be found in Ireland (compared to home market of most FDI donor countries choosing to locate in Ireland). The per-capita income was somewhat lower at the beginning of the 1990s than the donor country, meaning that vertical FDI can be expected on the basis of the location factors. These location factors for vertical FDI, however, can also be offered within the EU by the other cohesion countries, as have most eastern European countries since the eastward expansion. Compared to these countries, Ireland does not boast any location advantages for vertical FDI, even if we have to assume a certain development state as a necessary requirement for (horizontal and vertical) FDI (Zhang and Markusen 1998, p. 251). Presuming that simple production processes are prepared cheaply in a labour-abundant country in order to then be re-exported for processing (either to the donor country or a third country), vertical FDI are found to a lesser extent in Ireland. The high export orientation of the foreign firms in the whole EU zone and the high proportion of FDI in the high-tech sector only conditionally suggest vertical FDI.

The FDI in Ireland from Great Britain paint a very different picture: the export orientation is far lower than for the other foreign firms[23] and these exports primarily

[23]See Table A2 in Appendix.

go back to Great Britain (Barry et al. 1999, p. 52). The larger part of the British firms has already been in Ireland since the 1930s and the sectors can be found more in the middle to low technology sectors. The features of British firms consequently resemble Irish firms far more than the other foreign firms in Ireland. The aspects of horizontal FDI apply for these firms as there were still very high trade barriers in the location choice and they were effected to serve the market (O'connor 2001, p. 27). The proportion of British FDI, however, has relatively and absolutely declined in recent decades and now only accounts for 10% of the overall production by foreign firms in Ireland, meaning that they cannot explain the high inflows to Ireland since 1995.[24]

8.6 Consideration of the Regional Integration

The existing models cannot really explain the high inflows of FDI to Ireland. However, the consideration of EU integration could offer another possibility. An integration area particularly influences the location factors market size and trade costs as the internal trade barriers are reduced and the attainable market grows as a result of the lower transaction costs. Export-platform FDI combines the location factors of horizontal FDI with the location advantages of vertical FDI: the production affiliate serves the large-scale integration area, although the exact location is selected on the basis of cost appraisals (Ekholm et al. 2003, p. 1).

8.6.1 Horizontal Aspects

In Neary (2002)'s model, export-platform FDI are explained through trade barriers of different amounts for member and third countries. Referring back to Brainard's model of horizontal FDI, the intra-regional trade barriers drop to r and the inter-regional trade barriers remain t. In the case of serving two countries (of the same size) via a firm from a third country, an export profit of $\prod_{ex} = 2\pi(t)$ emerges. The return in the choice of a production in one of the two member states is now larger than for horizontal FDI. It now comprises the profit from serving the host country $(\pi(0) - f)$ and supplying the second country through exports with internal trade barriers $(\pi(r))$:$\prod_{FDI} = \pi(0) + \pi(r) - f$. The relative attractiveness of FDI compared to exports can be calculated as follows:

[24]See Table A2 in Appendix. The FDI inflows from United Kingdom were above all lower in the 1990s; see Fig. A3 in Appendix.

$$\prod_{FDI} - \coprod_{Ex} = \pi(0) + \pi(r) - f - 2\pi(t) = \pi(0) - \underbrace{f - \pi(t) + \pi(r)}_{\text{Decision without reg. integration (equation(8.1))}} - \pi(t) \quad (8.3)$$

Now, two yields are possible through an FDI decision: firstly, the savings of the trade costs as in Brainard's model (tariff-jumping-gain) and secondly the savings of the difference of the trade costs between supplying the market via the third country and that within the integration area (so-called export-platform-gain). As the internal trade tariff is lower than the external trade tariff ($r < t$) and the gain function is negatively dependent on the tariffs, always $\pi(r) - \pi(t) > 0$. This means that the FDI strategy is more attractive for a firm from a third country through the regional integration of two countries than exports. A second important conclusion is that whilst the reduction of the external trade barriers t leads to lower FDI, the reduction of the internal trade barriers r causes higher (export-platform) FDI. However, as long as the internal trade barriers are positive, it can still be worthwhile for MNE's with very low fixed costs to establish production facilities in both countries. Only in the case of a reduction of the internal trade costs r to zero does the incentive for the firms to make horizontal FDI in both countries disappear. Only export-platform FDI or exports from the third country then take place. According to this model, it is no longer the market size of the potential host country that is crucial but rather the size of the attainable market in the production location. For Ireland, the attainable market would be the whole European Union and thus very big.

The argumentation of the greater attractiveness of (export-platform) FDI compared to exports is no longer sustainable if the MNE already has production facilities in both member states. The regional integration can then even lead to a reduction of production plants if the second plant becomes inefficient (Pavelin and Barry 2005, p. 2). In a concentration of the production at one location, the investments would be expanded on site and redirected to the other location, meaning that in all there are no changes to the FDI inflows in the integration area. If the firm comes from one of the member states, it will – in this simple case – concentrate production on the domestic market and reduce the FDI (Buckley 2004, pp. 51).

In the case of serving the market of the whole integration area by firms from one of the member states or from a third country with only one production affiliate in a member state, the same argumentation as for horizontal FDI applies: the MNE decides whether to serve the second member country through exports or construct an additional production plant. As the trade costs are lower for regional integration than previously was the case, the goods can now be exported to the second country more cheaply and the FDI strategy becomes more unattractive. The MNE is more likely to opt for an extension of the existing production affiliate than the establishment of a new one as additional fixed costs would be incurred for an additional production affiliate.[25]

[25] I still assume that the capacity of an affiliate is unlimited. If there is a natural limit the firm could decide to set up a second plant.

Up to now, however, the MNE has been indifferent as to in which of the countries in the integration area it should make the FDI, whereby two countries of the same size are necessary. Only in the case of the existing production facilities in a member state would the location selection within the region already be made. The aspects of a vertical FDI are not yet necessary for the location selection within the integration area in this simple export-platform model due to cost considerations. Nevertheless, the EU is not as homogenous and Ireland in particular differs considerably from the founder member states. According the considerations so far, MNEs from third countries would be more likely to settle in the central countries of the EU as there is a greater demand there and no transport costs are incurred. MNEs from the central member states would be more likely to expand their production on site and not construct any additional production facilities in the new, peripheral member state. It also has to be clarified as to why a larger part of the multinational firms settles in Ireland as opposed to in one of the other EU nations.

8.6.2 Vertical Aspects

The particularity of Ireland's peripheral location is illustrative of the New Economic Geography (e.g. Krugman and Venables 1995). Here, the MNE does not choose the internationalisation strategy but rather the location of the production affiliate, in which the factor costs now assume a crucial role. The periphery is defined as a location where there is no demand for the produce, meaning that the entire production of the final product has to be exported in the central countries. The gain function of a firm with an affiliate in the integration area is composed of the following: $\prod_{FDI} = \pi(w,t) - f = px - (w + b + s)x - f$, with x for the production, p for price, w as a measure for the variable costs (labour costs per unit), b for the costs via trade barriers, s for transport costs per unit[26] and the fixed costs f for the construction of the affiliate. For production in the central country, the variables b and s would be absent from the equation as no costs would be incurred through trade barriers or presumably transport within the country. Prior to a regional integration, the trade barriers are high and presumably the unit labour costs lower in the peripheral country than in the central one as the periphery is less developed. The choice of a production in the periphery would be given if the following applied:

$$\begin{aligned} \Pi_{FDI_P} - \Pi_{FDI_C} &= px - (w_p + b + s)x - f - (px - w_c x - f) \\ &= (w_c - w_p)x - (b + s)x > 0 \end{aligned} \tag{8.4}$$

The firm's decision as to whether to construct the only affiliate in the peripheral location thus depends on the unit labour cost difference. As there are not any transport

[26]In the Export-platform model transport costs are part of the trade costs (t = b + s).

and trade costs for a production at the central location, the following has to apply: $w_c - w_p > b + s$. The unit labour cost difference has to be larger than the additional costs of transporting the entire production. In the case of very high trade barriers, the MNE is more likely to settle in the central country. Prior to Ireland's accession to the EU, most MNEs looking to supply the EU market would opt for a production affiliate in the central countries, which could also be observed in the 1960s.[27]

After integration, the trade costs b fall to zero for simplification, and thus the condition is shortened to: $w_c > w_p + s$. If the unit labour costs at the central location exceed those in the periphery plus transport costs, the MNE settles in the periphery. This is all the more probable the lower the (product-specific) transport costs are. These so-called weightless goods primarily involve products from the high technology industry. For firms from third countries that do not have production facilities in the integration area yet, the peripheral location is more attractive than the central location through the integration.

A similar consideration to that made for vertical FDI in Sect. 8.3 is now made for FDI from the member states: the choice of location within the integration area is made in virtue of different factor costs. The above (8.3) thus only has to be altered so that no additional fixed costs for an additional production plant arise here for the concentration of the production.

$$\prod_{FDI} - \prod_{C} = px - (w_p + b + s)x - f - (px - w_c x) > 0 \tag{8.5}$$

Here, the requirement for FDI in the other member state reads: $w_c > w_p + s + f/x$. FDI from the member states then take place if the labour costs of the centre exceed the low labour costs of the periphery, transport costs and the additional fixed costs per production unit. The incentive for firms from member states to invest in the periphery is smaller here than for firms from third countries, but it is greater than before the regional integration.

Decreasing internal trade barriers are therefore particularly positive in the attraction of (new) FDI from third countries for the peripheral regions of an integration area (Goerg and Ruane 2000, pp. 410). Furthermore, the different market sizes and factor endowments could be integrated here.

The locational factors for export-platform FDI are summarised in Table 8.3 and compared to those in Ireland.

8.6.3 *Impact of Regional Integration on Ireland*

The abovementioned approaches can explain a large part of the FDI in Ireland: firstly, inter-regional FDI, from the USA in particular, account for over 60% of the FDI to Ireland. Secondly, the foreign firms have a high export share in the EU and a

[27]In the 1960s, Ireland still had very low FDI inflows.

Table 8.3 Location determinants for export-platform FDI

Determinants	Export platform	In Ireland
Available market	Large	Large
Development stage	Similar	Similar
Relative factor costs	Different	Different
Trade barriers, extern	High	Low
Trade barriers, intern	Low	Low
Geographical distance	High	High/low

low export share back in the donor countries, which reinforces the export-platform model. Thirdly, the sectors with high FDI inflows produce so-called weightless goods. The global improvement of the information and communication paths offer Ireland additional support as an export-platform: the increasingly low transport and communication costs notionally bring Ireland closer to the EU and reduce the peripheral location of Ireland within the EU (Krugman 1997, p. 47).[28] The choice of Ireland as a location over other inexpensive and peripheral EU locations such as Portugal, however, cannot be explained as yet; the different general location advantages for FDI such as taxes, good business climate, and language then appear to play a decisive role.

Additionally, reallocations and the restructuring of existing production plants are carried out in the integration area (Buckley 2004, pp. 50). The reduction of the transaction costs and the possibility to serve the whole integration area does not necessarily make the parallel production in two member states profitable any more. This leads to the expansion of an existing affiliate in the low cost location and a reduction in the number of production plants in the more expensive locations. However, formerly concentrated firms in a member state can relocate parts of their production to another, cheaper member country through the lower trade costs and thus result in FDI in the low cost member state. As in the case of additional FDI from third countries, Ireland would not be the lowest in pure consideration of the factor costs in the EU: Ireland's competitive position in the labour-intensive production areas is worsened by the cohesion countries Portugal and Greece, not to mention the new Eastern European member states.[29] The dropping factor cost advantages, however, are compensated by increasing location advantages in Ireland (Krugman 1997, p. 47). Consequently, Ireland could benefit from the restructuring and reallocation processes as the country can produce relatively inexpensively and at the same time qualitatively high compared to the rest of the EU. This could be a reason for Ireland's high FDI from the EU (Table 8.4).

[28]The geographical and cultural proximity to a host country are crucial determinants for a potential investor.

[29]The EU-Enlargement was indeed in 2004, but preferential agreements between the EU and individual states exist. In addition to the announcement of EU-accession these cause to the effects explained earlier before the accession in 2004.

8.7 Conclusion

In all, certain location factors can be derived from the models explained for the different forms of FDI. Whilst the market conditions of country like the market size or the per-capita income assume a central role in the models for horizontal FDI, in the case of vertical FDI it is the factor conditions labour or trade costs that are crucial elements in the decision in favour of or against a country. The location factors for vertical and horizontal FDI were examined in Ireland but could not fully explain the high FDI inflows. Only the FDI from Great Britain can be explained with the traditional models. The models to explain export-platform FDI, however, create a consolidation of the location factors in Ireland. The most important reasons for investing in Ireland also include the crucial factors for export-platform FDI. Consequently, horizontal aspects primarily explain FDI from third countries into the EU, whilst vertical aspects explain FDI from the other member states and the location of FDI within the EU.

The aim of this article was to provide an overview of the models from location-specific perspectives. The examination of location factors for different forms of FDI in a country firstly can be helpful in facilitating the difficult investigation of the FDI form in a country. Secondly, considerations of the effects of FDI incentives on different FDI modes could be initiated. The usual practice of active FDI promotion could consequently support the crucial location factors of the desired FDI more purposefully. However, all in all, the significance of further location factors that have not been considered in detail here, such as agglomeration advantages or low tax rates, increases. An analysis of these factors and possible different influences on the FDI forms could paint a different picture again to explain FDI inflows.

Appendix

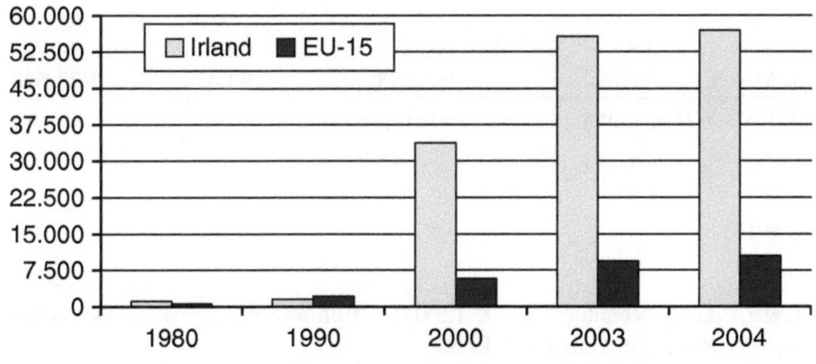

Fig. 8.1 FDI-stock per capita (in US-$), 1980–2004
Source: FDI-Data from UNCTAD (2005), pp. 308; Population data from Eurostat; Own calculation

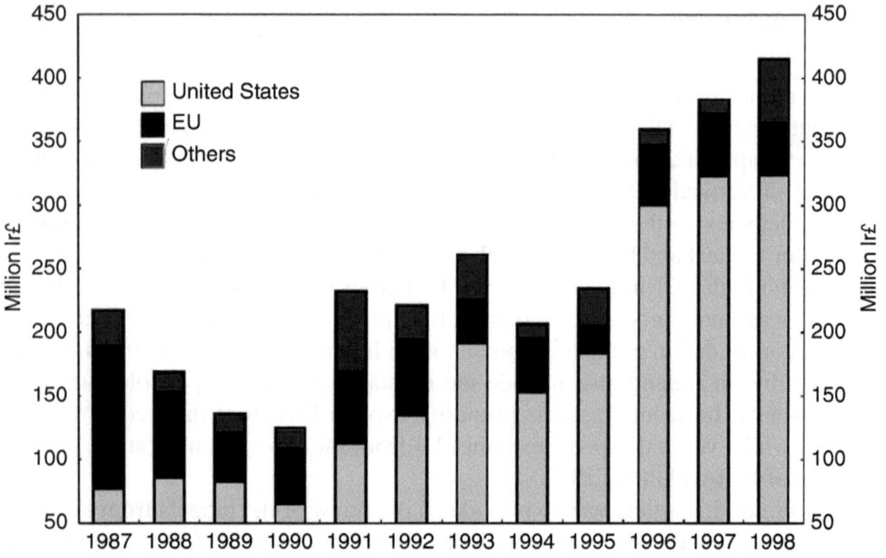

Fig. 8.2 FDI-Inflows from OECD-countries to Ireland
Source: OECD (2001), p. 21

Table 8.4 Domestic and foreign firms in manufacturing, 2000

Owner's nationality	Share of plants in Ireland (in %)	Total persons engaged (in %)	Gross output (in %)	Percent of gross output exported
Irish	87.5	51.3	23.5	51.10
Complete Foreign	12.4	48.7	76.5	91.70
Other EU	5.9	14.1	8.8	69.60
of which:				
UK	2	4.5	3.5	51.50
Germany	1.7	4.1	2	91.30
Non-EU	6.5	34.5	67.7	94.60
of which:				
USA	5.3	30.4	62.6	94.70
Total (No./in Mio. €)	5.256	252.353	94.472	77.648

Source: UNCTAD WID country profile, own compilation

References

Barba Navaretti, G., & Venables, A. J. (2004). *Multinational firms in the world economy*. Princeton, NY: Princeton University Press.

Barry, F. (1999). *Understanding Ireland's economic growth*. Basingstoke: Macmillan.

Barry, F. (2004). Export-platform FDI: the Irish experience. *EIB Papers, 9*, 8–37.

Barry, F., Bradley, J., & O'malley, E. (1999). Indigenous and foreign industry: characteristics and performance. In F. BARRY (Ed.), *Understanding Ireland's economic growth*. Basingstoke: Macmillan.

Barry, F., Goerg, H., & McDowell, A. (2003). Outward FDI and the investment development path of a late industrializing economy. Evidence from Ireland. *Regional Studies, 37*, 341–349.

Brainard, S.L. (1993), A simple theory of multinational corporations and trade with a trade-off between proximity and concentration, NBER Working Paper No. 4269.

Buckley, P. J. (2004). Regional integration and FDI in a globalized world economy. In L. Oxelheim & P. N. Ghauri (Eds.), *EU and the race for FDI in Europe*. Amsterdam: Elsevier.

Buckley, P. J., & Casson, M. (1976). *The future of the multinational enterprise*. London: Macmillan.

Carr, D. L., Markusen, J. R., & Maskus, K. E. (2001). Estimating the knowledge-capital model of the multinational enterprise. *American Economic Review, 91*, 693–708.

Dunning, J. H. (1981). Explaining the international direct investment position of countries: towards a dynamic or developmental approach. *Weltwirtschaftliches Archiv, 117*, 30–64.

Dunning, J. H. (1993). *Multinational enterprises and the global economy*. Wokingham: Addison-Wesley.

Ekholm, K., Forslid, R. and Markusen, J.R. (2003), Export-Platform Foreign Direct Investment, NBER Working Paper No. 9517.

Ethier, W. F., & Markusen, J. R. (1996). Multinational firms, technology diffusion and trade. *Journal of International Economics, 41*, 1–28.

Goerg, H., & Ruane, F. (2000). European integration and peripherality: lessons from the Irish experience. *The World Economy, 23*, 405–421.

Gray, A. W. (1997). *International perspectives on the Irish economy*. Dublin: Indecon Economic Consultants.

Helpman, E. (1984). A simple theory of international trade with multinational corporations. *Journal of Political Economy, 92*, 451–471.

Helpman, E., Melitz, M. J., & Yeaple, S. R. (2004). Exports versus FDI with heterogeneous firms. *American Economic Review, 94*, 300–316.

Hymer, S. H. (1976). *The international operations of national firms: a study of direct foreign investment*. Cambridge: MIT Press.

Krugman, P. (1997). Good news from Ireland: a geographical perspective. In A. W. Gray (Ed.), *International perspectives on the Irish economy*. Dublin: Indecon Economic Consultants.

Krugman, P., & Venables, A. J. (1995). Globalization and the inequality of Nations. *Quarterly Journal of Economics, 110*, 857–880.

Markusen, J. R. (1984). Multinationals, multi-plant economies, and the gains from trade. *Journal of International Economics, 16*, 205–226.

Markusen, J. R. (2002). *Multinational firms and the theory of international trade*. Cambridge: MIT Press.

Markusen, J. R., & Venables, A. J. (1998). Multinational firms and the new trade theory. *Journal of International Economics, 46*, 183–203.

Markusen, J. R., & Venables, A. J. (2000). The theory of endowment, intra-industry and multinational trade. *Journal of International Economics, 52*, 209–234.

Neary, J. P. (2002). Foreign direct investment and the single market. *The Manchester School, 70*, 291–314.

O'connor, T. (2001), FDI and indigenous industry in Ireland: review of evidence, ESRC Programme Working Paper No. 22/01.

OECD. (2001). *Economic surveys – Ireland 2001*. Paris: OECD Press.

Pavelin, S., & Barry, F. (2005). The single market and the geographical diversification of leading firms in the EU. *The Economic and Social Review, 36*, 1–17.

Pontes, J. P. (2001). Location of FDI in a regional integration area. *Economic Bulletin, 8*, 1–9.

Protsenko, A. (2004). *Vertical and horizontal foreign direct investment in transition countries*. München: Diss.

Roller, A. (1999). *Multinationale Unternehmen in Irland*. Wiesbaden: Gabler.

UNCTAD (1998), World Investment Report 1998: Trends and Determinants, New York, Genf: United Nations Publications.

UNCTAD (2002), World Investment Report 2002: Transnational Corporations and the Export Competitiveness, New York, Genf: United Nations Publications.
UNCTAD (2005), World Investment Report 2005: TNCs and the Internalization of R&D, New York, Genf: United Nations Publications.
Vernon, R. (1966). International investment and international trade in the product cycle. *Quarterly Journal of Economics, 10*, 190–207.
Zhang, K. H., & Markusen, J. R. (1998). Vertical multinationals and host country characteristics. *Journal of Development Economics, 59*, 233–252.

Chapter 9
Aspects of Market Integration in a Transition Economy

Julius Horvath and Katarina Lukacsy

9.1 Introduction

Within an international context, market integration studies are related – among others – to issues of the law of one price, dispersion of prices, pricing-to-market, and purchasing power parity. The most important conclusion one can draw from this work is that some types of friction provide considerable barriers to the integration of markets within a nation as well as across nations. A number of studies found that the speed of price convergence depends upon geographical distance, information costs, good and location specifics, currency fluctuations and national political borders.

Most retail markets are characterized by price dispersion; the important question is the extent of this dispersion. One reason for price dispersion is the degree to which the products considered in different markets actually differ from each other, i.e. the extent of product differentiation. Another reason lies in the degree of information quality at the disposal of consumers. In other words, even if goods are perfectly homogenous one might find price dispersion if the consumers are not aware of this fact.[1]

This study discusses price dispersion problems in the context of the Slovak economy and is structured in the following way. Section 9.2 provides a short description of the behaviour of final consumer prices across Slovakia, with an emphasis on dispersion of prices and their convergence. Section 9.3 discusses

[1]For example, Salop and Stiglitz (1977) consider a model in which one group of consumers is aware of price dispersion and the other is not. Consequently, one group always buys at low-priced stores and others buy randomly, which is the source of price dispersion.

This research is a part of the project "Financial Market Integration, Structural Change, Foreign Direct Investment and Economic Growth in the EU25" Number-2006-1623/001-001: The authors are solely responsible for the contents, which might not represent the opinion of the Community. The Community is not responsible for any use that might be made of data appearing in this publication.

J. Horvath (✉) and K. Lukacsy
Central European University, Budapest, Hungary
e-mail: horvathj@ceu.hu

P.J.J. Welfens and C. Ryan (eds.), *Financial Market Integration and Growth*,
DOI 10.1007/978-3-642-16274-9_9, © Springer-Verlag Berlin Heidelberg 2011

price dispersion in the context of more than one country, and Sect. 9.4 provides concluding observations.

9.2 Market Integration Within Slovakia

Markets function in space. At the national level, in an integrated market,[2] macroeconomic policies matter as they affect incentives at micro-level. If the national market consists of a number of non-integrated markets national policy might affect micro incentives in a way not expected by macro-policy-makers. Furthermore, integrated markets might transmit better signals needed for growth. "For example, without good access to distant markets that can absorb excess local supply, firms' adoption of improved production technologies will tend to cause producer prices to drop, erasing the gains from technological change and thereby dampening incentives for firms to adopt new technologies that can stimulate growth."[3]

One seems to observe puzzling missed arbitrage opportunities across space. Not only in developing countries are arbitrage opportunities not used due to inadequate communication and infrastructure, but one also finds unused arbitrage opportunities within more advanced economies. We do not have a clear expectation about market integration in the transition countries, i.e. whether the extent of unused arbitrage opportunities is comparable to more or less advanced economies.[4]

In this paper we do not use the spatial integration model, which takes into consideration both the behaviour of prices and trade flows. Rather, due to data limitation we use an intuitive concept of market integration which contends that as prices reach equilibrium across markets, the market is then integrated (or has a tendency for integration). Thus price equilibrium between two markets is seen as a sign of market integration, even if no trade flows occur between these two markets. On the other hand, even if trade flows occur but prices have a tendency not to equilibrate, we consider these markets to not be integrated.

9.2.1 *First Glimpse*

We use two data sets in this study.[5] The first data set contains monthly frequency nominal prices for over 600 final goods and services from 38 Slovak districts over

[2]Stigler and Sherwin (1985) consider that "a market for a good is the area within which the price of a good tends to uniformity, allowance being made for transportation costs".

[3]Barrett (2005, p. 1).

[4]Berkowitz and Dejong (1998) show that the lack of market integration in Russia reflects some 'hidden' division of this country into regional economies, at least in the first half of the 1990s.

[5]Both data sets were obtained from the Statistical Office of the Slovak Republic.

the time period starting in January 1997 and ending in December 2001.[6] The data are thus three dimensional, with the dimensions being time, commodity, and district.[7] Having disaggregated data on actual consumer prices for different types of products, we avoid aggregation problems associated with using sector level price indices.

The second data set – used later in this section – contains the same type of data, however only for two districts and a limited number of homogenous goods, but for a longer time span, January 1997–December 2006.

We begin with an illustrative presentation of data. As transport costs, price stickiness and other good-specific factors, non-competitive markets and other obstacles to arbitrage do exist in national markets, we expect differences in nominal prices across locations. The purpose of the illustration below is to provide a first glimpse at the character of these differences.

Figure 9.1 describes price dispersion for well-defined, homogenous brand-name tradable products, Fig. 9.2 for heterogeneous service products. As one would expect the price dispersion is significantly greater for heterogeneous as compared to homogenous products. Finally, Figs. 9.3 and 9.4 describe price dispersion for a pair of goods: matches and gasoline. One linkage to consumer search theory is the inverse relationship between per unit search costs and purchase frequency, which is clearly visible in both the gasoline and the matches markets.

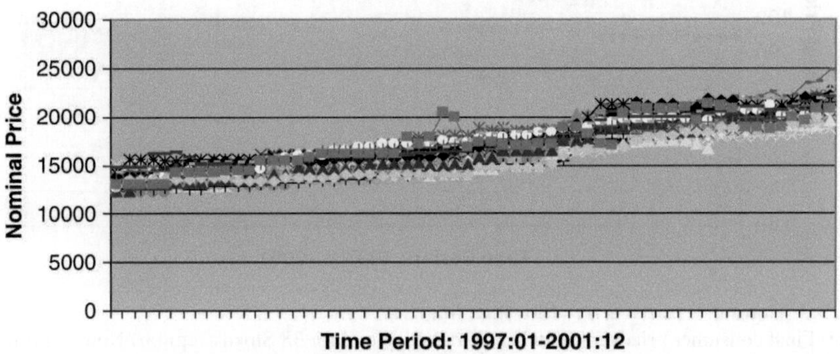

Fig. 9.1 Consumer prices across Slovakia: Cheese 'Niva'
Note: Final consumer monthly prices for Niva, Slovak cheese brand, for 38 Slovak regions. Nominal price is in 1/100 of Slovak koruna. The time period is 1997:01 till 2001:12. The figure is based on 2,280 observations

[6]Different subsets of this data set have been used in studies of Coricelli and Horvath (2006), Horvath and Vidovic (2005).

[7]The data collected in the sample are taken from the capital cities of the districts. The data set includes tradable and non-tradable goods and services, homogenous and heterogeneous products. The data set contains actual prices, and not quoted prices or price indices. For the empirical analysis, we create district specific cross-store averages from the individual prices, since store identifiers are not available.

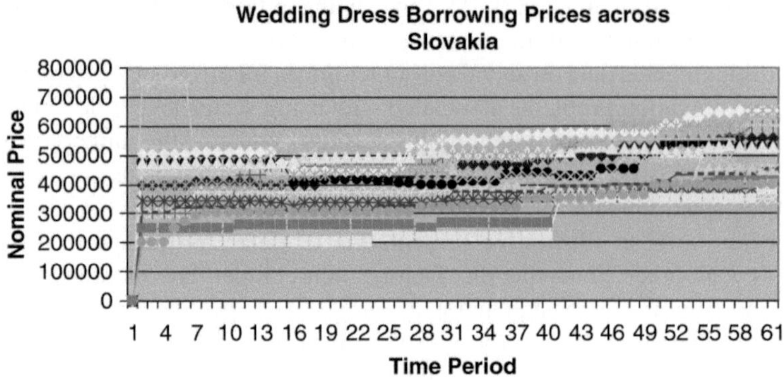

Fig. 9.2 Consumer prices across Slovakia: Borrowing wedding dress
Note: Final consumer prices for services, wedding dress borrowing price for 38 Slovak regions. Nominal Price is in 1/100 of Slovak koruna. The time period is 1997:01 till 2001:12. The figure is based on 2,280 observations

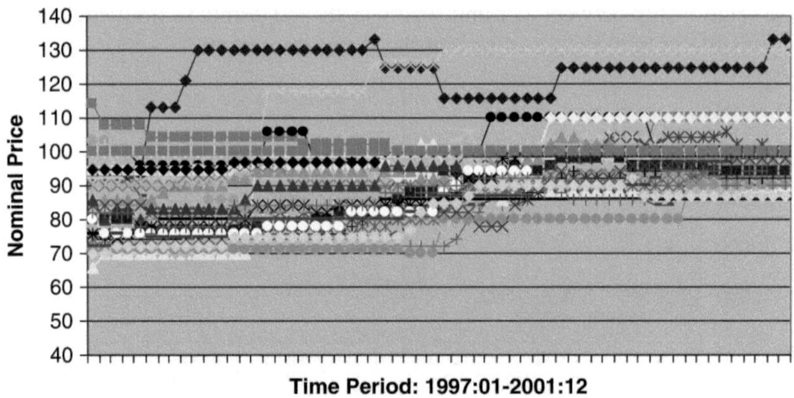

Fig. 9.3 Consumer prices across Slovakia: Matches
Note: Final consumer prices for matches, a tradable good for 38 Slovak regions. Nominal Price is in 1/100 of Slovak koruna. The time period is 1997:01 till 2001:12. The figure is based on 2,280 observations

Significant price deviations are also observed when we calculate the ratio of maximum price to minimum price, or the ratio of the maximum price to mean price in a given month. The *max–min* relative price is lowest for gasoline and tobacco products and highest for apartment painting and some other services and heterogeneous goods. The market of gasoline – homogenous product in a highly competitive oligopolistic market – is extremely integrated, the difference between the maximum and minimum average price across districts being only about 3% and the *max-mean* relative price ratio around 1%. The relative measure of dispersion (the coefficient of variation) is lower for more expensive and frequently purchased goods. For example, the coefficient of variation is 0.006 for gasoline, and 0.025 for cigarettes (Mars brand).

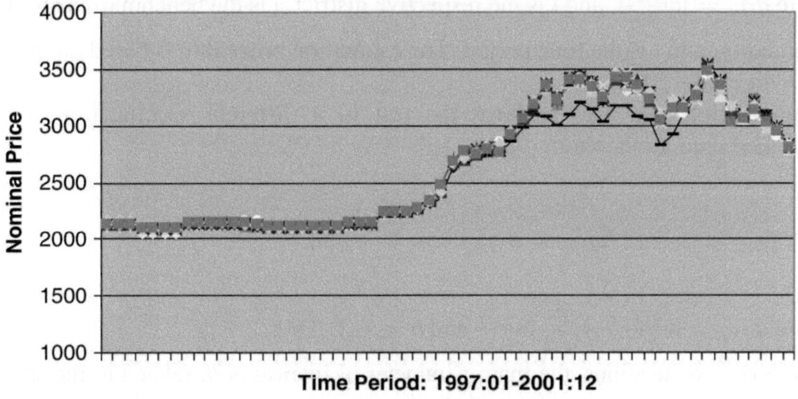

Fig. 9.4 Consumer prices across Slovakia: Gasoline 91-Octane
Note: Final consumer prices for gasoline 91-octane, a tradable good for 38 Slovak regions. Nominal Price is in 1/100 of Slovak koruna. The time period is 1997:01 till 2001:12. The figure is based on 2,280 observations

9.2.2 *Towards the Law of One Price*

Market integration is connected to the law of one price. Engel and Rogers (1995) observe that "one of the most direct implications of rational behavior is that two identical goods selling in the same market should have the same price." One expects the law of one price to hold in financial and currency markets, because arbitrage in these markets is more explicit. However, there is a plethora of reasons which might prevent the law of one price to hold in final consumer markets. Wolf (2003) lists these reasons into four groups: different tax rates facing wholesalers and retailers in various locations different transportation costs from factory to wholesalers and from wholesalers to retailers; different local costs across wholesalers and retailers and different mark-ups charged by producers to wholesalers, by wholesalers to retailers, and by retailers to purchasers In addition, the degree of failure of the law of one price also depends on the distance between locations.

The previous section provided some provisional evidence that in markets for final goods and services, price differences do not disappear at such a rate as is observed in exchange rate or financial markets. However, this does not preclude the tendency of prices to converge at different speeds. Literature dealing with this issue – i.e., Parsley and Wei (1996) – estimates the speed of adjustment of prices towards law of one price using the following (9.1)

$$\Delta q_{i,k,t} = \beta q_{i,k,t-1} + \sum_{m=1}^{s(k)} \gamma_m \Delta q_{i,k,t-m} + \varepsilon_{i,k,t} \tag{9.1}$$

where $q_{i,k,t} = \ln(\frac{p_{i,k,t}}{p_{j,k,t}})$, and i is the respective district, j is the benchmark district, k is commodity, and t is the time period. The estimation procedure is based on the work of Levin et al. (2002).

In addition, we also perform the test in a different specification, i.e. for demeaned data as shown in (9.2).

$$\Delta\tilde{q}_{i,k,t} = \beta\tilde{q}_{i,k,t-1} + \sum_{m=1}^{s(k)} \gamma_m \Delta\tilde{q}_{i,k,t-m} + \varepsilon_{i,k,t} \tag{9.2}$$

where $\tilde{q}_{ij,k,t} = \ln\frac{p_{i,k,t}}{p_{j,k,t}} - \frac{1}{T}\sum_{b=1}^{T} \ln\frac{p_{i,k,b}}{p_{j,k,b}}$ and $b = 1, 2, ...60$.

In both specifications, the main parameter of interest is β, related to the speed of convergence. Under the null hypothesis of no convergence, β is equal to zero, meaning that shocks to $q_{i,k,t}$ are permanent. β greater than zero implies the relative price on the left hand side of (9.1) and (9.2) has possible explosive divergence. Convergence implies a negative value of β. To obtain the auto-regressive coefficient, one would need to add one to the value of β. The closer the estimate of β to zero, the longer the estimated half-life of a disturbance and the more likely it is that the data contains unit root.

Table 9.1 reports the summary of these test results for Slovak data and compares them with results from similar studies on the US and Hungary. The adjustment among Slovakian districts is slower for non-perishable goods and for services than the corresponding results obtained in Parsley and Wei (1996). However, adjustment is fastest for perishable goods independent of the benchmark. Median values for the half-life of the price convergence are considerable lower if specification (9.2) is used.

We note that in specification (1) the β coefficient is positive in 34 cases out of 157 cases for non-perishable goods; in 6 cases out of 49 cases for perishable goods; and in 8 cases out of 24 cases for services. In these cases, there is no evidence for convergence towards the law of one price. However, using specification (2), the β coefficient becomes negative and the presence of the unit root is rejected in all cases.

Table 9.1 Retail price convergence: Slovakia, Hungary and the USA

	Slovakia specification (1)	USA specification (1)	Slovakia specification (2)	Hungary specification (2)
Non-perishable products	29.56	15.84	5.68	3.56
Perishable products	9.82	12.18	1.98	3.65
Services	79.62	46.21	7.34	10.93

Note: Half-life is an un-weighted median value calculated in months. Horvath and Vidovic (2005) perform the analysis for 157 non-perishable final products, 49 perishable products and 24 services. In both specifications Bratislava is the benchmark, results with Banska Bystrica as a benchmark have a bit faster adjustment. Hungary data are from Ratfai (2006). Data for Hungary services contains a mean instead of median. Data for the United States are from Parsley and Wei (1996). In Slovak case benchmark cities were Bratislava and Banska Bystrica; in study of Hungarian consumer price convergence benchmark location was Budapest; in the US study the benchmark was New Orleans

Horvath and Vidovic (2005) also regress the mean log-difference for all the commodities on the variable of distance to the benchmark and size of the individual city. Results show that the size variable is an important determinant of the level of mean log-differences in prices, i.e. the higher the population of the main city in the district, the higher the price levels. The distance from the benchmark district does not seem to be significant.

9.2.3 Market Integration Between the Most and the Least Developed Cities

In this section, we consider market integration of two distinct cities. We have chosen two cities to illuminate the division of Slovakia into the advanced western and less advanced eastern part. Table 9.2 provides a first glimpse into the differences between the western and eastern regions.

In addition to the western/eastern division, one also observes clear differences between Bratislava and other cities. World Bank (2002) compares the Slovak regional GDP per capita at purchasing power and finds that in 1999, the Bratislava region was approximately equal to the European Union average, while the remaining regions were around 50% or below the European Union average. The Presov region was the poorest at around one-third of the EU average.

In this section, we consider Bratislava to represent the 'west' and Svidnik from the Presov region to represent the 'east' of Slovakia. Our data consists of average final goods retail monthly prices for 14 consumer products for the time span from January 1997 to December 2006. These products are: plastic bucket 10 l; 60 W bulb, one piece; matches one box; towel, cotton, one piece; synthetic paint, 1 kg; cocoa powder, 0.1 kg; fresh egg, one piece; rice, 1 kg; apartment painting; photo development; glass window repair; meat beef soup, 0.33 l; DVD rental, 1 day; and a wedding dress rental, for 3 days.

Table 9.2 Differences between western and eastern regions in Slovakia

District name	Unemployment rate	Urbanization index in %	Average monthly salary in Slovak koruna	GDP per capita, Slovak koruna current prices
Western regions of Slovakia				
Bratislava	4.1	96	24,860	228,304
Trnava	7.2	64	17,610	120,428
Trencin	6.0	65	16,383	101,709
Zilina	11.1	57	16,437	88,076
Eastern regions of Slovakia				
Kosice	20.2	39	17,930	93,810
Presov	19.2	35	14,087	69,790

Source: Statistical Office of the Slovak Republic

Note: Data for the year of 2006; urbanization measured as a share of inhabitants living in cities and towns

Table 9.3 Basic statistics relative prices

Product	Mean price differential	Variability of price differential	Coefficient of variation
Tradable goods			
Plastic bucket	0.16088	0.08701	0.07387
Bulb	0.16174	0.05787	0.10387
Matches	0.33588	0.11247	0.22341
Cotton towel	0.44621	0.07989	0.36632
Synthetic paint	0.27255	0.06766	0.20489
Food products			
Cocoa powder	0.12760	0.07089	0.05671
Eggs	0.19685	0.10641	0.09044
Rice	0.42426	0.09835	0.32591
Services			
Apartment painting	0.38527	0.21603	0.16924
Photo development	0.30595	0.26298	0.04297
Glass repair work	0.20606	0.17924	0.02682
Meat soup	0.75378	0.07685	0.67693
DVD rental	0.34214	0.11636	0.22578
Wedding dress rental	0.40413	0.09507	0.30906

We define the product-level bilateral relative price as

$$p^i_{j,k,t} = \left| \log \frac{p_{i,j,t}}{p_{i,k,t}} \right|$$

where price of good i is defined for location j (Bratislava) and location k (Svidnik). In Table 9.3 we present price differential variability and mean absolute price differential. On average, prices were higher in Bratislava than in Svidnik.

In Table 9.3 we examine the dispersion in prices of 14 relatively homogeneous products between two distinct districts. In this sample, the greatest mean price differential is in meat soup served in restaurants, probably due to non-tradable local components. The mean price differential between the prices of meat soup in restaurants is considerably higher than between tradable goods such as plastic buckets and bulbs; for other services, this value does not show any clear pattern.

Individual goods mean price differential to a large extent seem to reflect significant income differences in these two locations. This effect is then mitigated probably by the fact that in Bratislava, retail store chains are already exposed to a fierce competition, while in Svidnik – especially in the first years of investigation – individual shops prevailed, with retail markets less exposed to competition.[8]

[8]We also experiment with the idea that a higher proportion of families with lower income in Svidnik should most likely lead to lower dispersion in prices in Svidnik for each individual good. However, interestingly while for most of the goods this expectation holds, there are still goods (4 out of 10) for which the standard deviation of nominal prices is higher in Svidnik than in Bratislava.

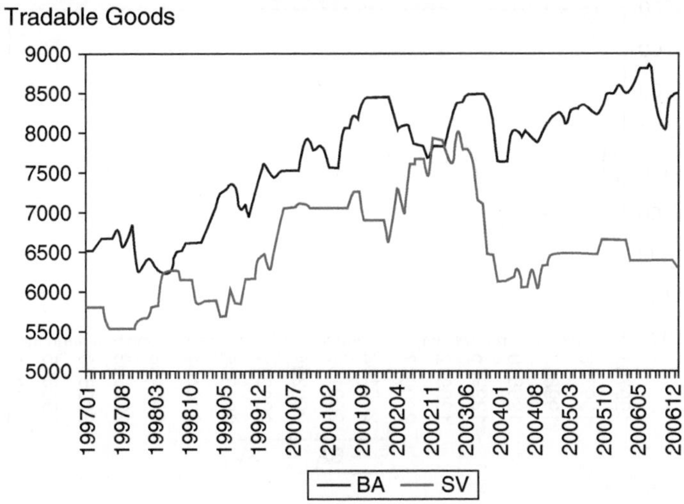

Fig. 9.5 Plastic bucket

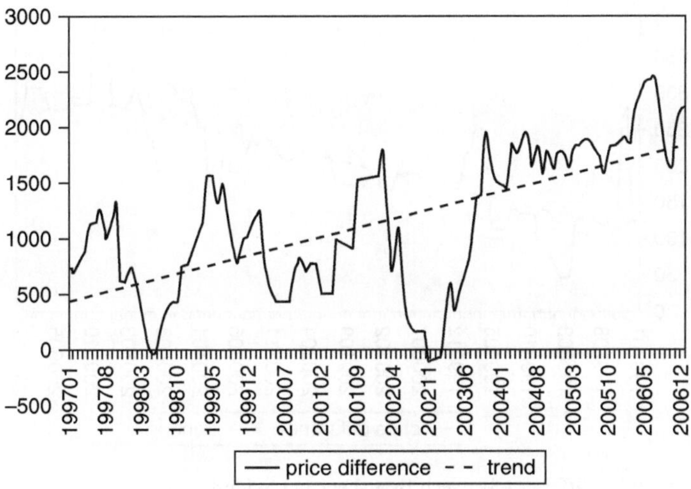

Fig. 9.6 Plastic bucket: price difference between Bratislava and Svidnik

Figures 9.5–9.30 plot monthly average prices for each individual product in both regions – Bratislava (BA) and Svidnik (SV). We present these figures in the following manner; the first figure plots the actual behavior of retail prices in both regions, full line for Bratislava and dashed for Svidnik. The second figure plots the difference of the two prices together with a fitted trend (dashed) line. Figures 9.5–9.30 plot monthly prices for the period from January 1997 to December 2006. Tradable Goods.

Figures 9.5–9.30 plot the behavior of retail prices for selected products in two Slovak cities, the most developed region, Bratislava and one of the least developed,

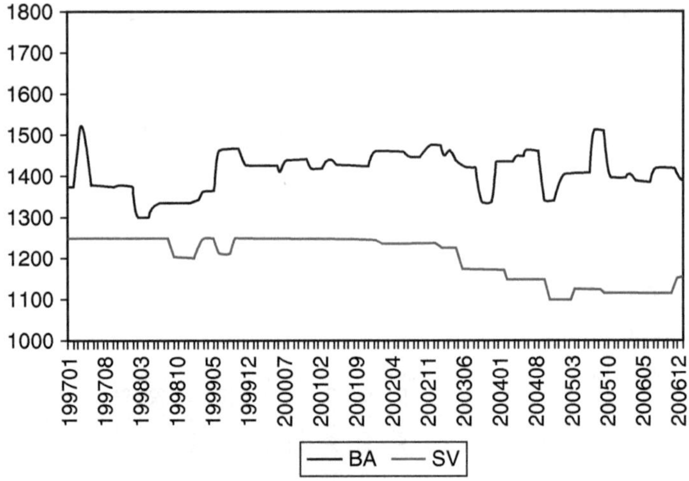

Fig. 9.7 Bulb

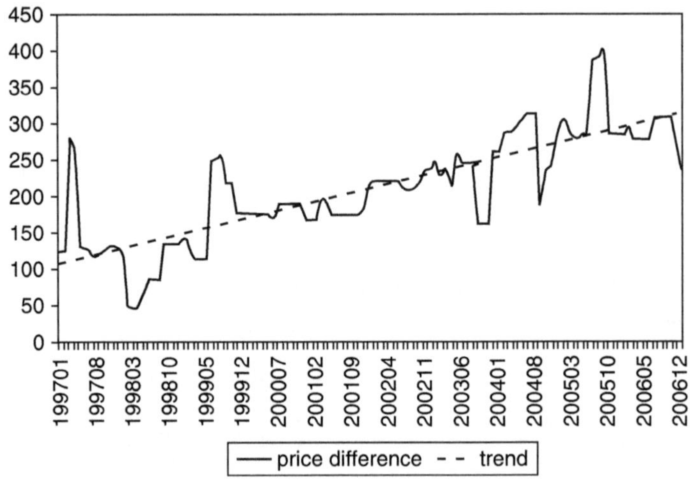

Fig. 9.8 Bulb: price difference between Bratislava and Svidnik

Svidnik. Retail prices for all 14 products are typically higher (sometimes much higher) in Bratislava. However, prices are higher in Svidnik in rare cases. For some goods, the price difference seems to have an increasing trend, this is especially pronounced for services (wedding dress rental, meat soup in restaurant, and photo development) but also for food products and some tradable goods. These differences seem to persist for at least several years and cannot be considered as merely transitory. This provides sketchy evidence for a low degree of spatial market integration between these two distinct cities. However, detailed analysis would be

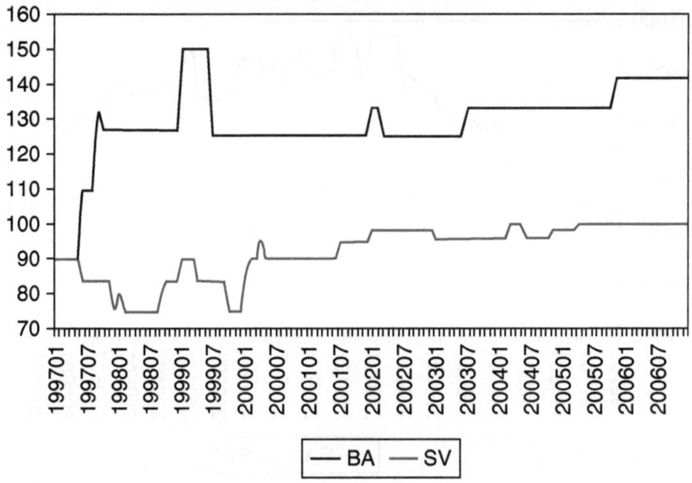

Fig. 9.9 Matches

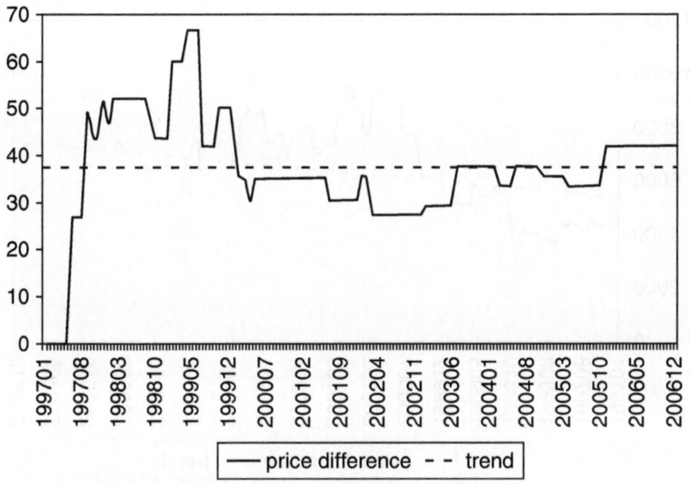

Fig. 9.10 Matches: price difference between Bratislava and Svidnik

needed, which is outside the scope of this study. In the following section, we deal with dispersion of prices across borders.

9.3 Market Integration: Across Borders

In the last decades, we observe decline of trade barriers world-wide. In addition, transportation and communication costs of trade are on the decline. These effects might increase the degree of market integration. However, even if all explicit trade

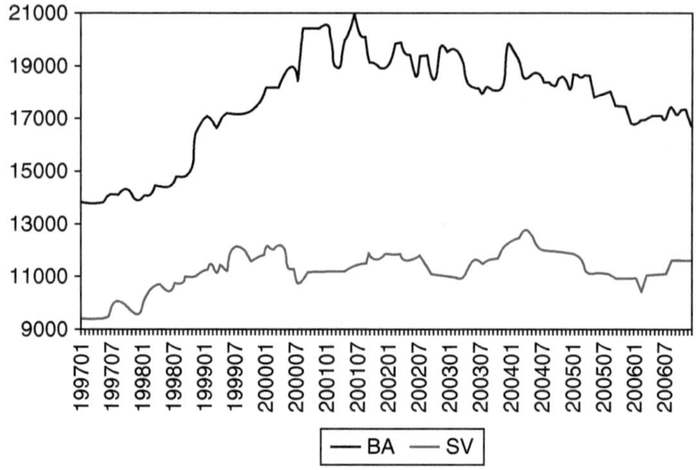

Fig. 9.11 Cotton towel

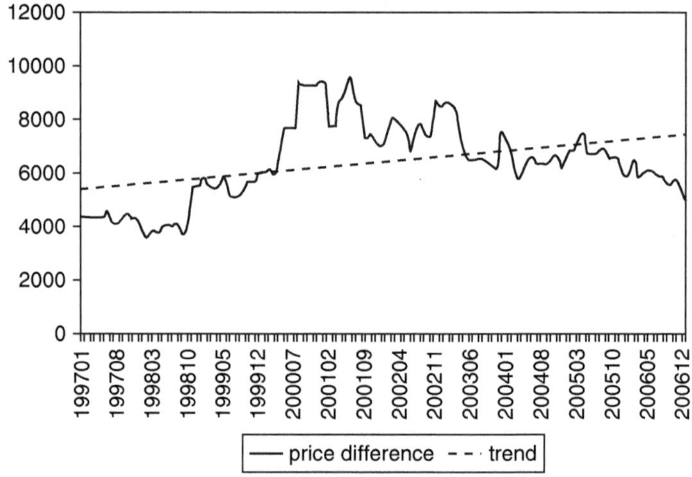

Fig. 9.12 Cotton towel: price difference between Bratislava and Svidnik

barriers disappear markets might not get fully integrated due to implicit barriers such as national borders.[9]

[9]Some authors are skeptical to claims about tendency of markets for integration. For example, Knetter (1994) shows that German firms charge significantly higher prices to Japanese importers than to other markets; i.e. they price-to-market. Under perfect separation of locations price discrimination is feasible, and no possibility of consumers arbitraging differences in final goods prices appears; Engel and Rogers (1995).

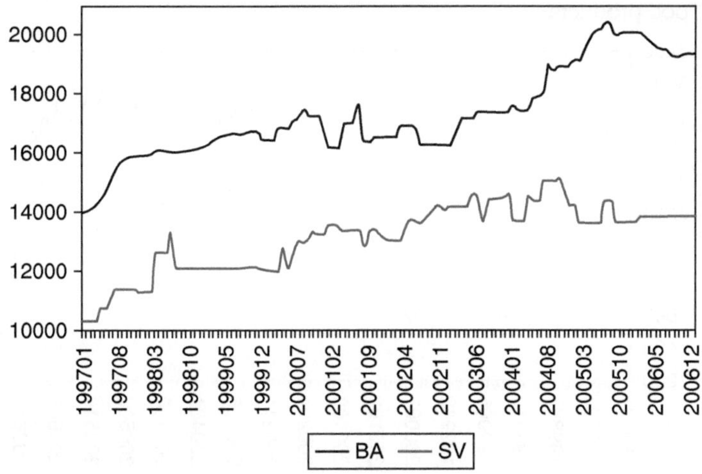

Fig. 9.13 Synthetic paint

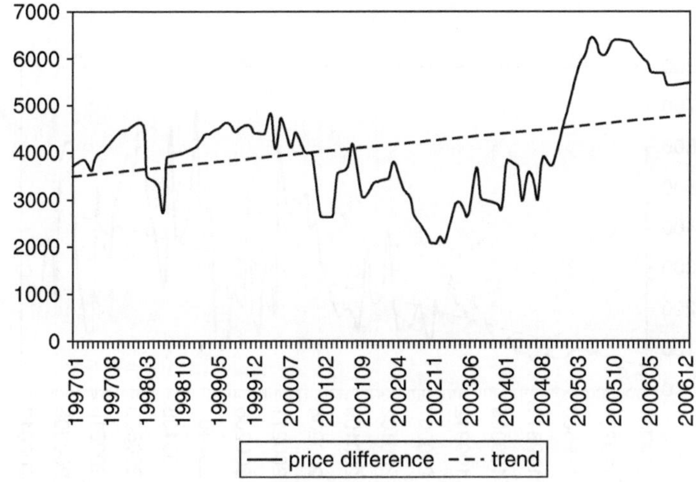

Fig. 9.14 Synthetic paint: price difference between Bratislava and Svidnik

Engel and Rogers (1996) analyze border effects in the context of consumer price dispersion. They consider all final consumer goods as non-traded, as tradable goods contain non-traded service components (marketing, distribution, and others).[10]

[10]Consumer final prices contain costs associated with distribution and marketing. These costs have either a strong local component (store rent, local salesmen wages, etc.) or strong regional component (when for example within a region one location unit shares similar packaging, distribution and other service system for final consumer goods). For 1992, estimates suggest that producers of final goods on average receive 60% of the final retail price; Wolf (2003).

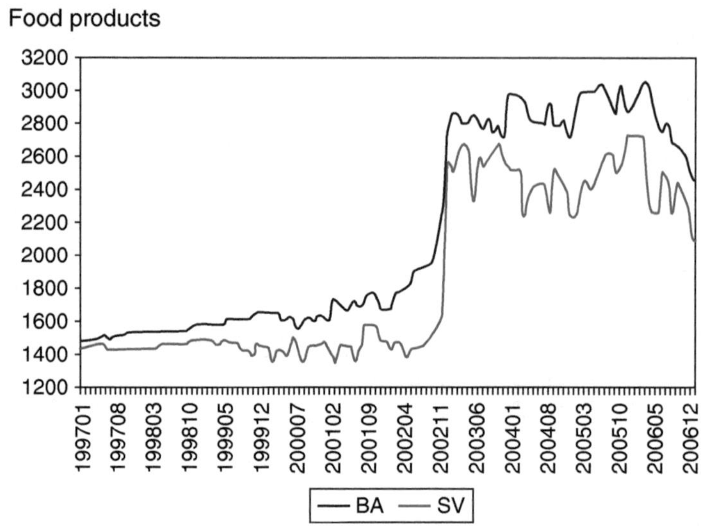

Fig. 9.15 Cocoa powder

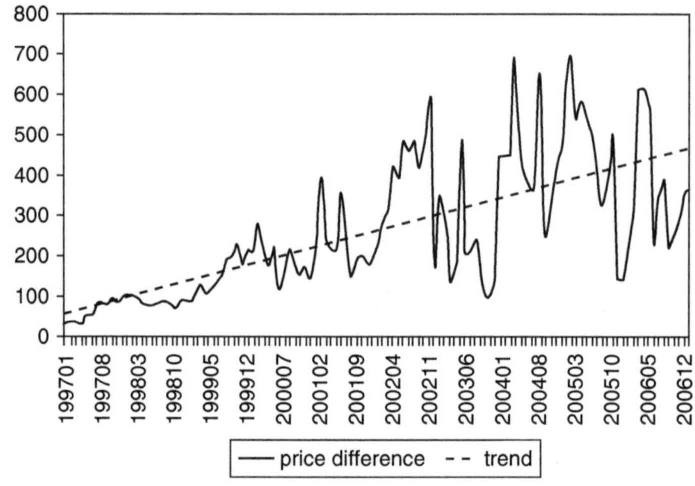

Fig. 9.16 Cocoa powder: price difference between Bratislava and Svidnik

In addition, all goods contain a tradable intermediate component. Thus, p_j^i, the price of the final product i, sold in location j, equals:

$$p_j^i = \beta_j^i \alpha_j^i (w_j^i)^{\gamma_i} (q_j^i)^{1-\gamma_i} \tag{9.3}$$

where β_j^i is the mark-up over costs, α_j^i is the total productivity of the final-goods sector, w_i^j is the price of the non-traded service; γ_i is the share of non-traded service in final output; and q_j^i is the price of traded intermediate input.

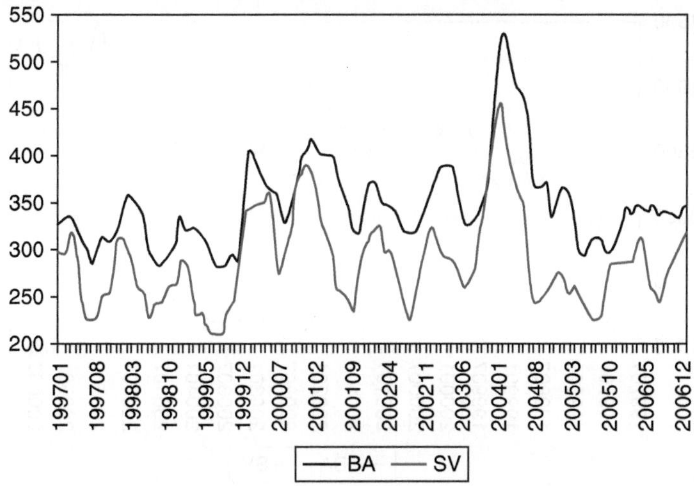

Fig. 9.17 Eggs

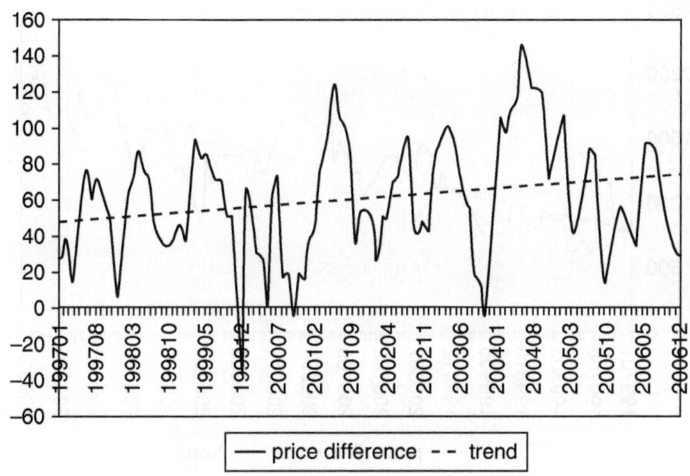

Fig. 9.18 Eggs: price difference between Bratislava and Svidnik

Engel and Rogers (1996) provide arguments for why borders matter in consumer pricing: locations farther apart might have less similar cost structures; total productivity of final-goods sector might differ at various locations; these effects might be exacerbated between distant regions and even more across borders; price variation of goods might differ if cities lie across borders; mark-ups might differ across borders; non-traded market services might be more integrated within a country than

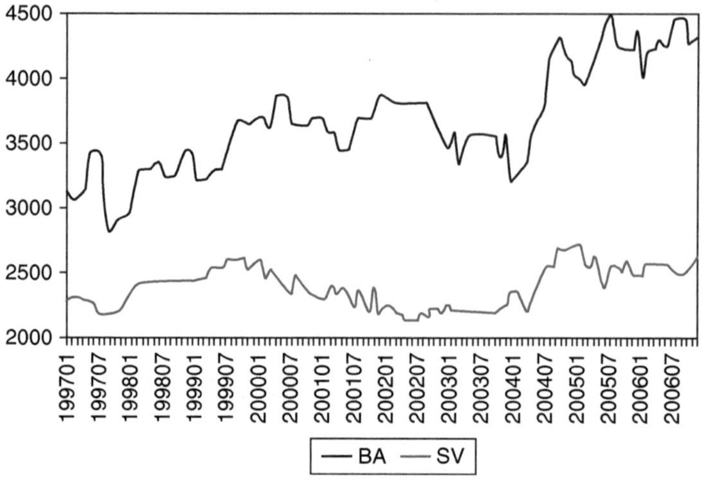

Fig. 9.19 Rice

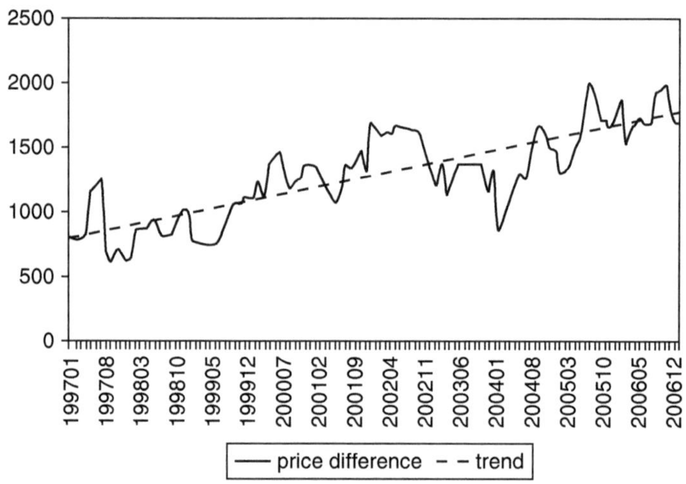

Fig. 9.20 Rice: price difference between Bratislava and Svidnik

across countries; national labor markets are more separated than local labor markets within the country; if nominal exchange rates are highly variable then cross-border prices would fluctuate along with the exchange rate, but the within-country prices would be stable.

In this context the border effect means that after controlling for distance and other trade costs, a substantial difference in the behavior of prices across two

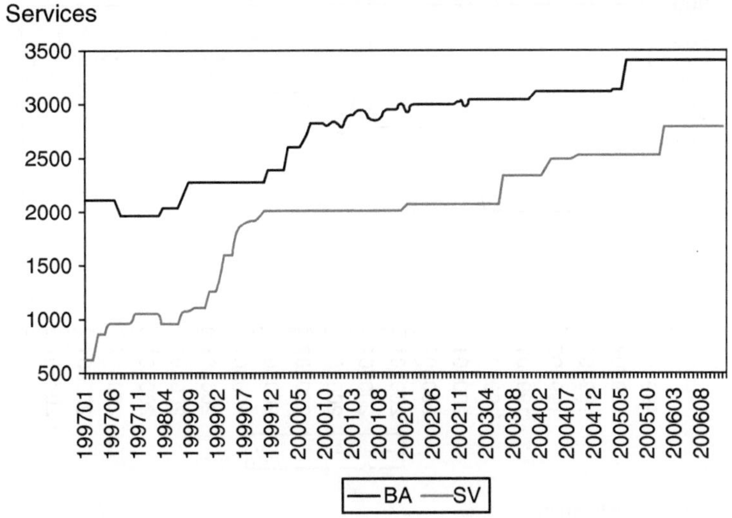

Fig. 9.21 Apartment painting

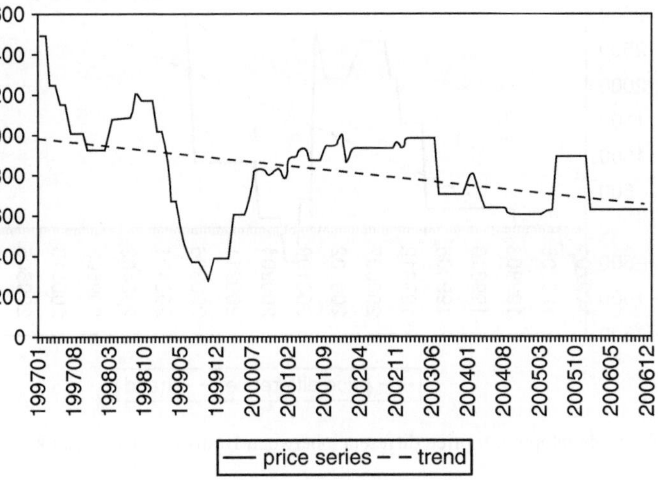

Fig. 9.22 Apartment painting: price difference between Bratislava and Svidnik

countries remains as compared to the behavior of prices within these countries. In other words, one defines border effect as the extent to which the law of one price holds in the intra-national as compared to inter-national environment after controlling for distance and other effects. It is thus important to isolate the border effect statistically, and this issue is dealt with in Sect. 9.3.1.

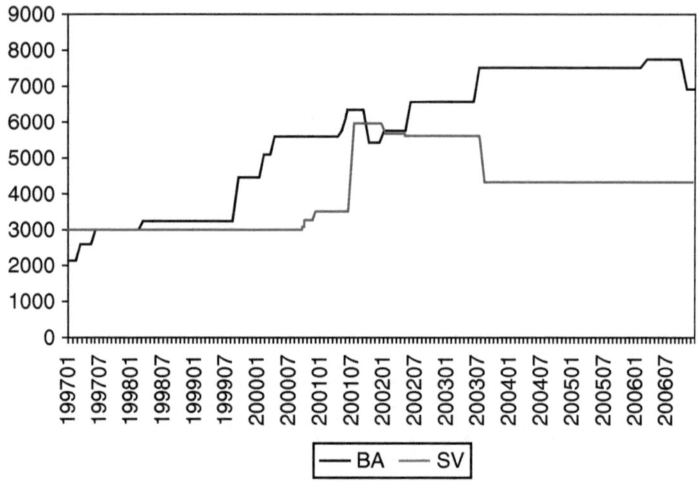

Fig. 9.23 Photo development

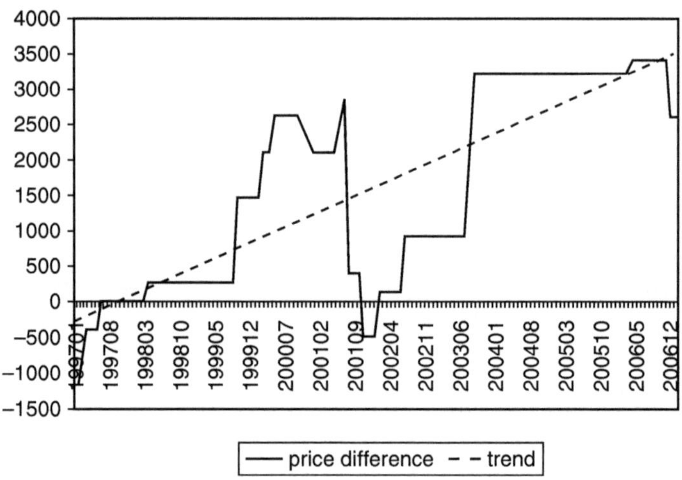

Fig. 9.24 Photo development: price difference between Bratislava and Svidnik

9.3.1 How to Isolate the Border Effect[11]

Define the real exchange rate as

$$Q^i_{j,k,t} = \frac{P^i_{j,t}}{SP^i_{k,t}} \tag{9.4}$$

[11]This exposition follows Engel and Rogers (1996) and Gorodnichenko and Tesar (2005).

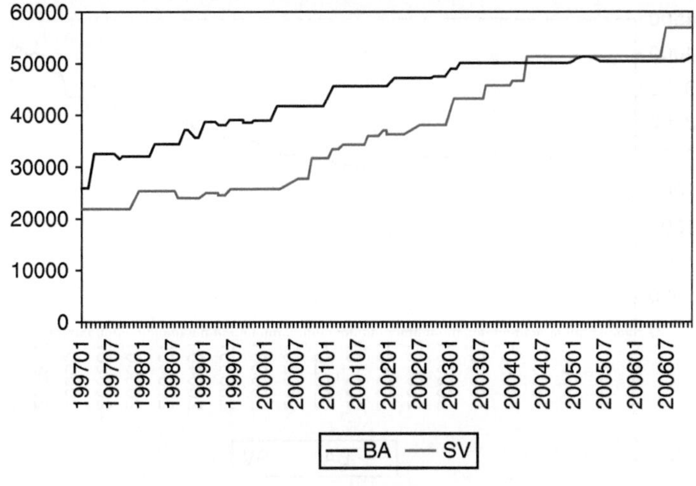

Fig. 9.25 Glass repair work

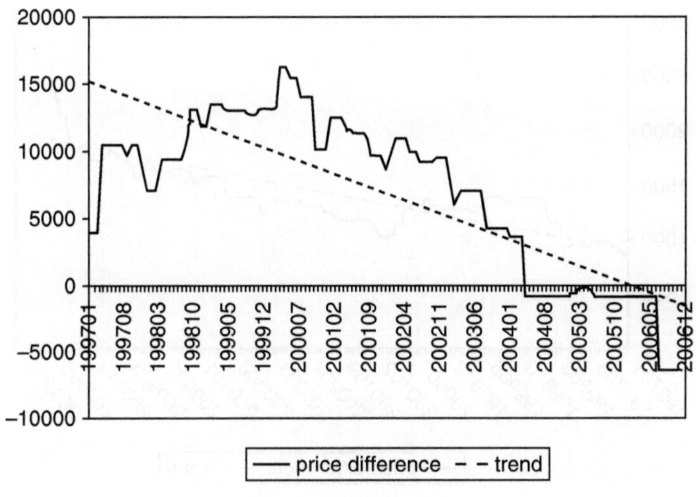

Fig. 9.26 Glass repair work: price difference between Bratislava and Svidnik

where P is the nominal price of good i in location j, or location k, at time t, and S is a nominal exchange rate. Furthermore, define $T^i_{j,k,t}$ as the cost of trade between location j and k, at time t, per unit of good i. Define the law of one price as:

$$\frac{1}{T^i_{j,k,t}} \leq Q^i_{j,k,t} \leq T^i_{j,k,t} \tag{9.5}$$

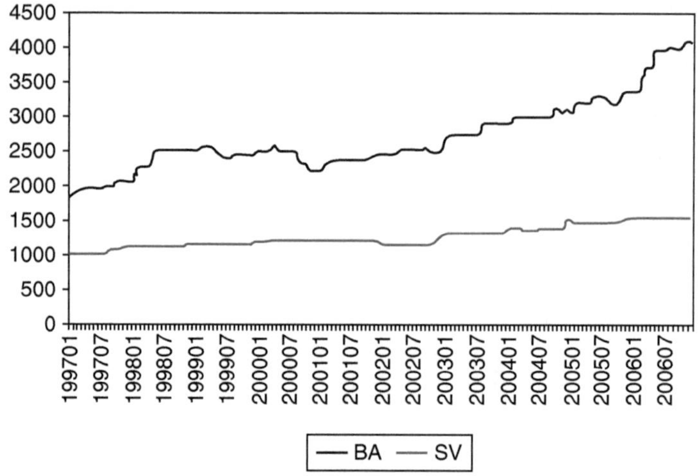

Fig. 9.27 Meat soup

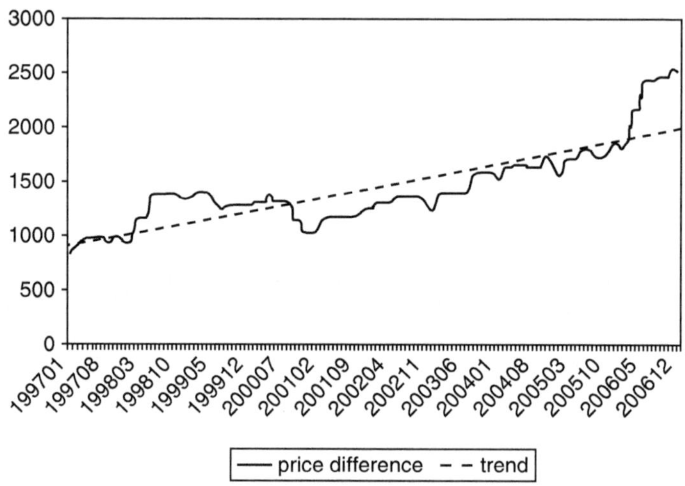

Fig. 9.28 Meat soup: price difference between Bratislava and Svidnik

Transfer (9.5) into logs to obtain:

$$-t^{i}_{j,k} \leq q^{i}_{j,k,t} \leq t^{i}_{j,k} \tag{9.6}$$

i.e., the price differential between two locations adjusted by nominal exchange rate cannot be higher than the cost of trade between these two locations.

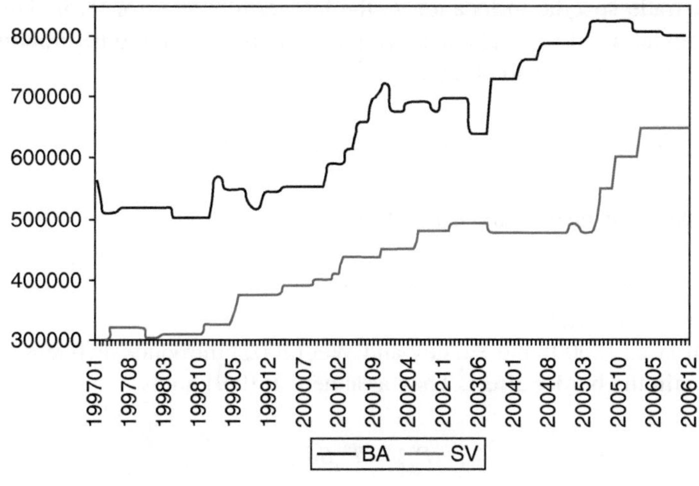

Fig. 9.29 Wedding dress rental

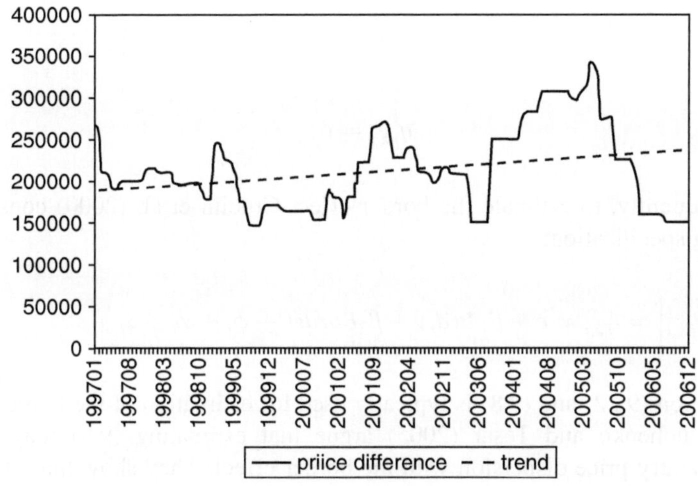

Fig. 9.30 Wedding dress rental: price difference between Bratislava and Svidnik

Assume that the cost of trade has following form:

$$T^i_{j,k} = e^{c+\beta_1 \ln d_{j,k}+\beta_2 \ln Border+\phi_i+\alpha_j+\alpha_k+\varepsilon^i_{j,k}} \tag{9.7}$$

where c is constant; $d_{j,k}$ is the distance between locations j and k; *Border* equals to one if locations are separated by a border, and to zero otherwise. Furthermore, φ_i represents costs of trade specific to good i; α_j costs of trade specific to location j, and

α_k cost of trade specific to location k; the last term is an error term. Time series standard deviation of the real exchange rate, $q^i_{j,k,t}$ is assumed to be proportional to the log of the trade costs to obtain:

$$\sigma(q^i_{j,k,t}) = c + \beta_1 \ln d_{j,k} + \beta_2 \, Border + \phi_i + \alpha_j + \alpha_k + \varepsilon^i_{j,k} \tag{9.8}$$

Panel data are needed for estimation of (9.8), but estimation itself is cross-sectional. The distance equivalent of the border is measured in Engel and Rogers (1996) as $e^{\frac{\beta_2}{\beta_1}}$, and in Parsley and Wei (2001) as $\bar{d}e^{\frac{\beta_2}{\beta_1}-1}$, where $\bar{d}$ is the average distance between cities.

Crucini et al. (2000) and Parsley and Wei (2002) introduce different specification to obtain the border effect. They assume that (9.9) holds,

$$P^i_{j,t} = T^i_{j,t} S_t P^i_{k,t} \tag{9.9}$$

$$Q^i_{j,k,t} = \frac{P^i_{j,t}}{SP_{k,t}} = T^i_{j,k,t} \tag{9.10}$$

in logs

$$q^i_{j,k,t} = t^i_{j,k,t} \tag{9.11}$$

Consequently, to estimate the border effect Crucini et al. (2000) consider the following specification:

$$\left| q^i_{j,k,t} \right| = t^i_{j,k,t} = c + \beta_1 \ln d_{j,k} + \beta_2 Border + \phi_i + \alpha_k + \alpha_j + \varepsilon^k_{k.j} \tag{9.12}$$

Specification (9.12) and (9.8) is typically used for estimation of the border effect.

Gorodnichenko and Tesar (2005) argue that estimating (9.8) may confuse within-country price dispersion with the border effect. They show that the border dummy in (9.8) measures the inter-country volatility as compared to the average intra-country volatility, which under some conditions might lead to bias.

Yin-Wong and Lai (2006) show that if foreign and domestic prices have similar volatility, then the inter-country versus intra-country analysis would yield unbiased border effect estimates. However, such cross-country homogeneity is typically violated in actual data. In a case with heterogeneity in foreign and domestic price volatility, Yin-Wong and Lai (2006) show that a symmetric sampling strategy, under which the same number of cities is sampled from each country, can be used to secure the unbiased border effect estimates. Yin-Wong and Lai (2006) devise a method which enables the quantification of the exact contribution of exchange rate fluctuations on the border effect.

9.3.2 *Empirical Evidence*

Engel and Rogers (1996) use consumer price index data disaggregated into 14 categories of goods for 9 Canadian and 14 U.S. cities for the period from June 1978 to December 1994. They isolate the border effect using the procedure described in the previous section, measuring prices as 2-month differences and measuring volatility as the standard deviation of the relative price series. The authors find substantial differences between the intra-national price volatilities, i.e. the price volatility among U.S. cities was considerable larger than the price volatility among Canadian cities. However, the price volatility was highest among American–Canadian city pairs.[12] Moreover, they find strong evidence that distance explains a large portion of price dispersion across cities for most goods. Most importantly, the coefficients on the dummy variable for the border are of the hypothesized sign and highly significant for all goods.[13]

The border effect might be significant, because it picks up the effect of nominal exchange rate volatility. To tackle the problem, Engel and Rogers (1996) construct real prices by dividing the nominal price ratios by the aggregate city price indexes; with this, the border effect significance remains. They also consider calculating the individual goods prices in each city relative to the national-level producer price index. Again, the results remain qualitatively similar to previous regressions. These results for the U.S. and Canada are puzzling, since free trade prevails between them and in addition, they share a common language as well as similar cultural and political traditions, but still the border effect remains significant.

Beck and Weber (2001) test the importance of borders in European markets. Their data contain monthly price indexes for 86 locations in seven European countries.[14] The sample period for aggregated data is from January 1991 to December 2002, and for the disaggregated data January 1995 to December 2002. They measure real price volatility as the 2-month change in log of relative prices. In their results, price volatility is lower for intra-county city pairs than for inter-country city pairs.[15] Beck and Weber (2001) estimate (9.8) and find that border

[12]For the pooled sample of goods crossing the border adds to the average standard deviation of prices between pairs of cities; in order to generate that much volatility by distance, the cities would have to be 75,000 miles apart; Engle and Rogers (1996).

[13]To check robustness of their results Engle and Rogers (1996) also consider a filtered measure of the real exchange rate when regressing the log of the relative price on seasonal monthly dummies and 6 monthly lags; then they take the 2-month-ahead in-sample forecast error from this regression as the measure of the real exchange rate. They also report results when the distance function is quadratic, again with robust results confirming the existence of a border effect. They also assess the importance of the free trade agreement between the two countries on the border effect but the size of the border coefficient has not diminished.

[14]These countries are Germany (West and East), Austria, Finland, Italy, Spain, Portugal and Switzerland.

[15]One interesting result of Beck and Weber (2001) is that relative price volatility between Germany and Austria is lower than the within-country price volatility in Portugal.

dummy is positive and significant for aggregated as well as disaggregated price data. They interpret these results as evidence in favor of European-market segmentation. In a second step, they estimate (9.8) including the exchange rate variables. While the effect of the border dummy weakens, it still remains significant. After including dummies for all country pairs, Beck and Weber (2001) find that the smallest border effect is at the German–Austrian border and the biggest at the Italian–Swiss border. Beck and Weber (2001) are also interested in determining whether the border effect weakens after the introduction of euro. Their findings support weakening of the border effect after the common currency is introduced, however the border dummy still remains significant even if smaller in size.[16] "The EMU is found to have greatly reduced but not completely eliminated the importance of intra-EMU borders."[17]

Engel et al. (2005) re-examine the border effect using actual data for different U.S. and Canadian cities instead of price index data as in Engel and Rogers (1996). Their dataset contains annual prices of 100 narrowly defined consumer goods (with almost half representing food products, and the remaining being clothing items, durables, non-tradable services and miscellaneous products) in 13 U.S. and 4 Canadian cities from 1990 to 2002. Engel et al. (2005) estimate specification (9.12). Accordingly, distance is no longer significant, which is in contrast to the findings of Engel and Rogers (1996), which demonstrated that distance remained significant across different specifications. Engel et al. (2005) estimate the same specifications for different sub-periods and for different groups of goods. The border dummy is significant and has the correct sign, but it nevertheless varies in magnitude.

Rogers and Smith (2001) compare the border effect between the United States, Mexico, and Canada. They use monthly and semi-monthly price data for the period from January 1980 to December 1997 for 14 U.S. cities, 10 Canadian cities, and 14 Mexican cities. They divide the total sample period into two sub-periods to differentiate between the stable and volatile periods of the peso-dollar exchange rates. In the full sample the border dummy is highly significant, yet when the volatility of the exchange rate is included, the border dummies somewhat lose their explanatory power. In sub-sample results – which differentiate between the stable and unstable peso periods – the coefficients of the border dummy are notably smaller. Rogers and Smith (2001) also compare border effects before and after the NAFTA agreement. The US–Mexico border dummy for the full period is larger than for the post NAFTA period, indicating that the removal of explicit trade barriers helped decrease the border effect.

Furthermore, Ceglowski (2003) finds that Canadian provincial borders account for a significant fraction of the discrepancy in prices across provinces. Shiue (2005) uses grain prices in France, Switzerland, the Habsburg Empire of Austria, and 15 Bavarian cities for the years 1815–1855 to assess the size of border effect in the

---

[16]Beck and Weber (2001) also estimate the importance of the border effect between East and West Germany. They find that after the German unification the border effect has principally disappeared.

[17]Beck and Weber (2001), p. 21.

context of the German Zollverein. Their main conclusion is that the estimated border effect for Europe in the mid-nineteenth century is small when compared to estimates using contemporary data.

Horvath et al. (2008) evaluate the importance of national borders in price setting in Hungary and Slovakia. Their sample draws on data of monthly prices of 20 homogenous goods and services observed in a total of 56 regional locations over a period of 56 months. The data set contains prices of four categories of consumer-products: durable goods, meat products, other food products, and services. For each product, they examine relative price volatility measured within and across countries. The volatility of prices is quite similar at district pairs in Hungary and in Slovakia, yet cross-border district pairs show much higher volatility. [18] This pattern appears most pronounced in the pooled data; high volatility in cross-border city pairs holds for most individual products as well.

Horvath et al. (2008) estimate (9.8) separately for each product. While the results for distance are less pronounced, the estimated parameters show strong evidence for the border effect, i.e. after controlling for distance and district-specific fixed effects, coefficients on the border dummy are significantly positive in all individual cases. Furthermore, they investigate factors which might explain the border effect. Formal trade barriers between Hungary and Slovakia appear to be low and declining over time. They explore three alternative approaches to account for the border effect: language, nominal exchange rates and cross-country heterogeneity.

Their results show that differences in the language spoken are not responsible for international price differentials between districts located in different countries. In order to assess the importance of the nominal exchange rate, they ask whether the border remains important when the real exchange rate is proxied by the relative real price, a variable free of fluctuations in nominal exchange rates. They obtain such relative real prices and re-estimate the system obtaining results similar to the ones obtained in the baseline specification. The border coefficient remains significant in all individual and pooled cases; that is, nominal exchange rates do not appear to be responsible for generating border effects.

In summary, Horvath et al. (2008) show that national borders have an independent, sizeable, and statistically significant impact on relative price variability. At the same time, the impact of transportation costs is much less pronounced. These results are robust in accounting for nominal exchange rate variability, differences in local culture as represented by language spoken and cross-country heterogeneity in relative price variability. In other words, the impact of borders seems substantial. After controlling for distance, language, city and goods specific effects, locations

[18] Gorodnichenko and Tesar (2006) demonstrate that the border effect estimates in some studies confounds the impact of the true border and the extent of cross-country heterogeneity in relative price variability. Since in the Slovak and Hungarian data set the authors observe similar time-series variability in relative prices, this analysis is able to get around the country heterogeneity problem in a natural way.

on opposite sides of the border feature substantially higher price differences than do locations on either side of the border.

9.4 Conclusion

This paper deals with problems of market integration. We present illustrative evidence about the extent of market integration within Slovakia. It seems that goods specifics are important with integration stronger for homogenous tradable products than for services and heterogeneous products. We also find evidence for convergence to the law of one price, with speed of convergence relatively low. Furthermore, evidence about market integration across borders is reviewed and discussed in the context of the importance of the border effect between Slovakia and Hungary.

References

Barrett B.C., (2005), "Spatial Market Integration," entry. In L.E. Blume and S.N. Durlauf (Ed.), *The New Palgrave Dictionary of Economics 2nd edition*, London: Palgrave Macmillan, forthcoming.

Beck, G., & Weber, A. (2001). How Wide Are European Borders, Center for Financial Studies, Frankfurt, Working Paper Series 2001/07.

Berkowitz, D. & Dejong, D. N. (1998), "Russia's Internal Border," The William Davidson Institute, Working Paper No. 189.

Ceglowski, J. (2003). The law of one price: intranational evidence for Canada. *Canadian Journal of Economics, 36*(2), 373–400.

Coricelli, F. and Horvath R. (2006). "Price setting behavior: micro evidence on Slovakia," CEPR DP 5445, January.

Crucini, M.J., Telmer C.I. & Zachariadis, M. (2000), "Dispersion in Real Exchange Rates," Department of Economics, Vanderbilt University, Working Paper 00-W13.

Engel, C. & Rogers, J.H. (1995), "Regional patterns in the law of one price: the roles of geography vs. currencies," NBER WP 5395, December.

Engel, C., & Rogers, J. H. (1996). How wide is the border? *The American Economic Review, 86* (5), 1112–1125.

Engel, C., Rogers, J. H., & Wang, S.-Y. I. (2005). Revisiting the border: an assessment of the law of one price using very disaggregated consumer price data. In R. Driver, P. Sinclair, & C. Thoenissen (Eds.), *Exchange rates, capital flows and policy* (pp. 187–203). London: Routledge.

Gorodnichenko, Y. & Tesar, L. (2005). A Re-Examination of the Border Effect, NBER Working Paper Series, Working Paper 11706, http://www.nber.org/papers/w11706.

Horvath, J., Ratfai, A., & Dome, B. (2008), "Border effects in small transition economies". *Economics Systems*, forthcoming.

Horvath, J., & Vidovic, S. (2005). The law of one price: evidence from a small transition economy. *Jahrbuch für Wirtschaftswissenschaften, (Review of Economics), 56*(3), 257–284.

Knetter, M.N. (1994), "Why are retail prices in Japan so high? Evidence from German export prices," NBER WP 4894.

Levin, A., Lin, C.-F., & Chu, C. (2002). Unit root in panel data: asymptotic and finite-sample properties. *Journal of Econometrics, 108*, 1–24.

Parsley, D. C., & Wei, S.-J. (1996). Convergence to the law of one price without trade barriers or currency fluctuations. *The Quarterly Journal of Economics, 111*, 1211–1236.

Parsley, D. C., & Wei, S.-J. (2001). Explaining the border effect: the role of exchange rate variability, shipping costs, and geography. *Journal of International Economics, 55*, 87–105.

Parsley, D.C., and Wei, S.-J. (2002), "Currency arrangements and goods market integration: a price based approach," mimeo, http://129.3.20.41/eps/if/papers/0211/0211004.pdf.

Ratfai, A. (2006). How fast is convergence to the law of one price? Very. *Economics Bulletin, 6* (10), 1–12.

Rogers, J.H. & Smith H.P. (2001), "Border Effects within the NAFTA Countries," Board of Governors of the Federal Reserve System, International Finance Discussion Papers No. 698, March.

Salop, S., & Stiglitz, J. (1977). Bargains and ripoffs: a model of monopolistically competitive price dispersion. *Review of Economic Studies, 44*, 493–510.

Shiue, C. H. (2005). *From political fragmentation towards a customs union: border effects of the German Zollverein, 1815 to 1855*. TX, USA: University of Texas.

Stigler, G., & Sherwin, R. (1985). The extent of the market. *Journal of Law and Economics, 28*, 555–585.

Wolf, H. C. (2000). Intranational home bias in trade. *Review of Economics and Statistics, 82*(4), 555–563.

Wolf, H. (2003) "International relative prices: facts and interpretation," in HM treasury, prices and EMU 2003, Appendix D: mimeo, pp. 53–73.

World Bank (2002), Slovak Republic Development Policy Review, November, Main Report, Poverty Reduction and Economic Management Unit, Europe and Central Asia Region.

Yin-Wong C. & Lai K.S. (2006) "A reappraisal of the border effect on relative price volatility," CEEifo Working Paper No. 1640, January.

[illegible]

Chapter 10
Trade and FDI Related Effects of the Monetary Union and Structural Adjustment in the Central European New Member States of the EU[1]

Kalman Dezseri

10.1 Introduction

10.1.1 Emerging Trade and FDI Related Effects in the Process of Integration

The EU is the world's largest market, with vast natural, technological and human resources. It encompasses 27 countries and about 500 million people with different needs to be satisfied and resources to offer. The EU is the largest trading bloc of countries of the world. The total trade turnover with other countries of the world and the intra-trade among the EU member states makes up about 40% of global trade. The flows of foreign direct investments are closely connected to the trade patterns. The EU member states also compete strongly to attract investment that can yield benefit from the potential of these resources.

The structures of trade turnover and their changes in time are fundamentally determined by factor endowments. One of the fundamental elements of international trade theories, the Heckscher–Ohlin theorem gives explanation how the differences in relative factor endowments determine the comparative advantage and international trade specialisation of economies. According to this theorem, a country will export goods whose production requires the intensive use of that country's relatively abundant and cheap factor(s), and it will import goods whose production requires the intensive use of its relatively scarce and expensive factor(s). The development of production capacities are financed from domestic and foreign savings. Foreign capital has roles of increasing importance in every economy. Attracting foreign capital to finance investments is vital for development and economic growth of countries.

[1]The paper was finalized in 2008.

K. Dezseri
Department of European Integration, Institute for World Economics of the Hungarian Academy of Sciences, Budapest, Hungary

P.J.J. Welfens and C. Ryan (eds.), *Financial Market Integration and Growth*,
DOI 10.1007/978-3-642-16274-9_10, © Springer-Verlag Berlin Heidelberg 2011

The competition among countries for FDI is of course largely individual, but there can be common regional interests and patterns. In spite of the fact that the EU member states together are becoming a single market offering a wide range of opportunities located in a safe, stable, modern economy, there are investments that may not be ideally suited for one of the member states but may find a proper place in another. The central European new member states provide new investment opportunities with partly or significantly different conditions. There is a changing pattern of relocation of FDI flows coming into the EU-27 from the rest of the world, and there is another changing pattern of relocation of FDI within the EU-27, that is, between the old and new member states.

From the point of view of new member states (EU-10), in the process of joining the EMU three phases can be distinguished regarding types and intensity of the trade and FDI related effects. These three phases are the following; phase A: pre-accession period, phase B: being member of the EU but not of the EMU (third stage), and phase C: from introducing the Euro onwards.

Phase A: One of the fundamental principles of the EU is the free movement of goods. As foreign trade rules and the functioning of economies of the ten Central European countries were liberalised to a very large extent during the period of transition to market economy, even prior to the EU accession, trade turnover increased substantially and growing values of foreign direct investment flowed into these countries. The trade between the EU-15 and EU-10 was not fully liberalised as exports in food and agricultural products from the Central European countries into the EU-15 were largely restricted. In spite of this restriction, the comparative advantage in 2003 already reflected free trade to a large extent.

Phase B: Actual EU membership brought some new aspects following 2004 and 2007 in the case of the eight Central European countries and Bulgaria and Romania, respectively. Due to the accession the still existing trade barriers were further decreased or were fully eliminated between member states, and especially between the new ones. Consequently, it further enhanced trade relations in Europe. As the EU-15 is much more important for the EU-10 as an export market than vice versa, the new member states could gain more from the lower trade barriers than the EU-15 did.

As EU members, the Central European countries are already eligible for funding from EU structural and cohesion funds. These funds can be used to improve infrastructure and enhance competitiveness. The new member states will gain from an improvement in their infrastructure and transport connections with their major export markets within the EU. The free movement of labour with the incumbent EU countries will also be fully liberalised.

EU membership, on the one hand, increases the competition faced by the new member states' manufacturing industries and strengthens the competitiveness of these countries on the other. They certainly can boost the economic growth of these countries. FDI also can play an important role in this process. The clustering of certain types of know-how in a particular region can have the effect of attracting further investments into sectors that use similar know-how. Declining transport costs are also likely to enhance the comparative advantage of the new member states.

Phase C: The final phase is the participation of the EU-10 in monetary integration. There are already 15 EU member states which use the same currency and by implication strive to develop and follow monetary and fiscal policies designed to ensure the safety and predictability of their money. Even the non-Eurozone EU member states co-operate in other ways to enhance the common business environment. Laws, regulations, tax policies and infrastructure projects aim at modernising the whole European marketplace. A few years on, we may expect some of the new member states to join the EMU, which will further lower financial barriers to trade and capital flow (e.g. exchange rate risk, etc.). In the course of the next decade, all EU-10 member states will gradually join the Eurozone, and this fact will certainly further reinforce the trade and FDI related effects.

10.2 Foreign Direct Investment Outflow and Inflow of the EU-25

International FDI flows are usually influenced or directed and oriented by various economic, political and social factors. The more decisive ones can be grouped into eight main categories: market and business vitality, human resources, research and innovation, infrastructure, administrative environment, costs and taxation, energy and sustainable development, internet and information communication technology readiness.[2] On the basis of these factors, the relative position of Europe vis-à-vis the other leading economies as well as its main competitors in the global economy can be evaluated. The main trends of FDI outflow and inflow show that the EU is an important investor in the other countries of the world, but at the same time it can attract significant amounts of foreign investments.

FDI outflow from the EU-25 grew from EUR 142.2 billion in 2004 to EUR 171.8 billion in 2005 and from EU-27 to 260.2 billion in 2006. This change in value meant about a 26% increase between 2001 and 2005, and the total amount of FDI outflows represented approximately 1.6% of the total GDP of the EU-25. This upturn came after a substantial decrease between 2001 and 2002 when the value of FDI outflow dropped by 56% from EUR 306.1 billion to 133.9 billion. The value of FDI outflow was rather stable in the course of 2003 and 2004.

FDI inflow into the EU from the rest of the world continuously declined between 2001 and 2004. Then, the trend changed, and there has been an upturn since 2005. The increase represented 77% of the value of the preceding year. Regarding the EU-27, the amount of FDI inflow reached EUR 127.0 billion, which made up about 0.9% of the total GDP in 2005 and EUR 157.1 billion in 2006. The EU has been a net investor in the global economy, as FDI outflow exceeded inflow by about EUR 100 billion since 2005 (Table 10.1).

[2]IFA and IG (2007).

Table 10.1 Extra EU-25 FDI flows between 2001 and 2005 and EU-27 FDI flows between 2004 and 2006 (in billion EUR)

	2001	2002	2003	2004	2005	2006
Outflows from EU-25	306.1	133.9	135.9	145.9	240.1	268.9
(−) EU-27				142.2	234.5	260.2
Inflows into EU-25	145.9	126.6	125.3	56.7	126.7	156.1
(+) EU-27				58.3	127.0	157.1
Balance	−160.2	−7.3	−10.6	−89.2	−113.4	−112.8
				−83.9	−107.5	−103.1

Source: Eurostat and Eurostat Statistics in Focus 41/2008

The FDI outflow from the EU-25 was mainly oriented towards the USA and Switzerland. In the case of the USA, the outflow increased from EUR 15.5 billion in 2004 to 72 billion in 2006 representing 10.9 and 27.7%, respectively, of the total FDI amount. The value of outflow into the other parts of the world also increased but to a lesser extent. The outflow into EU's candidate countries (Bulgaria, Croatia, Romania, and Turkey) more than doubled, from EUR 4.3 billion in 2003 to EUR 10.3 billion in 2005. The share of these countries in the total EU-25 FDI outflows increased from 3.2 to 6%, respectively. Substantial increases in FDI outflow could be recorded towards Japan until 2005 amounting EUR 11.9 billion and representing 5.1%, which was followed by a substantial fall to EUR 0.5 billion in 2006. The FDI outflows towards China reached its peak in 2004 when it amounted EUR 15.2 billion, representing 10.7% of the total FDI outflow, and it declined during the following 2 years to EUR 8.9 billion, representing 3.4% only. The FDI outflow increased towards the eastern neighbours of the EU (particularly to the Ukraine and Russia). The FDI flow towards Russia increased from EUR 6 billion to 10.4 billion between 2004 and 2006, but its share has remained around 4%. Meanwhile, the value of FDI flow from the EU-25 into Latin-America decreased to a significant extent.

The FDI inflow into the EU-25 came mainly from the USA (around 19.8% in 2005 and 48.1% in 2006) and from Switzerland (around 28.5% in 2004 and 10.6% in 2006), followed by Japan (8.7%) and Canada (4.5%). Russia's share increased very rapidly. The larger part of these amounts was invested in EU-15 and a smaller part only in the central European new member states.

In the same years, the distribution of the EU FDI stocks among the main economic activities remained almost unchanged and quite similar for both outward and inward FDI stocks. The largest share is investment in services (outward 69%, inward 76%), followed by manufacturing (both outward and inward 19%) and other activities (12 and 6%, respectively). Within the service sector financial intermediation remained the predominant activity (outward 64%, inward 46%), followed by business services (outward 17%, inward 19.6%) and telecommunication (outward 6%, inward 9.8%).

Contrary to perceptions, which prevailed prior to the accession of the ten countries in May 2004, there has not been a diversion of massive FDI flows away from the EU-15 old member states. During the late 1990s and early 2000s, the

Table 10.2 EU-25 FDI flows (in EUR billion)

	2001	2002	2003	2004	2005	2006
Outwards flows to extra-EU-25	306.1	133.9	135.9	145.9	240.1	268.9
From EU-15	305.3 (99.7%)	133.7 (99.9%)	134.1 (99.0%)	144.2 (98.8%)	235.8 (98.2%)	256.7 (95.5%)
From new member states	0.9 (0.3%)	0.2 (0.1%)	1.8 (1.0%)	1.7 (1.2%)	4.3 (1.8%)	12.2 (4.5%)
Inward flows from extra-EU-25	145.9	126.6	125.3	56.7	126.7	156.1
To EU-15	142.1 (97.4%)	123.4 (97.5%)	122.3 (97.6%)	52.9 (93.3%)	122.6 (96.8%)	143.6 (92.0%)
To new member states	3.8 (2.6%)	3.2 (2.5%)	3.0 (2.4%)	3.8 (6.7%)	4.1 (4.2%)	12.5 (8.0%)
Net outward flows	160.2	7.3	10.6	89.2	113.4	112.8
From EU-15	163.2	10.3	11.8	91.3	113.2	113.1
From new member states	−2.9	−3.0	−1.2	−2.1	0.2	−0.3
Intra-EU-25 flows	365.5	361.1	251.5	201.4	434.3	429.1
From EU-15 to new member States	17.2 (4.7%)	13 (3.6%)	7.9 (6.8%)	18 (8.9%)	26.2 (6.0%)	28 (6.5%)
From new member states to EU-15	0.1 (0.0%)	0.6 (0.2%)	1 (0.4%)	0.6 (0.3%)	1.2 (0.3%)	8.3 (1.9%)
Between EU-15 member States	346.2 (94.7%)	345.8 (95.8%)	242.3 (96.3%)	178.3 (88.5%)	397.1 (91.4%)	387.4 (90.3%)
Between EU-10 new member States	2 (0.5%)	1.7 (0.5%)	0.3 (0.1%)	4.5 (2.2%)	9.8 (2.3%)	5.4 (1.3%)

Source: Eurostat database

combined inflow into the ten new members remained considerably lower than those into such old EU member states as France and Germany and, more recently, Ireland and Spain (see Table 10.2). The EU-15 accounted for 93–97.5% of the inward flow from the world into the EU-25, and their total share in the combined outflow of the EU-25 was about 98–99.9%.

10.3 FDI Inflow into the New Member States

Since the mid-1990s, the FDI inflow into the ten then accession countries has come to account for a fraction of those flowing into the EU-15. It was a mere 2.4% only in 2003, down from a high of 10.6% in 1995. While a part of the low inflow during the early 2000s can be explained by such short-term factors as the end of the series of large privatisation deals. There were waves of privatisation – first in Hungary, then in Poland and, last in the Czech Republic and Slovakia. The gap between the actual and potential FDI flow is, however, too large to be explained by this factor alone. The low figures of inflow into the EU-10 suggest basically two things. First, a large untapped FDI potential still exists in the new member states. Second, concerted policy efforts are needed between the origin and destination countries of capital flow to speed up both the integration of the economies of the new member states into the enlarged EU and the process of economic catching-up of them with the development level of the 15 older member states.

It is worth mentioning that nominal values of the FDI flow from the EU-15 to the new member states and their shares within the total FDI flow within the EU-25 have been fluctuating since 2000 but accounted about EUR 28 billion in 2006. This amount represented about 6.5% of the total FDI flow of the EU-25. The share of the FDI flow from the new member states to the EU-15, however, grew rapidly to 1.9% between 2001 and 2006. The FDI flow of EU-25 has been dominated by intra EU-15 flows as the EU-15 accounted for about 90–96% of it. A relatively new phenomenon is the FDI flow among the new member states. During the period between 2001 and 2006 its value more than tripled; however, its share is still very insignificant (the largest share was 2.3% of the total FDI flow of the EU-25 in 2004).

Forecasts suggested that the value of FDI inflows to the EU-10 would grow after the EU accession of these countries. Based on more recent data, it is quite certain now that the FDI inflow to the eight new EU member states (NMS-8) declined slightly. In 2006, the whole Central and East European region[3] received 33% more FDI than in 2005 (in current euro terms, Table 10.3), but the FDI inflow into EU-10 increased by only 11%. This resulted in a decline in the share of the new EU

Table 10.3 Overview of FDI in Central European new EU member states (EU-10)

	FDI inflows (EUR million)								Per capita	
	2000	2001	2002	2003	2004	2005	2006	Forecast 2007	Inflow 2006	Stock 2006
Czech Rep.	5,404	6,296	9,012	1,863	4,007	9,374	4,752	5,000	463	5,719
Hungary	2,998	4,391	3,185	1,888	3,633	6,099	4,874	4,000	484	6,170
Poland	10,334	6,372	4,371	4,067	10,292	7,703	11,093	12,000	291	2,361
Slovakia	2,089	1,768	4,397	1,914	2,441	1,694	3,324	3,000	617	3,338
Slovenia	149	412	1,722	271	665	445	303	400	151	3,133
NMS-5	20,974	19,240	22,687	10,002	21,039	25,315	24,346	24,400	370	3,571
Estonia	425	603	307	822	776	2,349	1,282	1,300	954	9,232
Latvia	447	147	269	270	513	582	1,303	1,300	569	2,515
Lithuania	412	499	772	160	623	826	1,426	1,300	420	2,462
NMS-8	22,258	20,489	24,035	13,799	22,950	29,072	28,357	28,300	389	3,590
Bulgaria	1,103	903	980	1,851	2,736	3,103	4,104	4,000	533	2,047
Romania	1,147	1,294	1,212	1,946	5,183	5,213	9,082	7,000	421	1,432
NMS-10	24,508	22,685	26,226	15,051	30,869	37,387	41,544	39,300	407	3,019
CEE total	30,048	29,409	33,255	27,180	47,682	58,121	77,060	77,300	236	1,625

Source: WIIW

[3]The whole Central and Eastern European region includes the EU-10 + 2, the six Western Balkans countries (Albania, Bosnia and Herzegovina, Croatia, Macedonia, Montenegro, Serbia) and four eastern neighbouring countries (Belarus, Moldova, Russia, Ukraine).

member states in the total amount of FDI which flew into Central and Eastern Europe. It meant that the sub-regional distribution of inflows changed quite significantly. Specifically, only 36% was invested in the NMS-8 in 2006, which had joined the EU in 2004, compared to 50% in the previous year. The shift of new FDI to the Eastern and to the Southern parts of Europe reflected the emergence of new investment opportunities. It did not imply declining interests in the NMS-8, despite the fact that the FDI inflow into the NMS-8 was marginally lower in 2006 than in the preceding years.

Looking at the figures of the NMS-8 only, we can see that the declines in FDI flow into some of them were compensated by increases in other countries of the group. In the case of the Czech Republic, Hungary and Estonia, the decline of FDI inflow could be anticipated, because record values in 2005 were to a large extent driven by non-recurrent or unique privatization deals of large amounts. In the absence of privatisation of similar size, FDI inflows returned to about the previous levels or trends that are still higher than they were in 2004. There is no ground to argue that these countries lost their attractiveness.

In the case of Poland, Latvia and Lithuania, FDI inflows reached their all-time highest levels. Slovakia also recorded substantial increases. These countries have been lagging behind the others in terms of FDI per capita, so their catching-up could be expected. In fact, Poland, which was the largest FDI recipient in 2006 and has the largest population among the EU-10, accumulating however approximately 40% less FDI stock per capita than the forerunners (the Czech Republic or Hungary). Slovenia has continued to be the least frequented location for FDI among the EU-10. Privatisation by foreigners was modest, and the Slovenian economy is mainly dominated by domestic capital.

In Bulgaria and Romania, FDI is booming. Prior to their accession to the EU in 2007, the FDI inflows reached peaks in 2006. These records are partially due to the on-going privatization, and also to new investments in trade, real estate and other services. The EU membership turned out to be a stability anchor for foreign investors attracted by improving business conditions. The FDI surge is also related to the high economic growth rates of these two countries.

The global trend of FDI flows in 2007 was characterised by further expansion. Optimism can be justified as far as the EU-10 countries are concerned (Table 10.3). Nevertheless, ups and downs in privatisation-related FDI may cause fluctuations in the total inflow into the Central European region. Almost certainly, Bulgaria and Romania are not going to reach the previous year's levels, while Poland may strengthen its position. Even if a conservative forecast does not indicate increasing overall inflows, this should not be interpreted as stagnation, because there are several privatisation contracts under final negotiation. These deals will certainly modify the forecasted figures upwards. No significant change can be expected for the development of relocations. The four more developed new EU member states – the Czech Republic, Hungary, Poland and Slovakia – will continue to receive the bulk of the efficiency-seeking FDI, and Romania will be increasingly more often the destination of such investments. The other countries will not likely become major targets of efficiency-seeking FDI.

10.4 Some Important Features of FDI Flow into the New Member States

FDI flows are driven basically by two motives. Relocation seeks either the potential of local markets or utilising the efficiency. They are the local market-seeking (horizontal)[4] and the efficiency-seeking (vertical)[5] FDI flows. Contrary to the previous two types of foreign investments, the FDI flow into the service sector focuses on the demand of the local market of the host country. In most cases supplying any services requires the presence of the specific company in the targeted market.

FDI flow into larger host countries and in the service sector is in general driven by market-seeking motives. In the case of medium size countries and especially in small countries, FDI flow is characterised by efficiency-seeking investments. The size and frequency of such investments have increased and have concentrated on the manufacturing industry.

It is obvious that investors do not follow a single motive, but rather a multiple set of market, efficiency and strategic motives. One of the most important factors is the difference between labour costs. There are investments which are driven by the differences between unskilled labour costs and there are investments, which aim at benefiting from differences of skilled labour costs prevailing in various countries. There are, of course, other factors (successful previous co-operation, good opportunity) which can and may likewise determine and influence investment decisions of foreign companies.

Three categories can be identified when classifying the efficiency-seeking FDI inflows into the new member states:

(a) A relocation of existing facilities in the EU-15 member states into the new member states or consolidation of existing unprofitable sites
(b) Investment as an alternative option of domestic investment
(c) A combination of market-seeking, efficiency-seeking and strategic considerations
(d) FDI has generally several features which have favourable and adverse impacts on an economy. Among the favourable impacts, the most important ones are that FDI adds to productive capacities, improves efficiency and is also attracted by soaring consumption. The adverse impacts can be both macroeconomic (e.g. imbalances of the main balances, etc.) or microeconomic (e.g. adverse impact of stronger competition on domestic industry, etc.) (Table 10.4).

---

[4]The local market-seeking FDI flows are usually directed into the manufacturing industries. They look for potential effects on relocation via substituting exports by local productions. The liberalisation process in the new member states during the last 15 years opened new market opportunities for foreign investors, which boosted the market-seeking FDI flow into these economies.

[5]The efficiency-seeking FDI flows are also directed into the manufacturing industries but these investments aim at utilising the factor costs differences. On the basis of this advantage a strong export orientation can be built up. The efficiency-seeking FDI flow represents the main potential for relocation.

Table 10.4 Changes in attractiveness of manufacturing sectors of new member states for FDI between since 1993

Industry categories	Structural shares		Export propensity	Foreign penetration	Attractiveness for FDI
	Value added	Employment			
High technology	Medium Increasing fast	Low Increasing slow	Very high Increasing fast	Very high Increasing fast	Increasing Fast
Medium high technology	High Increasing	High Increasing slow	Very high Increasing fast	Very high Increasing fast	Increasing
Medium low technology	Medium Decreasing	Medium Stagnating	Low-medium Increasing slow	Very high Increasing fast	Stagnating
Low technology	Medium Decreasing fast	High Decreasing fast	Low-medium Increasing slow	High Increasing fast	Decreasing

Source: Hunya (2005)

Regarding the EU-10 countries some important features could be observed. In the cases of some EU-10 countries, the expanding foreign trade deficits with the other EU member states point out that FDI still generates more imports than exports. This happened in Bulgaria and Romania. The Baltic States and Slovenia similarly maintain high and growing trade deficits with the other EU member states, which indicates that they are attracting less FDI of the efficiency-seeking type and are hardly benefiting from production re-location.

Ten years ago market-seeking FDI dominated the capital inflow into the Central European countries. The situation has since changed. Since 2000 more or less, the trade balances of the Czech Republic, Hungary, Slovakia, and more recently also that of Poland with the EU-15, have turned positive. Knowing that most of the exports of these countries is generated by affiliates of the foreign companies located in the EU-10 countries, the export success may be regarded as a result of FDI. In addition to the local-market-oriented activities such as telecom, construction and financial intermediation, manufacturing and a part of services are of the efficiency-seeking, export-oriented type investments.

Foreign trade-surplus-generating FDI may be interpreted as production relocation in the broad sense. There are only a few examples of production relocation in the narrow sense. Companies rarely close a production site in a country and transfer productive asset to another country where operation costs are lower. However as for production enlargement, the location search is open to low-cost new member states. For instance, new automobile manufacturing facilities in Europe were mainly built in some of the new member states over the last 5 years. European companies utilise the advantage of internationalisation and benefit thereby from production in different locations. Companies of non-EU countries, when they relocate their production into the EU, often choose a location in a new member state (e.g., the surge of Japanese electronics investments in Poland and other countries). (See the country tables in Appendix.)

Regarding the sectoral distribution of the FDI in the EU-10, different trends could be observed. In the FDI stock of Hungary, Slovakia, Slovenia and Lithuania, manufacturing represented about 40% at the end of 2005. The share of this sector was of somewhat lower but still of high significance (36–38%) in the case of the Czech Republic, Poland and Romania. As for the rest of the EU-10, Bulgaria, Estonia and Latvia, the manufacturing sector was not a significant target of FDI inflow. In most countries, the weight of manufacturing is declining whereas the shares of investments in financial intermediation, real estate and other business activities are increasing. These sectors are mostly local-market oriented but also include some export-oriented, off-shore services (e.g., R&D, accounting service, customer call centre, and other service centre, etc.).[6]

10.5 Trade Related FDI in the New Member States

Since the late 1990s, investors in central European countries have been faced with new challenges. Changing locational characteristics in these countries have mainly brought about these challenges. Export demand became the main driving force of manufacturing FDI compared to the situation prevailed during the previous years, when it was local market penetration which drove FDIs. Therefore, it is important to know the relations between the comparative advantages of the central European new EU member states and the pattern of FDI inflows. The result would shed light on the export propensity of FDI in the new member states.

Theoretical considerations and approaches have shown that economic integration or trade liberalisation in general has substantial effects on the location of economic activities. Differences in comparative advantage across countries determine specialisation patterns at the inter-country level, while at intra-national level the forces of new economic geography are at work. The former mechanism works even in the absence of factor mobility across nations – trade and international factor mobility are substitutes – whereas the latter works when factors of production are mobile and trade is not costless.

Another aspect is that a combination of trade costs and scale economies generates agglomeration forces that encourage geographical clustering of production and economic activities in general. This clustering may create regions with many economic activities and others with very few or almost none. Moreover, agglomeration forces may lead to sectoral clustering: one sector clusters into one region while other sectors cluster in other regions. The geographical distribution of economic activities is then very concentrated in each sector but dispersed at the level of all sectors.

[6]This group of investments makes up an increasing portion of new FDI, but they cannot be properly identified in the statistics.

When trade costs become relatively low and previously non-tradable tasks of production or non-tradable product component become tradable, the location of production becomes irrelevant. This, in turn, tends to lead to industrialisation in one of the geographical areas and de-industrialisation in the other. The latter phase is unbundling industrial production into smaller parts as components or different tasks within a production process can be made in different locations not necessarily close to each other. Especially, the second phase affects tasks that can be easily codified or transmitted electronically.

Empirical analyses use a method to approach potential unbundling. This method utilises data on international trade flows and evaluates different countries comparative advantage. Unbundling is likely to be more intense between countries that have similar specialisation patterns and are located relatively close to each other. The latter can be justified by arguing that although distance has lost a part of its relevance it is still a significant ingredient in gravity models. Similar specialisation patterns lead to increasing intra-industry trade that is often based on input–output linkages within production chain. Agglomeration forces are then at work at an inter-country level not only at an intra-country level, as overlap in comparative advantage might lead to regions not necessarily bounded by national borders.

High-tech industries and some central European new EU member states serve as an example. Abundance in skilled labour might shift tasks from high-wage countries to low-wage countries when their wage gap exceeds their productivity gap. This, in turn, leads to a wage and income convergence between the two countries. The trade relations between some old and new EU member states serve as good examples.

Concentrating on comparative advantage and evaluating the specialisation patterns of the old and new EU member states during the latter half of the 1990s and early 2000s, the concept of revealed comparative advantage (RCA) is investigated. The basic logic behind RCA is to evaluate comparative advantage on the basis of a country's specialisation in (net) exports relative to some reference group. The most general point of reference would be the world as a whole or intra-EU trade. On the basis of these data, some conclusions can be drawn on how globalisation has affected specialisation patterns, and some of the differences and similarities can be shown among them.

Comparative advantage can be evaluated by analysing trade flows. This reveals countries' specialisation patterns and hence their revealed comparative advantage, though not the source of this advantage. The measure of revealed comparative advantage (RCA) is the Balassa index (BI).[7] RCA alone, however, only shows which goods countries tend to specialise in their trade. It does not reveal the origins of comparative advantage. Another theoretical approach does this, however. According to the Heckscher–Ohlin theorem, a given country's comparative

[7]This index is calculated as the ratio of the share of a given product in a country's exports to another country or region to the share of the same product in that country or region's total exports. If the ratio is greater than one for given product the country is said to have RCA in exports of that good.

advantage (or disadvantage) is determined by its production factor endowments (labour, capital, technology). A country has a comparative advantage in those sectors that intensively use those productive factors which are abundant in the country. Cross-country trade patterns are determined by differences in comparative advantage; a country will export goods whose production intensively uses those factors which are relatively abundant (and thus comparatively cheap) in that country before trade and import those goods whose production would require the use of relatively scarce (expensive) factors.

To be able to investigate the factor content of comparative advantage of the old and new member states, their traded goods are grouped into five categories[8] (from no.1 to no. 5). The division is made according to the factor intensity of their production. Traded goods are categorised, on the one hand, according to capital intensity (high, intermediate, low) and, on the other hand, according to skilled vs. unskilled labour intensity (Table 10.5).

The next step of the evaluation is the analysis of the differences and similarities of revealed comparative advantages (RCA) in trade between the EU-15 and the EU-10 central European new member states. The result is that the specialisation of the EU-10 is based on an intensive use of low-skilled labour. Except for some countries (e.g., the Czech Rep., Hungary and Estonia), the other seven countries are

Table 10.5 System of properties of the five industry classification categories

Intensity category	Human capital	Labour	Physical capital	Examples
1	Very high	High	Intermediate	High tech ind.
2	High	High	Low	Electrical equip.
3	Low	High	Low	Textiles
4	Low	Low	High	Automobile ind.
5	High	Low	High	Pulp and paper ind.

[8]This methodology and classification was proposed by Neven (1995).

Category 1 is characterised by a high share of wages in value added, very high average wages, and a very high proportion of white-collar workers. These are typically high-tech industries where human capital is used intensively in production.

Category 2 comprises production activities intensive in human capital, but low physical capital intensity. This category includes industries, which have a relatively low level of investment relative to value added, high wages, and a high share of wages in value added. Manufacturers of electrical machinery and equipment serve as an example from this category.

Category 3 includes production intensive in labour and which uses relatively little capital. Average wages are low, and there is a low level of investment and a high share of wages in value added. An example from this category is textiles and apparel industry.

Category 4 includes industries that are intensive in labour and capital. These industries have a high level of investment, relatively low wages, a low proportion of white-collar workers, and an intermediate share of wages in value added. Automobile manufacturing, for instance, falls under this category.

Category 5 is dominated by the forest and food-processing industries that are intensive in both physical and human capital. Also the paper industry belongs to this category.

Table 10.6 (A) The share of the revealed comparative advantage sectors of the EU-10 in skill-capital-intensive product groups in 2004 and (B) changes in this share between 1993 and 2002

(A)						
Product groups	1	2	3	4	5	3 + 4
Bulgaria	4.4	6.7	48.8	35.8	4.2	84.6
Czech Rep.	12.9	23.8	10.7	51.3	1.3	62.0
Estonia	26.0	10.6	21.3	39.4	2.7	60.7
Hungary	25.8	17.8	11.3	44.3	0.8	55.6
Latvia	2.1	2.6	24.5	69.8	1.0	94.3
Lithuania	12.9	8.5	42.4	31.2	4.9	73.6
Poland	4.6	14.0	23.5	53.7	4.3	77.1
Romania	1.5	10.6	68.5	18.5	1.0	87.0
Slovakia	7.4	13.5	17.6	59.6	1.9	77.2
Slovenia	3.8	25.5	15.1	55.4	0.2	70.5
(B)						
Bulgaria	−4.0	−1.0	13.2	1.4	−9.5	14.5
Czech Rep.	5.5	11.9	−16.2	3.4	−4.6	−12.9
Estonia	20.6	3.4	−4.4	−18.6	−1.0	−23.0
Hungary	16.3	5.3	−27.6	10.5	−4.5	−17.1
Latvia	−3.2	1.1	8.4	−3.8	−2.5	4.6
Lithuania	−4.2	6.7	22.3	−15.9	−8.9	6.4
Poland	−1.0	7.8	−18.3	15.8	−4.3	−2.5
Romania	−1.4	7.3	−1.1	−3.3	−1.7	−4.3
Slovakia	−0.1	6.4	−16.0	16.4	−6.7	0.4
Slovenia	1.9	6.2	−19.9	12.9	−1.1	−7.0

Source: Kaitila (2004)

in the same or very similar positions as other trading partners of the EU-15 such as India, Russia and Turkey. The specialisation in the EU-10 seems to be characterised by a more intensive use of capital. Regarding the specialisation in activities which require high-skilled labour (category 1), the statistical figures of Hungary and Estonia show substantial differences compared to the other eight new member states. In the case of these two countries, there was an obvious shift from an intensive use of low-skilled to high-skilled labour as the determinant of the revealed comparative advantages (Table 10.6).[9]

Analysing the trends and deviations from the average revealed comparative advantages, the following lessons can be drawn. In the case of Estonia, Hungary and the Czech Rep., both the skill-intensity and the capital-intensity increased. The common feature of their development is that they have moved towards skill-intensive production. The skill intensity of the other new member states has not changed much. Meanwhile, the EU-15 has moved towards a more intensive use of both, namely skill and capital intensity of production increased. It is very interesting to see how much the substantial shift in skill intensity in Estonia, Hungary and

[9]Similar changes took place in the structure of these two countries as in the case of EU-15, Canada, Thailand or China, Mexico and Indonesia.

the Czech Rep. and less or no shift in the case of the other new member states influenced the inflows of FDI into these countries.

The calculation of the Balassa index on the basis of OECD statistics[10] for 8 out of the 10 new Central European EU member states reveals similar results for the period 1995–2004 (Table 10.7). Except for the three Baltic States, the other five countries (Czech Rep., Poland, Hungary, Slovakia and Slovenia) showed an increasing specialisation and revealed comparative advantages in ITC, high-technology and medium-high technology manufactures meanwhile their specialisation in medium-low technology and low technology manufactures decreased to various extents.

There are differences among the better performing new member states as well. The largest improvement was achieved by the Czech ITC manufacturers, with its revealed comparative advantage increasing about 5.5 times. The specialisation index of the Hungarian ITC manufactures was, however, much higher than the Czech one, although the initial state of the former was about three times better than the latter at the beginning of the period between 1995 and 2004.

There was substantial improvement in the revealed comparative advantage in favour of the more modern manufacturers in Slovakia and Slovenia as well, but it was less overwhelming in comparison to some of the Czech and Hungarian manufacture sectors' records. The revealed comparative advantage in Slovakia improved in all three more modern sectors (ICT, high-technology and medium-high technology manufactures). Meanwhile, the improvement concentrated on the high-technology and medium-high technology manufactures in Slovenia.

The Baltic States showed a very variable picture. Lithuania's revealed comparative advantage differed from the others, because its medium-high technology manufactures decreased and medium-low technology manufactures increased, and its specialisation in ITC and low technology manufactures did not show substantial changes or they rather fluctuated. Estonia revealed that comparative advantages moderately increased in the ICT and medium-high technology manufactures but decreased in high-technology, medium-low technology and low technology manufactures. Latvia was the worst performing economy among the Baltic States; the almost continuous changes did not result in any significant and permanent trend in specialisation.

The economic theory would suggest that the flow of FDI would grow faster into those countries where the skill intensity of production increases. One of the main reasons for this is that the possibility of intra-industry trade enhances. A very typical area of skill intensive industrial branch where there is much opportunity for intra-industry trade is the information technology. Thus, an increase in FDI in the information technology sector of the new member states and a substantial growth of the exports of this sector can be rationally expected. The relocation of production (FDI) might have various impacts on the economies. The most important impacts can be a reduction in the number of jobs in the country of origin of the FDI and increase in the number of jobs in the country of destination (job creation), changes in productivity and wages as well as in the structure of production and

[10]OECD Bilateral Trade Database.

Table 10.7 Balassa index

	1995	1996	1997	1998	1999	2000	2001	2002	2003	2004
Czech Republic										
High-technology manufactures	0.22	0.34	0.34	0.38	0.35	0.35	0.48	0.61	0.63	0.69
Medium-high technology manufactures	0.86	0.95	1.03	1.09	1.10	1.12	1.11	1.06	1.08	1.06
Medium-low technology manufactures	2.05	1.77	1.68	1.59	1.68	1.63	1.55	1.53	1.44	1.37
Low technology manufactures	1.24	1.16	1.12	1.08	1.10	1.13	1.04	0.98	0.93	0.92
ICT Manufactures (ICT)	0.21	0.37	0.35	0.45	0.39	0.49	0.72	0.99	1.05	1.16
Poland										
High-technology manufactures	0.17	0.22	0.26	0.28	0.26	0.24	0.27	0.30	0.29	0.27
Medium-high technology manufactures	0.59	0.62	0.65	0.68	0.72	0.87	0.85	0.85	0.87	0.93
Medium-low technology manufactures	2.02	1.89	1.76	1.84	1.82	1.69	1.79	1.84	1.72	1.65
Low technology manufactures	1.79	1.82	1.90	1.85	1.90	1.79	1.69	1.61	1.59	1.53
ICT Manufactures (ICT)	0.24	0.29	0.36	0.41	0.39	0.34	0.41	0.48	0.50	0.46
Hungary										
High-technology manufactures	0.49	0.42	1.12	1.07	1.08	1.18	1.18	1.30	1.45	1.56
Medium-high technology manufactures	0.77	0.75	0.91	1.02	1.04	1.03	1.04	0.99	0.99	0.96
Medium-low technology manufactures	1.35	1.29	0.86	0.77	0.71	0.67	0.67	0.62	0.60	0.59
Low technology manufactures	1.65	1.81	1.16	1.05	1.02	0.93	0.91	0.92	0.79	0.73
ICT Manufactures (ICT)	0.66	0.60	1.74	1.73	1.72	1.81	1.92	2.29	2.63	2.80
Slovakia										
High-technology manufactures			0.23	0.23	0.23	0.19	0.22	0.21	0.23	0.32
Medium-high technology manufactures			0.90	1.06	1.08	1.11	1.06	1.07	1.19	1.11
Medium-low technology manufactures			2.22	1.97	1.93	1.97	1.96	1.90	1.62	1.70
Low technology manufactures			1.10	1.03	1.10	1.11	1.16	1.18	1.03	1.00
ICT Manufactures (ICT)			0.26	0.28	0.29	0.25	0.32	0.32	0.37	0.56
Slovenia										
High-technology manufactures			0.32	0.31	0.30	0.32	0.29	0.34	0.44	0.51
Medium-high technology manufactures			0.93	1.01	0.97	1.00	1.02	1.06	1.03	1.03
Medium-low technology manufactures			1.35	1.30	1.49	1.46	1.49	1.42	1.40	1.32
Low technology manufactures			1.62	1.54	1.59	1.60	1.53	1.39	1.31	1.27
ICT Manufactures (ICT)			0.24	0.24	0.22	0.26	0.24	0.26	0.29	0.29
Lithuania										
High-technology manufactures			0.17	0.16	0.17	0.18	0.16	0.21	0.24	0.23

(*continued*)

Table 10.7 (continued)

	1995	1996	1997	1998	1999	2000	2001	2002	2003	2004
Medium-high technology manufactures			0.48	0.49	0.42	0.44	0.37	0.35	0.41	0.38
Medium-low technology manufactures			1.07	1.00	1.23	1.55	1.94	1.96	1.75	2.22
Low technology manufactures			2.89	3.01	3.13	3.01	2.82	2.76	2.70	2.41
ICT Manufactures (ICT)			0.32	0.22	0.22	0.21	0.21	0.26	0.37	0.36
Estonia										
High-technology manufactures			0.49	0.79	0.87	1.92	1.06	0.72	0.76	0.58
Medium-high technology manufactures			0.25	0.26	0.27	0.29	0.29	0.29	0.32	0.32
Medium-low technology manufactures			2.01	1.28	1.22	1.51	1.28	1.44	1.08	1.34
Low technology manufactures			2.07	2.17	2.21	2.13	1.88	1.88	1.85	1.53
ICT Manufactures (ICT)			0.72	1.22	1.38	2.91	1.73	1.30	1.41	1.07
Latvia										
High-technology manufactures			0.04	0.03	0.02	0.02	0.02	0.03	0.04	0.03
Medium-high technology manufactures			0.13	0.12	0.09	0.08	0.08	0.08	0.07	0.07
Medium-low technology manufactures			1.73	1,20	1.14	1.41	0.99	0.95	0.96	1.48
Low technology manufactures			2.08	2.34	2.51	2.32	1.94	1.80	1.73	1.44
ICT Manufactures (ICT)			0.02	0.03	0.02	0.03	0.02	0.05	0.06	0.07

Source: calculation on the basis of OECD Bilateral Trade Database

foreign trade (both exports and imports). Moreover, economic theory suggests that economic growth and convergence is faster in those countries where revealed comparative advantage shifts towards skilled-intensive direction.

10.6 Effects of Relocation

The relevant economic literature considers FDI flows as probably the most important factor of the relocation process between the old member states (EU-15) and the new member states. In this context, three issues are particularly important and relevant. They deal with various aspects of national economic policies and development:

(a) Does the relocation process result in a reduction in the production, export and employment of the country of origin of the capital?
(b) What is the actual and potential scale and nature of the relocation process?
(c) What are the structural characteristics of the relocation process?

Of course, these issues have differing relevance and importance for the economies of origin and economies of destination. The first issue is of vital interest to

EU-15 member states, because they are the main source of FDI inflows into the new member states. The second issue is relevant for both groups of EU member states. Meanwhile, the third issue is particularly important for the new member states because their economies are influenced by the FDI inflows, which definitively result in structural changes and create economic growth and development.

In the EU-15, increasing production costs drove investors to relocate or upgrade their subsidiaries in the new member states. Despite the widespread perception that changing locations automatically means job losses, jobs are not flowing to the new member states in the numbers believed. First of all, their relatively low level of FDI suggests that they cannot be a major source of the employment problem currently facing the EU-15. Secondly, the location of FDI projects is not a simple game of win-or-lose. The locations not chosen for a given activity can still retain business links with the new project (and thus create additional jobs). Thirdly, reorganisation itself is a two-way street: projects can be relocated from new member states to older EU members if the latter offer better agglomeration advantages (e.g., examples in the food industry).

The relatively low level of FDI in the new member states might also be due to a lack of vigorous home-country measures in the 15 older member states and at the level of the EU. Because of the perception that new member states represent a threat to jobs at home, no old member country has thus far felt obliged to suggest any programme of outward FDI promotion in new member countries. The gradual introduction of structural and cohesion funds into the new members – in the first year, they will be entitled to only 35% of what is provided to old members (a differentiated treatment favouring the rich over the poor) – could further handicap their efforts to attract FDI.

In the case of the new member states, the recent period of less than two decades is already long enough to observe changing trends and to specify phases in the flows of FDI. In the 1990s, trans-national companies relocated their low and low-medium-tech, export-oriented subsidiaries to the low-cost central European transition countries. When the labour costs in the central European new EU member states started to increase, the transnational companies once again moved their subsidiaries farther to the East and rarely upgraded their activities in the more advanced transition or new EU member states. There are some sectors, however in which exceptions can be found.

FDI inflows in the manufacturing industry of the new EU member states increasingly concentrated in the most industrialised industries such as the automotive industry and electrical engineering, which provide greater opportunities for upgrading and networking. The new EU member states successfully moved from low-tech to medium-high-tech industries, but their business performance in the high-tech sector has been uneven. Their performance was hindered or even aggravated by the recent crisis in the electronic industry.

In most of the EU-15 member states, there has been a long-time fear of FDI outflow into the new member states, because it was supposed that the shift of production abroad would cause home country exports and employment to fall. The evidence of the last 3 years has not confirmed this expectation. Economic analysis[11] found limited evidence of employment substitution within European multinational enterprises between their centres and their affiliates. In the case of Nordic countries, some employment substitution took place between the mother companies and their affiliates, but no convincing evidence was found for the Southern European and the central European new member states. These studies showed that employment relocation takes place between high wage locations only. Competition created by low wage countries (Southern European and central European new member states) did not contribute to any massive or substantial relocation of jobs from the EU-15 countries into former group of countries. There can be, of course, differences among countries as far as job relocation is concerned. There were countries, which were not exposed at all or to a very small extent only to the impact of job relocation, whereas other countries suffered more.[12]

The central European new EU member states have developed and improved on the key ingredients for becoming a major pole of attraction for FDI within the enlarged EU, partly during their early transition from centrally planned to market economies and partly during the accession negotiations. Within the enlarged EU, these countries offer both competitive production costs and relatively low tax burdens. In parallel with the accession negotiations, huge amounts were invested in improving the physical infrastructure – an effort that is expected to continue after accession. The main source of competitiveness of these countries is their labour skills, the driving force behind the most dynamic product segments of FDI.

One of the main advantages of EU membership of great value to firms locating within the new member states is the relatively unlimited access to a large customs union. Membership also increases the stability and safety of investments. The reasons why FDI has not yet increased more quickly in the new member states may be related to various factors. One of the most important ones is the still lacking monetary integration. Problems related to the existence of two currencies (e.g., differences in monetary policies, exchange rate risk, conversion costs, etc.) may hinder FDI flow in growing even more.

10.7 Relations Between FDI and Export

The effects of FDI on structural upgrading can be traced by using a combination of various approaches and sources of information. They may include microeconomic, sectoral and macroeconomic approaches. A microeconomic approach examines the

[11]Konings (2003 and 2004), Braconier, Ekholm (2000).

[12]According to the Dutch Ministry of Economic Affairs (2005) 1 to 1.5 % of jobs lost in the period between 1999 and 2004 could be directly attributed to job relocation. It made up about 9,000 jobs per year. Moreover, 52% of the relocated companies moved into the central European new member states.

relation between capability and competence of a subsidiary and its possibility for upgrading. The macroeconomic approach deals with the changes in the distribution of FDI stock particularly in the manufacturing sector. As FDI is probably the most prominent factor of the relocation process between EU-15 and EU-10, one of the key issues is the structural characteristic and its impact on export. From the point of view of changes in competitiveness, it is an important question whether the increasing FDI stock in the EU-10 has contributed to an improvement in the export performance of these countries.

In the WIIW, OECD and Eurostat databases, there are statistical data which can provide tools for a partial analysis. This is due to the fact that the data needed to the analysis is not complete. FDI and export data in NACE classification are unavailable for every country of the EU-10 group and for the whole period between the early 1990s and 2007. Thus, only the impact of FDI on the export performance of eight central-European countries (Czech Rep., Hungary, Poland, Slovakia, Slovenia and the three Baltic States) until their EU accession in 2004 can be analysed.

The EU-10 countries reported substantial increases in their FDI stocks. The FDI inflow into these countries more than quadrupled between 1995 and 2005, and this increase was almost twice as much as the world-wide FDI growth. It is therefore no wonder that FDI is a relatively important factor for the production of national income in these countries. The increase in exports was also substantial, however, a direct causality link between the two cannot be proven. It is nonetheless interesting that in all EU-10 countries, the increase in FDI stock was superior to the growth of export. In the case of the Czech Rep., the increase in exports was only slightly less than the growth of FDI stock. In the case of Hungary, Poland, Slovakia and Estonia, the ratio between the two growth rates was between 60 and 75%, which would indicate a relatively strong export orientation of the FDI in these countries. Contrary to these cases, the ratio of the two growth rates was less than 50% in Slovenia, Latvia and Lithuania, which would indicate a less export orientation and more domestic market orientation in general.

A comparison of the growth rates of the values of the various product groups both in Table 10.8 the cases of FDI stocks and exports can indicate the impact of FDI on export performance and changes in the revealed comparative advantage of each main sector. There are some similarities and several substantial differences among the patterns of the EU-10 countries. The most important similarity is that in all EU-10, there was substantial FDI inflow in the rubber and plastic products sector and due to the development of new production capacities, the export of these products also increased significantly. Another similarity is that in each country there was a sector which recorded a particularly high FDI stock increase, but export growth was relatively insignificant (e.g., wood and wood products in the Czech Rep. and Estonia, coke and refined petroleum products in Hungary, Poland and Slovakia, leather and leather products in Slovenia).

In the case of the Czech Rep., there were four product groups whose FDI inflow and export increased significantly in parallel. Two of them belong to the more

Table 10.8 Changes in the stock of FDI and export values by various sectors of the manufacturing industry (NACE categories)

	FDI stock	Export		FDI stock	Export
Czech Rep. (1997–2004)			Hungary (1998–2004)		
D Total	363%	345%	D Total	312%	237%
DA food products, beverages & tobacco	177%	256%	DA food products, beverages & tobacco	189%	165%
DB textiles and textile products	288%	189%	DB textiles and textile products	196%	116%
DC leather and leather products	99%	(*)	DC leather and leather products	121%	(*)
DD wood and wood products	1,786%	166%	DD wood and wood products	241%	140%
DE pulp, paper, pap.prod, publish.& printing	280%	376%	DE pulp, paper, pap.prod, publish.& printing	218%	209%
DF coke, refined petrol. prod.& nuclear fuel	169%	146%	DF coke, refined petrol. prod.& nuclear fuel	31,669%	167%
DG chemicals, chemical prod. & man-made fibr.	662%	404%	DG chemicals, chemical prod.& man-made fibr.	196%	175%
DH rubber and plastic products	191%	193%	DH rubber and plastic products	352%	174%
DI other non-metallic mineral products	651%	276%	DI other non-metallic mineral products	347%	316%
DJ basic metals & fabricated metal prod.	797%	377%	DJ basic metals & fabricated metal prod.	347%	316%
DK machinery and equipment n.e.c.	625%	593%	DK machinery and equipment n.e.c.	268%	305%
DL electrical and optical equipment	458%	409%	DL electrical and optical equipment	517%	223%
DM transport equipment	390%	282%	DM transport equipment	238%	201%
DN manufacturing n.e.c.			DN manufacturing n.e.c.		
Poland (1996–2004)			Slovakia (1997–2004)		
D Total	574%	319%	D Total	617%	366%
DA food products, beverages & tobacco	373%	316%	DA food products, beverages & tobacco	338%	238%
DB textiles and textile products	274%	119%	DB textiles and textile products	475%	190%
DC leather and leather products	–	(*)	DC leather and leather products	381%	(*)
DD wood and wood products	670%	213%	DD wood and wood products	776%	207%
DE pulp, paper, pap.prod, publish.& printing	–	458%	DE pulp, paper, pap.prod, publish.& printing	943%	347%
DF coke, refined petrol. prod.& nuclear fuel	1,837%	452%	DF coke, refined petrol. prod.& nuclear fuel	1,362%	753%
DG chemicals, chemical prod.& man-made fibr.	606%	216%	DG chemicals, chemical prod.& man-made fibr.	316%	165%
	470%	572%		2,069%	497%
DH rubber and plastic products	–	180%	DH rubber and plastic products	273%	161%
DI other non-metallic mineral products	908%	237%	DI other non-metallic mineral products	1,232%	233%

(*continued*)

Table 10.8 (continued)

	FDI stock	Export		FDI stock	Export
DJ basic metals & fabricated metal prod.	582%	443%	DJ basic metals & fabricated metal prod.	625%	472%
DK machinery and equipment n.e.c.	943%	450%	DK machinery and equipment n.e.c.	629%	585%
DL electrical and optical equipment	670%	632%	DL electrical and optical equipment	389%	548%
DM transport equipment	631%	302%	DM transport equipment	786%	438%
DN manufacturing n.e.c.			DN manufacturing n.e.c.		
Slovenia (1995–2004)			Estonia (1995–2004)		Export
D Total	450%	141%	D Total	322%	256%
DA food products, beverages & tobacco	127%	121%	DA food products, beverages & tobacco	204%	284%
DB textiles and textile products	188%	57%	DB textiles and textile products	245%	160%
DC leather and leather products	16,000%	(*)	DC leather and leather products	698%	(*)
DD wood and wood products	6,403%	66%	DD wood and wood products	1,215%	214%
DE pulp, paper, pap.prod, publish.& printing	293% –	76% 55%	DE pulp, paper, pap. prod, publish.& printing	459% 5%	262% 171%
DF coke, refined petrol. prod.& nuclear fuel	1,092%	157%	DF coke, refined petrol. prod.& nuclear fuel	85%	301%
DG chemicals, chemical prod.& man-made fibr.	1,678%	147%	DG chemicals, chemical prod.& man-made fibr.	663%	539%
DH rubber and plastic products	386%	105%	DH rubber and plastic products	251%	129%
DI other non-metallic mineral products	994%	157%	DI other non-metallic mineral products	289%	370%
DJ basic metals & fabricated metal prod.	305%	163%	DJ basic metals & fabricated metal prod.	428%	285%
DK machinery and equipment n.e.c.	229%	176%	DK machinery and equipment n.e.c.	938%	402%
DL electrical and optical equipment	183%	213%	DL electrical and optical equipment	4,208%	1,159%
DM transport equipment	98%	182%	DM transport equipment	324%	273%
DN manufacturing n.e.c.			DN manufacturing n.e.c.		
Latvia (1995–2004)			Lithuania (1995–2004)		
D Total	544%	254%	D Total	687%	347%
DA food products, beverages & tobacco	229%	264%	DA food products, beverages & tobacco	531%	302%
DB textiles and textile products	942%	180%	DB textiles and textile products	263%	300%
DC leather and leather products	46%	(*)	DC leather and leather products	1,268%	(*)
DD wood and wood products	1,114%	356%	DD wood and wood products	306%	216%
DE pulp, paper, pap.prod, publish.& printing	1,121% 0%	165% 249%	DE pulp, paper, pap.prod, publish.& printing	1,542% –	279% 424%

(*continued*)

Table 10.8 (continued)

	FDI stock	Export		FDI stock	Export
DF coke, refined petrol. prod.& nuclear fuel	1,171%	67%	DF coke, refined petrol. prod.& nuclear fuel	814%	157%
DG chemicals, chemical prod.& man-made fibr.	479%	849%	DG chemicals, chemical prod.& man-made fibr.	1,970%	1837%
DH rubber and plastic products	1,649%	188%	DH rubber and plastic products	390%	59%
DI other non-metallic mineral products	743%	192%	DI other non-metallic mineral products	1,003%	358%
DJ basic metals & fabricated metal prod.	242%	311%	DJ basic metals & fabricated metal prod.	2,285%	294%
DK machinery and equipment n.e.c.	926%	500%	DK machinery and equipment n.e.c.	1,075%	624%
DL electrical and optical equipment	17,453%	519%	DL electrical and optical equipment	426%	1,072%
DM transport equipment	1,184%	526%	DM transport equipment	519%	1,324%
DN manufacturing n.e.c.			DN manufacturing n.e.c.		

Source: calculation on the basis of the WIIW, Hunya (2008) and OECD data *Note*: (*) combined rate of increase in export of DB + DC

capital and technology intensive product groups: electrical and optical equipment, and transport equipment. The other two product groups are less technology intensive: food products and pulp, paper and paper products.

In Hungary, the FDI stock and the export increased correspondingly in the case of the machinery and equipment sector and electrical and optical equipment sector. In the other sectors, export growth was inferior to the growth of FDI stock.

The Polish case was characterised by the relatively fast increase in FDI and export on the one hand, in the more technically intensive electrical and optical equipment as well as transport equipment, and in the food products sector, which is less technically intensive, on the other hand.

In the case of Slovakia, exports increased to the largest extent in those sectors for which the FDI stock growth rates were about average. These sectors were machinery and equipment, electrical and optical equipment as well as transport equipment. They represent the fast growing car industry.

Slovenia was the extreme case where an increase in FDI stock did not really result in significant growth in the export of the same manufacturing sector.

The Baltic States represent a mixed picture. FDI stock increased relatively quickly in most of the sectors and the enlarged production capacities resulted in growing exports both in more technical intensive sectors, e.g. transport equipment, machinery equipment, and in labour or natural resource intensive sectors, e.g. food products, leather and leather products as well as wood and wood products.

The increase in FDI stock and export growth figures show relatively heterogeneous pictures in the EU-10 countries. The main characteristics meet the main points of the revealed comparative advantage analysis in general.

10.8 Conclusion

Despite the currently low levels of FDI in new EU member states, good prospects can be supposed in the medium and longer term. It is expected that despite the lack of policy support, investors will substantially increase their presence in the new member states, because it makes good business sense. Furthermore, awareness of the interdependence of welfare in the two parts of the enlarged EU might well increase. If perceptions change, home countries might give more serious consideration to the idea of promoting investment in the new member states.

Firms from outside the EU in particular are likely to increasingly locate their efficiency- and EU-market-seeking new FDI in the central European new member states. For them, the considerations of sunk costs and home-country pressure might be less relevant. They in turn could imitate the strategy of firms (e.g., Flextronics of Singapore) that have started using the central European countries prior to their EU accession as a regional export platform.[13]

Relocation is a means of home and host economies restructuring. It is a part of an increased reorganisation of production into international networks and has two levels. At the macroeconomic level, structural restructuring of the economies takes place, and at microeconomic level, firm restructuring happens.

The share of central European new member states in outward FDI stock of the EU-15 is still limited. In relative terms, the scope of relocation between the EU-15 and the new member states is narrow. Therefore, its potential for future growth (further penetration) is substantial.

The relocation of investment from EU-15 into the central European new member states is a fact, and it comprises mainly efficiency-seeking FDI in the manufacturing sector. There is no evidence, however, that this trend leads to the fall of exports and employment in the EU-15.

Relocation in the manufacturing sector is accompanied by increased imports of affiliates from their foreign parents and other foreign companies. The increased volume of imports may more than compensate for initial relocations.

Empirical findings mostly do not support the notion of home country exports and employment substitution by the affiliates. It is especially invalid for low wage production.

The central European new member states are losing their attractiveness as locations for low tech and medium low tech industries. Inward FDI in low and segments of medium high and high tech industries is gaining momentum.

EU-15 and the EU-10 will increasingly relocate their low tech and wage intensive activities to countries outside the EU, and the EU-15 will increasingly relocate some low-end segments of medium-high and high tech activities to the central European new member states. This may have stronger effects on employment substitution between parent firms and affiliates than low tech relocations in the past.

[13]These platforms have in part replicated the global production strategy with which such firms experimented in China.

Appendix

Table 10.9 FDI inflow (Eur Million)

	1999	2000	2001	2002	2003	2004	2005	2006
Czech Republic	5,933	5,404	6,296	9,012	1,863	4,007	9,374	4,752
Hungary	3,106	2,998	4,391	3,185	1,888	3,633	6,099	4,874
Poland	6,824	10,334	6,372	4,371	4,067	10,292	7,703	11,093
Slovakia	402	2,089	17,68	4,397	1,914	2,441	1,694	3,324
Slovenia	99	149	412	1,722	271	665	445	303
New Member States-5	16,364	20,974	19,240	22,687	10,002	21,039	25,315	24,346
Estonia	284	425	603	307	822	776	2,349	1,282
Latvia	325	447	147	269	270	513	582	1,303
Lithuania	457	412	499	772	160	623	826	1,426
Bulgaria	866	1,103	903	980	1,851	2,736	3,103	4,104
Romania	964	1,147	1,294	1,212	1,946	5,183	5,213	9,082
New Member States-10	19,260	24,508	22,685	26,226	15,051	30,869	37,387	41,544

Source: WIIW

Table 10.10 Inward FDI Stock, EUR million

	1999	2000	2001	2002	2003	2004	2005	2006
Czech Republic	17,479	23,323	30,717	36,884	35,852	42,035	51,424	58,813
Hungary	23,041	24,578	31,045	34,575	38,329	45,881	52,299	62,096
Poland	25,947	36,792	46,686	46,139	45,896	63,318	75,778	90,000[a]
Slovakia	3,174	5,112	6,327	8,185	9,504	11,281	13,333	18,000[a]
Slovenia	2,675	3,110	2,940	3,948	5,047	5,580	5,980	6,300[a]
New Member States-5	72,316	92,915	117,715	129,731	134,628	168,095	198,815	23,5209
Estonia	2,454	2,843	3,573	4,035	5,553	7,379	10,748	12,390
Latvia	1,782	2,241	2,648	2,679	2,630	3,315	4,213	5,745
Lithuania	2,050	2,509	3,023	3,818	3,968	4,690	6,921	8,333
Bulgaria	2,392	2,426	3,129	3,530	4,946	6,769	9,674	15,723
Romania	5,447	6,966	8,656	7,482	9,662	15,040	21,885	30,891
New Member States-10	86,439	109,900	138,744	151,274	161,386	205,287	252,257	308,291

[a]*Note*: WIIW estimate
Source: WIIW

Table 10.11 FDI inflow as a percentage of gross fixed capital formation

	1999	2000	2001	2002	2003	2004	2005	2006
Czech Republic	38.9	31.4	32.5	41.0	8.6	17.5	37.7	16.8
Hungary	28.8	24.5	32.2	19.6	11.5	19.7	30.3	24.9
Poland	17.8	23.5	14.5	11.1	11.6	27.9	17.4	20.5
Slovakia	7.1	36.7	26.3	61.9	26.2	29.9	16.6	28.7
Slovenia	1.9	2.8	7.7	32.1	4.7	10.3	6.6	3.9
New member States-5	21.7	24.8	21.6	25.2	11.6	22.7	23.8	20.1
Estonia	22.0	26.8	32.7	13.3	33.0	26.3	68.3	29.0
Latvia	21.0	22.0	6.0	11.0	11.0	17.0	15.0	24.0
Lithuania	20.3	17.8	18.3	25.3	4.6	15.4	17.9	26.0
Bulgaria	47.0	51.3	32.6	32.4	54.1	67.1	58.7	62.3
Romania	16.3	15.1	14.0	11.7	17.3	39.0	28.4	38.0
New member States-10	21.8	24.4	21.0	23.6	13.8	25.7	26.3	24.9

Source: WIIW

Table 10.12 Inward FDI stock as a percentage of GDP

	1999	2000	2001	2002	2003	2004	2005	2006
Czech Republic	31.0	37.9	44.5	46.1	44.3	48.2	51.6	52.0
Hungary	51.1	48.6	52.2	48.8	51.3	55.8	58.9	69.6
Poland	16.5	19.8	22.0	22.0	24.0	31.1	31.1	33.4
Slovakia	16.4	23.1	26.8	31.4	32.5	33.3	35.0	41.0
Slovenia	13.2	14.8	13.3	16.7	20.3	21.2	21.6	21.2
New Member States-5	24.2	27.3	30.4	31.6	33.6	38.8	39.9	43.1
Estonia	47.0	47.9	51.7	52.0	65.4	78.7	97.2	94.8
Latvia	26.1	26.8	28.5	27.1	26.5	29.9	32.7	35.8
Lithuania	20.0	20.3	22.3	25.4	24.1	25.9	33.6	35.1
Bulgaria	19.7	17.7	20.6	21.3	27.9	34.1	44.2	62.6
Romania	16.3	17.3	19.3	15.4	18.4	24.7	27.5	31.8
New Member States-10	23.6	26.1	29.1	29.8	31.9	37.2	39.2	42.8

Table 10.13 Inward FDIstock in NMS-10 by major home countries

	As of December 2005, share in %										
	CZ	HU	PL	SK	SI	EE	LV	LT	BG	RO	NMS-10
Austria	11.1	11.1	5.0	15.3	28.9	1.1	1.3	2.2	33.8	15.4	10.3
Belgium	4.0	1.9	3.5	1.0	3.5	0.3	0.5	0.2	3.1	1.3	1.8
Cyprus	1.2	0.7	1.2	2.2	0.3	0.8	1.2	0.9	4.0	3.7	1.4
Denmark	0.5	0.4	2.9	0.8	1.3	1.4	8.7	15.9	0.7	0.2	1.9
Finland	0.1	2.1	1.3	0.1	0.0	20.6	6.5	6.4	0.0	0.1	2.0
France	6.1	4.7	12.6	2.7	8.7	0.4	0.4	1.1	3.1	8.4	7.4
Germany	20.3	27.8	16.3	19.7	8.7	1.9	12.5	10.7	3.9	10.7	17.5
Greece	0.0	0.0	0.0	0.0	0.0	0.1		0.0	10.2	8.5	1.2
Hungary	0.2		0.1	7.0	0.5	0.0		0.1	5.8	1.9	0.8
Italy	0.8	1.6	3.6	7.0	5.8	0.6	0.2	0.5	6.9	6.9	3.0
Japan	1.4	1.5	0.8	0.3	0.3	0.1	0.2		0.4		0.9
Luxembourg	2.7	3.5	4.8	1.2	1.3	0.3	0.2	1.0		1.0	2.9
Netherlands	28.7	14.9	21.7	21.3	10.6	3.0	7.3	2.9	2.0	19.5	19.0
Norway	0.2	2.5	0.4			1.8	3.3	2.0	0.1	0.2	0.9
Russia	0.1	0.0	0.7	0.0	−0.1	1.7	8.1	24.6	0.9	0.0	1.2
Spain	6.0	1.8	1.8	0.4	0.1	0.2	0.0	0.0	0.7	0.6	2.3
Sweden	1.5	1.5	4.2	0.2	0.3	53.3	15.3	11.1	0.4	1.4	5.0
Switzerland	2.2	1.8	2.5	1.6	16.3	0.7	2.3	1.7	4.1	7.1	3.0
United Kingdom	3.2	6.8	3.4	6.6	1.6	2.1	2.2	2.7	6.8	0.2	3.9
United States	4.7	3.9	7.4	3.7	1.6	2.9	6.6	1.8	3.4	2.6	4.9
Other countries	5.0	11.6	5.7	8.8	10.4	6.7	23.1	14.3	9.8	10.2	8.9
EU-15	84.9	78.0	83.2	76.4	72.2	86.9	56.0	55.0	62.0	74.3	79.3
Total	100.0	100.0	100.0	100.0	100.0	100.0	100.0	100.0	100.0	100.0	100.0
Total, EUR mn	51,424	46,670	75,778	11,094	5,980	10,748	4,213	6,921	9,674	21,885	244,389

Source: WIIW

Table 10.14 Czech Republic: inward FDI stock by economic activity

NACE	Classification	2003	2004	2005	2006	2003	2004	2005	2006
		EUR million				In% of total			
A	Agriculture, hunting and forestry	8.7	79.3	93.8	−43.4	0.0	0.2	0.2	−0.9
B	Fishing								
C	Mining and quarrying	422.4	536.3	213.7	183.8	1.2	1.3	0.4	3.9
D	Manufacturing	15019.6	16849.5	19592.3	1746.1	41.9	40.1	38.1	36.7
E	Electricity, gas and water supply	2587.6	2805.5	2907.7	−197.0	7.2	6.7	5.7	−4.1
F	Construction	819.1	804.1	604.9	−27.8	2.3	1.9	1.2	−0.6
G	Wholesale, retail trade, repair of veh. etc.	4405.9	5429.1	5020.4	899.9	12.3	12.9	9.8	18.9
H	Hotels and restaurants	307.1	397.0	340.3	36.0	0.9	0.9	0.7	0.8
I	Transport, storage and communication	2131.4	2610.4	6238.6	−89.5	5.9	6.2	12.1	−1.9
J	Financial intermediation	6018.5	6921.3	9653.5	680.5	16.8	16.5	18.8	14.3
K	Real estate, renting & business activities	3213.1	4746.2	6322.4	1559.9	9.0	11.3	12.3	32.8
L	Public administr., defence, comp.soc.sec.	34.8	42.0			0.1	0.1		
M	Education	2.6	1.8	9.0		0.0	0.0	0.0	
N	Health and social work	59.6	48.3	81.9		0.2	0.1	0.2	
O	Other community, social & pers.services	810.3	764.4	345.9		2.3	1.8	0.7	
P	Private househ. With employed persons	11.3				0.0			
Q	Extra-territorial organizations and bodies	0.2				0.0			
	Other services				3.1				0.1
Total by activities		35852.0	42035.0	51424.4	4751.7	100.0	100.0	100.0	100.0
D Manufacturing industry									
DA	Food products, beverages and tobacco	1660.6	1798.9	1876.4	87.5	11.1	10.7	9.6	5.0
DB	Textiles and textile products	349.0	367.3	346.4	18.3	2.3	2.2	1.8	1.0
DC	Leather and leather products	16.8	7.6	5.5	0.3	0.1	0.0	0.0	0.0
DD	Wood and wood products	204.3	317.9	303.4		1.4	1.9	1.5	
DE	Pulp, paper & prod.; publish.& printing	884.3	1060.0	1174.4		5.9	6.3	6.0	
DD_DE	Wood, pulp, paper, publishing				123.1				7.1
DF	Coke, ref. Petroleum prod. & nuclear fuel	251.8	265.5	325.7	9.7	1.7	1.6	1.7	0.6
DG	Chemicals, prod.& man-made fibres	871.1	1106.2	1338.9	155.8	5.8	6.6	6.8	8.9

(*continued*)

Table 10.14 (continued)

NACE	Classification	2003	2004	2005	2006	2003	2004	2005	2006
		EUR million				In% of total			
DH	Rubber and plastic products	907.1	1120.6	1248.4	276.3	6.0	6.7	6.4	15.8
DI	Other non-metallic mineral products	1808.2	1668.4	1963.0	3.4	12.0	9.9	10.0	0.2
DJ	Basic metals & fabricated metal prod.	1660.9	2248.7	2477.5	309.9	11.1	13.3	12.6	17.7
DK	Machinery and equipment n.e.c.	798.9	1005.2	1360.5	170.8	5.3	6.0	6.9	9.8
DL	Electrical and optical equipment	2072.3	2376.4	2210.6	−62.6	13.8	14.1	11.3	−3.6
DM	Transport equipment	3407.6	3345.4	4740.1	650.4	22.7	19.9	24.2	37.3
DN	Manufacturing n.e.c.	126.8	161.6	221.6	3.2	0.8	1.0	1.1	0.2
D	Manufacturing industry total	15019.6	16849.5	19592.3	1746.1	100.0	100.0	100.0	100.0

Table 10.15 Hungary: inward FDI stock by economic activity

NACE	Classification	2003	2004	2005	2006	2003	2004	2005	2006
		EUR million				In % of total			
A	Agriculture, hunting and forestry	192.4	178.8	186.8		0.6	0.4	0.4	
B	Fishing	0.2	0.8	0.4		0.0	0.0	0.0	
C	Mining and quarrying	88.2	57.1	42.3		0.3	0.1	0.1	
D	Manufacturing	15204.6	17861.8	19307.9		45.7	44.2	41.4	
E	Electricity, gas and water supply	1345.5	1608.0	1949.8		4.0	4.0	4.2	
F	Construction	294.6	344.5	430.2		0.9	0.9	0.9	
G	Wholesale, retail trade, repair of veh. etc.	3250.4	4066.9	5439.6		9.8	10.1	11.7	
H	Hotels and restaurants	268.3	326.2	352.4		0.8	0.8	0.8	
I	Transport, storage and communication	2872.1	3988.7	4710.1		8.6	9.9	10.1	
J	Financial intermediation	3343.2	4261.6	4788.8		10.1	10.5	10.3	
K	Real estate, renting & business activities	5628.7	6797.8	8359.7		16.9	16.8	17.9	
	Other services	271.0	286.8	308.4		0.8	0.7	0.7	
	Pivate purchase and sales of real estate	479.5	647.0	793.8		1.4	1.6	1.7	
Total by activities		33238.9	40425.9	46670.2		100.0	100.0	100.0	
D Manufacturing industry									
DA	Food products, beverages and tobacco	1976.0	2092.6	1957.9		13.0	11.7	10.1	
DB	Textiles and textile products	269.0	330.1	252.7		1.8	1.8	1.3	
DC	Leather and leather products	56.6	54.1	46.4		0.4	0.3	0.2	
DD	Wood and wood products	150.7	190.3	197.6		1.0	1.1	1.0	
DE	Pulp, paper & prod.; publish.& printing	528.1	601.0	588.0		3.5	3.4	3.0	
DF	Coke, ref. Petroleum prod. & nuclear fuel	–0.2	586.8	875.4		0.0	3.3	4.5	
DG	Chemicals, prod.& man-made fibres	2523.1	2317.9	2523.8		16.6	13.0	13.1	
DH	Rubber and plastic products	512.1	646.2	630.9		3.4	3.6	3.3	
DI	Other non-metallic mineral products	591.3	669.6	784.5		3.9	3.7	4.1	
DJ	Basic metals & fabricated metal prod.	914.9	1188.5	1299.5		6.0	6.7	6.7	
DK	Machinery and equipment n.e.c.	862.4	1125.2	1030.6		5.7	6.3	5.3	
DL	Electrical and optical equipment	2981.1	3571.0	4160.0		19.6	20.0	21.5	
DM	Transport equipment	3761.7	4387.4	4855.6		24.7	24.6	25.1	
DN	Manufacturing n.e.c.	77.9	101.0	104.9		0.5	0.6	0.5	
D	Manufacturing industry total	15204.6	17861.8	19307.9		100.0	100.0	100.0	

Table 10.16 Poland: inward FDI stock by economic activity

NACE	Classification	2003	2004	2005	2006	2003	2004	2005	2006
		EUR million				In % of total			
A + B	Agriculture, hunting and forestry, fishing	188.9	286.3	344.3		0.4	0.5	0.5	
C	Mining and quarrying	135.3	141.5	83.6		0.3	0.2	0.1	
D	Manufacturing	16498.7	23824.6	27699.7		35.9	37.6	36.6	
E	Electricity, gas and water supply	1447.8	2267.2	2571.8		3.2	3.6	3.4	
F	Construction	887.4	1234.3	1338.9		1.9	1.9	1.8	
G	Wholesale, retail trade, repair of veh. etc.	8791.9	11407.5	13973.5		19.2	18.0	18.4	
H	Hotels and restaurants	288.3	361.2	405.6		0.6	0.6	0.5	
I	Transport, storage and communication	3929.8	4811.6	5979.2		8.6	7.6	7.9	
J	Financial intermediation	8678.6	12449.2	15385.8		18.9	19.7	20.3	
K	Real estate, renting & business activities	4274.0	6040.0	7598.4		9.3	9.5	10.0	
L + Q	Other services	746.6	400.8	285.0		1.6	0.6	0.4	
M	Other not elsewhere classified activities	28.7	93.8	112.0		0.1	0.1	0.1	
Total by activities		45896.0	63318.0	75778.0		100.0	100.0	100.0	
D Manufacturing industry									
DA	Food products, beverages and tobacco	3115.4	3778.0	4530.3		18.9	15.9	16.4	
DB	Textiles and textile products	237.6	334.4	323.5		1.4	1.4	1.2	
DC	Leather and leather products								
DD	Wood and wood products	1862.4	2847.2	2985.5		11.3	12.0	10.8	
DE	Pulp, paper & prod.; publish.& printing								
DF	Coke, ref. Petroleum prod. & nuclear fuel	35.0	56.2	68.9		0.2	0.2	0.2	
DG	Chemicals, prod.& man-made fibres	1871.7	2455.0	2562.6		11.3	10.3	9.3	
DH	Rubber and plastic products	1042.5	1473.9	1978.9		6.3	6.2	7.1	
DI	Other non-metallic mineral products								
DJ	Basic metals & fabricated metal prod.	887.5	2014.2	2430.0		5.4	8.5	8.8	
DK	Machinery and equipment n.e.c.	741.4	901.1	1355.8		4.5	3.8	4.9	
DL	Electrical and optical equipment	651.6	804.4	853.7		3.9	3.4	3.1	
DM	transport equipment	2760.5	4465.1	4930.1		16.7	18.7	17.8	
DN	Manufacturing n.e.c.								
	other not elsewhere classified activities	3293.1	4928.2	5680.4		20.0	20.7	20.5	
D	Manufacturing industry total	16498.7	23824.6	27699.7		100.0	100.0	100.0	

Table 10.17 Slovakia: inward FDI stock by economic activity

NACE	Classification	2003	2004	2005	2006	2003	2004	2005	2006
		EUR million				In % of total			
A	Agriculture, hunting and forestry	32.8	44.3	47.1	52.9	0.4	0.4	0.4	0.4
B	Fishing								
C	Mining and quarrying	65.8	65.9	69.8	79.1	0.8	0.6	0.6	0.6
D	Manufacturing	3029.0	4134.6	4490.5	5380.4	35.8	40.4	40.5	39.1
E	Electricity, gas and water supply	981.0	980.9	1011.2	1909.0	11.6	9.6	9.1	13.9
F	Construction	69.1	74.1	83.5	96.3	0.8	0.7	0.8	0.7
G	Wholesale, retail trade, repair of veh. etc.	1070.3	1318.7	1358.9	1584.9	12.6	12.9	12.2	11.5
H	Hotels and restaurants	46.9	53.1	62.0	68.6	0.6	0.5	0.6	0.5
I	Transport, storage and communication	867.6	936.2	1008.9	1161.6	10.2	9.2	9.1	8.4
J	Financial intermediation	1967.4	2160.1	2420.1	2649.4	23.2	21.1	21.8	19.2
K	Real estate, renting & business activities	274.0	374.9	460.3	691.5	3.2	3.7	4.1	5.0
L	Public administr., defence, comp.soc.sec.								
M	Education								
N	Health and social work	35.1	40.5	42.9	46.9	0.4	0.4	0.4	0.3
O	Other community, social & pers.services	27.7	39.2	39.1	45.3	0.3	0.4	0.4	0.3
P	Private househ. With employed persons								
Q	Extra-territorial organizations and bodies								
Total by activities		8466.8	10222.5	11094.3	13766.1	100.0	100.0	100.0	100.0
D Manufacturing industry									
DA	Food products, beverages and tobacco	390.0	498.9	495.5	551.6	12.9	12.1	11.0	10.3
DB	Textiles and textile products	39.0	42.3	49.1	70.1	1.3	1.0	1.1	1.3
DC	Leather and leather products	25.6	27.5	30.3	35.6	0.8	0.7	0.7	0.7
DD	Wood and wood products	32.0	48.7	53.5	64.1	1.1	1.2	1.2	1.2
DE	Pulp, paper & prod.; publish.& printing	138.5	145.2	146.4	174.5	4.6	3.5	3.3	3.2
DF	Coke, ref. Petroleum prod. & nuclear fuel	351.1	620.8	634.9	695.0	11.6	15.0	14.1	12.9
DG	Chemicals, prod.& man-made fibres	179.1	287.8	238.9	259.9	5.9	7.0	5.3	4.8
DH	Rubber and plastic products	100.7	177.9	184.8	235.7	3.3	4.3	4.1	4.4
DI	Other non-metallic mineral products	177.9	177.1	180.8	205.8	5.9	4.3	4.0	3.8
DJ	Basic metals & fabricated metal prod.	1005.3	1166.2	1140.5	1335.9	33.2	28.2	25.4	24.8
DK	Machinery and equipment n.e.c.	175.7	306.0	329.2	369.6	5.8	7.4	7.3	6.9
DL	Electrical and optical equipment	207.6	277.9	339.4	400.3	6.9	6.7	7.6	7.4
DM	Transport equipment	156.2	314.7	563.5	879.0	5.2	7.6	12.5	16.3
DN	Manufacturing n.e.c.	50.6	43.9	103.8	103.4	1.7	1.1	2.3	1.9
D	Manufacturing industry total	3029.0	4134.6	4490.5	5380.4	100.0	100.0	100.0	100.0

Table 10.18 Slovenia: inward FDI stock by economic activity

NACE	Classification	2003	2004	2005	2006	2003	2004	2005	2006
		EUR million				In % of total			
A	Agriculture, hunting and forestry	1.9	2.5	2.5		0.0	0.0	0.0	
B	Fishing								
C	Mining and quarrying	2.1	3.0	2.8		0.0	0.1	0.0	
D	Manufacturing	2446.2	2609.1	2614.7		48.5	46.8	43.7	
E	Electricity, gas and water supply	266.6	265.4	269.2		5.3	4.8	4.5	
F	Construction	−3.0	−1.1	17.0		−0.1	0.0	0.3	
G	Wholesale, retail trade, repair of veh. etc.	723.0	766.1	834.8		14.3	13.7	14.0	
H	Hotels and restaurants	15.1	17.3	25.9		0.3	0.3	0.4	
I	Transport, storage and communication	241.9	193.8	219.8		4.8	3.5	3.7	
J	Financial intermediation	827.0	1064.2	1179.3		16.4	19.1	19.7	
K	Real estate, renting & business activities	582.9	609.1	771.2		11.5	10.9	12.9	
L	Public administr., defence, comp.soc.sec.								
M	Education	0.3	0.3	0.3		0.0	0.0	0.0	
N	Health and social work	2.0	2.0	1.0		0.0	0.0	0.0	
O	Other community, social & pers. services	28.8	51.9	45.8		0.6	0.9	0.8	
	Other not elsewhere classified activities	−88.0	−4.0	−4.2		−1.7	−0.1	−0.1	
Total by activities		5046.8	5579.6	5980.1		100.0	100.0	100.0	
D Manufacturing industry									
DA	Food products, beverages and tobacco	71.2	51.8	17.0		2.9	2.0	0.7	
DB	Textiles and textile products	48.0	51.9	49.1		2.0	2.0	1.9	
DC	Leather and leather products	37.7	25.6	45.0		1.5	1.0	1.7	
DD	Wood and wood products	30.6	39.7	39.1		1.3	1.5	1.5	
DE	Pulp, paper & prod.; publish.& printing	246.4	315.6	298.1		10.1	12.1	11.4	
DF	Coke, ref. petroleum prod. & nuclear fuel								
DG	Chemicals, prod.& man-made fibres	1084.4	993.0	942.1		44.3	38.1	36.0	
DH	Rubber and plastic products	260.6	295.6	307.2		10.7	11.3	11.7	
DI	Other non-metallic mineral products	134.9	140.8	151.4		5.5	5.4	5.8	
DJ	Basic metals & fabricated metal prod.	107.4	130.3	118.4		4.4	5.0	4.5	
DK	Machinery and equipment n.e.c.	176.6	229.9	246.0		7.2	8.8	9.4	
DL	Electrical and optical equipment	119.4	133.9	132.0		4.9	5.1	5.0	
DM	Transport equipment	124.9	197.3	256.1		5.1	7.6	9.8	
DN	Manufacturing n.e.c.	4.1	3.7	13.2		0.2	0.1	0.5	
D	Manufacturing industry total	2446.2	2609.1	2614.7		100.0	100.0	100.0	

Table 10.19 Estonia: inward FDI stock by economic activity

NACE	Classification	2003	2004	2005	2006	2003	2004	2005	2006
		EUR million				In % of total			
A	Agriculture, hunting and forestry	15.2	38.7	57.0	66.9	0.3	0.5	0.5	0.5
B	Fishing	2.8	1.7	1.8	2.1	0.1	0.0	0.0	0.0
C	Mining and quarrying	20.9	34.3	38.4	45.6	0.4	0.5	0.4	0.4
D	Manufacturing	939.0	1234.9	1426.5	1735.9	16.9	16.7	13.3	14.0
E	Electricity, gas and water supply	124.8	96.2	232.0	252.0	2.2	1.3	2.2	2.0
F	Construction	128.9	94.3	128.4	179.5	2.3	1.3	1.2	1.4
G	Wholesale, retail trade, repair of veh. etc.	822.3	737.0	836.1	993.2	14.8	10.0	7.8	8.0
H	Hotels and restaurants	87.3	66.7	37.2	27.8	1.6	0.9	0.3	0.2
I	Transport, storage and communication	913.3	390.4	325.7	643.4	16.4	5.3	3.0	5.2
J	Financial intermediation	1453.3	2326.1	4916.8	5636.3	26.2	31.5	45.7	45.5
K	Real estate, renting & business activities	573.2	1675.6	1638.6	1639.8	10.3	22.7	15.2	13.2
L	Public administr., defence, comp.soc.sec.		0.0				0.0		
M	Education	1.4	1.8	2.0	1.6	0.0	0.0	0.0	0.0
N	Health and social work	5.6	4.5	5.0	11.9	0.1	0.1	0.0	0.1
O	Other community, social & pers.services	336.9	477.7	994.6	1031.6	6.1	6.5	9.3	8.3
	Other not elsewhere classified activities	128.4	198.8	108.3	122.4	2.3	2.7	1.0	1.0
Total by activities		5553.2	7378.5	10748.3	12389.9	100.0	100.0	100.0	100.0
D Manufacturing industry									
DA	Food products, beverages and tobacco	200.1	181.0	256.8	280.9	21.3	14.7	18.0	16.2
DB	Textiles and textile products	73.8	74.3	87.2	203.1	7.9	6.0	6.1	11.7
DC	Leather and leather products	1.5	4.2	2.0	1.7	0.2	0.3	0.1	0.1
DD	Wood and wood products	116.0	314.8	335.8	376.6	12.4	25.5	23.5	21.7
DE	Pulp, paper & prod.; publish.& printing	64.3	130.0	139.8	160.8	6.8	10.5	9.8	9.3
DF	Coke, ref. Petroleum prod. & nuclear fuel		0.1				0.0		
DG	Chemicals, prod.& man-made fibres	62.6	66.8	92.6	87.1	6.7	5.4	6.5	5.0
DH	Rubber and plastic products	25.1	28.8	35.3	47.4	2.7	2.3	2.5	2.7
DI	Other non-metallic mineral products	117.4	127.8	137.6	175.1	12.5	10.4	9.6	10.1

(*continued*)

Table 10.19 (continued)

NACE	Classification	2003	2004	2005	2006	2003	2004	2005	2006
		EUR million				In % of total			
DJ	Basic metals & fabricated metal prod.	58.8	68.3	74.6	107.5	6.3	5.5	5.2	6.2
DK	Machinery and equipment n.e.c.	16.1	16.0	21.5	21.5	1.7	1.3	1.5	1.2
DL	Electrical and optical equipment	71.1	107.6	119.8	148.7	7.6	8.7	8.4	8.6
DM	Transport equipment	77.3	59.3	60.5	60.8	8.2	4.8	4.2	3.5
DN	Manufacturing n.e.c.	54.6	55.2	62.3	64.0	5.8	4.5	4.4	3.7
	Other not elsewhere classified industries	0.3	0.6	0.7	0.8	0.0	0.1	0.1	0.0
D	Manufacturing industry total	939.0	1234.9	1426.5	1735.9	100.0	100.0	100.0	100.0

Table 10.20 Latvia: inward FDI stock by economic activity

NACE	Classification	2003	2004	2005	2006	2003	2004	2005	2006
		EUR million				In % of total			
A	Agriculture, hunting and forestry	41.5	62.0	61.3	70.4	1.6	1.9	1.5	1.2
B	Fishing	0.1	1.3	1.7	1.7	0.0	0.0	0.0	0.0
C	Mining and quarrying	17.1	17.1	21.6	28.3	0.7	0.5	0.5	0.5
D	Manufacturing	411.7	471.3	539.6	564.7	15.7	14.2	12.8	9.8
E	Electricity, gas and water supply	91.4	275.5	466.1	496.0	3.5	8.3	11.1	8.6
F	Construction	30.1	60.6	68.9	94.2	1.1	1.8	1.6	1.6
G	Wholesale, retail trade, repair of veh. etc.	472.3	533.9	586.7	734.5	18.0	16.1	13.9	12.8
H	Hotels and restaurants	33.4	42.2	40.0	54.5	1.3	1.3	0.9	0.9
I	Transport, storage and communication	328.5	517.1	489.8	510.0	12.5	15.6	11.6	8.9
J	Financial intermediation	397.6	538.7	890.2	1412.4	15.1	16.2	21.1	24.6
K	Real estate, renting & business activities	623.7	665.6	731.8	1023.5	23.7	20.1	17.4	17.8
L	Public administr., defence, comp.soc.sec.	1.8	1.4	1.0	0.6	0.1	0.0	0.0	0.0
M	Education	0.7	1.3	3.3	0.9	0.0	0.0	0.1	0.0
N	Health and social work	3.1	3.0	4.0	3.0	0.1	0.1	0.1	0.1
O	Other community, social & pers. services	26.0	37.6	56.9	71.4	1.0	1.1	1.4	1.2
	Other not elsewhere classified activities	151.2	86.8	250.5	678.4	5.7	2.6	5.9	11.8
Total by activities		2630.2	3315.4	4213.4	5744.5	100.0	100.0	100.0	100.0
D Manufacturing industry									
DA	Food products, beverages and tobacco	113.8	100.3	118.5	144.2	27.6	21.3	22.0	25.5
DB	Textiles and textile products	45.7	69.1	14.1	14.1	11.1	14.7	2.6	2.5
DC	Leather and leather products	0.6	1.0			0.1	0.2		
DD	Wood and wood products	94.1	106.1	136.6	135.9	22.9	22.5	25.3	24.1
DE	Pulp, paper & prod.; publish.& printing	19.4	25.9	28.3	22.5	4.7	5.5	5.2	4.0
DF	Coke, ref. Petroleum prod. & nuclear fuel								
DG	Chemicals, prod.& man-made fibres	34.3	19.2	18.8	8.3	8.3	4.1	3.5	1.5
DH	Rubber and plastic products	11.3	13.7	13.1	11.4	2.7	2.9	2.4	2.0
DI	Other non-metallic mineral products	38.9	74.8	139.7	152.7	9.4	15.9	25.9	27.0

(*continued*)

Table 10.20 (continued)

NACE	Classification	2003	2004	2005	2006	2003	2004	2005	2006
		EUR million				In % of total			
DJ	Basic metals & fabricated metal prod.	16.4	18.9	24.2	26.7	4.0	4.0	4.5	4.7
DK	Machinery and equipment n.e.c.	18.8	4.4	4.6	3.3	4.6	0.9	0.9	0.6
DL	Electrical and optical equipment	8.2	14.1	16.2	24.8	2.0	3.0	3.0	4.4
DM	Transport equipment	1.2	9.8	13.2	13.1	0.3	2.1	2.4	2.3
DN	Manufacturing n.e.c.	9.0	14.0	12.3	7.7	2.2	3.0	2.3	1.4
D	Manufacturing industry total	411.7	471.3	539.6	564.7	100.0	100.0	100.0	100.0

Table 10.21 Lithuania: inward FDI stock by economic activity

NACE	Classification	2003	2004	2005	2006	2003	2004	2005	2006
		EUR million				In % of total			
A + B	Agriculture, hunting and forestry, fishing	32.4	37.0	48.7	48.4	0.8	0.8	0.7	0.6
C	Mining and quarrying	33.4	40.6	46.3	45.1	0.8	0.9	0.7	0.5
D	Manufacturing	1233.8	1593.8	2739.1	3326.1	31.1	34.0	39.6	39.9
E	Electricity, gas and water supply	175.2	347.3	867.2	883.1	4.4	7.4	12.5	10.6
F	Construction	46.0	56.2	82.0	125.5	1.2	1.2	1.2	1.5
G	Wholesale, retail trade, repair of veh. etc.	710.6	748.4	763.7	891.8	17.9	16.0	11.0	10.7
H	Hotels and restaurants	65.2	56.5	61.5	55.1	1.6	1.2	0.9	0.7
I	Transport, storage and communication	678.9	672.1	946.6	904.4	17.1	14.3	13.7	10.9
J	Financial intermediation	624.3	677.1	852.7	1329.5	15.7	14.4	12.3	16.0
K	Real estate, renting & business activities	290.9	398.8	441.6	631.7	7.3	8.5	6.4	7.6
L	Public administr., defence, comp.soc.sec.								
M + N	Education Health and social work	6.9	7.2	8.3	11.9	0.2	0.2	0.1	0.1
O	Other community, social & pers. services	59.5	42.5	63.0	79.2	1.5	0.9	0.9	1.0
	Other not elsewhere classified activities	9.5	10.7			0.2	0.2		
	Private purchases and sales of real estate	1.1	1.4		1.7	0.0	0.0		0.0
Total by activities		3967.6	4689.7	6920.7	8333.5	100.0	100.0	100.0	100.0
D Manufacturing industry									
DA	Food products, beverages and tobacco	464.0	483.7	468.8	415.3	37.6	30.3	17.1	12.5
DB	Textiles and textile products	117.1	103.9	139.2	125.1	9.5	6.5	5.1	3.8
DC	Leather and leather products	3.7	2.4	0.6	0.4	0.3	0.2	0.0	0.0
DD	Wood and wood products	56.4	63.1	59.7	87.4	4.6	4.0	2.2	2.6
DE	Pulp, paper & prod.; publish.& printing	45.0	46.7	59.3	63.1	3.6	2.9	2.2	1.9
DF	Coke, ref. Petroleum prod. & nuclear fuel	158.7	271.6		1764.9	12.9	17.0		53.1
DG	Chemicals, prod.& man-made fibres	67.1	113.0		240.4	5.4	7.1		7.2
DH	Rubber and plastic products	34.1	164.3	199.2	203.5	2.8	10.3	7.3	6.1
DI	Other non-metallic mineral products	62.9	65.4	87.2	99.1	5.1	4.1	3.2	3.0
DJ	Basic metals & fabricated metal prod.	23.8	28.2	30.0	34.6	1.9	1.8	1.1	1.0

(continued)

Table 10.21 (continued)

NACE	Classification	2003	2004	2005	2006	2003	2004	2005	2006
		EUR million				In % of total			
DK	Machinery and equipment n.e.c.	15.1	21.3	81.0	65.2	1.2	1.3	3.0	2.0
DL	Electrical and optical equipment	97.5	125.9	96.6	84.1	7.9	7.9	3.5	2.5
DM	Transport equipment	70.3	75.5		92.8	5.7	4.7		2.8
DN	Manufacturing n.e.c.	18.2	29.0	37.0	50.4	1.5	1.8	1.4	1.5
	Other not elsewhere classified industries			1480.7				54.1	
D	Manufacturing industry total	1233.8	1593.8	2739.1	3326.1	100.0	100.0	100.0	100.0

Table 10.22 Bulgaria: inward FDI stock by economic activity

NACE	Classification	2003	2004	2005	2006	2003	2004	2005	2006
		EUR million				In % of total			
A	Agriculture, hunting and forestry	40.7	46.3	58.3		0.8	0.7	0.6	
B	Fishing	0.3	2.9	2.8		0.0	0.0	0.0	
C	Mining and quarrying	51.3	65.7	90.1		1.0	1.0	0.9	
D	Manufacturing	1754.0	1900.2	1242.2		35.5	28.1	12.8	
E	Electricity, gas and water supply	73.7	47.3	20.5		1.5	0.7	0.2	
F	Construction	75.9	164.2	368.1		1.5	2.4	3.8	
G	Wholesale, retail trade, repair of veh. etc.	871.5	1203.8	998.9		17.6	17.8	10.3	
H	Hotels and restaurants	84.9	108.3	110.1		1.7	1.6	1.1	
I	Transport, storage and communication	569.7	1207.5	2260.4		11.5	17.8	23.4	
J	Financial intermediation	925.5	1351.6	3376.8		18.7	20.0	34.9	
K	Real estate, renting & business activities	416.2	531.4	928.6		8.4	7.9	9.6	
L	Public administr., defence, comp.soc.sec.								
M	Education	0.2	0.7			0.0	0.0		
N	Health and social work	0.7	1.5	1.4		0.0	0.0	0.0	
O	Other community, social & pers. services	55.1	54.0	71.5		1.1	0.8	0.7	
	Other elsewhere not classified activities	26.5	83.4	144.7		0.5	1.2	1.5	
Total by activities		4946.2	6768.7	9674.3		100.0	100.0	100.0	

Table 10.23 Romania: inward FDI stock by economic activity

NACE	Classification	2003	2004	2005	2006	2003	2004	2005	2006
		EUR million				In % of total			
A + B	Agriculture, hunting and forestry, fishing	86.0	100.0	106.0		0.9	0.7	0.5	
C	Mining and quarrying	21.0	1225.0	1602.0		0.2	8.1	7.3	
D	Manufacturing	4917.0	6876.0	8170.0		50.9	45.7	37.3	
E	Electricity, gas and water supply	66.0	83.0	917.0		0.7	0.6	4.2	
F	Construction	212.0	166.0	179.0		2.2	1.1	0.8	
G	Wholesale, retail trade, repair of veh. etc.	1106.0	2185.0	3279.0		11.4	14.5	15.0	
H	Hotels and restaurants	109.0	29.0	42.0		1.1	0.2	0.2	
I	Transport, storage and communication	1563.0	1749.0	2685.0		16.2	11.6	12.3	
J	Financial intermediation	882.0	1711.0	3176.0		9.1	11.4	14.5	
K	Real estate, renting & business activities	674.0	848.0	1679.0		7.0	5.6	7.7	
L + Q	Other services	26.0	68.0	50.0		0.3	0.5	0.2	
Total by activities		9662.0	15040.0	21885.0		100.0	100.0	100.0	
D manufacturing industry									
DA	Food products, beverages and tobacco	935.0	1109.0	1427.0		19.0	16.1	17.5	
DBDC	Textiles and prod. Leather and prod.	427.0	503.0	575.0		8.7	7.3	7.0	
DD	Wood and wood products	274.0	507.0	615.0		5.6	7.4	7.5	
DE	Pulp, paper & prod.; publish.& printing								
DF	Coke, ref. petroleum prod. & nuclear fuel	394.0	387.0	896.0		8.0	5.6	11.0	
DG	Chemicals, prod.& man-made fibres								
DH	Rubber and plastic products								
DI	Other non-metallic mineral products	448.0	603.0	704.0		9.1	8.8	8.6	
DJ	Basic metals & fabricated metal prod.	1116.0	1981.0	1791.0		22.7	28.8	21.9	
DK	Machinery and equipment n.e.c.	435.0	274.0	348.0		8.8	4.0	4.3	
DL	Electrical and optical equipment	224.0	434.0	404.0		4.6	6.3	4.9	
DM	Transport equipment	527.0	860.0	1112.0		10.7	12.5	13.6	
DN	Manufacturing n.e.c.								
	Other not elsewhere classified industries	137.0	218.0	298.0		2.8	3.2	3.6	
D	Manufacturing industry total	4917.0	6876.0	8170.0		100.0	100.0	100.0	

Source: WIIW

Table 10.24 Czech rep. exports to the EU-15 (in thousand USD, current prices)

NACE	1993	1994	1995	1996	1997	1998	1999	2000	2001	2002	2003	2004
	6,387,572	5,625,030	7,395,082	1,262,2783	1,363,2948	18,661,380	1,856,4292	19,917,740	23,009,380	26,303,993	3,401,6748	45,793,659
A + B	238,833	301,863	345,929	294,785	286,685	269,191	345,395	271,298	260,634	298,655	396,707	437,008
C	279,288	233,760	289,366	362,392	251,090	245,792	217,731	174,938	209,031	199,977	230,358	298,074
D	5,568,604	4,864,736	6,562,619	1,174,6516	1,279,4625	17,839,672	17,735,344	19,153,579	2,221,1741	25,393,502	3,278,6326	44,138,896
DA	304,376	206,303	25,7974	309,479	302,851	297,423	273,105	309,060	363,051	371,181	462,750	774,104
DB-DC	659,173	543,815	645,944	1,258,718	1,286,585	1,527,456	1,497,862	1,506,116	1,632,863	1,671,032	1,945,927	2,437,517
DD	236,289	333,259	402,737	472,853	431,645	474,246	492,023	458,394	438,842	438,510	549,524	714,636
DE	183,845	152,319	244,882	336,187	332,614	440,449	504,972	590,409	628,551	755,556	1,051,517	1,251,291
DF	127,577	117,161	148,503	213,400	201,967	173,764	209,441	250,171	230,176	284,246	334,486	294,315
DG	612,328	470,202	671,563	908,042	845,830	902,480	818,378	913,373	924,790	907,135	1,217,851	1,686,572
DH	135,576	140,432	230,585	471,588	576,551	767,333	880,291	971,978	1,088,317	1,407,371	1,737,705	2,331,549
DI	531,115	404,706	452,194	729,925	607,822	735,537	76,2912	772,630	781,793	828,935	1,016,318	1,173,656
DJ	995,860	1,022,185	1,444,744	1,863,572	1,936,141	2,410,542	2,359,393	2,531,273	2,694,362	2,894,033	3,751,800	5,338,999
DK	506,065	442,813	654,433	1,496,671	1,583,760	2,345,191	2,185,558	2,310,372	2,747,897	3,138,580	4,327,508	5,965,164
DL	436,629	351,367	512,735	1,683,306	1,995,569	3,457,195	3,050,080	3,851,464	5,285,651	6,397,478	8,426,990	11,833,949
DM	549,551	390,706	528,807	1,303,278	1,998,961	3,258,341	3,775,476	3,740,835	4,301,309	5,006,871	6,406,458	8,184,094
DN	290,220	289,469	367,518	699,497	69,4330	1,049,713	925,855	947,505	1,094,140	1,292,573	1,557,493	1,954,676
E	25,317	25,078	30,116	60,337	69,018	78,997	79,415	156,163	154,645	221,654	329,687	424,018

Sources: OECD, STAN Bilateral Trade Database (BTD); International Trade by Commodity Statistics (ITCS), 2006

Table 10.25 Poland, exports to the EU-15 (in thousand USD, current prices)

NACE	1992	1993	1994	1995	1996	1997	1998	1999	2000	2001	2002	2003	2004
	8,470,333	9,619,118	11,748,917	1,585,2126	16,004,801	16,322,642	19,055,106	19,100,701	21,913,093	24,748,662	27,933,215	36,580,655	4,9657,513
A + B	468,811	378,551	403,622	477,840	419,387	381,477	410,930	357,790	332,008	352,410	391,284	565,341	855,014
C	728,509	805,195	802,544	730,680	758,562	802,633	712,170	592,829	619,639	813,120	792,653	654,043	1,163,991
D	7,014,308	8,295,793	10,419,685	14,505,740	14,702,896	14,803,488	17,755,629	17,951,034	20,709,627	23,292,114	26,391,923	34,816,799	46,877,020
DA	833,161	721,415	818,679	929,584	936,661	945,775	976,289	968,684	1,002,416	1,159,632	1,261,176	1,819,602	2,964,372
DB-DC	799,663	1,855,414	2,194,735	2,810,414	2,898,600	2,777,330	3,033,124	2,859,974	2,628,681	2,738,677	2,743,969	3,215,461	3,448,723
DD	505,383	478,845	643,429	815,414	752,210	794,759	889,798	920,290	897,177	841,873	922,572	1,253,682	1,603,068
DE	99,086	116,840	174,974	326,447	302,559	345,990	394,616	452,572	594,665	700,659	880,661	1,206,153	1,386,405
DF	230,640	201,146	258,669	343,532	263,016	324,763	316,681	289,919	489,163	591,077	570,280	662,110	1,188,230
DG	725,371	519,726	650,517	1,008,032	896,988	870,069	948,480	849,770	1,099,487	1,013,619	1,140,293	1,563,808	1,938,914
DH	116,535	141,479	189,426	296,633	346,008	371,586	445,418	554,827	633,012	806,100	1,044,965	1,496,862	1,980,518
DI	267,580	302,020	396,569	488,988	511,098	453,718	484,319	491,255	470,354	530,607	570,857	773,573	920,874
DJ	1,574,337	1,455,976	2,050,229	2,808,907	2,423,622	2,532,478	2,678,045	2,550,165	2,848,819	2,883,449	3,053,667	4,032,256	5,754,619
DK	450,628	377,580	462,415	703,818	799,412	819,014	993,488	1,082,869	1,243,368	1,491,402	1,791,947	2,557,061	3,541,984
DL	363,933	424,785	607,273	968,080	1,292,470	1,661,007	2,221,108	2,381,317	2,552,145	2,973,325	3,559,227	4,579,301	5,817,722
DM	626,791	1,118,450	1,143,399	1,837,585	1,948,947	1,540,360	2,794,675	2,833,198	4,395,169	5,476,126	6,482,069	8,485,710	12,309,093
DN	421,200	582,117	829,371	1,168,306	1,331,305	1,366,639	1,579,588	1,716,194	1,855,171	2,085,568	2,370,240	3,171,220	4,020,796
E	25,836	51,127	64,477	69,800	65,326	65,987	81,954	90,399	79,114	106,141	144,800	222,970	231,546

Sources: OECD, STAN Bilateral Trade Database (BTD); International Trade by Commodity Statistics (ITCS), 2006

Table 10.26 Hungary, exports to the EU-15 (in thousand USD, current prices)

NACE	1992	1993	1994	1995	1996	1997	1998	1999	2000	2001	2002	2003	2004
	6,668,567	5,173,591	6,814,279	8,079,624	8,249,981	13,602,278	16,781,607	19,067,766	21,116,589	22,651,183	25,782,435	31,668,565	39,304,972
A + B	474,076	376,609	452,131	501,977	466,775	419,928	490,491	433,839	402,995	478,998	578,727	655,171	880,656
C	8,367	6,451	5,650	7,621	8,525	8,024	7,510	7,310	6,882	6,740	6,870	8,120	13,946
D	6,106,496	4,721,410	6,248,947	7,427,371	7,685,886	12,999,945	16,122,262	18,484,286	20,543,488	21,821,257	24,831,925	30,866,018	38,143,741
DA	944,643	757,676	816,353	833,797	903,476	818,653	789,148	779,732	711,194	807,207	825,506	1,074,920	1,299,269
DB-DC	1,643,837	1,105,502	1,379,569	1,427,466	1,567,268	1,583,403	1,754,226	1,822,930	1,717,945	1,787,264	1,786,962	1,980,513	2,037,983
DD	1,430,88	98,188	121,810	157,642	167,721	185,616	213,695	239,698	228,364	218,131	249,759	287,132	299,784
DE	91,825	63,400	90,776	82,642	108,187	136,806	170,674	195,645	209,526	231,580	231,567	320,223	357,442
DF	232,083	220,990	251,973	256,735	276,159	224,232	215,434	197,070	208,267	281,155	294,830	298,756	360,688
DG	575,459	454,189	542,689	706,231	594,039	641,315	747,805	662,353	771,834	740,560	815,974	1,104,709	1,466,720
DH	138,317	127,077	176,139	218,139	228,584	297,046	362,090	404,992	453,995	480,221	523,189	686,540	917,895
DI	161,944	154,466	151,543	169,548	174,608	189,815	217,435	227,120	217,152	214,823	231,695	352,977	381,463
DJ	597,719	445,407	686,254	952,527	863,455	1,008,448	1,076,065	1,010,033	1,123,022	1,112,921	1,154,884	1,397,748	1,867,467
DK	484,610	384,685	501,984	676,473	715,575	924,453	1,042,071	1,136,205	1,263,951	1,497,472	1,832,473	2,486,154	3,288,760
DL	713,369	632,108	1,010,023	1,458,307	1,485,094	4,624,676	5,564,243	6,628,218	8,410,068	8,667,193	10,169,540	13,218,032	16,948,176
DM	199,812	129,076	339,977	257,860	256,288	1,962,068	3,487,125	4,553,779	4,628,601	5,072,551	5,474,306	6,551,245	7,782,377
DN	172,522	146,843	175,374	228,139	271,754	387,679	482,233	626,440	599,513	635,697	1,241,058	859,556	970,304
E	0	0	0	0	0	82,747	79,624	77,086	66,629	0	0	5,642	9,030

Sources: OECD, STAN Bilateral Trade Database (BTD); International Trade by Commodity Statistics (ITCS), 2006

Table 10.27 Slovakia, exports to the EU-15 (in thousand USD, current prices)

ISIC Rev.3	1992	1993	1994	1995	1996	1997	1998	1999	2000	2001	2002	2003	2004
						4,540,074	5,966,042	5,974,612	6,968,634	7,554,326	8,765,652	13,316,282	16,477,581
A + B						84,785	64,719	92,402	74,645	92,190	91,683	111,086	153,373
C						18,472	17,433	12,890	11,968	11,999	15,421	19,577	37,334
D						440,9523	5,854,439	5,838,967	6,849,321	7,408,841	8,610,249	13,098,365	16,146,026
DA						73,468	63,975	50,283	60,542	71,090	66,420	81,853	174,617
DB-DC						663,930	727,260	756,633	762,164	809,125	957,481	1,142,307	1,264,590
DD						115,838	122,910	128,189	130,968	129,992	152,447	194,147	240,189
DE						172,166	185,481	203,425	261,217	320,380	351,150	425,801	597,917
DF						82,101	75,232	129,927	224,291	204,926	229,938	288,255	617,911
DG						387,704	382,903	289,515	362,625	350,220	420,617	470,864	639,599
DH						139,763	153,251	164,320	178,862	255,074	373,084	543,217	695,183
DI						159,525	161,513	164,231	161,983	173,746	190,896	228,317	257,591
DJ						765,239	781,454	691,377	795,259	928,541	986,749	1,326,721	1,779,512
DK						347,690	445,237	558,818	649,314	771,926	820,668	1,236,375	1,642,597
DL						491,968	685,029	746,408	840,716	987,659	1,161,003	1,834,604	2,877,009
DM						851,795	1,892,095	1,787,429	2,155,916	2,081,193	2,435,788	4,505,522	4,666,321
DN						158,337	178,099	168,414	265,466	324,969	464,006	820,382	692,991
E						0	0	0	54	6,243	6,337	25,681	29,249

Sources: OECD, STAN Bilateral Trade Database (BTD); International Trade by Commodity Statistics (ITCS), 2006

Table 10.28 Slovenia, exports to the EU-15 (in thousand USD, current prices)

NACE	1993	1994	1995	1996	1997	1998	1999	2000	2001	2002	2003	2004
			5,578,007	5,496,002	5,308,675	5,816,612	5,667,244	5,609,809	5,713,676	6,132,035	7,372,354	8,296,855
A + B			44,033	36,950	35,503	33,831	28,061	24,647	20,835	24,856	30,344	41,373
C			2,255	2,179	1,958	5,821	5,895	7,025	8,619	3,404	4,498	5,238
D			5,509,529	5,432,517	5,242,245	5,740,269	5,609,398	5,547,591	5,560,873	5,950,927	7,140,390	7,745,279
DA			70,560	82,474	74,577	816,88	83,490	71,552	67,899	56,917	77,381	85,195
DB-DC			977,197	913,142	836,844	773,023	665,360	588,512	586,772	557,169	580,213	553,808
DD			284,487	243,194	209,902	226,022	218,751	195,455	176,927	181,478	211,855	187,972
DE			285,634	225,600	200,164	198,623	176,320	194,723	174,140	172,267	204,830	217,162
DF			4,431	10,862	8,024	875	2,685	161	483	1,187	1,437	2,449
DG			268,136	230,991	212,864	223,772	245,965	265,072	259,240	285,087	383,318	421,523
DH			222,086	207,143	176,344	203,850	209,011	207,796	225,365	250,851	330,462	326,519
DI			163,710	173,781	155,254	168,786	162,783	145,390	150,250	158,152	182,852	172,013
DJ			741,203	729,734	733,066	732,299	797,047	828,488	815,864	819,548	1,000,123	1,162,145
DK			752,858	755,770	741,835	846,770	808,447	776,717	831,447	906,837	1,161,663	1,225,178
DL			540,436	561,647	563,521	600,544	612,524	691,775	669,666	748,948	950,264	948,558
DM			819,932	882,933	867,173	1,179,426	1,046,186	1,045,449	1,050,776	1,252,372	1,407,829	1,744,364
DN			378,737	415,146	462,474	504,427	580,674	536,131	553,869	559,615	647,929	687,454
E			0	0	6	4,583	731	734	87,849	119,269	150,301	163,846

Sources: OECD, STAN Bilateral Trade Database (BTD); International Trade by Commodity Statistics (ITCS), 2006

Table 10.29 Estonia, exports to the EU-15 (in thousand USD, current prices)

NACE	1993	1994	1995	1996	1997	1998	1999	2000	2001	2002	2003	2004
			1,234,593	1,468,748	1,799,149	1,915,442	2,096,451	3,167,715	2,857,827	2,881,065	3,612,615	4,335,966
A + B			91,253	91,227	145,083	181,762	192,777	154,543	123,237	130,399	148,148	124,170
C			54,159	39,020	41,170	61,019	74,190	117,721	166,241	90,190	129,140	137,481
D			999,874	1,277,604	1,529,457	1,590,771	1,746,748	2,809,677	2,490,617	2,622,846	3,294,758	3,909,192
DA			37,502	47,708	61,009	59,176	58,383	66,367	77,322	91,168	121,010	173,086
DB-DC			236,844	285,732	309,619	346,315	344,833	368,563	385,509	426,893	525,227	493,901
DD			127,013	173,430	203,706	203,693	251,607	277,283	281,953	325,899	445,925	435,919
DE			15,340	14,663	16,651	20,645	21,834	28,576	30,183	34,502	43,404	43,563
DF			120,993	260,396	366,193	175,274	150,168	303,094	261,991	377,068	259,782	624,432
DG			73,390	72,248	48,766	54,300	42,987	62,245	60,369	46,371	74,327	146,623
DH			10,223	10,358	11,497	16,335	21,314	30,200	31,966	44,573	60,746	61,917
DI			21,861	20,229	28,145	23,526	27,324	27,382	27,302	25,881	38,931	36,276
DJ			108,424	90,968	92,103	114,891	123,265	142,072	172,820	172,853	269,421	341,168
DK			28,365	37,916	49,602	58,172	68,390	67,943	85,242	83,308	130,359	141,310
DL			144,909	167,594	234,394	370,995	477,485	1,250,459	839,920	697,150	918,852	941,923
DM			9,568	16,508	1,4455	2,2493	25,317	40,207	65,099	93,500	148,939	167,497
DN			65,126	79,853	93,290	124,879	133,825	145,008	170,579	201,808	256,313	254,928
E			0	0	0	0	0	0	0	0	0	0

Sources: OECD, STAN Bilateral Trade Database (BTD); International Trade by Commodity Statistics (ITCS), 2006

Table 10.30 Latvia, exports to the EU-15 (in thousand USD, current prices)

NACE	1993	1994	1995	1996	1997	1998	1999	2000	2001	2002	2003	2004
			1,556,950	1,642,058	1,680,959	1,599,351	1,639,201	1,853,432	1,885,347	1,983,654	2,394,940	3,165,076
A + B			180,660	127,303	152,356	206,304	164,852	179,891	158,456	206,114	237,250	256,806
C			195,813	224,779	204,421	113,694	144,664	103,660	227,931	171,358	101,003	110,943
D			1,069,694	1,201,633	1,219,515	1,228,643	1,299,187	1,524,962	1,466,817	1,582,286	2,036,317	2,721,392
DA			30,023	26,343	33,302	33,961	34,402	35,063	56,738	45,027	51,518	79,253
DB-DC			155,109	175,349	197,285	252,651	269,584	271,273	270,437	271,898	313,618	279,085
DD			224,388	297,911	419,735	475,064	545,300	584,192	552,350	602,204	788,070	797,776
DE			7,866	1,179	1,395	2,360	3,428	2,550	4,043	6,026	12,888	12,941
DF			377,566	547,567	374,097	220,673	204,902	356,674	242,844	241,674	313,471	941,148
DG			94,437	41,502	51,985	46,706	32,178	32,632	44,461	48,165	45,748	63,134
DH			2,834	1,914	3,014	4,119	4,642	8,343	10,293	14,818	21,905	24,051
DI			12,499	12,898	10,436	16,757	15,863	11,159	12,281	17,090	21,372	23,523
DJ			105,609	35,685	41,485	71,500	77,206	95,168	11,7622	142,646	210,242	202,654
DK			11,727	128,88	11,810	16,817	18,284	20,532	26,016	31,029	35,526	36,450
DL			14,142	18,775	28,638	30,996	23,136	27,510	29,147	38,240	58,543	70,710
DM			4,443	3,968	11,068	6,350	5,604	6,235	7,788	14,337	26,023	23,072
DN			29,023	25,655	35,250	50,608	64,599	72,983	92,652	108,825	136,988	152,717
E			0	0	0	0	0	0	0	0	7	0

Sources: OECD, STAN Bilateral Trade Database (BTD); International Trade by Commodity Statistics (ITCS), 2006

Table 10.31 Lithuania, exports to the EU-15 (in thousand USD, current prices)

NACE	1993	1994	1995	1996	1997	1998	1999	2000	2001	2002	2003	2004
			1,284,740	1,468,777	1,521,064	1,625,089	1,751,409	2,073,636	2,445,180	2,633,746	3,475,100	4,103,976
A + B			53,541	34,961	47,801	47,936	58,687	54,247	71,439	86,853	94,404	101,378
C			21,498	31,630	19,380	21,447	30,015	16,313	69,511	105,547	241,228	172,256
D			1,041,501	1,265,671	1,328,864	1,425,723	1,503,647	1,805,316	2,152,305	2,326,967	3,011,259	3,614,632
DA			89,441	93,049	92,916	92,705	85,019	115,639	158,965	154,501	225,982	270,402
DB-DC			289,868	391,563	492,261	572,314	602,364	624,711	714,287	765,238	869,166	868,322
DD			121,420	181,438	184,564	158,454	155,928	159,517	161,705	190,246	271,510	262,694
DE			4,194	2,461	1,755	1,948	3,544	3,224	3,186	6,398	9,922	1,708
DF			147,934	140,266	110,481	74,405	106,150	212,007	424,851	383,478	347,018	627,944
DG			185,423	213,878	177,442	199,896	158,608	211,068	184,444	204,372	289,329	290,485
DH			4,762	6,891	10,331	13,632	18,817	20,911	21,350	34,212	62,801	87,488
DI			19,543	24,564	26,577	24,953	29,134	23,837	21,950	11,895	14,338	11,445
DJ			50,319	33,007	35,939	44,289	60,486	91,406	92,473	92,804	144,471	180,388
DK			18,742	20,960	25,018	32,470	38,571	37,241	40,092	47,102	60,545	55,067
DL			68,393	101,346	107,633	128,089	133,290	144,236	154,494	187,907	348,511	426,661
DM			12,826	24,181	28,221	34,036	39,169	58,514	48,545	59,891	61,146	137,534
DN			27,911	32,001	35,365	48,392	72,509	102,729	125,669	188,338	304,993	369,555
E			0	0	0	0	0	0	0	0	0	0

Sources: OECD, STAN Bilateral Trade Database (BTD); International Trade by Commodity Statistics (ITCS), 2006

References

Algieri, B. (2004), Trade Specialisation Patterns: The Case of Russia, BOFIT Discussion Papers 19/2004.

Balassa, B. (1965). Trade liberalization and revealed comparative advantage. *The Manchester School of Economic and Social Studies, 33*, 99–123.

Baldwin, R. (2006), Globalisation: a great unbundling, report to the Prime Minister's Office, August 2006.

Braconier, Henrik, Ekholm, Karolina, (2000), "Swedish Multinationals and Competition from High- and Low-Wage Locations," *Review of International Economics*, Blackwell Publishing, vol. 8(3), 448–461, August

Braconier, Henrik, Ekholm, Karolina, (2001), "Foreign Direct Investment in Central and Eastern Europe: Employment Effects in the EU," *CEPR Discussion Papers* 3052, C.E.P.R. Discussion Papers.

Hunya, Gabor (2007), Shift to East. WIIW Database on FDI in Central, East and Southeast Europe (2008): FDI statistical database.

IFA and IG (Investment in France Agency, Investment in Germany) (2007), The European Attractiveness Scoreboard.

Kaitila, V. (2001), Accession Countries' Comparative Advantage in the Internal Market A Trade and Factor Analysis, BOFIT Discussion Papers 3/2001.

Kaitila, V. (2004), The Factor Intensity of Accession and EU15 Countries' Comparative Advantage in the Internal Market, The Research Institute of Finnish Economy, Discussion Papers 926.

Neven, D. (1995), Trade Liberalization with Eastern Nations: How Sensitive? In: R. Faini, R. Portes (Eds.), European Union Trade with Eastern Europe: Adjustments and Opportunities, CEPR.

Widgrén (2000), Comparative Advantage, Intra-Industry Trade and Location in the Northern Dimension, In: K.E.O. Alho (Ed.), Economics of the Northern Dimension. The Research Institute of the Finnish Economy B 166.

Widgrén, M. (2003), Revealed comparative advantage in trade between the European Union and Baltic countries, V. Pettai, J. Zielonka (Eds.): The Road to the European Union, Manchester University Press.